Exam 70-642: *TS: Windows Server® 2008 Network Infrastructure, Configuring*

Objective	Chapter	Lesson
Configuring IP Addressing and Services (24 percent)		
Configure IPv4 and IPv6 addressing.	1	2, 3
Configure Dynamic Host Configuration Protocol (DHCP).	4	1, 2
Configure routing.	5	1
Configure IPsec.	6	1
Configuring Name Resolution (27 percent)		
Configure a Domain Name System (DNS) server.	2	2
Configure DNS zones.	3	1
Configure DNS records.	3	1
Configure DNS replication.	3	2
Configure name resolution for client computers.	2	3
Configuring Network Access (22 percent)		
Configure remote access.	7	3
Configure Network Access Protection (NAP).	8	2
Configure network authentication.	7	2, 3
Configure wireless access.	7	2
Configure firewall settings.	8	1
Configuring File and Print Services (13 percent)		
Configure a file server.	11	1, 2
Configure Distributed File System (DFS).	11	2
Configure shadow copy services.	11	2
Configure backup and restore.	11	3
Manage disk quotas.	11	2
Configure and monitor print services.	12	1
Monitoring and Managing a Network Infrastructure (14 percent)		
Configure Windows Server Update Services (WSUS) server settings.	9	1, 2
Capture performance data.	10	1, 2
Monitor event logs.	10	1
Gather network data.	10	1, 2, 3

Note: Exam objectives are subject to change at any time without prior notice and at Microsoft's sole discretion. Please visit the Microsoft Learning Certification Web site (*www.microsoft.com/learning/mcp/*) for the most current listing of exam objectives.

MCTS Self-Paced Training Kit (Exam 70-642): Configuring Windows Server® 2008 Network Infrastructure

J.C. Mackin and
Tony Northrup

PUBLISHED BY
Microsoft Press
A Division of Microsoft Corporation
One Microsoft Way
Redmond, Washington 98052-6399

Library of Congress Control Number: 2008923628

Printed and bound in the United States of America.

1 2 3 4 5 6 7 8 9   QWT   3 2 1 0 9 8

Distributed in Canada by H.B. Fenn and Company Ltd.

A CIP catalogue record for this book is available from the British Library.

Microsoft Press books are available through booksellers and distributors worldwide. For further information about international editions, contact your local Microsoft Corporation office or contact Microsoft Press International directly at fax (425) 936-7329. Visit our Web site at www.microsoft.com/mspress. Send comments to tkinput@microsoft.com.

Acquisitions Editor: Ken Jones
Developmental Editor: Laura Sackerman
Project Editor: Denise Bankaitis
Editorial Production: nSight, Inc.
Technical Reviewer: Rozanne Murphy Whalen
Cover: Tom Draper Design

Body Part No. X14-33192

For Miss Hare.

—Tony Northrup

For Joe Loverro.

—J.C. Mackin

About the Authors

J.C. Mackin

J.C. Mackin (MCITP, MCTS, MCSE, MCDST, MCT) is a writer, consultant, and trainer who has been working with Microsoft networks for more than a decade. Books he has previously authored or coauthored include *MCSA/MCSE Self-Paced Training Kit (Exam 70-291): Implementing, Managing, and Maintaining a Microsoft Windows Server 2003 Network Infrastructure; MCITP Self-Paced Training Kit (Exam 70-443): Designing a Database Server Infrastructure Using Microsoft SQL Server 2005;* and *MCITP Self-Paced Training Kit (Exam 70-622): Supporting and Troubleshooting Applications on a Windows Vista Client for Enterprise Support Technicians.* He also holds a master's degree in Telecommunications and Network Management.

When not working with computers, J.C. can be found with a panoramic camera photographing medieval villages in Italy or France.

Tony Northrup

Tony Northrup (MVP, MCSE, MCTS, and CISSP) is a Windows consultant and author living in Phillipston, Massachusetts. Tony started programming before Windows 1.0 was released, but has focused on Windows administration and development for the last fifteen years. He has written more than a dozen books covering Windows networking, security, and development. Among other titles, Tony is coauthor of *Windows Server 2008 Networking And Network Access Protection (NAP)* and the *Windows Vista Resource Kit.*

When he's not consulting or writing, Tony enjoys photography, remote-controlled flight, and golf. Tony lives with his cat, Sam, and his dog, Sandi. You can learn more about Tony by visiting his technical blog at *http://www.vistaclues.com* or his personal website at *http://www.northrup.org.*

Contents at a Glance

Table of Contents

What do you think of this book? We want to hear from you!

Microsoft is interested in hearing your feedback so we can continually improve our books and learning resources for you. To participate in a brief online survey, please visit:

www.microsoft.com/learning/booksurvey/

What do you think of this book? We want to hear from you!

Microsoft is interested in hearing your feedback so we can continually improve our books and learning resources for you. To participate in a brief online survey, please visit:

www.microsoft.com/learning/booksurvey/

Acknowledgments

This book was put together by a team of respected professionals, and we, the authors, would like to thank them each for the great job they did. At Microsoft, Ken Jones worked out our contracts, Laura Sackerman was our developmental editor, and Denise Bankaitis was our project editor. Carol Whitney at nSight, Inc., was the project manager, coordinating the many other people who worked on the book. Among those, Joe Gustaitis was our copy editor, who was responsible for making sure the book is readable and consistent, and Kenzie Grubitz and Paul Connelly provided additional proofreading.

Rozanne Murphy Whalen provided a technical review to help make the book as accurate as possible. Angela Montoya was our graphic artist, processing screenshots and converting our rough diagrams into the polished art you'll see throughout the book. Terrie Cundiff was our desktop publisher, largely responsible for creating a great presentation in the printed book. Chris Cecot created the index that you'll find at the back of the book.

Many people helped with this book, even though they weren't formally part of the team. I'd like to thank my friends, especially Tara Banks, Kristin Cavour, Bob Dean, Tracy Evans, Ashley Fontaine, Chris and Diane Geggis, Kaitlyn Harekut, Bob Hogan, Jeff Klein, Natasha Lee, Hayley Phillips, and Stephanie Wunderlich for helping me enjoy my time away from the keyboard.

It makes a huge difference when you consider the people you work with to be friends. Having a great team not only improves the quality of the book, it makes it a more enjoyable experience. Writing this book was my most enjoyable project yet, and I hope I get the chance to work with everyone in the future.

–TN

Introduction

This training kit is designed for information technology (IT) professionals who work in the complex computing environment of medium-sized to large companies and who also plan to take the Microsoft Certified Technology Specialist (MCTS) 70-642 exam. We assume that before you begin using this kit you have a solid foundation-level understanding of Microsoft Windows server operating systems and common Internet technologies.

By using this training kit, you will learn how to do the following:

- Configure IP addressing, routing, and IPsec
- Configure name resolution using Domain Name System (DNS)
- Configure remote and wireless network access
- Configure Network Access Protection (NAP)
- Configure file and print services
- Monitor and manage a network infrastructure

Lab Setup Instructions

Most of the exercises in this training kit require two computers or virtual machines running Windows Server 2008 using the default settings. (The exercises in Chapter 6, "Protecting Network Traffic with IPSec," require a third such computer or virtual machine.) All lab computers must be physically connected to the same network for most lessons. However, some lessons will describe different network configurations. We recommend that you use an isolated network that is not part of your production network to perform the practice exercises in this book.

To minimize the time and expense of configuring physical computers, we recommend that you use virtual machines for the computers. To run computers as virtual machines within Windows, you can use Virtual PC 2007, Virtual Server 2005 R2, Hyper-V, or third-party virtual machine software. To download Virtual PC 2007, visit *http://www.microsoft.com/windows/downloads/virtualpc*. For more information about Virtual Server 2005 R2, visit *http://www.microsoft.com/virtualserver*. For more information about Hyper-V, visit *http://www.microsoft.com/hyperv*.

IMPORTANT In Virtual PC, assign the adapters to Local Only

Using Virtual PC is the simplest way to prepare the computers for this training kit. To isolate the lab computers within a single network in Virtual PC, configure the settings in each virtual machine so that Adapter 1 is assigned to Local Only. Some exercises need Internet access, which will require you to connect the network adapter to an external network.

Preparing the Windows Server 2008 Computers

Perform the following steps to prepare the first Windows Server 2008 computer for the exercises in this training kit.

Perform a Default Installation of Windows Server 2008

On the three lab computers, perform a default installation of Windows Server 2008. Do not add any roles or adjust the networking settings.

Name the Computers

In the Control Panel, use System to specify the computer name of the first computer as **dcsrv1**, the second computer as **boston**, and the third computer as **binghamton**.

Using the CD

The companion CD included with this training kit contains the following:

■ **Practice tests** You can reinforce your understanding of how to configure Windows Server 2008 network infrastructure by using electronic practice tests you customize to meet your needs from the pool of Lesson Review questions in this book. Or you can practice for the 70-642 certification exam by using tests created from a pool of 200 realistic exam questions, which give you many practice exams to ensure that you are prepared.

■ **An eBook** An electronic version (eBook) of this book is included for when you do not want to carry the printed book with you. The eBook is in Portable Document Format (PDF), and you can view it by using Adobe Acrobat or Adobe Reader.

Digital Content for Digital Book Readers: If you bought a digital-only edition of this book, you can enjoy select content from the print edition's companion CD. Visit *http://go.microsoft.com/fwlink /?LinkId=114594* to get your downloadable content. This content is always up-to-date and available to all readers.

How to Install the Practice Tests

To install the practice test software from the companion CD to your hard disk, do the following:

- Insert the companion CD into your CD drive and accept the license agreement.
- A CD menu appears.

NOTE If the CD menu does not appear

If the CD menu or the license agreement does not appear, AutoRun might be disabled on your computer. Refer to the Readme.txt file on the CD-ROM for alternate installation instructions.

- Click Practice Tests and follow the instructions on the screen.

How to Use the Practice Tests

To start the practice test software, follow these steps:

- Click Start\All Programs\Microsoft Press Training Kit Exam Prep.
- A window appears that shows all the Microsoft Press training kit exam prep suites installed on your computer.
- Double-click the lesson review or practice test you want to use.

NOTE Lesson reviews vs. practice tests

Select the (70-642) TS: Windows Server 2008 Network Infrastructure, Configuring lesson review to use the questions from the "Lesson Review" sections of this book. Select the (70-642) TS: Windows Server 2008 Network Infrastructure, Configuring practice test to use a pool of 200 questions similar to those that appear on the 70-642 certification exam.

Lesson Review Options

When you start a lesson review, the Custom Mode dialog box appears so that you can configure your test. You can click OK to accept the defaults, or you can customize the number of questions you want, how the practice test software works, which exam objectives you want the questions to relate to, and whether you want your lesson review to be timed. If you are retaking a test, you can select whether you want to see all the questions again or only the questions you missed or did not answer.

After you click OK, your lesson review starts.

■ To take the test, answer the questions and use the Next, Previous, and Go To buttons to move from question to question.

■ After you answer an individual question, if you want to see which answers are correct—along with an explanation of each correct answer—click Explanation.

■ If you prefer to wait until the end of the test to see how you did, answer all the questions and then click Score Test. You will see a summary of the exam objectives you chose and the percentage of questions you got right overall and per objective. You can print a copy of your test, review your answers, or retake the test.

Practice Test Options

When you start a practice test, you choose whether to take the test in Certification Mode, Study Mode, or Custom Mode:

■ **Certification Mode**   Closely resembles the experience of taking a certification exam. The test has a set number of questions. It is timed, and you cannot pause and restart the timer.

■ **Study Mode**   Creates an untimed test in which you can review the correct answers and the explanations after you answer each question.

■ **Custom Mode**   Gives you full control over the test options so that you can customize them as you like.

In all modes the user interface you see when you are taking the test is basically the same but with different options enabled or disabled depending on the mode. The main options are discussed in the previous section, "Lesson Review Options."

When you review your answer to an individual practice test question, a "References" section is provided that lists where in the training kit you can find the information that relates to that question and provides links to other sources of information. After you click Test Results to score your entire practice test, you can click the Learning Plan tab to see a list of references for every objective.

How to Uninstall the Practice Tests

To uninstall the practice test software for a training kit, use Add Or Remove Programs option (Windows XP) or the Program And Features option (Windows Vista and Windows Server 2008) in Windows Control Panel.

Microsoft Certified Professional Program

The Microsoft certifications provide the best method to prove your command of current Microsoft products and technologies. The exams and corresponding certifications are developed to validate your mastery of critical competencies as you design and develop, or implement and support, solutions with Microsoft products and technologies. Computer professionals who become Microsoft-certified are recognized as experts and are sought after industrywide. Certification brings a variety of benefits to the individual and to employers and organizations.

MORE INFO **All the Microsoft certifications**

For a full list of Microsoft certifications, go to *www.microsoft.com/learning/mcp*.

Technical Support

Every effort has been made to ensure the accuracy of this book and the contents of the companion CD. If you have comments, questions, or ideas regarding this book or the companion CD, please send them to Microsoft Press by using either of the following methods:

- E-mail: tkinput@microsoft.com
- Postal mail at:

  Microsoft Press
  Attn: *MCTS Self-Paced Training Kit (Exam 70-642): Configuring Windows Server 2008 Network Infrastructure*, Editor
  One Microsoft Way
  Redmond, WA 98052-6399

For additional support information regarding this book and the CD-ROM (including answers to commonly asked questions about installation and use), visit the Microsoft Press Technical Support website at *www.microsoft.com/learning/support/books*. To connect directly to the Microsoft Knowledge Base and enter a query, visit *http://support.microsoft.com/search*. For support information regarding Microsoft software, connect to *http://support.microsoft.com*.

Find additional content online As new or updated material that complements your book becomes available, it will be posted on the Microsoft Press Online Windows Server and Client Web site. Based on the final build of Windows Server 2008, the type of material you might find includes updates to book content, articles, links to companion content, errata, sample chapters, and more. This Web site will be available soon at *www.microsoft.com/learning/books/online/serverclient* and will be updated periodically.

Chapter 1

Understanding and Configuring IP

Like any communication system, computer networks rely on a set of standards that allow communicators to send, receive, and interpret messages. For the Internet, Windows networks, and virtually all other computer networks, that underlying set of standards is the suite of protocols known collectively as Transmission Control Protocol/Internet Protocol (TCP/IP), the core of which is IP.

In this chapter, you learn the fundamentals of IP and how to configure Windows Server 2008 to connect to IP networks.

Exam objectives in this chapter:
- Configure IPv4 and IPv6 addressing.

Lessons in this chapter:

Before You Begin

To complete the lessons in this chapter, you must have:

- Two virtual machines or physical computers, named Dcsrv1 and Boston, that are joined to the same isolated network and on which Windows Server 2008 is installed. Neither computer should have any server roles added.
- A basic understanding of Windows administration.

Real World

JC Mackin

The *Ipconfig* command is the most basic tool in the network administrator's troubleshooting toolbox. If you are helping a user who cannot connect to the Internet, for example, typing **ipconfig** at a command prompt would most likely be the first thing you'd do to find out whether the computer is assigned a valid address. The output of *Ipconfig* has remained the same since Windows NT, and if you've been working as a network support specialist, you'd never expect to see anything unusual when you type this basic command.

However, Windows Vista and Windows Server 2008 now provide IPv6 information along with the traditional IPv4 information in the Ipconfig output. This might not sound like a big deal, but IPv6 can look pretty scary if you're not familiar with it, and the last thing you want is to be in a position where a user can detect fear on your face when you're troubleshooting his or her computer.

You might even be tempted to disable IPv6 to avoid exposing your ignorance and—ironically—to prevent it from "slowing down the network" (which it doesn't ever do). It's true that IPv6 isn't needed today, but despite any inclination we might have to live in IPv6 denial, there's no question that it will be used more and more in the coming years. There's just no avoiding it because there is no other solution proposed to deal with the problem of IPv4 address exhaustion, and that problem isn't going to disappear. IPv6 isn't intruding into your Windows networking life because you need it now but because you will need it soon, and for that reason, you need to start getting comfortable with it now. The good news is that there isn't much you need to know before you can once again read the complete Ipconfig output with complete confidence. To learn about IPv6 and the new Ipconfig output, see Lesson 3, "Understanding IP Version 6 (IPv6) Addressing."

Lesson 1: Understanding and Configuring Network Connections

Network connections in Windows are software interfaces that use TCP/IP and associated services to communicate over a network. This lesson helps you understand the concepts and features of TCP/IP, how you can configure Windows Server 2008 network connections, and how to troubleshoot network connections by using basic TCP/IP utilities.

> **After this lesson, you will be able to:**
> - Understand the four layers in the TCP/IP protocol suite.
> - View and configure the IP configuration of a local area connection.
> - Understand the concept of a network broadcast.
> - Troubleshoot network connectivity with TCP/IP utilities.
>
> **Estimated lesson time: 100 minutes**

What Are Network Layers?

Network layers are conceptual steps in network communication that are performed by standards-based programs called *protocols*. As an analogy, consider an assembly line. If a factory uses an assembly line to create a product that is assembled, coated, packaged, boxed, and labeled, for example, you could view these five sequential functions as vertically stacked layers in the production process, as shown in Figure 1-1. Following this analogy, the protocols in the assembly line are the specific machines or procedures used to carry out the function of each layer. Although each protocol is designed to accept a specific input and generate a specific output, you could replace any protocol within the system as long as it remained compatible with the neighboring machines on the assembly line.

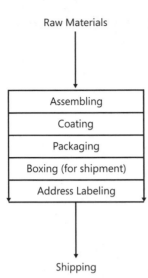

Figure 1-1   A layered view of assembly-line production

In a way, network communications really do resemble the creation of packaged products on an assembly line because computers communicate with one another by creating and sending encapsulated (wrapped) packages called *packets*. Unlike assembly-line production, however, communication between computers is bidirectional. This means that the networking layers taken together describe a way both to construct *and deconstruct* packets. Each layer, and each specific protocol, must be able to perform its function in both directions. In the assembly line example, such a bidirectional model could be illustrated as shown in Figure 1-2.

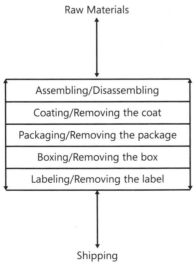

Figure 1-2   Layers in a bidirectional, "assembly-disassembly" line

In computer networking, the layered model traditionally used to describe communications is the seven-layer Open Systems Interconnect (OSI) model, shown in Figure 1-3. You can see that each of these seven layers was originally designed to perform a step in communication, such as presenting or transporting information.

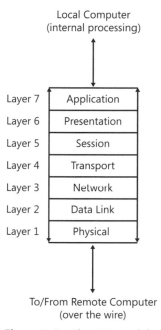

Figure 1-3   The OSI model of network communications

Although the protocols that originally instantiated the OSI model were never adopted in practice, the names, and especially the numbers, of the layers of the model survive to this day. As a result, even though TCP/IP is based on its own model, not the OSI model, the four TCP/IP networking layers are often defined in terms of their relationship to the OSI model, as shown in Figure 1-4.

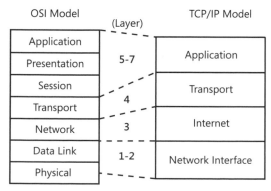

Figure 1-4   The TCP/IP networking layers are mapped to the OSI model

Exploring the Layers of the TCP/IP Networking Model

The idea of a layered networking model allows for the possibility that individual protocols at any layer can be replaced as long as the replacement protocols work seamlessly with the protocols at neighboring layers. Such a change has in fact recently happened with TCP/IP in Windows networks. Windows Server 2008 and Windows Vista have introduced a new implementation of the TCP/IP protocol stack known as the Next Generation TCP/IP stack. New protocols have been added to the stack, but this upgraded version of TCP/IP is still based on the same four-layer model.

Figure 1-5 shows the protocols that in new Microsoft networks work at the four layers of the TCP/IP model.

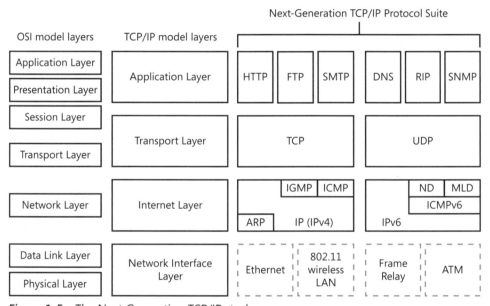

Figure 1-5   The Next Generation TCP/IP stack

NOTE **TCP/IP layer numbers**

Although you will sometimes see the layers of the TCP/IP model assigned their own numbers independent of the OSI model, this book's terminology reflects the layer number usage that is far more current.

Layer 2

Layer 2, also called the *Network Interface Layer* or *Data Link Layer*, is the step in the communication process that describes a specific set of standards for network adapters, hardware addresses (such as MAC addresses) assigned to those adapters, cabling type, hubs, switches, associated physical standards, and associated messaging protocols. The function of this layer is to deliver messages from one device to the next, and its protocols allow communications to occur between computers separated only by hubs, switches, and cabling. Examples of standards defined at the Network Interface Layer include Ethernet and Token Ring.

Layer 3

Also called the *Network Layer* or *Internet Layer*, Layer 3 is the step in the communication process during which a source and destination software address is added to the packet and during which the packet is routed to the remote network destination beyond the "earshot" of a physical signal. The main protocol that operates at Layer 3 is IP, and the device that operates at this layer is a *router*. Routers stop physical propagations (broadcasts) of messages on a network, read the software address assigned in Layer 3 of a packet, and then forward the message along an appropriate pathway toward its destination.

Layer 3 is where the main changes have appeared in Microsoft's new implementation of TCP/IP. Traditionally, IPv4 is the only protocol to appear at this layer. In the Next Generation TCP/IP stack, however, the IPv4 and IPv6 protocols now co-occupy Layer 3.

- **IPv4**   IPv4, or simply IP, is responsible for addressing and routing packets between hosts that might be dozens of network segments away. IPv4 relies on 32-bit addresses, and because of this relatively small address space, addresses are rapidly becoming depleted in IPv4 networks.

- **IPv6**   IPv6 uses 128-bit addresses instead of the 32-bit addresses used with IPv4, and, as a result, it can define many more addresses. Because few Internet routers are IPv6 compatible, IPv6 today is used over the Internet with the help of tunneling protocols. However, IPv6 is supported natively in Windows Vista and Windows Server 2008 LANs.

Both IPv4 and IPv6 are enabled by default. As a result of this dual-IP architecture, computers can use IPv6 to communicate if the client, server, and network infrastructure support it but also communicate with computers or network services that support only IPv4.

Layer 4

Layer 4, or the *Transport Layer* of the TCP/IP model, is the step in the communication process during which the terms of sending and receiving data are determined. Layer 4 also serves to tag data as being destined for a general application, such as e-mail or the Web.

TCP and UDP are the two Transport Layer protocols within the TCP/IP suite.

- **TCP**   TCP receives data from the Application Layer and processes the data as a stream of bytes. These bytes are grouped into segments that TCP then numbers and sequences for delivery to a network host. TCP acknowledges received data and arranges for data to be resent when such an acknowledgment is not received.

  When TCP receives a stream of data from a network host, it sends the data to the application designated by the TCP port number. TCP ports enable different applications and programs to use TCP services on a single host, as shown in Figure 1-6. Each program that uses TCP ports listens for messages arriving on its associated port number. Data sent to a specific TCP port is thus received by the application listening at that port.

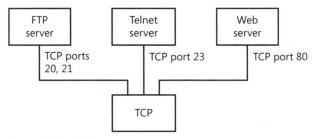

Figure 1-6   TCP ports

- **UDP**   Many network services (such as DNS) rely on UDP instead of TCP as a transport protocol. UDP enables fast transport of datagrams by eliminating the reliability features of TCP, such as delivery guarantees and sequence verification. Unlike TCP, UDP is a *connectionless* service that provides only best-effort delivery to network hosts. A source host that needs reliable communication must use either TCP or a program that provides its own sequencing and acknowledgment services.

Layer 7

Layer 7, or the *Application Layer* of the TCP/IP model, is the step in the communication process during which end-user data is manipulated, packaged, and sent to and from Transport Layer ports. Application Layer protocols often describe a user-friendly method of presenting, naming, sending, or receiving data over TCP/IP. Common examples of Application Layer protocols native to the TCP/IP suite include HTTP, Telnet, FTP, Trivial File Transfer Protocol (TFTP), Simple Network Management Protocol (SNMP), DNS, Post Office Protocol 3 (POP3), Simple Mail Transfer Protocol (SMTP), and Network News Transfer Protocol (NNTP).

TCP/IP Encapsulation

By encapsulating data with each of the four layers described above, TCP/IP creates a packet as shown in the simplifed example in Figure 1-7. In the figure, an e-mail message of "Hello" is encapsulated with POP3 email (Layer 7), TCP (Layer 4), IP (Layer 3), and Ethernet (Layer 2) headers.

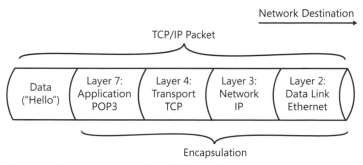

Figure 1-7   An example of a TCP/IP packet

NOTE   The number of protocols in each packet varies

The packet shown in Figure 1-7 is simplified because not every packet really includes data encapsulated by exactly four protocols. Many packets, for example, are designed to provide end-to-end communication only for lower layers such as TCP and therefore include fewer protocols. Other packets can have more than four protocols if they include more than one protocol at a given layer. For example, ICMP, IP, and ARP can all be used at Layer 3 within a single packet.

Quick Check
1. At which networking layer is Ethernet found?
2. What do routers do to network broadcasts by default?
Quick Check Answers
1. Layer 2.
2. Routers block broadcasts by default.

Configuring Networking Properties for a Windows Vista or Windows Server 2008 Client

Windows Server 2008 includes two main areas in which to configure client networking properties: Network and Sharing Center and Network Connections. The following section describes these areas within the Windows Server 2008 interface and the settings that you can configure in them.

Network and Sharing Center

Network and Sharing Center is the main network configuration tool in Windows Server 2008. To open the Network and Sharing Center, from the Start Menu, right-click Network, and then select Properties. Alternatively, in the Notification area, right-click the network icon, and then select Network And Sharing Center from the shortcut menu. As a third option, you can also find the Network and Sharing Center by browsing to Control Panel\Network and Internet\Network and Sharing Center.

Network and Sharing Center is shown in Figure 1-8.

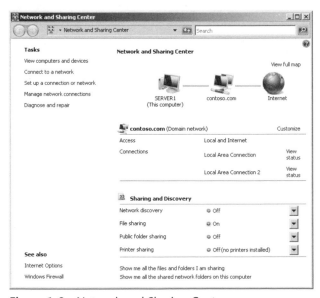

Figure 1-8   Network and Sharing Center

You can use the Network and Sharing Center to perform functions such as setting the network location, viewing the network map, configuring Network Discovery, configuring file and printer sharing, and viewing the status of network connections. These various properties are described in the following list.

■ **Network Location**   The network location setting is a parameter that is set for all Windows Vista and Windows Server 2008 computers. All clients running these operating systems are assigned to one of three network locations: Public, Private, and Domain. Different network properties are then automatically enabled or disabled in a manner based on the network location to which the machine has been assigned. For example, the Network Map is enabled by default in some locations and disabled by default in others.

By default, all clients are assigned to the Public location type. For a computer in a Public network, Windows Firewall is turned on, Network Discovery is turned off, file and printer sharing is turned off, and the Network Map is turned off.

When you assign a computer to the Private network location, Network Discovery and the Network Map feature are turned on. File sharing is turned off by default, but unlike the Public location type, you can enable file sharing on a single computer assigned to a private network without changing the default settings for all computers assigned to a private network.

When a computer running Windows Vista joins an Active Directory directory service domain, it automatically configures the existing network for the Domain network location type. The Domain network location type resembles the Private network location type except that with the Domain network location, the configuration for Windows Firewall, Network Discovery, and Network Map can be determined by Group Policy settings.

■ **Network Map**   The Network Map allows you to see the devices on your local LAN and how these devices are connected to each other and to the Internet. An example Network Map output is shown in Figure 1-9.

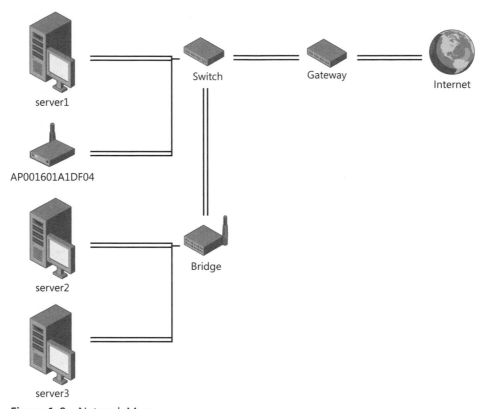

Figure 1-9   Network Map

Network Map relies on two components:

❑ The Link Layer Topology Discovery (LLTD) Mapper component queries the network for devices to include in the map.

❑ The LLTD Responder component responds to the queries from the Mapper I/O.

Although these components are included only in Windows Vista and Windows Server 2008, you can install a Responder component on computers running Windows XP so that they will appear on a Network Map on other computers.

Exam Tip   Remember that to make a computer running Windows XP appear on the Network Map, you have to install the LLTD Responder on that computer.

Network Map in a Domain profile

The Network Map feature is disabled by default when you select the Domain profile. However, you can enable it through Group Policy.

■ **File Sharing** When this feature is turned on, Windows Firewall allows standard users to choose whether to share files or folders in their profiles—that is, files and folders under %systemroot%\Users\%username%. Administrators can share any file or folder on the computer.

IMPORTANT File sharing enables Ping

Enabling file sharing also creates the firewall exceptions for Internet Control Message Protocol (ICMP), the protocol used in the Ping, Pathping, and Tracert utilities. If you leave file sharing disabled, therefore, the local computer by default will not respond to pings. Remember this point both for the 70-642 exam and for real-world administration!

■ **Public Folder Sharing** Enabling this feature automatically shares the folder found at %systemroot%\Users\Public. Enabling public folder sharing also automatically turns on file sharing.

■ **Printer Sharing** Enabling this feature shares the printers that are installed on the local computer so they can be used from other computers on the network. Selecting the Printer Sharing option automatically enables file sharing.

■ **Password Protected Sharing** This option is available only on computers that are not joined to a domain. Turning this option on restricts access to shared resources to only those users who have valid accounts on the local computer.

Viewing Network Connections

Windows Server 2008 automatically detects and configures connections associated with network adapters installed on the local computer. These connections are then displayed in Network Connections, along with any additional connections, such as dial-up connections, that you have added manually by clicking the Set Up A Connection Or Network option in Network and Sharing Center.

You can open Network Connections in a number of ways. First, select the *Server Manager* node in Server Manager, and then click View Network Connections. In the Initial Configuration Tasks window, you can click Configure Networking. In the Network and Sharing Center, you can click Manage Network Connections. Finally, from the command line, Start Search box, or Run box, you can type the command **ncpa.cpl** or **control netconnections.**

Viewing Default Components of Network Connections Connections by themselves do not allow network hosts to communicate. Instead, the network clients, services, and protocols *bound to* a connection are what provide connectivity through that connection. The General tab of a connection's properties dialog box shows the clients, services, and protocols bound to that connection.

Figure 1-10 shows the default components installed on a Windows Server 2008 local area connection. The check box next to each component indicates that the component is bound to the connection.

Figure 1-10   Default components for a connection

- **Network Clients**   In Windows, *network clients* are software components, such as Client For Microsoft Networks, that allow the local computer to connect with a particular network operating system. By default, Client For Microsoft Networks is the only network client bound to all local area connections. Client For Microsoft Networks allows Windows client computers to connect to shared resources on other Windows computers.

- **Network Services**   Network services are software components that provide additional features for network connections. File And Printer Sharing For Microsoft Networks and QoS Packet Scheduler are the two network services bound to all local area connections by default. File And Printer Sharing For Microsoft Networks allows the local computer to share folders for network access. QoS Packet Scheduler provides network traffic control, including rate-of-flow and prioritization services.

- **Network Protocols**   Computers can communicate through a connection only by using network protocols bound to that connection. By default, four network protocols are installed and bound to every network connection: IPv4, IPv6, the Link-Layer Topology Discovery (LLTD) Mapper, and the LLTD Responder.

Viewing Advanced Connection Settings   To view advanced connection settings, open the Network Connections window and from the Advanced menu, select Advanced Settings, as shown in Figure 1-11.

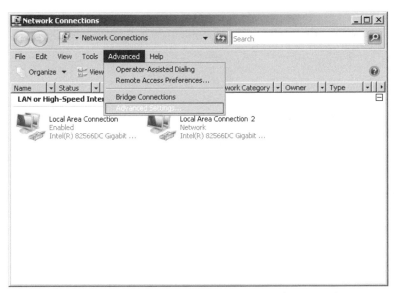

Figure 1-11   Opening Advanced Settings in Network Connections

The Advanced Settings dialog box, shown in Figure 1-12, displays the order (priority) of each connection. By adjusting the order of the connections, you can configure the computer to attempt network communication through various available connections in the order you define. You can also adjust the binding order of the services used for each connection.

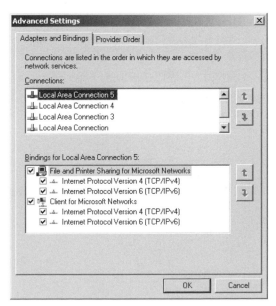

Figure 1-12   Advanced Settings dialog box

Provider Order Tab   The Provider Order tab of the Advanced Settings dialog box, shown in Figure 1-13, displays the order in which the connection will attempt to communicate with other computers using the various network providers, such as a Microsoft Windows Network or Microsoft Terminal Services. Note that the network provider order specified in this dialog box applies to all network connections.

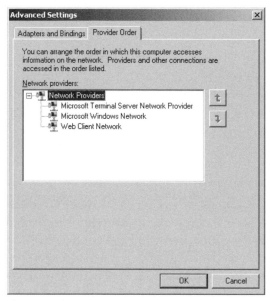

Figure 1-13   Provider Order tab

Bridging Network Connections

In some cases, you might want to combine multiple network connections on a given computer so that Windows will treat these connections as if they were on the same network (in one broadcast domain). For example, you might want to share a single wireless access point (WAP) with multiple and varying connection topologies, as shown in Figure 1-14.

In this example, an Internet connection is joined to a single WAP. The WAP then communicates with the wireless network interface card (NIC) in the server. Additionally, the server has an Ethernet connection and a Token Ring connection attached to other networks.

When you enable *network bridging* on this connection, all points entering the server (wireless, Token Ring, and Ethernet) appear on the same network. Hence, they can all share the wireless connection and get out to the Internet.

To bridge the networks, press Ctrl as you select multiple network connections on the server. Then, right-click and select Bridge Networks, as shown in Figure 1-15.

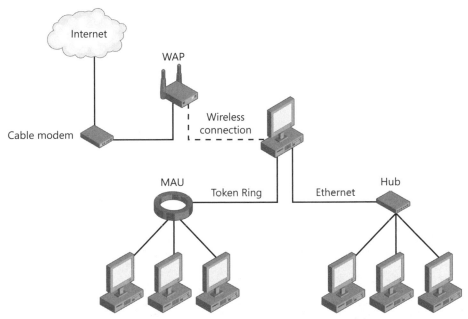

Figure 1-14 Example of a network that can leverage network bridging

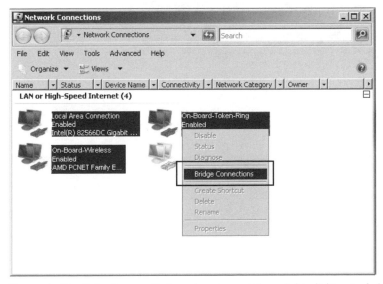

Figure 1-15 Selecting multiple networks and then right-clicking to bridge them

When you configure network bridging, you allow traffic from the wireless, Ethernet, and Token Ring NIC to share the same network space. Hence, a single wireless NIC can be the outbound gateway to disparate networks.

Viewing an Address Configuration

The IP configuration of a connection consists, at a minimum, of an IPv4 address and subnet mask or an IPv6 address and subnet prefix. Beyond these minimal settings, an IP configuration can also include information such as a default gateway, DNS server addresses, a DNS name suffix, and WINS server addresses.

To view the IP address configuration for a given connection, you can use either the *Ipconfig* command or the Network Connection Details dialog box.

To use *Ipconfig*, type **ipconfig** at a command prompt. You will see an output similar to that shown in Figure 1-16.

Figure 1-16   Viewing an IP address

To open the Network Connection Details dialog box, first right-click the connection in Network Connections, and then select Status from the shortcut menu, as shown in Figure 1-17.

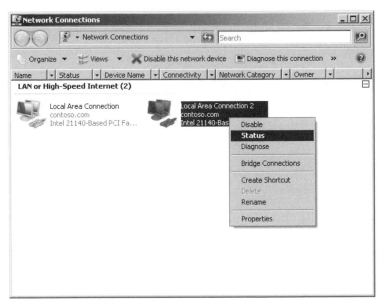

Figure 1-17   Opening the Local Area Connection Status dialog box

Then, in the Local Area Connection Status dialog box, click the Details button, as shown in Figure 1-18.

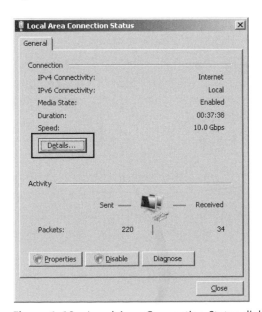

Figure 1-18   Local Area Connection Status dialog box

This last step opens the Network Connection Details dialog box, shown in Figure 1-19.

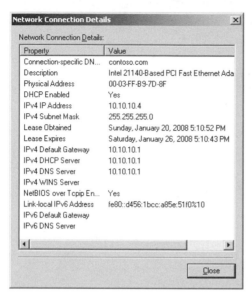

Figure 1-19   Network Connection Details dialog box

Assigning an IP Configuration Manually

A network connection can be assigned an IP configuration manually or automatically. This next section explains how to assign an IPv4 and IPv6 configuration manually.

Assigning an IPv4 Configuration Manually   A manually configured address is known as a static address because such an address remains constant even after the computer reboots. Such static addresses are appropriate for critical infrastructure servers such as domain controllers, DNS servers, DHCP servers, WINS servers, and routers.

You can manually assign a static address and other IPv4 configuration parameters to a network connection by using the Internet Protocol Version 4 (TCP/IP) Properties dialog box. To access this dialog box, open the properties of the network connection for which you want to assign an IPv4 configuration. In the connection's properties dialog box, double-click the Internet Protocol Version 4 (TCP/IPv4) from the list of components.

The Internet Protocol Version 4 (TCP/IPv4) Properties dialog box is shown in Figure 1-20.

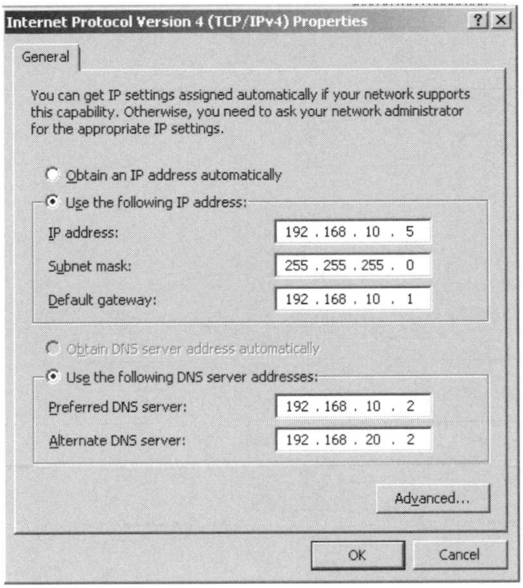

Figure 1-20 Manually assigning an IPv4 configuration for a network connection

By default, network connections are configured to obtain an IP address and DNS server address automatically. To configure a static IP address, therefore, you need to select the Use The Following IP Address option and then specify an IP address, a subnet mask, and (optionally) a default gateway. To assign a static DNS server assignment to the connection, select the Use The Following DNS Server Addresses option, and then specify a preferred and (optionally) alternate DNS server address.

Assigning an IPv6 Configuration Manually   In most cases, you do not need to configure an IPv6 address manually because static IPv6 addresses are normally assigned only to routers and not to hosts. Typically, an IPv6 configuration is assigned to a host through autoconfiguration.

However, you can set an IPv6 address manually by using the Internet Protocol Version 6 (TCP/IPv6) Properties dialog box. To open this dialog box, in the properties of the network connection, double-click Internet Protocol Version 6 (TCP/IPv6). The Internet Protocol Version 6 (TCP/IPv6) dialog box is shown in Figure 1-21.

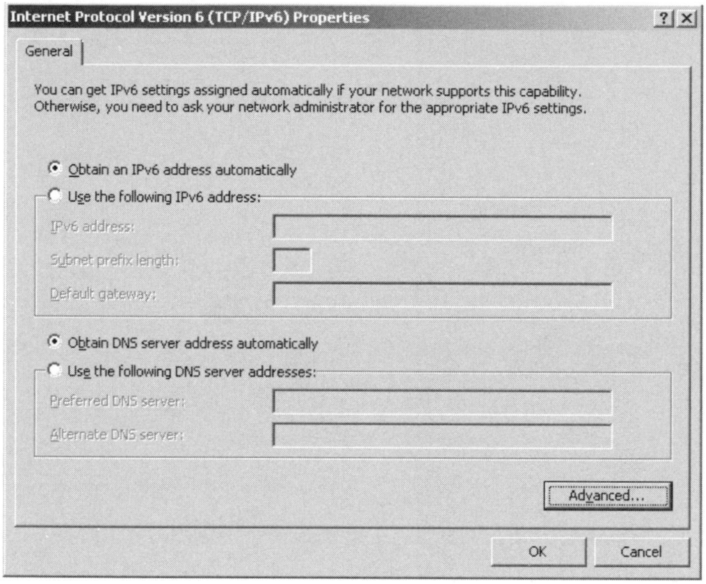

Figure 1-21   The Internet Protocol Version 6 (TCP/IPv6) dialog box

As with IPv4, network connections are configured to obtain an IPv6 address automatically and to obtain a DNS server address automatically. To configure a static IPv6 address, select the Use The Following IPv6 Address option and specify an IPv6 address, subnet prefix length (typically 64), and (optionally) a default gateway. Note that if you configure a static IPv6 address, you must also specify a static IPv6 DNS server address.

Configuring IPv4 and IPv6 Settings Manually from the Command Prompt   You can use the Netsh utility to assign an IP configuration to a connection from the command prompt.

To assign a static IPv4 address and subnet mask to a connection from the command propt, type the following, where *Connection_Name* is the name of the connection (such as Local Area Connection), *Address* is the IPv4 address, and *Subnet_Mask* is the subnet mask.

```
netsh interface ip set address "Connection_Name" static Address Subnet_Mask
```

For example, to set the IPv4 address of the Local Area Connection to 192.168.33.5 with a subnet mask of 255.255.255.0, you would type the following:

```
netsh interface ip set address "local area connection" static 192.168.33.5 255.255.255.0
```

If you also want to define a default gateway along with the IPv4 configuration, you can add that information to the end of the command. For example, to configure the same IPv4 address for the local area connection with a default gateway of 192.168.33.1, type the following:

```
netsh interface ip set address "local area connection" static 192.168.33.5 255.255.255.0
192.168.33.1
```

NOTE Alternate Netsh syntax

There are many acceptable variations in Netsh syntax. For example, you can type **netsh interface ipv4** instead of **netsh interface ip**. For more information, use Netsh Help.

To assign a static IPv6 address to a connection from the command prompt, type the following, where *Connection_Name* is the name of the connection and *Address* is the IPv6 address.

```
netsh interface ipv6 set address "Connection_Name" Address
```

For example, to assign an address of 2001:db8:290c:1291::1 to the Local Area Connection (leaving the default subnet prefix of 64), type the following:

```
netsh interface ipv6 set address "Local Area Connection" 2001:db8:290c:1291::1
```

The Netsh utility includes many other options for configuring both IPv4 and IPv6. Use Netsh Help for more information on the options and syntax.

Configuring an IPv4 Connection to Receive an Address Automatically

By default, all connections are configured to receive an IPv4 address automatically. When configured in this way, a computer owning this type of a connection is known as a DHCP client.

As a result of this setting, all network connections will obtain an IPv4 address from a DHCP server if one is available. If no DHCP server is available, a connection will automatically assign itself any alternate configuration that you have defined for it. If you have defined no alternate configuration, the connection will automatically assign itself an Automatic Private IP Addressing (APIPA) address for IPv4.

To configure a connection to obtain an IPv4 address automatically, select the appropriate option in the Internet Protocol Version 4 (TCP/IPv4) Properties dialog box, as shown in Figure 1-22.

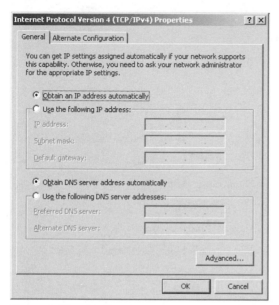

Figure 1-22   Configuring a connection to obtain an IPv4 address automatically (the default setting)

You can also use the Netsh utility to configure a client to obtain an IPv4 address automatically. To do so, at the command prompt type the following, where *Connection_Name* is the name of the network connection:

```
netsh interface ip set address "Connection_Name" dhcp
```

For example, to configure the Local Area Connection to obtain an address automatically, type the following:

```
netsh interface ip set address "Local Area Connection" dhcp
```

Understanding DHCP-assigned Addresses   DHCP-assigned addresses always take priority over other automatic IPv4 configuration methods. A host on an IP network can receive an IP address from a DHCP server when a DHCP server (or DHCP Relay Agent) is located within broadcast range.

A network broadcast is a transmission that is directed to all local addresses. Such a broadcast propagates through all Layer 1 and Layer 2 devices (such as cables, repeaters, hubs, bridges, and switches) but is blocked by Layer 3 devices (routers). Computers that can communicate with one another through broadcasts are said to be located in the same broadcast domain.

A network broadcast is illustrated in Figure 1-23.

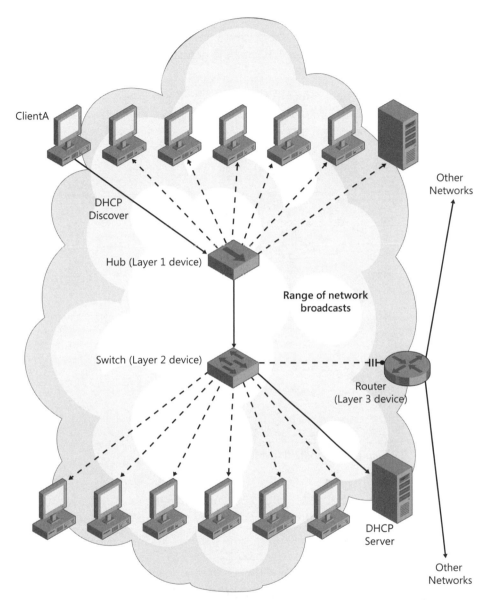

Figure 1-23   ClientA can obtain an IP address from the DHCP server because the two computers lie within the same broadcast domain. Note that the broadcast range extends only as far as the router.

Defining an Alternate Configuration   If no DHCP server is available within a client's broadcast range, a client that has been configured to obtain an address automatically will default to an alternate configuration if you have defined one.

You can assign an alternate configuration to a connection by selecting the Alternate Configuration tab in the Internet Protocol Version 4 (TCP/IPv4) Properties dialog box. This tab is shown in Figure 1-24. Note that the alternate configuration allows you to specify an IP address, subnet mask, default gateway, DNS server, and WINS server.

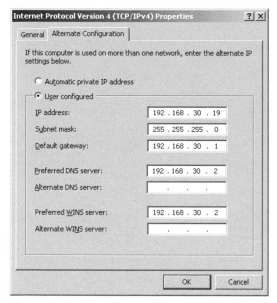

Figure 1-24   Defining an alternate IP configuration

Because an alternate configuration allows a computer to be assigned a specific and detailed IP configuration when no DHCP server can be found, defining an alternate configuration is useful for portable computers that move between networks with and without DHCP servers.

Exam Tip   You need to undertand the benefit of alternate configurations for the 70-642 exam.

Understanding Automatic Private IP Addressing (APIPA)   *APIPA* is an automatic addressing feature useful for some ad hoc or temporary networks. Whenever a Windows computer has been configured to obtain an IP address automatically and when no DHCP server or alternate configuration is available, the computer uses APIPA to assign itself a private IP address in the range of 169.254.0.1 and 169.254.255.254 and a subnet mask of 255.255.0.0.

By default, all network connections are set to default to APIPA when no DHCP server can be reached. This setting is shown in Figure 1-25.

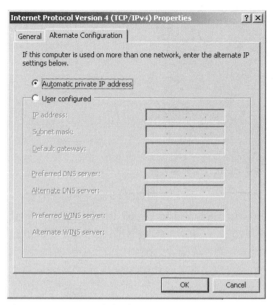

Figure 1-25 By default, network connections are configured to default to an APIPA address in the absence of a DHCP server

The APIPA feature is very useful because it enables two or more Windows computers located in the same broadcast domain to communicate with one another without requiring a DHCP server or any user configuration. It also allows DHCP clients to communicate in the event of a DHCP failure. If the DHCP server later becomes available, the APIPA address is replaced by one obtained from the DHCP server.

Exam Tip   When two client computers can see each other but cannot connect to anything else on the network (or the Internet), suspect APIPA. Either there is a problem with your network's DHCP server or there is a faulty connection to the DHCP server.

Although an APIPA address enables some local network communication, the limitations of being assigned such an address are significant. Connections assigned APIPA addresses can communicate only with other computers using APIPA addresses within broadcast range on the network; such computers cannot access the Internet. Note also that through APIPA you cannot configure a computer with a DNS server address, a default gateway address, or a WINS server address.

An APIPA address configuration is shown in Figure 1-26.

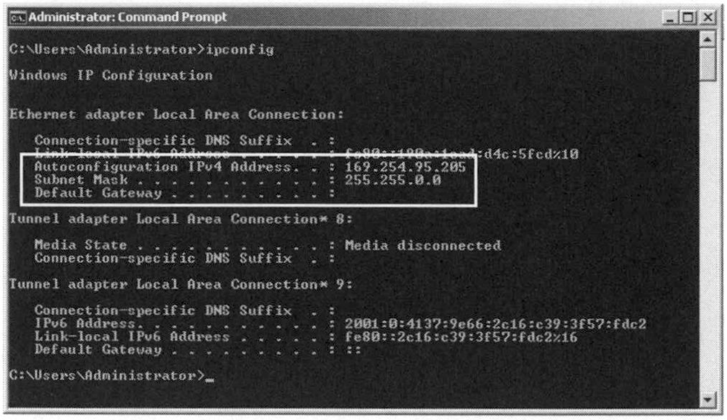

Figure 1-26   An APIPA address is a sign of a network problem

Repairing a Network Connection with *Ipconfig /renew* and the Diagnose Feature   If a connection has been assigned an APIPA address, it is typically a sign that the connection has not properly obtained an IP address from a DHCP server. Because connections assigned with APIPA addresses can communicate only with nearby computers that have also been assigned APIPA addresses, such addresses are usually undesirable. You should expect limited or no connectivity for a connection that has been assigned such an APIPA address.

If a connection has been assigned an APIPA address and no DHCP server is available on the network, you can either install a DHCP server or assign the connection a static IP configuration or alternate configuration.

If a connection has been assigned an APIPA address on a network on which a DHCP server is already operative, you should first try either to renew the IP configuration or to use the Diagnose feature with the connection. To renew the IP configuration, type **ipconfig /renew** at a command prompt. To use the Diagnose feature, in Network Connections, right-click the connection to which an APIPA address has been assigned, and then select Diagnose from the shortcut menu. You will then be given a chance to repair the connection.

Should this strategy fail to provide the host with a new IP address, you should then verify that the DHCP server is functioning properly. If the DHCP server is functioning, proceed to investigate hardware problems, such as faulty cables, hubs, and switches, that might be occuring between between the DHCP server and client.

NOTE   Renewing an IPv6 configuration

To renew an IPv6 configuration, type **ipconfig/renew**.

Troubleshooting Network Connectivity with Ping, Tracert, PathPing, and Arp   If neither the Diagnose feature nor the *Ipconfig /renew* command solves a network problem, you should use utilities such as Ping, Tracert, PathPing, and Arp to troubleshoot the connection. A description of these four utilities is described in the next section.

- **Ping**   Ping is the key tool used to test network connectivity. To use the Ping utility, at a command prompt, type **ping** *remote_host,* where *remote_host* is the name or IP address of a remote computer, server, or router to which you want to verify connectivity. If the remote computer replies to the ping, you know that connectivity to the remote host has been verified.

   Figure 1-27 showns a successful attempt to ping a server named server1.

Figure 1-27   A successful ping demonstrating that the local computer can communicate with server1

IMPORTANT   ICMP, firewalls, and Ping

The Ping, Tracert, and Pathping utilities all rely on a Layer 3 messaging protocol named Internet Control Message Protocol (ICMP). ICMP is, however, blocked by default by Windows Firewall in Windows Vista and Windows Server 2008, and it is also blocked by some routers and stand-alone firewalls. Consequently, to perform adequate troubleshooting of network connectivity, you need to ensure that ICMP is not blocked by the remote host. To enable a firewall exception for ICMP in Windows Vista and Windows Server 2008, enable File Sharing in Network and Sharing Center.

- **Tracert**   Tracert is a network utility that you can use to trace a path to a network destination and test the status of each router along the way. For example, if the path from

ServerA to ServerE crosses RouterB, RouterC, and RouterD, you can use Tracert to test whether each of those intermediate routers (as well as the destination ServerE) can respond to ICMP messages. The purpose of this test is to determine the location of any break in connectivity that might lie between the local computer and a remote destination.

To use the Tracert utility, at a command prompt, type **tracert** *remote_host,* where *remote_host* is the name or address of a destination computer, server, or router to which you want to trace a path.

An output of Tracert is shown below. Notice that the -d switch is used to speed up the test by preventing each IP address from being resolved to a name.

```
C:\Users\jcmackin>tracert -d 69.147.114.210

Tracing route to 69.147.114.210 over a maximum of 30 hops

  1      1 ms     <1 ms     <1 ms   192.168.2.1
  2    822 ms    708 ms    659 ms   67.142.148.2
  3    708 ms    649 ms    658 ms   67.142.131.209
  4    632 ms    619 ms    629 ms   67.142.131.254
  5    726 ms    698 ms    619 ms   67.142.128.246
  6    732 ms    679 ms    709 ms   65.46.24.177
  7    713 ms    650 ms    679 ms   207.88.81.245
  8    732 ms    719 ms    719 ms   71.5.170.41
  9    957 ms    739 ms    719 ms   71.5.170.34
 10    734 ms    736 ms    677 ms   64.212.107.85
 11    723 ms    690 ms    862 ms   64.208.110.166
 12    824 ms    849 ms    739 ms   216.115.101.137
 13    781 ms    799 ms    869 ms   216.115.101.152
 14    822 ms    719 ms    678 ms   216.115.108.72
 15    759 ms    709 ms    799 ms   216.115.108.61
 16    724 ms    819 ms   1479 ms   68.142.238.65
 17    775 ms    859 ms    739 ms   69.147.114.210

Trace complete.
```

- **PathPing**   PathPing is similar to Tracert except that PathPing is intended to find links that are causing *intermittent* data loss. PathPing sends packets to each router on the way to a final destination over a period of time and then computes the percentage of packets returned from each hop. Since PathPing shows the degree of packet loss at any given router or link, you can use PathPing to pinpoint which routers or links might be causing network problems.

To use the PathPing utility, at a command prompt type **PathPing** *remote_host,* where *remote_host* is the name or address of a destination computer, server, or router on whose path to which you want to test intermittent data loss.

The following shows a sample PathPing output:

```
D:\>pathping -n testpc1
Tracing route to testpc1 [7.54.1.196]
over a maximum of 30 hops:
0 172.16.87.35
1 172.16.87.218
2 192.168.52.1
3 192.168.80.1
4 7.54.247.14
5 7.54.1.196
Computing statistics for 25 seconds...
Source to Here This Node/Link
Hop RTT Lost/Sent = Pct Lost/Sent = Pct Address
0 172.16.87.35
0/ 100 = 0% |
1 41ms 0/ 100 = 0% 0/ 100 = 0% 172.16.87.218
13/ 100 = 13% |
2 22ms 16/ 100 = 16% 3/ 100 = 3% 192.168.52.1
0/ 100 - 0% |
3 24ms 13/ 100 = 13% 0/ 100 = 0% 192.168.80.1
0/ 100 = 0% |
4 21ms 14/ 100 = 14% 1/ 100 = 1% 7.54.247.14
0/ 100 = 0% |
5 24ms 13/ 100 = 13% 0/ 100 = 0% 7.54.1.196
Trace complete.
```

Notice how the output above first lists the five hops on the path to the specified destination and then computes the percentage of data lost over each of these hops. In this case, PathPing shows that data loss at a rate of 13% is occurring between the local computer (172.16.87.35) and the first hop (172.16.87.218).

■ **Arp**   Arp is the name of both a utility and a protocol. The Address Resolution Protocol (ARP) is used to translate the IPv4 (software) address of a computer or router in broadcast range to the MAC (hardware) address of an actual interface across the network. In other words, the ARP protocol enables a computer to communicate physically with a neighboring computer or router represented by an IPv4 address. The Arp utility performs a related function. You can use it to display and manage a computer's ARP cache, which stores the IPv4-address-to-MAC-address mappings of other computers on the local network.

Because the connection to a computer within broadcast range depends on an accurate IPv4-address-to-MAC-address mapping of that computer in the local ARP cache, the Arp utility can help you fix network problems when an inaccurate mapping is the cause. For example, by displaying the cache with the ***arp -a*** command, you could reveal a problem—for example, with two neighboring virtual machines that have assigned themselves the same virtual MAC address. (This is fairly common.) You could also use the ***arp -d*** command to delete an entry in the ARP cache of a computer or virtual machine whose MAC address has just changed and that you know to be invalid.

In rare cases, you can also the Arp utility to reveal a local hacker's attempt to poison your ARP cache by associating some or all local IPv4 addresses, most notably the local router's IPv4 address, with the hacker's own MAC address. This is a well-known technique that allows the hacker to secretly route your network connections through the hacker's computer.

An example of a poisoned ARP cache is shown in Figure 1-28. Notice how the IPv4 addresses 192.168.2.1, 192.168.2.52, and 192.168.2.53 are all associated with the same MAC address. If the hacker's own computer were represented as 192.168.2.52, this ARP cache would enable all connections to 192.168.2.1 and 192.168.2.53 to be intercepted. If 192.168.2.1 represented the IPv4 address of the local router, all Internet communications could be intercepted.

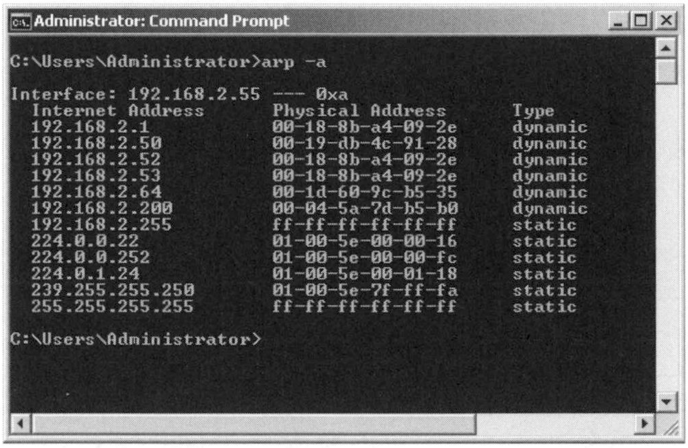

```
Administrator: Command Prompt                                    _ □ ×

C:\Users\Administrator>arp -a

Interface: 192.168.2.55 --- 0xa
  Internet Address      Physical Address      Type
  192.168.2.1           00-18-8b-a4-09-2e     dynamic
  192.168.2.50          00-19-db-4c-91-28     dynamic
  192.168.2.52          00-18-8b-a4-09-2e     dynamic
  192.168.2.53          00-18-8b-a4-09-2e     dynamic
  192.168.2.64          00-1d-60-9c-b5-35     dynamic
  192.168.2.200         00-04-5a-7d-b5-b0     dynamic
  192.168.2.255         ff-ff-ff-ff-ff-ff     static
  224.0.0.22            01-00-5e-00-00-16     static
  224.0.0.252           01-00-5e-00-00-fc     static
  224.0.1.24            01-00-5e-00-01-18     static
  239.255.255.250       01-00-5e-7f-ff-fa     static
  255.255.255.255       ff-ff-ff-ff-ff-ff     static

C:\Users\Administrator>
```

Figure 1-28   A poisoned ARP cache

NOTE   Is a duplicate MAC address listing in the ARP cache always a sign of a problem?

Unless you have assigned two or more IPv4 addresses to a single network adapter somewhere on your local network (which is rarely done but is possible), each IPv4 address in the ARP cache should be associated with a unique physical address.

NOTE   IPv6 prevents Arp cache poisoning

To resolve IP-to-MAC address mappings, IPv6 uses a protocol named Neighbor Discovery (ND) instead of the ARP protocol used by IPv4. For this reason, a nice benefit of an all-IPv6 network is that it prevents the possibility of Arp cache poisoning.

PRACTICE **Configuring TCP/IP Addresses**

In this practice, you configure a static IP address for the local area connections on Dcsrv1, an alternate address for the local area connection on Boston, and finally a static address on Boston by using the command line. Until now these connections have been assigned APIPA addresses. After configuring these addresses, you enable file sharing on both computers and test connectivity with Ping.

This practice assumes that you have performed the computer lab setup as described in the Introduction to this book. On Dscrv1, Local Area Connection must be connected to the private lab network and *Local Area Connection 2 must be disabled*. On Boston, the Local Area Connection must be connected to the same private lab network.

No server roles should be installed on either computer.

▶ **Exercise 1   Verifying Your Current IP Address**

In this exercise, you review the current IP configuration on Dcsrv1.

1. Log on to Dcsrv1 as an administrator.
2. Open a command prompt by clicking Start and then choosing Command Prompt.
3. At the command prompt, type **ipconfig,** and then press Enter. This command is used to show your IP address configuration.

    The output shows your network connections. Below "Ethernet adapter Local Area Connection" and next to Autoconfiguration IPv4 Address, you will see the address of 169.254.y.z, where y and z refer to the host ID currently assigned to that connection. The subnet mask is the default of 255.255.0.0. Because a default Windows Server 2008 installation specifies that the IP address of the host is assigned automatically, in the absence of a DHCP server, the host uses an APIPA address (assuming no alternate configuration has been defined). Note also that the same connection has been assigned a link-local IPv6 address beginning with fe80::. This address is the IPv6 equivalent of an APIPA address.

    Finally, you will also see tunnel adapter local area connections. These are associated with IPv6 and will be described in more detail in Lesson 3, "Understanding IPv6 Addressing."

▶ **Exercise 2   Configuring a Manual Address**

In this exercise, you assign a static IP address to the Local Area Connection on Dcsrv1. A static IP address is needed for computers that will later host network infrastructure services such as DNS or DHCP.

1. While you are still logged on to Dcsrv1 as an administrator, at the command prompt, type **ncpa.cpl.**

2. In the Network Connections window, right-click Local Area Connection, and then choose Properties. This connection faces the private lab network.

3. In the Local Area Connections Properties dialog box, in the This Connection Uses The Following Items area, double-click Internet Protocol Version 4 (TCP/IPv4).

4. In the General tab of the Internet Protocol Version 4 (TCP/IPv4) Properties dialog box, select Use The Following IP Address.

5. In the IP Address text box, type **192.168.0.1.**

6. Select the Subnet Mask text box to place your cursor inside it. The subnet mask 255.255.255.0 appears in the Subnet Mask text box. Click OK.

7. In the Local Area Connection Properties dialog box, click OK.

8. At the command prompt, type **ipconfig**.

   You will see the new static IPv4 address associated with the Local Area Connection.

▶ **Exercise 3   Defining an Alternate Configuration**

In this exercise, you alter the IP configuration on Boston so that in the absence of a DHCP server on the private lab network, Boston assigns the addresss 192.168.0.200 to the Local Area Connection.

1. Log on to Boston as an administrator.

2. In Server Manager, click View Network Connections.

3. In Network Connections, open the properties of the Local Area Connection.

4. In the Local Area Connection Properties dialog box, open the properties of Internet Protocol Version 4 (TCP/IPv4).

   In the General tab of the Internet Protocol (TCP/IP) Properties dialog box, notice that Obtain An IP Address Automatically and Obtain DNS Server Address Automatically are selected.

5. Click the Alternate Configuration tab.

   Automatic Private IP Address is selected. Because no DHCP server is available and this setting is enabled by default, Boston has automatically assigned the Local Area Connection an APIPA address.

6. Select User Configured.

7. In the IP Address text box, type **192.168.0.200**.

8. Click the Subnet Mask text box to place the cursor inside it. The default subnet mask of 255.255.255.0 appears in the Subnet Mask text box. Leave this entry as the default subnet mask.

   You have just defined an alternate IP address configuration of 192.168.0.200/24 for Boston. You can use this configuration until you configure a DHCP server for your network.

9. Click OK.

10. In the Local Area Connection Properties dialog box, click OK.

11. Open a command prompt and type **ipconfig /all**.

    In the Ipconfig output, will see the new alternate address assigned to Boston. Note also that Autoconfiguration Enabled is set to Yes.

▶ **Exercise 4   Configuring a Static IPv4 Address from a Command Prompt**

In the following exercise, you use the command prompt to configure for Boston a static IPv4 address of 192.168.0.2 and a subnet mask of 255.255.255.0.

1. While you are logged on to Boston as an administrator, open an elevated command prompt. (This step is not necessary if you are logged on with the account named Administrator. You can open an elevated command prompt by clicking Start, right-clicking Command Prompt, and then choosing Run As Administrator.)

2. At the command prompt, type the following:

   ```
   netsh interface ip set address "local area connection" static 192.168.0.2 255.255.255.0
   ```

3. At the command prompt, type **ipconfig**.

   The Ipconfig output reveals the new IPv4 address.

▶ **Exercise 5   Enabling File Sharing**

In Windows Server 2008, you need to enable file sharing before the local computer will respond to pings. For this reason, you now perform this step in Network and Sharing Center on both Dcsrv1 and Boston.

1. While you are logged on to Dcsrv1 as an administrator, open Network and Sharing Center by right-clicking the network icon in the Notification Area and then choosing Network And Sharing Center. (The Notification Area is the area on the right side of the Taskbar.)

2. In Network and Sharing Center, in the Sharing And Discovery area, click the button marked Off that is next to File Sharing.

3. Select the option to turn on file sharing, and then click Apply.

   A dialog box appears asking whether you want to turn on file sharing for all public networks.

4. Click Yes, Turn On File Sharing For All Public Networks.

   Note that this option is only recommended for test networks.

5. Repeat steps 1 through 4 on Boston.

▶ **Exercise 6   Verifying the Connection**

In this exercise, you verify that the two computers can now communicate over the private lab network.

1. While you are logged on to Boston as Administrator, open a command prompt.
2. At the command prompt, type ping **192.168.0.1**.

   The output confirms that Dcsrv1 and Boston are communicating over IP.
3. Log off both computers.

Lesson Summary

- Transmission Control Protocol/Internet Protocol (TCP/IP) defines a four-layered architecture, including the Network Interface or Data Link Layer, the Internet or Network Layer, the Transport Layer, and the Application Layer. Because of their position within the OSI networking model, these layers are also known as Layer 2, Layer 3, Layer 4, and Layer 7, respectively.

- Network and Sharing Center is the main network configuration tool in Windows Server 2008. You can use the Network and Sharing Center to perform functions such as setting the network location, viewing the network map, configuring Network Discovery, configuring file and printer sharing, and viewing the status of network connections.

- By using the properties of a network connection, you can configure a computer with a static address or with an automatically configured address. Automatically configured addresses are obtained from a DHCP server if one is available.

- When a connection is configured to obtain an address automatically and no DHCP server is available, that connection by default will assign itself an address in the form 169.254.x.y. You can also define an alternate configuration that the connection will assign itself in the absence of a DHCP server.

- Certain basic TCP/IP utilities are used to test and troubleshoot network connectivity. These utilities include Ipconfig, Ping, Tracert, PathPing, and Arp.

Lesson Review

The following questions are intended to reinforce key information presented in this lesson. The questions are also available on the companion CD if you prefer to review them in electronic form.

NOTE   Answers

Answers to these questions and explanations of why each answer choice is correct or incorrect are located in the "Answers" section at the end of the book.

---

1. A user in your organization complains that she cannot connect to any network resources. You run the *Ipconfig* command on her computer and find that the address assigned to the Local Area Connection is 169.254.232.21.

    Which of the following commands should you type first?

    A. Ipconfig /renew

    B. ping 169.254.232.21

    C. tracert 169.254.232.21

    D. Arp -a

2. Which of the following address types is best suited for a DNS server?

    A. DHCP-assigned address

    B. APIPA address

    C. Alternate configuration address

    D. Manual address

Lesson 2: Understanding IP Version 4 (IPv4) Addressing

IPv4 is by far the most popular networking protocol in use. Although connecting computers to an established IPv4 network is straightforward (and often entirely automatic), to implement, configure, and troubleshoot IPv4, you need to understand basic concepts about IPv4 addressing.

After this lesson, you will be able to:

- Understand the structure of an IPv4 address, including the network ID and host ID.
- Understand the function of a subnet mask.
- Convert a subnet mask between its dotted-decimal and slash notations.
- Convert an 8-bit value between binary and decimal notations.
- Understand the function of a default gateway in IP routing.
- Understand and recognize the private IPv4 address ranges.
- Understand the concept of an address block.
- Determine the number of addresses in a given address block.
- Determine the address block size needed for a given number of addresses.
- Understand the benefits of subnetting.

Estimated lesson time: 180 minutes

The Structure of IPv4 Addresses

IPv4 addresses are 32 bits in length and are composed of 4 *octets* of 8 bits apiece. The usual representation of an IPv4 address is in *dotted-decimal* notation, with each of the four numbers— for example, 192.168.23.245—representing an octet separated from another by a period (dot). This common dotted-decimal notation, however, is only ever displayed for human benefit. Computers actually read IPv4 addresses in their native 32-bit binary notation such as

11000000 10101000 00010111 11110101

This point becomes important if you want to understand how IPv4 works.

IPv4 is an addressing system—a system to help *find* devices—and not merely an identification system. Every IPv4 address on a network must be unique, but an address cannot be assigned randomly to a networked device because that would provide no way of finding the device. The way that IPv4 achieves both uniqueness and findability is by dividing addresses into two parts: the *network ID* and the *host ID*.

Network ID and Host ID

The first part of an IPv4 address is the *network ID*. The job of the network ID is to identify a particular network within a larger IPv4 internetwork (such as the Internet). The last part of an IPv4 address is the *host ID*. The host ID identifies an IPv4 host (a computer, router, or other IPv4 device) within the network defined by the network ID.

NOTE Network ID + Host ID = 32 bits

If n = the number of bits in the network ID and h = the number of bits in the host ID, n + h is equal to 32.

Figure 1-29 shows a sample view of an IPv4 address (131.107.16.200) as it is divided into network ID and host ID sections. The letters w, x, y, and z are often used to designate the four octets within an IPv4 address. In this example, the network ID portion (131.107) is indicated by octets w and x. The host ID portion (16.200) is indicated by octets y and z.

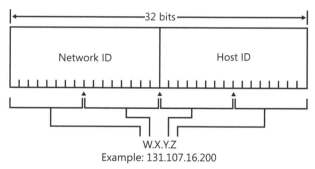

Figure 1-29   Network and host IDs

IPv4 Addresses and ZIP+4 Compared   This system of dividing the IPv4 address into a network ID and a host ID is reminiscent of the "ZIP+4" system used by most post offices in the United States Postal System. This system is used to route and deliver mail to individual post office boxes across the country.

NOTE ZIP+4

For the purposes of our analogy, we will assume that the +4 digits only ever represent individual post office boxes.

Taken together, the 5-digit ZIP code (also known as a postal code) and the 4-digit box number represent a unique 9-digit ZIP+4 address similar in structure and function to the 32-bit IPv4 address. The first part of the ZIP+4 address—the five-digit zip code—represents a findable area, not a unique address. The second part represents a specific 4-digit mailbox within the 5-digit ZIP code area, a mailbox to which the post office represented by the ZIP code has the responsibility to deliver mail.

However, ZIP+4 addresses are much simpler than IPv4 addresses in one respect. When you look at a ZIP+4 address, you know for certain which part of the address represents the post office (the ZIP code) and which part represents the individual mailbox (the +4). The dividing line between them never changes. The first five digits and the last four digits always have the same function.

The tricky thing about IPv4 addresses is that the size of the network ID and the size of the host ID vary. Just by looking at an IPv4 address such as 192.168.23.245, you cannot determine which of the 32 bits are used for the network ID and which are used for the host ID. To do this, you need an additional piece of information. That piece of information is the subnet mask.

Subnet Masks

The subnet mask is used to determine which part of a 32-bit IPv4 address should be considered its network ID. For example, when we write 192.168.23.245/24, the /24 represents the subnet mask and indicates that the first 24 of the 32 bits in that IPv4 address should be considered its network ID. For the IPv4 address 131.107.16.200 shown in Figure 1-29 above, the first 16 bits according to the picture are used for the network ID. Therefore, the appropriate subnet mask to be used by a host assigned that address is /16.

The two subnet masks we have just mentioned—/16 and /24—are relatively easy to interpret. Because their values are divisible by 8, these subnet masks indicate that the network ID is composed of, respectively, the the first two complete octets and the first three complete octets of an IPv4 address. In other words, the network ID of a host assigned the address 131.107.16.200 /16 is 131.107, and the host's network address is therefore 131.107.0.0. The network ID of a host assigned the address 192.168.23.245/24 is 192.168.23, and host's network address is therefore 192.168.23.0. However, subnet masks are not always divisible by 8 and are not always so easy to interpret, as we shall see.

Subnet Mask Notations   We have been discussing subnet masks in slash notation—also known as Classless Inter Domain Routing (CIDR) notation or network prefix notation. Slash notation is a common way of referring to subnet masks both on the 70-642 exam and in the real world. However, subnet masks are represented just as commonly in 32-bit dotted-decimal notation.

In dotted-decimal notation, the subnet mask takes the form of a 32-bit IPv4 address. For example, the subnet mask /16 is represented in dotted-decimal notation as 255.255.0.0, and the subnet mask /24 is represented in dotted-decimal notation as 255.255.255.0.

To translate a subnet mask between slash notation and its dotted-decimal equivalent, you first have to translate the slash notation to binary notation. To begin, take the value after the slash in slash notation—for example, the 16 in /16—and represent it as an equivalent number of ones in binary notation, with a space after each 8 bits or octet.

11111111 11111111

Then, to complete the 32-bit subnet mask in binary notation, add a string of 0s until the values of all 32 bits are represented (again with a space after each 8 bits):

11111111 11111111 00000000 00000000

Finally, convert this binary notation into dotted-decimal notation. Because 11111111 is the binary equivalent of the decimal 255 and 00000000 is the binary equivalent of the decimal 0, you can represent each octet as either 255 or 0. For this reason, /16 is equivalent to 255.255.0.0.

NOTE   How do you convert binary into dotted-decimal?

For information on converting between binary and decimal notations, see the section entitled "Converting between Binary and Decimal Notations" later in this lesson.

IMPORTANT   What happened to address classes?

You might occasionally hear that a /8 address is called *Class A*, a /16 address is called *Class B*, and a /24 address is called *Class C*. These terms refer to an older system of IPv4 routing that is no longer used, even though its vocabulary is sometimes used informally. The 70-642 exam does not use these terms because they are technically defunct.

Subnet Mask Mid-range Values   The subnet masks we have been looking at in dotted-decimal notation have octets whose values are represented as either 255 or 0. This limits our discussion to only three possible subnet masks: /8 (255.0.0.0), /16 (255.255.0.0), and /24 (255.255.255.0). In fact, these are the most common subnet masks used for addresses on the Internet (especially /24 or 255.255.255.0).

However, both on the 70-642 exam and in the real world, you will also encounter subnet masks such as /25 or /22 which, when expressed in dotted-decimal notation, include a midrange value octet such as 128 or 252. This situation arises whenever the length of a network ID (expressed in bits) is not divisible by 8.

For example, Figure 1-30 shows the binary representation of the IPv4 address 192.168.14.222 with a subnet mask of /24 or 255.255.255.0. For this address, the network ID is represented by the first 24 bits (first three octets), and the host ID is represented by the last 8 bits (the last octet).

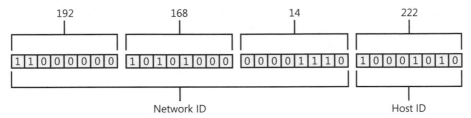

Figure 1-30   An IPv4 address with a /24 subnet mask

Now, consider the same IPv4 address with a 26-bit subnet mask, as shown in Figure 1-31. In this example, the network ID uses the first two bits from the last octet. Although this arrangement is more difficult to visualize in decimal form because the last octet is partially dedicated to the network ID and partially dedicated to the host ID, in binary the network ID is simply a 26-bit number, whereas the host ID is a 6-bit number.

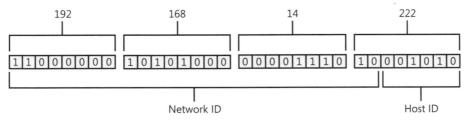

Figure 1-31   The same IPv4 address with a /26 subnet mask

Table 1-1 compares the slash, binary, and dotted-decimal notations for all subnet masks from /8 to /30. These are the only subnet masks you are ever likely to see. However, the subnet masks you will encounter most frequently (both on the 70-642 exam and in the real world) are in the /16 to /28 range.

IMPORTANT   Study this table

This table presents information that most network administrators are expected to understand. Be sure to spend as much time as necessary browsing this table until you are comfortable with subnet mask values and how the three notations relate to one another.

Table 1-1   Subnet Mask Notations Compared

Slash Notation	Binary Notation	Dotted Decimal Notation
/8	11111111 00000000 00000000 00000000	255.0.0.0
/9	11111111 10000000 00000000 00000000	255.128.0.0
/10	11111111 11000000 00000000 00000000	255.192.0.0
/11	11111111 11100000 00000000 00000000	255.224.0.0

Table 1-1   Subnet Mask Notations Compared

Slash Notation	Binary Notation	Dotted Decimal Notation
/12	11111111 11110000 00000000 00000000	255.240.0.0
/13	11111111 11111000 00000000 00000000	255.248.0.0
/14	11111111 11111100 00000000 00000000	255.252.0.0
/15	11111111 11111110 00000000 00000000	255.254.0.0
/16	11111111 11111111 00000000 00000000	255.255.0.0
/17	11111111 11111111 10000000 00000000	255.255.128.0
/18	11111111 11111111 11000000 00000000	255.255.192.0
/19	11111111 11111111 11100000 00000000	255.255.224.0
/20	11111111 11111111 11110000 00000000	255.255.240.0
/21	11111111 11111111 11111000 00000000	255.255.248.0
/22	11111111 11111111 11111100 00000000	255.255.252.0
/23	11111111 11111111 11111110 00000000	255.255.254.0
/24	11111111 11111111 11111111 00000000	255.255.255.0
/25	11111111 11111111 11111111 10000000	255.255.255.128
/26	11111111 11111111 11111111 11000000	255.255.255.192
/27	11111111 11111111 11111111 11100000	255.255.255.224
/28	11111111 11111111 11111111 11110000	255.255.255.240
/29	11111111 11111111 11111111 11111000	255.255.255.248
/30	11111111 11111111 11111111 11111100	255.255.255.252

Subnet Mask Octet Values   If you want to understand IPv4 addressing, you need to memorize the sequence of nine specific values that can appear in a subnet mask octet. Learning these values and their ordered sequence will help you in real-world situations as well as on the 70-642 exam, especially when you need to determine the size of an existing or planned network. To a large degree, in fact, the ability to perform such calculations in one's head is expected of a good network administrator. (This process is described later in this lesson in the section entitled "Determining the Number of Addresses Per Address Block.")

Use Table 1-2 below to help you memorize the values. Begin by covering the top row of the table. After you can recite without hesitation the decimal value associated with any number of 1-bits or binary value chosen at random from the bottom two rows, proceed to cover up the bottom two rows. When you can recite without hesitation the number of 1-bits associated with any decimal value chosen at random from the top row, proceed to memorize the sequence of decimal values from left to right and right to left.

Subnet Mask Octet Values

Decimal value	0	128	192	224	240	248	252	254	255
# of 1-bits	0	1	2	3	4	5	6	7	8
Binary value	00000000	10000000	11000000	11100000	11110000	11111000	11111100	1111110	11111111

You should know these sequences forward and backward so well that you can look at a number such as 192 and know that when moving from left to right, this value is the second after 0 and is therefore *2 bits removed to the right from* the 0 octet value. In the same way, you need to be able to look at 248 and know that when moving from right to left, it is three places before 255 and is therefore *three bits removed to the left from 255.*

Converting Between Binary and Decimal Notations

It's not often that you need to convert between base-two and base-ten notations, and if you do, you could use a scientific calculator. However, when you don't have access to a calculator, it's good to know how to perform these conversions manually. It will certainly also help you understand the logic of IP addressing.

The key to understanding binary notation is to understand the value of each bit place. As with our base ten system, in which each place holds different values such as ones, tens, hundreds, and so on, a base two system holds potential values in each bit place that increase from right to left.

Table 1-3 shows the scientific and decimal notation associated with each bit place within a binary octet. Notice that, as you move from right to left and begin with the eighth bit's potential value of 1, each successive bit represents double the potential value of the previous bit, with a maximum value of 128 for the leftmost bit. Knowing this pattern allows you to recall easily the potential value of each bit place.

Table 1-3   Potential Values in a Binary Octet

Bit Place	1st Bit	2nd Bit	3rd Bit	4th Bit	5th Bit	6th Bit	7th Bit	8th Bit
Scientific notation	2^7	2^6	2^5	2^4	2^3	2^2	2^1	2^0
Decimal notation	128	64	32	16	8	4	2	1

Note that these numbers represent only the values that are held when the bit places contain a "1." When an octet contains a 0 in any bit place, the value of the bit is null. For example, if the first (leftmost) bit place is filled with a bit value of 1, the equivalent decimal value is 128. Where the bit value is 0, the equivalent decimal value is 0 as well. If all the bit places in an octet are filled with ones (1), the equivalent decimal value is 255. If all the bit places are filled with zeroes (0), the equivalent decimal value is 0.

Binary-to-Decimal Conversion Example   The following binary string represents an octet that could be used in an IPv4 address:

10000011

To understand the decimal equivalent of this binary octet, draw a simple conversion table, such as the one below, in which to enter the bit values of the octet:

128	64	32	16	8	4	2	1
1	0	0	0	0	0	1	1

By then using this table as a reference, you can perform simple addition of each bit place's decimal equivalent value to find the decimal sum for this octet string, as follows:

128 + 2 + 1 = 131

Because the sum is 131, the first octet of the example IPv4 address is expressed as 131 in decimal form.

Decimal-to-Binary Conversion Example   You convert an octet from decimal to binary form by drawing the conversion chart and then adding a 1 in the octet's bit places from left to right until the desired target decimal value is achieved. If, by adding a 1, your total would exceed the target decimal value, simply note a 0 in that bit place instead and move to the next bit place. There is always exactly one combination of 1s and 0s of that will yield the target value.

For example, suppose you want to convert the octet value 209 into binary form. First draw the conversion table on scratch paper, as shown below:

128	64	32	16	8	4	2	1

Next, consider the potential value of the first (leftmost) bit place. Is 128 less than 209? Because it is, you should write a 1 beneath the 128 on your scratch paper and then write a 128 off to the side to keep tally of the running subtotal.

128	64	32	16	8	4	2	1	Subtotal
1								128

Move to the next potential value. Is 128+64 less than 209? The sum of these values is only 192, so again, you should write a 1 beneath the 64 and then a 64 to your running subtotal.

128	64	32	16	8	4	2	1	Subtotal
1	1							128
								+64
								=192

The next potential value is 32, but if you were to add a 1 here, you would achieve a subtotal of 224. This exceeds the target total of 209, so you must place a zero in the third bit place of the octet and not add anything to your running subtotal.

128	64	32	16	8	4	2	1	Subtotal
1	1	0						128
								+64
								=192

Next, the fourth bit potential value is 16; adding this value to 192 results in a subtotal of 208. Is 208 less than 209? Because it is, you should add a 1 beneath the 16 and a 16 to your running subtotal.

128	64	32	16	8	4	2	1	Subtotal
1	1	0	1					128
								64
								+16
								=208

Because you only need to add a value of 1 to achieve the target value of 209, placing a 1 in the eighth bit place will complete the translation of the octet.

128	64	32	16	8	4	2	1	Subtotal
1	1	0	1	0	0	0	1	128
								64
								16
								+1
								=209

The first octet is therefore written as follows in binary notation:

11010001

Understanding Routing and Default Gateways

The calculation of the network ID by using the subnet mask is a vital step in IPv4 communication because the network ID essentially tells a computer how to send an IPv4 packet toward a destination. When a computer on a network needs to send a packet to a remote address, the computer compares its own network ID to that of the destination network ID specified in the IPv4 packet. (To determine these network IDs, the computer always uses its locally configured subnet mask.) If the two network IDs match, the message is determined to be local and is broadcast to the local subnet. If the two network IDs do not match, the computer sends the packet to an address known as the default gateway. The router found at this default gateway address then forwards the IPv4 datagram in a manner determined by its routing tables.

Figure 1-32 illustrates this process of IP routing. In the figure, a computer whose address is 192.168.100.5/24 needs to send an IP packet destined for the address 192.168.1.10. Because the network IDs of the two addresses do not match, the computer sends the packet to the router specified by the default gateway address. This router consults its routing tables and sends the packet to the router connected to the 192.168.1.0 network. When the router connected to this network receives the packet, the router broadcasts the packet over the local subnet. The destination computer at the address 192.168.1.10 responds to the broadcast and receives the packet for internal processing.

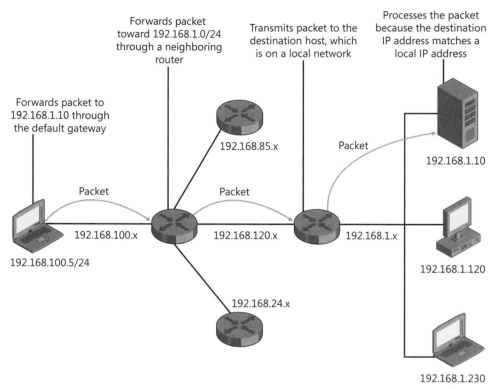

Figure 1-32   Routing an IP packet over an internetwork

Remember also these essential points about routing and default gateways:

■ A default gateway must share the same network ID and be located within the same broadcast domain as the hosts it is serving.

■ If a host has no default gateway setting configured, that host will be unable to connect to the Internet or to any computers beyond broadcast range. For example, a private internal server that occasionally needs to download content from the Internet needs to have a default gateway configured.

■ Leaving the default gateway setting unconfigured on a host prevents access to that host from all points beyond the local subnet. In certain situations, therefore, you might in fact want to leave the default gateway setting unconfigured for security reasons.

Understanding IPv4 Address Ranges

You can divide IPv4 unicast addresses into Public, Private, and APIPA ranges. Whereas APIPA addresses are only used for temporary addresses or isolated computers, public and private ranges are divided into blocks that can be assigned to entire networks. These public and private ranges, along with the concept of address blocks in general, are described in the following section.

Using Public IPv4 Addresses

Every IPv4 address on the public Internet is unique. To allow networks to obtain unique addresses for the Internet, the Internet Assigned Numbers Authority (IANA) divides up the nonreserved portion of the IPv4 address space and delegates responsibility for address allocation to a number of regional registries throughout the world. These registries include Asia-Pacific Network Information Center (APNIC), American Registry for Internet Numbers (ARIN), and Réseaux IP Européens Network Coordination Centre (RIPE NCC). The regional registries then allocate *blocks* of addresses to a small number of large Internet service providers (ISPs) that then assign smaller blocks to customers and smaller ISPs.

Using Private IPv4 Addresses

The IANA has also reserved a certain number of IPv4 addresses that are never used on the global Internet. These private IPv4 addresses are used for hosts that require IPv4 connectivity but that do not need to be seen on the public network. For example, a user connecting computers in a home TCP/IPv4 network does not need to assign a public IPv4 address to each host. The user can instead take advantage of the address ranges shown in Table 1-4 to provide addresses for hosts on the network.

Table 1-4   Private Address Ranges

Starting Address	Ending Address
10.0.0.0	10.255.255.254
172.16.0.0	172.31.255.254
192.168.0.0	192.168.255.254

Hosts addressed with a private IPv4 address can connect to the Internet through a server or router performing Network Address Translation (NAT). The router performing NAT can be a Windows Server 2008 computer or a dedicated routing device. Windows Server 2008 and Windows Vista also include the Internet Connection Sharing (ICS) feature, which provides simplified NAT services to clients in a private network.

Exam Tip   You need to be able to understand and recognize the private IP ranges for the exam.

Understanding Address Blocks and Subnets

Most organizations use a combination of public and private addresses. Often, public addresses are assigned to publicly available servers and private addresses are assigned to client computers, but there are many exceptions. What is certain is that every organization that wants to communicate on the Internet must have at least one public address. This public address can then be leveraged by many clients through NAT and private address ranges.

Typically, your ISP assigns you one public IPv4 address for each computer directly connected to the Internet. Although small organizations might be able to get by with only a single public IPv4 address, many organizations need far more than that. Organizations needing more than one public address purchase those addresses from their ISP as a block.

An *address block* is the complete group of individual IP addresses that shares any single network ID. For example, an organization may purchase from an ISP a /24 address block with network ID 206.73.118. The range of addresses associated with this address block would thus be 206.73.118.0 – 206.73.118.255.

NOTE   What is address space?

The range of addresses associated with a given address block is also known as the block's *address space*.

It is essential to understand that the addresses within an address block comprise a single network, and unless the network is subnetted—a possibility we will consider later in this lesson—that address block will serve a *single broadcast domain* with a single router or way out of the network. The *default gateway* is the address within the same broadcast domain and assigned to that router.

Stated another way, an address block by default is designed to serve a single *subnet*. A subnet is a group of hosts within a single broadcast domain that share the same network ID and the same default gateway address.

Figure 1-33 displays a network served by the address block 206.73.118.0/24.

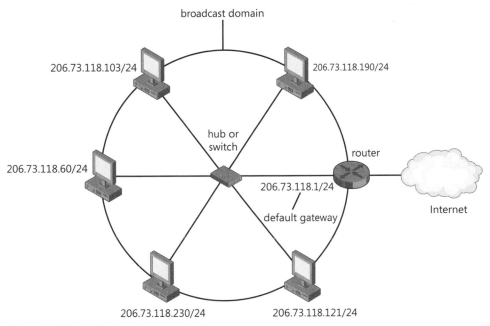

Figure 1-33   A single-subnet network

NOTE   **What's the difference between a network and a subnet?**

The terms network and subnet are often used interchangeably. The difference between them is that a subnet always refers to a single broadcast domain that is undivided. The term network, meanwhile, can refer to a single subnet or a group of interconnected subnets.

Determining the Number of Addresses Per Address Block

If your company purchases a block of addresses from an ISP, the size of that address block will typically be referred to by its subnet mask. To understand this terminology, then, you need to know how to translate the value of a subnet mask into a specific number of addresses.

To determine the number of addresses in any block, you can start with a single point of memorization: A /24 network (subnet mask 255.255.255.0) always contains 256 addresses. From this point you can determine the number of addresses in a network simply by halving or doubling 256 as the string of one-bits in the subnet mask is moved to the right or to the left of /24. For example, if a /24 network has 256 addresses, a /25 network (subnet mask 255.255.255.128) must have 128 addresses (half of 256). Continuing the trend, a /26 network must have 64 addresses (half that of /25). Moving in the other direction, if a /24 network has 256 addresses, a /23 network (subnet mask 255.255.254.0) must have 512 (double 256) and a /22 must have 1024 (double that of /23).

Suppose that you need to determine the size of a /27 subnet (that is, the size of a subnet whose subnet mask is 255.255.255.224). You would start as always with the knowledge that /24 = 256, and then, seeing that the subnet mask of /27 is three bits removed to the right from /24, you would merely halve 256 three times in a row to yield 128, then 64, and finally 32. Therefore, a /27 network must have 32 addresses per subnet.

Now suppose that you need to determine the size of a network with a subnet mask of 255.255.248.0. If you have memorized the sequence of the subnet mask octet values, you will see that this subnet mask is three bits removed to the left from 255.255.255.0. This means that you should double 256 three times in a row to yield 512, 1024, and finally 2048. Therefore, a network with a subnet mask of 255.255.248.0 must have 2048 addresses.

Finally, note that when you are given a subnet mask between 255.255.255.0 and 255.255.255.255, you have another option for determining subnet size that you might find even easier than the halving method: simply subtract the value of the final octet from 256. For example, if you need to determine the size of a network whose subnet mask is given as 255.255.255.240, you could simply perform the calculation 256 − 240 = 16. Therefore, an address block with a subnet mask of 255.255.255.240 includes 16 possible addresses. Note that the difference will always equal a power of two (specifically, 1, 2, 4, 8, 16, 32, 64, or 128).

Table 1-5 presents a list of the nine most common subnet sizes. Use the list to help you practice using the halving and doubling technique for determining subnet sizes.

Exam Tip   Expect to see several questions on the 70-642 exam in which you are given a subnet mask value and need to determine the size of a network. The subnet mask might be given in either the dotted-decimal or slash notation form. To answer these questions correctly, use the halving-and-doubling or the subtract-from-256 method.

Quick Check
  ■ Does an address block get bigger or smaller when its subnet mask is lengthened?
Quick Check Answer
  ■ Smaller

Table 1-5   Common Address Blocks Sizes

Slash Notation	Dotted-decimal Notation	Addresses per Block
/20	255.255.240.0	5096
/21	255.255.248.0	2048
/22	255.255.252.0	1024
/23	255.255.254.0	512
/24	**255.255.255.0**	**256**
/25	255.255.255.128	128
/26	255.255.255.192	64
/27	255.255.255.224	32
/28	255.255.255.240	16

Determining Host Capacity per Block   The host capacity of an address block is the number of addresses that can be assigned to computers, routers, and other devices. In every address block assigned to a single broadcast domain and subnet, exactly two addresses are reserved for special use: the all-zeroes host ID, which is reserved for the entire subnet, and the all-ones host ID, which is reserved for the broadcast address of the subnet. This means that the host capacity of an undivided address block is always two fewer than the number of addresses in that network.

For example, the network 192.168.10.0/24 has 256 addresses. The specific address 192.168.10.0 is reserved for the network address, and 192.168.10.255 is reserved for the network broadcast address. This leaves 254 addresses that can be assigned to network hosts.

Determining Block Size Requirements

If you are designing a network for a given number of computers, you might have to determine an appropriate subnet mask for that network. For example, if you are building a new departmental local area network (LAN) with 20 computers that will be connected to the corporate network, you need to plan for that LAN by requesting a /27 or larger address block from a network engineer in charge of addressing in your company. (This is because a /27 network can accommodate 32 addresses and 30 computers.) The network engineer can then assign you a block such as 10.25.0.224/27 within a larger address space, such as 10.0.0.0 /8 used by the corporate network.

To determine block size requirements in terms of a subnet mask, first determine the number of addresses needed by adding two to the number of computers. Then, you can use the halving-and-doubling technique to find the smallest address block that can accommodate your network requirements.

For example, if you are planning a network with 15 computers, you need 17 addresses. Using the halving technique, you know that a /24 network provides 256 addresses, a /25 network provides 128 addresses, and so on. If you continue counting in this fashion, you will determine that a /27 network is the smallest network size that can provide the 17 addresses you need. To help you perform this calculation, you can count on your fingers, use a scratch pad, or just memorize the values in Table 1-5.

If you need to express the subnet mask in dotted-decimal notation and the required block size is less than 256, you also have the option of using the subtract-from-256 method. To use this method, subtract targeted subnet mask octet values from 256 to find the smallest subnet mask that can meet your address space requirements. For example, if you need to obtain a block of five addresses, you can perform the calculations 256 – 252=4 (too small) and 256 – 248=8 (large enough). This calculation thus determines that a subnet mask of 255.255.255.248 defines a network large enough to accommodate your needs. To help you perform this calculation, you should use a scratch pad.

Exam Tip   Expect to see more than one question on the 70-642 exam in which you are given a specific number of computers and need to determine a subnet mask that will accommodate those computers. The answer choices might present subnet masks in either dotted-decimal or slash notation. Note that when the answer choices present subnet masks between 255.255.255.0 and 255.255.255.255, it is easy to use the subtract-from-256 method. Just take the value of the last octet in each answer choice and subtract it from 256; this will determine the address block size for that answer choice.

What Is Subnetting?

Subnetting refers to the practice of logically subdividing a network address space by extending the string of 1-bits used in the subnet mask of a network. This extension enables you to create multiple subnets or broadcast domains within the original network address space.

For example, let's assume that you have purchased from your ISP the address block 131.107.0.0 /16 for use within your organization. Externally, the ISP then uses the /16 (255.255.0.0) subnet mask on its routers to forward to your organization IPv4 packets that have been addressed to *131.107.y.z*.

Let us then assume in a first scenario that within your organization you configure the subnet mask at its original 255.255.0.0 value on all internal hosts. In this case, all IPv4 addresses within the address space, such as 131.107.1.11 and 131.107.2.11, for example, are logically seen by hosts to share the same network ID (131.107) and to belong to the same subnet. All hosts within this address space therefore attempt to communicate with one another by means of a broadcast. The configuration in this first scenario requires that internal to the network, only devices such as hubs, switches, and wireless bridges that do not block broadcasts can be used.

However, if in another scenario you decide to alter the subnet mask used within your organization to /24 or 255.255.255.0, internal hosts will read the addresses 131.107.1.11 and 131.107.2.11 as having different network IDs (131.107.1 vs. 131.107.2) and consider these addresses as belonging to different subnets. Whenever a host then attempts to send an IPv4 datagram to a host on another subnet, it sends the datagram to its default gateway, at which address a router is responsible for forwarding the packet toward its destination.

For example, to communicate with each other, the hosts assigned the addresses 131.107.1.11/ 24 and 131.107.2.11/24 send IPv4 packets to their respective default gateways, an address which must lie within the same broadcast domain. The router owning the default gateway address is then responsible for routing the IP packet toward the destination subnet. Hosts external to the organization continue to use the /16 subnet mask to communicate with hosts within the network.

Figure 1-34 and Figure 1-35 illustrate these two possible versions of the network.

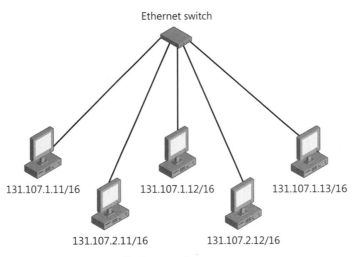

Figure 1-34   A /16 address space not subnetted

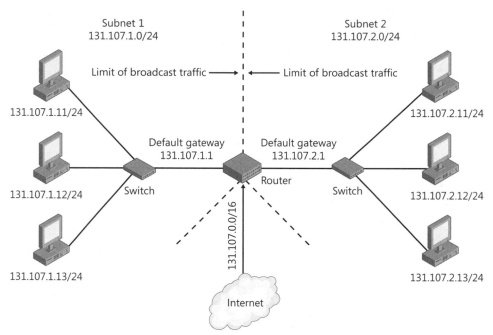

Figure 1-35   Subnetted /16 address space

Whereas the original /16 network address space in Figure 1-34 consisted of a single subnet including up to 65,534 (2^{16} – 2) hosts, the new subnet mask configured in Figure 1-35 allows you to subdivide this original space into 256 (2^8) subnets with as many as 254 (2^8 – 2) hosts each.

Advantages of Subnetting

Subnetting is often used to accommodate a divided physical topology or to restrict broadcast traffic on a network. Other advantages of subnetting include improved security (by restricting unauthorized traffic behind routers) and simplified administration (by delegating control of subnets to other departments or administrators).

Accommodating Physical Topology

Suppose you are designing a campus network with 200 hosts spread over four buildings—Voter Hall, Twilight Hall, Monroe Hall, and Sunderland Hall. You want each of these four buildings to include 50 hosts. If your ISP has allocated to you the /24 network 208.147.66.0, you can use the addresses 208.147.66.1 – 208.147.66.254 for your 200 hosts. However, if these hosts are distributed among four physically separate locations, the distances among them might be too great to allow the hosts to communicate with one another by means of a local network broadcast. By extending the subnet mask to /26 and borrowing two bits from the host ID portion of your address space, you can divide the network into four logical subnets. You can then use a router in a central location to connect the four physical networks. Figure 1-36 illustrates this scenario.

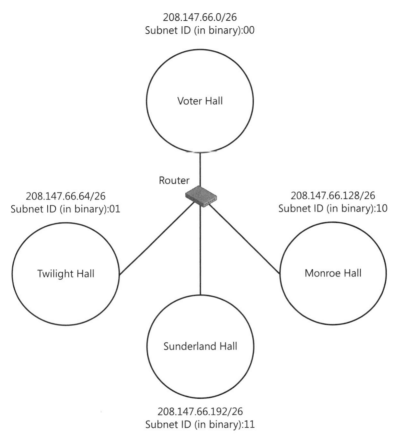

Figure 1-36 Subnetting in a divided physical topology

Restricting Broadcast Traffic

A *broadcast* is a network message sent from a single computer and propagated to all other devices on the same physical network segment. Broadcasts are resource-intensive because they use up network bandwidth and request the attention of every network adapter and processor on the LAN.

Routers block broadcasts and protect networks from becoming overburdened with unnecessary traffic. Because routers also define the logical limits of subnets, subnetting a network allows you to limit the propagation of broadcast traffic within that network.

NOTE   VLANs are an alternative to subnetting

As a means to restrict broadcast traffic in large networks, virtual LAN (VLAN) switches are becoming an increasingly popular alternative to subnetting. Through VLAN software that integrates all the VLAN switches on the network, you can design broadcast domains in any manner, independent of the network's physical topology.

The Subnet ID

Every 32-bit IPv4 address consists of a host ID and a network ID. When you obtain an address block from your ISP (or from your central network administrator in a multibranch network), that address block contains a single network ID that cannot be changed. In other words, if you are given a /16 network, for example, the values of the first 16 bits of your address block are not configurable. It is only the remaining portion—the portion reserved for the host ID—that represents your configurable address space.

When you decide to subnet your network, you are essentially taking some of your configurable address space from the host ID and moving it to the network ID, as shown in Figure 1-37. This string of bits you use to extend your network ID internally within your organization (relative to the original address block) is known as the subnet ID.

The example provided in Figure 1-37 is easy to visualize and understand because both the original and modified subnet masks (/16 and /24) are divisible by 8. However, this is not always the case. For example, you might be granted a /23 address block whose address space you decide to subnet with a /26 subnet mask.

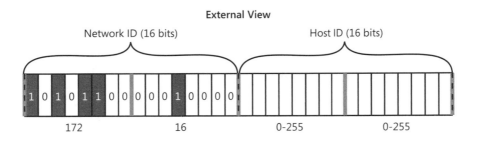

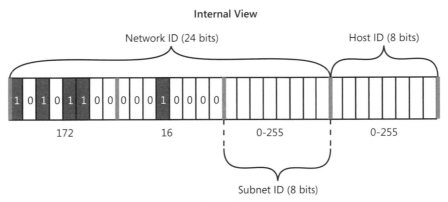

Figure 1-37   The Subnet ID is taken from the Host ID

Determining the Number of Subnets

It is sometimes necessary to determine how many logical subnets have been created by a given subnet mask. To determine the number of subnets in a given network, use the formula

$$s = 2^b$$

where s = the number of subnets and b = the number of bits in the subnet ID. To calculate the number of bits of the subnet ID, use the following formula:

$$b = n_{int} - n_{ext}$$

where n_{int} is the length (in bits) of the network ID used internally within the organization, and n_{ext} is the length of the original network ID assigned externally to the entire address block.

Here is an example. If you work in a large organization, a central network engineer at the office headquarters might grant you the 10.10.100.0/24 address block for use within your branch office. In this scenario, then, your n_{ext} = 24. If you decide to modify the subnet mask internally to /27, your n_{int} = 27. Therefore, b = 27-24 = 3, and s = 2^3 = 8. Therefore, by changing the subnet mask internally from /24 to /27 (255.255.255.224), you generate eight subnets.

In this example, calculating the number of subnets available is easy because we have been given the external and internal subnet mask values in slash notation. If you are given the subnet mask values in dotted-decimal notation, your best bet is to first translate those subnet masks to slash notation.

For example, if you have purchased a 255.255.252.0 address block from your ISP, you might decide to subnet the address space by using a subnet mask of 255.255.255.0 internally. Because 255.255.252.0 =/22 and 255.255.255.0 =/24, b = 24 − 22 = 2 and s= 2^2 = 4. Therefore, by changing the subnet mask internally from 255.255.252.0 to 255.255.255.0, you generate four subnets.

Using Variable-Length Subnet Masks (VLSMs)

It is possible to configure subnet masks so that one subnet mask is used externally and *multiple subnet masks* are used internally. Doing this can allow you to use your network address space more efficiently.

For example, if your /24 address block needs one subnet to accommodate 100 computers, a second subnet to accommodate 50 computers, and a third subnet to accommodate 20 computers, this arrangement cannot be designed with traditional subnet mask options. As Table 1-6 shows, any single default mask fails to accommodate either enough subnets or enough hosts per subnet to meet all your network needs.

Table 1-6   Traditional Options for Subnetting a /24 Address Block

Network Address	Subnets	Hosts per Subnet
Internal subnet mask: 255.255.255.0	1	254
Internal subnet mask: 255.255.255.128	2	126
Internal subnet mask: 255.255.255.192	4	62
Internal subnet mask: 255.255.255.224	8	30

In situations such as these, you can assign different subnet masks to different subnets. This option will allow you to accommodate your specific network needs without having to acquire new address space from your provider.

Figure 1-38 illustrates how you can use subnet masks of various lengths to accommodate three subnets of 100, 50, and 20 hosts, respectively. This particular network configuration will allow for up to four more subnets to be added later.

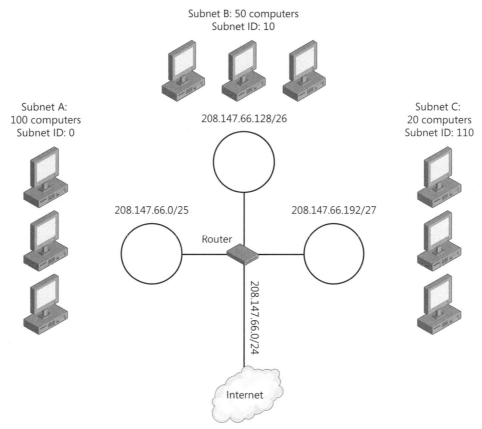

Figure 1-38   Using variable-length subnet masks for flexible subnetting

When you use VLSMs to divide your network into subnets of varying sizes, the address block is divided up a specific way. If you have a /22 network, for example, you can use VLSMs to divide the network into one /23 network, one /24 network, one /25 network, and so on. If, on the other hand, you have a /24 network as in the example presented in Table 1-7, you can use VLSMs to divide it up into one /25 network, one /26 network, one /27 network, and so on.

Also, note that whenever you use VLSMs, a *specific pattern* of subnet IDs composed of 1s and a single trailing 0 must be used. The trailing 0 in each subnet ID prevents the address space in each subnet from overlapping with the address space in other subnets. When the subnet IDs with VLSMs are fixed in the specific pattern shown in Table 1-7, subnets do not overlap, and the addresses can be interpreted unambiguously.

Table 1-7   Variable-length Subnet IDs

Subnet Number	Subnet ID (Binary)	Subnet Mask	Hosts per Subnet	Example Subnet Address
1	0	255.255.255.128	126	208.147.66.0/25
2	10	255.255.255.192	62	208.147.66.128/26
3	110	255.255.255.224	30	208.147.66.192/27
4	1110	255.255.255.240	14	208.147.66.224/28
5	11110	255.255.255.248	6	208.147.66.240/29
6	111110	255.255.255.252	2	208.147.66.248/30
7	111111	255.255.255.252	2	208.147.66.252/30

Maximizing Available Address Space

In Table 1-7, notice that the seventh and final subnet listed is the same size as the sixth and is distinguished by an all-1s subnet ID instead of by the trailing 0 used with the other subnet IDs. As an alternative to using the maximum seven subnets presented, you could define the all-1s subnet ID at any level in the table to replace all the subnets listed below that subnet. For example, you could define a subnet ID of 11 to replace subnets 3 through 7 listed in the table.

Exam Tip   Just about everyone considers VLSMs confusing. If you see a question on VLSMs on the 70-642 exam, and you very well might, it will probably be the toughest question you will face on the whole test. To handle such questions, first try to eliminate incorrect answer choices whose subnet masks do not match the appropriate incremental pattern. Then, try to eliminate answer choices whose address ranges do not properly correspond to the pattern of 1s with a single trailing 0. You might need to perform decimal-to-binary conversions to get the answer correct. Most of all, though, make sure you don't spend too much time on a VLSM question. Eliminate what you can, and if you don't have an answer within 3 minutes or so, take your best guess and move on.

PRACTICE Learning to Work with Address Blocks

In this practice, you perform exercises that help solidify your understanding of address blocks, subnet masks, and host capacity.

▶ **Exercise 1   Choosing an Appropriate Subnet Mask**

You are adding a new server to each of the following subnets. Given the addresses of the existing computers on that subnet, determine which subnet mask you should assign the new server.

1. Which subnet mask would you assign to the new server?

Subnet 1:Existing Computers
10.2.12.1
10.2.41.23
10.2.41.100
10.2.41.101

Answer Choices:

- **A.** 255.0.0.0 (/8)
- **B.** 255.255.0.0 (/16)
- **C.** 255.255.255.0 (/24)

   Answer: B

2. Which subnet mask would you assign to the new server?

Subnet 2: Existing Computers
192.168.34.1
192.168.34.55
192.168.34.223
192.168.34.5

Answer Choices:

- **A.** 255.0.0.0 (/8)
- **B.** 255.255.0.0 (/16)
- **C.** 255.255.255.0 (/24)

   Answer: C

▶ Exercise 2   Converting Subnet Masks to Dotted-Decimal Notation

Convert the following subnet masks in slash notation to dotted-decimal by using your familiarity with the /16 subnet mask, the /24 subnet mask, and the nine possible subnet mask octet values. Write the final answer in each space provided.

Slash Notation	Dotted-decimal
/18	
/28	
/21	
/30	

Slash Notation	Dotted-decimal
/19	
/26	
/22	
/27	
/17	
/20	
/29	
/23	
/25	

Answer:

Slash Notation	Dotted-decimal
/18	255.255.192.0
/28	255.255.255.240
/21	255.255.248.0
/30	255.255.255.252
/19	255.255.224.0
/26	255.255.255.192
/22	255.255.252.0
/27	255.255.255.224
/17	255.255.128.0
/20	255.255.240.0
/29	255.255.255.248
/23	255.255.254.0
/25	255.255.255.128

▶ **Exercise 3   Converting Subnet Masks to Slash Notation**

Using your familiarity with 255.255.0.0, 255.255.255.0, and with the nine possible values in a subnet mask octet, convert the following subnet masks in dotted-decimal notation to slash notation. Write the final answer in each space provided.

Dotted-decimal	Slash Notation
255.255.240.0	
255.255.255.248	

Dotted-decimal	Slash Notation
255.255.192.0	
255.255.255.128	
255.255.248.0	
255.255.255.224	
255.255.252.0	
255.255.128.0	
255.255.255.252	
255.255.224.0	
255.255.254.0	
255.255.255.192	
255.255.255.240	

Answer:

Dotted-decimal	Slash Notation
255.255.240.0	/20
255.255.255.248	/29
255.255.192.0	/18
255.255.255.128	/25
255.255.248.0	/21
255.255.255.224	/27
255.255.252.0	/22
255.255.128.0	/17
255.255.255.252	/30
255.255.224.0	/19
255.255.254.0	/23
255.255.255.192	/26
255.255.255.240	/28

▶ Exercise 4   **Determining the Host Capacity of Networks**

For each of the given address blocks below, determine the number of hosts that can be supported. Use either the halving-and-doubling or subtract-from-256 technique, as appropriate. Write down the answer in the space provided in the right column. (Hint: remember to subtract two from the total number of addresses to determine the number of supported hosts.)

Address Block	Number of Supported Hosts
131.107.16.0/20	
10.10.128.0 Subnet mask: 255.255.254.0	
206.73.118.0/26	
192.168.23.64 Subnet mask: 255.255.255.224	
131.107.0.0 Subnet mask: 255.255.255.0	
206.73.118.24/29	
10.4.32.0/21	
172.16.12.0/22	
192.168.1.32 Subnet mask: 255.255.255.128	
131.107.100.48/28	
206.73.118.12 Subnet mask: 255.255.255.252	
10.12.200.128/25	
192.168.0.0 Subnet mask: 255.255.248.0	
172.20.43.0/24	
131.107.32.0 Subnet mask 255.255.255.240	
10.200.48.0 Subnet mask: 255.255.240.0	
192.168.244.0/23	
10.0.0.0 /30	
172.31.3.24 Subnet mask: 255.255.255.248	
206.73.118.32/27	
131.107.8.0 Subnet mask: 255.255.252.0	
192.168.0.64 Subnet mask: 255.255.255.192	

Answer:

Address Block	Number of Supported Hosts
131.107.16.0/20	4,094
10.10.128.0 Subnet mask: 255.255.254.0	510
206.73.118.0/26	62
192.168.23.64 Subnet mask: 255.255.255.224	30
131.107.0.0 Subnet mask: 255.255.255.0	254
206.73.118.24/29	6
10.4.32.0/21	2046
172.16.12.0/22	1022
192.168.1.32 Subnet mask: 255.255.255.128	126
131.107.100.48/28	14
206.73.118.12 Subnet mask: 255.255.255.252	2
10.12.200.128/25	126
192.168.0.0 Subnet mask: 255.255.248.0	2046
172.20.43.0/24	254
131.107.32.0 Subnet mask 255.255.255.240	14
10.200.48.0 Subnet mask: 255.255.240.0	4094
192.168.244.0/23	510
10.0.0.0 /30	2
172.31.3.24 Subnet mask: 255.255.255.248	6
206.73.118.32/27	30
131.107.8.0 Subnet mask: 255.255.252.0	1022
192.168.0.64 Subnet mask: 255.255.255.192	62

► **Exercise 5   Determining Network Size Requirements in Slash Notation Terms**

Each of the values in the left column of the table below refers to a number of computers that a given network must support. In the corresponding space in the right column, specify with a subnet mask in slash notation the smallest network address size that will accommodate those computers.

The first row is provided as an example.

(Hint: remember to add two to the number of hosts in order to determine the number of addresses needed.)

Number of Network Hosts	Subnet Mask (/n)
18	/27
125	
400	
127	
650	
7	
2000	
4	
3500	
20	
32	

Answer:

Number of Network Hosts	Subnet Mask (/n)
125	/25
400	/23
127	/24
650	/22
7	/28
2000	/21
4	/29
3500	/20
20	/27
32	/26

▶ **Exercise 6   Determining Network Size Requirements in Terms of a Dotted-Decimal Subnet Mask**

Each of the values in the left column of the table below refers to a number of computers that a given network must support. In the corresponding space in the right column, specify with a subnet mask in dotted-decimal notation the smallest network size that will accommodate those computers.

The first row is provided as an example.

(Hint: remember to add two to the number of hosts in order to determine the number of addresses needed. Then, use the halving-and-doubling or subtract-from-256 technique.)

Number of Network Hosts	Subnet Mask (w.x.y.z)
100	255.255.255.128
63	
1022	
6	
1100	
12	
150	
2500	
20	
300	
35	

Answer:

Number of Network Hosts	Subnet Mask (w.x.y.z)
63	255.255.255.128
1022	255.255.252.0
6	255.255.255.248
1100	255.255.248.0
12	255.255.255.240
150	255.255.255.0
2500	255.255.240.0
20	255.255.255.224

Number of Network Hosts	Subnet Mask (w.x.y.z)
300	255.255.254.0
35	255.255.255.192

Lesson Summary

- An IPv4 address is a 32-bit number divided into four octets. One part of the IPv4 address represents a network ID, and the other part represents the host ID.

- The subnet mask is used by an IP host to separate the network ID from the host ID in every IP address. The subnet mask can appear in slash notation, such as /24, or dotted-decimal notation, such as 255.255.255.0. As a network administrator you need to be able to translate between these two forms of the IPv4 subnet mask.

- The calculation of the network ID by using the subnet mask tells a computer what to do with an IP packet. If the destination network ID of an IP packet is local, the computer broadcasts the packet on the local network. If the destination network ID is remote, the computer sends the packet to the default gateway.

- The IANA has reserved certain ranges of IP addresses to be used only within private networks. These ranges include 10.0.0.0 to 10.255.255.254, 17.16.0.0 to 17.31.255.254, and 192.168.0.0 to 192.168.255.254.

- You can obtain blocks of IP addresses from your provider. The block will be defined as a single address with a subnet mask, such as 131.107.1.0/24. As a network administrator, you need to be able to determine how many addresses are contained in address blocks defined in this manner. To meet your own needs for addresses, you also need to specify an appropriately sized address block in these terms.

- An address block can be subdivided into multiple subnets, each with its own router. To achieve this, you need to lengthen the subnet mask within your organization so that computers see subnet IDs as distinct.

Lesson Review

The following questions are intended to reinforce key information presented in this lesson. The questions are also available on the companion CD if you prefer to review them in electronic form.

NOTE Answers

Answers to these questions and explanations of why each answer choice is correct or incorrect are located in the "Answers" section at the end of the book.

---

1. How many computers can you host in an IPv4 network whose address is 172.16.0.0/22?

    A. 512

    B. 1024

    C. 510

    D. 1022

2. You work as a network administrator for a research lab in a large company. The research lab includes six computers for which central computing services has allocated the address space 172.16.1.0/29. You now plan to add 10 new computers to the research network. Company policy states that each network is granted address space only according to its needs.

    What should you do?

    A. Ask to expand the network to a /28 address block.

    B. Ask to expand the network to a /27 address block.

    C. Ask to expand the network to a /26 address block.

    D. You do not need to expand the network because a /29 network is large enough to support your needs.

Lesson 3: Understanding IP Version 6 (IPv6) Addressing

IPv4 provides 4.3 billion unique possible addresses. This might sound like a large number, but because of the exponential growth of the Internet, the IPv4 address space is expected to become exhausted in the near future.

IPv6 was designed primarily to resolve this problem of IPv4 address exhaustion. In place of the 32-bit addresses used by IPv4, IPv6 uses 128-bit addresses. This larger IPv6 address space therefore provides 2^{128} or 3.4 undecillion (3.4×10^{38}) unique addresses. Compared to the number of IPv4 addresses, this number is staggeringly large. If each address were a grain of sand, you could comfortably fit all IPv4 addresses into a small moving truck, but to fit all IPv6 addresses, you would need a container the size of 1.3 million Earths—or the entire Sun.

IPv6 is enabled by default in both Windows Vista and Windows Server 2008, and it requires virtually no configuration. However, you still need to become familiar with the various types and formats of IPv6 addresses. This lesson introduces you to IPv6 by describing its addresses and the transition technologies used in mixed IPv4/IPv6 networks.

After this lesson, you will be able to:
- Recognize various types of IPv6 addresses, such as global, link-local, and unique local addresses.
- Understand IPv6 transition technologies such as ISATAP, 6to4, and Teredo.

Estimated lesson time: 50 minutes

Introducing IPv6 Addresses

Although there are other improvements in IPv6 compared to IPv4, such as built-in Quality of Service (QoS), more efficient routing, simpler configuration, and improved security, the increased address space of IPv6 is by far its most important feature. This large address space can be seen in its long addresses.

IPv6 addresses are written by using eight blocks of four hexadecimal digits. Each block, separated by colons, represents a 16-bit number. The following shows the full notation of an IPv6 address:

2001:0DB8:3FA9:0000:0000:0000:00D3:9C5A

You can shorten an IPv6 address by eliminating any leading zeroes in blocks. By using this technique, you can shorten the representation of the preceding address to the following:

2001:DB8:3FA9:0:0:0:D3:9C5A

You can then shorten the address even further by replacing all adjacent zero blocks as a single set of double colons (":"). You can do this only once in a single IPv6 address.

2001:DB8:3FA9::D3:9C5A

Because IPv6 addresses consist of eight blocks, you can always determine how many blocks of zeroes are represented by the double colons. For example, in the previous IPv6 address, you know that three zero blocks have been replaced by the double colons because five blocks still appear.

The Structure of IPv6 Addresses

Unicast IPv6 addresses are divided into two parts: a 64-bit network component and a 64-bit host component. The network component identifies a unique subnet, and the IANA assigns these numbers to ISPs or large organizations. The host component is typically either based on the network adapter's unique 48-bit Media Access Control (MAC) address or is randomly generated.

For unicast addressing, IPv6 does not support variable length subnet identifiers, and the number of bits used to identify a network in a unicast IPv6 host address is always 64 (the first half of the address). It is therefore unnecessary to specify a subnet mask when representing a unicast address; a network identifier of /64 is understood.

IPv6 addresses, however, do use network prefixes expressed in slash notation, but only to represent routes and address ranges, not to specify a network ID. For example, you might see an entry such as "2001:DB8:3FA9::/48" in an IPv6 routing table.

NOTE   **Unicast, multicast, and anycast in IPv6**

Unicast refers to the transmission of a message to a single point, as opposed to broadcast (sent to all local network points), multicast (sent to multiple points), and anycast (sent to any one computer of a set of computers). Unlike IPv4, IPv6 does not rely on network broadcasts. Instead of broadcasts, IPv6 uses multicast or anycast transmission.

How Do IPv6 Computers Receive an IPv6 Address?

IPv6 was designed from the beginning to be easier to configure than IPv4. Although manual configuration is still an option (and is required for routers), computers will almost always have their IPv6 configurations automatically assigned. Computers can receive IPv6 addresses either from neighboring routers or from DHCPv6 servers. Computers also always assign themselves an address for use on the local subnet only.

Understanding IPv6 Address Types

IPv6 currently defines three types of addresses: global addresses, link-local addresses, and unique local addresses. The following section explains these three address types.

Global Addresses

IPv6 global addresses (GAs) are the equivalent of public addresses in IPv4 and are globally reachable on the IPv6 portion of the Internet. The address prefix currently used for GAs is 2000::/3, which translates to a first block value between 2000-3FFF in the usual hexadecimal notation. An example of a GA is 2001:db8:21da:7:713e:a426:d167:37ab.

The structure of a GA, shown in Figure 1-39, can be summarized in the following manner:

- The first 48 bits of the address are the global routing prefix specifying your organization's site. (The first three bits of this prefix must be 001 in binary notation.) These 48 bits represent the public topology portion of the address, which represents the collection of large and small ISPs on the IPv6 Internet and which is controlled by these ISPs through assignment by the IANA.

- The next 16 bits are the subnet ID. Your organization can use this portion to specify up to 65,536 unique subnets for routing purposes inside your organization's site. These 16 bits represent the site topology portion of the address, which your organization has control over.

The final 64 bits are the interface ID and specify a unique interface within each subnet. This interface ID is equivalent to a host ID in IPv4.

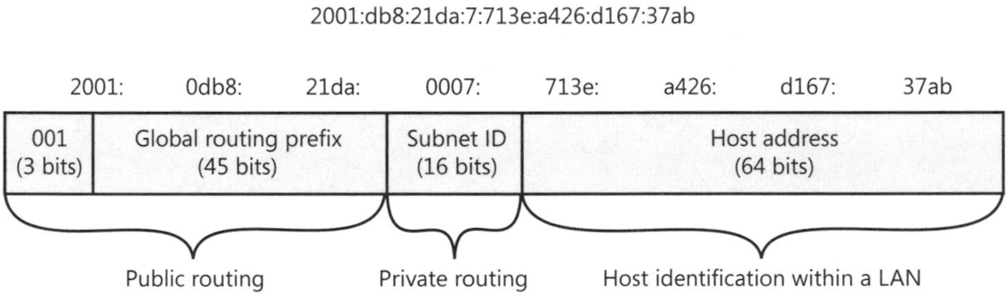

2001:db8:21da:7:713e:a426:d167:37ab

2001:	0db8:	21da:	0007:	713e:	a426:	d167:	37ab
001 (3 bits)	Global routing prefix (45 bits)		Subnet ID (16 bits)	Host address (64 bits)			

Public routing   Private routing   Host identification within a LAN

Figure 1-39   A global IPv6 address

Link-local Addresses

Link-local addresses (LLAs) are similar to Automatic Private IP Addressing (APIPA) addresses (169.254.0.0/16) in IPv4 in that they are self-configured, nonroutable addresses used only for communication on the local subnet. However, unlike an APIPA address, an LLA remains assigned to an interface as a secondary address even after a routable address is obtained for that interface.

LLAs always begin with "fe80". An example LLA is fe80::154d:3cd7:b33b:1bc1%13, as shown in the following Ipconfig output:

```
Windows IP Configuration

    Host Name . . . . . . . . . . . . : server1
    Primary Dns Suffix  . . . . . . . :
    Node Type . . . . . . . . . . . . : Hybrid
    IP Routing Enabled. . . . . . . . : No
    WINS Proxy Enabled. . . . . . . . : No
    DNS Suffix Search List. . . . . . : contoso.com

Ethernet adapter Local Area Connection :

    Connection-specific DNS Suffix  . : contoso.com
    Description . . . . . . . . . . . : Intel(R) 82566DC Gigabit Network Connection - Virtual
Network
    Physical Address. . . . . . . . . : 00-1D-60-9C-B5-35
    DHCP Enabled. . . . . . . . . . . : Yes
    Autoconfiguration Enabled . . . . : Yes
    Link-local IPv6 Address . . . . . : fe80::154d:3cd7:b33b:1bc1%13(Preferred)
    IPv4 Address. . . . . . . . . . . : 192.168.2.99(Preferred)
    Subnet Mask . . . . . . . . . . . : 255.255.255.0
    Lease Obtained. . . . . . . . . . : Wednesday, February 06, 2008 9:32:16 PM
    Lease Expires . . . . . . . . . . : Wednesday, February 13, 2008 3:42:03 AM
    Default Gateway . . . . . . . . . : 192.168.2.1
    DHCP Server . . . . . . . . . . . : 192.168.2.10
    DNS Servers . . . . . . . . . . . : 192.168.2.10
                                        192.168.2.201
    NetBIOS over Tcpip. . . . . . . . : Enabled
```

The structure of such an LLA, illustrated in Figure 1-40, can be summarized as follows:

- The first half of the address is written as "fe80::" but can be understood as fe80:0000:0000:0000.

- The second half of the address represents the interface ID.

- Each computer tags an LLA with a zone ID in the form "%ID". This zone ID is *not part of the address* but changes relative to each computer. The zone ID in fact specifies the network interface that is connected, either locally or across the network, to the address.

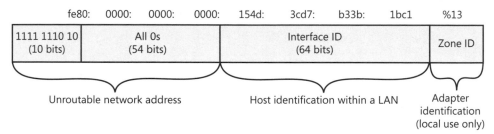

Figure 1-40   A link-local IPv6 address

What Are the Zone IDs After Link-local Addresses?

Because all LLAs share the same network identifier (fe80::), you cannot determine which interface an LLA is bound to merely by looking at the address. Therefore, if a computer running Windows has multiple network adapters connected to different network segments, it distinguishes the networks by using a numeric zone ID following a percent sign after the IP address, as the following examples demonstrate:

- fe80::d84b:8939:7684:a5a4%7
- fe80::462:7ed4:795b:1c9f%8
- fe80::2882:29d5:e7a4:b481%9

The two characters after each address indicate that the preceding networks are connected to the zone IDs 7, 8, and 9, respectively. Although zone IDs can occasionally be used with other types of addresses, you should always specify the zone ID when connecting to LLAs.

Remember also that zone IDs are relative to the sending host. If you want to ping a neighboring computer's LLA, you have to specify the neighbor's address along with the Zone ID of *your* computer's network adapter that faces the neighbor's computer. For example, in the command **ping fe80::2b0:d0ff:fee9:4143%3**, the address is of the neighboring computer's interface, but the "%3" corresponds to the zone ID of an interface on the local computer.

In Windows Vista and Windows Server 2008, the zone ID for an LLA is assigned on the basis of a parameter called the *interface index* for that network interface. You can view a list of interface indexes on a computer by typing **netsh interface ipv6 show interface** at a command prompt.

Unique Local Addresses

Unique local addresses (ULAs) are the IPv6 equivalent of private addresses in IPv4 (10.0.0.0/8, 172.16.0.0/12, and 192.168.0.0/16). These addresses are routable between subnets on a private network but are not routable on the public Internet. They allow you to create complex internal networks without having public address space assigned. Such addresses begin with "fd". An example of a ULA is fd65:9abf:efb0:0001::0002.

The structure of a ULA can be summarized in the following way:

- The first seven bits of the address are always 1111 110 (binary) and the eighth bit is set to 1, indicating a local address. This means that the address prefix is fd00::/8 for this type of address. (Note that in the future the prefix fc00::/8 might also be used for ULAs.)
- The next 40 bits represent the global ID and is a randomly generated value that identifies a specific site within your organization.
- The next 16 bits represent the subnet ID and can be used for further subdividing the internal network of your site for routing purposes.
- The last 64 bits are the interface ID and specify a unique interface within each subnet.

A ULA is illustrated in Figure 1-41.

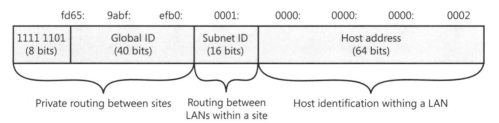

Figure 1-41   A unique local IPv6 address

Exam Tip   Expect to see more than one question on the 70-642 exam about IPv6 address types. These questions are easy if you just remember that GAs are equivalent to IPv4 public addresses, LLAs are equivalent to APIPA addresses, and ULAs are equivalent to IPv4 private addresses.

NOTE   **What are site-local addresses?**

Site-local addresses in the feco::/10 address prefix also provide private routing on IPv6 networks, but they have recently been deprecated (officially set on a path toward obsolescence) by RFC 3879.

States of an IPv6 Address

IPv6 hosts typically configure IPv6 addresses by interacting with an IPv6-enabled router and performing IPv6 address autoconfiguration. Addresses are in a *tentative* state for the brief period of time between first assigning the address and verifying that the address is unique. Computers use duplicate address detection to identify other computers that have the same IPv6 address by sending out a Neighbor Solicitation message with the tentative address. If a computer responds, the address is considered invalid. If no other computer responds, the address is considered unique and valid. A valid address is called *preferred* within its valid lifetime assigned by the router or autoconfiguration. A valid address is called *deprecated* when it exceeds its lifetime. Existing communication sessions can still use a deprecated address.

IMPORTANT   Loopback addresses in IPv4 and IPv6

In IPv4, the address 127.0.0.1 is known as the loopback address and always refers to the local computer. The loopback address in IPv6 is ::1. On a computer with any IPv4 or IPv6 address, you can ping the loopback address to ensure that TCP/IP is functioning correctly.

IPv6 Transition Technologies

IPv6 has a new header format, and IPv4 routers that have not been designed to support IPv6 cannot parse the fields in the IPv6 header. Therefore, organizations must upgrade their routers before adopting IPv6. Layer 2 protocols are not affected, so layer 2 switches and hubs don't need to be upgraded and computers on a LAN can communicate using existing network hardware.

NOTE   Can Internet routers handle IPv6?

Few routers on the Internet today are IPv6-compatible. However, a specific public wide area network uses IPv6 as its Network Layer protocol. This network is known as the IPv6 Internet. Currently, the IPv6 Internet is made of both IPv6 native links and tunneled links over the IPv4 Internet.

Transition technologies, including the Next Generation TCP/IP stack in Windows, ISATAP, 6to4, and Teredo allow IPv6 to be used across a routing infrastructure that supports only IPv4. These technologies are described below.

Next Generation TCP/IP

The most fundamental transition technology is the architecture of the Next Generation TCP/IP stack, which is native to Windows Vista and Windows Server 2008. With this technology, computers can use IPv6 to communicate if the client, server, and network infrastructure support it. However, they can also communicate with computers or network services that support only IPv4.

Intra-site Automatic Tunnel Addressing Protocol (ISATAP)

ISATAP is a tunneling protocol that allows an IPv6 network to communicate with an IPv4 network through an ISATAP router, as shown in Figure 1-42.

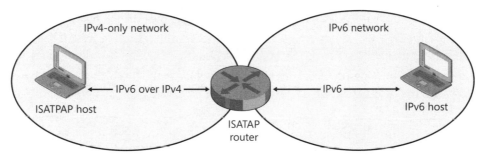

Figure 1-42 ISATAP routers allows IPv4-only and IPv6-only hosts to communicate with each other

ISATAP allows IPv4 and IPv6 hosts to communicate by performing a type of address translation between IPv4 and IPv6. In this process, all ISATAP clients receive an address for an ISATAP interface. This address is composed of an IPv4 address encapsulated inside an IPv6 address.

ISATAP is intended for use within a private network.

NOTE Tunnel Adapter Local Area Connection* 8

Installations of Windows Server 2008 include an ISATAP tunnel interface by default. Usually this interface is assigned to Tunnel Adapter Local Area Connection* 8.

6to4

6to4 is a protocol that tunnels IPv6 traffic over IPv4 traffic through 6to4 routers. 6to4 clients have their router's IPv4 address embedded in their IPv6 address and do not require an IPv4 address. Whereas ISATAP is intended primarily for intranets, 6to4 is intended to be used on the Internet. You can use 6to4 to connect to IPv6 portions of the Internet through a 6to4 relay even if your intranet or your ISP supports only IPv4.

A sample 6to4 network is shown in Figure 1-43.

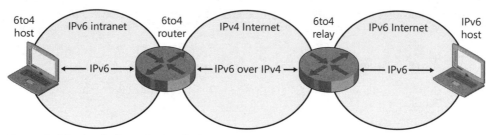

Figure 1-43   6to4 allows IPv6-only hosts to communicate over the Internet

Teredo

Teredo is a tunneling protocol that allows clients located behind an IPv4 NAT device to use IPv6 over the Internet. Teredo is used only when no other IPv6 transition technology (such as 6to4) is available.

Teredo relies on an infrastructure, illustrated in Figure 1-44, that includes Teredo clients, Teredo servers, Teredo relays, and Teredo host-specific relays.

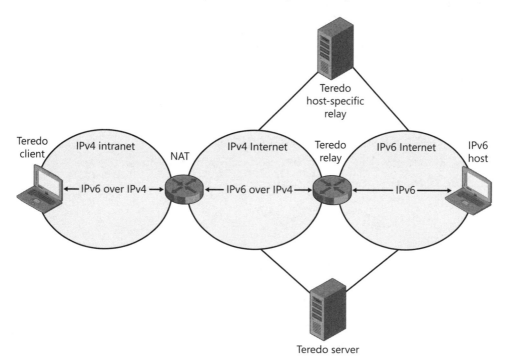

Figure 1-44   Teredo allows hosts located behind IPv4 NAT to use IPv6 over the Internet to communicate with each other or with IPv6-only hosts

- **Teredo client** A Teredo client is computer that is enabled with both IPv6 and IPv4 and that is located behind a router performing IPv4 NAT. The Teredo client creates a Teredo tunneling interface and configures a routable IPv6 address with the help of a Teredo server. Through this interface, Teredo clients communicate with other Teredo clients or with hosts on the IPv6 Internet (through a Teredo relay).

- **Teredo server** A Teredo server is a public server connected both to the IPv4 Internet and to the IPv6 Internet. The Teredo server helps perform the address configuration of the Teredo client and facilitates initial communication either between two Teredo clients or between a Teredo clients and an IPv6 host.

  To facilitate communication among Windows-based Teredo client computers, Microsoft has deployed Teredo servers on the IPv4 Internet.

- **Teredo relay** A Teredo relay is a Teredo tunnel endpoint. It is an IPv6/IPv4 router that can forward packets between Teredo clients on the IPv4 Internet and IPv6-only hosts.

- **Teredo host-specific relay** A Teredo host-specific relay is a host that is enabled with both IPv4 and IPv6 and that acts as its own Teredo relay. A Teredo host-specific relay essentially enables a Teredo client that has a global IPv6 address to tunnel through the IPv4 Internet and communicate directly with hosts connected to the IPv6 Internet.

  Windows Vista and Windows Server 2008 include Teredo host-specific relay functionality, which is automatically enabled if the computer has a GA assigned. If the computer does not have a GA, Teredo client functionality is enabled.

NOTE Tunnel Adapter Local Area Connection* 9

Installations of Windows Server 2008 include a Teredo tunnel interface by default. Usually this interface is assigned to Tunnel Adapter Local Area Connection* 9.

Quick Check

1. Which technology is designed to allow an IPv4-only LAN to communicate with an IPv6-only LAN?
2. Which technology allows an IPv4-only host to communicate with the IPv6 Internet?

Quick Check Answers

1. ISATAP
2. 6to4

PRACTICE Testing IPv6 Connectivity

In this practice, you will review IPv6 information in the *Ipconfig* output, ping a computer's IPv6 LLA, and then specify a ULA for both Dcsrv1 and Boston.

▶ **Exercise 1   Reading *Ipconfig* Output**

In this exercise, you will use the *Ipconfig /all* command on the Boston computer to review IPv6 settings.

1. Log on to Boston. At a command prompt, type **ipconfig /all.**
2. Review the output, and then answer the following questions:

   a. How many local area connections are assigned to your computer?

   Answer: If only one network adapter is connected to Boston, there should be three local area connections (software interfaces) at this time: one for the Local Area Connection corresponding to the physical network adapter, one for an ISATAP tunnel interface, and one for a Teredo tunnel interface.

   b. Which local area connection corresponds to a physical adapter on the network?

   Answer: The first local area connection.

   c. Which local area connection corresponds to a software interface for ISATAP?

   Answer: The second local area connection on a one-adapter computer will normally be assigned to ISATAP, but your particular configuration may vary.

   Note that because Boston is not communicating with an ISATAP router, the media state for this interface is shown to be disconnected.

   d. Which local area connection corresponds to a software interface for Teredo?

   Answer: The third local area connection on a one-adapter computer will normally be assigned to Teredo, but your particular configuration may vary.

   Note that because Boston is not communicating on the Internet, it cannot obtain a Teredo address. The media state is therefore described as disconnected.

   e. What does the "*" signify when it appears after "Local Area Connection"?

   Answer: The asterisk signifies that the local area connection represents an interface for a tunneled connection.

   f. How many IPv6 addresses have been assigned to the computer?

   Answer: One.

   g. What do the following addresses represent?

   ```
   fec0:0:0:ffff::1%1
   fec0:0:0:ffff::2%1
   fec0:0:0:ffff::3%1
   ```

Answer: These site-local addresses are used for the autodiscovery of DNS servers when no specific DNS server address has been assigned to the local computer. To facilitate DNS autodiscovery, you can assign these addresses to the DNS servers in your organization.

▶ **Exercise 2   Pinging a Link-local IPv6 Address**

In this exercise, you will test IPv6 connectivity from Boston to Dcsrv1 by pinging Dcsrv1's IPv6 address. To do so, you will also specify the Boston adapter's zone ID.

1. Log on to Dcsrv1. At a command prompt, type **ipconfig.**

   Note the link-local IPv6 address assigned to Dcsrv1.

2. If you are not able to view the monitors of Dcsrv1 and Boston side by side, write down the LLA of Dcsrv1's local area connection on a piece of scratch paper. Do not copy the zone ID (the "%" sign with a number following it).

3. Log on to Boston and open a command prompt.

4. At the command prompt, type **ipconfig.**

   Note the link-local Ipv6 address assigned to Boston and note the zone ID appended to it. You will use this zone ID in the next step.

5. At the command prompt, type **ping** *IPv6addressZoneID*, where IPv6address = Dcsrv1's IPv6 address and ZoneID = the zone ID assigned to the local area connection on Boston. For example, if the LLA on Dcsrv1 is fe80::1d63:a395:1442:30f0 and the zone ID assigned to the LLA in Boston's local area connection is %10, type the following:

   `ping fe80::1d63:a395:1442:30f0%10`

6. You will see four replies from Dcsrv1's IPv6 address.

▶ **Exercise 3   Assigning a Unique Local Address**

In this exercise, you assign a ULA to the local area connection on both Dcsrv1 and Boston.

1. While you are logged on to Dcsrv1 as an administrator, open the Run box, type **ncpa.cpl**, and then press Enter.

2. Open the properties of the local area connection, and then double-click Internet Protocol Version 6 (TCP/IPv6).

3. In the Internet Protocol Version 6 (TCP/IPv6) Properties dialog box, select Use The Following IPv6 Address, and then specify the following settings:

   IPv6 address: fd00::1

   Subnet prefix length: 64

   Default gateway: (leave empty)

   Preferred DNS server: (leave empty)

   Alternate DNS server: (leave empty)

4. Click OK.

5. In the Local Area Connection Properties dialog box, click OK.

6. Perform steps 1-5 on Boston, specifying an IPv6 address of fd00::2.

7. On Boston, open a command prompt, and type **ping fd00::1**.

    You will see four replies from the address fd00::1.

8. At the command prompt, type **ipconfig**, and then answer the following questions:

    a. What is the name assigned to the address fd00::2?

        Answer: IPv6 Address

    b. Is a LLA still specified?

        Answer: Yes. Unlike APIPA addresses in IPv4, LLAs in IPv6 are not replaced by other addresses.

9. Log off both computers.

Lesson Summary

- IPv6 is a technology designed to resolve the problem of IPv4 address exhaustion, although it also provides other advantages, such as improved security and simpler configuration.

- IPv6 addresses are 128-bit numbers written as eight four-digit hexadecimal blocks, but the notation can be shortened. Leading zeroes within any block can be omitted, and once per address any adjacent all-zero blocks can be replaced by a double colon ":".

- IPv6 hosts can obtain their address from a neighboring IPv6 router, from a DHCPv6 server, or from autoconfiguration.

- For unicast traffic, the first half of an IPv6 address is the network identifier and the second half of the address is the interface (host) identifier.

- Three types of addresses are used for unicast traffic. Global addresses (GAs), which begin with a 2 or 3, are routable on the IPv6 Internet. Link-local addresses (LLAs), which begin with fe80::, are not routable and are randomly assigned to each interface. Unique local addresses (ULAs), which begin with "fd", are routable within a private network but not on the IPv6 Internet.

- Transition technologies have been defined to allow IPv4 and IPv6 to interoperate. With ISATAP, a special router negotiates directly between an IPv4-only and an IPv6-only LAN. 6to4 enables IPv6-only hosts to tunnel over an IPv4 network such as the Internet. Teredo is a host-based technology that is used when no other option is available. It uses Internet servers to help create IPv6 tunnels over the Internet.

Lesson Review

The following questions are intended to reinforce key information presented in this lesson. The questions are also available on the companion CD if you prefer to review them in electronic form.

NOTE Answers

Answers to these questions and explanations of why each answer choice is correct or incorrect are located in the "Answers" section at the end of the book.

---

1. You want an IPv6 address for a server that you want to connect to the IPv6 Internet. What type of IPv6 address do you need?
   - **A.** A global address
   - **B.** A link-local address
   - **C.** A unique local address
   - **D.** A site-local address

2. You want to create a test IPv6 network in your organization. You want the test network to include three subnets.

   What type of IPv6 addresses do you need?
   - **A.** Global addresses
   - **B.** Link-local addresses
   - **C.** Unique local addresses
   - **D.** Site-local addresses

Chapter Review

To further practice and reinforce the skills you learned in this chapter, you can

- Review the chapter summary.
- Review the list of key terms introduced in this chapter.
- Complete the case scenario. This scenario sets up a real-world situation involving the topics of this chapter and asks you to create solutions.
- Complete the suggested practices.
- Take a practice test.

Chapter Summary

- IP provides routing and addressing for virtually all computer networks in the world. Windows clients by default are configured to obtain an IP address automatically. In this default configuration, the clients obtain an IPv4 address from a DHCP server if one is available. If one is not available, they assign themselves an address that offers only limited connectivity. Critical infrastructure servers, however, should be assigned addresses manually.

- To troubleshoot connectivity problems on IP networks, you should use tools such as Ipconfig, Ping, Tracert, PathPing, and Arp.

- If you need to implement IPv4 on a network or troubleshoot connectivity in a large network, you need to understand how IPv4 addressing works. An IPv4 address is a 32-bit number that can be broken down into a network ID and host ID, and the subnet mask is used to determine which is which.

- Some IP address ranges are reserved for use in private networks: 10.0.0.0–10.255.255.255, 172.16.0.0–172.31.255.254, and 192.168.0.0–192.168.255.254.

- Groups of addresses are known as address blocks, which you can obtain from your provider. To understand address blocks, you need to understand how many addresses are associated with each subnet mask. Two addresses in every subnet are reserved for special uses, so you always need at least two more addresses than computers for each subnet.

- Public IPv4 addresses are becoming exhausted, and the only long-term solution is a replacement protocol called IPv6, which is just beginning to be implemented. IPv6 addresses are 128-bit addresses. Global IPv6 addresses are usable on public networks. Unique local addresses are routable but are usable only on private networks, and link-local addresses are autoconfigured addresses that provide only limited connectivity.

Key Terms

Do you know what these key terms mean? You can check your answers by looking up the terms in the glossary at the end of the book.

- address block
- Automatic Private IP Addressing (APIPA)
- broadcast
- IPv4
- IPv6
- Network Address Translation (NAT)
- private address ranges
- subnet mask

Case Scenarios

In the following case scenario, you will apply what you've learned in this chapter. You can find answers to these questions in the "Answers" section at the end of this book.

Case Scenario: Working with IPv4 Address Blocks

You work as a network administrator for a company with 100 employees. Your company currently uses a total of six public IP addresses for its public servers and routers, all of which are hosted in a perimeter network on the company premises.

1. What is the smallest size address block that can support the servers and routers in your perimeter network? (Express the network size in slash notation and dotted-decimal notation.)

2. You have decided to deploy three new servers in the perimeter network and assign them each a public IP address. If your provider sells addresses in blocks only, what size block should you request to enable you to host all of your public servers on a single subnet? Express the size of the network with a subnet mask in both slash notation and dotted-decimal notation.

3. What is the maximum number of servers or routers you could deploy in this new address block?

Suggested Practices

To help you successfully master the exam objectives presented in this chapter, complete the following tasks.

Configure IP Addressing

- **Practice**   In a physical or virtual environment, assign two neighboring computers a subnet mask of 255.255.255.252. Assign one computer an address of 192.168.0.1. Assign the second computer an address of 192.168.0.2 and ensure that the two computers can ping each other. Then, increment the address of the second computer and attempt to ping again. At what point does the connection break between the two? Use this method to determine the complete address range of the 192.168.0.0/30 block.

  On two neighboring computers, disable IPv4, and then manually assign them unique local IPv6 addresses. Verify connectivity by using Ping.

Take a Practice Test

The practice tests on this book's companion CD offer many options. For example, you can test yourself on just one exam objective, or you can test yourself on all the 70-642 certification exam content. You can set up the test so that it closely simulates the experience of taking a certification exam, or you can set it up in study mode so that you can look at the correct answers and explanations after you answer each question.

MORE INFO   Practice tests

For details about all the practice test options available, see the "How to Use the Practice Tests" section in this book's Introduction.

Chapter 2
Configuring Name Resolution

Name resolution is the essential, endlessly repeated process of converting computer names to addresses on a network. In Microsoft Windows networks, the primary name resolution system is Domain Name System (DNS), which is also the name resolution system of the Internet. DNS has a hierarchical structure that allows it to support networks of any size, and because DNS relies on point-to-point communication, it is blind to physical topology. DNS does not help clients resolve the names merely of computers that happen to be nearby; it helps clients resolve the names of all computers registered in the DNS server, regardless of location.

The DNS infrastructure is one of the most important areas of concern for Windows administration, but DNS is not the only name resolution system used in Windows. For reasons of history as well as user convenience, Windows relies on other name resolution systems in specific circumstances.

As a network administrator, you need to understand all name resolution systems. This chapter introduces them to you and gives the proper emphasis to DNS.

Exam objectives in this chapter:
- Configure a Domain Name System (DNS) server.
- Configure name resolution for client computers.

Lessons in this chapter:

Before You Begin

To complete the lessons in this chapter, you must have:

- Two networked computers running Windows Server 2008 and named Dcsrv1 and Boston, respectively
- Assigned the IPv4 address 192.168.0.1/24 to Dcsrv1 and 192.168.0.2/24 to Boston
- Assigned the IPv6 address fd00::1 to Dcsrv1 and fd00::2 to Boston
- Enabled file sharing on both computers

Real World

JC Mackin

DNS has served as the principal naming and name resolution provider in Windows networks since Windows 2000, but the older set of services that used to be responsible for names—NetBIOS—has been slow to disappear.

DNS upstaged NetBIOS for a good reason. NetBIOS networks resemble a world in which no family names exist and in which, to avoid ambiguity, everyone's given name has to be completely different from everyone else's. Because every computer in a NetBIOS network has only a single name tag, Windows networks before Windows 2000 were difficult to manage on a large scale. Aside from its lack of large-scale manageability, NetBIOS also has the limitation of providing too much transparency into corporate networks. If you watch the traffic on a NetBIOS network, you can see that it is noisy and, because of the information it broadcasts, not particularly secure. Finally, NetBIOS is incompatible with IPv6, a characteristic that will eventually restrict its deployment.

Despite these limitations, NetBIOS is enabled on network connections by default to this day. Why? It's true that some deployed network applications still rely on NetBIOS names, but many network administrators have kept NetBIOS enabled for another reason: before Windows Vista, NetBIOS provided the only means to perform simple network browsing. Many users learned years ago to connect to network resources by clicking Network Neighborhood or My Network Places, and they never got out of the habit. You couldn't do that without NetBIOS until now.

Finally, with Windows Vista and Windows Server 2008, browsing the network through the Network icon in Start Menu can work through a new name resolution service called Link Local Multicast Name Resolution, or LLMNR. LLMNR doesn't require any support, but even it has a significant limitation: it doesn't allow you to use to browse to computers beyond the local subnet.

Is it time for you to start disabling NetBIOS on network connections? If your network includes computers running only Windows Vista and Windows Server 2008, it's a good idea to begin testing network functionality with NetBIOS disabled. If users complain about their inability to browse to network locations, you know it's still too early for you to make the switch to a NetBIOS-less network.

Lesson 1: Understanding Name Resolution in Windows Server 2008 Networks

When we connect to a computer, we normally specify it by a name such as www.microsoft.com or FileSrvB. However, computer names such as these are used only for human benefit. For a connection to be established to a remote computer, the name we specify must be translated into an IP address to which packets can be routed. In computer terminology, to *resolve* a computer name means to translate the name into an address, and the process in general is called *name resolution*.

Name resolution is one of the most important components in a network infrastructure. To be a Windows network administrator, you need to understand how names are resolved so that you can configure and troubleshoot this essential feature. In addition, it is a topic that is heavily tested on the 70-642 exam.

This lesson introduces the various name resolution methods used in Windows Server 2008 networks.

After this lesson, you will be able to:
- Understand the function of Link Local Multicast Name Resolution (LLMNR)
- Understand NetBIOS Name Resolution methods
- Understand the components in a DNS infrastructure
- Understand the steps in a DNS query

Estimated lesson time: 120 minutes

Name Resolution Methods in Windows

Windows Server 2008 networks include no fewer than three name resolution systems: DNS, Link Local Multicast Name Resolution (LLMNR), and NetBIOS. Of these three, DNS is by far the most important because it is the name resolution method used to support Active Directory Domain Services, as well as the method used to resolve all Internet names. DNS is in fact the preferred name resolution method in Windows networks and is used whenever it is available.

However, because of the way that DNS works, it is not by itself sufficient to provide name resolution services for all Windows networks. A DNS infrastructure requires network-wide configuration for both servers and clients. Most small and informal networks lack such a DNS infrastructure. As a result, DNS cannot be used to resolve, for example, the names of computers in a workgroup with only default installations of Windows Server 2008. The other two name resolution services—LLMNR and NetBIOS—are the ones used in workgroups such as these.

The next sections describe these two fallback name resolution mechanisms.

What Is Link Local Multicast Name Resolution (LLMNR)?

LLMNR is the name resolution method enabled by Network Discovery, a feature you can turn on in the Network and Sharing Center, as shown in Figure 2-1. LLMNR is used only in Windows Vista and Windows Server 2008.

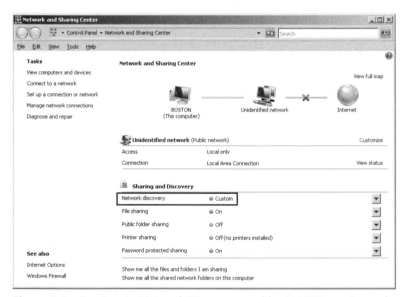

Figure 2-1 Turning on Network Discovery enables LLMNR queries and responses

LLMNR uses multicasting to resolve IPv6 addresses to the names of computers found on the local subnet only. When LLMNR is available, it is used before NetBIOS. Consequently, LLMNR is the name resolution method used for a single subnet that has no DNS infrastructure, that contains computers running only Windows Vista or Windows Server 2008, and that has both IPv6 and Network Discovery enabled on its computers.

For example, suppose that you are working on a computer named ClientA that is running Windows Vista and that has both IPv6 and Network Discovery enabled. If you want to connect to ClientB by typing a Universal Naming Convention (UNC) path in the form \\ClientB and DNS is not implemented on the network, your computer will first use LLMNR to attempt to resolve the name ClientB so that your computer can connect.

ClientA uses LLMNR to resolve this name by first checking the LLMNR cache of previously resolved names on the local computer. If no matching entry is found, ClientA sends an LLMNR Name Query Request packet over IPv6 to the IPv6 multicast address of FF02::1:3. All IPv6 hosts on the network that have Network Discovery enabled listen to traffic sent to this multicast address. If ClientB is located on the same subnet and has Network Discovery enabled, the computer hears the query and responds to ClientA by providing its IPv6 address. ClientA can then establish a connection to ClientB.

This process is illustrated in Figure 2-2.

NOTE LLMNR over IPv4

LLMNR also sends out name resolution requests over IPv4 (specifically, to the address 224.0.0.252), but at the time of this writing, Windows Server 2008 and Windows Vista clients are designed not to answer those requests by default.

As a name resolution mechanism, LLMNR offers a few important advantages. The first is that it requires no configuration to resolve computer names on the local subnet. The second is that, unlike NetBIOS, it is compatible with IPv6. Essentially, therefore, LLMNR is the only name resolution protocol that works without configuration for IPv6-only Windows networks. The third advantage is that, compared to NetBIOS, it is a much smaller service and therefore has a reduced attack surface.

However, LLMNR also has a number of significant disadvantages, the first of which is that it does not resolve the names of computers running Windows Server 2003, Windows XP, or any earlier version of Windows. In addition, LLMNR in practice does not enable connectivity to clients in a Windows IPv4-only network. Furthermore, you have to enable Network Discovery on all computers in the subnet for the LLMNR to work, so even though it doesn't require configuration, it doesn't resolve the names of neighboring computers by default. A final and significant disadvantage of LLMNR is that it cannot be used to resolve the names of computers beyond the local subnet.

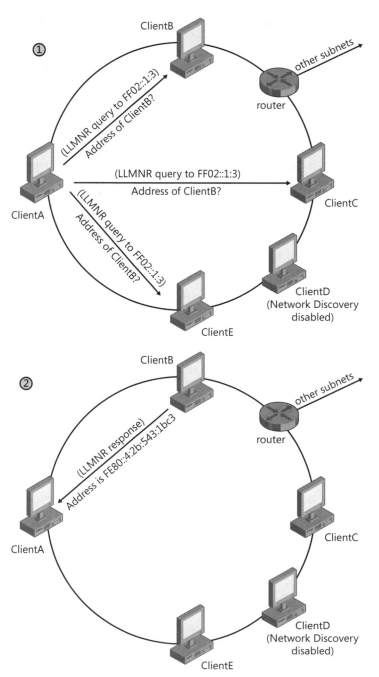

Figure 2-2 LLMNR resolves names by sending a name query to an IPv6 multicast address

---

NOTE   Disabling LLMNR on a network

You can disable LLMNR for many computers at a time by using Group Policy. In a Group Policy object (GPO), navigate to Computer Configuration\Policies\Administrative Templates\Network\DNS Client, and then search for the policy setting named Turn Off Multicast Name Resolution.

Exam Tip   You need to understand the basics of LLMNR for the 70-642 exam.

What Is NetBIOS Name Resolution?

NetBIOS, or NetBIOS-over-TCP/IP (NetBT or NBT), is a legacy protocol and naming system used for compatibility with older Windows network services. Although NetBIOS can be disabled in certain network situations, as a network administrator you will still generally need to be able to configure, manage, and troubleshoot NetBIOS name resolution.

NetBIOS provides the only name resolution in Windows that works by default on an IPv4 network without DNS. For example, in a home wireless network you can connect to other computers by specifying their names in a UNC such as \\Comp3 without enabling Network Discovery and even when Comp3 is running an older operating system such as Windows XP. NetBIOS also enables you to ping a name such as Comp3 and receive a response from the IPv4 address of that computer.

Figure 2-3 provides an example of NetBIOS name resolution. Windows will always try to resolve a name first by using DNS, but if DNS is not available, Windows will try LLMNR and NetBIOS. In this case you know that Windows has used NetBIOS to resolve the name because no DNS domain, such as mydomain.com, has been appended to the computer name (which DNS always does) and because the response has come from an IPv4 address. (An IPv6 address response would signify LLMNR.)

Figure 2-3   No domain name has been appended to the computer name "boston," and the response displays an IPv4 address. These two details prove that Windows has resolved the name by using NetBIOS.

NetBIOS Name Resolution Methods

NetBIOS includes three name resolution methods: broadcasts, WINS, and the Lmhosts file.

NetBIOS broadcasts   The first name resolution mechanism enabled by NetBIOS is the use of NetBIOS broadcasts over IPv4. Local area connections in Windows have NetBIOS enabled by default; as a result, a computer that needs to resolve a name will send out broadcasts to the local network requesting the owner of that name to respond with its IPv4 address. This process is illustrated in Figure 2-4.

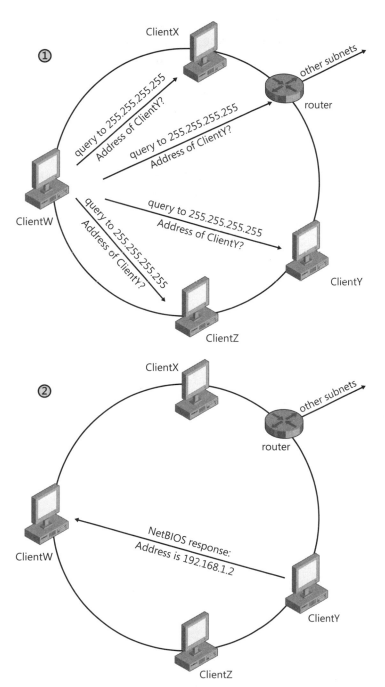

Figure 2-4   NetBIOS broadcasts, shown in this figure, represent the only name resolution method enabled by default in Windows networks

WINS   A WINS server is essentially a directory of computer names such as "Client2" and "ServerB" and their associated IP addresses. When you configure a network connection with the address of a WINS server, you perform two steps in one. First, you enable the computer to look up computer names that cannot be resolved by DNS or LLMNR, and, second, you register the local computer's name in the directory of the WINS server.

The most important advantage of WINS is that it enables NetBIOS name resolution beyond the local subnet.

Lmhosts File   The Lmhosts file is a static, local database file that is stored in the directory %SystemRoot%\System32\Drivers\Etc and that maps specific NetBIOS names to IP addresses. Recording a NetBIOS name and its IP address in the Lmhosts file enables a computer to resolve an IP address for the given NetBIOS name when every other name resolution method has failed.

You must manually create the Lmhosts file. For this reason it is normally used only to resolve the names of remote clients for which no other method of name resolution is available—for example, when no WINS server exists on the network, when the remote client is not registered with a DNS server, and when the client computer is out of broadcast range.

Enabling and Disabling NetBIOS

NetBIOS is enabled by default for IPv4 on every local area connection. To change NetBIOS settings, first open the properties of a local area connection. Then open the properties of Internet Protocol Version 4 (TCP/IPv4) and click the Advanced button to open the Advanced TCP/IP Settings dialog box. In this dialog box, click the WINS tab, shown in Figure 2-5.

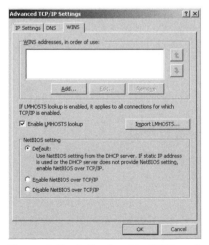

Figure 2-5   Adjusting NetBIOS settings

As shown in Figure 2-5, a local area connection will by default allow a DHCP server to assign its NetBIOS setting. A NetBIOS setting from DHCP does not merely enable or disable NetBIOS. The DHCP server can also configure a client as a specific NetBIOS node type.

NetBIOS Node Types

The exact mechanism by which NetBIOS names are resolved to IP addresses depends on the NetBIOS node type that is configured for the computer. Four node types exist:

- **broadcast or b-node**   This node type uses broadcast NetBIOS name queries for name registration and resolution. B-node has two drawbacks: broadcasts disturb every node on the network and routers typically do not forward broadcasts, so only NetBIOS names on the local network can be resolved. This node type is most similar to LLMNR in its functionality.
- **point-to-point or p-node**   This node type uses point-to-point communications with a WINS server to resolve names. P-node does not use broadcasts; instead, it queries the name server directly.
- **mixed or m-node**   This node type uses broadcasts first (b-node) and then uses WINS queries (p-node) if broadcasts are not successful.
- **hybrid or h-node**   This node type uses WINS queries first (p-node) and then uses broadcasts (b-node) if the name server is unavailable or if the name is not registered in the WINS database. To reduce IP broadcasts, these computers also use an Lmhosts file to search for name–to–IP address mappings before using B-node IP broadcasts.

By default, Windows clients are configured in hybrid or h-node. You can determine the current node status assigned to a Windows computer by viewing the output of *Ipconfig /all*, as shown below. Note that the Node Type setting on this computer is set to Hybrid.

```
C:\Users\Administrator>ipconfig /all

Windows IP Configuration

    Host Name . . . . . . . . . . . . : dcsrv1
    Primary Dns Suffix  . . . . . . . :
    Node Type . . . . . . . . . . . . : Hybrid
    IP Routing Enabled. . . . . . . . : No
    WINS Proxy Enabled. . . . . . . . : No

Ethernet adapter Local Area Connection:

    Connection-specific DNS Suffix  . :
    Description . . . . . . . . . . . : Microsoft VMBus Network Adapter
    Physical Address. . . . . . . . . : 00-15-5D-02-40-08
    DHCP Enabled. . . . . . . . . . . : No
    Autoconfiguration Enabled . . . . : Yes
```

```
    IPv6 Address. . . . . . . . . . : fd00::1(Preferred)
    Link-local IPv6 Address . . . . : fe80::1d63:a395:1442:30f0%10(Preferred)
    IPv4 Address. . . . . . . . . . : 192.168.0.1(Preferred)
    Subnet Mask . . . . . . . . . . : 255.255.255.0
    Default Gateway . . . . . . . . :
    DNS Servers . . . . . . . . . . : fec0:0:0:ffff::1%1
                                      fec0:0:0:ffff::2%1
                                      fec0:0:0:ffff::3%1
    NetBIOS over Tcpip. . . . . . . : Enabled

Tunnel adapter Local Area Connection* 8:

    Media State . . . . . . . . . . : Media disconnected
    Connection-specific DNS Suffix  . :
    Description . . . . . . . . . . : isatap.{F69512CF-ED15-4D1F-93BF-96D3A3F9A
AOF}
    Physical Address. . . . . . . . : 00-00-00-00-00-00-00-E0
    DHCP Enabled. . . . . . . . . . : No
    Autoconfiguration Enabled . . . . : Yes

Tunnel adapter Local Area Connection* 9:

    Media State . . . . . . . . . . : Media disconnected
    Connection-specific DNS Suffix  . :
    Description . . . . . . . . . . : Teredo Tunneling Pseudo-Interface
    Physical Address. . . . . . . . : 02-00-54-55-4E-01
    DHCP Enabled. . . . . . . . . . : No
    Autoconfiguration Enabled . . . . : Yes
```

Exam Tip   Expect to see a question about node types on the 70-642 exam.

Advantages and Disadvantages of NetBIOS

As a name resolution mechanism, the biggest advantages of NetBIOS are, first, that it resolves the names of neighboring computers by default and without requiring any user configuration and, second, that it is enabled on all versions of Windows. In addition, when you add a WINS server to your name resolution infrastructure, NetBIOS can be used (like DNS and unlike LLMNR) to resolve the names of computers in neighboring subnets. (This is a particularly important option when those remote computers are not registered in a DNS zone.) Other advantages of NetBIOS are that it is easier to manage and configure than DNS and that, unlike LLMNR, it works on familiar IPv4 hosts.

The biggest limitation of NetBIOS is that, although it provides a useful backup method for resolving computers within broadcast range and in small networks, it is impractical for very large networks. In NetBIOS, each computer is assigned only a single name or tag, and if you use WINS to enable NetBIOS name resolution across subnets, each computer name on the entire network has to be unique. Another disadvantage of NetBIOS is that it is not recommended for high-security areas. NetBIOS advertises information about network services, and this information can theoretically be used to exploit the network. Finally, NetBIOS is not compatible with IPv6 networks.

Exam Tip   When you have multiple WINS servers in a large organization, you must configure replication among them so that each WINS database remains up-to-date. In most cases, you want to configure *push-pull replication* among all WINS servers (often in a star configuration) so that they can efficiently and effectively update one another.

What Is DNS Name Resolution?

DNS enables you to locate computers and other resources by name on an IP internetwork. By providing a hierarchical structure and an automated method of caching and resolving host names, DNS removes many of the administrative and structural difficulties associated with naming hosts on the Internet and large private networks.

DNS Namespace

The naming system on which DNS is based is a hierarchical and logical tree structure called the *DNS namespace*. The DNS namespace has a unique root that can have any number of subdomains. In turn, each subdomain can have more subdomains. For example, the root "" (empty string) in the Internet namespace has many top-level domain names, one of which is com. The domain com can, for example, have a subdomain for the Lucerne Publishing company, lucernepublishing.com, which in turn can have a further subdomain for manufacturing called mfg.lucernepublishing.com. Organizations can also create private networks and use their own private DNS namespaces that are not visible on the Internet.

Domain Names

You can identify every node in the DNS domain tree by a *fully qualified domain name*, or FQDN. The FQDN is a DNS domain name that has been stated unambiguously to indicate its location relative to the root of the DNS domain tree. For example, the FQDN for the finance1 server in the lucernepublishing.com domain is constructed as finance1.lucernepublishing.com., which is the concatenation of the host name (finance1) with the primary DNS suffix (lucernepublishing.com) and the trailing dot (.). The trailing dot is a standard separator between the top-level domain label and the empty string label corresponding to the root. (In everyday usage and applications such as Web browsers, the trailing dot is usually dropped, but the DNS Client service adds it during actual queries.)

The DNS root (the topmost level) of the Internet domain namespace is managed by the Internet Corporation for Assigned Names and Numbers (ICANN). ICANN coordinates the assignment of identifiers that must be globally unique for the Internet to function, including Internet domain names, IP address numbers, and protocol parameter and port numbers.

Beneath the root DNS domain lie the top-level domains, also managed by ICANN. Three types of top-level domains exist:

- **Organizational domains**   These domains are named using a code that indicates the primary function or activity of the organizations contained within the DNS domain. Some organizational domains can be used globally, although others are used only for organizations in the United States. Most organizations located in the United States are contained within one of these organizational domains. The best-known organizational domains are .com, .net, .edu, and .org. Other top-level organizational domains include .aero, .biz, .info, .name, and .pro.

- **Geographical domains**   These domains are named using the two-character country and region codes established by the International Organization for Standardization (ISO) 3166, such as .uk (United Kingdom) or .it (Italy). These domains are generally used by organizations outside the United States, but this is not a requirement.

- **Reverse domains**   These are special domains, named in-addr.arpa, that are used for IP-address-to-name resolution (referred to as reverse lookups).

IMPORTANT   Top-level domains

For the most up-to-date information about these new top-level domains, consult *http:// www.icann.org/tlds*.

Beneath the top-level domains, ICANN and other Internet naming authorities, such as Network Solutions or Nominet (in the United Kingdom), delegate domains to various organizations, such as Microsoft (microsoft.com) or Carnegie Mellon University (cmu.edu). These organizations connect to the Internet, assign names to hosts within their domains, and use DNS servers to manage the name-to-IP-address mappings within their portion of the namespace. These organizations can also delegate subdomains to other users or customers. Internet service providers (ISPs), for example, receive a delegation from ICANN and can delegate subdomains to their customers.

Private Domain Namespace

In addition to the top-level domains on the Internet, organizations can also have a *private namespace*: a DNS namespace based on a private set of root servers independent of the Internet's DNS namespace. Within a private namespace, you can name and create your own root server or servers and any subdomains as needed. Private names cannot be seen or resolved on the Internet. An example of a private domain name is mycompany.local.

DNS Components

DNS relies on the proper configuration of DNS servers, zones, resolvers, and resource records.

DNS Servers

A *DNS server* is a computer that runs a DNS server program, such as the DNS Server service in Windows Server or Berkeley Internet Name Domain (BIND) in UNIX. DNS servers contain DNS database information about some portion of the DNS domain tree structure and resolve name resolution queries issued by DNS clients. When queried, DNS servers can provide the requested information, provide a pointer to another server that can help resolve the query, or respond that the information is unavailable or does not exist.

A server is *authoritative* for a domain when that server relies on locally hosted database data (as opposed to merely cached information from other servers) in order to answer queries about hosts within a given domain. Such servers define their portion of the DNS namespace.

Servers can be authoritative for one or more levels of the domain hierarchy. For example, the root DNS servers on the Internet are authoritative only for the top-level domain names, such as .com. As a result, servers authoritative for .com are authoritative only for names within the .com domain, such as lucernepublishing.com. However, within the Lucerne Publishing namespace, the server or servers authoritative for lucernepublishing.com can also be authoritative for both example.lucernepublishing.com and widgets.example.lucernepublishing.com.

DNS Zones

A *DNS zone* is a contiguous portion of a namespace for which a server is authoritative. A server can be authoritative for one or more zones, and a zone can contain one or more contiguous domains. For example, one server can be authoritative for both microsoft.com and lucernepublishing.com zones, and each of these zones can include one or more subdomains.

Contiguous domains, such as .com, lucernepublishing.com, and example.lucernepublishing.com, can become separate zones through the process of delegation, through which the responsibility for a subdomain within the DNS namespace is assigned to a separate entity.

Zone files contain the data for the zones for which a server is authoritative. In many DNS server implementations, zone data is stored in text files; however, DNS servers running on Active Directory domain controllers can also store zone information in Active Directory.

NOTE   What are forward and reverse lookup zones?

Zones can occur in one of two varieties: forward lookup zones and reverse lookup zones. A forward lookup zone is the main type of zone, in which names are resolved to IP addresses. In a reverse lookup zone, an IP address is resolved to a name. Zone types are discussed in more detail in Chapter 3, "Configuring a DNS Zone Infrastructure."

DNS Resolvers

A *DNS resolver* is a service that uses the DNS protocol to query for information from DNS servers. DNS resolvers communicate with either remote DNS servers or the DNS server program running on the local computer. In Windows Server 2008, the function of the DNS resolver is performed by the DNS Client service. Besides acting as a DNS resolver, the DNS Client service provides the added function of caching DNS mappings.

Resource Records

Resource records are DNS database entries that are used to answer DNS client queries. Each DNS server contains the resource records it needs to answer queries for its portion of the DNS namespace. Resource records are each described as a specific record type, such as IPv4 host address (A), IPv6 host address (AAAA, pronounced "quad-A"), alias (CNAME), pointer (PTR), and mail exchanger (MX). These records are covered in more detail in Lesson 1 of Chapter 3, "Configuring a DNS Zone Infrastructure."

Understanding How a DNS Query Works

When a DNS client needs to look up a name used by an application, it queries DNS servers to resolve the name. Each query message the client sends contains the following three pieces of information:

- A DNS domain name, stated as an FQDN. (The DNS Client service adds the suffixes necessary to generate an FQDN if the original client program does not provide them.)
- A specified query type, which can specify either a resource record by type or a specialized type of query operation.
- A specified class for the DNS domain name. (For the DNS Client service, this class is always specified as the Internet [IN] class.)

For example, the name could be specified as the FQDN for a particular host computer, such as host-a.example.microsoft.com., and the query type could be specified as a search for an A resource record by that name. You can think of a DNS query as a client asking a server a two-part question, such as, "Do you have any A resource records for a computer named hostname.example.microsoft.com?" When the client receives an answer from the server, the client reads the received A resource record and learns the IP address of the computer name originally queried for.

DNS Resolution Methods

DNS queries resolve in a number of different ways. In a basic scenario, the DNS client contacts a DNS server, which then uses its own database of resource records to answer a query. However, by referring to its cache first, a DNS client can sometimes answer a query without contacting a server at all. Another way that DNS queries are often resolved is through recursion. Using this process, a DNS server can query other DNS servers on behalf of the requesting client in order to resolve the FQDN. When the DNS server receives the answer to the query, it then sends an answer back to the client. A final method by which DNS queries are resolved is through iteration. Through this process the client itself attempts to contact additional DNS servers to resolve a name. When a client does so, it uses separate and additional queries based on referral answers from DNS servers. A client typically performs iteration only when a DNS server has been specifically configured not to perform recursion.

DNS Query Steps

In general, the DNS query process occurs in two stages:

- A name query begins at a client computer and is passed to the DNS Client service for resolution.
- When the query cannot be resolved locally, the DNS Client service passes the query to a DNS server.

Both of these processes are explained in more detail in the following sections.

Step 1: The Local Resolver   Figure 2-6 presents an overview of the default DNS query process, in which a client is configured to make recursive queries to a server. In this scenario, if the DNS Client service cannot resolve the query from locally cached information (which itself is preloaded with name-to-address mappings from the Hosts file), the client makes only a single query to a DNS server, which is then responsible for answering the query on behalf of the client.

In the figure, queries and answers are represented by Qs and As. The higher numbered queries are made only when the previous query is unsuccessful. For example, Q2 is performed only when Q1 is unsuccessful.

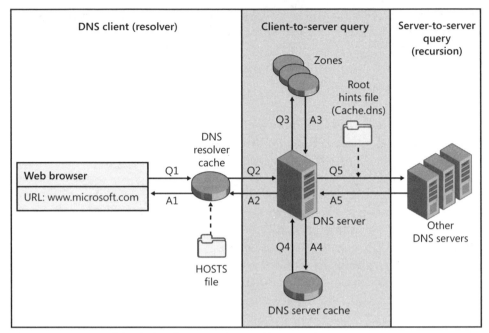

Figure 2-6   A possible chain of events triggered by a DNS name query

The query process begins when a DNS domain name is used in a program on the local computer. In the example shown in Figure 2-6, a Web browser calls the FQDN www.microsoft.com. The request is then passed to the DNS Client service (the DNS resolver cache) to resolve this name by using locally cached information. If the queried name can be resolved, the query is answered and the process is completed.

The local resolver cache can include name information obtained from two possible sources:

- If a Hosts file is configured locally, any host-name-to-address mappings from that file are loaded into the cache when the DNS Client service is started and whenever the Hosts file is updated. In Windows Server 2008, the Hosts file is essentially provided as a means to add entries to the resolver cache dynamically.

- Resource records obtained in answered responses from previous DNS queries are added to the cache and kept for a period of time.

If the query does not match an entry in the cache, the resolution process continues with the client querying a DNS server to resolve the name.

Quick Check

- If a computer needs to resolve a DNS name, what is the first method it attempts to use?

Quick Check Answer

- A computer first checks the resolver cache to answer a query.

Step 2: Querying a DNS Server   The DNS Client service uses a server search list ordered by preference. This list includes all preferred and alternate DNS servers configured for each of the active network connections on the system. The client first queries the DNS server specified as the preferred DNS server in the connection's Internet Protocol (TCP/IP) Properties dialog box. If no preferred DNS servers are available, alternate DNS servers are used. Figure 2-7 shows a sample list of preferred and alternate DNS servers, as configured in Windows Server 2008.

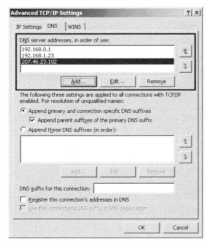

Figure 2-7   Preferred and alternate servers

When a DNS server receives a query, it first checks to see whether it can answer the query authoritatively—that is, on the basis of information contained in a locally configured zone on the server. If the queried name matches a corresponding resource record in local zone information, the server answers authoritatively, using this information to resolve the queried name.

If no zone information exists for the queried name, the server then checks to see whether it can resolve the name by using locally cached information from previous queries. If a match is found here, the server answers with this information. Again, if the preferred server can answer with a positive matched response from its cache to the requesting client, the query is completed.

Quick Check

1. When a DNS server receives a query, how does it first attempt to resolve the name?
2. If a DNS server cannot resolve a query by using the first method, which method will it use next?

Quick Check Answers

1. A DNS server first attempts to resolve a query by using resource records stored in a locally configured zone.
2. If a DNS server cannot resolve a query by using zone data, it attempts to answer the query by using cached information.

Understanding Recursion

If the queried name does not find a matched answer at its preferred server—either from its cache or zone information—the query process continues in a manner dependent on the DNS server configuration. In the default configuration, the DNS server performs recursion to resolve the name. In general, *recursion* in DNS refers to the process of a DNS server querying other DNS servers on behalf of an original querying client. This process, in effect, turns the original DNS server into a DNS client.

If recursion is disabled on the DNS server, the client itself performs iterative queries by using root hint referrals from the DNS server. *Iteration* refers to the process of a DNS client making repeated queries to different DNS servers.

Root Hints

To perform recursion properly, the DNS server first needs to know where to begin searching for names in the DNS domain namespace. This information is provided in the form of *root hints*, a list of preliminary resource records used by the DNS service to locate servers authoritative for the root of the DNS domain namespace tree.

By default, DNS servers running Windows Server 2008 use a preconfigured root hints file, Cache.dns, that is stored in the WINDOWS\System32\Dns folder on the server computer. The contents of this file are preloaded into server memory when the service is started and contain pointer information to root servers for the DNS namespace. Figure 2-8 shows the default root hints file.

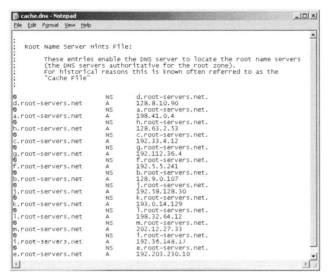

Figure 2-8   Root hints file

In Windows Server 2008, the root hints file already contains addresses of root servers in the Internet DNS namespace. Therefore, if you are using the DNS Server service in Windows Server 2008 to resolve Internet-based DNS names, the root hints file needs no manual configuration. If, however, you are using the DNS service on a private network, you can edit or replace this file with similar records that point to your own internal root DNS servers. Furthermore, for a computer that is hosting a root DNS server you should not use root hints at all. In this scenario, Windows Server 2008 automatically deletes the Cache.dns file used for root hints.

Query Example

The following example illustrates default DNS query behavior. In the example, the client queries its preferred DNS server, which then performs recursion by querying hierarchically superior DNS servers. The DNS client and all DNS servers are assumed to have empty caches.

In Figure 2-9 a client somewhere on the Internet needs to resolve the name example.lucerne-publishing.com to an IP address.

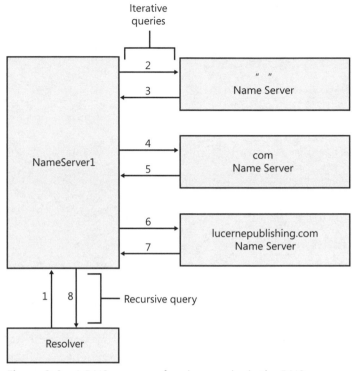

Figure 2-9   A DNS server performing queries in the DNS namespace to resolve a name on behalf of a client

When the DNS Client service on the client computer begins the query process, the following events take place:

1. The client contacts NameServer1 with a query for example.lucernepublishing.com.

2. NameServer1 checks its cache and zones for the answer but does not find it, so it contacts a server authoritative for the Internet (that is, a root server) with a query for example.lucernepublishing.com.

3. The server at the root of the Internet does not know the answer, so it responds with a referral to a server authoritative for the .com domain.

4. NameServer1 contacts a server authoritative for the .com domain with a query for example.lucernepublishing.com.

5. The server authoritative for the .com domain does not know the exact answer, so it responds with a referral to a server authoritative for the lucernepublishing.com domain.

6. NameServer1 contacts the server authoritative for the lucernepublishing.com domain with a query for example.lucernepublishing.com.

7. The server authoritative for the lucernepublishing.com domain does know the answer. It responds with the requested IP address.

8. NameServer1 responds to the client query with the IP address for example.lucernepublishing.com.

Quick Check

1. When would a DNS server contact a root server?
2. If a DNS server contacts a root server to resolve the name "www.contoso.com" and the root server cannot answer the query, how does the original server know which server to query next?

Quick Check Answers

1. A DNS server contacts a root server when it cannot answer a query with its own cached or authoritative data.
2. The root server responds to the DNS server with a referral for the address of the DNS server authoritative for the ".com" domain. The DNS server then contacts this server for which it has received a referral.

Understanding How Caching Works

Both the DNS Client service and the DNS Server service maintain caches. Caching provides a way to improve DNS performance and to substantially reduce DNS-related query traffic on the network.

DNS Client Cache

The DNS client cache is also called the DNS resolver cache. Whenever the DNS Client service starts, all host-name-to-IP-address mappings contained in a static file named Hosts are preloaded into the DNS resolver cache. The Hosts file can be found in WINDOWS \System32 \Drivers\Etc.

NOTE How is the Hosts file used?

Whenever you add an entry to the Hosts file, that entry is immediately loaded into the DNS resolver cache.

In addition to the entries in the Hosts file, the DNS resolver cache also includes entries the client has received in response to a query from DNS servers. The DNS resolver cache is emptied whenever the DNS Client service is stopped.

Exam Tip   For the 70-642 exam, you need to know the difference between the Hosts file and the Lmhosts file. The Hosts file helps resolve host names (essentially DNS names) to IP addresses, and the Lmhosts file helps resolve NetBIOS names to IP addresses.

DNS Server Cache

As DNS servers make recursive queries on behalf of clients, they temporarily cache resource records. These cached records contain information acquired in the process of answering queries on behalf of a client. Later, when other clients place new queries that request information matching cached resource records, the DNS server can use the cached information to answer these queries.

The DNS server cache is cleared whenever the DNS Server service is stopped. In addition, you can clear the DNS server cache manually in the DNS console—the administrative tool used for DNS administration—by right-clicking the server icon in the console tree and then choosing Clear Cache. Finally, you can clear the server cache at the command line by typing the command **Dnscmd /clearcache** at a command prompt.

Time to Live Values   A Time to Live (TTL) value applies to all cached resource records, whether in the DNS resolver cache or the DNS server cache. As long as the TTL for a cached resource record does not expire, a DNS resolver or server can continue to use that record to answer queries. By default, the TTL is 3600 seconds (1 hour), but you can adjust this parameter at both the zone and record levels.

PRACTICE Exploring Automatic Name Resolution in Local Networks

In this practice, you explore the name resolution mechanisms that are available in Windows networks before a DNS server is installed and configured. By turning on and off various features and then attempting to connect to a computer in three ways (ping, UNC path, and the Network window), you will learn which features enable which functionality.

To begin the exercises in this practice, on Dcsrv1 and Boston, File Sharing must be turned on and Network Discovery must be turned off. Only a single local area connection should be enabled on both computers. Dcsrv1 should be assigned the IPv4 address 192.168.0.1/24 and the IPv6 address fd00::1. Boston should be assigned the IPv4 address 192.168.0.2/24 and the IPv6 address fd00::2.

▶ **Exercise 1   Testing Automatic Name Resolution on an IPv4-only Workgroup without NetBIOS or Network Discovery**

In this exercise, for the local area connections on both Dcsrv1 and Boston, you disable the IPv6 protocol and NetBIOS in IPv4.

1. Log on to Boston as an administrator.

2. In the Initial Configuration Tasks window, click Configure Networking. If the Initial Configuration Tasks window is not open, you can instead open Server Manager and then click View Network Connections. (Note also that you can always open the Initial Configuration Tasks window by typing **oobe** in the Run box.)

3. In Network Connections, open the properties of Local Area Connection.

4. In the Local Area Connection Properties dialog box, clear the Internet Protocol Version 6 (TCP/IPv6) check box.

5. Double-click the Internet Protocol Version 4 (TCP/IPv6) check box.

6. In the Internet Protocol Version 4 (TCP/IPv4) Properties dialog box, click the Advanced button, and then click the WINS tab in the Advanced TCP/IP Settings dialog box.

7. In the WINS tab, select Disable NetBIOS Over TCP/IP, and then click OK.

NOTE   NetBIOS is for IPv4 only

NetBIOS does not exist within IPv6. It's a feature found in IPv4 Windows networks only.

---

8. In the Internet Protocol Version 4 (TCP/IPv4) Properties dialog box, click OK.

9. In the Local Area Connection Properties dialog box, click OK.

10. Restart the computer.

11. Perform steps 1 through 10 on Dcsrv1. When both computers have finished restarting, proceed to step 12.

12. Log on to Boston as an administrator. At a command prompt on Boston, type **ping dcsrv1**.

    You receive a message indicating that the Ping request could not find the host. Without NetBIOS, Boston has no way to resolve the name dcsrv1 on an IPv4-only network for which DNS has not been configured.

13. At the command prompt on Boston, type **ping 192.168.0.1**.

    You receive a response from 192.168.0.1. You can determine that connectivity is established between the two computers; the problem is name resolution only.

14. From the Run box, type **\\dcsrv1**, and then press Enter.

    A Network Error message appears, indicating that Windows cannot access \\dcsrv1.

NOTE UNC paths

This type of network path to a remote computer is known as a UNC path.

---

15. Click Cancel to dismiss the Network Error message.
16. From the Run box, type **\\192.168.0.1**, and then press Enter.

    A connection is established, indicated by an open window displaying the shared folders on Dcsrv1. At this time only the Printers folder is shared.
17. From the Start Menu, choose Network.

    The Network window displays no computers. In the window, a yellow band displays a message indicating that Network Discovery is turned off.
18. Close all open windows.

▶ **Exercise 2   Testing Automatic Name Resolution on an IPv4/IPv6 Workgroup with Both NetBIOS and Network Discovery Disabled**

In this exercise, you leave NetBIOS disabled and enable IPv6. You then observe functionality for Ping, UNC path connectivity, and the Network window.

1. On both Boston and Dcsrv1, in the properties of Local Area Connection, enable IPv6 by selecting the Internet Protocol Version 6 (TCP/IPv6) check box.
2. Restart both computers.
3. Log on to Boston as an administrator. At a command prompt, type **ping dcsrv1**.

    You receive a message indicating that the Ping request could not find the host. IPv6 by itself does not facilitate name resolution.
4. At the command prompt, type **ping fd00::1**.

    You receive a response, indicating that you can now ping Dcsrv1 by its IPv6 address in addition to its IPv4 address.
5. From the Run box, type **\\dcsrv1**, and then press Enter.

    A Network Error message appears, indicating that Windows cannot access \\dcsrv1.

    By itself, IPv6 does not enable you to use a UNC path connect to a computer specified by name.
6. Click Cancel to dismiss the Network Error message.
7. From the Run box, type **\\fd00--1.ipv6-literal.net**, and then press Enter.

    The fd00--1.ipv6-literal.net window opens, displaying the Printers share on Dcsrv1. This is the syntax you must use to connect to a computer by specifying its IPv6 address in a

UNC path. Notice that in the IPv6 UNC path you replace each of the colons in the original IPv6 address with a hyphen and append the suffix ".ipv6-literal.net" to the address.

8. From the Start Menu, choose Network.

   The Network window still displays no computers.

9. Close all open windows.

NOTE IPv6 by itself does not enable name resolution

Because no name resolution was exhibited in this last exercise even when IPv6 was enabled together with IPv4, we do not need to test name resolution in an IPv6-only network with Network Discovery disabled. In an IPv6-only subnet without Network Discovery or DNS, you cannot ping a computer by name, connect to a computer by specifying its UNC, or see it listed in the Network window.

▶ **Exercise 3   Testing Automatic Name Resolution on an IPv4-only Workgroup with NetBIOS Enabled and Network Discovery Disabled**

In this exercise, you disable IPv6 and enable NetBIOS on both computers. Then you observe functionality for Ping, UNC path connectivity, and the Network window.

1. On Boston, open the properties of Local Area Connection, and then clear the Internet Protocol Version 6 (TCP/IPv6) check box.

2. Double-click Internet Protocol Version 4 (TCP/IPv4).

3. In the Internet Protocol Version 4 (TCP/IPv4) Properties dialog box, click the Advanced button, and then click the WINS tab in the Advanced TCP/IP Settings dialog box.

4. In the NetBIOS Setting area, select Default, and then click OK.

   This option enables NetBIOS unless a DHCP server disables it.

5. Click OK to close the Internet Protocol Version 4 (TCP/IPv4) Properties dialog box, and then click OK to close the Local Area Connection Properties dialog box.

6. Restart the computer.

7. Perform steps 1 through 6 on Dcsrv1. When both computers have finished restarting, proceed to step 8.

8. Log on to Boston as an administrator.

9. At a command prompt, type **ping dcsrv1**.

   You receive a reply from the IPv4 address of 192.168.0.1. This response demonstrates that NetBIOS resolves computer names in an IPv4-only subnet without a DNS server.

10. From the Run box, type **\\dcsrv1**, and then press Enter.

    The dcsrv1 window opens, displaying the Printers share on Dcsrv1. We can determine from this step that NetBIOS resolves local computer names specified in a UNC.

11. From the Start menu, choose Network.

    The Network window is still empty. In Windows Server 2008 networks, NetBIOS is not used to display computers in the Network window.

12. Close all open windows.

▶ **Exercise 4   Testing Automatic Name Resolution on an IPv4/IPv6 Workgroup with NetBIOS Enabled and Network Discovery Disabled**

In this exercise, you enable IPv6 on both computers and observe the behavior.

1. On both computers, open the properties of Local Area Connection, and then enable IPv6 by selecting the Internet Protocol Version 6 (TCP/IPv6) check box.

2. Restart both computers.

3. Log on to Boston as an administrator.

4. From a command prompt, type **ping dcsrv1**.

    You receive a response. Notice that with NetBIOS enabled and Network Discovery disabled, the response is from the IPv4 address of Dcsrv1, even though both IPv4 and IPv6 are enabled. Later you will observe the circumstances under which this behavior will change.

5. From the Start Menu, choose Network.

    The Network window is still empty.

    We do not need to check for UNC path connectivity because we know this will work when NetBIOS is enabled. Adding a protocol or a service (in this case IPv6) never removes name resolution functionality.

6. Close all open windows.

▶ **Exercise 5   Enabling Network Discovery**

In this exercise, you will enable Network Discovery on both Boston and Dscrv1. In the remaining exercises you will observe the functionality enabled by this feature.

1. On Boston, open Network And Sharing Center.

2. In the Sharing And Discovery area, click the Off button next to Network Discovery.

3. Select Turn On Network Discovery, and then click Apply.

    A Network Discovery message appears, asking whether you want to turn on Network Discovery for all Public networks.

4. Click Yes, Turn On Network Discovery For All Public Networks.

    Note that this option is only recommended for test environments.

5. Restart the computer.

6. Perform steps 1–5 on Dcsrv1.

▶ Exercise 6   **Testing Automatic Name Resolution on an IPv4-only Workgroup with Network Discovery Enabled and NetBIOS Disabled**

In this exercise, you disable IPv6 and NetBIOS in IPv4. You then observe the distinctive behavior that results from this configuration.

1. Using the instructions given in the previous exercises, on Local Area Connection on both computers, disable both IPv6 and NetBIOS in IPv4. After you perform this step, restart both computers.

2. When both computers finish restarting, log on to Boston as an administrator.

3. At the command prompt, type **ping dcsrv1**.

    You receive a message indicating that the Ping request could not find the host.

    In an IPv4-only network, you need NetBIOS to be able to ping a computer by name. Network Discovery does not provide this functionality.

4. In the Run box, **type \\dcsrv1**, and then press Enter.

    In an IPv4-only network, you cannot connect to a computer by specifying its name in a UNC pathname unless NetBIOS is enabled. Network Discovery does not enable this functionality in IPv4 networks.

5. From the Start Menu, choose Network.

    The Network window displays either Boston, or Dcsrv1, or both. Both will eventually appear if you refresh the screen.

    Network Discovery is the feature that populates the Network window in IPv4.

6. When Dcsrv1 appears in the Network window, double-click its icon.

    You receive a message indicating that Windows cannot access \\DCSRV1. Double-clicking a computer in the Network window is functionally equivalent to attempting to connect by specifying the computer's name in a UNC. Even if you can see a computer listed in the Network window, you cannot connect to it because NetBIOS is disabled in this IPv4-only network.

7. Close all open windows.

▶ Exercise 7   **Testing Automatic Name Resolution on an IPv4-only Workgroup with Both Network Discovery and NetBIOS Enabled**

In this exercise, you enable NetBIOS and observe the change in name resolution behavior.

1. Using the instructions provided in the previous exercises, on the Local Area Connection on both computers, enable NetBIOS in IPv4 by selecting the NetBIOS setting of Default in the WINS tab of the Advanced TCP/IP Settings dialog box. (Leave IPv6 disabled for the connection.) After you perform this step, restart both computers.

2. When both computers finish restarting, log on to Boston as an administrator.

3. From the Start Menu, choose Network.

4. When Dcsrv1 appears in the Network window, double-click its icon.

    The DCSRV1 window opens, displaying the Printers share on Dcsrv1.

    This combination of features provides full name resolution functionality for IPv4 work-groups. With both NetBIOS and Network Discovery enabled, in an IPv4-only subnet without DNS we can ping a computer by name, connect to a computer by specifying its UNC, or browse to it by using the Network window.

5. Close all open windows.

▶ **Exercise 8   Testing Automatic Name Resolution on an IPv6-only Workgroup with Network Discovery Enabled**

In this exercise you enable IPv6 and disable IPv4 (and therefore NetBIOS). You then observe name resolution behavior in the IPv6-only network with Network Discovery enabled.

1. On Boston, open the properties of Local Area Connection.

2. In the Local Area Connection properties dialog box, enable IPv6 by selecting the Internet Protocol Version 6 (TCP/IPv6) check box.

3. Disable IPv4 by clearing the Internet Protocol Version 4 (TCP/IPv4) check box.

4. In the Local Area Connection Properties dialog box, click OK.

5. Restart the computer.

6. Perform steps 1–5 on Dcsrv1.

7. When both computers finish restarting, log on to Boston as an administrator.

8. From a command prompt, type **ping dcsrv1**.

    You receive a response from the link-local IPv6 address on Dcsrv1.

    As this step shows, Network Discovery provides name resolution services for IPv6 that it does not provide for IPv4. In an IPv4 network, you need to have NetBIOS enabled to ping a computer by name.

9. In the Run box, type **\\dcsrv1**, and then press Enter.

    Again, this procedure shows that Network Discovery provides services for IPv6 that it does not provide for IPv4. In an IPv4-only network, you need NetBIOS to connect to another computer by specifying its name in a UNC. In an IPv6-only network, you need Network Discovery to perform this same task.

10. From the Start Menu, choose Network.

11. When Dcsrv1 appears in the Network window, double-click its icon.

    The DCSRV1 window opens, displaying the Printers share on Dcsrv1.

Network Discovery essentially provides the name resolution services for IPv6 that NetBIOS provides for IPv4. In addition, Network Discovery populates the Network window for both IPv4 and IPv6.

12. Close all open windows.

▶ **Exercise 9   Testing Automatic Name Resolution on an IPv4/IPv6 Workgroup with Both NetBIOS and Network Discovery Enabled**

In this exercise, you enable IPv4. You then ping Dcsrv1 from Boston and observe a difference in the Ping output.

1. Use the instructions provided in the previous exercises to enable IPv4 on the Local Area Connection on both computers. Verify that both NetBIOS and IPv6 remain enabled.

2. Restart both computers.

3. At the command prompt, type **ping dcsrv1**.

   You receive a response from the link-local IPv6 address on Dcsrv1. Note that when IPv6, IPv4, Network Discovery, and NetBIOS are all enabled in a subnet without DNS, LLMNR is used to resolve names, and it does so by first resolving the name to an IPv6 address.

4. Shut down both computers.

Lesson Summary

- To resolve a name means to translate the name of a computer to an IP address.

- Windows networks can perform name resolution by using any of three separate name resolution systems. DNS is the preferred name resolution service and is by far the most common, especially in large networks. However, because of the way DNS is designed, it requires configuration.

- LLMNR is the name resolution method used for a single subnet that has no DNS infrastructure, that contains computers running only Windows Vista or Windows Server 2008, and that has both IPv6 and Network Discovery enabled on its computers.

- NetBIOS is a legacy protocol and naming system used for compatibility with older Windows network services. NetBIOS provides the only name resolution in Windows that works by default on a network without DNS. NetBIOS can resolve names by using network broadcasts, a WINS server, or a local Lmhosts file. NetBIOS is compatible only with IPv4 and not with IPv6.

- DNS provides a hierarchical name structure. In DNS, an FQDN is a domain name that has been stated unambiguously to indicate its location relative to the root of the DNS domain tree. An example of an FQDN is Client1.east.fabrikam.com.

- A *DNS zone* is a portion of a namespace for which a server is authoritative. When a server hosts a zone such as fabrikam.com, the zone contains resource records that map names to IP addresses within that namespace. For example, the DNS server hosting the fabrikam.com zone can authoritatively resolve names like client1.fabrikam.com and server2.fabrikam.com.

- In general, a DNS client that needs to resolve a DNS name first checks its local cache for the answer. If it doesn't find the answer, the DNS client queries its preferred DNS server. If the DNS server cannot resolve the query through authoritative or cached data, the DNS server will attempt to resolve the query by performing iterative queries against the DNS namespace, beginning with the root server.

Lesson Review

The following questions are intended to reinforce key information presented in this lesson. The questions are also available on the companion CD if you prefer to review them in electronic form.

NOTE Answers

Answers to these questions and explanations of why each answer choice is correct or incorrect are located in the "Answers" section at the end of the book.

1. After the address of a certain client computer is updated, you notice that a local DNS server is resolving the name of the computer incorrectly from cached information. How can you best resolve this problem?

    A. At the DNS server, type the command **dnscmd /clearcache**.

    B. Restart the DNS Client service on the client computer.

    C. At the client computer, type **ipconfig /flushdns**.

    D. Restart all DNS client computers.

2. You are working on a Windows Server 2008 computer named WS08A. You cannot connect to computers running Windows XP on the local network by specifying them by name in a UNC path such as \\computer1.

    What can you do to enable your computer to connect to these computers by specifying them in a UNC?

    A. Enable IPv6 on WS08A.

    B. Disable IPv6 on WS08A.

    C. Enable Local Link Multicast Name Resolution (LLMNR) on WS08A.

    D. Enable NetBIOS on WS08A.

Lesson 2: Deploying a DNS Server

Active Directory domains require DNS servers in order to enable all domain members to resolve the names of computers and services. In most Windows networks, in fact, DNS servers are hosted on the Active Directory domain controllers themselves. Deploying a new DNS server in such a case requires very little administrative expertise, but you still need to know how to customize a DNS deployment to meet the particular needs of your organization.

This lesson introduces you to DNS server deployment and configuration. Whereas the topic of creating and configuring zones is covered in Chapter 3, "Configuring a DNS Zone Infrastructure," this lesson focuses on configuring server-wide properties and features.

After this lesson, you will be able to:
- Deploy a DNS server on a new Active Directory domain controller
- Deploy a DNS server on a computer that is not a domain controller
- Deploy a DNS server on a Server Core installation of Windows Server 2008
- Configure DNS server properties
- Understand when to configure DNS forwarding

Estimated lesson time: 60 minutes

Deploying a DNS Server on a Domain Controller

Active Directory Domain Services (AD DS), which provides the unified management structure for all accounts and resources in a Windows network, is tightly integrated with DNS. In Active Directory, DNS is required for locating resources like domain controllers, and DNS zone data can optionally be stored within the Active Directory database.

When you deploy a DNS server within an Active Directory domain, you typically do so on a domain controller. Deploying DNS servers on domain controllers enables the zone to benefit from additional features, such as secure dynamic updates and Active Directory replication among multiple DNS servers. The best way to deploy a DNS server on a domain controller, in turn, is to install it at the same time as you install the domain controller.

To promote a server to a domain controller for a new or existing domain, run Dcpromo.exe. This program first installs the AD DS binaries (the data elements common to all Active Directory domains) and then launches the AD DS Installation Wizard. The wizard prompts you for the name of the Active Directory domain, such as Fabrikam.com, for which you are installing the domain controller. The name you give to the Active Directory domain then becomes the name of the associated DNS zone. This page in the AD DS Installation Wizard is shown in Figure 2-10.

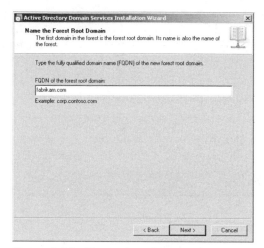

Figure 2-10 The Active Directory domain name becomes a DNS zone name

NOTE What is the Active Directory Domain Services server role?

Installing the AD DS binaries can require up to five minutes, and because of this time requirement you might prefer to install the AD DS binaries as a separate step before running *Dcpromo*. To do so, use the Add Roles Wizard to add the Active Directory Domain Services server role. Note that this server role does not provide any functionality until you run *Dcpromo*.

Later in the wizard you are given an opportunity to install a DNS server on the same domain controller. This option is selected by default, as shown in Figure 2-11.

If you do choose to install a DNS Server along with the new domain controller, the DNS server and the hosted forward lookup zone will automatically be configured for you. You can review or manage these settings in DNS Manager, as shown in Figure 2-12, after the AD DS Installation Wizard completes. To open DNS Manager, click Start, point to Administrative Tools, and then choose DNS.

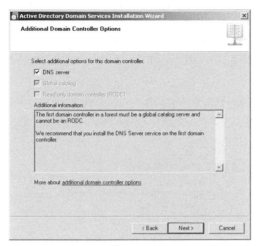

Figure 2-11   Installing a DNS server along with an Active Directory domain controller

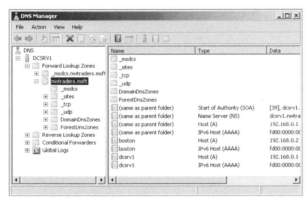

Figure 2-12   *Dcpromo* can automatically configure a locally hosted DNS server with a forward lookup zone for the domain

Quick Check
- What is the main function of *Dcpromo*?

Quick Check Answer
- It is used to promote a server to a domain controller.

Deploying a DNS Server on a Stand-alone or Member Server

Your name resolution infrastructure might require you to install a DNS server on a stand-alone server or on a member server in an Active Directory domain. In this case you will need to install a DNS server without using *Dcpromo*.

To install a DNS server, use the Add Roles Wizard available in Server Manager or the Initial Configuration Tasks window. Then, in the wizard, select the DNS Server role (as shown in Figure 2-13) and follow the prompts.

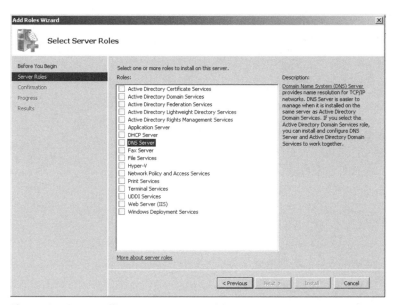

Figure 2-13   Installing a DNS server without AD DS

Installing the DNS server separately from AD DS requires you to configure the DNS server manually afterward. The main task in configuring a DNS server manually is to add and configure one or more forward lookup zones. To add a forward lookup zone, right-click the Forward Lookup Zones folder in the DNS Manager console tree, and then choose New Zone, as shown in Figure 2-14.

For more information about creating, configuring, and managing DNS zones, see Chapter 3, "Configuring a DNS Zone Infrastructure."

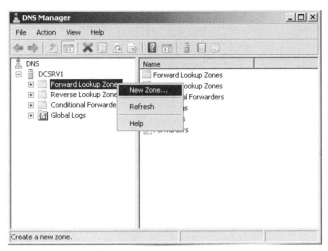

Figure 2-14   Adding a New Zone

Deploying a DNS Server on a Server Core Installation of Windows Server 2008

You can install a DNS server on a Server Core installation of Windows Server 2008 along with AD DS by using *Dcpromo*, in which case the DNS server can be installed and configured automatically. You also have the option of installing the DNS server as a stand-alone or member server.

To install a DNS server along with a domain controller on a Server Core installation, use *Dcpromo*. However, no wizard is available to facilitate the process. You must specify an answer file with the *Dcpromo* command.

To install the Active Directory Domain Services role on a Server Core installation, at the command prompt type **dcpromo /unattend:<*unattendfile*>**, where *unattendfile* is the name of a Dcpromo.exe unattend or answer file.

You can create the Dcpromo answer file by running *Dcpromo* on another computer that is running a full installation of Windows Server 2008. On the last (Summary) page of the wizard, before the installation is actually performed, you are given an opportunity to export settings to an answer file, as shown in Figure 2-15. You can then cancel out of the wizard and use the answer file with *Dcpromo* on the Server Core installation.

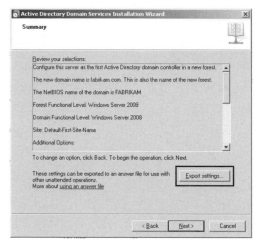

Figure 2-15   Creating an answer file for *Dcpromo*

If you want to install a DNS server on a stand-alone or member server running a Server Core installation of Windows Server 2008, type the following command:

```
start /w ocsetup DNS-Server-Core-Role
```

To remove the role, type the following:

```
start /w ocsetup DNS-Server-Core-Role /uninstall
```

After you have installed the DNS server on a Server Core installation, whether by using *Dcpromo* or the *Start /w ocsetup* command, you can configure and manage the server by connecting to it through DNS Manager on another computer.

To connect to another server from DNS Manager, right-click the root (server name) icon in the DNS Manager console tree, and then choose Connect To DNS Server, as shown in Figure 2-16.

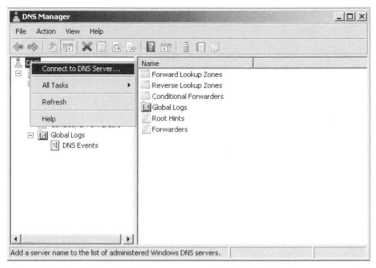

Figure 2-16   Using DNS Manager on a full installation to manage a DNS server installed on a Server Core installation

Configuring a Caching-only DNS Server

All DNS servers include a cache of query responses. Although a DNS server initially contains no cached information, cached information is obtained over time as client requests are serviced. When a client queries a DNS server with a name resolution request, the DNS server first checks its cache to see if it already has the answer stored. If the server can respond with information from resource records found in the local cache, the server response to the client is much faster.

Cached records stay alive in the server cache until they exceed their TTL value, until the the DNS Server service is restarted, or until the cache is cleared manually.

Caching-only servers do not host any zones and are not authoritative for any particular domain. However, the mere availability of a DNS server cache that is shared by clients can be useful in certain network scenarios.

For example, if your network includes a branch office with a slow wide area network (WAN) link between sites, a caching-only server can improve name resolution response times because after the cache is built, traffic across the WAN link decreases. DNS queries are resolved faster, which can improve the performance of network applications and other features. In addition, the caching-only server does not perform zone transfers, which can also be network-intensive in WAN environments. In general, a caching-only DNS server can be valuable at a site where DNS functionality is needed locally but where administering domains or zones is not desirable.

Exam Tip   You can use a caching-only server when you want to improve name resolution for a branch office that has little technical expertise on its local staff. For example, if the headquarters for Contoso.com is in New York and a branch office is in Albany, you might not want to host a copy of the Contoso.com zone at the Albany office because managing that zone would require too much technical expertise. However, a caching-only server, which requires no technical expertise to maintain, would allow users in the Albany office to channel their DNS queries through a single server and create a large pool of cached queries. Repeated queries could then be resolved from the local server cache instead of through queries across the Internet, thereby improving response times.

By default, the DNS Server service acts as a caching-only server. Caching-only servers thus require little or no configuration.

To install a caching-only DNS server, complete the following steps:

1. Install the DNS server role on the server computer.
2. Do not create any zones.
3. Verify that server root hints are configured or updated correctly.

Configuring Server Properties

The DNS server properties dialog box allows you to configure settings that apply to the DNS server and all its hosted zones. You can access this dialog box in DNS Manager by right-clicking the icon of the DNS server you want to configure and then choosing Properties.

Interfaces Tab

The Interfaces tab allows you to specify which of the local computer's IP addresses the DNS server should listen to for DNS requests. For example, if your server is multihomed (has more than one network adapter) and uses specific addresses for the local network and others for the Internet connection, you can prevent the DNS server from servicing DNS queries from the public interface. To perform this task, specify that the DNS server listen only on the computer's internal IP addresses, as shown in Figure 2-17.

By default, the setting on this tab specifies that the DNS server listens on all IP addresses associated with the local computer.

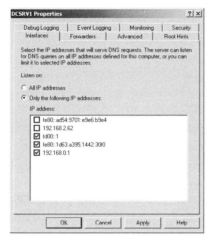

Figure 2-17   You can configure a multihomed DNS server to provide service to one network only. In this figure, the selected addresses are all associated with the same network adapter.

Root Hints Tab

The Root Hints tab contains a copy of the information found in the WINDOWS\System32 \Dns\Cache.dns file. For DNS servers answering queries for Internet names, this information does not need to be modified. However, when you are configuring a root DNS server (named ".") for a private network, you should delete the entire Cache.dns file. (When your DNS server is hosting a root server, the Root Hints tab is unavailable.)

In addition, if you are configuring a DNS server within a large private namespace, you can use this tab to delete the Internet root servers and specify the root servers in your network instead.

NOTE   Updating the root servers list

Every few years the list of root servers on the Internet is slightly modified. Because the Cache.dns file already contains so many possible root servers to contact, it is not necessary to modify the root hints file as soon as these changes occur. However, if you do learn of the availability of new root servers, you can choose to update your root hints accordingly. As of this writing, the last update to the root servers list was made on November 1, 2007. You can download the latest version of the named cache file from InterNIC at *ftp://rs.internic.net/domain/named.cache*.

Figure 2-18 shows the Root Hints tab.

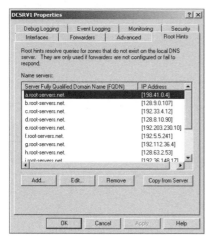

Figure 2-18   Root Hints tab

Forwarders Tab

The Forwarders tab allows you to configure the local DNS server to forward DNS queries it receives to upstream DNS servers, called *forwarders*. Using this tab, you can specify the IP addresses of upstream DNS servers to which queries should be directed if the local DNS server cannot provide a response through its cache or zone data. For example, in Figure 2-19 all queries that cannot be resolved by the local server will be forwarded to the DNS server 192.168.2.200. When, after receiving and forwarding a query from an internal client, the local forwarding server receives a query response from 192.168.2.200, the local forwarding server passes this query response back to the original querying client.

In all cases, a DNS server that is configured for forwarding uses forwards only after it has determined that it cannot resolve a query using its authoritative data (primary or secondary zone data) or cached data.

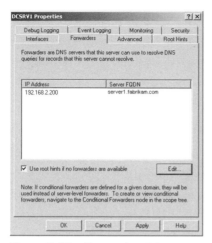

Figure 2-19   Forwarders tab

When to Use Forwarders   In some cases network administrators might not want DNS servers to communicate directly with external servers. For example, if your organization is connected to the Internet through a slow link, you can optimize name resolution performance by channeling all DNS queries through one forwarder, as shown in Figure 2-20. Through this method, the server cache of the DNS forwarder has the maximum potential to grow and reduce the need for external queries.

Another common use of forwarding is to allow DNS clients and servers inside a firewall to resolve external names securely. When an internal DNS server or client communicates with external DNS servers by making iterative queries, the ports used for DNS communication with all external servers must normally be left open to the outside world through the firewall. However, by configuring a DNS server inside a firewall to forward external queries to a single DNS forwarder outside your firewall and by then opening ports only for this one forwarder, you can resolve names without exposing your network to outside servers. Figure 2-21 illustrates this arrangement.

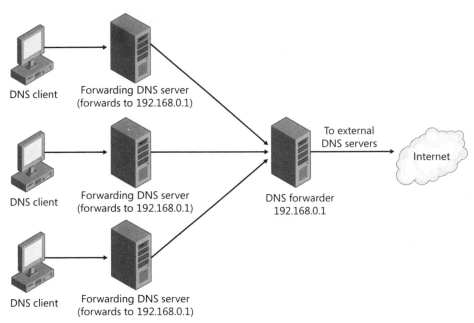

Figure 2-20 Using forwarding to consolidate caching

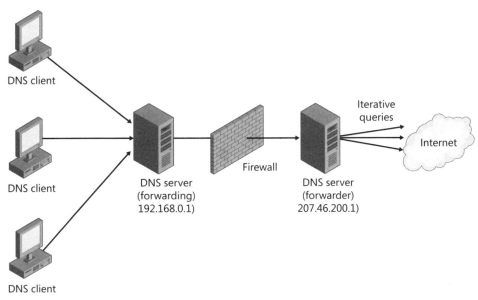

Figure 2-21 Secure iteration with forwarders

Finally, a third use of DNS forwarders is within an Active Directory forest hierarchy. When you have an Active Directory forest with multiple domains, DNS delegations naturally enable client queries within parent domains to resolve the names of resources in child (sub) domains. However, without forwarding there is no built-in mechanism that allows clients in child domains to resolve queries for names in parent domains. To enable this necessary functionality, DNS servers in the child domains of multidomain forests are typically configured to forward unresolved queries to the forest root domain DNS server or servers, as shown in Figure 2-22.

Forwarding to the root domain DNS servers in an organization in this way enables client queries originating in child domains to resolve names of resources not only in the root domain, but also in all the domains in the forest.

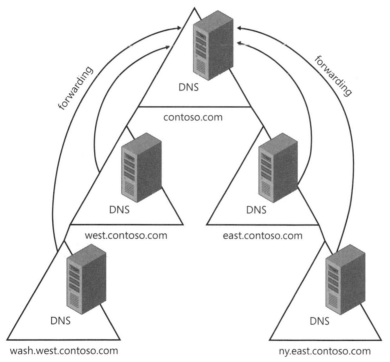

Figure 2-22   Forwarding queries within an Active Directory forest

When to Use Conditional Forwarding   The term *conditional forwarding* describes a DNS server configuration in which queries for specific domains are forwarded to specific DNS servers.

One of the many scenarios in which conditional forwarding is useful is when two separate networks merge. For example, suppose the Contoso and Fabrikam companies have separate networks with Active Directory domains. After the two companies merge, a 128-Kbps leased line is used to connect the private networks. For clients in each company to resolve queries for names in the opposite network, conditional forwarding is configured on the DNS servers in both domains. Queries to resolve names in the opposite domain will be forwarded to the DNS server in that domain. All Internet queries are forwarded to the next DNS server upstream beyond the firewall. This scenario is depicted in Figure 2-23.

Note that conditional forwarding is not the only way to provide name resolution in this type of merger scenario. You can also configure secondary zones and stub zones, which are described in Chapter 3, "Configuring a DNS Zone Infrastructure." These zone types provide basically the same name resolution service that conditional forwarding does. However, conditional forwarding minimizes zone transfer traffic, provides zone data that is always up-to-date, and allows for simple configuration and maintenance.

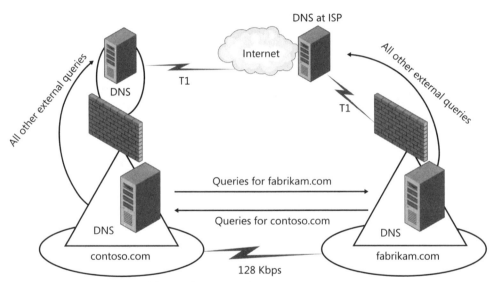

Figure 2-23   A conditional forwarding scenario

To configure conditional forwarding for a domain, you do not use the DNS server properties dialog box. You use the Conditional Forwarders container in the DNS Manager console tree. To add a conditional forwarder, right-click the Conditional Forwarder container, and then choose New Conditional Forwarder, as shown in Figure 2-24.

Then, in the New Conditional Forwarder dialog box that opens, specify the domain name for which DNS queries should be forwarded along with the address of the associated DNS server. The New Conditional Forwarder dialog box is shown in Figure 2-25.

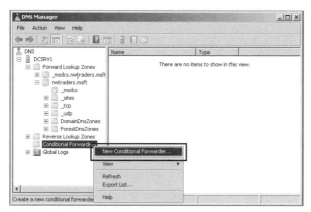

Figure 2-24   Adding a conditional forwarder

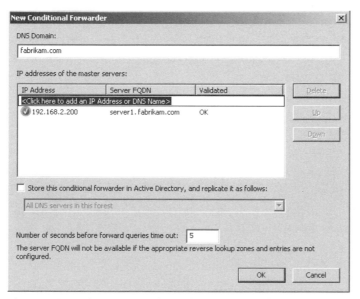

Figure 2-25   The New Conditional Forwarder dialog box

Exam Tip   You will almost certainly see a question about conditional forwarding on the 70-642 exam. Understand its purpose and scenarios in which it might be useful.

PRACTICE Exploring DNS in an Active Directory Environment

In this practice, you create an Active Directory domain named Nwtraders.msft. During the process of creating this Active Directory domain, a DNS server is created for hosting the zone lookup information for Nwtraders.msft. You then explore this zone information along with the DNS server settings, create a domain administrator account for personal use, add the Boston computer to the domain, and observe the new DNS records created for Boston.

▶ **Practice 1   Creating a Domain Controller**

In this exercise, you use the Dcpromo program to create a domain controller for a new Active Directory domain named Nwtraders.msft.

1. Log on to Dcsrv1 with the account named Administrator.

2. In the Run box, type **dcpromo**, and then press Enter.

    A message appears indicating the Active Directory Domain Services binaries are being installed. After the binaries have been installed, the Active Directory Domain Services Installation Wizard appears.

3. On the Welcome page of the Active Directory Domain Services Installation Wizard, read all the text on the page, and then click Next.

4. On the Operating System Compatibility page, click Next.

5. On the Choose A Deployment Configuration page, select Create A New Domain In A New Forest, and then click Next.

6. On the Name The Forest Root Domain page, type **nwtraders.msft**, and then click Next.

    The forest name is verified to ensure that it is unique on the network, and then the NetBIOS name is verified.

7. On the Set Forest Functional Level page, select the Windows Server 2008 functional level, read the text in the Details section, and click Next.

8. On the Additional Domain Controller Options page, verify that DNS Server is selected, read the text in the Additional Information section, and click Next.

    A dialog box appears and informs you that a delegation for this server cannot be created. You receive this message because you are creating a new DNS root domain and not a subdomain (for example, in the Internet namespace).

9. Click Yes to continue.

10. On the Location For Database, Log Files, And SYSVOL page, review the default settings, and then click Next.

11. On the Directory Services Restore Mode Administrator Password page, read all the text on the page, and then type a password of your choice in the Password and Confirm Password fields.

12. Click Next.

13. On the Summary page, review the summary information (especially the DNS server information), and then click Export Settings.

    You should always choose this option because it generates an answer file that you can later modify to use with Dcpromo on a Server Core installation. If you want to promote a Server Core installation to a domain controller, you must specify such an answer file.

14. In the Save Unattend File dialog box, specify a name, such as DCunattend, and then save the text file in the default location (the Documents folder).

    A message box appears, informing you that the settings were successfully exported.

15. Click OK.

16. On the Summary page of the Active Directory Domain Services Installation Wizard, click Next.

    The Active Directory Domain Services Installation Wizard dialog box appears while the DNS Server and Active Directory Domain Services are installed and configured.

    When the installation completes, the Completing page of the Active Directory Domain Services Installation Wizard appears.

17. Click Finish.

    A dialog box appears informing you that you need to restart your computer for the changes take effect.

18. Click Restart Now.

▶ **Practice 2   Reviewing DNS Server Information**

In this exercise, you review the DNS server configuration on Dcsrv1.

1. After Dcsrv1 finishes restarting, log on to Nwtraders from Dcsrv1 as Administrator.

   After a few moments the Initial Configuration Tasks window appears.

2. If the Select Features page of the Add Features Wizard appears, click Cancel and then Yes to confirm the cancel.

3. In the Initial Configuration Tasks window, verify that the computer name is now *dcsrv1.nwtraders.msft* and that the domain is *nwtraders.msft*.

4. Open the DNS Manager console by clicking Start, pointing to Administrative Tools, and then choosing DNS.

5. In the DNS Manager console tree, navigate to DCSRV1\Forward Lookup Zones\nwtraders.msft.

   In the details pane, two records have been created for dcsrv1—a Host (A) record and an IPv6 Host (AAAA) record. These records point to the IPv4 and IPv6 addresses, respectively, of Dcsrv1.

6. Spend a few minutes browsing the contents of the other folders in the nwtraders.msft zone.

   Notice that many of the records in the zone are SRV records. These records point clients to the domain controller (Dcsrv1) when they query DNS for the location of a specific service such as Kerberos (which provides network authentication) or Lightweight Directory Access Protocol (LDAP). LDAP finds objects in Active Directory.

7. In the DNS Manager console tree, right-click the *DCSRV1* node, and then choose Properties.

8. In the DCSRV1 Properties dialog box, review the information in the Interfaces tab.

   If your DNS server has multiple network interfaces or multiple addresses, you can use this tab to limit the sources of requests to which the server will respond.

9. Click the Forwarders tab.

10. Read the text in the tab, and then click the Edit button.

11. In the Edit Forwarders dialog box, read the text on the page.

    You would use this tab to specify a DNS server (a forwarder) to which unanswered queries should be forwarded. In a large organization, for example, the DNS servers for subdomains like east.contoso.local could forward queries to DNS server authoritative for the root zone (contoso.local) in the private DNS namespace.

12. Click Cancel to close the Edit Forwarders dialog box.

13. In the DCSRV1 Properties dialog box, click the Root Hints tab.

14. Read the text on the tab.

    Note that these name servers are the root DNS servers for the Internet. In a large organization, you might choose to replace this list with the root servers in your private namespace. (In such a case, the DNS servers in the corporate network could no longer resolve Internet names, but users could still connect to the Internet through the use of proxy servers.)

15. Click the Monitoring tab.

16. In the Monitoring tab, select the check box to test a simple query, and then click Test Now.

    In the Test Results area, an entry appears indicating that the simple query has passed.

    Do not perform the recursive test now. The recursive test would fail because this server is not yet configured with Internet access and cannot connect to the root servers.

17. In the DCSRV1 Properties dialog box, click Cancel.

18. In the DNS Manager console tree, select and then right-click the Conditional Forwarders container, and then choose New Conditional Forwarder. (If the option appears dimmed, select the Conditional Forwarders container, and then right-click it again.)

19. In the New Conditional Forwarder dialog box, read all the text.

    Note that you use this dialog box to specify the addresses of remote DNS servers to which queries for specific domain names should be forwarded.

20. In the New Conditional Forwarder dialog box, click Cancel.

21. Minimize all open windows.

▶ **Practice 3   Creating a Personal Administrator Account**

In this exercise, you create a domain administrator account to use in future exercises.

1. Open Active Directory Users And Computers by clicking Start, pointing to Administrative Tools, and then choosing Active Directory Users And Computers.

2. In the Active Directory Users And Computers console tree, navigate to nwtraders.msft \Users.

3. Right-click the Users container, point to New, and then choose User.

4. In the New Object - User wizard, complete the fields by using a domain name of your choosing for a personal administrator account.

5. Click Next.

6. On the second page of the New Object - User wizard, type a password of your choosing in the Password and Confirm Password fields, select or clear any options, and then click Next.

7. On the third page of the New Object - User wizard, click Finish.

8. In the Active Directory Users And Computers console, locate the user account you have just created in the details pane.

9. Right-click your new user account, and then choose Add To A Group.

10. In the Select Groups dialog box, type **domain admins**, and then press Enter.

    A message box appears indicating that the operation was successfully completed.

11. Click OK.

12. Close Active Directory Users And Computers.

▶ **Practice 3   Adding Boston to the Nwtraders Domain**

In this exercise, you join Boston to the Nwtraders domain.

1. Log on to Boston as an administrator, and then open an elevated command prompt. (To open an elevated command prompt, right-click Command Prompt in the Start Menu, and then choose Run As Administrator. If you are logged on with the account named Administrator, you can merely open a Command Prompt because this prompt is already elevated by default.)

2. At the command prompt, type **netsh interface ip set dnsserver "local area connection" static 192.168.0.1**.

3. When the prompt reappears, type **netsh interface ipv6 set dnsserver "local area connection" static fd00::1**.

    These two commands configure Boston to look for the Nwtraders.msft domain by querying Dcsrv1.

4. When the prompt reappears, minimize or close the command prompt.

5. In the Initial Configuration Tasks window, click Provide Computer Name And Domain.

    If the Initial Configuration Tasks is not open, you can open it by typing **oobe** in the Run box.

6. In the System Properties dialog box, click Change.

7. In the Member Of area of the Computer Name/Domain Changes dialog box, select Domain, and then type **nwtraders.msft** in the associated text box.

8. Click OK.

    A Windows Security prompt opens.

9. In the Windows Security prompt, specify the user name and password of your domain administrator account, and then click OK.

    After several moments (up to a minute), a message box appears welcoming you to the nwtraders.msft domain.

10. Click OK.

    A message appears indicating that you must restart your computer to apply these changes.

11. Click OK.

12. In the System Properties dialog box, click Close.

    A message appears again indicating that you must restart your computer.

13. Click Restart Now.

▶ **Practice 4   Verifying New Zone Data**

In this exercise you verify that new resource records have been created in the Nwtraders.msft zone.

1. After Boston has finished restarting, switch to Dcsrv1.

2. While you are logged on to Dcsrv1 as a domain administrator, open DNS Manager.

3. In the console tree, navigate to the nwtraders.msft forward lookup zone.

4. Right-click the nwtraders.msft container, and then choose Refresh.

Two records have been created for Boston—a Host (A) record mapped to 192.168.0.2 and an IPv6 Host (AAAA) record mapped to fd00::2.

5. Log off Dcsrv1.

Lesson Summary

- In most Windows networks, DNS servers are hosted on Active Directory domain controllers. You can install a DNS server together with a domain controller by running Dcpromo.exe. To install a DNS server without a domain controller, use the Add Roles Wizard to add the DNS Server role.

- You can install a DNS server on a Server Core installation of Windows Server 2008. To do so on a domain controller, use *Dcpromo* and specify an answer file by using the command **dcpromo /unattend:<*unattendfile*>**. To install a stand-alone DNS server on a Server Core installation, type **start /w ocsetup DNS-Server-Core-Role**.

- The DNS server properties dialog box allows you to configure settings that apply to the DNS server and all its hosted zones.

- The Interfaces tab allows you to specify which of the local computer's IP addresses the DNS server should listen to for DNS requests. The Root Hints tab allows you to modify default root servers for the DNS namespace. The Forwarders tab allows you to specify the IP addresses of upstream DNS servers to which queries should be directed if the local DNS server cannot provide a response through its cache or zone data.

- You can use the DNS Manager console to configure conditional forwarding. In conditional forwarding, queries for specific domains are forwarded to specific DNS servers.

Lesson Review

The following questions are intended to reinforce key information presented in this lesson. The questions are also available on the companion CD if you prefer to review them in electronic form.

NOTE Answers

Answers to these questions and explanations of why each answer choice is correct or incorrect are located in the "Answers" section at the end of the book.

---

1. You are configuring a new DNS server in your organization. You want to configure the new DNS server to specify the root servers in your organization as its root servers. What should you do?

    A. Replace the Cache.dns file with a new version specifying the company root servers.

    B. Configure a HOSTS file with the names and addresses of the root servers in your organization.

    C. Configure an Lmhosts file with the names and addresses of the root servers in your organization.

    D. Configure the new DNS server to forward queries to the root servers in your organization.

2. Your company includes a headquarters office in New York and a branch office in Sacramento. These offices host the Active Directory domains ny.lucernepublishing.com and sac.lucernepublishing.com, respectively. You want users in each office to be able to resolve names and browse the internal network of the other office. You also want users in each network to resolve Internet names. How should you configure the DNS servers in each office?

    A. Configure root servers in the New York office, and then configure the Sacramento servers to forward queries to the root servers in New York.

    B. Configure the DNS server in each office to forward queries to an external forwarder.

    C. Use conditional forwarding to configure the parent DNS servers in the New York office to forward queries destined for the sac.lucernepublishing.com to the Sacramento DNS servers. Configure the parent DNS servers in the Sacramento office to forward queries destined for the ny.lucernepublishing.com to the New York DNS servers.

    D. Configure the parent DNS servers in the New York office to forward queries to the parent DNS server in the Sacramento office. Configure the parent DNS servers in the Sacramento office to forward queries to the parent DNS server in the New York office.

Lesson 3: Configuring DNS Client Settings

A DNS infrastructure requires configuration for clients as well as for servers. In a typical business network, DNS clients are configured through settings inherited through DHCP or from Active Directory domain membership. However, for computers with static IP configurations, as well as for some outside of an Active Directory environment, you need to define DNS client settings manually. This lesson describes the DNS settings that affect a computer's ability to resolve DNS names successfully and to have its own name resolved by other querying computers.

> **After this lesson, you will be able to:**
> - Configure a DNS client with a DNS server list
> - Configure a suffix search list
> - Configure a DNS client with a primary DNS suffix
> - Configure a DNS client with a connection-specific DNS suffix
> - Configure a DNS client to register its name and address with a DNS server
>
> **Estimated lesson time: 45 minutes**

Specifying DNS Servers

The most important configuration parameter for a DNS client is the DNS server address. When a client performs a DNS query, the client first directs that query toward the address specified as the client's preferred DNS server. If the preferred DNS server is unavailable, a DNS client then contacts an alternate DNS server, if one is specified. Note that the client does not contact an alternate DNS server when the preferred server is available yet merely unable to resolve a query.

You can configure a DNS client with a prioritized list of as many DNS server addresses you choose, either by using DHCP to assign the list or by manually specifying the addresses. With DHCP, you can configure clients with a DNS server list by using the 006 DNS Server option and then configuring the clients to obtain a DNS server address automatically in the TCP/IPv4 Properties dialog box, as shown in Figure 2-26. (This is the default setting.)

MORE INFO DHCP options

DHCP options are discussed in Chapter 4, "Creating a DHCP Infrastructure."

To configure a DNS server list manually, you can use the TCP/IPv4 Properties dialog box if you want to configure the local client with one or two DNS servers (a preferred and an alternate).

However, if you want to configure a longer list, click the Advanced button, and then select the DNS tab. Use the Add button to add servers to the prioritized list of DNS servers, as shown in Figure 2-27.

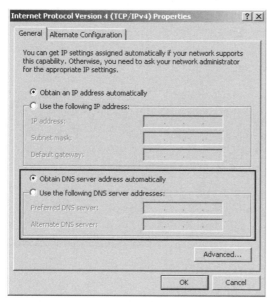

Figure 2-26 By default, IPv4 hosts are configured to obtain a DNS server address through DHCP

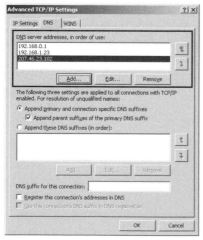

Figure 2-27 Configuring a prioritized list of DNS servers for a client to contact

Specifying a Computer Name and DNS Suffixes

When you install Windows Server 2008 on a computer or server, a computer name is generated automatically if you do not specify one in an answer file. You can later change this computer name after installation by using the System Properties dialog box (which you can open through the System control panel or by typing the **sysdm.cpl** command). In DNS, this same computer name is called a host name and is analogous to a person's first name or given name. An example of such a computer name or host name is ClientA. You can determine the computer's host name by typing the command **hostname** at a command prompt.

However, a client can take the fullest advantage of DNS name resolution services when it is configured with not just a host name, but also with a primary DNS suffix, which is analogous to a person's last name or surname (family name). The host name together with the primary DNS suffix creates the *full computer name*. For example, a computer named ClientA with a primary DNS suffix of contoso.com is configured with a full computer name of ClientA.contoso.com. Normally, the primary DNS suffix corresponds to the name of a primary (read-write) zone hosted on the locally specified preferred DNS server. For example, the client named ClientA.contoso.com would normally be configured with the address of a DNS server hosting the contoso.com zone.

The primary DNS suffix serves two specific functions. First, it enables a client to automatically register its own host record in the DNS zone whose name corresponds to the primary DNS suffix name. This host record enables other computers to resolve the name of the local DNS client. Second, the DNS client automatically adds the primary DNS suffix to DNS queries that do not already include a suffix. For example, on a computer configured with the DNS suffix fabrikam.com, the command **ping dcsrv1** would effectively be translated to **ping dcsrv1.fabrikam.com.** This appended query, demonstrated in Figure 2-28, would then be sent to the DNS server.

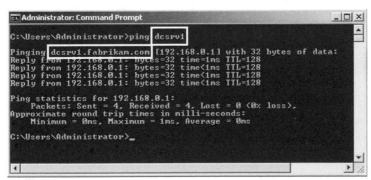

Figure 2-28   A computer configured with a DNS suffix appends that suffix to host names in its DNS queries

Joining a computer to an Active Directory domain automatically configures the domain name as the computer's primary DNS suffix. To configure a primary DNS suffix outside of an Active Domain, click Change in the Computer Name tab in the System Properties dialog box, and then click More in the Computer Name / Domain Changes dialog box. This procedure opens the DNS Suffix And NetBIOS Computer Name dialog box, shown in Figure 2-29.

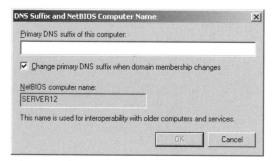

Figure 2-29 Manually configuring a DNS suffix

Configuring a Connection-specific DNS Suffix

Besides being assigned a primary DNS suffix, a computer can also be assigned a *connection-specific suffix* from a DHCP server or from a manual configuration. This type of suffix is associated with a particular network connection only. From a DHCP server, the connection-specific suffix is assigned through the 015 DNS Domain Name option. You can assign a connection-specific suffix manually for any particular network connection in the DNS tab of the Advanced TCP/IP Settings dialog box, as shown in Figure 2-30.

A connection-specific suffix is useful if a computer has two network adapters and you want to distinguish the two routes to that computer by name. For example, in Figure 2-31 a computer named Host-A is connected to two subnets through two separate adapters. The first adapter, assigned the address 10.1.1.11, is connected to Subnet 1 by a slow (10-MB) Ethernet connection. This slow connection is assigned a connection-specific DNS suffix of public.example.microsoft.com. The second adapter, assigned the address 10.2.2.22, is connected to Subnet 2 by a Fast Ethernet (100-MB) connection. This fast connection is assigned a connection-specific DNS suffix of backup.example.microsoft.com.

Computers on both subnets can connect to Host-A through either adapter. However, when computers specify the address host-a.public.example.microsoft.com, their connections are resolved and then routed to Host-A through the slow link. When they specify host-a.backup.example.com, their connections are resolved and then routed to Host-A through the fast link.

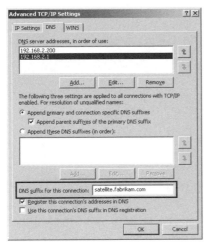

Figure 2-30 Assigning a connection-specific DNS suffix

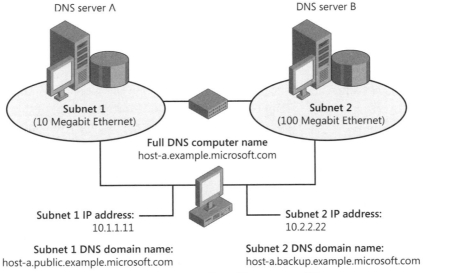

Figure 2-31 Using a connection-specific suffix to name different routes to a computer

Configuring a Suffix Search List

For DNS clients, you can configure a DNS domain suffix search list that extends or revises their DNS search capabilities. By adding suffixes to the list, you can search for short, unqualified computer names in more than one specified DNS domain. Then, if a DNS query fails, the DNS Client service can use this list to append other name suffix endings to your original name and repeat DNS queries to the DNS server for these alternate FQDNs.

Default DNS Suffix Searches

By default, the DNS Client service first attaches the primary DNS suffix of the local computer to the unqualified name. If the query fails to resolve this name, the DNS Client service then adds any connection-specific suffix that you have assigned to a network adapter. Finally, if these queries are also unsuccessful, the DNS Client service adds the parent suffix of the primary DNS suffix.

For example, suppose the full computer name of a multihomed computer is computer1 .domain1.microsoft.com. The network adapters on Computer1 have been assigned the connection-specific suffixes subnet1.domain1.microsoft.com and subnet2.domain1.microsoft.com, respectively. If on this same computer you type **computer2** into the Address text box in Internet Explorer and then press Enter, the local DNS Client service first tries to resolve the name Computer2 by performing a query for the name computer2.domain1.microsoft.com. If this query is unsuccessful, the DNS Client service queries for the names computer2.subnet1 .domain1.microsoft.com and computer2.subnet2.domain1.microsoft.com. If this query does not succeed in resolving the name, the DNS Client service queries for the name computer2 .microsoft.com.

Custom DNS Suffix Search Lists

You can customize suffix searches by creating a DNS suffix search list in the Advanced TCP/ IP Settings dialog box, as shown in Figure 2-32.

The Append These DNS Suffixes option lets you specify a list of DNS suffixes to add to unqualified names. If you enter a DNS suffix search list, the DNS Client service adds those DNS suffixes in order and does not try any other domain names. For example, if the suffixes appearing in the search list in Figure 2-32 are configured and you submit the unqualified, single-label query "coffee," the DNS Client service first queries for coffee.lucernepublishing.com and then for coffee.eu.lucernepublishing.com.

You can also configure a DNS suffix search list through Group Policy. You can find this setting in a GPO by navigating to Computer Configuration\Policies\Administrative Tools\Network \DNS Client and then configuring the policy setting named DNS Suffix Search List.

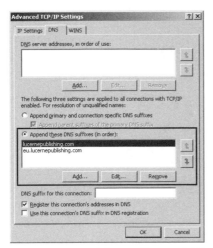

Figure 2-32 Adding suffixes to DNS queries

Configuring Dynamic Update Settings

When configured to do so, DNS servers running on Windows Server 2008 can accept dynamic registration and updates of the A (host), AAAA (IPv6 host), and PTR (pointer) resource records. The registration and updates themselves must be performed either by a DNS client or by a DHCP server (on behalf of a DNS client).

NOTE **What are host and pointer records?**

A host record in a forward lookup zone is a record that returns the address of a computer when you query using its name. It is the most important resource record type. A pointer record provides the opposite service: it is found only in a reverse lookup zone and returns the name of a computer when you query using its IP address. For more information about zone types and resource records, see Chapter 3, "Configuring a DNS Zone Infrastructure."

Dynamic updates for particular clients can occur only when those clients are configured with a primary or connection-specific DNS suffix that matches the zone name hosted by the preferred DNS server. For example, for the record of a computer named Client1 to be dynamically updated in the lucernepublishing.com zone, the FQDN of that computer must be client1.lucernepublishing.com and the client must specify as its preferred DNS server the IP address of a DNS server hosting a primary zone named lucernepublishing.com.

Default Client Update Behavior

Figure 2-33 shows the default DNS registration settings for a DNS client, which are found in the DNS tab of the Advanced TCP/IP Settings dialog box.

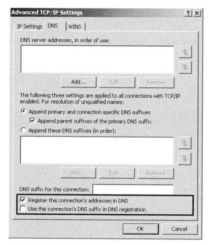

Figure 2-33   Default DNS client registration settings

Update Behavior for Host Records   The setting named Register This Connection's Addresses In DNS, when enabled, configures a client to attempt to register both A and AAAA records with its preferred DNS server. For these Host record registrations to succeed, a number of conditions must be met. First, a primary DNS suffix must also be assigned to the local computer, either manually or through Active Directory membership. Second, the preferred DNS server specified for the client must host a primary zone that matches the name of the client's primary DNS suffix. Finally, the primary zone hosted at the preferred DNS server must be configured to allow the type of dynamic updates that the client can perform: either secure updates (only from domain members) or both secure and nonsecure updates (from either domain members or non-domain-joined computers).

NOTE   **Automatic addressing and automatic DNS updates**

DNS clients never attempt to register IPv4 APIPA addresses or IPv6 link-local addresses with a DNS server.

The setting named Use This Connection's DNS Suffix In DNS Registration configures the local computer to attempt to register the A and AAAA records for any connection-specific DNS suffixes that are assigned to the associated network connection. Note that the connection-specific

DNS suffix does not actually have to appear in the DNS Suffix For This Connection text box; the connection-specific suffix can instead be inherited from a DHCP server (specifically from the 015 DNS Domain Name option). Enabling this setting therefore configures a DHCP client that has been assigned a DNS domain name from DHCP to register an A and AAAA record with its preferred DNS server. For these registrations to succeed, the DNS domain name inherited from the DHCP server must match the name of a primary zone hosted on the preferred DNS server and the primary zone hosted at the preferred DNS server must be configured to allow the type of dynamic updates that the client can perform. Note also that if a client is already configured with a primary DNS suffix that matches this connection-specific DNS suffix, enabling this setting does not force the registration of any additional Host records.

For all host records, you can attempt to force a registration in DNS by typing the command **Ipconfig /registerdns** at an elevated command prompt.

Update Behavior for Pointer Records   For statically addressed clients, the update behavior for PTR records is the same as that for Host (A or AAAA) records: Statically addressed DNS clients always attempt to register and update their Pointer records in a DNS server when the Register This Connection's Addresses In DNS setting is enabled. You can attempt to force a registration in DNS of PTR records for a statically addressed client by typing *Ipconfig /registerdns* at an elevated command prompt on the client. For the registration to succeed, however, some conditions must be met. First, the DNS client must be configured with an appropriate primary DNS suffix, and then the client's preferred DNS server must be hosting appropriately configured forward and reverse lookup zones.

The PTR record update behavior of DHCP clients differs from that of statically addressed clients, and the PTR update behavior of DHCP clients in a workgroup environment differs from the behavior of those in an Active Directory environment. The following section explains the PTR update behavior of DHCP clients in these two environments.

In a workgroup environment, DHCP clients have their PTR records updated by the DHCP server. To force an update, you can run the command *Ipconfig /renew*. For this registration to succeed, a number of conditions must be met. First, both the DNS client *and the DNS server* must be configured with the address of the DNS server as the preferred DNS server. Second, the DNS client must have the Register This Connection's Addresses In DNS setting enabled. Third, the DNS client must be configured with an appropriate DNS suffix, either specified manually as a primary DNS suffix or assigned automatically from the DHCP server. Finally, the DNS server must host appropriately configured forward and reverse lookup zones.

In an Active Directory environment, DHCP clients update their own PTR records. To force an update, you can run either the *Ipconfig /registerdns* or the *Ipconfig /renew* commands. For such an update to succeed, the Use This Connection's DNS Suffix In DNS Registration setting must be enabled. (To enable this setting, you must first enable the Register This Connection's Addresses In DNS setting.) Finally, for a PTR record to be updated successfully in an AD DS environment, the client's preferred DNS server must host appropriately configured forward and reverse lookup zones.

NOTE   Using Group Policy to register connection-specific names

You can use Group Policy to force computers on a network to register connection-specific DNS names. In a GPO, navigate to Computer Configuration\Policies\Administrative Templates\Network \DNS Client. Search for the policy setting named Register DNS Records With Connection-specific DNS Suffix and configure the setting as Enabled.

Exam Tip   To force a DNS client to attempt dynamic registration of its resource records, type **ipconfig /registerdns** at a command prompt.

> ## Quick Check
>
> - By default, does a client with a domain name assigned by DHCP attempt to register its address in DNS?
>
> ## Quick Check Answer
>
> - No.

Viewing and Clearing the DNS Client Cache

The *DNS client cache,* also known as the DNS resolver cache, is maintained on all DNS clients. DNS clients check this resolver cache before they attempt to query a DNS server. New entries are added to the resolver cache whenever a DNS client receives a query response from a DNS server.

To view the DNS client cache, type **ipconfig /displaydns** at a command prompt. The output of this command includes any entries loaded from the local Hosts file, as well as any recently obtained resource records for name queries resolved by the system.

To clear the DNS client cache, you can type **ipconfig /flushdns** at the command prompt. Alternatively, you can restart the DNS Client service by using the Services console, which is an administrative tool accessible through the Start menu.

Exam Tip   For the exam, remember that you sometimes need to run *Ipconfig /flushdns* on your computer before you can see the benefit of having fixed a DNS problem elsewhere on the network. For example, if a Windows client has cached a negative response from a DNS server to an earlier query, the client will continue to receive a negative response even if the DNS server can now resolve the query. To fix such a problem, flush the DNS client cache by executing *Ipconfig /flushdns* on the Windows computer. This command forces the Windows client to contact the DNS server again instead of just responding with the cached negative response.

PRACTICE **Managing the DNS Client Cache**

In this practice, you use the *Ipconfig* command with the /flushdns and /displaydns switches to clear and display the DNS client cache.

▶ **Exercise   Exploring the DNS Resolver (Client) Cache**

In this exercise, you observe the behavior of the DNS client cache.

1. Log on to Nwtraders from Boston as a domain administrator.

2. At a command prompt, type **ipconfig /flushdns**.

   At the command prompt, a message appears indicating that the DNS Resolver Cache has been flushed.

3. At a command prompt, type **ipconfig /displaydns**.

   The contents of the cache are displayed. Notice that it is not completely empty. The four records that appear by default include a PTR record for the IPv6 localhost address of ::1, a PTR record for the IPv4 localhost address of 127.0.0.1, an A record that maps the name localhost to the IPv4 address 127.0.0.1, and an AAAA record that maps the name localhost to the IPv6 address ::1. The addresses 127.0.0.1 and ::1 are special addresses that always point to the local computer.

4. At the command prompt, type **ping dcsrv1**.

   You receive a response from the IPv6 address of Dcrsv1. Note that the primary DNS suffix of the local computer, nwtraders.msft, has been appended to the name "dcsrv1." This DNS suffix was assigned to Boston when Boston joined the Nwtraders domain.

5. At the command prompt, type **ipconfig /displaydns**.

   Beneath the same heading of dcsrv1.nwtraders.msft, two new records appear in the cache: an A record and an AAAA record. Note that the A record is associated with Dcsrv1's IPv4 address and the AAAA record is associated with Dcrv1's IPv6 address.

6. At the command prompt, type **ipconfig /flushdns**.

7. At the command prompt, type **ipconfig /displaydns**.

   The output reveals that the two new records have been flushed from the cache.

8. Close all open windows.

Lesson Summary

- When a client performs a DNS query, the client first directs that query toward the address specified as the client's preferred DNS server. If the preferred DNS server is unavailable, a DNS client then contacts an alternate DNS server, if one is specified. You can configure a DNS client with a prioritized list of as many DNS server addresses you choose, either by using DHCP to assign the list or by manually specifying the addresses.

- In DNS, the computer name is called a host name. This is a single-tag name that you can discover by typing the command **hostname** at a command prompt.

- DNS client settings affect a computer's ability to resolve DNS names successfully and to have the client's own name resolved by other querying computers.

- A client can take the fullest advantage of DNS name resolution services when it is configured with a primary DNS suffix. The primary DNS suffix enables a client to automatically register its own host record in the DNS zone whose name corresponds to the primary DNS suffix name. The client also appends the primary DNS suffix to DNS queries that do not already include a suffix. A connection-specific suffix applies only to connections through a specific network adapter.

- You can configure a DNS client to specify a list of DNS suffixes to add to unqualified names. This list is known as a DNS suffix search list.

- DNS clients can register their own records in DNS only when the clients are configured with a primary or connection-specific DNS suffix that matches the zone name hosted by the preferred DNS server. By default, DNS clients assigned static addresses attempt to register both host and pointer records. DNS clients that are also DHCP clients attempt to register only host records.

Lesson Review

The following questions are intended to reinforce key information presented in this lesson. The questions are also available on the companion CD if you prefer to review them in electronic form.

NOTE Answers

Answers to these questions and explanations of why each answer choice is correct or incorrect are located in the "Answers" section at the end of the book.

1. You are a network administrator for an organization whose network is composed of two Active Directory domains, east.cpandl.com and west.cpandl.com. Users in each domain can already connect to resources in the opposing domain by specifying an FQDN, such as client1.west.cpandl.com You now want users in the east.cpandl.com domain also to be able to connect to computers in the west.cpandl.com domain by specifying those computers with a single name tag in a UNC path, such as \\WestSrv1.

   What can you do to enable this functionality?

   A. Use conditional forwarding to configure the DNS server in the east.cpandl.com domain to forward queries for names in the west.cpandl.com domain to the DNS servers in the west.cpandl.com domain.

   B. Use Group Policy in the east.cpandl.com domain to configure network clients with a DNS suffix search list. Add the domain suffix west.cpandl.com to the list.

   C. On the clients in the east.cpandl.com domain, configure TCP/IP properties of the local area connection to use the connection's DNS suffix in DNS registration.

   D. You do not need to do anything. The DNS suffix of the opposing will automatically be appended to single-tag name queries.

2. A computer named ClientA.nwtraders.com is not registering its DNS record with a DNS server. ClientA is configured with a static IP address and with the IP address of the DNS server authoritative for nwtraders.com domain. The TCP/IP properties for the local area connection on ClientA have been left at the default settings.

   What can you do to ensure that ClientA registers its own record with the DNS server?

   A. Configure a connection-specific suffix.

   B. Enable the option to use the connection's DNS suffix in DNS registration.

   C. Enable the option to register the connection's addresses in DNS.

   D. Configure a primary DNS suffix.

Chapter Review

To further practice and reinforce the skills you learned in this chapter, you can

- Review the chapter summary.
- Review the list of key terms introduced in this chapter.
- Complete the case scenarios. These scenarios sets up a real-world situation involving the topics of this chapter and asks you to create solutions.
- Complete the suggested practices.
- Take a practice test.

Chapter Summary

- DNS is the preferred name resolution service in Windows networks. However, because of the way DNS is designed, it requires configuration.
- DNS provides a hierarchical name structure. In DNS, an FQDN is a domain name that has been stated unambiguously to indicate its location relative to the root of the DNS domain tree. An example of an FQDN is Client1.east.fabrikam.com.
- When a DNS client queries for a name, it first checks its local cache for the answer. If it doesn't find the answer, the DNS client queries its preferred DNS server. If the DNS server doesn't know the answer, it will attempt to resolve the query by performing iterative queries against the DNS namespace, beginning with the root server.
- In most Windows networks, DNS servers are hosted on Active Directory domain controllers. You can install a DNS server together with a domain controller by running Dcpromo.exe. To install a DNS server without a domain controller, use the Add Roles Wizard to add the DNS Server role.
- DNS client settings affect a computer's ability to resolve DNS names successfully and to have the client's own name resolved by other querying computers.

Key Terms

Do you know what these key terms mean? You can check your answers by looking up the terms in the glossary at the end of the book.

- Domain Name System (DNS)
- dynamic updates
- forwarder
- forwarding

- fully qualified domain name (FQDN)
- host name
- HOSTS
- iteration
- Link Local Multicast Name Resolution (LLMNR)
- Lmhosts
- name resolution
- NetBIOS
- primary DNS suffix
- recursion
- referrals
- resolver
- root hints
- Time to Live (TTL)
- WINS server
- zone

Case Scenarios

In the following case scenarios, you will apply what you've learned in this chapter. You can find answers to these questions in the "Answers" section at the end of this book.

Case Scenario 1: Troubleshooting DNS Clients

You work as a network administrator for a company named Contoso Pharmaceuticals. You have recently deployed a number of Windows Vista clients in a research workgroup. The workgroup is isolated on its own subnet, which is physically connected to the larger corporate network.

You have deployed a DHCP server in the research workgroup to assign these computers an IP address, a default gateway, a DNS server, and the DNS domain name of contoso.com. The preferred DNS server address assigned to the clients belongs to a DNS server hosting a primary zone for the contoso.com domain. The zone is configured to accept both secure and nonsecure dynamic updates.

1. None of the clients in the research workgroup is successfully registering DNS records with the DNS server. Which TCP/IP setting can you enable to ensure that these dynamic registrations occur?

2. Certain network computers running Windows XP are configured as WINS clients yet are unable to browse to the research subnet by using the My Network Places icon. Which setting can you configure on the Windows Vista clients to enable them to be seen by the Windows XP clients? Assume that the default settings have been left for all options not assigned by DHCP.

Case Scenario 2: Deploying a Windows Server

You work as a network support specialist for a company named Fabrikam.com. You are planning to deploy a new DNS server in a branch office to improve name resolution response times.

1. There are no administrators at the branch office. You want to deploy a DNS server that will not require any administration but that will help resolve the queries of computers on the Internet. What kind of DNS server should you deploy?

2. You also want the new DNS server to be able to resolve names on the internal Fabrikam.com network at the main office. How can you achieve this without hosting a zone named Fabrikam.com on the branch office network?

Suggested Practices

To help you successfully master the exam objectives presented in this chapter, complete the following tasks.

Configure a DNS Server

Use this exercise to practice deploying DNS servers manually (without *Dcpromo*) and to practice configuring conditional forwarding.

■ **Practice** In a test network, deploy two DNS servers outside of an Active Directory environment. Configure zones for each server with domain names of your choice. Configure both servers with conditional forwarding so that each server forwards queries to the other server when appropriate. Test the configuration.

Configure Name Resolution for Clients

Perform this practice to become more familiar with client update behavior. To prepare for this practice, you need to enable dynamic updates in the primary zones hosted on each DNS server.

■ **Practice**   Using the same test described in the previous practice, configure a DNS client to register its own host records with one of the DNS servers without specifying a primary DNS suffix for the client computer.

Take a Practice Test

The practice tests on this book's companion CD offer many options. For example, you can test yourself on just one exam objective, or you can test yourself on all the 70-642 certification exam content. You can set up the test so that it closely simulates the experience of taking a certification exam, or you can set it up in study mode so that you can look at the correct answers and explanations after you answer each question.

MORE INFO   **Practice tests**

For details about all the practice test options available, see the "How to Use the Practice Tests" section in this book's Introduction.

Chapter 3
Configuring a DNS Zone Infrastructure

Deploying a DNS server is a fairly simple procedure, especially on a domain controller. However, DNS is a multifeatured service, and to manage and troubleshoot it adequately you need to become familiar with configuring DNS zones. Zones are the databases in which DNS data is stored, and different types of zones have different features. Common to all zone types is the requirement that data be kept consistent among zones in a common namespace, and to achieve this goal you need to configure zone replication or zone transfers.

A DNS zone infrastructure essentially consists of the various servers and hosted zones that communicate with one another in a way that ensures consistent name resolution. This chapter introduces you to the types of zones that make up a DNS infrastructure, the options for zone replications and transfers among them, and the configurable settings within zones that you need to understand in order to manage DNS effectively on your network.

Exam objectives in this chapter:
- Configure DNS zones.
- Configure DNS records.
- Configure DNS replication.

Lessons in this chapter:

Before You Begin

To complete the lessons in this chapter, you must have

- Two networked computers running Windows Server 2008.
- The first computer must be a domain controller named Dcsrv1 in a domain named nwtraders.msft. Dcsrv1 must be assigned the static address 192.168.0.1/24 with the DNS server specified as the same address. Dcsrv1 includes the server roles Active Directory Domain Services and DNS Server.
- The second computer must be named Boston.nwtraders.msft and must be assigned the address 192.168.0.2/24. Its DNS server must be specified as 192.168.0.1. Finally, Boston must be joined to the Nwtraders.msft domain.

> ## Real World
>
> *JC Mackin*
>
> DNS Manager is the main administration tool for DNS servers, but if you need to manage DNS for your job, it's a good idea to become familiar with some other DNS tools as well. Of all the alternate tools available, the Dnscmd command-line tool is the most important and the most powerful. By typing **dnscmd** at a command prompt, you can see all 40 or so of its subcommands. Some of the most important of these include **dnscmd /clear cache**, which clears the server cache; **dnscmd /enumdirectorypartitions**, which shows the application directory partitions available on the local server; and **dnscmd /info** (which provides a basic overview of the DNS server configuration).
>
> If your network includes Active Directory–integrated zones, you should also review tools for managing Active Directory replication. If you want to test replication on a domain controller, type **dcdiag /test:replications**. If you want to show replication partners, type **repadmin /showrepl**. Finally, if you want to force replication with another domain controller, use the Active Directory Sites and Services console to browse to the NTDS settings beneath your server, right-click the connection object in the details pane, and click Replicate Now.

Lesson 1: Creating and Configuring Zones

A zone is a database that contains authoritative information about a portion of the DNS namespace. When you install a DNS server with a domain controller, the DNS zone used to support the Active Directory domain is created automatically. However, if you install a DNS server at any other time, either on a domain controller, domain member server, or stand-alone server, you have to create and configure zones manually.

This lesson describes the steps required to create and configure a zone, as well as the underlying concepts you need to understand in order to configure a zone properly.

After this lesson, you will be able to:
- Create and configure DNS zones.
- Create and configure resource records.

Estimated lesson time: 120 minutes

Creating Zones

A DNS zone is a database containing records that associate names with addresses for a defined portion of a DNS namespace. Although a DNS server can use cached information from other servers to answer queries for names, it is only through a locally hosted zone that a DNS server can answer queries authoritatively. For any portion of a DNS namespace represented by a domain name such as "proseware.com," there can only be one authoritative source of zone data.

To create a new zone on a DNS server, you can use the New Zone Wizard in DNS Manager. To launch this wizard, right-click the server icon in the DNS Manager console tree, and then choose New Zone, as shown in Figure 3-1.

The New Zone Wizard includes the following configuration pages:

- Zone Type
- Active Directory Zone Replication Scope
- Forward or Reverse Lookup Zone
- Zone Name
- Dynamic Update

The sections that follow describe the configuration concepts related to these five wizard pages.

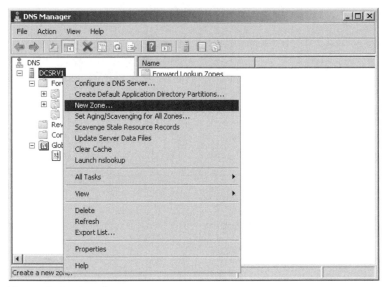

Figure 3-1   Creating a new zone

Choosing a Zone Type

The Zone Type page of the New Zone Wizard, shown in Figure 3-2, enables you to create your choice of a primary zone, a secondary zone, or a stub zone. If you are creating a primary or stub zone on a domain controller, you also have the option to store zone data in Active Directory.

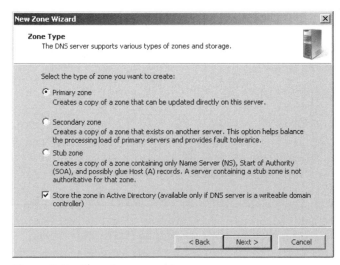

Figure 3-2   Choosing a zone type

Primary Zones   A primary zone is the main type of DNS zone. A primary zone provides original read-write source data that allows the local DNS server to answer DNS queries authoritatively about a portion of a DNS namespace.

When the local DNS server hosts a primary zone, the DNS server is the primary source for information about this zone, and the server stores the master copy of zone data in a local file or in Active Directory Domain Services (AD DS). When the zone is stored in a file instead of Active Directory, by default the primary zone file is named *zone_name*.dns, and this file is located in the %systemroot%\System32\Dns folder on the server.

Secondary Zones   A secondary zone provides an authoritative, read-only copy of a primary zone or another secondary zone.

Secondary zones provide a means to offload DNS query traffic in areas of the network where a zone is heavily queried and used. Additionally, if the zone server hosting a primary zone is unavailable, a secondary zone can provide name resolution for the namespace until the primary server becomes available again.

The source zones from which secondary zones acquire their information are called *masters*, and the data copy procedures through which this information is regularly updated are called *zone transfers*. A master can be a primary zone or other secondary zone. You can specify the master of a secondary zone when the secondary zone is created through the New Zone Wizard. Because a secondary zone is merely a copy of a primary zone that is hosted on another server, it cannot be stored in AD DS.

Stub Zones   A stub zone is similar to a secondary zone, but it contains only those resource records necessary to identify the authoritative DNS servers for the master zone. Stub zones are often used to enable a parent zone like proseware.com to keep an updated list of the name servers available in a delegated child zone, such as east.proseware.com. They can also be used to improve name resolution and simplify DNS administration.

Storing the Zone in Active Directory   When you create a new primary or stub zone on a domain controller, the Zone Type page gives you the option to store the zone in Active Directory. In Active Directory–integrated zones, zone data is automatically replicated through Active Directory in a manner determined by the settings you choose on the Active Directory Zone Replication Scope page. In most cases this option eliminates the need to configure zone transfers to secondary servers.

Integrating your DNS zone with Active Directory has several advantages. First, because Active Directory performs zone replication, you do not need to configure a separate mechanism for DNS zone transfers between primary and secondary servers. Fault tolerance, along with improved performance from the availability of multiple read/write primary servers, is automatically supplied by the presence of multimaster replication on your network. Second, Active

Directory allows for single properties of resource records to be updated and replicated among DNS servers. Avoiding the transfer of many and complete resource records decreases the load on network resources during zone transfers. Finally, Active Directory–integrated zones also provide the optional benefit of requiring security for dynamic updates, an option you can configure on the Dynamic Update page.

NOTE **Read-only domain controllers and Active Directory–integrated zones**

For traditional domain controllers, the copy of the zone is a read-write copy. For read-only domain controllers (RODCs) the copy of the zone will be read-only.

Standard Zones   By default, on the Zone Type page the option to store the zone in Active Directory is selected when you are creating the zone on a domain controller. However, you can clear this check box and instead create what is called a standard zone. A standard zone is also the only option for a new zone when you are creating the zone on a server that is not a domain controller; in this case the check box on this page cannot be selected.

As opposed to an Active Directory–integrated zone, a standard zone stores its data in a text file on the local DNS server. Also unlike Active Directory–integrated zones, with standard zones you can configure only a single read-write (primary) copy of zone data. All other copies of the zone (secondary zones) are read-only.

The standard zone model implies a single point of failure for the writable version of the zone. If the primary zone is unavailable to the network, no changes to the zone can be made. However, queries for names in the zone can continue uninterrupted as long as secondary zones are available.

Choosing an Active Directory Zone Replication Scope

On the Active Directory Zone Replication Scope page of the New Scope Wizard, you can choose which domain controllers in your network will store the zone. This page, shown in Figure 3-3, appears only when you have configured the zone to be stored in Active Directory. Note that the choice of where you store the zone determines the domain controllers among which the zone data will be replicated.

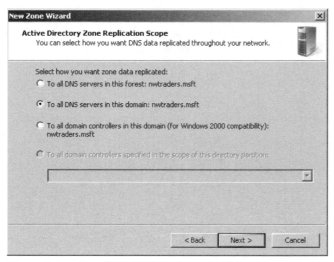

Figure 3-3   Choosing the domain controllers to store the zone

You have four choices:

- Store the zone in all domain controllers that are also DNS servers in the entire Active Directory forest.
- Store the zone in all domain controllers that are also DNS servers in the local Active Directory domain.
- Store the zone in all domain controllers in the local Active Directory domain (used for compatibility with Windows 2000).
- Store the zone in all domain controllers specified in the scope of a custom Active Directory directory partition.

These options are described in more detail in Lesson 2, "Configuring Zone Replication and Transfers."

Creating a Forward or Reverse Lookup Zone

On the Forward Or Reverse Lookup Zone page of the New Zone Wizard, you determine whether the new zone you are creating should act as a forward or reverse lookup zone. This page is shown in Figure 3-4.

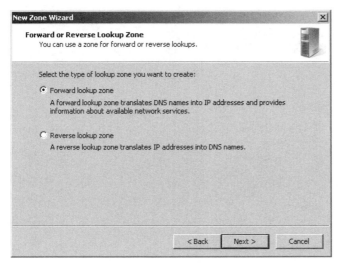

Figure 3-4   Choosing a forward or reverse lookup zone

In forward lookup zones, DNS servers map fully qualified domain names (FQDNs) to IP addresses. In reverse lookup zones, DNS servers map IP addresses to FQDNs. Forward lookup zones thus answer queries to resolve FQDNs to IP addresses, and reverse lookup zones answer queries to resolve IP addresses to FQDNs. Note that forward lookup zones adopt the name of the DNS domain name for whose names you want to provide resolution service, such as "proseware.com." Reverse lookup zones are named by a reverse order of the first three octets in the address space for which you want to provide reverse name resolution service *plus* the final tag "in-addr.arpa." For example, if you want to provide reverse name resolution service for the subnet 192.168.1.0/24, the name of the reverse lookup zone will be "1.168.192.in-addr.arpa." Within a forward lookup zone, a single database entry or record that maps a host name to an address is known as a *host* or *A* record. In a reverse lookup zone, a single database entry that maps an address host ID to a host name is known as *pointer* or *PTR* record.

A forward lookup zone is illustrated in Figure 3-5, and a reverse lookup zone is illustrated in Figure 3-6.

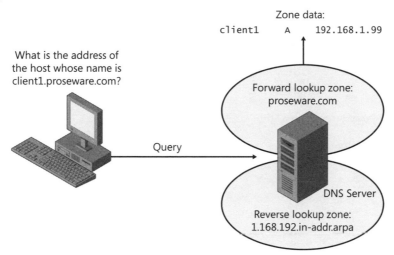

Figure 3-5   A forward lookup zone

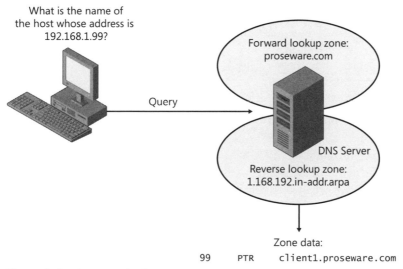

Figure 3-6   A reverse lookup zone

NOTE   The Configure A DNS Server Wizard

To create forward and reverse lookup zones at one time, you can use the Configure A DNS Server Wizard. To open this wizard, right-click the server icon in the DNS Manager console tree, and then choose Configure A DNS Server.

Choosing a Zone Name

The Zone Name page of the New Zone Wizard enables you to choose a name for the forward lookup zone you are creating. (Reverse lookup zones have specific names corresponding to the IP address range for which they are authoritative.) The Zone Name page is shown in Figure 3-7.

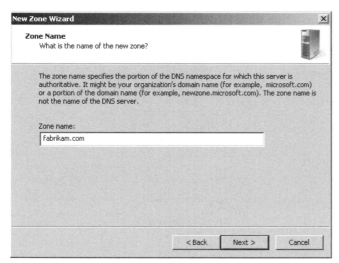

Figure 3-7   Choosing a zone name

In general, if the zone you are creating is going to be providing name resolution for an Active Directory domain, you want the zone to match the name of that Active Directory domain. For example, if your organization includes two Active Directory domains named proseware.com and east.proseware.com, your name resolution infrastructure should include two zones with names that match those Active Directory domains.

If you are creating a zone for a DNS namespace outside of an Active Directory environment, you should supply the name of your organization's Internet domain name, such as fabrikam.com.

NOTE   Adding a DNS server to a domain controller

If you want to add a DNS server to an existing domain controller, you normally want to add a copy of the primary zone providing name resolution for the local Active Directory domain. To achieve this, merely create a zone whose name corresponds to the name of the existing zone in the local Active Directory domain, and the new zone will be populated with data from other DNS servers in the domain.

Configuring Dynamic Update Settings

DNS client computers can register and dynamically update their resource records with a DNS server. By default, DNS clients that are configured with static IP addresses attempt to update host (A or AAAA) and pointer (PTR) records and DNS clients that are DHCP clients attempt to update only host records. In a workgroup environment, the DHCP server updates the pointer record on behalf of the DHCP client whenever the IP configuration is renewed.

For dynamic DNS updates to succeed, the zone in which the client attempts to register or update a record must be configured to accept dynamic updates. Two types of dynamic updates can be allowed:

- **Secure updates** Allow registrations only from Active Directory domain member computers and updates only from the same computer that originally performed the registration
- **Nonsecure updates** Allow updates from any computer

The Dynamic Update page of the New Zone Wizard enables you to specify whether the zone you are creating should accept secure, nonsecure, or no dynamic updates. The Dynamic Update page is shown in Figure 3-8.

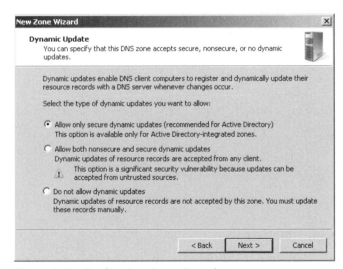

Figure 3-8 Configuring dynamic updates on a zone

Exam Tip To manually force a DNS client to perform a dynamic update, use the *Ipconfig /registerdns* command.

Quick Check

■ What are the server requirements for storing a zone in Active Directory?

Quick Check Answer

■ The server needs to be a domain controller.

Examining Built-in Resource Records

When you create a new zone, two types of records required for the zone are automatically created. First, a new zone always includes a Start of Authority (SOA) record that defines basic properties for the zone. All new zones also include at least one NS record signifying the name of the server or servers authoritative for the zone. Figure 3-9 shows a new zone populated by these two records.

The following section describes the functions and features of these two resource records.

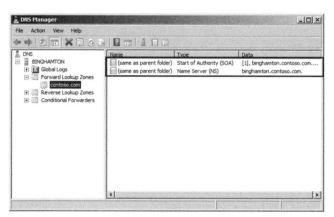

Figure 3-9   A new zone always includes at least an SOA and an NS record

Start of Authority (SOA) Records

When a DNS server loads a zone, it uses the SOA resource record to determine basic and authoritative properties for the zone. These settings also determine how often zone transfers are performed between primary and secondary servers.

If you double-click the SOA record, you open the Start Of Authority (SOA) tab of the zone properties dialog box, shown in Figure 3-10.

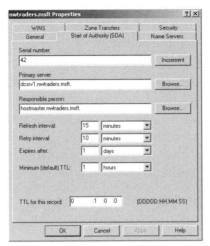

Figure 3-10   SOA record settings

In this tab you can modify the following settings:

- **Serial Number**   The Serial Number text box in the Start Of Authority (SOA) tab contains the revision number of the zone file. This number increases each time a resource record changes in the zone or when you manually increment the value in this tab by clicking Increment.

    When zones are configured to perform zone transfers to one or more secondary servers, the secondary servers query the master server intermittently for the serial number of the zone. This query is called the *SOA query*. If, through the SOA query, the serial number of the master zone is determined to be equivalent to the serial number stored on the secondary, no transfer is made. However, if the serial number for the zone at the master server is greater than that at the requesting secondary server, the secondary server initiates a transfer.

    NOTE   Forcing a zone transfer on the master

    When you click the Increment button, you force a zone transfer.

- **Primary Server**   The Primary Server text box in the Start Of Authority (SOA) tab contains the full computer name for the primary DNS server of the zone. This name must end with a period.

- **Responsible Person**   When this text box is configured, it contains the name of a responsible person (RP) resource record that specifies a domain mailbox name for a zone administrator. The name of the record entered into this field should always end with a period. The name "hostmaster" is used in this field by default.

- **Refresh Interval**   The value you configure in the Refresh Interval field determines how long a secondary DNS server waits before querying the master server for a zone renewal. When the refresh interval expires, the secondary DNS server requests a copy of the current SOA resource record for the zone from its master server source, which then answers this SOA query. The secondary DNS server then compares the serial number of the source server's current SOA resource record (as indicated in the master's response) with the serial number of its own local SOA resource record. If they are different, the secondary DNS server requests a zone transfer from the primary DNS server. The default value for this setting is 15 minutes.

Exam Tip   Increasing the refresh interval decreases zone transfer traffic.

- **Retry Interval**   The value you configure in the Retry Interval box determines how long a secondary server waits before retrying a failed zone transfer. Normally, this time is less than the refresh interval. The default value is 10 minutes.

- **Expires After**   The value you configure in the Expires After box determines the length of time that a secondary server, without any contact with its master server, continues to answer queries from DNS clients. After this time elapses, the data is considered unreliable. The default value is one day.

- **Minimum (Default) TTL**   The value you configure in the Minimum (Default) TTL box determines the default Time to Live (TTL) that is applied to all resource records in the zone. The default value is one hour.

  TTL values are not relevant for resource records within their authoritative zones. Instead, the TTL refers to the cache life of a resource record in nonauthoritative servers. A DNS server that has cached a resource record from a previous query discards the record when that record's TTL has expired.

- **TTL For This Record**   The value you configure in this text box determines the TTL of the present SOA resource record. This value overrides the default value setting in the preceding field.

  After you create it, an SOA resource record is represented textually in a standard zone file in the manner shown in this example:

```
@ IN SOA computer1.domain1.local. hostmaster.domain1.local. (
   5099    ; serial number
   3600    ; refresh (1 hour)
```

```
600      ; retry (10 mins)
86400    ; expire (1 day)
60  )    ; minimum TTL (1 min)
```

Exam Tip   Make sure you understand all the settings and concepts related to the Start Of Authority (SOA) tab.

Name Server Records

A name server (NS) record specifies a server that is authoritative for a given zone. When you create a zone in Windows Server 2008, every server hosting a primary copy of an Active Directory–integrated zone will have its own NS record appear in the new zone by default. If you are creating a standard primary zone, an NS record for the local server appears in the zone by default.

However, you need to manually add NS records for servers hosting secondary zones on a primary copy of the zone.

Creating an NS record requires a different procedure than creating other resource record types does. To add an NS record, double-click any existing NS record in DNS Manager. This step opens the Name Servers tab of the zone properties dialog box, shown in Figure 3-11. In the Name Servers tab, click the Add button to add the FQDN and IP address of the server hosting the secondary zone of the local primary zone. When you click OK after adding the new server, a new NS record pointing to that server appears in DNS Manager.

Figure 3-11   Adding an NS record to specify a server hosting a secondary zone

---

NOTE   Enabling transfers to secondary zones

Note that a secondary zone will not be recognized as a valid name server until it contains a valid copy of zone data. For the secondary zone to obtain this data, you must first enable zone transfers to that server by using the Zone Transfers tab in the zone properties dialog box. This tab is discussed in more detail in Lesson 2, "Configuring Zone Replication and Transfers."

After you create the record, a line such as the following appears in the standard zone file:

```
@ NS  dns1.lucernepublishing.com.
```

In this record, the "@" symbol represents the zone defined by the SOA record in the same zone file. The complete entry, then, effectively maps the lucernepublishing.com domain to a DNS server named dns1.lucernepublishing.com.

Creating Resource Records

Beyond the SOA and NS records, some other resource records are also created automatically. For example, if you choose to install a new DNS server when promoting a server to a domain controller, many SRV records for AD DS services are automatically created in the locally hosted zone. In addition, through dynamic updates many DNS clients automatically register host (A or AAAA) and pointer (PTR) records in a zone by default.

Even though many resource records are created automatically, in a production environment you usually need to create some resource records manually as well. Such records might include (Mail Exchanger) MX records for mail servers, Alias (CNAME) records for Web servers or application servers, and host records for servers or clients that cannot perform their own updates.

To add a resource record for a zone manually, right-click the zone icon in the DNS Manager console, and then choose the type of resource record you want to create from the shortcut menu. Figure 3-12 demonstrates the creation of a new MX record.

After you make your selection from the shortcut menu, a new dialog box appears in which you can specify the name of the record and the computer associated with it. Figure 3-13 shows the New Resource Record dialog box that appears for the creation of a new MX record. Note that only host records associate the name of a computer with the actual IP address of the computer. Most record types associate the name of a service or alias with the original host record. As a result, the MX record shown in Figure 3-13 relies on the presence in the zone of a host record named SRV12.nwtraders.msft.

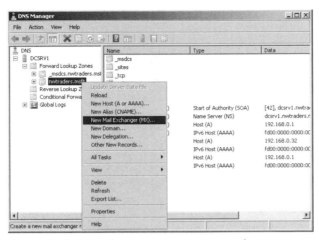

Figure 3-12 Creating a new resource record

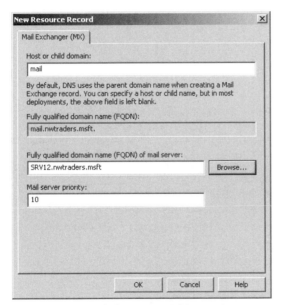

Figure 3-13 Defining a new MX record

Record Types

The most common resource records you need to create manually include the following:

- Host (A or AAAA)
- Alias (CNAME)
- Mail exchanger (MX)
- Pointer (PTR)
- Service location (SRV)

Host (A or AAAA) Resource Records   For most networks, host resource records make up the majority of resource records in a zone database. These records are used in a zone to associate computer names (host names) to IP addresses.

After you create them in the DNS Manager console, an A resource record that maps the host name server1.lucernepublishing.com to the IPv4 address 192.168.0.99 and an AAAA resource record that maps the same name to the IPv6 address fd00:0:0:5::8 would be represented textually within the standard zone file lucernepublishing.com.dns in the following way:

```
;
;  Zone records
;

server1                 A              192.168.0.99
                        AAAA               fd00:0:0:5::8
```

Even when dynamic updates are enabled for a particular zone, in some scenarios it might be necessary to add host records manually to that zone. For example, in Figure 3-14 a company named Contoso, Inc., uses the domain name contoso.com for both its public namespace and its internal Active Directory domain. In this case the public Web server named www.contoso.com is located outside the Active Directory domain and performs updates only on the public DNS server authoritative for contoso.com. Internal clients, however, point their DNS requests toward internal DNS servers. Because the A record for www.contoso.com is not updated dynamically on these internal DNS servers, the record must be added manually for internal clients to resolve the name and connect to the public Web server.

Another case in which you might need to add host records manually is when you have a UNIX server on your network. For example, in Figure 3-15 a company named Fabrikam, Inc., uses a single Active Directory domain named fabrikam.com for its private network. The network also includes a UNIX server named App1.fabrikam.com that runs an application critical to the company's daily operations. Because UNIX servers cannot perform dynamic updates, you need to add a host record for App1 on the DNS server hosting the fabrikam.com zone. Otherwise, users will not be able to connect to the application server when they specify it by FQDN.

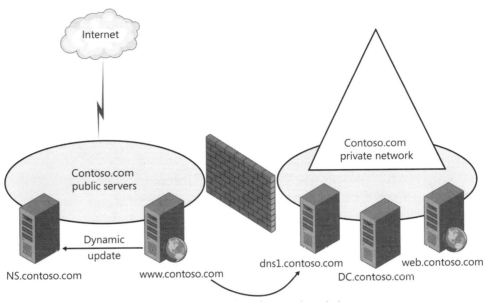

Figure 3-14 Adding a host record for a public Web server

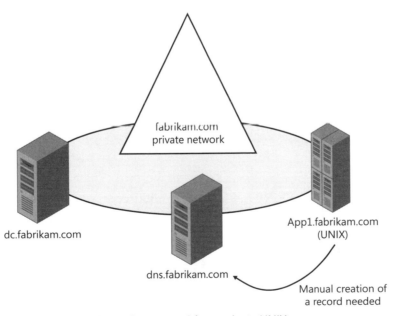

Figure 3-15 Adding a host record for a private UNIX server

Exam Tip   If you can ping a computer by IP address but not by name, the computer might be missing a host record in DNS. You can attempt to remedy this situation by executing the *Ipconfig /registerdns* command at that computer—but only if the client computer is running Windows 2000 or later.

Alias (CNAME) Resource Records   Alias (CNAME) resource records are sometimes called *canonical names*. These records allow you to use more than one name to point to a single host. For example, the well-known server names (ftp, www) are typically registered using CNAME resource records. These records map the host name specific to a given service (such as ftp.lucernepublishing.com) to the actual A resource record of the computer hosting the service (such as server-boston.lucernepublishing.com).

CNAME resource records are also recommended for use in the following scenarios:

- When a host specified in an A resource record in the same zone needs to be renamed
- When a generic name for a well-known server such as www needs to resolve to a group of individual computers (each with individual A resource records) that provide the same service (for example, a group of redundant Web servers)

After you create it in the DNS Manager console, a CNAME resource record that maps the alias ftp.lucernepublishing.com to the host name ftp1.lucernepublishing.com would be represented textually within the lucernepublishing.com.dns standard zone file as follows:

```
ftp             CNAME      ftp1.lucernepublishing.com.
```

MX Resource Records   The mail exchanger (MX) resource record is used by e-mail applications to locate a mail server within a zone. It allows a domain name such as lucernepublishing.com, specified in an e-mail address such as joe@lucernepublishing. com, to be mapped to the A resource record of a computer hosting the mail server for the domain. This type of record thus allows a DNS server to handle e-mail addresses in which no particular mail server is specified.

Multiple MX records are often created to provide fault tolerance and failover to another mail server when the preferred server listed is not available. Multiple servers are given a server preference value, with the lower values representing higher preference. After you create them in the DNS Manager console, such MX resource records would be represented textually within the lucernepublishing.com.dns zone file as follows:

```
@          MX     1     mailserver1.lucernepublishing.com.
@          MX     10    mailserver2.lucernepublishing.com.
@          MX     20    mailserver3.lucernepublishing.com.
```

NOTE What does the "@" symbol mean?

In this example, the @ symbol represents the local domain name contained in an e-mail address.

PTR Resource Records   The pointer (PTR) resource record is used in reverse lookup zones only to support reverse lookups, which perform queries to resolve IP addresses to host names or FQDNs. Reverse lookups are performed in zones rooted in the in-addr.arpa domain. PTR resource records can be added to zones manually or automatically.

After you create it in the DNS Manager console, a PTR resource record that maps the IP address 192.168.0.99 to the host name server1.lucernepublishing.com would be represented textually within a zone file as follows:

```
99              PTR     server1.lucernepublishing.com.
```

NOTE Why is the PTR record named 99?

In a reverse lookup zone, the last octet of an IPv4 address is equivalent to a host name. The 99 therefore represents the name assigned to the host within the 0.168.192.in-addr.arpa zone. This zone corresponds to the 192.168.0.0 subnet.

SRV Resource Records   Service location (SRV) resource records are used to specify the location of specific services in a domain. Client applications that are SRV-aware can use DNS to retrieve the SRV resource records for given application servers.

Windows Server 2008 Active Directory is an example of an SRV-aware application. The Netlogon service uses SRV records to locate domain controllers in a domain by searching the domain for the Lightweight Directory Access Protocol (LDAP) service.

If a computer needs to locate a domain controller in the lucernepublishing.com domain, the DNS client sends an SRV query for the name:

```
_ldap._tcp.lucernepublishing.com.
```

The DNS server then responds to the client with all records matching the query.

Although most SRV resource records are created automatically, you might need to create them through the DNS Manager console to add fault tolerance or troubleshoot network services. The following example shows the textual representation of two SRV records that have been configured manually in the DNS Manager console:

```
_ldap._tcp  SRV    0  0 389    dc1.lucernepublishing.com.
            SRV    10 0 389    dc2.lucernepublishing.com.
```

In the example, an LDAP server (domain controller) with a priority of 0 (highest) is mapped to port 389 at the host dc1.lucernepublishing.com. A second domain controller with a lower priority of 10 is mapped to port 389 at the host dc2.lucernepublishing.com. Both entries have a 0 value in the weight field, which means that no load balancing has been configured among servers with equal priority.

Enabling DNS to Use WINS Resolution

You can use the WINS tab in the properties of a zone to specify a WINS server that the DNS Server service can contact to look up names not found through DNS queries. When you specify a WINS server in the WINS tab in the properties of a forward lookup zone, a special WINS resource record pointing to that WINS server is added to the zone. When you specify a WINS server in the WINS tab in a reverse lookup zone, a special WINS-R resource record pointing to that WINS server is added to the zone.

For example, if a DNS client queries for the name ClientZ.contoso.com and the preferred DNS server cannot find the answer through any of its usual sources (cache, local zone data, queries to other servers), the server then queries the WINS server specified in the WINS record for the name "CLIENTZ." If the WINS server responds with an answer to the query, the DNS server returns this response to the original client.

Exam Tip   For the 70-642 exam, you need to understand the function of the WINS and WINS-R records in a DNS zone.

Aging and Scavenging

Aging in DNS refers to the process of using timestamps to track the age of dynamically registered resource records. *Scavenging* refers to the process of deleting outdated resource records on which timestamps have been placed. Scavenging can occur only when aging is enabled. Together, aging and scavenging provide a mechanism to remove stale resource records, which can accumulate in zone data over time. Both aging and scavenging are disabled by default.

Enabling Aging   To enable aging for a particular zone, you have to enable this feature both at the server level and at the zone level.

To enable aging at the server level, first open the Server Aging/Scavenging Properties dialog box by right-clicking the server icon in the DNS Manager console tree and then choosing Set Aging/Scavenging For All Zones, as shown in Figure 3-16. Next, in the Server Aging/Scavenging Properties dialog box that opens, select the Scavenge Stale Resource Records check box. Although this setting enables aging and scavenging for all new zones at the server level, it does not automatically enable aging or scavenging on existing Active Directory–integrated zones at the server level. To do that, click OK, and then, in the Server Aging/Scavenging Confirmation dialog box that appears, enable the option to apply these settings to existing Active Directory–integrated zones, as shown in Figure 3-17.

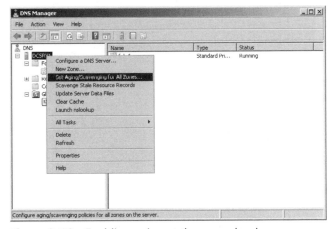

Figure 3-16   Enabling aging at the server level

Figure 3-17   Enabling aging on Active Directory–integrated zones

To enable aging and scavenging at the zone level, open the properties of the zone and then, in the General tab, click Aging, as shown in Figure 3-18. Then, in the Zone Aging/Scavenging Properties dialog box that opens, select the Scavenge Stale Resource Records check box, as shown in Figure 3-19.

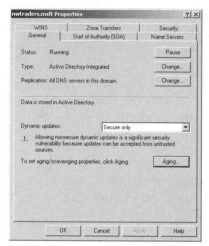

Figure 3-18   Accessing aging properties for a zone

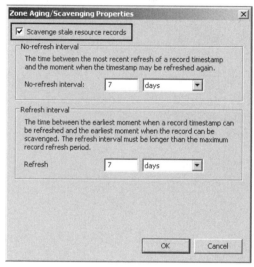

Figure 3-19   Enabling aging and scavenging at the zone level

Timestamping   The DNS server performs aging and scavenging by using timestamps values set on resource records in a zone. Active Directory–integrated zones perform timestamping for dynamically registered records by default, even before aging and scavenging are enabled. However, primary standard zones place timestamps on dynamically registered records in the zone only after aging is enabled. Manually created resource records for all zone types are assigned a timestamp of 0; this value indicates that they will not be aged.

Modifying Zone Aging/Scavenging Properties The Zone Aging/Scavenging Properties dialog box enables you to modify two key settings related to aging and scavenging: the no-refresh interval and the refresh interval.

- **Modifying the no-refresh interval** The *no-refresh interval* is the period after a timestamp during which a zone or server rejects a timestamp refresh. The no-refresh feature prevents the sever from processing unnecessary refreshes and reduces unnecessary zone transfer traffic. The default no-refresh interval is seven days.

- **Modifying refresh intervals** The *refresh interval* is the time after the no-refresh interval during which timestamp refreshes are accepted and resource records are not scavenged. After the no-refresh and refresh intervals expire, records can be scavenged from the zone. The default refresh interval is seven days. Consequently, when aging is enabled, dynamically registered resource records can be scavenged after 14 days by default.

Exam Tip You need to understand the no-refresh and refresh intervals for the 70-642 exam. Remember also that the refresh interval should be equal to or greater than the no-refresh interval.

Performing Scavenging Scavenging in a zone is performed either automatically or manually. For scavenging to be performed automatically, you must enable automatic scavenging of stale resource records in the Advanced tab of DNS server properties dialog box, as shown in Figure 3-20.

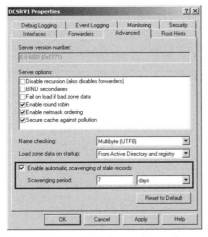

Figure 3-20 Enabling automatic scavenging on a DNS server

When this feature is not enabled, you can perform manual scavenging in zones by right-click-ing the server icon in the DNS Manager console tree and then choosing Scavenge Stale Resource Records, as shown in Figure 3-21.

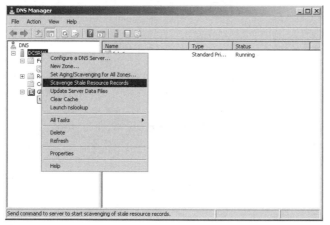

Figure 3-21   Performing manual scavenging for zones

Quick Check

■ What kind of zones do not automatically perform timestamping on dynamically created resource records?

Quick Check Answer

■ Standard zones

Using a GlobalNames Zone

Windows Server 2008 includes a new feature that enables all DNS clients in an Active Directory forest to use single-label name tags such as "Mail" to connect to specific server resources located anywhere in the forest. This feature can be useful when the default DNS suffix search list for DNS clients would not enable users to connect quickly (or connect at all) to a resource by using a single-label name.

To support this functionality, the DNS Server role in Windows Server 2008 includes capability for a GlobalNames zone. The GlobalNames zone does not exist by default, but by deploying a zone with this name you can provide access to selected resources through single-label names without relying on WINS. These single-label names typically refer to records for important, well-known, and widely used servers—servers that are already assigned static IP addresses.

Figure 3-22 shows a GlobalNames zone with a record for a server with a single-label name of Mail.

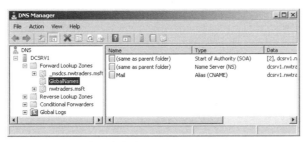

Figure 3-22   The GlobalNames zone

Deploying a GlobalNames Zone

The GlobalNames zone is compatible only with DNS servers running Windows Server 2008. Therefore, it cannot replicate to servers running earlier versions of Windows Server.

There are three basic steps in deploying a GlobalNames zone:

- **Enable GlobalNames zone support**   You can perform this step before or after you create the zone, but you must perform it on every DNS server to which the GlobalNames zone will be replicated.

  At an elevated command prompt, type the following:

  ```
  dnscmd . /config /enableglobalnamessupport 1
  ```

  In this case the "." is used to represent the local server. If you want to enable Global-Names zone support on a remote server, substitute the "." for the remote server name.

- **Create the GlobalNames zone**   The next step in deploying a GlobalNames zone is to create the zone on a DNS server that is a domain controller running Windows Server 2008. The GlobalNames zone is not a special zone type; rather, it is simply an Active Directory–integrated forward lookup zone that is called GlobalNames. When you create the zone, make sure to select the option to replicate zone data to all DNS servers in the forest. (This option appears on the Active Directory Zone Replication Scope page of the New Zone Wizard.)

- **Populate the GlobalNames zone**   For each server that you want to be able to provide single-label name resolution for, create an alias (CNAME) resource record in the Global-Names zone. The name you give each CNAME record represents the single-label name that users will use to connect to the resource. Note that each CNAME record points to a host record in another zone.

Exam Tip   Expect to see a question about the GlobalNames zone on the 70-642 exam.

> **Quick Check**
>
> ■ Why would you use a GlobalNames zone?
>
> **Quick Check Answer**
>
> ■ To facilitate the resolution of single-label computer names in a large network.

PRACTICE Deploying a GlobalNames Zone

In this practice, you will create the GlobalNames Zone to enable connectivity to a specific single-label name throughout an Active Directory forest.

▶ Exercise 1   Enabling the GlobalNames Zone

In this exercise, you will enable the GlobalNames zone on Dcsrv1. In a production environment you would need to perform this step on every DNS server in the forest.

1. Log on to Nwtraders from Dcsrv1 as a domain administrator.
2. Open an elevated command prompt.
3. At the command prompt, type **dnscmd . /config /enableglobalnamessupport 1**.
   Note the space in this command after the "."
4. You receive an output message indicating that the Registry property was successfully reset.

▶ Exercise 2   Creating the GlobalNames Zone

In this exercise, you will create a new DNS forward lookup zone named GlobalNames on Dcsrv1.

1. While you are logged on to Nwtraders from Dcsrv1 as a domain administrator, open DNS Manager.
2. In the DNS Manager console tree, right-click the Forward Lookup Zones container, and then choose New Zone.
3. On the Welcome page of the New Zone Wizard, read the text, and then click Next.
4. On the Zone Type page, read all of the text on the page. Then, leaving the default selections of Primary and Store The Zone In Active Directory, click Next.
5. On the Active Directory Zone Replication Scope page, select To All DNS Servers In This Forest, and then click Next.

6. On the Zone Name page, type **GlobalNames**, and then click Next.

7. On the Dynamic Update page, select the Do Not Allow Dynamic Updates option, and then click Next.

   You should choose the option because dynamic updates are not supported with the GlobalNames zone.

8. On the Completing The New Zone Wizard page, read the text, and then click Finish.

   In the DNS Manager console tree, the new GlobalNames zone appears.

▶ **Exercise 3   Adding Records to the GlobalNames Zone**

In this exercise, you will add records to the GlobalNames zone so that you can later test its functionality.

1. While you are still logged on to Nwtraders from Dcsrv1 as a domain administrator, in the DNS Manager console tree right-click the GlobalNames zone, and then choose New Alias (CNAME).

2. In the New Resource Record dialog box, in the Alias Name text box, type **mail**.

3. In the Fully Qualified Domain Name (FQDN) For Target Host text box, type **dcsrv1.nwtraders.msft**, and then click OK.

   A new alias (CNAME) record with the name "mail" now appears in the GlobalNames zone.

▶ **Exercise 4   Testing the GlobalNames Zone**

In this exercise, you will attempt to resolve the name of the new record you have created. The GlobalNames zone is used to resolve single-name tags anywhere in an Active Directory forest.

1. Log on to Nwtraders from Boston as a domain administrator.

2. Open an elevated command prompt.

3. At the command prompt, type **ping mail**.

   Boston translates the name "mail" to dcsrv1.nwtraders.msft and then pings the address of that server. You know that this name has been resolved from the GlobalNames zone because there is no record in the Nwtraders.msft zone for a host or alias named "mail."

4. Log off both Dcsrv1 and Boston.

Lesson Summary

■ A DNS zone is a database containing records that associate names with addresses for a defined portion of a DNS namespace. To create a new zone on a DNS server, you can use the New Zone Wizard in DNS Manager. The New Zone Wizard enables you to choose a zone type, specify a forward or reverse lookup zone, set the zone replication scope, name the zone, and configure options for dynamic updates.

■ A primary zone provides original read-write source data that allows the local DNS server to answer DNS queries authoritatively about a portion of a DNS namespace. A secondary zone provides an authoritative, read-only copy of a primary zone or another secondary zone. A stub zone is similar to a secondary zone, but it contains only those resource records necessary to identify the authoritative DNS servers for the master zone.

■ When you create a new primary or stub zone on a domain controller, the Zone Type page gives you the option to store the zone in Active Directory. There are several advantages to integrating your DNS zone with Active Directory, including ease of management, the availability of multiple primary zones, and improved security.

■ When you do not store a zone in Active Directory, the zone is called a standard zone and zone data is stored in text files on the DNS server.

■ When you create a new zone, two types of records required for the zone are automatically created: an SOA record and at least one NS record. The SOA record defines basic properties for the zone. NS records determine which servers hold authoritative information for the zone.

■ *Aging* in DNS refers to the process of using timestamps to track the age of dynamically registered resource records. *Scavenging* refers to the process of deleting outdated resource records on which timestamps have been placed.

Lesson Review

The following questions are intended to reinforce key information presented in this lesson. The questions are also available on the companion CD if you prefer to review them in electronic form.

NOTE   Answers

Answers to these questions and explanations of why each answer choice is correct or incorrect are located in the "Answers" section at the end of the book.

---

1. You want to prevent a certain host (A) record from being scavenged. The record belongs to a portable computer named LaptopA that connects to the network only infrequently. LaptopA obtains its address from a DHCP server on the network.

   Which of the following steps would best enable you to achieve this goal?

   A. Disable scavenging on the zone in which the record has been created.

   B. Disable scavenging on the server with which the computer registers its record.

   C. Assign the computer a static address.

   D. Create a record for LaptopA manually.

2. You are a network administrator for a company named Fabrikam, Inc. The DNS server for the network is located on a member server named Dns1 in the Fabrikam.com Active Directory domain. Dns1 provides name resolution for the Fabrikam.com domain only.

   Occasionally, you see DNS records for unauthorized computers in the Fabrikam.com zone. These computers do not have accounts in the Fabrikam.com Active Directory domain.

   What steps should you take to prevent unauthorized computers from registering host records with the DNS server? (Choose three. Each answer represents part of the solution.)

   A. Re-create the zone on a domain controller.

   B. Choose the option to store the zone in Active Directory.

   C. Clear the option to store the zone in Active Directory.

   D. Configure the zone not to accept dynamic updates.

   E. Configure the zone to accept secure and nonsecure dynamic updates.

   F. Configure the zone to accept secure updates only.

Lesson 2: Configuring Zone Replication and Transfers

In an organization, you need not only to configure DNS on an individual server but also to design DNS for the entire network. DNS queries are common, and you want to place DNS servers in a way that keeps the processing workload for these servers at a manageable level, that reduces unnecessary network traffic between servers and clients, and that minimizes the latency time for DNS servers to respond to clients. For all but the smallest organizations, achieving these goals requires you to deploy more than one DNS server.

When you deploy more than one DNS server in an organization, achieving data consistency among these servers becomes an essential aspect of configuring and managing DNS on your network. And in order for multiple DNS servers in an organization to provide synchronized and current information to clients, you need to configure zone replication and transfers.

Zone replication refers to the synchronization of zone data for Active Directory–integrated zones. Zone transfers refer to the synchronization of zone data between any master and a secondary standard zone. These two mechanisms are based on completely different technologies and produce a separate set of considerations for configuration.

After this lesson, you will be able to:
- Configure a zone replication scope appropriate to your network.
- Create a new directory partition and enlist a server in that partition.
- Understand the benefits of a secondary zone.
- Implement a secondary zone.
- Understand the benefits of stub zones.
- Implement a stub zone.
- Enable zone transfers to secondary and stub zones.

Estimated lesson time: 90 minutes

Configuring Zone Replication for Active Directory–Integrated Zones

You can install Active Directory–integrated zones only on domain controllers on which the DNS Server role is installed. Active Directory–integrated zones are generally preferable to standard zones because they offer multimaster data replication, simpler configuration, and improved security and efficiency. With Active Directory–integrated storage, DNS clients can send updates to any Active Directory–integrated DNS server. These updates are then copied to other Active Directory–integrated DNS servers by means of Active Directory replication.

Replication and Application Directory Partitions

DNS data for any particular zone can be replicated among domain controllers in a number of ways, depending on the application directory partition on which the DNS zone data is stored.

A partition is a data structure in Active Directory that distinguishes data for different replication purposes. By default, domain controllers include two application directory partitions reserved for DNS data: DomainDnsZones and ForestDnsZones. The DomainDnsZones partition is replicated among all domain controllers that are also DNS servers in a particular domain, and the ForestDnsZones partition is replicated among all domain controllers that are also DNS servers in every domain in an Active Directory forest.

Each of these application directory partitions is designated by a DNS subdomain and an FQDN. For example, in an Active Directory domain named east.nwtraders.msft and whose root domain in the Active Directory forest is nwtraders.msft, the built-in DNS application partition directories are specified by these FQDNs: DomainDnsZones.east.nwtraders.msft and ForestDnsZones.nwtraders.msft.

You can see evidence of these partitions when you browse DNS Manager, as shown in Figure 3-23. Note that the ForestDnsZones name is located in the nwtraders.msft zone. Note also that each zone includes a DomainDnsZones name that points to the partition that is replicated only within each local domain.

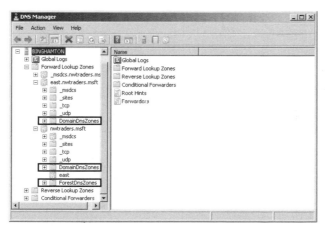

Figure 3-23 You can see evidence of the built-in directory partitions for DNS within an Active Directory–integrated zone

Aside from these two application directory partition types, you can also create a custom or user-defined application directory partition with a name of your own choosing. You can then configure a zone to be stored in this new structure that you have created. By default, the new application directory partition exists only on the server on which you created the partition, but you can enlist other servers in the partition so that replication of its data contents are copied to those particular servers you choose.

The replication pattern displayed by these three application data partition types—Domain-DnsZones, ForestDnsZones, and a custom partition—is illustrated in Figure 3-24.

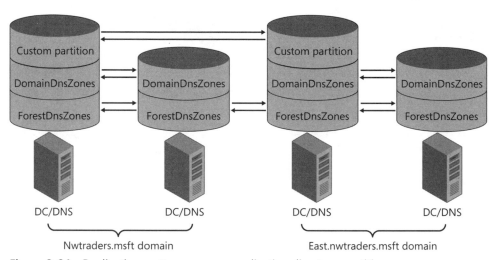

Figure 3-24   Replication patterns among application directory partitions

Storing DNS Data in the Domain Partition   The final storage option for an Active Directory–integrated zone is to store the zone in the domain partition along with all remaining data for a domain. In this configuration the DNS data does not replicate merely to domain controllers that are also DNS servers; it replicates to all domain controllers in general in the local domain. This option is not ideal because it generates unnecessary replication traffic. However, you need to use it if you want your DNS data to be replicated to computers running Windows 2000 Server.

Choosing Zone Replication Scope

The partition in which a zone is stored effectively determines the replication scope for that zone. Replication scope is set when an Active Directory–integrated zone is first created. When you use Dcpromo to promote a server to a domain controller in a new domain, the new Active Directory–integrated zone created for the domain is stored automatically in the

DomainDnsZones partition. However, when you create a new zone by using the New Zone Wizard instead, you are given an opportunity on the Active Directory Zone Replication Scope page to choose the partition in which to store the zone, as shown in Figure 3-25.

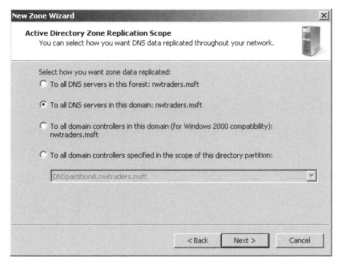

Figure 3-25 Choosing zone replication scope for a new zone

The four options presented on the Active Directory Zone Replication Scope page are the following:

- **To All DNS Servers In This Forest** This option stores the new zone in the ForestDns-Zones partition. Every domain controller in the entire forest and on which the DNS Server role is installed will receive a copy of the zone.
- **To All DNS Servers In This Domain** This option stores the new zone in the DomainDns-Zones partition. Every domain controller in the local domain and on which the DNS Server role is installed will receive a copy of the zone.
- **To All Domain Controllers In This Domain** This option stores the zone in the domain partition. Every domain controller in the local domain will receive a copy of the zone, regardless of whether the DNS Server role is installed on that domain controller.
- **To All Domain Controllers Specified In The Scope Of This Directory Partition** This option stores the zone in the user-created application directory partition specified in the associated drop-down list box. For a domain controller to fall within the scope of such a directory partition, you must manually enlist that domain controller in the partition.

After a new zone is created, you can choose to change the replication scope for the zone at any time. To do so, in the General tab of the properties of the zone, click the Change button associated with replication, as shown in Figure 3-26.

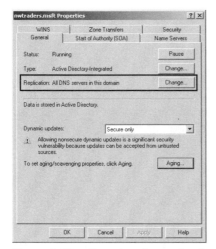

Figure 3-26 Changing the replication scope of an existing zone

This step opens the Change Zone Replication Scope dialog box, which, as shown in Figure 3-27, provides the same zone replication scope options that the New Zone Wizard does.

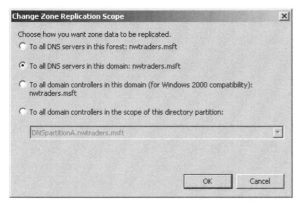

Figure 3-27 Modifying the replication scope for an existing zone

When deciding which replication scope to choose, consider that the broader the replication scope, the greater the network traffic caused by replication. For example, if you choose to have Active Directory–integrated DNS zone data replicated to all DNS servers in the forest, this setting produces greater network traffic than does replicating the DNS zone data to all DNS servers in the local domain only. On the other hand, replicating zone data to all DNS servers in a forest can improve forest-wide name resolution performance and increase fault tolerance.

NOTE   Re-creating DomainDnsZones and ForestDnsZones

If either of the default application directory partitions is deleted or damaged, you can re-create them in DNS Manager by right-clicking the server node and choosing Create Default Application Directory Partitions.

Creating Custom Application Directory Partitions

You can create your own custom application directory partitions for use with DNS and then enlist selected domain controllers in your network to host replicas of this partition.

To accomplish this task, first create the partition by typing the following command:

```
dnscmd servername /createdirectorypartition FQDN
```

Then enlist other DNS servers in the partition by typing the following command:

```
dnscmd servername /enlistdirectorypartition FQDN
```

For example, to create an application directory partition named DNSpartitionA on a computer named Server1 in the Active Directory domain contoso.com, type the following command:

```
dnscmd server1 /createdirectorypartition DNSpartitionA.contoso.com
```

NOTE   Use a dot (".") for the local server name

You can substitute a "." for the server name if you are executing the command on the same server on which you want to create the partition.

To enlist a computer named Server2 in the application directory partition, type the following command:

```
dnscmd server2 /enlistdirectorypartition DNSpartitionA.contoso.com
```

NOTE   Who can create a custom application directory partition?

You must be a member of the Enterprise Admins group to create an application directory partition.

After you create a new application directory partition, that partition will appear as an option in the drop-down list box both on the Active Directory Zone Replication Scope page of the New Zone Wizard and in the Change Zone Replication Scope dialog box. To store a zone in the new partition, choose To All Domain Controllers Specified In The Scope Of This Directory Partition and then select the partition in the drop-down list box.

Exam Tip   Expect to be tested on application directory partition concepts, as well as on the options in the Change Zone Replication Scope dialog box.

Using Zone Transfers

When all of your DNS servers are located on domain controllers, you will normally want to use Active Directory replication to keep zone data consistent among all DNS servers. However, this option is not available when you install a DNS server on a computer that is not a domain controller. In such cases you cannot store the zone in Active Directory and instead must use a standard zone that stores data in a local text file on each DNS server. If your organization requires multiple DNS servers, then the source data can be copied to read-only secondary zones hosted on other servers. In order to keep data consistent and up-to-date between a primary and any secondary zones, you need to configure zone transfers.

Zone transfers are essentially pull operations initiated on secondary zones that copy zone data from a master zone, which itself can be a primary or another secondary. In fact, the master zone for a secondary zone need not even be another standard zone—you can configure a secondary zone for an Active Directory–integrated primary zone. This arrangement might be suitable, for example, if you have two sites, one in New York and one in Los Angeles, each with its own Active Directory domain. In each domain you might want to provide name resolution for the opposite domain without installing a new domain controller and managing replication traffic between the two sites.

Such an infrastructure is illustrated in Figure 3-28.

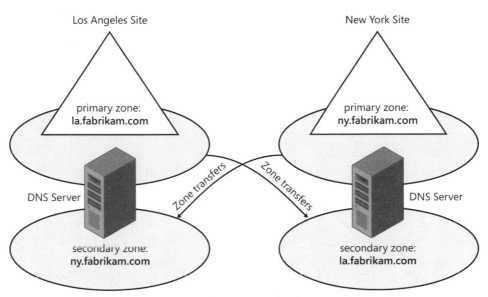

Figure 3-28   A DNS infrastructure with zone transfers between sites

Zone Transfer Initiation

Any of three events can trigger zone transfers on secondary zones:

■ They can be triggered when the refresh interval of the primary zone's SOA resource record expires.

■ They can be triggered when a server hosting a secondary zone boots up.

   In these first two cases the secondary server initiates a query to find out whether any updates in the zone have occurred. This information is determined by comparing the serial number (specified in the SOA record) of the secondary zone to the serial number of the master zone. If the master zone has a higher serial number, the secondary zone initiates a transfer from the master.

■ They are triggered when a change occurs in the configuration of the primary zone and this primary zone is configured to notify a secondary zone of zone updates.

Enabling Zone Transfers

By default, zone transfers are disabled from any zone, and you must enable them in the Zone Transfers tab of the zone properties dialog box, as shown in Figure 3-29. After you have selected the option to allow zone transfers from the zone, you have a choice of three suboptions:

- **To Any Server**   This option is the least secure. Because a zone transfer is essentially a copy of zone data, this setting allows anyone with network access to the DNS server to discover the complete contents of the zone, including all server and computer names along with their IP addresses. This option should therefore be used only in private networks with a high degree of security.

- **Only To Servers Listed On The Name Servers Tab**   This option restricts zone transfers only to secondary DNS servers that have an NS record in the zone and are therefore already authoritative for zone data.

- **Only To The Following Servers**   This option allows you to specify a list of secondary servers to which you will allow zone transfers. The secondary servers do not need to be identified by an NS record in the zone.

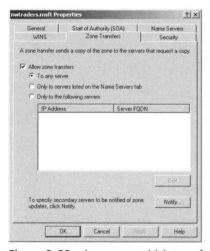

Figure 3-29   A zone on which transfers have been enabled

Configuring Notifications

The Zone Transfers tab also allows you to configure notification to secondary servers whenever a change occurs at the primary zone. Because zone transfers are pull operations, they cannot be configured to push new data to secondary zones. Instead, when a modification occurs in zone data, the primary zone sends a notification to any specified servers hosting secondary zones. When the secondary zone receives this notification, it initiates a zone transfer.

To configure notifications, click Notify in the Zone Transfers tab when zone transfers are enabled. This action opens the Notify dialog box, shown in Figure 3-30, in which you can specify secondary servers that should be notified whenever a zone update occurs at the local master server. By default, when zone transfers are enabled, all servers listed in the Name Servers tab are automatically notified of zone changes.

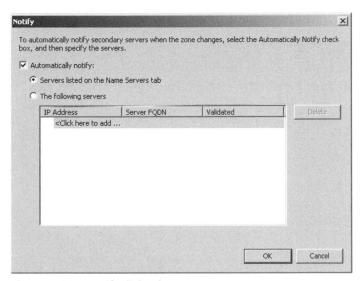

Figure 3-30   Notify dialog box

Manaully Updating a Secondary Zone

By right-clicking a secondary zone in the DNS Manager console tree, you can use the shortcut menu to perform the following secondary zone update operations:

- **Reload**   This operation reloads the secondary zone from the local storage.
- **Transfer From Master**   The server hosting the local secondary zone determines whether the serial number in the secondary zone's SOA resource record has expired and then pulls a zone transfer from the master server.
- **Reload From Master**   This operation performs a zone transfer from the secondary zone's master server regardless of the serial number in the secondary zone's SOA resource record.

Implementing Stub Zones

A *stub zone* is a copy of a zone that contains only the most basic records in the master zone. The purpose of a stub zone is to enable the local DNS server to forward queries to the name servers authoritative for the master zone. In this way a stub zone is functionally identical to a zone delegation. However, because stub zones can initiate and receive zone transfers from the master (delegated) zone, stub zones provide the added benefit of informing parent zones of updates in the NS records of child zones.

An example of a stub zone is shown in Figure 3-31.

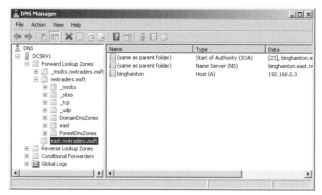

Figure 3-31   East.nwtraders.msft is a stub zone of a child zone hosted on remote server

---

NOTE   **What is a delegated zone?**

A delegated zone is a child zone (such as east.nwtraders.msft) of a parent zone (such as nwtraders.msft) that is typically hosted on its own DNS server. With delegations, the parent zone includes an NS record for the server hosting the child zone, so when the parent receives queries for names in the child zone, those queries get redirected to the server specified in that NS record. It is unlikely that you will see any questions about delegations on the 70-642 exam.

You can use stub zones to:

- **Keep delegated zone information current**   By updating a stub zone for one of its child zones regularly, the DNS server that hosts both the parent zone and the stub zone will maintain a current list of authoritative DNS servers for the child zone.

- **Improve name resolution**   Stub zones enable a DNS server to perform recursion using the stub zone's list of name servers without having to query the Internet or an internal server within the local DNS namespace. When stub zones are deployed for this reason, they are deployed not between parent and child zones but across domains in a large Active Directory forest or DNS namespace.

Stub Zone Example

Suppose that you are an administrator for the DNS server named Dns1.contoso.com, which is authoritative for the zone Contoso.com. Your company includes a child Active Directory domain, India.contoso.com, for which a delegation has been performed. When the delegation is originally performed, the child zone (which is Active Directory–integrated) contains only two authoritative DNS servers: 192.168.2.1 and 192.168.2.2. Later, administrators of the India.contoso.com domain deploy additional domain controllers and install the DNS Server role on these new domain controllers. However, these same administrators do not notify you of the addition of more authoritative DNS servers in their domain. As a result, Dns1.contoso.com is not configured with the records of the new DNS servers authoritative for India.contoso.com and continues to query only the two DNS servers that were defined in the original delegation.

You can remedy this problem by configuring Dns1.contoso.com to host a stub zone for India.contoso.com. As a result of this new stub zone, Dns1 learns through zone transfers about the new name servers authoritative for the India.contoso.com child zone. Dns1 is thus able to direct queries for names within the India.contoso.com namespace to all of that child zone's authoritative DNS servers.

This example is illustrated in Figure 3-32.

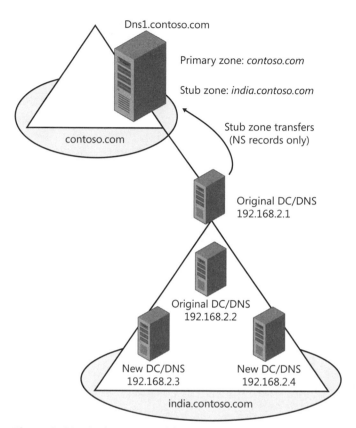

Figure 3-32   Stub zones enable a parent domain to keep an updated list of name servers in a child domain

Other Uses for Stub Zones

Another use for stub zones is to facilitate name resolution across domains in a manner that avoids searching the DNS namespace for a common parent server. Stub zones can thus replace secondary zones when achieving DNS connectivity across domains is important but providing data redundancy for the master zone is not. Also note that stub zones improve name resolution and eliminate the burden on network resources that would otherwise result from large zone transfers.

Exam Tip   Expect to see a question about stub zones on the 70-642 exam. Understand that you can use them to keep an updated list of name servers in a remote zone and to improve name resolution across domains.

Quick Check

1. True or False: you can perform a delegation only from a parent zone to a child zone.
2. Why does a stub zone improve name resolution when it is implemented across domains in a large forest or other DNS namespace?

Quick Check Answers

1. True.
2. A stub zone provides a DNS server with the names of servers that are authoritative for a given zone. When this information is stored locally, the DNS server does not need to query other servers to find the authoritative servers for that zone. The process of resolving a name in that zone is therefore more efficient.

PRACTICE **Creating an Application Directory Partition for DNS**

In this practice, you will create a custom application directory partition and then modify the Nwtraders.msft zone to store data in that partition. (Note that zone data can only be stored in directory partitions for Active Directory–integrated zones.)

▶ **Exercise 1 Creating the New Application Directory Partition**

In this exercise, you will create an application directory partition on Dcsrv1.

1. Log on to Nwtraders from Dcsrv1 as a domain administrator.
2. At an elevated command prompt, type the following:

```
dnscmd . /createdirectorypartition DNSpartitionA.nwtraders.msft
```

This command creates an application directory partition that will replicate in Active Directory only to domain controllers that you enlist in the partition. You do not need to enlist the local server in the partition.

▶ **Exercise 2 Storing Zone Data in the New Application Directory Partition**

In this exercise, you will modify the properties of the Nwtraders.msft zone so that its data is stored in the new application directory partition you have just created.

1. While you are logged on to Nwtraders from Dcsrv1 as a domain administrator, open DNS Manager.
2. In the DNS Manager console tree, expand the Forward Lookup Zones folder, select and then right-click the Nwtraders.msft zone, and then choose Properties.

3. In the General tab of the Nwtraders.msft Properties dialog box, click the Change button for replication. This button is found directly to the right of the text "Replication: All DNS Servers In This Domain."

4. In the Change Zone Replication Scope dialog box that opens, select To All Domain Controllers In The Scope Of This Directory Partition.

5. In the associated drop-down list box, select DNSpartitionA.nwtraders.msft, and then click OK.

6. In the Nwtraders.msft Properties dialog box, click OK.

   The Nwtraders.msft zone data is now stored in the new application directory partition you have created on Dcsrv1. Other domain controllers that are DNS servers in the Nwtraders.msft forest will receive a copy of the Nwtraders.msft primary zone only if you later enlist those servers in the new partition by using the following command:

   ```
   dnscmd <server name> /enlistdirectorypartition DNSpartitionA.nwtraders.msft
   ```

PRACTICE   Deploying a Secondary Zone

In this practice, you will create a secondary DNS zone for Nwtraders.msft on the Boston server. Because the Boston server is not a domain controller, it cannot host an Active Directory-integrated copy of the Nwtraders.msft primary zone. In a production environment you might choose to install a secondary zone when you want to install a DNS server without installing a domain controller.

▶ Exercise 1   Adding the DNS Server Role

In this exercise, you will install the DNS server role on the Boston server.

1. Log on to Nwtraders from Boston as a domain administrator.

2. If the Initial Configuration Tasks window appears, click Add Roles. Otherwise, open Server Manager and click Add Roles in the details pane.

3. On the Before You Begin page of the Add Roles Wizard, click Next.

4. On the Select Server Roles page, select the DNS Server check box, and then click Next.

5. On the DNS Server page, read all of the text, and then click Next.

6. On the Confirm Installation Selections page, click Install.

7. After the installation completes, on the Installation Results page, click Close.

▶ **Exercise 2   Creating the Secondary Zone**

In this exercise, you will create a secondary zone named Nwtraders.msft on Boston.nwtraders.msft.

1. While you are still logged on to Nwtraders from Boston as a domain administrator, open DNS Manager.

2. Expand the DNS Manager console tree.

3. In the DNS Manager console tree, select and then right-click the Forward Lookup Zones folder, and then choose New Zone.

   The Welcome page of the New Zone Wizard appears.

4. Click Next.

5. On the Zone Type page, read all of the text, and then select Secondary Zone.

   Note that the option to store the zone in Active Directory is dimmed. This choice is unavailable because the local computer is not a domain controller.

6. Click Next.

7. On the Zone Name page, in the Zone Name text box, type **nwtraders.msft**. Click Next.

8. On the Master DNS Servers page, read the text on the page.

9. In the Master Servers area, type **192.168.0.1**, and then press Enter.

10. Wait about 30 seconds for the name DCSRV1 to appear beneath the Server FQDN heading in the Master Servers area. Click Next.

11. On the Completing The New Zone Wizard page, click Finish.

    The new zone now appears in DNS Manager.

12. In the DNS Manager console tree, select the Nwtraders.msft forward lookup zone.

    An error message that appears in the details pane indicates that the zone is not loaded by the DNS server. The problem is that you have not enabled zone transfers in the properties of the primary zone on Dcsrv1.

▶ **Exercise 3   Enabling Zone Transfers to the Secondary Zone**

In this exercise, you will enable zone transfers to the Boston computer from Dcsrv1.

1. Log on to Nwtraders from Dcsrv1 as a domain administrator.

2. Open DNS Manager.

3. Expand the DNS Manager console tree.

4. Right-click the Nwtraders.msft forward lookup zone, and then choose Properties.

5. In the Nwtraders.msft Properties dialog box, click the Zone Transfers tab.

6. In the Zone Transfers tab, select the Allow Zone Transfers check box.

7. Verify that To Any Server is selected, and then click OK.

▶ **Exercise 4   Transfer the Zone Data**

In this exercise, you will load the zone data from the primary zone to the secondary zone. You will perform this exercise while logged on to Nwtraders from the Boston computer as a domain administrator.

1. On Boston, in the DNS Manager console tree, right-click the Nwtraders.msft forward lookup zone, and then choose Transfer From Master. If you see an error, wait 15 seconds, and then press F5 or select Refresh from the Action menu.

2. The Nwtraders.msft zone data eventually appears in the details pane of DNS Manager. Note that the application directory partition DNSpartitionA appears above DomainDNS-Zones and ForestDNSZones.

▶ **Exercise 5   Creating an NS Record for the Server Hosting the Secondary Zone**

In this exercise, you will create an NS record for the Boston DNS server in the primary zone. Note that you cannot create an NS record for a secondary zone server from within the secondary zone itself because a secondary zone is a read-only copy of the zone.

You perform this exercise while logged on to Nwtraders from Dcsrv1 as a domain administrator.

1. On Dcsrv1, in the DNS Manager console tree, select the Nwtraders.msft zone.

    In the details pane, note that the only name server (NS) record included in the zone points to dcsrv1.nwtraders.msft. The fact that there is only one such NS record means that even if the DNS domain were connected to a larger DNS namespace, information about names in the Nwtraders.msft domain will always originate from Dcsrv1.

2. In the detail pane, double-click the NS record.

    The Nwtraders.msft Properties dialog box opens, and the Name Servers tab is selected.

3. Click the Add button.

4. In the New Name Server Record dialog box, in the Server Fully Qualified Domain Name (FQDN) text box, type **boston.nwtraders.msft**, and then click Resolve.

    The name is resolved to an IPv6 address and an IPv4 address.

5. In the New Name Server Record dialog box, click OK.

6. In the Nwtraders.msft Properties dialog box, click the Zone Transfers tab.

7. Select Only To Servers Listed On The Name Servers Tab.

    This setting provides security for the zone by restricting copies (transfers) of the zone data to only authorized servers.

8. In the Nwtraders.msft Properties dialog box, click OK.

    In the details pane of DNS Manager, a new NS record appears that points to boston.nwtraders.msft.

9. Close all windows and log off both servers.

Lesson Summary

- Zone replication refers to the synchronization of zone data for Active Directory–integrated zones. Zone transfers refer to the synchronization of zone data between any master and a secondary standard zone.

- A partition is a data structure in Active Directory that distinguishes data for different replication purposes. By default, domain controllers include two application directory partitions reserved for DNS data: DomainDnsZones and ForestDnsZones. The DomainDnsZones partition is replicated among all domain controllers that are also DNS servers in a particular domain, and the ForestDnsZones partition is replicated among all domain controllers that are also DNS servers in every domain in an Active Directory forest.

- You can also create a user-defined directory partition with a name of your choice. You can then configure a zone to be stored in this new structure that you have created.

- The partition in which a zone is stored effectively determines the replication scope for that zone.

- Zone transfers are essentially pull operations initiated on secondary zones that copy zone data from a master zone, which itself can be a primary zone or another secondary zone. By default, zone transfers are disabled from any zone and you must enable them in the Zone Transfers tab of the zone properties dialog box.

- You can use stub zones to keep delegated zone information current or to improve name resolution across domains in a large DNS namespace.

Lesson Review

The following questions are intended to reinforce key information presented in this lesson. The questions are also available on the companion CD if you prefer to review them in electronic form.

NOTE Answers

Answers to these questions and explanations of why each answer choice is correct or incorrect are located in the "Answers" section at the end of the book.

---

1. You are a network administrator for a large company named Northwind Traders that has many branch offices worldwide. You work at the New York office, which has its own Active Directory domain, ny.us.nwtraders.msft.

   Recently you have noticed that when users in the New York office want to connect to resources located in the uk.eu.nwtraders.msft domain, name resolution for computer names in the remote domain is very slow. You want to improve name resolution response times for names within uk.eu.nwtraders.msft domain by keeping an updated list of remote name servers authoritative for that domain name. You also want to minimize zone transfer traffic.

What should you do?

    A. Create a stub zone of the uk.eu.nwtraders.msft domain on the DNS servers at the New York office.

    B. Configure conditional forwarding so that queries for names within the uk.eu.nwtraders.msft domain are automatically forwarded to the name servers in that domain.

    C. Create a secondary zone of the uk.eu.nwtraders.msft domain on the DNS servers at the New York office.

    D. Perform a delegation of the uk.edu.nwtraders.msft domain on the DNS servers at the New York office.

2. You have recently migrated a DNS zone named Contoso.com to a domain controller running Windows Server 2008. You have selected the option to store the zone in Active Directory, but you find that the zone does not appear on a domain controller named DC2000 that is running Windows 2000 Server in the same domain. DC2000 is already configured with the DNS server component.

    You want the zone to appear on all domain controllers in the Contoso.com domain. What should you do?

    A. Choose the option to store the zone in all DNS servers in the forest.

    B. Choose the option to store the zone in all DNS servers in the domain.

    C. Choose the option to store the zone in all domain controllers in the domain.

    D. Create a new directory partition, and then choose the option to store the zone in the new partition.

Chapter Review

To further practice and reinforce the skills you learned in this chapter, you can

- Review the chapter summary.
- Review the list of key terms introduced in this chapter.
- Complete the case scenario. This scenario sets up a real-world situation involving the topics of this chapter and asks you to create solutions.
- Complete the suggested practices.
- Take a practice test.

Chapter Summary

- A zone is a database that contains authoritative information about a portion of the DNS namespace. Zones are created on DNS servers. Primary zones provide the original read-write source data for a zone. Secondary zones are read-only copies of a zone. Stub zones contain only the names of servers containing primary or secondary zones.
- When you create a zone on a domain controller, you have the option to store the zone in Active Directory. This option offers a number of benefits, including reduced administration, improved security for dynamic updates, and multiple primary servers. If you do not store a zone in Active Directory, the zone is known as a standard zone and the zone file is a text file. In standard zones there is only one copy of the primary zone.
- Aging and scavenging provide a mechanism for removing stale resource records in a zone.
- The GlobalNames zone enables the resolution of single-label names in a multidomain forest.
- An application directory partition is a type of data structure used by DNS to store data for Active Directory–integrated zones. By default, every domain controller includes application directory partitions called DomainDnsZones and ForestDnsZones. These partitions are replicated among all domain controllers in the domain and the forest, respectively. You can also create custom application directory partitions and enlist chosen servers in the partition. You can choose to store a zone in any of these partitions. This decision affects what is called the replication scope of the zone.
- Zone transfers keep DNS data consistent between secondary zones and a master zone, which is usually a primary zone.

Key Terms

Do you know what these key terms mean? You can check your answers by looking up the terms in the glossary at the end of the book.

- aging
- application directory partition
- master zone
- primary zone
- replication
- scavenging
- secondary zone
- stub zone
- zone
- zone transfers

Case Scenarios

In the following case scenario you will apply what you've learned in this chapter. You can find answers to these questions in the "Answers" section at the end of this book.

Case Scenario 1: Managing Outdated Zone Data

You work as a domain administrator for Fabrikam, Inc. Your responsibilities include managing the Active Directory and network infrastructure, including DNS. The DNS servers for the Fabrikam.com domain are all installed on domain controllers.

1. Recently you have noticed that some records in the Fabrikam.com zone refer to computers that were removed from the network several months ago. What is the best way to remove these stale records?
2. What is the best way to prevent such data from accumulating in the future?
3. You want to allow records to remain in the zone for 21 days without being scavenged. However, you want to prevent timestamps from being refreshed for the first seven days after each record is first created in the zone. How should you configure the No-Refresh and the Refresh intervals?

Case Scenario 2: Configuring Zone Transfers

You are a network administrator for City Power and Light, whose network is composed of a single Active Directory domain, Cpandl.com. The Cpandl.com zone is stored in Active Directory.

At the company headquarters the Cpandl.com domain controllers host the DNS zones for the domain. The Cpandl.com network also includes several branch offices.

1. The Rochester office does not include a DNS server. You want to improve name resolution of computer names in the Cpandl.com domain, but you don't want to host a domain controller at the Rochester site. Minimizing zone transfer traffic is not a priority. What should you do?

2. You want zone transfers to the Rochester office to occur whenever a change occurs in the zone data. How can you enable this functionality?

Suggested Practices

To help you successfully master the exam objectives presented in this chapter, complete the following tasks.

Configure a DNS Infrastructure

The following practices will deepen your understanding of DNS replication within multi-domain forests. They both require three computers, but you can still perform these practices easily by using virtual machine software such as Virtual PC.

- **Practice 1**   Using virtual machines, create an Active Directory forest with two domain controllers in a domain named Contoso.com and one domain controller in a child domain called East.contoso.com. Choose the option to store both DNS zones in all DNS servers in the forest. View the zone data and then add a record manually to each zone. Force replication by using Active Directory Sites and Services.

- **Practice 2**   Using the same three-computer network, create a custom application directory partition on the domain controller in the East.contoso.com domain. Configure the zone to store its data in the newly created partition. Enlist only one of the domain controllers in the Contoso.com domain in the partition. Reboot each computer and then verify that the zone data is stored on only two of the three servers.

Take a Practice Test

The practice tests on this book's companion CD offer many options. For example, you can test yourself on just one exam objective, or you can test yourself on all the 70-642 certification exam content. You can set up the test so that it closely simulates the experience of taking a certification exam, or you can set it up in study mode so that you can look at the correct answers and explanations after you answer each question.

MORE INFO   Practice tests

For details about all the practice test options available, see the "How to Use the Practice Tests" section in this book's Introduction

---

Chapter 4
Creating a DHCP Infrastructure

Dynamic Host Configuration Protocol (DHCP) allows you to assign IP addresses, subnet masks, and other configuration information to client computers on a local network. When a DHCP server is available, computers that are configured to obtain an IP address automatically request and receive their IP configuration from that DHCP server upon booting.

This chapter introduces you to DHCP concepts as well as to the steps you need to take to deploy and configure a DHCP server on your network.

Exam objectives in this chapter:
- Configure Dynamic Host Configuration Protocol (DHCP).

Lessons in this chapter:

Before You Begin

To complete the lessons in this chapter, you must have

- Two networked computers running Windows Server 2008.
- The first computer must be a domain controller named Dcsrv1 in a domain named nwtraders.msft. Dcsrv1 must be assigned the static address 192.168.0.1/24 with the DNS server specified as the same address. Dcsrv1 includes the server roles Active Directory Domain Services and DNS Server.
- The second computer must be named Boston.nwtraders.msft and must be assigned the address 192.168.0.2/24. Its DNS server must be specified as 192.168.0.1. Finally, Boston must be joined to the Nwtraders.msft Active Directory domain.

Real World

JC Mackin

Believe it or not, some network administrators to this day shun DHCP and assign addresses manually to all of their clients. I know an administrator for a major university, for example, who has static addresses assigned to over 100 computers spread among several floors of a large campus building. To keep track of addresses, he uses an old spiral notebook. I hope he doesn't lose it.

There is usually a halfway decent argument presented in favor of this old-fashioned approach: in some environments client addresses really do need to be permanent. DHCP, however, is not incompatible with permanent addressing. DHCP reservations can be used to associate each client permanently to an address. In addition, the benefits of using DHCP reservations over static addresses are substantial: reserved addresses can be centrally managed, they are far less likely to be misconfigured, and they enable you to make global IP configuration changes easily.

In truth, the biggest hurdle most static-addressing-enamored administrators have with creating reservations is that doing so for every computer seems time-consuming and impractical. Reservations, after all, require you to know the MAC address of the computer whose address you want to reserve. Normally, if you needed to configure 100 DHCP reservations, you would need several hours just to go around typing **Ipconfig /all** and then scribbling down hardware addresses.

Fortunately, the Getmac command-line tool built into Windows Server 2008 enables you to obtain the MAC addresses of remote computers easily. By using this tool, you should be able to configure a DHCP reservation from scratch in no more than 30 seconds—even if you don't know a remote computer's name.

To begin, if you want to avoid typing computer names for every reservation, make sure that your DNS server is hosting a remote lookup zone with dynamic updates enabled. After every client reboots, the PTR record of each client should be registered in this reverse lookup zone.

Next, use the *Getmac* command with the /s switch to specify a remote computer, and then pipe the output into the clipboard to avoid having to type out the MAC address manually.

For example, to create a DHCP reservation for the computer whose address is currently 192.168.0.99, open the New Reservation dialog box from the DHCP console, and then type the following command at a command prompt:

```
getmac /s 192.168.0.99 | clip
```

Next, open Notepad and press the keystroke Ctrl+V. This operation pastes the output from the previous Getmac operation. From Notepad you can then copy the hardware address and paste it into the MAC Address text box of the New Reservation dialog box. In the same dialog box, just type the IP address you want to assign and a name for the reservation, click Add, and you're done.

This technique significantly lowers the hurdle for migrating from static addressing to DHCP reservations. In almost all cases it's a worthwhile switch.

Lesson 1: Installing a DHCP Server

Every computer needs an address to communicate on an IP network, and this address can be provided either manually or automatically. For IPv4, the great majority of devices on a network receive their configurations automatically through a DHCP server. DHCP servers can also assign IPv6 addresses, but this arrangement is not as common because IPv6 hosts by default configure their own addresses.

The actual procedure of installing and configuring a DHCP server is simple, but you still need to understand DHCP concepts in order to implement and manage DHCP on your network. This lesson introduces you not only to the initial configuration steps required to deploy a DHCP server but also to these basic DHCP concepts.

> **After this lesson, you will be able to:**
> - Deploy a DHCP server.
> - Configure a server DHCP scope.
> - Configure DHCP scope options.
>
> **Estimated lesson time: 45 minutes**

Understanding DHCP Address Assignment

The function of a DHCP server is to assign IP addresses to computers. More specifically, when a computer without an IPv4 address is configured to obtain an address automatically, that computer, upon booting, broadcasts DHCP Discover packets on the network. These DHCP Discover messages are then transmitted through all neighboring cables, hubs, and switches. If a DHCP server lies within broadcast range of the computer, that server receives the message and responds by providing the client computer with an IPv4 address configuration. This configuration includes at least an IPv4 address, a subnet mask, and usually other settings as well (such as a default gateway and DNS server).

The actual negotiation between a DHCP client and a DHCP server occurs in four stages, illustrated in Figure 4-1 and described in the following section.

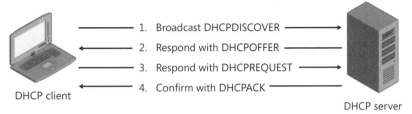

Figure 4-1   The DHCP address assignment process

1. Broadcast DHCP Discover

    In this first stage the client broadcasts a DHCP Discover message to the local network to identify any available DHCP servers. This broadcast reaches only as far as the nearest router (unless the router is configured to forward it.)

2. Respond with DHCP Offer

    If a DHCP server is connected to the local network and can provide the DHCP client with an IP address assignment, it sends a unicast DHCP Offer message to the DHCP client. The DHCP Offer message contains a list of DHCP configuration parameters and an available IP address from the DHCP scope. If the DHCP server has an IP address reservation that matches the DHCP client's MAC address, it offers the reserved IP address to the DHCP client.

3. Respond with DHCP Request

    In the third stage of DHCP negotiation, the DHCP client responds to the DHCP Offer message and requests the IP address contained in this DHCP Offer message. Alternatively, the DHCP client might request the IP address that was previously assigned.

4. Confirm with DHCP Ack

    If the IP address requested by the DHCP client is still available, the DHCP server responds with a DHCP Ack acknowledgement message. The client can now use the IP address.

Understanding Address Leases

Every DHCP server maintains a database of addresses that the server can distribute to clients. When a DHCP server assigns a computer an address, it assigns that address in the form of a lease that lasts six or eight days by default (depending on the method used to configure the server). The DHCP server keeps track of leased addresses so that no address is assigned to two clients.

To prevent an IP address from being indefinitely assigned to a client that has disconnected from the network, DHCP servers reclaim addresses at the end of the DHCP lease period. Halfway through a DHCP lease, the DHCP client submits a lease renewal request to the DHCP server. If the DHCP server is online, the DHCP server typically accepts the renewal, and the lease period restarts. If the DHCP server is not available, the DHCP client tries to renew the DHCP lease again after half the remaining lease period has passed. If the DHCP server is not available when 87.5 percent of the lease time has elapsed, the DHCP client attempts to locate a new DHCP server and possibly acquire a different IP address.

If the DHCP client shuts down normally, or if an administrator runs the command *Ipconfig /release*, the client sends a DHCP Release message to the DHCP server that assigned the IP address. The DHCP server then marks the IP address as available and can reassign it to a different DHCP client. If the DHCP client disconnects suddenly from the network and does not have the opportunity to send a DHCP Release message, the DHCP server will not assign the IP address to a different client until the DHCP lease expires. For this reason, it's important to use a shorter DHCP lease period (for example, six hours instead of six days) on networks where clients frequently connect and disconnect—such as in wireless networks.

Understanding DHCP Scopes

Before your DHCP server can provide IP address leases to clients, a range of IP addresses must be defined at the DHCP server. This range, known as a scope, defines a single physical subnet on your network to which DHCP services are offered. So, for example, if you have two subnets defined by the address ranges 10.0.1.0/24 and 192.168.10.0/24, your DHCP server should be directly connected to each subnet (unless a DHCP Relay Agent is used) and must define a scope for each of these subnets and associated address ranges. Scopes also provide the principal method for the server to manage the distribution and assignment of IP addresses and options to clients on the network.

Understanding DHCP Options

DHCP options provide clients with additional configuration parameters, such as DNS or WINS server addresses, along with an address lease. For example, when the TCP/IP properties of a client computer have been configured to obtain a DNS server address automatically, that computer relies on DHCP options configured at the DHCP server to acquire a DNS server address (or list of addresses).

More than 60 standard DHCP options are available. For an IPv4 configuration, the most common of these include the following:

- **003 Router** A preferred list of IPv4 addresses for routers on the same subnet as DHCP clients. The client can then contact these routers as needed to forward IPv4 packets destined for remote hosts.
- **006 DNS Servers** The IP addresses for DNS name servers that DHCP clients can contact and use to resolve a domain host name query.
- **015 DNS Domain Name** An option that specifies the domain name that DHCP clients should use when resolving unqualified names during DNS domain name resolution. This option also allows clients to perform dynamic DNS updates.
- **044 WINS/NBNS Servers** The IPv4 addresses of primary and secondary WINS servers for the DHCP client to use.
- **046 WINS/NBT Node Type** A preferred NetBIOS name resolution method for the DHCP client to use—such as b-node (0x1) for broadcast only or h-node (0x8) for a hybrid of point-to-point and broadcast methods.
- **051 Lease** An option that assigns a special lease duration only to remote access clients. This option relies on user class information advertised by this client type.

DHCP options are usually assigned to an entire scope, but they can also be assigned at the server level and apply to all leases within all scopes defined for a DHCP server installation. Finally, they can also be assigned on a per-computer basis at the reservation level.

Exam Tip   You need to understand these six DHCP options for the 70-642 exam.

Adding the DHCP Server Role

To install and configure a DHCP server on a computer running Windows Server 2008, first deploy a server on the physical subnet for which you want to provide addressing. Be sure to assign the server a static IP address that will be compatible with the address range planned for the local subnet. For example, if you want to assign computers addresses in the range of 10.1.1.0/24, you could assign the DHCP server the address 10.1.1.2/24.

After you have assigned the server a static address, use the Add Roles Wizard to add the DHCP Server role on the computer. You can launch the Add Roles Wizard in the Initial Configuration Tasks window or in Server Manager.

When you select the DHCP Server role check box on the Select Server Roles page of the Add Roles Wizard, as shown in Figure 4-2, the wizard presents you with the following configuration pages:

- Select Network Connection Bindings
- Specify IPv4 DNS Server Settings
- Specify IPv4 WINS Server Settings
- Add Or Edit DHCP Scopes
- Configure DHCPv6 Stateless Mode
- Specify IPv6 DNS Server Settings
- Authorize DHCP Server

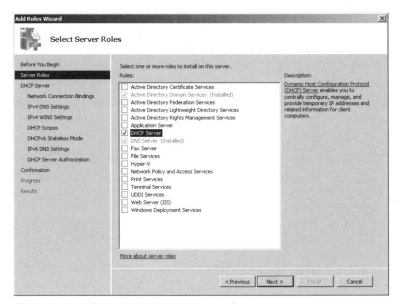

Figure 4-2   Selecting the DHCP Server role

The sections that follow describe the configuration options presented on these seven wizard pages.

Selecting Network Connection Bindings

On the Select Network Connection Bindings page of the Add Roles Wizard, shown in Figure 4-3, you specify the network adapter or adapters that the DHCP server will use to service clients. If your DHCP server is multihomed, this page gives you an opportunity to limit DHCP service to one network only. Remember also that the IP address tied to the adapter must be a manually assigned address and that the addresses you assign to clients from the server must be on the same logical subnet as this statically assigned address (unless you are using a DHCP Relay Agent to provide service to a remote subnet).

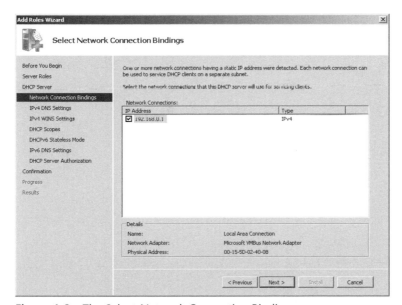

Figure 4-3   The Select Network Connection Bindings page

Specifying IPv4 DNS Server Settings

The Specify IPv4 DNS Server Settings page of the Add Roles Wizard, shown in Figure 4-4, essentially provides you an opportunity to configure the 015 DNS Domain Names and the 006 DNS Servers options for all scopes that you will create on the DHCP server.

The 015 DNS Domain Names option enables you to set a DNS suffix for the client connections obtaining an address lease from the DHCP server. This DNS suffix is specified by the value that you supply in the Parent Domain text box on the Specify IPv4 DNS Server Settings page.

The 006 DNS Servers option enables you to configure a DNS server address list for the client connections obtaining an address lease from the DHCP server. Although the option itself does not limit the number of addresses you can specify, the Specify IPv4 DNS Server Settings page allows you to configure only two. The value you specify in the Preferred DNS Server IPv4 Address corresponds to the first address in the DNS server list, and the Alternate DNS Server IPv4 Address value corresponds to the second DNS server address in the list assigned to each DHCP client.

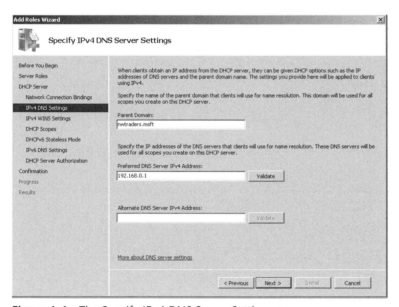

Figure 4-4 The Specify IPv4 DNS Server Settings page

Specifying IPv4 WINS Server Settings

Shown in Figure 4-5, the Specify IPv4 WINS Server Settings page enables you to configure the 044 WINS/NBNS Server option, in which you can assign a WINS server list to clients. To configure this option, select WINS Is Required For Applications On This Network, and then specify a preferred and (optionally) an alternate WINS server address.

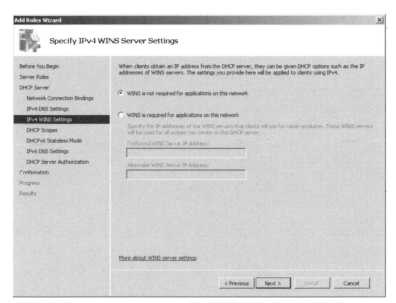

Figure 4-5   The Specify IPv4 WINS Server Settings page

Adding DHCP Scopes

The Add Or Edit DHCP Scopes page, shown in Figure 4-6, enables you to define or edit scopes on the DHCP server.

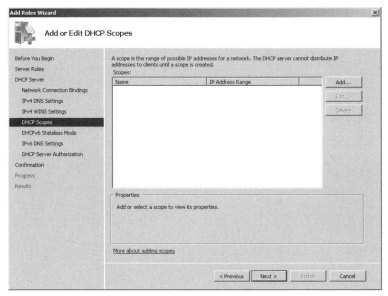

Figure 4-6 The Add Or Edit DHCP Scopes page

A scope is an administrative grouping of IP addresses for computers on a subnet that use the DHCP service. Each subnet can have only a single DHCP scope with a single continuous range of IP addresses.

To add a new scope, click the Add button. This opens the Add Scope dialog box, shown in Figure 4-7.

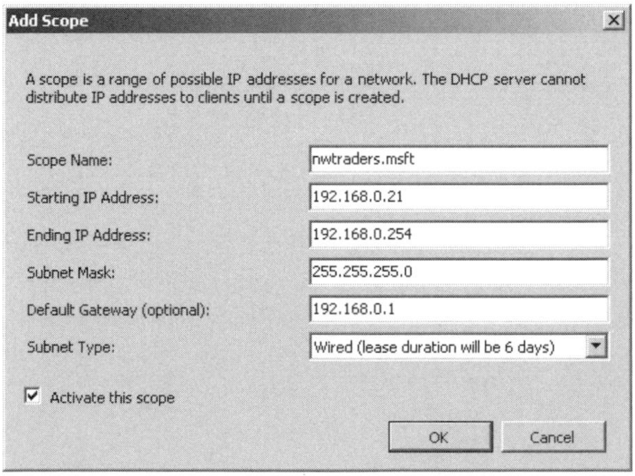

Figure 4-7 The Add Scope dialog box

The process of creating a scope is the most important aspect of configuring a DHCP server. The following list describes the features that you can configure for a scope by using this dialog box.

- **Scope Name** This value has no effect on DHCP clients. It is merely a name you can use to label the scope as it appears in the DHCP console.
- **Starting and Ending IP Address** When defining the IP address range of a scope, you should use the consecutive addresses that make up the subnet for which you are enabling the DHCP service. However, you should also be sure to exclude from this defined range any statically assigned addresses for existing or planned servers on your network. For example, on the same subnet you need to assign a static IP address to the local DHCP server, router (default gateway), and any DNS servers, WINS servers, and domain controllers.

  To exclude these addresses, you can simply choose to limit the scope range so that it does not include any of the static addresses assigned to servers. For example, in the subnet 192.168.0.0/24 you can keep the addresses 192.168.0.1 through 192.168.0.20 for your statically addressed servers, such as your DHCP server, your DNS server, your WINS server, your router, and other servers whose addresses should not change. You can then define the addresses 192.168.0.21 through 192.168.0.254 as the range for the subnet's DHCP scope.
- **Subnet Mask** The subnet mask that you choose here is the subnet mask that will be assigned to DHCP clients that receive an address lease through this scope. Be sure to choose the same subnet mask as the one configured for the DHCP server itself.
- **Default Gateway (optional)** This field effectively enables you to configure the 003 Router option, which assigns a default gateway address to the DHCP clients that receive an address lease through this scope.
- **Subnet Type** This setting essentially allows you to assign one of two lease durations to the scope. By default, the scope is set to the Wired subnet type, which configures a lease duration of six days. The alternative setting is Wireless, for which the lease duration is eight hours.
- **Activate This Scope** A scope will lease out addresses only if it is activated. By default, this option to activate the new scope is enabled.

Configuring DHCPv6 Stateless Mode

DHCPv6 refers to DHCP for IPv6, and stateless mode refers to the default addressing mode for IPv6 hosts, in which addresses are configured without the help of a DHCP server while options can still be obtained from the DHCP server. When an IPv6 host is configured to obtain an address automatically, instead of using a DHCP server, the host in stateless mode self-configures an address compatible with the local subnet by exchanging Router Solicitation and Router Advertisement messages with a neighboring IPv6 router.

However, on the Configure DHCPv6 Stateless Mode page, shown in Figure 4-8, you can disable stateless mode on the DHCP server and enable it to respond to IPv6 hosts that have been enabled for stateful addressing. When stateful addressing is then enabled on IPv6 hosts, they request an address and potentially other IPv6 configuration options (such as DNS server addresses) from a DHCP server by using the DHCPv6 protocol.

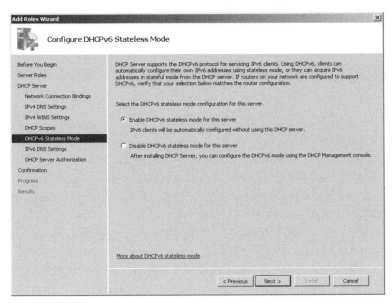

Figure 4-8   Configuring DHCPv6 stateless mode

If you choose to disable stateless addressing on the DHCP server on the Configure DHCPv6 Stateless Mode page, you will later need to create a scope for an IPv6 address range by using the DHCP console. To do so, right-click the *IPv6* node in the DHCP console tree, choose New Scope as shown in Figure 4-9, and then follow the prompts in the New Scope Wizard.

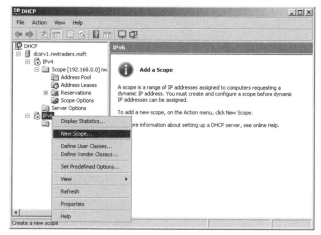

Figure 4-9   Creating a scope for DHCPv6 clients

NOTE   Enabling stateful addressing for IPv6 hosts

To enable stateful addressing on an IPv6 host, type the following command:

`netsh interface ipv6 set interface `*interface_name*` managedaddress=disabled`

To enable the IPv6 host to obtain DHCP options from a DHCPv6 server, type the following command:

`netsh interface ipv6 set interface `*interface_name*` otherstateful=enabled`

For more information about DHCPv6 addressing, consult the DHCP server information within the Windows Server 2008 online technical library at *http://technet2.microsoft.com/windowsserver2008/en /servermanager/dhcpserver.mspx*.

Exam Tip   It is unlikely that you will see any questions about DHCPv6 on the 70-642 exam.

Configuring IPv6 DNS Server Settings

When you leave the Enable DHCPv6 Stateless Mode For This Server option selected, the Configure IPv6 DNS Server Settings page appears. You can use the Configure IPv6 DNS Server Settings page to specify a DNS server address for IPv6 clients enabled for configuration of DHCP options. This page resembles the Specify IPv4 DNS Server Settings page except that you must specify a DNS server by its IPv6 address.

Authorizing DHCP Server

The Authorize DHCP Server page, shown in Figure 4-10, gives you an opportunity to authorize a DHCP server for use in an Active Directory domain.

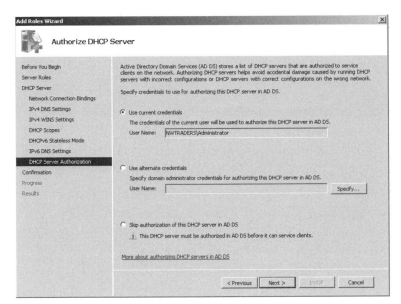

Figure 4-10   Authorizing a DHCP server

In Active Directory domain environments, a DHCP server will not issue IP addresses to clients unless the server is authorized. Requiring servers to be authorized reduces the risk that a user will accidentally or intentionally create a DHCP server that assigns invalid IP address configurations to DHCP clients, which might prevent the clients from accessing network resources.

If a server requires authorization, you will see a red arrow pointing downward next to the IPv4 or IPv6 icon in the DHCP console, as shown in Figure 4-11.

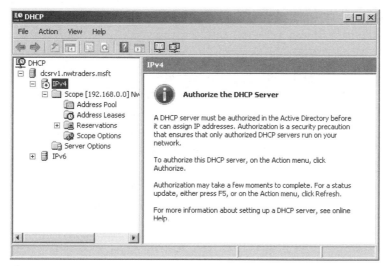

Figure 4-11   A DHCP Server that needs to be authorized

Quick Check

■ (Fill in the blanks.) Before a DHCP server in a domain environment can lease addresses from an existing scope to any DHCP clients, you first need to _____ the server and _____ the scope.

Quick Check Answer

■ authorize, activate

PRACTICE **Deploying a DHCP Server**

In this practice, you will use the Add Roles Wizard to add the DHCP Server role and configure a scope for IPv4 on Dcsrv1. You will then configure the Boston computer as a DHCP client and observe the output.

▶ **Exercise 1   Adding the DHCP Server Role**

In this exercise, you will add the DHCP Server role on Dcsrv1.

1. Log on to Nwtraders from Dcsrv1 as a domain administrator.

2. In the Initial Configuration Tasks window (or Server Manager), click Add Roles. The Add Roles Wizard opens.

3. On the Before You Begin page, click Next.

4. On the Select Server Roles page, select the DHCP Server check box.

5. On the Select Server Roles page, click Next.

6. On the DHCP Server page, read all of the text on the page, and then click Next.

7. On the Select Network Connection Bindings page, read all of the text on the page. Then, verify that the check box next to 192.168.0.1 is selected and click Next.

8. On the Specify IPv4 DNS Server Settings page, read all of the text on the page. Then, verify that nwtraders.msft is specified as the parent domain and that 192.168.0.1 is specified as the preferred DNS server IPv4 address. Click Next.

9. On the Specify IPv4 WINS Server Settings page, read all of the text on the page. Then, leave the selection specifying that WINS is not required for applications on the network and click Next.

10. On the Add Or Edit DHCP Scopes page, read all of the text on the page, and then click Add.

    The Add Scope dialog box appears.

11. Use the following information to complete the fields in the Add Scope dialog box:

    Scope Name: **Nwtraders.msft IPv4**

    Starting IP Address: **192.168.0.20**

    Ending IP Address: **192.168.0.254**

    Subnet Mask: **255.255.255.0**

    Default Gateway (optional): **192.168.0.1**

    Subnet Type: Wired (lease duration will be six days)

    Activate this scope: Enabled

12. After you have entered the appropriate values in the Add Scope dialog box, click OK.

13. On the Add Or Edit DHCP Scopes page, click Next.

14. On the Configure DHCPv6 Stateless Mode page, read all of the text on the page. Then, leave the Enable DHCPv6 Stateless Mode For This Server option selected and click Next.

15. On the Specify IPv6 DNS Server Settings page, read all of the text on the page. Then, verify that nwtraders.msft is specified as the parent domain and that fd00::1 is specified as the preferred DNS server IPv6 address. Click Next.

16. On the Authorize DHCP Server page, read all of the text on the page. Then, verify that the Use Current Credentials option is selected and click Next.

17. On the Confirm Installation Selections page, review the selections, and then click Install.

    When the installation completes, the Installation Results page appears.

18. On the Installation Results page, click Close.

▶ **Exercise 2   Enabling DHCP on the Client**

In this exercise, you will configure the Boston computer as a DHCP client for IPv4.

1. Log on to Nwtraders from Boston as a domain administrator.

2. Open an elevated command prompt.

3. At the command prompt, type the following:

   `netsh interface ipv4 set address "local area connection" dhcp`

4. After the command completes successfully and the prompt reappears, type the following:

   `netsh interface ipv4 set dnsserver "local area connection" dhcp`

5. After the command completes successfully and the prompt reappears, type **ipconfig /all**. The *Ipconfig* output shows that DHCP is enabled and that Boston has received a new IP address, 192.168.0.20.

6. Log off both computers.

Lesson Summary

- When a computer without an IPv4 address is configured to obtain an address automatically, the computer, upon booting, broadcasts DHCP Discover packets on the network. If a DHCP server lies within broadcast range of the computer, that server will receive the message and respond by providing the client computer with an IPv4 address configuration. This configuration includes at least an IPv4 address and a subnet mask and usually other settings as well (such as a default gateway and DNS server).

- When a DHCP server assigns a computer an address, it assigns that address in the form of a lease. The DHCP server keeps track of leased addresses so that no address is assigned to two clients.

- Before your DHCP server can provide IP address leases to clients, a range of IP addresses must be defined at the DHCP server. This range, known as a scope, defines a single physical subnet on your network to which DHCP services are offered.

- DHCP options provide clients with additional configuration parameters, such as DNS or WINS server addresses, along with an address lease.

- To deploy a DHCP server, use the Add Roles Wizard to add the DHCP Server role. The Add Roles Wizard guides you through an initial DHCP configuration and enables you to select network bindings, specify DNS and WINS server addresses, add DHCP scopes, configure DHCPv6 stateless mode, and specify IPv6 DNS server settings.

Lesson Review

The following questions are intended to reinforce key information presented in this lesson. The questions are also available on the companion CD if you prefer to review them in electronic form.

NOTE Answers

Answers to these questions and explanations of why each answer choice is correct or incorrect are located in the "Answers" section at the end of the book.

---

1. After you deploy a DHCP server for the 192.168.1.0/24 subnet, you find that none of the DHCP clients can communicate beyond the local subnet when they specify the IP address of a computer on the company network. Statically assigned computers can successfully communicate beyond the local subnet.

   How can you configure the DHCP server to enable DHCP clients to communicate beyond the local subnet?

   A. Configure the 003 Router option.

   B. Configure the 006 DNS Servers option.

   C. Configure the 015 Domain Name option.

   D. Configure the 044 WINS/NBNS Servers option.

2. You want to deploy a DHCP server on a computer named Dhcp1.nwtraders.msft. To this server you have configured a static address of 10.10.0.5/24 and assigned a DNS server address of 10.10.1.1. On Dhcp1 you configure a scope within the range 10.10.1.0/24. You then activate the scope and authorize the server, but the server does not successfully lease any addresses to computers on the local subnet. When you verify the addresses of the clients on the subnet, you find that they are all assigned addresses in the 169.254.0.0/16 range.

   You want the DHCP server to lease addresses to client computers on the local subnet only. Which of the following actions will most likely fix the problem?

   1. Configure the clients as DHCP clients.

   2. Enable the DHCP client service on Dhcp1.

   3. Change the address of Dhcp1 and redeploy the DHCP server.

   4. Run the command *Ipconfig /registerdns* on Dhcp1.

Lesson 2: Configuring a DHCP Server

Although using the Add Roles Wizard enables you to deploy a DHCP server with basic installation options, you can use the main DHCP management tool, the DHCP console, to finish the configuration.

This lesson describes the key features of a DHCP server that you can configure after deployment by using the DHCP console.

After this lesson, you will be able to:

- Create scope reservations.
- Create scope exclusions.
- Configure DHCP scope options.

Estimated lesson time: 30 minutes

Performing Post-installation Tasks

After you add the DHCP Server role, you can perform further configuration tasks by using the DHCP console. These tasks include configuring exclusions, creating address reservations, adjusting the lease duration of a scope, and configuring additional scope or server options. Each of these tasks is described below.

Creating Address Exclusions

An *exclusion range* is a set of one or more IP addresses that is included within the range of a defined scope but that you do not want to lease to DHCP clients. Exclusion ranges ensure that the DHCP server does not assign addresses that are already assigned manually to servers or other computers.

For example, you might define a new scope whose address range is 192.168.0.10–192.168.0.254. Within the subnet serviced by the DHCP server, however, you might have a number of preexisting servers whose static addresses might lie within this range—for example, between 192.168.0.200 and 192.168.0.210. Or you might have servers with isolated static addresses, such as 192.168.0.99. By setting an exclusion for these addresses, you specify that DHCP clients are never offered these addresses when they request a lease from the server.

To add an exclusion range, in the DHCP console tree navigate to DHCP \ *<server node>* \ IPv4 \ Scope \ Address Pool. Right-click the Address Pool folder, and then choose New Exclusion Range, as shown in Figure 4-12.

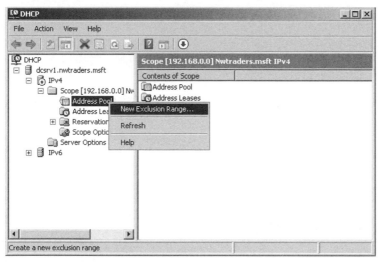

Figure 4-12 Adding exclusions

Then, in the Add Exclusion dialog box that opens, configure the range of addresses that you want to exclude from the address range within the scope you have defined. If you want to exclude a single address, specify the Start IP Address and the End IP Address as the same address. The Add Exclusion dialog box is shown in Figure 4-13.

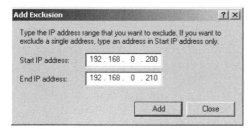

Figure 4-13 Adding an exclusion range

If you have more than one contiguous range of addresses that you need to exclude or separate individual addresses, such as 192.168.0.25 and 192.168.0.200, that need to be excluded, you need to create more than one exclusion range to exclude all of the necessary addresses.

Creating Reservations

You use a *reservation* to create a permanent address lease assignment by the DHCP server by associating an IP address with a MAC address. Reservations ensure that a specified hardware device on the subnet can always use the same IP address without relying on a manually configured address. For example, if you have defined the range 192.168.0.11–192.168.0.254 as your DHCP scope, you can then reserve the IP address 192.168.0.100 within that scope for the network adapter whose hardware address is 00-b0-d0-01-18-86. Every time the computer hosting this adapter boots, the server recognizes the adapter's MAC address and leases the address 192.168.0.100.

The advantage of a reservation, compared to a manually configured address, is that it is centrally managed and less likely to be configured incorrectly. The disadvantage of a reservation is that its address is assigned late in the boot process and depends on the presence of a DHCP server, which is unsuitable for certain infrastructure servers, such as DNS servers. However, some servers, such as application servers, print servers, and even some domain controllers, benefit from a permanent address but you do not need to configure this address manually.

To create a reservation, in the DHCP console tree navigate to DHCP \ *server node* \ IPv4 \ Scope \ Reservations. Right-click the Reservations folder, and then choose New Reservation, as shown in Figure 4-14.

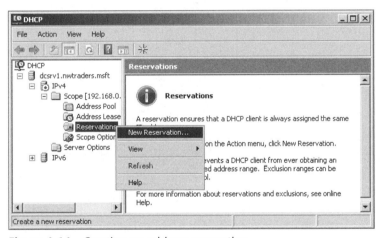

Figure 4-14   Creating an address reservation

Then, in the New Reservation dialog box that opens, specify a name, IP address, and MAC address for the reservation. For the reservation configured in Figure 4-15, the DHCP server will recognize DHCP requests originating from the hardware address 00-15-5D-02-40-08 and will then assign the IP address 192.168.0.30 to that MAC address.

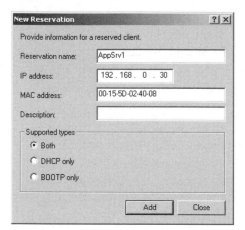

Figure 4-15 Creating an address reservation

Adjusting Lease Durations

You can modify the lease duration to be used for assigning IP address leases. For most local area networks (LANs), the default value of six days is acceptable but can be further increased if computers seldom move or change locations. In cases where addresses are sparse and in cases where users connect for brief periods of time, you should shorten the lease duration. Be especially careful with configuring unlimited lease times. You can configure these in small networks when addresses are abundant, but you should use this setting with caution.

To adjust the length of a lease duration, open the properties of the scope whose lease duration you want to adjust. You can adjust the lease duration in the General tab in the Lease Duration For DHCP Clients area, shown in Figure 4-16.

NOTE Deleting leases

In the DHCP console, the *Address Leases* node displays which IP addresses are currently leased to which clients. If you want to end the lease for a given address or client, you can simply delete that lease by right-clicking the lease and then choosing Delete. Normally, if you want to end the lease of any particular computer, you can use the *Ipconfig /release* command on that computer. However, by using the DHCP console, you can end the leases of many clients at once. This option is useful, for example, if you want many clients to obtain a new address (because of new exclusions or reservations affecting those clients). Another case in which deleting many leases is useful is when you want to assign a newly defined DHCP option to many clients. By deleting the address leases, the DHCP clients will be forced to renew their leases and obtain the new addresses or new options.

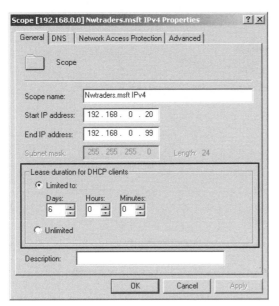

Figure 4-16   Adjusting the lease duration for a scope

Configuring Additional DHCP Options

You can assign options at the server level, the scope level, and the reservation level. Options defined at the server level are inherited by all scopes configured on the server. Options defined at the scope level are inherited by all leases and reservations within the scope. Options defined at the reservation level apply to that reservation only. At all three levels the DHCP options available are the same.

Exam Tip   You need to understand this concept of options inheritance for the 70-642 exam. For example, if you want an option to apply to all scopes, leases, and reservations, you should define the scope at the server level. To do so, right-click the Server Options folder in the DHCP console tree, and then choose Configure Options.

Although the Add Roles Wizard enables you to define a small number of server and scope options, the full range of DHCP options can be configured in the DHCP console. To see the built-in options that you can configure, in the DHCP console navigate to DHCP \ *<server node>* \ IPv4 \ Scope \ Scope Options. Right-click the Scope Options folder, and then choose Configure Options, as shown in Figure 4-17.

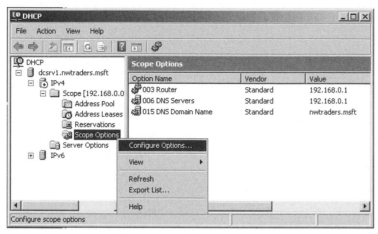

Figure 4-17   Configuring options for an existing scope

Then use the Scope Options dialog box to choose an option for the scope, as shown in Figure 4-18.

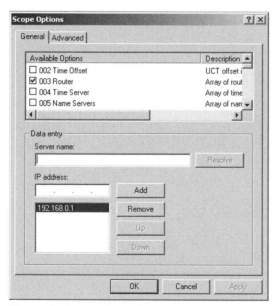

Figure 4-18   Configuring options for an existing scope

NOTE Browse the DHCP options

On the 70-642 exam you won't be tested on any DHCP options beyond those covered in the section entitled "Understanding DHCP Options" in Lesson 1 of this chapter. However, browsing the long list of options made available through the DHCP console helps you get a feel for what DHCP options are and how you might use them in a production environment.

Understanding DHCP Options Classes

An *options class* is a client category that enables the DHCP server to assign options only to particular clients within a scope. When an options class is added to the server, clients of that class can be provided class-specific options. Options classes can be of two types:

- Vendor classes are used to assign vendor-specific options to DHCP clients identified as a vendor type. For example, you can configure clients that can be identified as running Windows 2000 to enable or disable NetBIOS. A vendor class is generally not configurable in the sense that the class identification is built into the software of the client. An administrator typically does not need to populate the class by enabling a setting on the client.

- User classes are used to assign options to any set of clients identified as sharing a common need for similar DHCP options configuration. These classes are configurable. Administrators can create new user classes, which they then populate by configuring a setting on clients they choose.

NOTE What is the Default User class?

The Default User class is a class to which all DHCP clients belong and the class in which all options are created by default. If you want an option to apply to all DHCP clients, regardless of their class identification, leave the option configured for the Default User class. Note, however, that particular options assigned through the Default User class can be overridden by options defined in other classes. For example, if the Default User class defines both a WINS server and DNS server address, and a custom user class named special WINS defines only a WINS server, a client assigned to special WINS will obtain the WINS server address from special WINS and the DNS server address from the Default User Class.

Implementing User Classes

User classes enable you to apply a particular configuration of DHCP options to any subset of DHCP clients you define. To implement a user class, you first define the class at the DHCP server by assigning an ID and a set of options for the class. Then you assign selected client computers to that class by using the *Ipconfig /setclassid* command. When these clients subsequently communicate with DHCP servers, they announce their class ID and inherit the options of that class along with the options of the default user class. If no class ID is manually configured in this way, the client inherits the options merely of the default user class.

A custom user class is helpful when you need to assign distinct options to distinct sets of client computers. For example, your network might require certain clients to be assigned a special default gateway that allows them to bypass the company firewall. In this example you could configure options to distribute the unique default gateway to the security-exempt class.

To create a custom or new user class, begin by right-clicking the IPv4 icon in the DHCP console and choosing Define User Classes, as shown in Figure 4-19.

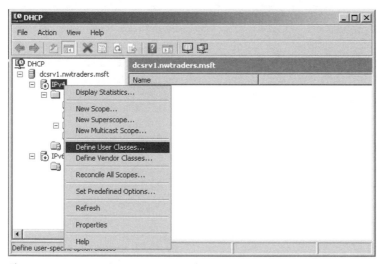

Figure 4-19 Creating a new user class

This step opens the DHCP User Classes dialog box. In this dialog box, shown in Figure 4-20, you can see that three user classes are predefined: Default Routing And Remote Access Class, Default Network Access Protection Class, and Default BOOTP Class. Beyond these three, the Default User Class is the implicit class to which all clients belong by default.

You can create a new user class by clicking the Add button in the DHCP User Classes dialog box. This step opens the New Class dialog box, shown in Figure 4-21. In this dialog box, you merely need to name the class and then set an ID string of your choice for the class. (Use the ASCII field to define the string.)

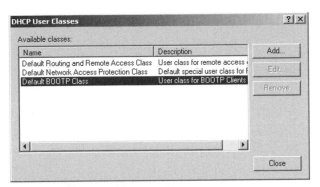

Figure 4-20   Available user classes

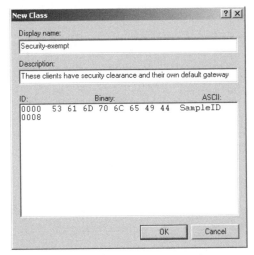

Figure 4-21   Defining a new user class

After defining a new class and specifying an ID string for that class, the new user class appears in the User Class drop-down list box in the the Advanced Tab of the Scope Options dialog box, as shown in Figure 4-22. You can then select that user class and define a set of options that will be assigned only to members of the class.

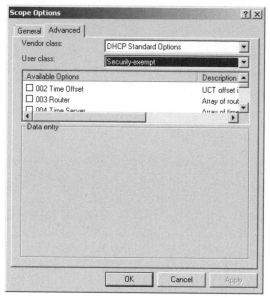

Figure 4-22 Configuring options for a custom user class

Finally, you need to populate the class. For the desired computers to inherit the options of the new class, you need to set the class ID of appropriate client computers to match the ID you have defined for that class at the DHCP server. You can do this by executing the *Ipconfig /setclassid* command at a command prompt at each client computer.

For example, to configure a connection named "Local Area Connection" with the class ID named "SampleID," type the following command:

```
ipconfig /setclassid "local area connection" SampleID
```

After you run this command on a DHCP client, the client will inherit the options defined for that class in addition to the options defined for the default user class. If the two options conflict, such as with the definition of a default gateway, the option defined for the more specific class takes precedence over the setting defined for the Default User class.

Installing and Configuring DHCP on a Server Core Installation

To configure a DHCP server on a Server Core installation of Windows Server 2008, first install the DHCP Server role by typing the following command:

```
start /w ocsetup DHCPServerCore
```

Even though this command installs the DHCP Server role, it does not automatically start the DHCP Server service or configure the service to start automatically by default upon booting. To start the service for the first time, use the following command:

```
net start dhcpserver
```

To configure the DHCP service to start automatically, type the following command. (Be sure to include the space after the equal sign.)

```
sc config dhcpserver start= auto
```

After the DHCP Server role is installed on the Server Core installation, you will need to configure it. To add scopes and configure the server, you can simply connect to the server from the DHCP console on a computer running a full installation of Windows Server 2008. You can then add scopes and perform all configurations remotely as if the server were local. Alternatively, you can create and configure scopes on the Server Core installation itself by using the Netsh utility at the command prompt.

If you want to configure a Server Core installation as a DHCP client for IPv4, type the following command, where "local area connection" is the name of the connection on the network:

```
netsh interface ipv4 set address "local area connection" dhcp
```

To configure the server to obtain a DNS server address through DHCP, type the following:

```
netsh interface ipv4 set dnsserver "local area connection" dhcp
```

Note that these two final commands need to be executed only if the setting has been changed from the default. As with all installations of Windows, a Server Core installation of Windows Server 2008 is a full DHCP client by default.

Quick Check

■ When you configure DHCP options for the Default User class, which clients are assigned these options?

Quick Check Answer

■ All clients, except when a client is assigned a class-specific option that conflicts with an option defined for the Default User class. In this case the class-specific option takes precedence.

PRACTICE **Creating an Exclusion Range**

In this practice, you will create an exclusion range on Dcsrv1 that prevents the DHCP server from leasing a particular set of addresses.

▶ **Exercise 1   Creating an Exclusion Range**

In this exercise, you will you will create an exclusion range on Dcsrv1 for the address range 192.168.0.200–192.168.0.210.

1. Log on to Nwtraders from Dcsrv1 as a domain administrator.
2. Open the DHCP console by clicking Start, pointing to Administrative Tools, and then choosing DHCP.
3. In the DHCP console tree, navigate to DHCP \ dcsrv1.nwtraders.msft \ IPv4 \ Scope [192.168.0.0.] Nwtraders.msft \ Address Pool.
4. Right-click the Address Pool folder, and then choose New Exclusion Range.
   The Add Exclusion dialog box opens.
5. In the Add Exclusion dialog box, type **192.168.0.200** and **192.168.0.210** in the Start IP Address and End IP Address boxes, respectively.
6. Click Add, and then click Close.
   In the details pane you can see that the address range you have configured is now listed. The icon next to the range includes a red X, and the description associated with the range is "IP Addresses excluded from distribution."
7. Log off Dcsrv1.

Lesson Summary

- After you deploy a DHCP server, you might want to perform additional configuration by using the DHCP console. For example, you can create exclusion ranges, create reservations, adjust the lease duration, and configure additional options.

- An exclusion is an address within a scope's address range that cannot be leased to DHCP clients. You can use exclusions to make a scope's address range compatible with static addresses already assigned to computers on a network.

- A DHCP reservation is a particular address that a DHCP server assigns to a computer owning a particular MAC address.

- An *options class* is a client category that enables the DHCP server to assign options only to particular clients within a scope. Vendor classes are used to assign vendor-specific options to DHCP clients identified as a vendor type. User classes are used to assign options to any set of clients identified as sharing a common need for similar DHCP options configuration.

- The Default User class is a class to which all DHCP clients belong and the class in which all options are created by default.
- You can create a custom user class when you need to assign distinct options to distinct sets of client computers. After you create a custom user class and assign options to it, you can assign a client to a class by using the *Ipconfig /setclassid* command.

Lesson Review

The following questions are intended to reinforce key information presented in this lesson. The questions are also available on the companion CD if you prefer to review them in electronic form.

NOTE Answers

Answers to these questions and explanations of why each answer choice is correct or incorrect are located in the "Answers" section at the end of the book.

---

1. You are deploying a DHCP server on your network to supply addresses in the 192.168.1.0/24 range. You have 200 DHCP client computers on the local subnet.

   The subnet includes a DNS server on the network with a statically assigned address of 192.168.1.100. How can you create a scope on the DHCP server that does not conflict with the existing DNS server address?

   A. Use the 006 DNS Servers option to assign to clients the address of the DNS server.

   B. Create a reservation that assigns the address 192.168.1.100 to the DNS server.

   C. Configure two address ranges in the DHCP scope that avoids the address 192.168.1.100.

   D. Create an exclusion for the address 192.168.1.100.

2. Which of the following commands should you run to install a DHCP server on a Server Core installation of Windows Server 2008?

   A. sc config dhcpserver start= auto

   B. start /w ocsetup DHCPServer

   C. net start DHCPServer

   D. servermanagercmd -install dhcp

Chapter Review

To further practice and reinforce the skills you learned in this chapter, you can

- Review the chapter summary.
- Review the list of key terms introduced in this chapter.
- Complete the case scenario. This scenario sets up a real-world situation involving the topics of this chapter and asks you to create solutions.
- Complete the suggested practices.
- Take a practice test.

Chapter Summary

- DHCP servers provide clients with IP addresses. DHCP clients are those that have been configured to receive an address automatically. When such clients have no address, they send a network broadcast requesting the service of a DHCP server. If a DHCP server lies within broadcast range, it will answer the request and provide the client with an address from an address range you configure.

- Each range of contiguous addresses that can be assigned to DHCP clients is known as a scope.

- Addresses are leased to clients for a finite amount of time. The DHCP server keeps track of leased addresses in a local database.

- DHCP options are configuration settings that a DHCP server can assign to clients, settings such as a default gateway address and DNS server address.

- You can deploy a DHCP server by using the Add Roles Wizard to add the DHCP Server role. When you choose this role, the Add Roles Wizard gives you an opportunity to configure the basic features of a DHCP server. These features include a DHCP scope and basic DHCP options.

- You can also configure a DHCP server by using the DHCP console after you run the Add Roles Wizard. You can use the DHCP console to add new scopes, create exclusion ranges, create reservations, adjust the lease duration, and configure additional options.

Key Terms

Do you know what these key terms mean? You can check your answers by looking up the terms in the glossary at the end of the book.

- Default User class
- exclusion
- lease
- option
- options class
- reservation
- user class
- vendor class

Case Scenarios

In the following case scenarios, you will apply what you've learned in this chapter. You can find answers to these questions in the "Answers" section at the end of this book.

Case Scenario 1: Deploying a New DHCP Server

You have just deployed a new DHCP server in your organization, whose network consists of a single subnet. After you finish running the Add Roles Wizard, you find that although all company computers can communicate with each other, only the computers with static addresses can communicate with the Internet. You confirm that the problem is not related to name resolution.

1. What configuration change can you make in the new scope that will enable the clients to communicate beyond the local subnet?

2. What step can you take in the DHCP console to force this configuration change to take effect?

Case Scenario 2: Configuring DHCP Options

Your network includes a DHCP server connected to both a wired subnet and a wireless subnet. The DHCP server uses a separate scope to provide addressing for each of the two subnets. For the wired subnet the DHCP leases addresses in the range 192.168.10.0/24, and for the wireless subnet the DHCP server leases addresses in the range 192.168.20.0/24. These two subnets share many configuration options, including the same DNS domain name, the same DNS server list, and the same WINS server.

1. At what level should you configure the DHCP options specifying a domain name, DNS server, and WINS server?

2. You want to configure a special connection-specific DNS suffix for 30 of the 200 DCHP clients on the wired subnet. How can you best achieve this by using DHCP options?

Suggested Practice

To help you successfully master the exam objectives presented in this chapter, complete the following task.

Configure DHCP

This practice helps solidify your understanding of DHCP server concepts on your home network. If you do not have a home network, you can perform these exercises in a virtual environment instead.

- **Practice** Remove DHCP services from any devices on your network, and then deploy a new DHCP server on a server running Windows Server 2008 on your home network. On the DHCP server, configure a scope with options for a DNS server and a default gateway. Run the *Ipconfig /release* and *Ipconfig /renew* commands on every client to ensure that they obtain addresses from the new DHCP server.

  Using the DHCP console, create a new user class with a name and class ID of your choice. Configure a special DHCP option for the class, such as an extended DNS server list or a WINS server address. Use the *Ipconfig /setclassid* command to assign the class ID to a client. Use *Iponfig /renew* to obtain a new address lease on the same client and observe the effects.

  Create a DHCP reservation for another client on your network. In the reservation, specify a particular address in the middle of the IP address range of the scope. Then, configure DHCP options for the reservation. Use *Ipconfig /renew* to observe how the client is assigned the address specified and the option defined in the reservation.

Take a Practice Test

The practice tests on this book's companion CD offer many options. For example, you can test yourself on just one exam objective, or you can test yourself on all the 70-622 certification exam content. You can set up the test so that it closely simulates the experience of taking a certification exam, or you can set it up in study mode so that you can look at the correct answers and explanations after you answer each question.

MORE INFO   Practice tests

For details about all the practice test options available, see the "How to Use the Practice Tests" section in this book's Introduction.

Chapter 5
Configuring IP Routing

IP networks, including home networks, enterprise intranets, and the Internet, consist of a series of interconnected *routers*. Routers forward traffic to computers, to other routers, and finally to a destination computer. At the most basic, client computers send all communications through a single router known as the default gateway. If you connect multiple routers to a single subnet, however, you might need to configure more complex routing for computers on the subnet. Additionally, computers running Windows Server 2008 can act as routers.

Exam objectives in this chapter:
- Configure routing.

Lessons in this chapter:

Before You Begin

To complete the lessons in this chapter, you should be familiar with Microsoft Windows networking and be comfortable with basic network configuration, including configuring IP settings. You will also need a computer named Dcsrv1 that has at least one network interface, connected to a network with a router that is connected to the Internet.

NOTE   Computer and domain names

The computer and domain names you use will not affect these practices. The practices in this chapter refer to these computer names for simplicity, however.

Real World

Tony Northrup

For the exam it's important to understand how to configure Windows Server 2008 as a router. In the real world you'll almost never use computers as routers. Hardware-based routers offer better performance with a lower purchase cost and cheaper maintenance. More important, they offer much better reliability. Because routers are designed to be only routers (whereas Windows Server 2008 is designed to be everything from a Web server to a mail server), much less can go wrong.

Lesson 1: Routing

This lesson provides an overview of routing concepts, describes how to troubleshoot routing problems using PathPing and TraceRt, and then shows you how to configure static routing.

> **After this lesson, you will be able to:**
> - Describe routing concepts.
> - Use PathPing and TraceRt to examine network routes.
> - Describe and configure routing protocols.
> - Use static routing to configure access to networks that cannot be reached through a default gateway.
>
> **Estimated lesson time: 45 minutes**

Routing Overview

Figure 5-1 shows a typical enterprise intranet consisting of three locations, each with four routers. As you can see, any of the example computers can communicate with any other computer by forwarding communications between routers.

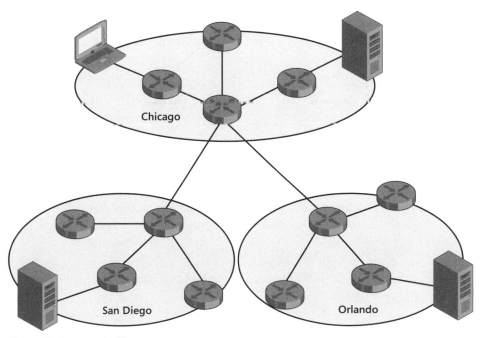

Figure 5-1   A typical intranet

As you know from earlier chapters, every computer must have a unique IP address. A router has an IP address, too, and must have a unique IP address assigned to every network interface. Figure 5-2 shows the Chicago network from Figure 5-1 with more detail, showing sample IP addresses for every router interface.

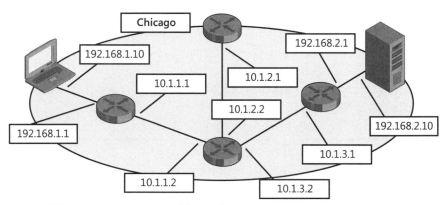

Figure 5-2   A routed network with IP addresses

On the network shown in Figure 5-2, imagine that the mobile computer on the left needs to connect to the server on the right. In this example the mobile computer has the IP address 192.168.1.10. The router on the same subnet has the IP address 192.168.1.1 and would be configured as the default gateway on the mobile computer. To communicate from the mobile computer to the server, the process would be:

1. The mobile computer sends a packet with a source IP address of 192.168.1.10 and a destination IP address of 192.168.2.10. The mobile computer compares the destination IP address to the network ID of the local subnet and determines that the packet must be sent to a remote network. Because remote networks are always accessed through routers, the mobile computer forwards the packet to the default gateway with the IP address 192.168.1.1. *Gateway* is just another term for router.

2. When the default gateway receives the packet, it checks the destination address, 192.168.2.10. It examines its routing table and determines that the next *hop* (a term for a router in a path) is the router with the IP address 10.1.1.2. So it forwards the packet to 10.1.1.2.

3. When the router with IP address 10.1.12 receives the packet, it also checks the destination IP address, 192.168.2.10, and determines that the next hop toward the destination is the router with the IP address 10.1.3.1.

4. When the router with IP address 10.1.3.1 receives the packet, it checks the destination IP address, 192.168.2.10, and determines that it has a network interface that is directly

connected to the destination network. So it forwards the packet directly to the server by sending it on the server's local area network.

If the server responds to the client, the packet flows back through each of the routers to the client.

How It Works: Layer 2 and Layer 3 Addresses

The destination IP address (a Layer 3 address) of the packet never changes; it is always set to the IP address of the target computer. To forward packets to a router without changing the destination IP address, computers use the MAC address (a Layer 2 address). Therefore, as the packet is forwarded between networks, the source and destination IP addresses never change. However, the source and destination MAC addresses are rewritten for every network between the client and server.

Examining Network Routes

You can use the PathPing and TraceRt commands to determine how packets travel between your computer and a destination. Both tools provide similar results; TraceRt provides a quicker response, and PathPing provides a more detailed and reliable analysis of network performance. The following demonstrates how PathPing displays a route to the *www.microsoft.com* destination:

```
Tracing route to www.microsoft.com [10.46.19.190]
over a maximum of 30 hops:
  0  d820.hsd1.nh.contoso.com. [192.168.1.199]
  1  c-3-0-ubr01.winchendon.ma.boston.contoso.com [10.165.8.1]
  2  ge-1-2-ur01.winchendon.ma.boston.contoso.com [10.87.148.129]
  3  ge-1-1-ur01.gardner.ma.boston.contoso.com [10.87.144.225]
  4  vlan99.csw4.NewYork1.Fabrikam.com [10.68.16.254]
  5  ae-94-94.ebr4.NewYork1.Fabrikam.com [10.69.134.125]
  6  ae-2.ebr4.SanJose1.Fabrikam.com [10.69.135.185]
  7  ae-64-64.csw1.SanJose1.Fabrikam.com [10.69.134.242]
  8  ge-2-0-0-51.gar1.SanJose1.Fabrikam.com [10.68.123.2]
  9      *       *       *
Computing statistics for 450 seconds...
             Source to Here   This Node/Link
Hop  RTT     Lost/Sent = Pct  Lost/Sent = Pct  Address
  0                                             d820.hsd1.nh.contoso.com. [192.168.1.199]
                               0/ 100 =   0%  |
  1   10ms     0/ 100 =   0%   0/ 100 =   0%  c-3-0-ubr01.winchendon.ma.boston.contoso.com
[10.165.8.1]
                               0/ 100 =   0%  |
  2   11ms     0/ 100 =   0%   0/ 100 =   0%  ge-1-2-ur01.winchendon.ma.boston.contoso.com
[10.87.148.129]
                               0/ 100 =   0%  |
```

```
  3    13ms      0/ 100 =   0%      0/ 100 =   0%  ge-1-1-ur01.gardner.ma.boston.contoso.com
[10.87.144.225]
                                    0/ 100 =   0%   |
 14    40ms      0/ 100 =   0%      0/ 100 =   0%  vlan99.csw4.NewYork1.Fabrikam.com [10.68.16.254]
                                    0/ 100 =   0%   |
 15    40ms      0/ 100 =   0%      0/ 100 =   0%  ae-94-94.ebr4.NewYork1.Fabrikam.com [10.69.134.125]
                                    0/ 100 =   0%   |
 16   107ms      0/ 100 =   0%      0/ 100 =   0%  ae-2.ebr4.SanJose1.Fabrikam.com [10.69.135.185]
                                    0/ 100 =   0%   |
 17   108ms      0/ 100 =   0%      0/ 100 =   0%  ae-64-64.csw1.SanJose1.Fabrikam.com [10.69.134.242]
                                    0/ 100 =   0%   |
 18   104ms      0/ 100 =   0%      0/ 100 =   0%  ge-2-0-0-51.gar1.SanJose1.Fabrikam.com
[10.68.123.2]

Trace complete.
```

Notice that PathPing shows the data in two sections. The first section shows the route from the source to the destination. The second section takes longer to generate and shows the latency in milliseconds (ms) to each router.

In this example the last line of the first section shows three asterisk (*) symbols. This occurs when a node does not respond to the Internet Control Message Protocol (ICMP) requests. Servers are often configured to not respond to ICMP, so they will not appear in the list, even though they might be online and responding to other requests.

Routing Protocols

Although you can manually configure each router with a list of destination networks and the next hop for each network, routing protocols simplify configuration and allow routers to automatically adjust when network conditions change (for example, if a router or network connection fails).

When a router is connected to a network and the router has a routing protocol enabled, the routing protocol announces a list of networks to which it is directly connected. The router also listens for announcements from neighboring routers so that it can learn how to reach specific remote networks. This is illustrated in Figure 5-3.

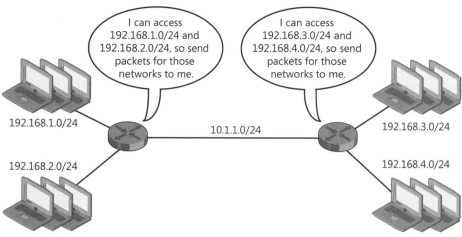

Figure 5-3   Using routing protocols

Exam Tip   For the exam, know what routing protocols do and when they should be used. You don't need to understand the details of how they function, however.

Windows Server 2008 (as well as earlier versions of Windows) support Routing Internet Protocol (RIP) version 2, a popular routing protocol. The sections that follow describe how to enable routing and how to configure RIP. Earlier versions of Windows supported the Open Shortest Path First (OSPF) routing protocol, which has been removed from Windows Server 2008.

Installing Routing and Remote Access Services

To install Routing And Remote Access Services, which includes tools for configuring Windows Server 2008 as a router, follow these steps:

1. Click Start, and then choose Server Manager.
2. In the left pane, select Roles, and then, in the right pane, click Add Roles.
3. If the Before You Begin page appears, click Next.
4. On the Select Server Roles page, select the Network Policy And Access Services check box, and then click Next.
5. On the Network Policy And Access Services page, click Next.
6. On the Select Role Services page, select the Routing And Remote Access Services check box. The wizard automatically selects the Remote Access Service and Routing check boxes. Click Next.

7. On the Confirmation page, click Install.

8. After the Add Roles Wizard completes the installation, click Close.

9. In the console tree of Server Manager, expand Roles, expand Network Policy And Access Services, and then select Routing And Remote Access. Right-click Routing And Remote Access, and then choose Configure And Enable Routing And Remote Access.

    The Routing And Remote Access Server Setup Wizard appears.

10. On the Welcome To The Routing And Remote Access Server Setup Wizard page, click Next.

11. On the Configuration page, select Custom Configuration, and then click Next.

12. On the Custom Configuration page, select the LAN Routing check box, and then click Next.

13. If the Routing And Remote Access dialog box appears, click Start Service.

14. On the Completing The Routing And Remote Access Server Wizard page, click Finish.

Now you can configure RIP, as described in the following section, or use graphical tools to configure static routes, as discussed later in this lesson.

Configuring RIP

When you enable RIP, you allow Windows Server 2008 to advertise routes to neighboring routers and to automatically detect neighboring routers and remote networks. To enable RIP, follow these steps:

1. In Server Manager, right-click Roles\Network Policy And Access Services\Routing And Remote Access\IPv4\General, and then choose New Routing Protocol.

2. In the New Routing Protocol dialog box, select RIP Version 2 For Internet Protocol, and then click OK.

3. Right-click Roles\Network Policy And Access Services\Routing And Remote Access \IPv4\RIP, and then choose New Interface.

4. In the New Interface For RIP Version 2 For Internet Protocol dialog box, select the interface you want to advertise with RIP. Then click OK.

    The RIP Properties dialog box appears.

5. Configure RIP settings to match those of neighboring routers. The default settings will work in most environments. You can adjust settings using the four tabs of the RIP Properties dialog box:

    ❑ **General** Select whether RIP v1 or RIP v2 is used and whether authentication is required.

    ❑ **Security** Choose whether to filter router advertisements. Because a routing protocol could be used to advertise a route to a malicious computer, RIP could be used as part of a man-in-the-middle attack. Therefore, you should restrict the advertised routes that will be accepted whenever possible.

❑ **Neighbors**   Allows you to manually list the neighbors that the computer will communicate with.

❑ **Advanced**   Configure announcement intervals and time-outs, as well as other infrequently used settings.

6. Click OK.

RIP is now enabled on the selected interface. Repeat this process for every interface that will have routing enabled.

Static Routing

On most networks, client computers need to be configured with a single default gateway that handles all communications to and from the subnet. Sometimes, for redundancy, network administrators might place two default gateways on a single subnet. Whether you use single or multiple default gateways, you do not need to configure static routing—simply configure the default gateways using standard network configuration techniques such as DHCP.

Exam Tip   For the exam, know that a router's IP address must always be on the same subnet as the computer.

If a computer needs to use different routers to communicate with different remote networks, you need to configure static routing. For example, in the network shown in Figure 5-4, the client computer would have a default gateway of 192.168.1.1 (because that leads to the Internet, where most IP address destinations reside). However, an administrator would need to configure a static route for the 192.168.2.0/24 subnet that uses the gateway at 192.168.1.2.

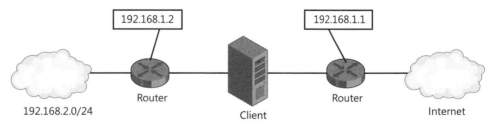

Figure 5-4   A network that requires static routing

Typically, you would do this configuration using the command-line tool Route. For the example shown in Figure 5-4, you could allow it to access the 192.168.2.0/24 network by running the following command:

```
route -p add 192.168.2.0 MASK 255.255.255.0 192.168.1.2
```

After running the command, the computer would route traffic destined for the 192.168.2.0/24 subnet through the router at 192.168.1.2. All other communications would be sent through the default gateway. The next section provides more information about using the Route command to configure static routing, and the following section describes how to use Routing And Remote Access to configure static routes using graphical tools.

NOTE   **On-demand network connections**

Dial-up networks and virtual private networks (VPNs) change a client's routing configuration automatically. Depending on how the connection is configured, either they change the default gateway so that all traffic travels through the on-demand connection, or they establish temporary routes so that just the traffic destined for the private network is sent through the on-demand connection. Either way, you shouldn't have to manually configure the routing.

Configuring Static Routing with the *Route* Command

You can use the *Route* command to examine and configure static routing from a command prompt. To view the *routing table*, run the *Route Print* command. Output resembles the following:

```
===========================================================================
Interface List
28 .......................... ContosoVPN
 7 ...00 15 c5 08 82 f3 ...... Broadcom NetXtreme 57xx Gigabit Controller
 8 ...00 13 02 1e e6 59 ...... Intel(R) PRO/Wireless 3945ABG Network Connection
 1 .......................... Software Loopback Interface 1
16 ...00 00 00 00 00 00 00 e0  isatap.hsd1.nh.comcast.net.
13 ...00 00 00 00 00 00 00 e0  6T04 Adapter
18 ...00 00 00 00 00 00 00 e0  Microsoft 6to4 Adapter
 9 ...02 00 54 55 4e 01 ...... Teredo Tunneling Pseudo-Interface
30 ...00 00 00 00 00 00 00 e0  Microsoft ISATAP Adapter #2
19 ...00 00 00 00 00 00 00 e0  isatap.hsd1.nh.comcast.net.
===========================================================================

IPv4 Route Table
===========================================================================
Active Routes:
Network Destination        Netmask          Gateway       Interface  Metric
          0.0.0.0          0.0.0.0      192.168.1.1   192.168.1.198     25
          0.0.0.0          0.0.0.0      192.168.1.1   192.168.1.199     10
         10.0.0.0        255.0.0.0          On-link   192.168.2.102     21
   10.255.255.255  255.255.255.255          On-link   192.168.2.102    266
   71.121.128.170  255.255.255.255      192.168.1.1   192.168.1.199     11
        127.0.0.0        255.0.0.0          On-link       127.0.0.1    306
        127.0.0.1  255.255.255.255          On-link       127.0.0.1    306
  127.255.255.255  255.255.255.255          On-link       127.0.0.1    306
      192.168.1.0    255.255.255.0          On-link   192.168.1.198    281
      192.168.1.0    255.255.255.0          On-link   192.168.1.199    266
    192.168.1.198  255.255.255.255          On-link   192.168.1.198    281
```

```
       192.168.1.199   255.255.255.255         On-link      192.168.1.199   266
       192.168.1.255   255.255.255.255         On-link      192.168.1.198   281
       192.168.1.255   255.255.255.255         On-link      192.168.1.199   266
         192.168.2.0     255.255.255.0      192.168.1.2      192.168.1.198    26
         192.168.2.0     255.255.255.0      192.168.1.2      192.168.1.199    11
         192.168.2.0     255.255.255.0    192.168.2.100      192.168.2.102    11
       192.168.2.102   255.255.255.255         On-link      192.168.2.102   266
           224.0.0.0       240.0.0.0             On-link         127.0.0.1   306
           224.0.0.0       240.0.0.0             On-link     192.168.1.198   281
           224.0.0.0       240.0.0.0             On-link     192.168.1.199   266
     255.255.255.255   255.255.255.255         On-link         127.0.0.1   306
     255.255.255.255   255.255.255.255         On-link     192.168.1.198   281
     255.255.255.255   255.255.255.255         On-link     192.168.1.199   266
     255.255.255.255   255.255.255.255         On-link     192.168.2.102   266
===========================================================================
Persistent Routes:
  Network Address          Netmask  Gateway Address  Metric
         10.0.0.0        255.0.0.0         On-link      11
      192.168.2.0    255.255.255.0     192.168.1.2       1
===========================================================================


IPv6 Route Table
===========================================================================
Active Routes:
 If Metric Network Destination      Gateway
  9     18 ::/0                     On-link
  1    306 ::1/128                  On-link
  9     18 2001::/32                On-link
  9    266 2001:0:4137:9e66:2020:7c1:e7c0:b11e/128
                                    On-link
  8    281 fe80::/64                On-link
  9    266 fe80::/64                On-link
 19    266 fe80::5efe:192.168.1.198/128
                                    On-link
 19    266 fe80::5efe:192.168.1.199/128
                                    On-link
 30    266 fe80::5efe:192.168.2.102/128
                                    On-link
  8    281 fe80::462:7ed4:795b:1c9f/128
                                    On-link
  9    266 fe80::2020:7c1:e7c0:b11e/128
                                    On-link
  1    306 ff00::/8                 On-link
  9    266 ff00::/8                 On-link
  8    281 ff00::/8                 On-link
===========================================================================
Persistent Routes:
  None
```

The routing table lists destination networks and the interface or router used to access it. Windows maintains separate routing tables for IPv4 and IPv6.

Although the routing table is complex, looking for specific details makes it easier to interpret. Most networks exclusively use IPv4, which means you should focus on the IPv4 Route Table section. Within that section:

- Routes with a Netmask of 0.0.0.0 show the default gateway.
- The Persistent Routes section displays any static routes to remote networks that have been added.
- Routes with a Netmask of 255.255.255.255 indentify an interface and can be ignored.
- A network destination of 127.0.0.0 or 127.0.0.1 shows a loopback interface, which you can ignore.
- A network destination of 224.0.0.0 is a multicast address. Multicasting is rarely used.

For example, consider the following line from the Route Print output:

```
10.0.0.0        255.0.0.0        On-link      192.168.2.102      21
```

This indicates that the computer is configured to send traffic destined for the 10.0.0.0/8 network (a network of 10.0.0.0 with a subnet mask of 255.0.0.0) to the router at 192.168.2.102, rather than to the default gateway.

The following line of output shows that the default gateway is configured to be 192.168.1.1 (for the interface with the IP address 192.168.1.198). You can tell it's the default gateway because the subnet mask is set to 0.0.0.0, which would match all destination networks—assuming no more specific route exists.

```
0.0.0.0         0.0.0.0         192.168.1.1   192.168.1.198     25
```

Examining just the previous two static routes, you can determine that a connection to the IP address 10.12.55.32 would be sent to the router at 192.168.2.102. However, a connection to the IP address 172.18.39.75 would be routed through 192.168.1.1—the default gateway.

MORE INFO   **Routers on the local network**

Routers must always be on the same subnet as a computer. For example, a computer with the IP address 192.168.1.10 and a subnet mask of 255.255.255.0 could have a router with the IP address 192.168.1.1. However, a router with the IP address 192.168.2.1 would be invalid because the router is on a different subnet—and to communicate with a remote subnet, a computer needs to send the packets to a router.

To add static routes from the command line, use the Route Add command. For example, if a neighboring router with the IP address 192.168.1.2 provides access to the network 10.2.2.0 /24 (which would have a network mask of 255.255.255.0), you would run the following command to add a static route to the network:

```
route -p add 10.2.2.0 MASK 255.255.255.0 192.168.1.2
```

When using the Route Add command, the –p parameter makes a route persistent. If a route is not persistent, it will be removed the next time you restart the computer.

Quick Check

1. When are static routes required?
2. What command would you use to configure a static route?

Quick Check Answers

1. Static routes are required when multiple gateways are connected to the local network, and one or more of them does not act as a default gateway.
2. You would use the **route add** command.

Configuring Static Routing with Routing and Remote Access

After installing Routing And Remote Access Services, you can view the IP routing table by right-clicking Roles\Network Policy And Access Services\Routing And Remote Access\IPv4\Static Routes and then choosing Show IP Routing Table. As shown in Figure 5-5, Routing And Remote Access displays the static routing table (which does not include any dynamic routes added from RIP).

DCSRV1 - IP Routing Table					
Destination	Network mask	Gateway	Interface	Metric	Protocol
0.0.0.0	0.0.0.0	192.168.1.1	Local Area Connection	276	Network management
127.0.0.0	255.0.0.0	127.0.0.1	Loopback	51	Local
127.0.0.1	255.255.255.255	127.0.0.1	Loopback	306	Local
192.168.1.0	255.255.255.0	0.0.0.0	Local Area Connection	276	Network management
192.168.1.190	255.255.255.255	0.0.0.0	Local Area Connection	276	Network management
192.168.1.255	255.255.255.255	0.0.0.0	Local Area Connection	276	Network management
224.0.0.0	240.0.0.0	0.0.0.0	Local Area Connection	276	Network management
255.255.255.255	255.255.255.255	0.0.0.0	Local Area Connection	276	Network management

Figure 5-5 The static routing table

To add static routes, follow these steps:

1. In Server Manager, right-click Roles\Network Policy And Access Services\Routing And Remote Access\IPv4\Static Routes, and then choose New Static Route.

2. In the IPv4 Static Route dialog box, select the network interface that will be used to forward traffic to the remote network. In the Destination box, type the network ID of the destination network. In the Network Mask box, type the subnet mask of the destination network. In the Gateway box, type the IP address of the router that packets for the destination network should be forwarded to. Adjust the Metric only if you have multiple paths to the same destination network and want the computer to prefer one gateway

over the others; in this case, configure the preferred routes with lower metrics. Figure 5-6 illustrates how to configure a static route. Click OK.

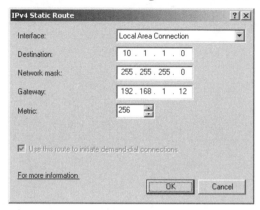

Figure 5-6   Adding a static route

Routing And Remote Access adds the static route, which is displayed in the details pane.

To remove static routes, right-click the route, and then choose Delete.

PRACTICE Analyzing and Configuring Routing

In this practice, you examine real-world network routes and then use the Route command to configure static routes on a computer.

▶ **Exercise 1   Using PathPing and TraceRt**

In this exercise, you will use PathPing and TraceRt to examine the list of routers used to connect your computer to the Web server at *www.microsoft.com*.

1. Log on to Dcsrv1 or on to any computer (even an earlier version of Windows) with an Internet connection.

2. At a command prompt, run the command **pathping www.microsoft.com**.

3. While *PathPing* is computing statistics, open a second command prompt and run the command **tracert www.microsoft.co**.

4. In the TraceRt window, examine the router names and IP addresses. The list shows every router used to carry communications from your computer to the Web server at *www.microsoft.com*. Notice the latency time for each hop—routers that are farther away probably have higher latency because packets must travel a farther distance, and through more routers, before reaching the router. Notice that the last several lines of the TraceRt output show the message Request Timed Out. This message is generated because the Web server at *www.microsoft.com* is configured to not reply to ICMP messages.

5. When PathPing has completed computing statistics, examine the output. The router names and IP addresses should match those displayed by PathPing. The latency information is more detailed and accurate than TraceRt, however, because it was computed over a longer period of time.

▶ **Exercise 2   Configuring Static Routes**

In this exercise, you must configure your network as shown in Figure 5-7. Then you will configure Dcsrv1 with a static route to forward traffic to the 192.228.79.0/24 subnet instead of the default gateway.

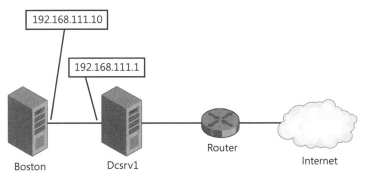

Figure 5-7   A practice routing architecture

The steps in this exercise use the IP addresses shown in Figure 5-7. However, you can substitute Dcsrv1's IP address with any valid IP address on your network. You can substitute the router's IP address given in the exercise with your default gateway's IP address. You can substitute the default gateway's IP address given in the exercise with any unused IP address on your network—in this scenario the default gateway does not physically exist.

With the network and IP address settings configured, follow these steps to configure Dcsrv1 with a static route:

1. On Dcsrv1, run the following command. *PathPing* should return a Destination Host Unreachable message because the default gateway does not exist.

    ```
    PathPing 192.228.79.201
    ```

NOTE   The sample IP address

The IP address in this example is one of the root DNS servers that happens to respond to ICMP requests. Root DNS servers will use the same IP addresses indefinitely. Because this server responds to ICMP requests, you can use PathPing to verify connectivity to it.

---

2. Next, you will configure a static route for a specific subnet that sends traffic for that subnet to your router. Run the following command to add a static route:

    ```
    route -p add 192.228.79.0 MASK 255.255.255.0 192.168.111.1
    ```

3. Run **Route Print** at the command prompt and verify that the static route has been added.

4. Repeat the *PathPing* command from step 1. Now you should be able to communicate with the IP address. Notice that the first router reported by PathPing is the gateway IP address you specified in step 2.

    You've configured a static route to the 192.228.79.0/24 subnet, simulating the addition of a second router on your subnet. Because your default gateway doesn't exist in this scenario, communications to all other networks will fail. In a production environment, however, communications to other networks would be sent successfully through the default gateway and to the destination.

5. You can now return Dcsrv1 to its original network configuration.

Lesson Summary

- Routing allows routers to forward traffic between each other to allow clients and servers on different subnets to communicate.

- *PathPing* and *TraceRt* allow you to identify the routers between a source and destination. Both tools are also useful for identifying routing problems.

- Routers use routing protocols to communicate available routes, as well as to communicate changes such as failed links. Windows Server 2008 supports RIP v2, which you can enable by installing the Routing And Remote Access Services role service.

- You can use static routing to allow computers with multiple routers connected to their subnet to forward traffic with different destinations to the correct router.

Lesson Review

You can use the following questions to test your knowledge of the information in Lesson 1, "Routing." The questions are also available on the companion CD if you prefer to review them in electronic form.

NOTE   Answers

Answers to these questions and explanations of why each answer choice is correct or incorrect are located in the "Answers" section at the end of the book.

---

1. Currently, client computers on the 192.168.1.0/24 subnet are configured with the default gateway 192.168.1.1. You connect a second router to both the 192.168.1.0/24 subnet and the 192.168.2.0/24 subnet. You would like clients on the 192.168.1.0/24 subnet to connect to the 192.168.2.0/24 subnet using the new router, which has the IP address 192.168.1.2. What command should you run?

    A. route add 192.168.2.0 MASK 255.255.255.0 192.168.1.1

    B. route add 192.168.2.0 MASK 255.255.255.0 192.168.1.2

    C. route add 192.168.1.2 MASK 255.255.255.0 192.168.2.0

    D. route add 192.168.1.1 MASK 255.255.255.0 192.168.2.0

2. You are experiencing intermittent connectivity problems accessing an internal Web site on a remote network. You would like to view a list of routers that packets travel through between the client and the server. Which tools can you use? (Choose all that apply.)

    A. PathPing

    B. Ping

    C. Ipconfig

    D. TraceRt

3. You configure a computer running Windows Server 2008 with two network interfaces. Each of the interfaces is connected to different subnets. One of those subnets has four other routers connected to it, and each router provides access to different subnets. You would like the computer running Windows Server 2008 to automatically identify the routers and determine which remote subnets are available using each router. What should you do?

    A. Enable NAT on the interface.

    B. Enable OSPF on the interface.

    C. Enable RIP on the interface.

    D. Add a static route to the interface.

Chapter Review

To further practice and reinforce the skills you learned in this chapter, you can

- Review the chapter summary.
- Review the list of key terms introduced in this chapter.
- Complete the case scenarios. These scenarios set up real-world situations involving the topics of this chapter and ask you to create a solution.
- Complete the suggested practices.
- Take a practice test.

Chapter Summary

- Routing allows communications to be forwarded between subnets. On most networks configuring computers with a default gateway is sufficient. On more complex networks with multiple routers that provide access to different remote networks, you need to configure static routing. By installing the Routing And Remote Access Services role service, you can use Windows Server 2008 as a router, including the RIP version 2 routing protocol.

Key Terms

Do you know what these key terms mean? You can check your answers by looking up the terms in the glossary at the end of the book.

- gateway
- hop
- router
- routing table

Case Scenarios

In the following case scenarios, you will apply what you've learned about how to plan and configure routing. You can find answers to these questions in the "Answers" section at the end of this book.

Case Scenario 1: Adding a Second Default Gateway

You are a systems administrator for City Power & Light. Recently, the default gateway for the subnet used by your customer support staff failed. The network was offline for several hours until the default gateway was replaced.

Network engineering has since added a second default gateway. Now you need to configure client computers to connect through the second default gateway if the first default gateway is unavailable.

Answer the following question for your manager:

1. How can you configure the client computers to use the second default gateway?

Case Scenario 2: Adding a New Subnet

You are a systems administrator working for Humongous Insurance. Recently, network administration added a new subnet, 192.168.2.0/24, that will be used for internal servers. Although client computers on the 192.168.1.0/24 subnet can access the new subnet through their default gateway of 192.168.1.1, the route is less than ideal because traffic must pass through two routers instead of just one. This network is illustrated in Figure 5-8.

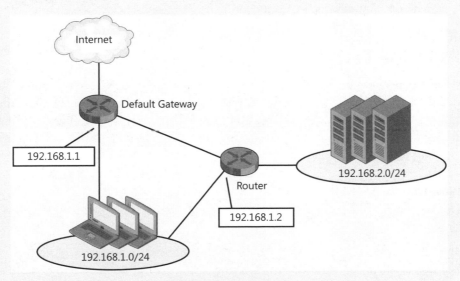

Figure 5-8   A sample network architecture

Answer the following questions for your manager:

1. Is there any way client computers on the 192.168.1.0/24 subnet can send traffic for the 192.168.2.0/24 subnet through the new router while sending traffic destined for every other network through the current default gateway?

2. What command should we run on the client computers?

Suggested Practices

To successfully master the Configure Routing exam objective, complete the following tasks.

- **Practice 1**   Use *PathPing* to check the path to several of your favorite Web sites. Which Web sites are near and which are far? Can you determine from the names of the routers where communications move from one Internet service provider (ISP) to another?

- **Practice 2**   Run the *Route Print* command at a command prompt. Examine each line until you understand the purpose of every route.

- **Practice 3**   If you have access to multiple routers and computers, connect two or more routers to a single subnet. Use static routing, configured using both command-line and graphical tools, to configure appropriate routes for each network.

- **Practice 4**   Repeat Practice 3, but configure IPv6 routing.

Take a Practice Test

The practice tests on this book's companion CD offer many options. For example, you can test yourself on just the content covered in this chapter, or you can test yourself on all the 70-642 certification exam content. You can set up the test so that it closely simulates the experience of taking a certification exam, or you can set it up in study mode so that you can look at the correct answers and explanations after you answer each question.

MORE INFO   **Practice tests**

For details about all the practice test options available, see "How to Use the Practice Tests" in this book's Introduction.

Chapter 6

Protecting Network Traffic with IPSec

Internet Protocol Security (IPSec) protects networks by securing IP packets through encryption and through the enforcement of trusted communication. You can use IPSec to secure communication between two hosts or to secure traffic across the Internet in virtual private network (VPN) scenarios.

You can manage IPSec through Local Security Policy, Group Policy, or command-line tools.

Exam objectives in this chapter:
- Configure IPSec.

Lessons in this chapter:

Before You Begin

To complete the lessons in this chapter, you must have

- A Windows Server 2008 domain controller named dcsrv1.nwtraders.msft.
- A computer named boston.nwtraders.msft that is running Windows Server 2008 and that is a member of the Nwtraders domain (file sharing must be enabled on this computer).
- A computer named binghamton.nwtraders.msft that is running Windows Server 2008 and that is a member of the Nwtraders domain.
- A basic understanding of Microsoft Windows networking and Group Policy.

Real World

JC Mackin

From an administrator's point of view, Windows Server 2008 introduces a few modest but noteworthy enhancements to IPSec. The most important of these changes is the addition of connection security rules, which facilitate implementing IPSec for authenticated communication on a network. Connection security rules aren't heavily tested on the 70-642 exam, but they are a useful addition to your real-world expertise.

Connection security rules first appeared as an option for individual computers in Windows Vista, but with Windows Server 2008, you now have the option of enforcing connection security rules through a Group Policy object (GPO) (in the *Windows Firewall with Advanced Security* node).

By default, connection security rules do not encrypt data but only provide protection against spoofed data, altered data, and replay attacks. I would recommend leaving connection security rules to perform these default functions and instead using IPSec Policies when you need encryption. The biggest advantage of connection security rules is, after all, their simplicity, and when you create custom rules with expanded functionality, you negate the main benefit of the feature.

Lesson 1: Configuring IPSec

IP Security (IPSec) is a means to protect network data by ensuring its authenticity, its confidentiality, or both. In Windows Server 2008 networks, you typically implement IPSec through Group Policy, either through IPSec Policies or through connection security rules.

After this lesson, you will be able to:
- Deploy IPSec on a network through Group Policy.

Estimated lesson time: 70 minutes

What Is IPSec?

IPSec is essentially a way to provide security for data sent between two computers on an IP network. IPSec is not just a Windows feature; the Windows implementation of IPSec is based on standards developed by the Internet Engineering Task Force (IETF) IPSec working group.

IPSec protects data between two IP addresses by providing the following services:

- Data Authentication
  - ❑ Data origin authentication. You can configure IPSec to ensure that each packet you receive from a trusted party in fact originates from that party and is not spoofed.
  - ❑ Data integrity. You can use IPSec to ensure that data is not altered in transit.
  - ❑ Anti-replay protection. You can configure IPSec to verify that each packet received is unique and not duplicated.
- Encryption
  - ❑ You can use IPSec to encrypt network data so that the data is unreadable if captured in transit.

In Windows Server 2008 and Windows Vista, IPSec is enforced either by IPSec Policies or connection security rules. IPSec Policies by default attempt to negotiate both authentication and encryption services. Connection security rules by default attempt to negotiate only authentication services. However, you can configure IPSec Policies and connection security rules to provide any combination of data protection services.

NOTE   IPSec beyond Windows

Because IPSec is an interoperable standard, it can be implemented to secure communications between Windows and non-Windows computers.

IPSec Policies

IPSec Policies define how a computer or group of computers handle IPSec communications. You can assign an IPSec Policy either to an individual computer by using Local Security Policy or to a group of computers by using Group Policy. Although you may define many IPSec Policies for use on a computer or network, only one policy is ever assigned to a computer at any given time.

Figure 6-1 shows a Group Policy object (GPO) in which an IPSec Policy is assigned.

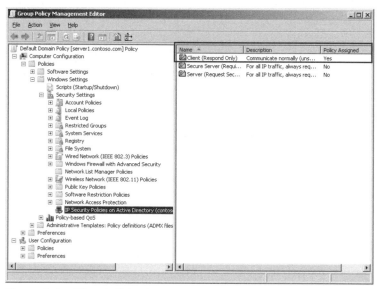

Figure 6-1   IPSec Policies in a GPO

Every IPSec Policy is composed of one or more IPSec Policy *rules* that determine when and how IP traffic should be protected. Each policy rule, in turn, is associated with one *IP filter list* and one *filter action*.

IP filter lists contain a set of one or more *IP filters* that capture IP traffic for an IPSec Policy. IP filters define a source or destination address, address range, computer name, TCP/UDP port, or server type (DNS, WINS, DHCP, default gateway). If traffic leaving or arriving at a computer on which a policy is assigned matches a filter in one of the assigned policy's policy rules, the filter action associated with that rule is applied. Possible filter actions for a rule include *block*, *permit*, or *negotiate security*. Note that when matching a source or destination address, the most specific IPSec filter always takes precedence.

NOTE How is security negotiated?

"Negotiate Security" is a general option for a filter action, but you can then specifically choose the way security is negotiated for that filter action. For example, should encryption or merely authentication (data integrity) be negotiated? What is the order of preference for encryption technologies or hashing algorithms? Is it okay to fall back to unsecured communications if no common protocol for security can be agreed upon? Because there are so many ways that you can choose to negotiate security for a filter action, it is possible to define many distinct rules for which the Negotiate Security option has been selected. Remember also that you can sucessfully negotiate security only when both ends of an IPSec connection can agree on the particular services and algorithms used to protect the data.

IPSec Policy Example Figure 6-2 illustrates an IPSec Policy and how that policy is composed of rules, filters, and filter actions. In the illustrated example, the IPSec Policy is made up of three rules. The first rule has priority because it defines traffic the most specifically—both by type (Telnet or Post Office Protocol 3 [POP3]) and by address (from 192.168.3.32 or 192.168.3.200). The second rule is the next most specific, defining traffic by type only (Telnet or POP3). The third rule is the least specific because it applies to all traffic and therefore has the lowest priority. As a result of the IPSec policy composed of these three rules, a computer to which this policy is assigned will attempt to authenticate (but not encrypt) all data aside from Telnet traffic and POP3 traffic. Telnet traffic and POP3 traffic by default are blocked unless they originate from 192.168.3.32 (for Telnet) or 192.168.3.200 (for POP3), in which case the traffic is allowed if encryption can be successfully negotiated.

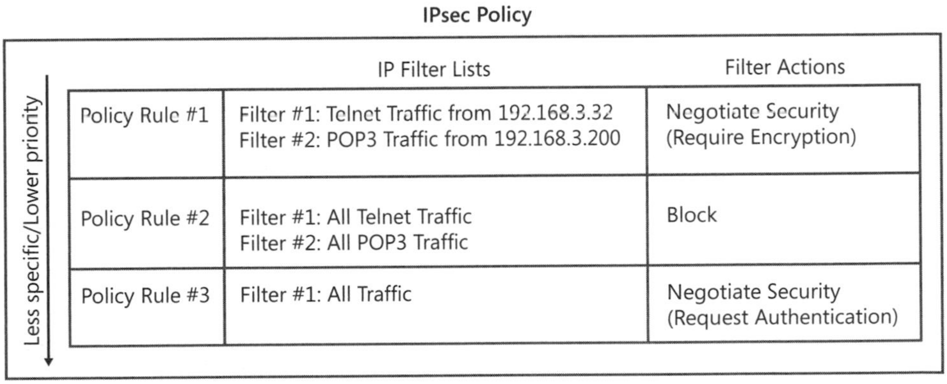

IPsec Policy

		IP Filter Lists	Filter Actions
	Policy Rule #1	Filter #1: Telnet Traffic from 192.168.3.32 Filter #2: POP3 Traffic from 192.168.3.200	Negotiate Security (Require Encryption)
	Policy Rule #2	Filter #1: All Telnet Traffic Filter #2: All POP3 Traffic	Block
	Policy Rule #3	Filter #1: All Traffic	Negotiate Security (Request Authentication)

Less specific/Lower priority

Figure 6-2 IPSec Policies, rules, filters, and filter actions

---

Quick Check

1. Does every IPSec Policy rule have an IP filter list?
2. In terms of its function within an IPSec Policy, what does a filter action do?

Quick Check Answers

1. Yes, even if the list has only one IP filter.
2. A filter action determines whether the traffic captured by an IP filter in a given policy rule is permitted, blocked, encrypted, or authenticated.

Connection Security Rules

You can also use connection security rules to configure IPSec settings for connections between computers. Like IPSec Policies, connection security rules evaluate network traffic and then block, allow, or negotiate security for messages based on the criteria you establish. Unlike IPSec Policies, however, connection security rules do not include filters or filter actions. The features provided by filters and filter actions are built into each Connection Security Rule, but the filtering capabilities in connection security rules are not as powerful as those of IPSec Policies. Connection security rules do not apply to *types* of IP traffic, such as IP traffic that passes over port 23. Instead, they apply to *all* IP traffic originating from or destined for certain IP addresses, subnets, or servers on the network.

A Connection Security Rule first authenticates the computers defined in the rule before they begin communication. It then secures the information sent between these two authenticated computers. If you have configured a Connection Security Rule that requires security for a given connection and the two computers in question cannot authenticate each other, the connection is blocked.

By default, connection security rules provide only data authentication security (data origin authentication, data integrity, and anti-replay security). For this reason, connection security rules are typically said to only *authenticate* connections. However, you can also configure data encryption for connection security rules so that the connections in question are truly *secured* and not merely authenticated.

You configure connection security rules for any computer in the Windows Firewall with Advanced Security (WFAS) console or the *WFAS* node in Server Manager. However, you can enforce specific WFAS settings for multiple clients on a network by using Group Policy. Figure 6-3 shows a GPO that defines connection security rules for many computers on a network.

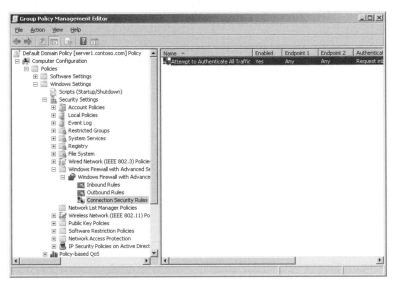

Figure 6-3   Defining connection security rules in Group Policy

---

NOTE **Exporting connection security rules**

By using the Export Policy and Import Policy functions in the WFAS console, you can create one set of connection security rules and export them to other computers or GPOs.

Security Associations

After two computers negotiate an IPSec connection, whether through IPSec Policies or connection security rules, the data sent between those computers is secured in what is known as a Security Association (SA). Security for an SA is provided by the two IPSec protocols—Authentication Header (AH) and Encapsulating Security Payload (ESP). These protocols provide data and identity protection for each IP packet in an SA. AH provides data origin authentication, data integrity, and anti-replay protection for the entire IP packet. ESP provides *data encryption*, data origin authentication, data integrity, and anti-replay protection for the ESP payload. To secure data within any SA, you can use either AH alone, ESP alone, or AH and ESP together.

Exam Tip   You need to know the basic difference between AH and ESP for the 70-642 exam. If you need encryption, use ESP. If you just need to authenticate the data origin or verify data integrity, use AH.

How IPSec Connections Are Established

To establish SAs dynamically between IPSec peers, the Internet Key Exchange (IKE) protocol is used. IKE establishes a mutually agreeable policy that defines the SA—a policy that includes its security services, protection mechanisms, and cryptographic keys between communicating peers. In establishing the SA, IKE also provides the keying and negotiation for the IPSec security protocols AH and ESP.

To ensure successful and secure communication, IKE performs a two-phase negotiation operation, each with its own SAs. Phase 1 negotiation is known as *main mode* negotiation, and Phase 2 is known as *quick mode* negotiation. The IKE main mode SAs are used to secure the second IKE negotiation phase. As a result of the second IKE negotiation phase, quick mode SAs are created. These quick mode SAs are the ones used to protect application traffic.

You can summarize the steps for establishing an IPSec connection in the following way:

1. Set up a main mode SA.
2. Agree upon the terms of communication and encryption algorithm.
3. Create a quick mode SA.
4. Send data.

Using IPSec in Tunnel Mode

IPSec by default operates in *transport mode*, which is used to provide end-to-end security between computers. Transport mode is also used in most IPSec-based VPNs, for which the Layer Two Tunneling Protocol (L2TP) protocol is used to tunnel the IPSec connection through the public network.

However, when a particular VPN gateway is not compatible with L2TP/IPSec VPNs, you can use IPSec in *tunnel mode* instead. With tunnel mode, an entire IP packet is protected and then encapsulated with an additional, unprotected IP header. The IP addresses of the outer IP header represent the tunnel endpoints, and the IP addresses of the inner IP header represent the ultimate source and destination addresses.

NOTE Tunnel Mode Is Rarely Used

IPSec tunnel mode is supported as an advanced feature. It is used in some gateway-to-gateway tunneling scenarios to provide interoperability with routers, gateways, or end-systems that do not support L2TP/IPSec or Point-to-Point Tunneling Protocol (PPTP) connections. IPSec tunnels are not supported for remote access VPN scenarios. For remote access VPNs, use L2TP/IPSec or PPTP. These VPNs are discussed in Chapter 7, "Connecting to Networks."

An illustration of an IPSec tunnel is shown in Figure 6-4.

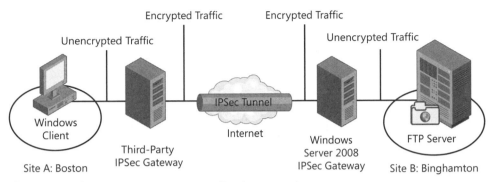

Figure 6-4 Gateway-to-gateway tunneling between sites

Exam Tip You need to understand the basics of IPSec tunnel mode for the 70-642 exam.

Authentication Methods for IPSec

An essential concept in implementing IPSec is that IPSec requires a shared authentication mechanism between communicating computers. You can use any of these three methods to authenticate the hosts communicating through IPSec:

- **Kerberos (Active Directory)** Because Kerberos is the default authentication protocol in an Active Directory environment, the easiest way to configure authentication for IPSec is to implement IPSec within a single Active Directory forest. When the two IPSec endpoints can be authenticated by Active Directory, the security foundation for IPSec requires no configuration beyond joining the hosts to the domain. Note that if your network environment includes a Kerberos realm outside of Active Directory, you can also use this Kerberos realm to provide authentication for IPSec communications.

- **Certificates** If you need to implement IPSec in a production environment in which Kerberos authentication is not available, you should use a certificate infrastructure to authenticate the IPSec peers. In this solution, each host must obtain and install a computer certificate from a public or private certification authority (CA). The computer certificates do not need to originate from the same CA, but each host must trust the CA that has issued the certificate to the communicating peer.

- **Preshared Key** A preshared key is a password shared by peers and used both to encrypt and decrypt data. In IPSec, you can also specify a preshared key on endpoints to enable encryption between hosts. Although this authentication method enables

IPSec SAs to be established, preshared keys do not provide the same level of authentication that certificates and Kerberos do. In addition, preshared keys for IPSec are stored in plaintext on each computer or in Active Directory, which reduces the security of this solution. For these reasons, it is recommended that you use preshared keys only in nonproduction environments such as test networks.

Exam Tip   You need to understand IPSec authentication mechanism for the 70-642 exam. Remember that Kerberos authentication is preferable in an Active Directory environment. Outside of an Active Directory environment, a certificate infrastructure is your best option.

Assigning a Predefined IPSec Policy

In Group Policy, three IPSec Policies are predefined. You can thus configure an IPSec Policy for a domain or OU by assigning any one of the following predefined policies:

- **Client (Respond Only)**   When you assign this policy to a computer through a GPO, that computer will never initiate a request to establish an IPSec communications channel with another computer. However, any computer to which you assign the Client policy will negotiate and establish IPSec communications when requested by another computer. You typically assign this policy to intranet computers that need to communicate with secured servers but that do not need to protect all traffic.

- **Server (Request Security)**   You should assign this policy to computers for which encryption is preferred but not required. With this policy, the computer accepts unsecured traffic but always attempts to secure additional communications by requesting security from the original sender. This policy allows the entire communication to be unsecured if the other computer is not IPSec-enabled. For example, communication to specific servers can be secure while allowing the server to communicate in an unsecured manner to accommodate a mixture of clients (some of which support IPSec and some of which do not).

- **Secure Server (Require Security)**   You should assign this policy to intranet servers that require secure communications, such as a server that transmits highly sensitive data.

To assign an IPSec Policy within a GPO, select the *IP Security Policies* node, right-click the chosen policy in the Details pane, and then choose Assign from the shortcut menu, as shown in Figure 6-5.

You can assign only one IPSec Policy to a computer at a time. If you assign a second IPSec Policy to a computer, the first IPSec Policy automatically becomes unassigned. If Group Policy assigns an IPSec Policy to a computer, the computer ignores any IPSec Policy assigned in its Local Security Policy.

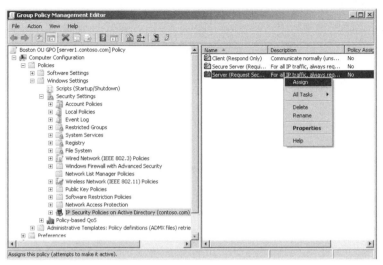

Figure 6-5   Assigning an IPSec Policy in a GPO

Exam Tip   Know the three predefined IPSec Policies.

Creating a New IPSec Policy

To create a new custom IPSec Policy, first open Local Security Policy or a GPO. In the console tree below Security Settings, right-click the *IP Security Policies* node, and then choose Create IP Security Policy, as shown in Figure 6-6. (You can find Security Settings in a GPO in the Computer Configuration\Policies\Windows Settings container.) This procedure launches the IP Security Policy Wizard.

The IP Security Policy Wizard simply gives you an opportunity to create an "empty" policy, to name that IPSec Policy, and to enable the Default Response Rule. (The Default Response Rule is read only by versions of Windows earlier than Windows Vista. For those operating systems the rule provides a default action for an IPSec Policy when no other IPSec Policy filters apply.)

After you have created the IPSec Policy, you can configure the policy through its properties. In the properties, you can add rules to the policy by clicking the Add button in the Rules tab in the Properties dialog box for the policy, as shown in Figure 6-7. This procedure launches the Create IP Security Rule Wizard.

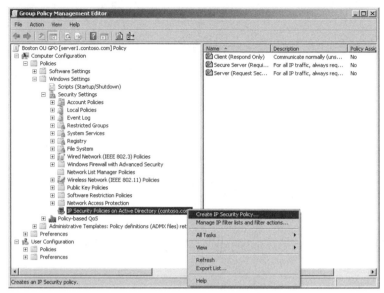

Figure 6-6   Creating a new IPSec Policy in a GPO

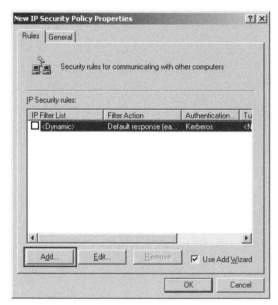

Figure 6-7   Launching the Create IP Security Rule Wizard

Using the Create IP Security Rule Wizard

The bulk of IPSec Policy configuration involves creating and configuring IPSec rules for that policy. To create and configure these rules, use the Create IP Security Rule Wizard (also known simply as the Security Rule Wizard).

The following section describes the five main pages of the Create IP Security Rule Wizard.

- **Tunnel Endpoint page**   Configure this page only when you want to use IPSec in tunnel mode.

- **Network Type page**   Use this page if you want to limit the rule to either the local area network or remote access connections.

- **IP Filter List page**   Use this page to specify the set of IP Filters you want to attach to the rule. In Group Policy, two IP filter lists are predefined for IPSec Policy rules: All ICMP Traffic and All IP Traffic. To create a new IP filter list, click the Add button on the IP Filter List page, as shown in Figure 6-8. This procedure opens the IP Filter List dialog box.

NOTE   What is ICMP traffic?

ICMP (Internet Control Message Protocol) is a messaging feature of IP that allows Ping and Tracert to function. ICMP traffic typically refers to Ping and Tracert traffic.

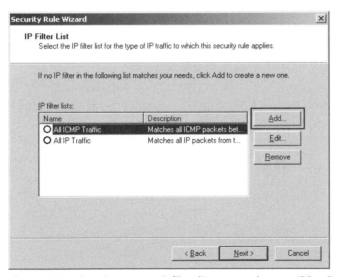

Figure 6-8   Creating a new IP filter list to attach to an IPSec Policy rule

To create a new IP filter to add to the new IP filter list you are creating, click the Add button in the IP Filter List dialog box, as shown in Figure 6-9. This procedure, in turn, launches the IP Filter Wizard.

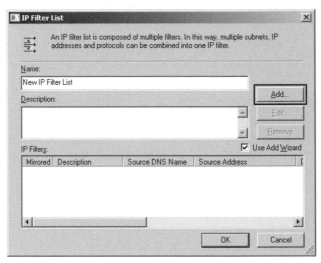

Figure 6-9   Creating a new IP filter to add to an IP filter list

Use the IP Filter Wizard to define IP traffic according to source and destination. You can specify a source and destination according to IP address, DNS name, server function (such as any DHCP server, DNS server, WINS server, or default gateway), and IP protocol type (including TCP/UDP port number).

You can also use the IP Filter Wizard to create a "mirrored" filter. A mirrored filter matches the source and destination with the exact opposite addresses so that, for example, you can easily configure a filter that captures POP3 traffic sent *to and from* the local address. To configure your filter as a mirrored filter, leave the Mirrored check box selected on the first page of the IP Filter Wizard, as shown in Figure 6-10.

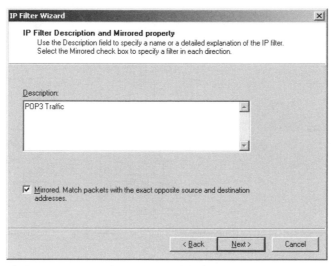

Figure 6-10   Creating a mirrored IP filter

- **Filter Action page**   After you have attached the desired IP filter list to the rule, you can specify a filter action for the rule in the Security Rule Wizard. In Group Policy, the following three IP filters are predefined for IPSec Policy rules:
    - ❑ Permit – This filter action permits the IP packets to pass through unsecured.
    - ❑ Request Security (Optional) – This filter action permits the IP packets to pass through unsecured but requests that clients negotiate security (preferably encryption).
    - ❑ Require Security – This filter action triggers the local computer to request secure communications from the client source of the IP packets. If security methods (including encryption) cannot be established, the local computer will stop communicating with that client.

To create a new filter action, click the Add button on the Filter Action page of the Security Rule Wizard, as shown in Figure 6-11. This procedure launches the Filter Action Wizard.

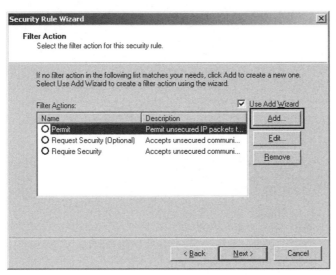

Figure 6-11   Creating a new filter action

■ **Authentication Method page**   Security can be negotiated only after the IPSec clients are authenticated. By default, IPSec rules rely on Active Directory directory service and the Kerberos protocol to authenticate clients. However, you can also specify a certificate infrastructure or a preshared key as a means to authenticate IPSec clients. To select the authentication method for IPSec, you can use the Authentication Method page of the Security Rule Wizard, as shown in Figure 6-12. (Note that this page does not appear if you select Permit on the Filter Action page.)

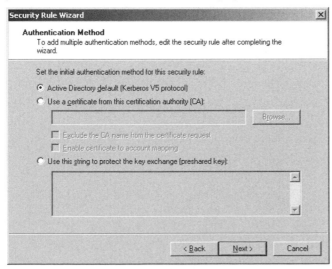

Figure 6-12   Specifying an authentication method for a new IPSec Policy rule

Managing IP Filter Lists and Filter Actions

The IP filters, IP filter lists, and filter actions you create for an IPSec rule can be shared with other IPSec rules. You can also create and configure these features outside of the Security Rule Wizard. To do so, right-click the *IP Security Policies* node in Local Security Policy or a GPO, and then choose Manage IP Filter Lists And Filter Actions, as shown in Figure 6-13.

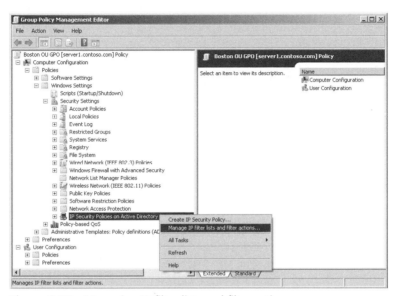

Figure 6-13 Managing IP filter lists and filter actions

Creating and Configuring a Connection Security Rule

To create a Connection Security Rule in a GPO, first browse to and expand Computer Configuration\Policies\Windows Settings\Security Settings\Windows Firewall With Advanced Security\Windows Firewall With Advanced Security – LDAP://*address*. Beneath this node, select and right-click the *connection security rules* node, and then, from the shortcut menu, choose New Rule.

This procedure, which launches the New Connection Security Rule Wizard, is shown in Figure 6-14.

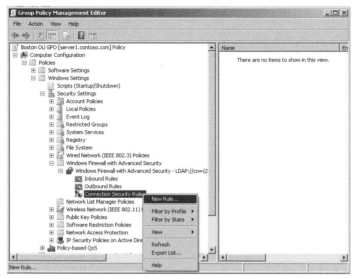

Figure 6-14   Creating a new Connection Security Rule

Using the New Connection Security Rule Wizard

The specific pages you see when you use the New Connection Security Rule Wizard depend on the type of rule you choose to create on the first page. The following section describes the six pages you find when creating a custom rule.

■ **Rule Type page**   As shown in Figure 6-15, the Rule Type page allows you to create any of five rule types.

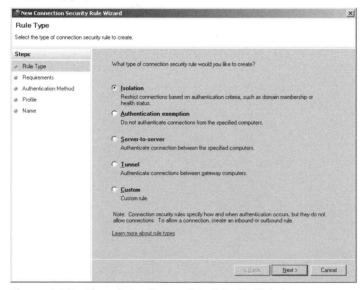

Figure 6-15   Choosing a Connection Security Rule type

These five rule types are the following:

- **Isolation rule**   This is a general rule used to authenticate all traffic for select network *profiles* (network location types). When the network location defined for the local computer in Network and Sharing Center corresponds to one of the profiles selected for the rule, the local computer attempts to negotiate security as defined in the rule. The three profiles defined are Domain, Private, and Public.

Exam Tip   You can use an Isolation rule to configure "domain isolation." This term simply means that you can use connection security rules to block traffic from computers originating from outside the local Active Directory domain.

- **Authentication Exemption rule**   You can use this rule type to exempt specific computers or a group or range of IP addresses (computers) from being required to authenticate themselves, regardless of other connection security rules. You commonly use this rule type to grant access to infrastructure computers that the local computer must communicate with before authentication can be performed. It is also used for other computers that cannot use the form of authentication you configured for this policy and profile.

  To create an authentication exemption rule, you need only to specify the computers by name or IP address and then name the rule.

- **Server-To-Server rule**   This rule type allows you to authenticate the communications between IP addresses or sets of addresses, including specific computers and subnets.

- **Tunnel rule**   Use this rule type to configure IPSec tunnel mode for VPN gateways.

- **Custom rule**   Use this rule type to create a rule that requires special settings or a combination of features from the various rule types.

- **Endpoints page**   Use this page to specify the remote computers with which you want to negotiate an IPSec connection.

- **Requirements page**   Use this page to specify whether authenticated communication should be required or merely requested with the endpoints specified. As an alternative, you can require authentication for inbound connections but only request them for outbound connections. Finally, on this page, you can also configure an authentication exemption for the specified endpoints.

- **Authentication Method page**   This page allows you to specify the method by which computer endpoints are authenticated. The first option is Default. When you choose this option, the authentication method that the connection uses is the one specified for the profile in the Profile tabs in the properties of the *Windows Firewall with Advanced Security* node. Other authentication options you can select include Kerberos (Active Directory) authentication for both computers and users, Kerberos authentication for computers only, a computer certificate from a certificate infrastructure, and the Advanced authentication option. The Advanced option allows you to configure an order of preference of authentication methods for both users and computers. It also allows you to configure these authentication methods as optional.

- **Profile page**   The Profile page allows you to limit the local network location types to which the rule will apply. The profiles you can enable for the rule are Domain, Private, and Public.
- **Name page**   The Name page allows you to name the new Connection Security Rule and (optionally) to provide a description.

Configuring IPSec Settings for Connection Security Rules

You can define IPSec Settings in the *WFAS* node of a GPO or in the WFAS console. To access these settings, first open the properties of the *Windows Firewall with Advanced Security* node, as shown in Figure 6-16.

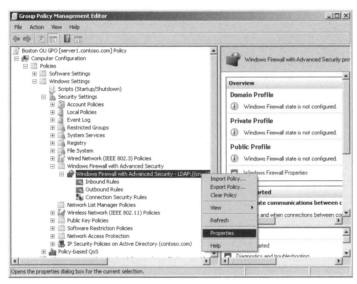

Figure 6-16   Opening Windows Firewall properties

Then, in the properties dialog box that opens, click the IPSec Settings tab, as shown in Figure 6-17.

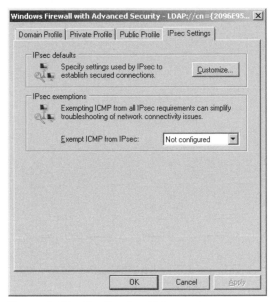

Figure 6-17   Configuring IPSec settings

Through this tab you can configure two aspects of IPSec: IPSec defaults and ICMP exemptions from IPSec.

- **IPSec defaults**   Clicking the Customize button opens the Customize IPSec Settings dialog box, as shown in Figure 6-18. From this dialog box, you can set new default parameters for key negotiation (exchange), for data protection, and for the authentication method.

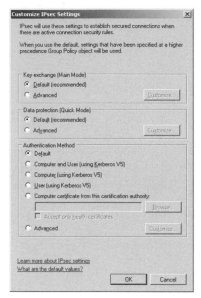

Figure 6-18 Setting IPSec defaults

For example, to configure data encryption for connection security rules, first select Advanced in the Data Protection area, and then click Customize. This procedure opens the Customize Data Protection Settings dialog box, as shown in Figure 6-19. Next, in this dialog box, select the Require Encryption For All Connection security rules That Use These Settings check box, and then click OK.

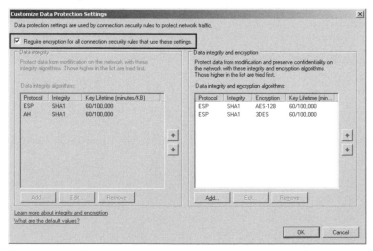

Figure 6-19 Requiring encryption for connection security rules

■ **Exempt ICMP from IPSec**   Use this setting in the IPSec Settings tab to prevent ICMP (Ping and Tracert) messages from being authenticated, encrypted, or both. Keeping ICMP messages unprotected allows you to perform basic network troubleshooting when IPSec cannot be successfully negotiated.

PRACTICE **Deploying IPSec Through IPSec Policies and Connection Security Rules**

In the first stage of this practice, you will install Telnet services and then configure an IPSec Policy to encrypt Telnet traffic between Boston.nwtraders.msft and Binghamton.nwtraders.msft. In the second stage, you will create a Connection Security Rule that authenticates all network traffic between the same two computers.

▶ **Exercise 1   Installing Telnet Services**

In this exercise, you will install Telnet services on both Boston and Binghamton computers.

1. Log on to Nwtraders from Boston as a domain administrator.
2. Insert the Windows Server 2008 Product DVD into the local hard disk drive.
3. In the Initial Configuration Tasks or Server Manager window, click Add Features. The Select Features page of the Add Features Wizard opens.
4. In the list of features, select both the Telnet Client and Telnet Server check boxes, and then click Next.
5. On the Confirm Installation Selections page of the Add Features Wizard, click Install.
6. After the installation has completed, click Close on the Installation Results page.
7. Open the Services console by clicking Start, pointing to Administrative Tools, and then choosing Services.
8. In the Services console, locate and then double-click Telnet to open its properties.
9. In the Telnet Properties dialog box, change the Startup Type to Automatic, and then click Apply.
10. In the Service Status area, click Start.
11. When the Service Status has changed to Started, click OK to close the Telnet Properties dialog box, and then close the Services console.
12. In the Search area of the Start Menu, type **lusrmgr.msc**, and then press Enter.
13. In the Local Users And Groups console tree, select the Groups folder.
14. In the Details pane, double-click TelnetClients.
15. In the TelnetClients Properties dialog box, click the Add button.

16. In the Select Users, Computers, Or Groups dialog box, in the Enter The Object Names To Select text box, type **Domain Admins**, and then click OK.

17. In the TelnetClients Properties dialog box, click OK.

18. Log off Boston.

19. Log on to Nwtraders from Binghamton, and then perform steps 2 through 18 on Binghamton.

▶ **Exercise 2   Creating an IPSec Policy**

In this exercise, you will create a GPO and an IPSec Policy that you will later configure to encrypt Telnet traffic in the Nwtraders.msft domain.

1. Log on to Nwtraders from Dcsrv1 as a domain administrator.

2. Open the Group Policy Management (GPM) console by clicking Start, pointing to Administrative Tools, and then choosing Group Policy Management.

3. In the GPM console tree, expand the Domains container, and then select the *Nwtraders .msft* node.

4. Right-click the *Nwtraders.msft* node and choose Create A GPO In This Domain, And Link It Here.

5. In the New GPO box, type **IPSec GPO**, and then click OK.

6. In the GPM console, in the Details pane, right-click the IPSec GPO, and then, from the shortcut menu, choose Edit.

7. In the Group Policy Management Editor window, navigate to Computer Configuration, Policies, Windows Settings, Security Settings, and IP Security Policies On Active Directory.

8. Right-click the *IP Security Policies On Active Directory* node, and then choose Create IP Security Policy on the shortcut menu.

    The IP Security Policy Wizard opens.

9. Click Next.

10. On the IP Security Policy Name page, type **Nwtraders IPSec Policy**.

11. In the Description field, type **This IPSec Policy encrypts Telnet traffic**.

12. Click Next.

13. On the Requests For Secure Communications Page, read all of the text on the page, and then click Next.

14. Click Finish.

    The Nwtraders IPSec Policy Properties dialog box appears.

15. Leave all windows open and continue to Practice 3.

▶ **Exercise 3   Creating an IPSec Policy Rule and Filter**

In this exercise, you will configure the newly created Nwtraders IPSec Policy with rules that require high security for Telnet traffic. In the process you will run the Security Rule Wizard, the IP Filter Wizard, and the Filter Action Wizard.

1. While you are still logged on to Dcsrv1, in the Nwtraders IPSec Policy Properties dialog box, click Add.

   The Create IP Security Rule Wizard opens. (This wizard is also called the Security Rule Wizard.)

2. Read all of the text on the first page, and then click Next.

3. On the Tunnel Endpoint page, read all of the text on the page, and then click Next.

4. On the Network Type page, read all of the text on the page, and then click Next.

5. On the IP Filter List page, read all of the text on the page, and then click the Add button.

   The IP Filter List dialog box opens.

6. In the Name text box, type **Encrypt Telnet Filter List**, and then click Add.

   The IP Filter Wizard opens.

7. Click Next.

8. On the IP Filter Description And Mirrored Property page, read all of the text on the page, and then click Next.

9. On the IP Traffic Source page, leave the default selection of Any IP Address, and then click Next.

10. On the IP Traffic Destination page, leave the default of Any IP Address, and then click Next.

11. On the IP Protocol Type page, select TCP from the Select A Protocol Type drop-down list box, and then click Next.

    Telnet runs on TCP port 23, so you need to specify both TCP and the appropriate port.

12. On the IP Protocol Port page, select To This Port, and then type **23** in the accompanying text box. (Leave From Any Port selected.)

13. Click Next, and then click Finish to close the IP Filter Wizard.

14. In the IP Filter List dialog box, click OK.

    The IP Filter List page of the Security Rule Wizard reappears.

15. In the IP Filter Lists area, select the Encrypt Telnet Filter List option button, and then click Next.

16. On the Filter Action page, read all of the text on the page, and then click Add.

    The Filter Action Wizard opens. Leave this wizard open and continue to Practice 4.

▶ **Exercise 4   Using the Filter Action Wizard**

In this exercise, you use the Filter Action Wizard to configure a custom filter action to apply to Telnet traffic. Although the default filter actions available in Group Policy are usually adequate for creating IPSec rules, it is a good idea to configure higher security for Telnet. In addition, you should be familiar with the IP Security Filter Action Wizard for the 70-642 exam.

1. On the Welcome To The IP Security Filter Action Wizard page, read all of the text on the page, and then click Next.

2. On the Filter Action Name page, in the Name text box, type **Require High Authentication and Encryption**.

3. In the Description field, type **Require AH authentication and 3DES encryption**.

4. Click Next.

5. On the Filter Action General Options page, ensure that Negotiate Security is selected, and then click Next.

6. On the Communicating With Computers That Do Not Support IPSec page, ensure that Do Not Allow Unsecured Communication is selected, and then click Next.

7. On the IP Traffic Security page, select Custom, and then click Settings.

8. In the Custom Security Method Settings dialog box, select the Data And Address Integrity Without Encryption (AH) check box.

9. In the Session Key Settings area, select both Generate A New Key Every check boxes.

10. Ensure that the Data Integrity And Encryption (ESP) check box is selected, and then click OK. (Also note that 3DES is the selected encryption algorithm.)

11. On the IP Traffic Security page, click Next.

12. On the Completing The IP Security Filter Action Wizard page, click Finish.

13. On the Filter Action page of the Security Rule Wizard, in the list of Filter Actions, select Require High Authentication And Encryption, and then click Next.

14. On the Authentication Method page of the Security Rule Wizard, leave the default as Active Directory Default (Kerberos V5 Protocol), and then click Next.

    The Completing The Security Rule Wizard page appears.

15. Click Finish.

16. In the Nwtraders IPSec Policy Properties dialog box, click OK.

17. In the Group Policy Management Editor, right-click the Nwtraders IPSec Policy, and then, from the shortcut menu, choose Assign.

18. On Boston and Binghamton, run the *Gpupdate* command at a command prompt.

▶ **Exercise 5   Testing the New IPSec Policy**

In this exercise, you will initiate a Telnet session from Boston to Binghamton. You will then verify that data authentication and encryption are applied to the Telnet session.

1. On Boston, open a command prompt.

2. At the command prompt, type **telnet Binghamton**.

3. A Telnet session to the Telnet server on Binghamton begins.

4. On Boston, from the Start Menu, point to Administrative Tools, and then choose Windows Firewall With Advanced Security.

5. In the WFAS console tree, expand the *Monitoring* node and expand the *Security Associations* node.

6. Beneath the *Security Associations* node, select the Main Mode folder, and then the Quick Mode folder. You will see that an SA appears in the Details pane when you select each folder. Spend a few moments browsing the information displayed about these SAs. If the quick mode SA disappears, enter a command such as **dir** at the Telnet prompt to reestablish it.

7. Answer the following question: How do you know that the quick mode SA is securing Telnet traffic in particular?

    Answer: Because the remote port is specified as port 23.

8. At the Telnet prompt, type **exit**.

    You now want to unlink the IPSec GPO so that it does not interfere with the next practice.

9. On Dcsrv1, open the GPM console.

10. In the GPM console tree, ensure that the Nwtraders.msft domain is selected.

11. In the Details pane, right-click the GPO named IPSec GPO, and then choose Link Enabled.

12. In the Group Policy Management message box, click OK to change the Link Enabled status.

13. Verify that the Link Enabled Status of IPSec GPO is now set to No.

14. At a command prompt on both Boston and Binghamton, run the *Gpupdate* command.

▶ **Exercise 6   Implementing IPSec Through Connection Security Rules**

In this exercise, you will configure connection security rules in the domain so that all IP traffic between those clients is authenticated.

1. If you have not already done so, log on to Nwtraders from Dcsrv1 as a domain administrator.

2. In the GPM console tree, beneath the Domains container, right-click the *Nwtraders.msft* node, and then click Create A GPO In This Domain, And Link It Here.

3. In the New GPO dialog box, type **Connection Security Rule GPO**, and then click OK.

4. In the GPM console, in the Details pane, right-click the Connection Security Rule GPO, and then, from the shortcut menu, choose Edit.

5. In the Group Policy Management Editor window, expand Computer Configuration, Policies, Windows Settings, Security Settings, Windows Firewall With Advanced Security, and then Windows Firewall With Advanced Security - LDAP://*address*.

   This last object in the GPO is known as the *WFAS* node.

6. Beneath the *WFAS* node, select Connection Security Rules.

7. Right-click the *Connection Security Rules* node, and then, from the shortcut menu, choose New Rule.

   The New Connection Security Rule Wizard appears.

8. On the Rule Type page, read all of the text on the page, and then, leaving the default selection of Isolation, click Next.

9. On the Requirements page, read all of the text on the page, and then click Next.

10. On the Authentication Method page, leave the default selection, and then click Next.

11. On the Profile page, leave the default selections, and then click Next.

12. On the Name page, type **Request Data Authentication**, and then click Finish.

13. On both Boston and Binghamton, run the *Gpupdate* command at a command prompt.

14. From the Start Menu of Binghamton, type **Boston** in Start Search, and then press Enter.

    A window appears that displays the Printers folder and any network shares available on Boston.

15. Open the WFAS console on Binghamton.

16. In the WFAS console tree, expand the *Monitoring* node and expand the *Security Associations* node.

17. Beneath the *Security Associations* node, select the Main Mode folder, and then the Quick Mode folder. You will now see that at least one SA appears in the Details pane when each folder is selected. Spend a few moments browsing the information displayed about these SAs.

18. Answer the following question: Which SA reveals that ESP confidentiality is None?

    Answer: The quick mode SA.

19. Answer the following question: Can you configure a Connection Security Rule that encrypts only Telnet traffic?

    Answer: No. Connection security rules are not port-specific.

You should now unlink the Connection Security Rule GPO you just created so that it does not interfere with any other practices in this book.

20. On DCSrv1, open the GPM console.

21. In the GPM console tree, ensure that the Nwtraders.msft domain is selected.

22. In the Details pane, right-click the GPO named Connection Security Rule GPO, and then choose Link Enabled.

23. In the Group Policy Management message box, click OK to change the Link Enabled status.

24. Verify that the Link Enabled Status of Connection Security Rule GPO is now set to No.

25. Shut down all three computers.

Lesson Summary

- IPSec allows you to protect network traffic by providing data authentication or encryption, or both. Security in IPSec is provided by two protocols, Authentication Header (AH) and Encapsulating Security Payload (ESP). AH provides data origin authentication, data integrity, and anti-replay protection for the entire IP packet. ESP provides data encryption, data origin authentication, data integrity, and anti-replay protection for the ESP payload.

- In Windows Server 2008, networks you can implement IPSec either through IPSec Policies or through connection security rules.

- IPSec by default operates in *transport mode*, which is used to provide end-to-end security between computers. Transport mode is also used in most IPSec-based virtual public networks (VPNs), for which the L2TP protocol is used to tunnel the IPSec connection through the public network. However, when a particular VPN gateway is not compatible with L2TP/IPSec VPNs, you can use IPSec in tunnel mode instead.

- IPSec Policies, which are deployed through Local Computer Policy or a GPO, are made up of a set of IPSec rules. Each IPSec rule in turn is comprised of one IP filter list and one filter action. The filter list defines the type of traffic to which the filter action is applied. Filter actions are allow, block, and negotiate security (authenticate, encrypt, or both).

- Connection security rules protect all traffic between particular sources and destinations. By default, connection security rules do not encrypt data but only ensure data integrity. You can configure connection security rules in the Windows Firewall with Advanced Security console on an individual computer or enforce them through a GPO.

Lesson Review

You can use the following questions to test your knowledge of the information in Lesson 1, "Securing Network Traffic." The questions are also available on the companion CD if you prefer to review them in electronic form.

NOTE   Answers

Answers to these questions and explanations of why each answer choice is correct or incorrect are located in the "Answers" section at the end of the book.

---

1. You want to require network communications to be encrypted in the Nwtraders.com domain. What should you do?

    A. Use IPSec with Authentication Header (AH).

    B. Use IPSec with Encapsulating Security Payload (ESP).

    C. Use IPSec with both AH and ESP.

    D. Use IPSec in tunnel mode.

2. You want to enforce IPSec communications between the Nwtraders.com domain and the Contoso.com domain. Both domains belong to the same Active Directory forest. Which authentication method should you choose for IPSec?

    A. Kerberos

    B. Certificates

    C. Preshared key

    D. NTLM

Chapter Review

To further practice and reinforce the skills you learned in this chapter, you can

- Review the chapter summary.
- Review the list of key terms introduced in this chapter.
- Complete the case scenario. This scenario sets up a real-world situation involving the topics of this chapter and asks you to create solutions.
- Complete the suggested practices.
- Take a practice test.

Chapter Summary

- IPSec allows you to protect network traffic by providing data authentication or encryption, or both.
- In Windows Server 2008 networks, you can implement IPSec either through IPSec policies or through connection security rules. As a means to deploy IPSec, IPSec policies are more powerful but are also more difficult to configure than connection security rules are.

Key Terms

Do you know what these key terms mean? You can check your answers by looking up the terms in the glossary at the end of the book.

- Authentication Header (AH)
- Encapsulating Security Payload (ESP)
- Internet Control Message Protocol (ICMP)
- Internet Protocol Security (IPSec)
- Kerberos
- Preshared Key
- Security Association (SA)
- Transport mode
- Tunnel mode

Case Scenario

In the following case scenario, you will apply what you've learned in this chapter. You can find answers to these questions in the "Answers" section at the end of this book.

Case Scenario: Implementing IPSec

You are a network administrator for a company whose network consists of a single Active Directory domain, Contoso.com. Recently, you have decided to implement mandatory IPSec-based data authentication to all finance servers.

1. What authentication method should you use for IPSec?
2. A manager in the Marketing department needs to connect to a finance server but cannot. Which predefined IPSec policy can you assign in Group Policy to allow users such as the Marketing manager to communicate with the finance servers? You do not want the IPSec policy to affect communications with other computers and servers that do not require security.

Suggested Practices

To help you successfully master the exam objectives presented in this chapter, complete the following tasks.

Deploy IPSec

- **Practice**   In an Active Directory domain, configure and assign an IPSec policy that requires the securest methods of authentication and encryption. Make a note of any disruptions or difficulty in network communication. Then, unassign the IPSec policy and deploy a Connection Security Rule through Group Policy that also requires the securest methods of authentication and encryption. Again, make a note of any disruptions or difficulty in network communication.

Watch a Webcast

- **Practice**   Watch the Webcast, "Deploying Internet Protocol Security (IPSec) with Windows Vista," by Chris Avis, available on the companion CD in the Webcasts folder. (You can find this Webcast also by browsing to *http://msevents.microsoft.com* and searching for Event ID 1032327282.)

Take a Practice Test

The practice tests on this book's companion CD offer many options. For example, you can test yourself on just one exam objective, or you can test yourself on all the 70-642 certification exam content. You can set up the test so that it closely simulates the experience of taking a certification exam, or you can set it up in study mode so that you can look at the correct answers and explanations after you answer each question.

MORE INFO Practice tests

For details about all the practice test options available, see the "How to Use the Practice Tests" section in this book's Introduction.

Chapter 7

Connecting to Networks

This chapter describes four common network connection scenarios:

- **Network Address Translation (NAT)**   A service that translates private IP addresses used on the Internet into a public IP address that can communicate on the Internet.
- **Wireless network**   A local area networking technology that provides connectivity without physical Ethernet cables.
- **Dial-up connections**   A remote access technology that uses the telephone circuits and modems to connect to the intranet.
- **Virtual Private Network (VPN) connections**   A remote access technology that tunnels encrypted traffic across the Internet to a VPN server, which forwards the communications to the intranet.

This chapter provides conceptual information for each of these scenarios and shows you exactly how Windows Server 2008 can support these scenarios while minimizing security risks.

Exam objectives in this chapter:
- Configure remote access.
- Configure network authentication.
- Configure wireless access.

Lessons in this chapter:

Before You Begin

To complete the lessons in this chapter, you should be familiar with Microsoft Windows networking and be comfortable with the following tasks:

- Adding roles to a Windows Server 2008 computer
- Configuring Active Directory domain controllers and joining computers to a domain
- Basic network configuration, including configuring IP settings

You will also need the following nonproduction hardware connected to test networks:

- A computer named Dcsrv1 that is a domain controller in the Nwtraders.msft domain. This computer must have two interfaces:
  - ❑ An interface connected to the Internet, with a public Internet IP address.
  - ❑ An interface connected to your private intranet. Configure this interface with the static, private IP address 10.0.0.1, a subnet mask of 255.255.255.0, no default gateway, and no DNS servers.

NOTE   Computer and domain names

The computer and domain names you use will not affect these exercises. The practices in this chapter, however, refer to these computer names for simplicity.

- A computer named Boston that is a member of the Nwtraders.msft domain. Boston can be running either Windows Vista or Windows Server 2008. Boston needs both a wired and a wireless network adapter. In Lesson 1, "Configuring Network Address Translation," Boston should have either interface connected to the private intranet network. In Lesson 2, "Configuring Wireless Networks," you will first connect it to the wired network and then to the wireless network. In Lesson 3, "Connecting to Remote Networks," you will connect it to the same network as the public interface of Dcsrv1.

NOTE   Network configuration

Both computers need to be connected to the private interface. If you are using two physical computers, you can connect them with a crossover Ethernet cable. If you are using two virtual machines, create a virtual network and connect one virtual network interface on each computer to the virtual network. Do not enable a Dynamic Host Configuration Protocol (DHCP) server on the internal network.

- A wireless access point that supports WPA-EAP authentication.

Real World

Tony Northrup

Because private IP addresses are private, different organizations can use the same IP address. Of course, this means that private IP addresses aren't routable on the public Internet—hence the need for NAT.

Here's the problem: if two companies merge, they will need to connect their private networks. If these companies use the same private IP address ranges, one of them is going to have to renumber the network. Renumbering networks is a huge task, requiring updating DHCP servers, updating DNS records, updating servers with static IP addresses, and refreshing client IP settings. And, perhaps worst of all, the work needs to happen after hours to minimize downtime—meaning you'll have several late nights changing IP settings and testing everything afterward.

To minimize the chance of private IP address conflicts, pick random networks from within the private ranges. For example, the network 10.252.83.0/24 is much less likely to be used than the network 192.168.1.0/24 because people tend to choose networks at the beginning of the address ranges.

Lesson 1: Configuring Network Address Translation

Today, the vast majority of intranets use private IP addressing. Private IP addresses are not routable on the public Internet, however. Therefore, to allow hosts with private IP addresses to communicate on the Internet, you need a Network Address Translation (NAT) server to forward traffic to the Internet while translating private IP addresses to public IP addresses.

This lesson describes how to configure a computer running Windows Server 2008 as a NAT server.

After this lesson, you will be able to:

- Describe the purpose of Network Address Translation.
- Configure Internet Connection Sharing to act as a NAT server with minimal configuration.
- Configure NAT using Routing And Remote Access to provide additional configuration options.
- Troubleshoot NAT problems.

Estimated lesson time: 35 minutes

Network Address Translation Concepts

The Internet was designed to provide every computer with a unique, public IP address. In recent years, however, the Internet has grown much larger than was ever anticipated. As a result, enough public IP addresses are simply not available.

NOTE   IPv6 and NAT

Because of the larger address space and improved private addressing design, IPv6 does not require NAT. Therefore, this lesson applies only to IPv4 networks.

As a result of the IP address shortage, Internet service providers (ISPs) typically assign a small number of public IP addresses to each organization with an Internet connection. For example, if an organization with 1000 computers purchases an Internet connection from the ISP, the ISP might assign the organization a total of four public IP addresses. Obviously, most of the organization's 1000 computers will need to share a public IP address.

Network Address Translation (NAT) allows one computer (or another type of network host, such as a router) with a public IP address to provide Internet access to hundreds or thousands of hosts on an internal network. The hosts on the internal network must have private IP addresses (as defined in Request for Comments [RFC] 1918) in one of the following address ranges:

- 192.168.0.0–192.168.255.255
- 172.16.0.0–172.31.255.255
- 10.0.0.0–10.255.255.255

Figure 7-1 illustrates how a NAT server can be placed on the boundary between the public Internet and a private intranet, translating the private IP addresses in outgoing connections into public IP addresses.

Although Windows Server 2008 can be used as a NAT server, most organizations choose dedicated network hardware to perform NAT. Many routers have NAT capabilities built-in, allowing you to configure NAT without purchasing additional hardware. If the NAT server ever goes offline, all clients will be unable to access the public Internet. Because of this, uptime is extremely important for a NAT server. Servers tend to have more downtime than dedicated network hardware because of the requirement to restart the server after installing updates, the higher risk of hardware failures (because of the more complex hardware configuration), and the higher risk of software failures (because of the instability that server applications can introduce).

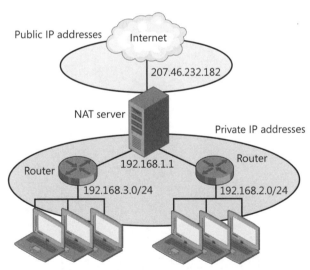

Figure 7-1 NAT architecture

Windows Server 2008 includes two NAT services:

- **Internet Connection Sharing (ICS)**   Primarily intended for home and small offices. ICS configuration can be performed with only a few clicks, but its configuration options are extremely limited.
- **Routing And Remote Access Services**   Intended for organizations with a routed intranet (meaning an intranet with multiple subnets).

The sections that follow describe each of these NAT technologies.

Exam Tip   For the exam, understand the differences between ICS and Routing And Remote Access Services. Focus most of your energy on Routing And Remote Access Services, however.

Configuring Internet Connection Sharing

Figure 7-2 shows a typical ICS architecture. The ICS computer has a public IP address (or an IP address that provides access to a remote network) on the external network interface. The internal network interface always has the IP address 192.168.0.1. Enabling ICS automatically enables a DHCP service that assigns clients IP addresses in the range 192.168.0.0/24. This DHCP service is not compatible with either the DHCP Server role nor the DHCP relay agent feature of Routing And Remote Access.

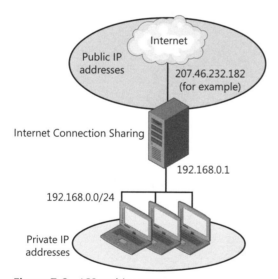

Figure 7-2   ICS architecture

Follow these steps to configure NAT using Internet Connection Sharing:

1. Configure the NAT server with two interfaces:

        ❏ An interface connected to the Internet, with a public Internet IP address

        ❏ An interface connected to your private intranet, with a static, private IP address

2. If you have previously enabled Routing And Remote Access, disable it before continuing.

3. Click Start, right-click Network, and then choose Properties.

   The Network And Sharing Center appears.

4. Under Tasks, click Manage Network Connections.

5. Right-click the network interface that connects to the Internet, and then click Properties.

6. Click the Sharing tab and select the Allow Other Network Users To Connect Through This Computer's Internet Connection check box.

7. If you want users on the Internet to access any servers on your intranet (such as a Web or e-mail server that has only a private IP address), click the Settings button. For each internal service, follow these steps:

        ❏ If the service appears in the Services list, select its check box. In the Service Settings dialog box, type the internal name or IP address of the server and click OK.

        ❏ If the service does not appear on the list or if it uses a nonstandard port number, click Add. Type a description for the service and the internal name or IP address of the server. Then, in both the External Port Number For This Service and Internal Port Number For This Service boxes, type the port number used by the server. Select either TCP or UDP, and then click OK.

NOTE **Using different internal and external port numbers**

The only time you should specify a different internal and external port number is if you want users on the Internet to use a different port number to connect to a server. For example, Web servers typically use port 80 by default. If you have an internal Web server using TCP port 81, you could provide an external port number of 80 and an internal port number of 81. Then, users on the Internet could access the server using the default port 80. If you have two Web servers on your intranet, each using TCP port 80, you can assign the external TCP port number 80 to only one of the servers. For the second server, you should assign a different external port number, such as 8080, but leave the internal port number set to 80.

---

8. Click OK.

Enabling ICS does not change the configuration of the Internet network interface, but it does assign the IP address 192.168.0.1 to the intranet network interface. Additionally, the computer will now respond to DHCP requests on the intranet interface only and assign clients IP addresses in the range 192.168.0.0/24. All clients will have 192.168.0.1 (the private IP address of the ICS computer) as both their default gateway and the preferred DNS server address.

You can also share a VPN or dial-up connection. This allows a single computer to connect to a remote network and to forward traffic from other computers on the intranet. To enable ICS for a remote access connection, follow these steps:

1. Click Start, right-click Network, and then choose Properties.
2. In the Network And Sharing Center, click Manage Network Connections.
3. In the Network Connections window, right-click the remote access connection, and then choose Properties.
4. Click the Sharing tab. Then, select the Allow Other Network Users To Connect Through This Computer's Internet Connection check box.
5. Optionally, select the Establish A Dial-Up Connection Whenever A Computer On My Network Attempts To Access The Internet check box. This automatically establishes a remote access connection if a computer on the intranet sends any traffic that would need to be forwarded to the remote network.
6. Optionally, click the Settings button to configure internal services that should be accessible from the remote network.
7. Click OK.

Configuring Network Address Translation Using Routing And Remote Access

Using Routing And Remote Access, you can enable full-featured NAT capabilities. The specific reasons to use Routing And Remote Access instead of ICS include:

- You can use internal networks other than 192.168.0.0/24.
- You can route to multiple internal networks.
- You can use a different DHCP server, including the DHCP Server role built into Windows Server 2008.
- ICS cannot be enabled on a computer that uses any Routing And Remote Access component, including a DHCP relay agent.

Enabling NAT

Follow these steps to configure NAT using Routing And Remote Access Services on a Windows Server 2008 computer:

1. Configure the NAT server with two interfaces:
   - ❏ An interface connected to the Internet, with a public Internet IP address
   - ❏ An interface connected to your private intranet, with a static, private IP address

2. In Server Manager, select the *Roles* object, and then click Add Roles. Add the Network Policy And Access Services role, with the Routing And Remote Access Services role service.

3. In Server Manager, right-click Roles\Network Policy And Access Services\Routing And Remote Access, and then choose Configure And Enable Routing And Remote Access.

4. On the Welcome To The Routing And Remote Access Server Setup Wizard page, click Next.

5. On the Configuration page, select Network Address Translation (NAT), and then click Next.

6. On the NAT Internet Connection page, select the interface that connects the server to the Internet. Then click Next.

7. On the Completing The Routing And Remote Access Server Setup Wizard page, click Finish.

The server is ready to forward packets from the internal network to the Internet.

Enabling DHCP

When you enable NAT, you can use any DHCP server. Typically, if you want to use a Windows Server 2008 computer as a DHCP server, you should add the DHCP Server role, as described in Chapter 4, "Installing and Configuring a DHCP Server," instead. The DHCP Server role provides a very full-featured DHCP server.

NAT does include a very limited, but functional, DHCP server capable of providing IP address configuration to DHCP clients on a single subnet. To configure the NAT DHCP server, follow these steps:

1. In Server Manager, right-click Roles\Network Policy And Access Services\Routing And Remote Access\IPv4\NAT, and then choose Properties.

2. In the Address Assignment tab, select the Automatically Assign IP Addresses By Using The DHCP Allocator check box, as shown in Figure 7-3.

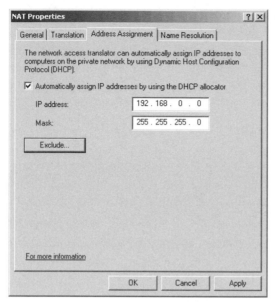

Figure 7-3 The NAT Properties dialog box

3. Type the private network address and subnet mask.

4. If you need to exclude specific addresses that are statically assigned to existing servers (other than the NAT server's private IP address), click the Exclude button and use the Exclude Reserved Addresses dialog box to list the addresses that will not be assigned to DHCP clients. Click OK.

5. Click OK twice to close the open dialog boxes.

You can view statistics for the DHCP server by right-clicking the Roles\Network Policy And Access Services\Routing And Remote Access\IPv4\NAT node in Server Manager and then choosing Show DHCP Allocator Information.

Enabling Forwarding of DNS Requests

To connect to the Internet, NAT clients need to be able to resolve DNS requests. You can provide this using the DNS Server role, as described in Chapter 3, "Configuring and Managing DNS Zones."

For small networks not requiring a DNS server, you can configure NAT to forward DNS requests to the DNS server configured on the NAT server. Typically, this is the DNS server at your ISP. To configure forwarding of DNS requests, follow these steps:

1. In Server Manager, right-click Roles\Network Policy And Access Services\Routing And Remote Access\IPv4\NAT, and then choose Properties.
2. In the Name Resolution tab, select the Clients Using Domain Name System (DNS) check box.
3. If the NAT server must connect to a VPN or dial-up connection for network access, select the Connect To The Public Network When A Name Needs To Be Resolved check box, and then select the appropriate demand-dial interface.
4. Click OK.

You can view statistics for the DNS server by right-clicking the Roles\Network Policy And Access Services\Routing And Remote Access\IPv4\NAT node in Server Manager and then choosing Show DNS Proxy Information.

Configuring Client Computers

To configure the client computers, perform the following tasks:

■ For computers on the same LAN as the NAT server's intranet interface, configure the default gateway as the NAT server's intranet IP address.

■ For other intranet LANs, configure routers to forward traffic destined for the Internet to the NAT server's intranet IP address.

■ Ensure that all clients can resolve Internet DNS names. The NAT server is often also configured as a DNS server, although this is not always the case. For more information about configuring DNS servers, refer to Chapter 2, "Configuring DNS and Name Resolution."

Troubleshooting Network Address Translation

By default, the Routing And Remote Access Services NAT component logs NAT errors to the System event log, which you can view in Server Manager at Diagnostics\Event Viewer\Windows Logs\System. All events will have a source of SharedAccess_NAT.

You can configure NAT to perform logging of warnings, perform verbose logging, or disable logging entirely. To configure NAT logging, in Server Manager, right-click the Roles\Network Policy And Access Services\Routing And Remote Access\IPv4\NAT node, and then choose Properties. In the General tab, select the desired logging level, and then click OK.

PRACTICE Configuring NAT

In this practice, you will configure two computers. In the first practice, you will configure a Windows Server 2008 computer as a NAT server. In the second practice, you will configure a second computer (which can be any operating system, although instructions are provided for Windows Vista or Windows Server 2008) to connect to the Internet through the NAT server.

These are the exact steps you would go through to configure NAT in scenarios such as:

- Using a Windows Server 2008 computer to provide Internet access for a small business.
- Configuring NAT for a regional office that has only a single public IP address.

▶ **Exercise 1   Configure a NAT Server**

In this exercise, you will configure Dcsrv1 as a NAT server to forward requests from an internal IP network to the Internet.

1. On Dcsrv1, add the Network Policy And Access Services role, with the Routing And Remote Access Services role service.

2. In Server Manager, right-click Roles\Network Policy And Access Services\Routing And Remote Access, and then choose Disable Routing And Remote Access (if necessary). Then, confirm the dialog box that appears. Disabling routing and remote access allows you to reconfigure it as if it were a newly configured computer.

3. In Server Manager, right-click Roles\Network Policy And Access Services\Routing And Remote Access, and then choose Configure And Enable Routing And Remote Access.

4. On the Welcome To The Routing And Remote Access Server Setup Wizard page, click Next.

5. On the Configuration page, select Network Address Translation, and then click Next.

6. On the NAT Internet Connection page, select the interface that connects the server to the Internet. Then click Next.

7. On the Completing The Routing And Remote Access Server Setup Wizard page, click Finish.

▶ **Exercise 2   Configure a NAT Client and Test the Connection**

In this exercise, you configure Boston as a NAT client, and then verify that the client can connect to the Internet.

1. Start the Boston computer and verify that it is connected to the private network and the network interface is configured to use DHCP.

2. If necessary, run **ipconfig /release** and **ipconfig /renew** at a command prompt to retrieve an IP address from the NAT DHCP server.

3. At a command prompt, run **ipconfig /all** to verify that the computer has an IP address in the 10.0.0.0/24 network and has 10.0.0.1 configured as both the default gateway and DNS server.

4. Open Internet Explorer and verify that you can connect to *http://www.microsoft.com*.

Lesson Summary

- If you have more computers than public IP addresses, you will need to assign hosts private IP addresses. To allow hosts with private IP addresses to communicate on the Internet, deploy a NAT server, with network interfaces attached both to the public Internet and your private intranet.

- ICS allows you to enable NAT on a server with just a few clicks. However, configuration options are very limited. For example, the internal interface must have the IP address 192.168.0.1. Additionally, you cannot use the DHCP Server role built into Windows Server 2008; instead, you must use the DHCP server component built into ICS.

- Routing And Remote Access provides a much more flexible NAT server than is available with ICS. Although configuration is slightly more complex than configuring ICS, you can start the configuration wizard by right-clicking Roles\Network Policy And Access Services\Routing And Remote Access in Server Manager and then choosing Configure and Enable Routing And Remote Access. After it's configured, you can choose to use the built-in DHCP server or add the DHCP Server role.

Lesson Review

You can use the following questions to test your knowledge of the information in Lesson 1, "Configuring Network Address Translation." The questions are also available on the companion CD if you prefer to review them in electronic form.

NOTE Answers

Answers to these questions and explanations of why each answer choice is correct or incorrect are located in the "Answers" section at the end of the book.

---

1. How does enabling ICS change the IP settings on a computer? (Choose all that apply.)
   A. The IP address of the internal network adapter is changed to 192.168.0.1.
   B. The IP address of the external network adapter is changed to 192.168.0.1.
   C. DHCP services are enabled on the internal network adapter.
   D. DHCP services are enabled on the external network adapter.

2. Which of the following scenarios are not likely to work with NAT without additional configuration?

    A. Clients on the Internet accessing a Web server on the intranet using HTTP

    B. Clients on the intranet downloading e-mail from an Exchange server on the Internet

    C. Clients on the intranet streaming video using a TCP connection from a server on the Internet

    D. Clients on the intranet accessing a Web server on the Internet using HTTPS

3. You are an administrator for a small business with a single server. All computers on the network need to share a single Internet connection. You configure a Windows Server 2008 computer with two network adapters. You connect one network adapter directly to the DSL modem provided by your ISP. You connect the second network adapter to a Layer 2-switch that all other computers are connected to. Then, you enable ICS on the Internet network adapter. What is the IP address of the internal network adapter?

    A. The public IP address provided by your ISP

    B. The DNS server address provided by your ISP

    C. 192.168.0.1

    D. 192.168.0.0

Lesson 2: Configuring Wireless Networks

Once thought to be the domain of coffee shops, wireless networks are now common in businesses, college campuses, and other large networks. Although the security risks are still significant, you can minimize the risk by carefully planning an infrastructure around the latest wireless security technologies, Windows Server 2008, and Remote Authentication Dial-In User Service (RADIUS). This chapter provides an overview of wireless technologies and shows you how to configure Windows Server 2008 to process authentication requests from wireless access points.

MORE INFO   Wireless networks

For a more detailed discussion of wireless networks, read Chapter 10, "IEEE 802.11 Wireless Networks," of *Windows Server 2008 Networking and Network Access Protection* from Microsoft Press, by Joseph Davies and Tony Northrup

---

> **After this lesson, you will be able to:**
> - Describe wireless networking and wireless authentication standards.
> - Choose between infrastructure and ad hoc wireless networking.
> - Configure a public key infrastructure (PKI) to enable wireless authentication using certificates.
> - Configure Windows Server 2008 as a RADIUS server to provide centralized, Active Directory–integrated authentication for wireless clients.
> - Manually or automatically connect wireless clients to your wireless networks.
>
> **Estimated lesson time: 90 minutes**

Wireless Networking Concepts

Wireless networks have changed the way people use their computers:

- Organizations can instantly network an entire building—including meeting rooms, common areas, and courtyards. This can increase productivity and provide more flexible work spaces. For some buildings, including historical landmarks, this might be the only legal way to network a facility.
- Business travelers can use their mobile computers to connect to the Internet from any place with a public wireless network (including hotels, airports, and coffee shops). They can use this Internet connection to establish a VPN connection to their organization's internal network (as described in Lesson 3, "Connecting to Remote Networks").

- People can network their homes in just a few minutes.

- Users with mobile computers can establish an ad hoc network while traveling and share resources without a network infrastructure.

Unfortunately, wireless networks have also introduced some problems:

- Because a physical connection isn't required, attackers can connect to wireless networks from outside your facility (such as from your parking lot, other offices in the same building, or even buildings hundreds of feet away).

- By default, most wireless access points use neither authentication nor encryption. This allows any attacker who can send and receive a wireless signal to connect to your network. Additionally, attackers can capture data as it crosses the network.

- Technologies such as Wired Equivalent Protection (WEP) and Wi-Fi Protected Access (WPA) provide both authentication and encryption for wireless networks. However, they're vulnerable to cracking attacks by attackers who can receive a wireless signal. Attackers with the right skill and equipment within a few hundred feet of a wireless access point can often identify the key used to connect to a WEP-protected wireless network.

Wireless Networking Standards

The following are the most commonly used wireless network technologies:

- **802.11b**   The original and still most common wireless network type. 802.11b advertises a theoretical network throughput of 11 Mbps, but 3–4 Mbps is more realistic. Because 802.11g and 802.11n are backward-compatible with 802.11b, an 802.11b client can connect to almost any network (albeit at the slower 802.11b speed).

NOTE 802.11

An 802.11 standard preceded 802.11b, but it was never widely used.

- **802.11g**   An update to 802.11b that advertises a theoretical network throughput of 54 Mbps (with 10–15 Mbps realistic bandwidth under good circumstances). You can use 802.11g network access points in one of two modes: mixed (which supports 802.11b clients but reduces bandwidth for all clients) or 802.11g-only (which does not support 802.11b clients but offers optimal bandwidth).

- **802.11n**   An update to 802.11g and 802.11b that provides improved range and performance claims of 250 Mbps (with a much smaller realistic bandwidth). In addition to providing backward compatibility with 802.11b and 802.11g, this standard is backward compatible with 802.11a. As of the time of this writing, 802.11n has not yet been standardized; however, many vendors have offered wireless access points with support for "pre-N" standards.

- **802.11a** An old standard that uses the 5.4 GHz range instead of the 2.4 GHz range used by 802.11b, 802.11g, and 802.11n. 802.11a originally competed with 802.11b, but it was not as popular and has now been largely abandoned.

Many vendors offer wireless access points that include proprietary extensions that offer better network performance when used with wireless network adapters from the same vendor. Although these proprietary extensions can improve performance, they don't work with network adapters made by other vendors. In enterprise environments where network adapters are often built into mobile computers, these extensions are typically not useful.

Wireless Security Standards

Wireless access points can require clients to authenticate before connecting to the network. This authentication also allows a private key to be established that can be used to encrypt wireless communications, protecting the data from being intercepted and interpreted. Windows wireless clients support all common wireless security standards:

- **No security** To grant guests easy access, you can choose to allow clients to connect to a wireless access point without authentication (or encryption). To provide some level of protection, some wireless access points detect new clients and require the user to open a Web browser and acknowledge a usage agreement before the router grants the user access to the Internet. Unfortunately, any communications sent across an unprotected wireless network can be intercepted by attackers who can receive the wireless signal (which typically broadcasts several hundred feet). Because almost all public wireless networks are unprotected, ensure that your mobile users understand the risks. If you allow users to connect to unprotected wireless networks, provide encryption at other layers whenever possible. For example, use Secure Sockets Layer (SSL) to protect communications with your e-mail server, require users to connect using an encrypted VPN, or require IPsec communications with encryption.

- **Wired Equivalent Protection (WEP)** WEP, available using either 64-bit or 128-bit encryption, was the original wireless security standard. Unfortunately, WEP has significant vulnerabilities because of weaknesses in the cryptography design. Potential attackers can download freely available tools on the Internet and use the tools to *crack* the key required to connect to the WEP network—often within a few minutes. Therefore, neither 64-bit nor 128-bit WEP can protect you against even unsophisticated attackers. However, WEP is sufficient to deter casual users who might connect to an otherwise unprotected wireless network. WEP is almost universally supported by wireless clients (including non-Windows operating systems and network devices, such as printers) and requires no additional infrastructure beyond the wireless access point. When connecting to a WEP network, users must enter a key or passphrase (though this process can be automated).

- **Wi-Fi Protected Access (WPA)**   Like WEP, WPA provides wireless authentication and encryption. WPA can offer significantly stronger cryptography than WEP, depending on how it is configured. WPA is not as universally supported as WEP, however, so if you have non-Windows wireless clients or wireless devices that do not support WEP, you might need to upgrade them to support WPA. Computers running Windows support WPA-PSK and WPA-EAP.

    ❑ WPA-PSK (for preshared key), also known as WPA-Personal, uses a static key, similar to WEP. Unfortunately, this static key means it can be cracked using brute force techniques. Additionally, static keys are extremely difficult to manage in enterprise environments; if a single computer configured with the key is compromised, you would need to change the key on every wireless access point. For that reason, WPA-PSK should be avoided.

    MORE INFO   Choosing a Preshared Key

    If you must use WPA-PSK, use a long, complex password as the preshared key. When attackers attempt to crack a WPA-PSK network, they will start with a precomputed rainbow table, which allows cracking tools to identify whether a WPA-PSK network is protected by a common value (such as a word in the dictionary) in a matter of minutes. If your preshared key isn't a common value, it probably won't appear in the rainbow table, and the attacker will have to resort to brute force methods, which can take much longer—typically hours, days, or weeks instead of seconds or minutes.

    ❑ WPA-EAP (Extensible Authentication Protocol), also known as WPA-Enterprise, passes authentication requests to a back-end server, such as a Windows Server 2008 computer running RADIUS. Network Policy Server (NPS) provides RADIUS authentication on Windows servers. NPS can pass authentication requests to a domain controller, allowing WPA-EAP protected wireless networks to authenticate domain computers without requiring users to type a key. WPA-EAP enables very flexible authentication, and Windows Vista and Windows Server 2008 enable users to use a smart card to connect to a WPA-Enterprise protected network. Because WPA-EAP does not use a static key, it's easier to manage because you don't need to change the key if an attacker discovers it and multiple wireless access points can use a single, central server for authentication. Additionally, it is much harder to crack than WEP or WPA-PSK.

- **WPA2** WPA2 (also known as IEEE 802.11i) is an updated version of WPA, offering improved security and better protection from attacks. Like WPA, WPA2 is available as both WPA2-PSK and WPA2-EAP.

Windows Vista, Windows Server 2003, and Windows Server 2008 include built-in support for WEP, WPA, and WPA2. Windows XP can support both WPA and WPA2 by installing updates available from Microsoft.com. Recent versions of Linux and the Mac OS are capable of supporting WEP, WPA, and WPA2. Network devices, such as printers that connect to your wireless network, might not support WPA or WPA2. When selecting a wireless security standard, choose the first standard on this list that all clients can support:

- WPA2-EAP
- WPA-EAP
- WPA2-PSK
- WPA-PSK
- 128-bit WEP
- 64-bit WEP

If all clients cannot support WPA-EAP or WPA2-EAP, consider upgrading those clients before deploying a wireless network.

Infrastructure and Ad Hoc Wireless Networks

Wireless networks can operate in two modes:

- **Infrastructure mode** A wireless access point acts as a central hub to wireless clients, forwarding traffic to the wired network and between wireless clients. All communications travel to and from the wireless access point. The vast majority of wireless networks in business environments are of the infrastructure type.
- **Ad hoc mode** Ad hoc wireless networks are established between two or more wireless clients without using a wireless access point. Wireless communications occur directly between wireless clients, with no central hub. For business environments, ad hoc wireless networks are primarily used when short-term mobile networking is required. For example, in a meeting room without wired networking, a Windows Vista user could connect a video projector to a computer, establish an ad hoc wireless network, and then share the video with other computers that connected to the ad hoc wireless network.

Because servers rarely participate in ad hoc wireless networks, this book does not discuss them in depth.

Configuring the Public Key Infrastructure

WEP and WPA-PSK rely on static keys for wireless authentication, and, as a result, they are both unsecure and unmanageable in enterprise environments. For better security and manageability, you will need to use WPA-EAP. The most straightforward approach to deploying WPA-EAP is to use a PKI to deploy certificates to both your RADIUS server and all wireless client computers.

To create a PKI and enable autoenrollment so that client computers have the necessary certificates to support WPA-EAP wireless authentication, follow these steps:

1. Add the Active Directory Certificate Services role to a server in your domain (the default settings work well for test environments).

2. In the Group Policy Management Console, edit the Group Policy object (GPO) used to apply wireless settings (or the Default Domain Policy). In the console tree, select Computer Configuration\Policies\Windows Settings\Security Settings\Public Key Policies.

3. In the Details pane, right-click Certificate Services Client – Auto-Enrollment, and then choose Properties.

4. In the Certificate Services Client – Auto-Enrollment Properties dialog box, from the Configuration Model drop-down list, select Enabled. Optionally, select the check boxes for other options related to autoenrollment, and then click OK.

Authenticating Wireless Networks Using Windows Server 2008

Windows wireless clients can authenticate using the following modes:

- **Computer only** Windows authenticates to the wireless network prior to displaying the Windows logon screen. Windows can then connect to Active Directory domain controllers and other network resources before the user logs on. No user authentication is required.

- **User only** Windows authenticates to the wireless network after the user logs on. Unless wireless Single Sign On is enabled (described later in this section), users cannot authenticate to the domain before connecting to the wireless network, however. Therefore, users can log on only if domain logon credentials have been cached locally. Additionally, domain logon operations (including processing Group Policy updates and logon scripts) will fail, resulting in Windows event log errors.

- **Computer and user** Windows authenticates prior to logon using computer credentials. After logon, Windows submits user credentials. In environments that use virtual LANs (VLANs), the computer's access to network resources can be limited until user credentials are provided (for example, the computer might be able to access only Active Directory domain controllers).

Windows Vista and Windows Server 2008 support wireless Single Sign On, which allows administrators to configure user authentication to the wireless network to occur before the user logs on. This overcomes the weaknesses of user-only authentication. To enable wireless Single Sign On, use the Wireless Network (IEEE 802.11) Policies Group Policy extension or run the *netsh wlan* command with appropriate parameters.

Configuring the RADIUS Server for Wireless Networks

You can use a Windows Server 2008 computer to authenticate wireless users by configuring the Windows Server 2008 computer as a RADIUS server and configuring your wireless access points to send authentication requests to the RADIUS server. This architecture is shown in Figure 7-4.

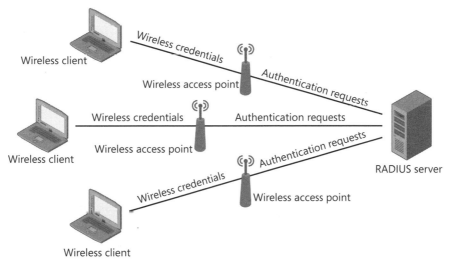

Figure 7-4   Wireless authentication to a RADIUS server

First, add the Network Policy And Access Services role (if it is not yet installed) by following these steps. If the server role is already installed, you can simply add the Routing And Remote Access Services role service by right-clicking Network Policy And Access Services in Server Manager, and then choosing Add Role Services.

1. Click Start, and then choose Server Manager.
2. In the console tree, select Roles, and then in the details pane, click Add Roles.
3. If the Before You Begin page appears, click Next.
4. On the Select Server Roles page, select the Network Policy And Access Services check box, and then click Next.

5. On the Network Policy And Access Services page, click Next.

6. On the Select Role Services page, select the Network Policy Server check box. Then, select the Routing And Remote Access Services check box. The Remote Access Service and Routing check boxes are automatically selected. Click Next.

7. On the Confirmation page, click Install.

8. After the Add Roles Wizard completes the installation, click Close.

Next, configure the Network Policy Server to allow your wireless access point as a RADIUS client.

1. In Server Manager, select Roles\Network Policy And Access Services\NPS. If this node does not appear, close and reopen Server Manager.

2. In the details pane, under Standard Configuration, select RADIUS Server For 802.1X Wireless Or Wired Connections. Then, click Configure 802.1X.

   The Configure 802.1X Wizard appears.

3. On the Select 802.1X Connections Type page, select Secure Wireless Connections, and then click Next.

4. On the Specify 802.1X Switches page, you will configure your wireless access points as valid RADIUS clients. Follow these steps for each wireless access point, and then click Next:

   a. Click Add.

   b. In the New RADIUS Client dialog box, in the Friendly Name box, type a name that identifies that specific wireless access point.

   c. In the Address box, type the host name or IP address that identifies the wireless access point.

   d. In the Shared Secret section, select Manual and type a shared secret. Alternatively, you can automatically create a complex secret by selecting the Generate option button and then clicking the Generate button that appears. Also, write the shared secret down for later use.

   e. Click OK.

5. On the Configure An Authentication Method page, from the Type drop-down list, select one of the following authentication methods, and then click Next:

   ❑ **Microsoft: Protected EAP (PEAP)**   This authentication method requires you to install a computer certificate on the RADIUS server and a computer certificate or user certificate on all wireless client computers. All client computers must trust the certification authority (CA) that issued the computer certificate installed on the RADIUS server, and the RADIUS server must trust the CA that issued the certificates that the client computers provide. The best way to do this is to use an enterprise PKI (such as the Active Directory Certificate Services role in Windows Server 2008). PEAP is compatible with the 802.1X Network Access Protection (NAP) enforcement method, as described in Chapter 8, "Configuring Windows Firewall and Network Access Protection."

❑ **Microsoft: Smart Card Or Other Certificate**   Essentially the same authentication method as PEAP, this authentication technique relies on users providing a certificate using a smart card. When you select this authentication method, Windows wireless clients prompt users to connect a smart card when they attempt to connect to the wireless network.

❑ **Microsoft: Secured Password (EAP-MSCHAP v2)**   This authentication method requires computer certificates to be installed on all RADIUS servers and requires all client computers to trust the CA that issued the computer certificate installed on the RADIUS server. Clients authenticate using domain credentials.

6. On the Specify User Groups page, click Add. Specify the group you want to grant wireless access to, and then click OK. Click Next.

7. On the Configure A Virtual LAN (VLAN) page, you can click the Configure button to specify VLAN configuration settings. This is required only if you want to limit wireless users to specific network resources, and you have created a VLAN using your network infrastructure. Click Next.

8. On the Completing New IEEE 802.1X Secure Wired And Wireless Connections And RADIUS Clients page, click Finish.

9. In Server Manager, right-click Roles\Network Policy And Access Services\NPS, and then choose Register Server In Active Directory. Click OK twice.

RADIUS authentication messages use UDP port 1812, and RADIUS accounting messages use UDP port 1813.

Quick Check

1. What is the strongest form of wireless network security supported by Windows Vista and Windows Server 2008?
2. Which server role is required to support authenticating wireless users to Active Directory?

Quick Check Answers

1. WPA2.
2. You must add the Network Policy And Access Services role to configure the server as a RADIUS server.

Configuring RADIUS Proxies

If you have existing RADIUS servers and you need a layer of abstraction between the access points and the RADIUS servers or if you need to submit requests to different RADIUS servers based on specific criteria, you can configure Windows Server 2008 as a RADIUS proxy. Figure 7-5 demonstrates a typical use.

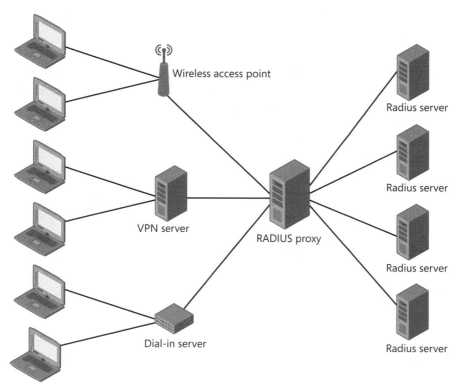

Figure 7-5 Sample RADIUS proxy architecture

The most common use of a RADIUS proxy is to submit requests to organization-specific RADIUS servers based on the realm identified in the RADIUS request. In this way, different organizations can manage their own RADIUS servers (and thus manage the user accounts that each RADIUS server authenticates). For example, if your organization has two domains that do not trust each other, you could have your wireless access points (or your VPN servers, as discussed in Lesson 3, "Connecting to Remote Networks") submit requests to your RADIUS proxy. The RADIUS proxy could then determine which domain's RADIUS proxy to forward the request to. You can also use a RADIUS proxy to load-balance requests across multiple RADIUS servers if one RADIUS server is unable to handle the load.

To configure a Windows Server 2008 computer as a RADIUS proxy, follow these conceptual steps:

1. Create a RADIUS server proxy group.
2. Create a connection request policy that forwards authentication requests to the remote RADIUS server group and define it at a higher priority than the default Use Windows Authentication For All Users connection request policy.

After you configure the connection request policy, the RADIUS proxy might send requests that match specific criteria to any server in a group. Therefore, you must create a separate group for each set of RADIUS servers that will receive unique authentication requests. RADIUS server groups can consist of a single RADIUS server, or they can have many RADIUS servers (assuming the RADIUS servers authenticate the same users).

At a detailed level, follow these steps to create a RADIUS server proxy group:

1. Add the Network Policy And Access Services role, as described in "Configuring the RADIUS Server for Wireless Networks" earlier in this lesson.
2. In Server Manager, right-click Roles\Network Policy And Access Services\NPS\RADIUS Clients And Servers\Remote RADIUS Server Groups, and then choose New.
   The New Remote RADIUS Server Group dialog box appears.
3. Type a name for the RADIUS server group.
4. Click the Add button.
   The ADD RADIUS Server dialog box appears.
5. In the Address tab, type the host name or IP address of the RADIUS server.
6. In the Authentication/Accounting tab, type the shared secret in the Shared Secret and Confirm Shared Secret boxes.
7. In the Load Balancing tab, leave the default settings if you are not performing load balancing or if all servers should receive the same number of requests. If you are load balancing among servers with different capacities (for example, if one RADIUS server can handle twice as many requests as the next), then adjust the Priority and Weight appropriately.
8. Click OK.
9. Repeat steps 4–8 to add RADIUS servers to the group.

Repeat steps 1–9 for every RADIUS server group. Then, follow these steps to create a connection request policy:

1. In Server Manager, right-click Roles\Network Policy And Access Services\NPS\Policies \Connection Request Policies, and then choose New.
   The Specify Connection Request Policy Name And Connection Type Wizard appears.

2. Type a name for the policy. In the Type Of Network Access Server list, select the access server type. If your access server provides a specific type number, click Vendor Specific, and then type the number. Click Next.

3. On the Specify Conditions page, click Add. Select the condition you want to use to distinguish which RADIUS server group receives the authentication request. To distinguish using the realm name, select User Name. Click Add.

4. Provide any additional information requested for the condition you selected, and then click OK.

5. Repeat steps 3 and 4 to add criteria. Then, click Next.

6. On the Specify Connection Request Forwarding page, select Forward Requests To The Following Remote RADIUS Server Group For Authentication. Then, select the RADIUS server group from the drop-down list. Click Next.

7. On the Configure Settings page, you can add rules to overwrite any existing attributes, or you can add attributes that might not exist in the original request. For example, you could change the realm name of an authentication request before forwarding it to a RADIUS server. This step is optional and is required only if you know that a destination RADIUS server has specific requirements that the original RADIUS request does not meet. Click Next.

8. On the Completing Connection Request Policy Wizard page, click Finish.

9. In Server Manager, right-click the new policy, and then choose Move Up to move the policy above any lower-priority policies, if necessary.

Repeat steps 1–9 to define unique criteria that will forward different requests to each RADIUS group, and your configuration of the RADIUS proxy is complete.

Monitoring RADIUS Server Logons

Like any authentication mechanism, it's important to monitor logons to wireless networks. The Windows Server 2008 RADIUS server provides several mechanisms. The most straightforward is the Security event log, viewable using the standard Event Viewer snap-in. Additionally, you can examine the RADIUS log file, which is formatted for compatibility with reporting software. For debugging or detailed troubleshooting, you can enable trace logging. The sections that follow describe each of these reporting mechanisms.

Using Event Viewer   If a wireless user attempts to authenticate to a wireless access point using WPA-EAP and the wireless access point is configured to use a Windows Server 2008 computer as the RADIUS server, the Network Policy Server service adds an event to the Security event log. Figure 7-6 shows a sample event. Events have a Task Category of Network Policy Server. Successful authentication attempts appear as Audit Success, and failed authentication attempts appear as Audit Failure.

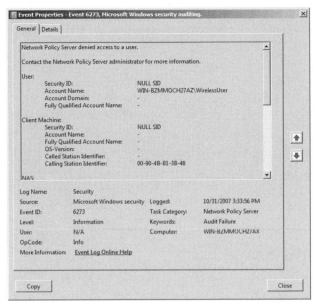

Figure 7-6 A failed authentication attempt logged to the Security event log

Analyzing the RADIUS Log File RADIUS is a standards-based authentication mechanism, and it also has a standards-based log file. By default, the RADIUS log (also known as the IAS log) is stored in %SystemRoot%\system32\LogFiles, with the filename IN<*date*>.log. However, you can also configure RADIUS logging to a database server.

Typically, you will not directly analyze the RADIUS log file. Instead, you will parse the file with software specifically designed to analyze RADIUS logs, including security auditing software and accounting software used for usage-based billing. Table 7-1 shows the first several fields in the RADIUS log file format. The remaining fields can vary depending on the wireless access point being used.

Table 7-1 RADIUS Log Fields

Field	Description
Server name	The computer name registered to the RADIUS server.
Service	This value is always "IAS."
Date	The date, in the format "MM/DD/YYYY."
Time	The time, in the format "hh:mm:ss."

Enabling Trace Logging on the Server   You can also enable extremely detailed trace logging, which is useful primarily when working with Microsoft support. To enable trace logging, run the following command:

```
netsh ras set tr * en
```

This will cause the network policy server to generate a log file named %SystemRoot%\Tracing\IASNAP.log. You can submit this log file to Microsoft support for detailed analysis.

MORE INFO   NAP logging

These log files should provide you with most of the information you need for both auditing and troubleshooting. If you need even more detailed information, read "The Definitive Guide to NAP Logging" at *http://blogs.technet.com/wincat/archive/2007/10/29/the-definitive-guide-to-nap-logging.aspx*.

Connecting to Wireless Networks

Users can manually connect to a wireless network, or you can use Group Policy settings to configure client computers to automatically connect to your wireless networks. The sections that follow provide step-by-step instructions for each of the two approaches.

Manually Connecting to a Wireless Network

From a Windows Vista or Windows Server 2008 computer, you can manually connect to wireless networks by following these steps:

1. Click Start, and then choose Connect To.
2. On the Connect To A Network Wizard page, click the wireless network you want to connect to, and then click Connect.

NOTE   Connecting to a network with a hidden SSID

If the network does not broadcast a service set identifier (SSID), click the Set Up A Connection Or Network link and follow the prompts that appear to provide the hidden SSID.

---

3. Click Enter/Select Additional Log On Information.
4. In the Enter Credentials dialog box, type the User Name **WirelessUser**. Then, type the password you specified for that user. Click OK.
5. After the client computer connects to the wireless network, click Close.

6. In the Set Network Location dialog box, select the network profile type. In domain environments, Work is typically the best choice. Provide administrative credentials if required, and then click OK.

7. Click Close.

Configuring Clients to Automatically Connect to Wireless Networks

You can also use Group Policy settings to configure computers to automatically connect to protected wireless networks without requiring the user to manually connect:

1. From a domain controller, open the Group Policy Management console from the Administrative Tools folder. Right-click the GPO that applies to the computers you want to apply the policy to, and then click Edit.

2. In the Group Policy Management Editor console, right-click Computer Configuration \Policies\Windows Settings\Security Settings\Wireless Network (IEEE 802.11) Policies, and then choose Create a New Windows Vista Policy.

NOTE Windows XP and Windows Vista policies

You can create either Windows Vista or Windows XP policies. Windows Vista policies are automatically applied to wireless clients running Windows Server 2008 and Windows Vista. Windows XP policies apply to clients running Windows XP with SP2 and Windows Server 2003. If no Windows Vista policy exists, computers running Windows Vista and Windows Server 2008 will apply the Windows XP policy.

---

3. In the General tab, click Add, and then click Infrastructure. You can also use this dialog box to configure ad hoc networks, although enterprises rarely use preconfigured ad hoc networks.

4. In the New Profile Properties dialog box, in the Connection tab, type a name for the wireless network in the Profile Name box. Then, type the SSID in the Network Name box and click Add. You can remove the default NEWSSID SSID.

5. In the New Profile Properties dialog box, click the Security tab. Click the Authentication list and select the wireless authentication technique and network authentication method for that SSID, as shown in Figure 7-7.

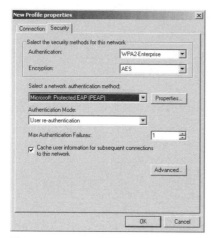

Figure 7-7   Configuring security settings for a wireless network using Group Policy

6. While still in the Security tab of the New Profile Properties dialog box, click Advanced. Optionally, select the Enable Single Sign On For This Network check box. Click OK.

7. Click OK again to return to the New Vista Wireless Network Policy Properties dialog box.

8. In the New Profile Properties dialog box, click OK.

9. In the New Vista Wireless Network Policy Properties dialog box, click OK.

Deploying Wireless Networks with WPA-EAP

Deploying a wireless network with WPA-EAP requires combining several technologies: wireless access points, Active Directory users and groups, a PKI, RADIUS, and Group Policy settings. Although deploying a protected wireless network can be complex, after you understand the individual components and how they fit together, it is reasonably straightforward.

To deploy a protected wireless network, follow these high-level steps:

1. Deploy certificates (preferably, using Active Directory Certificate Services).

2. Create groups for users and computers that will have wireless access and add members to those groups.

3. Configure RADIUS servers using NPS.

4. Deploy wireless access points and configure them to forward authentication requests to your RADIUS server.

5. Configure wireless clients using Group Policy settings.

6. Allow the client computers to apply the Group Policy and either manually or automatically connect them to the wireless network.

Best Practices for Wireless Networking

Adding wireless networks always introduces additional risk. However, you can keep that risk to a minimum by following these best practices:

- **Assign a short DHCP lease duration** For wireless networks, configure a DHCP lease duration of six hours or less. Wireless clients frequently connect and disconnect, and a short lease duration will minimize the number of IP addresses that are unavailable and unused at any given time. For more information, see Chapter 3, "Configuring and Managing DNS Zones."

- **Create a universal global group in Active Directory for users and computers with wireless access** You can then grant access to the universal global group and grant computers and users access to your wireless network by adding them as members of the group.

- **Broadcast the wireless SSID** Early in the adoption of wireless networks, many users disabled SSID broadcasts in a futile attempt to improve wireless security. Disabling SSID broadcasts prevents users from connecting to a wireless network without manual configuration. However, attackers can very easily connect to wireless networks that do not broadcast a SSID. Additionally, when Windows XP and earlier versions of Windows are configured to connect to a wireless network that does not broadcast a SSID, they can broadcast private information that might be useful to wireless attackers.

- **Do not use MAC filtering** MAC addresses uniquely identify network adapters. Most wireless access points support MAC filtering, which allows only computers with approved MAC addresses to connect to the wireless network. Keeping a MAC filtering list up-to-date is high maintenance, and you will need to update the list every time you replace a network adapter or purchase a new computer. Additionally, it does little to prevent attackers from connecting to your network because they can detect and impersonate an approved MAC address.

- **Require strong passwords when using Microsoft: Secured Password authentication** This security technique authenticates users with standard credentials. Therefore, it is only as strong as each user's password.

- **Use user and computer wireless authentication whenever possible** Additionally, if you cannot support computer authentication, enable Single Sign On for user authentication.

PRACTICE Configure WPA-EAP Authentication for a Wireless Access Point

In this practice, you enable WPA-EAP wireless authentication using Windows Server 2008, a wireless access point, and a wireless client. After you connect the client to the network, you will examine the event log on the RADIUS server.

▶ **Exercise 1 Install and Configure NPS**

In this exercise, you configure Dcsrv1 as a RADIUS server.

1. If you haven't already, use Server Manager to add the Active Directory Certificate Services role to the domain controller using the default settings.

2. Using Roles\Active Directory Domain Services\Active Directory Users And Computers in Server Manager, create a universal group named "Wireless Users." Then, create a user account named WirelessUser, with a complex password. Add the WirelessUser account to the Domain Users and Wireless Users groups. Copy the WirelessUser account to a second account named WirelessUser2. Then, add the computer account for your client computer to the Wireless Users group.

3. Click Start, and then choose Server Manager.

4. In the left pane, click Roles, and then in the details pane, click Add Roles.

5. If the Before You Begin page appears, click Next.

6. On the Select Server Roles page, select the Network Policy And Access Services check box, and then click Next.

NOTE Adding a role service

If the Network Policy And Access Services role is already installed, close the wizard, expand Roles in Server Manager, right-click Network Policy And Access Services, and then click Add Role Services.

---

7. On the Network Policy And Access Services page, click Next.

8. On the Role Services page, select the Network Policy Server check box. Then, select the Routing And Remote Access Services check box. The Remote Access Service and Routing check boxes are automatically selected. Click Next.

9. On the Confirmation page, click Install.

10. After the Add Roles Wizard completes the installation, click Close.

    Next, configure the network policy server to allow your wireless access point as a RADIUS client.

11. In Server Manager, click Roles\Network Policy And Access Services\NPS. If this node does not appear, close and reopen Server Manager.

12. In the Details pane, under Standard Configuration, select RADIUS Server For 802.1X Wireless Or Wired Connections. Then, click Configure 802.1X.

    The Configure 802.1X Wizard appears.

13. On the Select 802.1X Connections Type page, select Secure Wireless Connections. Click Next.

14. On the Specify 802.1X Switches page, you will configure your wireless access points as valid RADIUS clients. Follow these steps for each wireless access point, and then click Next:

    a. Click Add.

    b. In the New RADIUS client dialog box, in the Friendly Name box, type a name that identifies that specific wireless access point.

    c. In the Address box, type the host name or IP address that identifies the wireless access point.

    d. In the Shared Secret group, click the Generate option button. Then, click the Generate button. Copy the shared secret to your clipboard by selecting it and then pressing Ctrl+C. Also, write the key down for later use.

    e. Click OK.

15. On the Configure An Authentication Method page, click the Type list, and then select Microsoft: Protected EAP. Click Next.

16. On the Specify User Groups page, click Add. In the Select Group dialog box, type **Wireless Users,** and then click OK. Click Next.

17. On the Configure A Virtual LAN (VLAN) page, click Next. If you wanted to quarantine wireless clients to a specific VLAN, you could click Configure on this page, and then provide the details for the VLAN.

18. On the Completing New IEEE 802.1X Secure Wired And Wireless Connections And RADIUS Clients page, click Finish.

19. In Server Manager, right-click Roles\Network Policy And Access Services\NPS, and then click Register Server In Active Directory. Click OK twice.

Now, use Server Manager to examine the configuration of your new policy:

1. In Server Manager, expand Roles, expand Network Policy And Access Services, expand NPS, and then click Radius Clients. Notice that your wireless access point is listed in the Details pane. Double-click the wireless access point to view the configuration settings. Click OK.

2. Select the Network Policy And Access Services\NPS\Policies\Network Policies node. In the Details pane, notice that the Secure Wireless Connections policy is enabled with the Access Type set to Grant Access. Double-click Secure Wireless Connections to view its settings. In the Secure Wireless Connection Properties dialog box, select the Conditions tab and notice that the Wireless Users group is listed as a condition of type Windows Groups. Click the Add button, examine the other types of conditions you can add, and then click Cancel.

3. Select the Network Policy And Access Services\NPS\Accounting node. Notice that Windows Server 2008 saves the log file to the %SystemRoot%\system32\LogFiles\ folder by default. Click Configure Local File Logging and make note of the different types of events that are logged. Click OK.

▶ **Exercise 2   Configure the Wireless Access Point**

In this exercise, you configure your wireless access point to use WPA-EAP authentication. Because different wireless access points use different configuration tools, the steps will vary depending on the hardware you use.

1. Open the administrative tool you use to manage your wireless access point. This is often a Web page accessed by typing the wireless access point's IP address into the address bar of your Web browser.
2. Configure the wireless access point with a SSID of **Contoso**.
3. Set the wireless security setting to WPA-EAP (which might be listed as WPA-Enterprise) or, if supported, WPA2-EAP.
4. Set the RADIUS server IP address to your Windows Server 2008 computer's IP address.
5. For the shared secret, specify the shared secret that you generated in the Configure 802.1X Wizard.

Note that many wireless access points allow you to configure multiple RADIUS servers. Although not necessary for this practice, in production environments, you should always configure at least two RADIUS servers for redundancy. If you had only a single RADIUS server, wireless clients would be unable to connect if the RADIUS server was offline.

▶ **Exercise 3   Configure Wireless Network Group Policy Settings**

In this exercise, you configure Group Policy settings to allow clients to connect to the wireless network.

1. From Dcsrv1, open the Group Policy Management console from the Administrative Tools folder.
2. In the console tree, expand Forest, expand Domains, and expand your domain. Right-click Default Domain Policy, and then choose Edit.
3. In the Group Policy Management Editor console, right-click Default Domain Policy \Computer Configuration\Policies\Windows Settings\Security Settings\Wireless Network (IEEE 802.11) Policies, and then choose Create a New Windows Vista Policy.
4. In the General tab, click Add, and then click Infrastructure.
5. In the New Profile Properties dialog box, in the Connection tab, type **Contoso** in the Profile Name box. Then, type **CONTOSO** in the Network Name box and click Add. Click NEWSSID, and then click Remove.

6. In the New Profile Properties dialog box, click the Security tab and verify that Protected EAP security is selected. Then, click Advanced. In the Advanced Security Settings dialog box, select the Enable Single Sign On For This Network check box. Click OK twice.

7. In the New Vista Wireless Network Policy Properties dialog box, click OK.

8. In the Group Policy Management Console, select Default Domain Policy\Computer Configuration\Policies\Windows Settings\Security Settings\Public Key Policies.

9. In the Details pane, right-click Certificate Services Client – Auto-Enrollment, and then click Properties.

10. On the Certificate Services Client – Auto-Enrollment Properties dialog box, click the Configuration Model list, and then click Enabled. Select both available check boxes, and then click OK.

11. In the Details pane, right-click Certificate Path Validation Settings, and then click Properties.

12. In the Certificate Path Validation Properties dialog box, select the Define These Policy Settings check box, and then click OK.

▶ Exercise 4   **Connect to the Wireless Access Point**

In this exercise, you connect the Boston client computer to the WPA-EAP protected wireless network. You can use any Windows Vista or Windows Server 2008 computer that has a wireless network adapter. Technically, you could use a Windows XP wireless computer, too, but the steps would be different.

1. Connect the Boston client computer to a wired network. Then, run **gpupdate /force** to update the Group Policy settings.

2. Click Start, and then click Connect To.

3. On the Connect To A Network Wizard page, click the Contoso wireless network, and then click Connect.

4. After the client computer connects to the wireless network, click Close. The authentication was automatic because the client computer has the computer certificate installed.

5. In the Set Network Location dialog box, click Work. Provide administrative credentials if required, and then click OK.

6. Click Close.

7. Open Internet Explorer to verify that you can access network resources.

8. Restart the computer and log back on using the WirelessUser2 account. Notice that the computer automatically connected to the wireless network using computer authentication. This network access allowed the computer to connect to the domain controller and authenticate using the WirelessUser2 account, even though that account did not have previously cached credentials.

▶ **Exercise 5   View the Security Event Log**

In this exercise, you view the log entries generated during your authentication attempt.

1. On Dcsrv1, use Server Manager to browse to Diagnostics\Event Viewer\Windows Logs\Security.

2. Browse through the recent events to identify the successful authentication from the client computer and the user account.

3. Using Windows Explorer, open the %SystemRoot%\system32\LogFiles folder, and then double-click the IN<*date*>.log file. Examine the RADIUS log file and note the lines that correspond to your recent authentication attempts.

Lesson Summary

■ Wireless networks give users flexible connectivity that allows them to connect to the Internet (or, with a VPN, your internal network) from anywhere in your facilities and from coffee shops, airports, hotels, and their homes.

■ 802.11b was the original, widely adopted networking standard. Today, 802.11g and 802.11n are the wireless networking standards of choice because they provide greatly improved performance while still offering backward-compatibility with 802.11b.

■ Private wireless networks should always be protected with security. WEP is compatible with almost every wireless device, but a competent attacker can easily break the security. WPA-EAP (also known as WPA-Enterprise) provides very strong security and easy manageability.

■ Most wireless networks, especially those that provide access to an internal network or to the Internet, operate in infrastructure mode. In infrastructure mode, all wireless communications travel to and from a central wireless access point. For peer-to-peer networking without an infrastructure, you can also create ad hoc wireless networks.

■ You can use a PKI to issue certificates to client computers and your RADIUS servers. These certificates provide a manageable and scalable authentication mechanism well suited to enterprise environments. Windows Server 2008 includes the Active Directory Certificate Services role, which provides an Active Directory-integrated PKI. Using Group Policy settings, you can provide client computers with computer and user certificates using autoenrollment.

■ Typically, wireless access points aren't able to store a list of authorized users. Instead, the wireless access points submit requests to a central authentication server, known as a RADIUS server. Using NPS, Windows Server 2008 can provide a RADIUS server that authenticates credentials based on client certificates or user credentials.

■ Users can manually connect to wireless networks by clicking Start and then clicking Connect To. Alternatively, you can use Group Policy settings to configure client computers to automatically connect to wireless networks when they are in range.

Lesson Review

You can use the following questions to test your knowledge of the information in Lesson 2, "Configuring Wireless Networks." The questions are also available on the companion CD if you prefer to review them in electronic form.

NOTE Answers

Answers to these questions and explanations of why each answer choice is correct or incorrect are located in the "Answers" section at the end of the book.

1. You are currently planning a wireless deployment for an enterprise organization. Based on the physical layout of your facilities, you determine that you need 12 wireless access points for adequate coverage. You want to provide the best wireless performance possible, but you need to support wireless clients that are compatible with only 802.11b. Which wireless protocol should you choose?

   A. 802.11b

   B. 802.11g

   C. 802.11a

   D. 802.11n

2. You are a systems administrator at an enterprise help desk. A user calls to complain that she is unable to connect to the wireless network. After discussing her problem, you discover that the wireless access point is rejecting her credentials. You examine the wireless access point configuration and determine that it is submitting authentication requests to a RADIUS service running on a Windows Server 2008 computer. How can you determine the exact cause of the authentication failures?

   A. Examine the Security event log on the wireless client.

   B. Examine the System event log on the wireless client.

   C. Examine the Security event log on the computer running Windows Server 2008.

   D. Examine the System event log on the computer running Windows Server 2008.

3. To improve productivity for employees during meetings, your organization has decided to provide authentication and encrypted wireless network access throughout your facilities. The organization is not willing to sacrifice security, however, and requires the most secure authentication mechanisms available. You have recently upgraded all client computers to either Windows XP (with the latest service pack) or Windows Vista. Which wireless security standard should you use?

    A. 128-bit WEP

    B. WPA-PSK

    C. 64-bit WEP

    D. WPA-EAP

Lesson 3: Connecting to Remote Networks

Public wireless networks allow users to connect to the Internet. Although that's sufficient to allow users to catch up on the news, check a flight, or read a weather forecast, business users typically need access to their company's or organization's intranet resources. To allow your users to connect to internal servers in order to exchange documents, synchronize files, and read e-mail, you need to configure remote access.

Remote access typically takes one of two forms: dial-up connections or VPNs. Dial-up connections allow users to connect from anywhere with a phone line. However, dial-up connections offer poor performance, and maintaining dial-up servers can be costly. VPNs require both the client and server to have an active Internet connection. VPNs can offer much better performance, and costs scale much better than dial-up connections.

This lesson provides an overview of remote access technologies and step-by-step instructions for configuring remote access clients and servers.

> **After this lesson, you will be able to:**
> - Decide whether dial-up connections, VPN connections, or a combination of both best meet your remote access requirements.
> - Configure a Windows Server 2008 computer to act as a dial-up server, a RADIUS server for a separate dial-up server, or a dial-up client.
> - Configure a Windows Server 2008 computer to act as a VPN server or a VPN client.
>
> **Estimated lesson time: 45 minutes**

Remote Access Overview

You can provide remote network access to users with either dial-up connections or VPNs. Dial-up connections provide a high level of privacy and do not require an Internet connection, but performance might be too low to meet your requirements. VPNs can be used any time a user has an Internet connection, but they require you to expose your internal network infrastructure to authentication requests from the Internet (and, potentially, attacks).

The sections that follow provide an overview of dial-up and VPN connections.

Dial-up Connections

The traditional (and now largely outdated) remote access technique is to use a dial-up connection. With a dial-up connection, a client computer uses a modem to connect to a remote access server over a phone line. Figure 7-8 illustrates how connections are established, with each client requiring a separate physical circuit to the server.

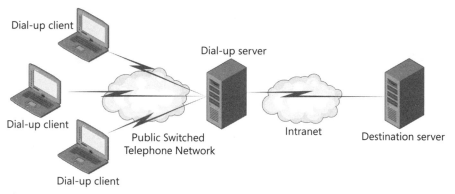

Figure 7-8   The architecture of dial-up remote access connections

Dial-up connections offer the following advantages:

■ **No Internet connection required**   Dial-up connections use a standard analog phone line to establish a network connection directly to your internal network. This means you do not need to expose your internal network to authentication requests from the Internet, unlike a VPN. In fact, you do not need to connect your internal network to the Internet at all—a common requirement for high-security networks.

■ **Minimal privacy risks**   Although dial-up connections lack encryption, the traffic crosses the public switched telephone network (PSTN), which many security experts consider to offer better privacy than the public Internet.

■ **Predictable performance**   Dial-up connections offer consistent, predictable performance because the connection is dedicated to a single client.

However, dial-up connections have the following drawbacks:

■ **High cost for scalability**   When planning to allow employees dial-up access, you need to have as many incoming phone lines and modems available as users who will simultaneously access the dial-up network. To support hundreds or thousands of users, the monthly costs of the telephone circuits can be very expensive, as can be the one-time costs of the modems required.

■ **Poor bandwidth**   Modems for traditional analog phone lines are technically rated for 56 Kbps of bandwidth, but typically, usable bandwidth is between 20 Kbps and 25 Kbps. That bandwidth makes simple tasks such as browsing the Web tedious and makes tasks such as listening to streaming video or audio impossible. Digital phone lines, such as Integrated Services Digital Network (ISDN) circuits, can offer true 128 Kbps bandwidth, but at a much higher cost.

Virtual Private Networks

Whereas dial-up connections use the PSTN to carry traffic to your internal network, VPNs traverse the public Internet. Because your organization probably already has an Internet connection, you might not need to purchase any additional bandwidth (unless you determine that your current bandwidth will not meet the needs of the users simultaneously connected using a VPN).

Figure 7-9 illustrates how connections are established, with each client requiring a separate Internet connection but the VPN server requiring only a single connection to the Internet (instead of a separate physical circuit per dial-up client).

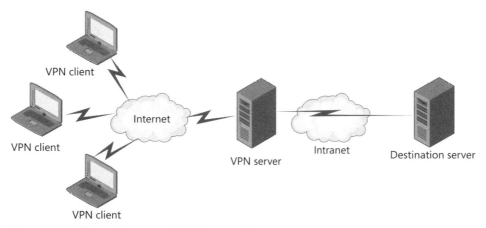

Figure 7-9 The architecture of VPN connections

VPNs offer the following advantages:

- **Higher bandwidth potential** Theoretically, VPN bandwidth can be as high as the client or VPN server's Internet connection (whichever is slower). In practice, because other services will probably use both connections and many other factors can limit bandwidth on the Internet, performance will be somewhat lower than the theoretical maximum. If the client has a broadband connection, however, bandwidth is likely to be much higher than a dial-up connection.

- **Minimal costs** Both the VPN server and the client need to be connected to the Internet. However, your organization probably has an existing Internet connection, and many home or traveling users have Internet access. Therefore, there are no connection costs associated with using a VPN, regardless of the number of incoming connections. If the number of incoming VPN connections requires more bandwidth than you have, you might need to purchase additional bandwidth from your ISP. However, this cost is likely to be far less than purchasing a similar number of telephone circuits and modems for dial-up connections.

However, VPNs have the following drawbacks:

- **Internet connection required**   You must connect the VPN server, and thus your internal network, to the Internet and allow incoming VPN traffic through any firewalls. Additionally, users must have an Internet connection to use a VPN. Organizations typically take one of two approaches:
  - ❏ Work with an ISP to arrange Internet access for all users, using either a dial-up connection or a broadband connection such as a cable modem or DSL.
  - ❏ Require employees to find their own ISPs. Many users currently have an Internet connection at home, and traveling users can often connect to the Internet using public hotspots or wireless broadband services.
- **Poor latency**   Even if the bandwidth is high, VPN connections often seem slow because of high *latency*. Latency is the delay that occurs when a packet travels from a client to a server. As Figure 7-9 shows, packets in a VPN have to travel across the Internet to the VPN server, across the intranet to the destination server, and back. The latency on a VPN connection can often be several times greater than the latency on a dial-up connection.
- **Poor efficiency with dial-up connections**   Although it's possible to dial up to the Internet and then connect to a VPN, the added overhead of the VPN, and the latency added by the Internet, offer even worse performance than using a dial-up connection directly to a remote access server. If users will be using a dial-up connection to access the Internet, they will receive much better performance dialing directly to your intranet.

Configuring Dial-up Connections

The sections that follow describe how to configure a computer running Windows Server 2008 as a either a dial-up server (as described in the following section, "Configuring the Dial-up Server") or a RADIUS server for a separate dial-up server (as described in the section entitled "Configuring the RADIUS Server for Dial-up Connections").

Configuring the Dial-up Server

To configure a server to accept incoming dial-up connections, first connect the modem hardware to the server and connect the modems to the telephone circuits. Then, add the Network Policy And Access Services role, as described in the previous lesson.

NOTE Configuring a dial-up server without a physical modem

For the purpose of experimentation, you can add a fake modem using the Add Hardware Wizard in Control Panel. Choose to manually select the hardware, and then select Standard 56000 Bps Modem in the Add Hardware Wizard.

Next, configure the Routing And Remote Access Service to accept dial-up connections by following these steps:

1. In Server Manager, right-click Roles\Network Policy And Access Services\Routing And Remote Access, and then choose Configure And Enable Routing And Remote Access.

   The Routing And Remote Access Server Setup Wizard appears.

2. On the Welcome To The Routing And Remote Access Server Setup Wizard page, click Next.

3. On the Configuration page, select Remote Access. Then, click Next.

4. On the Remote Access page, select the Dial-Up check box, and then click Next.

5. On the Network Selection page, select the network you want users to connect to after they dial in. Then, click Next.

6. On the IP Address Assignment page, select Automatically if there is already a DHCP server on the network. If you want the dial-up server to assign IP addresses from a pool not already assigned to a DHCP server, click From A Specified Range Of Addresses. Click Next.

7. If the Address Range Assignment page appears, click New, type an IP address range, and then click OK. Add as many address ranges as required. Click Next.

8. On the Managing Multiple Remote Access Servers page, you will choose how dial-up users are authenticated. If you have a separate RADIUS server, select Yes, Set Up This Server To Work With A RADIUS Server. If you want Routing And Remote Access to perform the authentication (which is fine for Active Directory domain authentication), select No, Use Routing And Remote Access To Authenticate Connection Requests. Then, click Next.

9. Click Finish. If prompted, click OK.

Next, you need to enable demand-dial routing on the server by following these steps:

1. In Server Manager, right-click Roles\Network Policy And Access Services\Routing And Remote Access, and then choose Properties.

2. In the General tab of the Routing And Remote Access Properties dialog box, do one or both of the following:

   ❑ To allow IPv4 dial-up clients (the most common scenario), select the IPv4 Router check box, and then select LAN And Demand-Dial Routing. Then, select the IPv4 Remote Access Server check box.

   ❑ To allow IPv6 dial-up clients, select the IPv6 Router check box, and then select LAN And Demand-Dial Routing. Then, select the IPv6 Remote Access Server check box.

3. If you are allowing IPv4 dial-up connections, click the IPv4 tab. Verify that the Enable IPv4 Forwarding check box is selected. If you want to assign IP addresses to clients using an existing DHCP sever, leave Dynamic Host Configuration Protocol selected. If you want the dial-up server to assign IP addresses from an address pool without having to install the DHCP server role, select Static Address Pool. Then, click the Add button to add the IP address ranges to assign addresses from. These IP address ranges should not overlap with other IP address ranges currently in use or assigned to an existing DHCP server.

4. If you are allowing IPv6 dial-up connections, click the IPv6 tab. Verify that Enable IPv6 Forwarding and Enable Default Route Advertisement are selected to allow the dial-up server to act as an IPv6 router. In the IPv6 Prefix Assignment box, type an IPv6 network prefix to be assigned to dial-up clients. If you are unsure of the network prefix, consult network administration.

5. In the PPP tab, notice that you can disable multilink connections (which allow users to dial-up using multiple modems and phone lines to increase bandwidth). You can also disable link control protocol (LCP) extensions or software compression if you have a compatibility problem, although such compatibility problems are rare.

6. In the Logging tab, notice that errors and warnings are logged by default. You can choose to enable more detailed logging by clicking Log All Events and selecting Log Additional Routing And Remote Access Information, or you can click Do Not Log Any Events to disable logging entirely.

7. Click OK.

8. If prompted to restart the router, click Yes. Restarting the router will disconnect any users.

Next, verify that the modems are configured to accept dial-up connections by following these steps:

1. In Server Manager, right-click Roles\Network Policy And Access Services\Routing And Remote Access\Ports, and then choose Properties.

2. In the Ports Properties dialog box, select your modem, and then click Configure. If your modem does not appear, use the Add Hardware Wizard (available from within Control Panel) to add it first.

3. In the Configure Device dialog box, as shown in Figure 7-10, select the Remote Access Connections check box. In the Phone Number For This Device box, type the phone number assigned to that modem. Click OK.

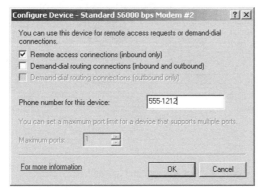

Figure 7-10   Configuring a modem to accept incoming connections

4. Repeat steps 2–3 for each modem you want to use to accept incoming dial-up connections.

5. In the Ports Properties dialog box, click OK.

The dial-up server is ready to accept dial-up connections. To view the status of all modems, select the Roles\Network Policy And Access Services\Routing And Remote Access\Ports node. To view the currently connected users, select the Roles\Network Policy And Access Services\Routing And Remote Access\Remote Access Clients node.

Configuring the RADIUS Server for Dial-up Connections

Dial-up servers function exactly like wireless access points or any other access point and can submit RADIUS requests to the computer running Windows Server 2008. Although users can dial directly into a modem attached to a dial-in server, most organizations that require more than one or two dial-up connections use dedicated hardware known as a modem bank. Modem banks accept dial-up connections and submit authentication requests to a RADIUS server in much the same way as a wireless access point.

Some organizations will have an ISP manage the modem bank and accept the dial-up connections. In this scenario, the ISP can typically configure its modem bank to send authentication requests to a RADIUS server (such as a Windows Server 2008 computer) on your internal network. In this way, users can log on to the dial-up connection using their Active Directory credentials, rather than requiring a separate set of credentials for the ISP. This also allows you to add and remove users without contacting the ISP. Figure 7-11 illustrates this scenario. In this case, have the ISP provide the realm name it is using for the modem bank.

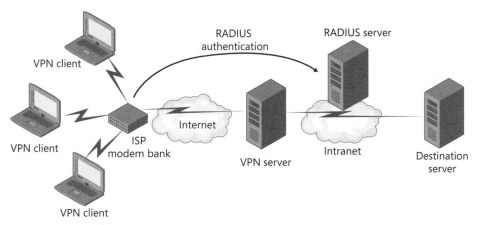

Figure 7-11   Outsourcing dial-up modems while controlling authentication

To configure a Windows Server 2008 computer to act as a RADIUS server for a modem bank or other dial-up server, follow these steps:

1. If you haven't already, create a user group for users who will be granted dial-up access. Then, configure the server with a static IP address.

2. In Server Manager, expand Roles, expand Network Policy And Access Services, and then select NPS.

3. In the details pane, under Standard Configuration, select RADIUS Server For Dial-Up Or VPN Connections. Then, click Configure VPN Or Dial-Up.

    The Configure VPN Or Dial-Up Wizard appears.

4. On the Select Dial-up Or Virtual Private Network Connections Type page, select Dial-Up Connections. Optionally, type a name. Click Next.

5. On the Specify Dial-Up Or VPN Server page, you will configure your modem banks as valid RADIUS clients. Follow these steps for each modem bank, and then click Next:

    a. Click Add.

    b. In the New RADIUS client dialog box, in the Friendly Name box, type a name that identifies that specific modem bank.

    c. In the Address box, type the host name or IP address that identifies the modem bank.

    d. In the Shared Secret group, click the Generate option button to have a complex shared secret automatically generated. Alternatively, you can click Manual and type your own shared secret twice. Write the key down for later use; you'll need to enter it when configuring your modem bank.

    e. Click OK.

6. On the Configure Authentication Methods page, select the authentication method you want to use. Click Next.

7. On the Specify User Groups page, click Add. In the Select Group dialog box, type the name of the group you created for users who are allowed to connect using dial-up, and then click OK. Click Next.

8. On the Specify IP Filters page, as shown in Figure 7-12, click the Input Filters button or the Output Filters button to filter traffic going to or from remote access clients (using either IPv4 or IPv6). Typically, this is not required for intranet scenarios. However, to limit security risks, you might use this capability to prevent dial-up users from accessing specific IP addresses or networks containing highly confidential resources. Alternatively, you could limit dial-up users to accessing only specific resources by selecting the Permit Only The Packets Listed Below option on the Inbound Filters or Outbound Filters dialog box and listing those networks dial-up users are allowed to access. Click Next.

Figure 7-12   The Specify IP Filters page

9. On the Specify Encryption Settings page, select the check boxes for the encryption levels that you want to support. Click Next.

10. On the Specify A Realm Name page, type the realm name provided by your ISP if your ISP is managing the modem bank. Otherwise, leave the Realm Name box blank. Click Next.

11. On the Completing New Dial-Up Or Virtual Private Network Connections And RADIUS Clients page, click Finish.

Configure the modem bank to submit RADIUS requests to your server with the shared secret you selected.

Configuring the Dial-up Client

From a Windows Vista or Windows Server 2008 computer, you can manually create a dial-up connection by following these steps:

1. Click Start, and then choose Connect To.

2. On the Connect To A Network page, click the Set Up A Connection Or Network link.

3. On the Choose A Connection Option page, select Set Up A Dial-Up Connection, and then click Next.

4. On the Set Up A Dial-up Connection page, type the dial-up phone number (including a 1, 9, or other dialing prefix that might be required by the phone system). Then, type the user name and password. If multiple users on the computer will use the same connection and you have administrative credentials, select the Allow Other People To Use This Connection check box. Click Connect.

    Windows will immediately attempt to connect.

5. After Windows is connected, click Close.

Configuring VPN Connections

Windows Server 2008 and Windows Vista support three VPN technologies:

■ **Point-to-Point Tunneling Protocol (PPTP)**   A Microsoft VPN technology that is now widely supported by non-Microsoft operating systems. PPTP uses Point-to-Point Protocol (PPP) authentication methods for user-level authentication and Microsoft Point-to-Point Encryption (MPPE) for data encryption. PPTP does not require a client certificate when using PEAP-MS-CHAP v2, EAP-MS-CHAP v2, or MS-CHAP v2 for authentication.

■ **Layer Two Tunneling Protocol (L2TP)**   An open standards VPN technology that is widely supported by both Microsoft and non-Microsoft operating systems. L2TP uses PPP authentication methods for user-level authentication and IPsec for computer-level peer authentication, data authentication, data integrity, and data encryption. L2TP requires both the VPN clients and servers to have computer certificates. Most organizations implement this using Active Directory Certificate Services, exactly as you configured in Lesson 2, "Configuring Wireless Networks." L2TP is the only VPN technology that can be used across the IPv6 Internet.

■ **Secure Socket Tunneling Protocol (SSTP)**   SSTP uses PPP authentication methods for user-level authentication and Hypertext Transfer Protocol (HTTP) encapsulation over a Secure Sockets Layer (SSL) channel for data authentication, data integrity, and data encryption. Using HTTP encapsulation allows SSTP to traverse many firewalls, NATs, and proxy servers that would cause PPTP and L2TP to fail. SSTP is supported only by Windows Server 2008 (as a VPN server or client) and Windows Vista with Service Pack 1 (as a VPN client). SSTP requires that the VPN server has a computer certificate installed and that clients trust the CA that issued the computer certificate. Most organizations implement this using Active Directory Certificate Services, exactly as you configured in Lesson 2, "Configuring Wireless Networks" (except that autoenrollment of client computers is not required).

By default, a Windows Server 2008 VPN server supports each of these three VPN technologies simultaneously, although you can selectively disable them. The sections that follow describe how to configure VPN servers and clients.

MORE INFO   VPN servers

For extremely detailed information about planning, configuring, and managing Windows Server 2008 VPN servers, read Chapter 12, "Remote Access VPN Connections," in *Windows Server 2008 Networking and Network Access Protection* by Joseph Davies and Tony Northrup (Microsoft Press, 2008).

Configuring the VPN Server

Configuring a VPN server is very similar to configuring a dial-up server. First, configure the VPN server with at least two network adapters. Connect one network adapter to the public Internet—this interface will accept incoming VPN connections and should have a static IP address. Connect the second network adapter to your intranet—this interface will forward traffic between the VPN and your network resources. Then, add the Network Policy And Access Services role, as described in "Configuring the RADIUS Server" in the previous lesson.

Next, you need to enable demand-dial routing on the server by following these steps:

1. In Server Manager, right-click Roles\Network Policy And Access Services\Routing And Remote Access, and then choose Configure And Enable Routing And Remote Access.

2. On the Welcome To The Routing And Remote Access Server Setup Wizard page, click Next.

3. On the Configuration page, select Remote Access, and then click Next.

4. On the Remote Access page, select the VPN check box, and then click Next.

5. On the VPN Connection page, select the network adapter that connects the server to the Internet. Then, click Next.

6. On the Network Selection page, select the interface that connects the server to the internal network.

7. On the IP Address Assignment page, select Automatically if there is already a DHCP server on the network. If you want the dial-up server to assign IP addresses from a pool not already assigned to a DHCP server, select From A Specified Range Of Addresses. Click Next.

8. If the Address Range Assignment page appears, click New, type an IP address range, and then click OK. Add as many address ranges as required. Click Next.

9. On the Managing Multiple Remote Access Servers page, you will choose how VPN users are authenticated. If you have a separate RADIUS server, select Yes. If you want Routing And Remote Access to perform the authentication (which is fine for Active Directory domain authentication), select No. Then, click Next.

10. Click Finish. If prompted, click OK.

Now you can click the Roles\Network Policy And Access Services\Routing And Remote Access\Ports node to view the list of VPN ports available to accept incoming VPN connections. By default, Windows Server 2008 creates 128 ports for each of the three VPN technologies. Each VPN connection requires a single port. To add or remove ports, right-click Ports, and then click Properties. In the Ports Properties dialog box, click the port type you want to adjust, and then click Configure.

When you configure a computer as a VPN server, Windows Server 2008 automatically configures a DHCP relay agent. If the VPN server is a DHCP client at the time the Routing And Remote Access Server Setup Wizard is run, the wizard automatically configures the DHCP Relay Agent with the IPv4 address of a DHCP server. If you need to change the IP address later, edit the DHCP relay agent properties using the Roles\Network Policy And Access Services\Routing And Remote Access\IPv4\DHCP Relay Agent node. For more information about DHCP, refer to Chapter 4, "Installing and Configuring a DHCP Server."

Configuring VPN Packet Filters

After configuring the VPN server to accept incoming VPN connections, you will no longer be able to ping the VPN server on the Internet interface because the Routing And Remote Access Server Setup Wizard creates filters to block all incoming traffic except incoming VPN connections. If you are running a Web server, e-mail server, or other services on the VPN server, you must manually add packet filters and exceptions for Windows Firewall to allow the traffic to and from the other services.

To change the inbound filters, follow these steps:

1. In Server Manager, select either Roles\Network Policy And Access Services\Routing And Remote Access\IPv4\General (for IPv4 traffic) or Roles\Network Policy And Access Services\Routing And Remote Access\IPv6\General (for IPv6 traffic).

2. In the Details pane, right-click your Internet interface, and then choose Properties. The properties dialog box for the network interface appears.

3. In the General tab, click the Inbound Filters button.

4. In the Inbound Filters dialog box, as shown in Figure 7-13, update, add, or remove filters as necessary. Then, click OK.

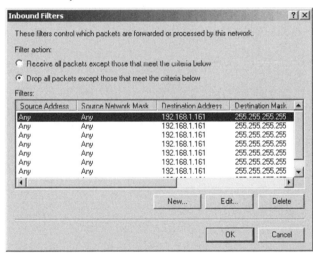

Figure 7-13   Configuring inbound filters

5. In the General tab, you can also click the Outbound Filters button to configure outbound packet filtering.

6. Click OK again.

Configuring the VPN Client

First, grant VPN users remote access. In Active Directory domain environments, you can do this by editing the user's properties, selecting the Dial-in tab, and then selecting Allow Access.

To connect a VPN client to your VPN server, follow these steps:

1. On the VPN client computer, click Start, and then choose Connect To.
    The Connect To A Network Wizard appears.
2. On the Disconnect Or Connect To Another Network page, click Set Up A Connection or Network.
3. On the Choose A Connection Option page, select Connect To A Workplace, and then click Next.
4. If the Do You Want To Use A Connection That You Already Have page appears, click No, Create A New Connection, and then click Next.
5. On the How Do You Want To Connect page, click Use My Internet Connection (VPN).
6. On the Type The Internet Address To Connect To page, type the IP address of your VPN server's network adapter that is connected to your internal network. Then, click Next.
7. On the Type Your User Name And Password page, type the user name, password, and domain. Select the Remember This Password check box. Then, click Connect.
8. After the connection is established, click Close.
9. On the Set Network Location page, choose the network profile type for the VPN. Typically, this should be Work.
10. When prompted, click Close.

In the future, you can connect to the VPN by clicking Start and clicking Connect To to open the Connect To A Network wizard. Then, click the VPN connection you created and click Connect.

Troubleshooting VPN Connection Problems

Windows Server 2008 adds VPN connection events to the System event log. As shown in Figure 7-14, these events have a Source of RemoteAccess and provide a description of any authentication errors.

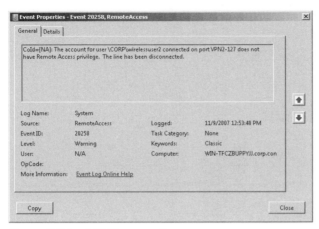

Figure 7-14 A VPN connection error

Configuring Connection Restrictions

Whether you configure dial-up, VPN, or wireless connections, you can configure network policies to control access based on time of day, day of week, user name, domain, or dozens of other factors. This can also be used to restrict wireless access—for example, to disable wireless networks after hours when attackers are more likely to be connecting than legitimate users.

To configure an existing network policy, follow these steps:

1. Click Start, and then click Server Manager.
2. In Server Manager, select Roles\Policies\Network Policies.
3. In the details pane, double-click the policy that you want to update.
   The properties dialog box for the connection appears.
4. Select the Conditions tab. This tab shows the default conditions that the wizard creates when you initially configured the server.
5. Click the Add button.
6. In the Select Condition tab, you can create conditions that must be matched before the policy applies to the connection. Select one of the following conditions, and then click Add. The most commonly used conditions (not including conditions related to NAP, which are discussed in Chapter 8, "Configuring Windows Firewall and Network Access Protection") are:
   - ❏ **Windows Groups, Machine Groups, and User Groups**   Requires the computer or user to belong to a specified group.
   - ❏ **Day And Time Restrictions**   Restricts connections based on day of week or time of day, as shown in Figure 7-15. This is useful if you allow dial-up connections only

after hours. You can also configure day and time restrictions using the Constraints tab.

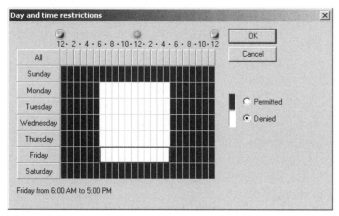

Figure 7-15 Restricting connections to specific days and times

❏ **Access Client IPv4 Address and Access Client IPv6 Address** Control access based on the IP address of the client when the Windows Server 2008 computer is acting as a VPN server. This condition is primarily useful for remote access VPN connections.

❏ **Client IPv4 Address and Client IPv6 Address** Control access based on the IP address of the client when the Windows Server 2008 computer is acting as a RADIUS server. This condition is primarily useful for remote access VPN connections.

❏ **NAS IPv4 Address and NAS IPv6 Address** Control access based on the IP address of the wireless access point (or other network access server).

❏ **Authentication Type, Allowed EAP Types, Framed Protocol, Service Type, and Tunnel Type** Require specific protocols or authentication methods. This condition is primarily useful for remote access VPN connections. You can also configure authentication method restrictions using the Constraints tab.

❏ **Calling Station ID** When caller ID exists for a dial-up connection, this allows you to accept connections only from a specific phone number. This is primarily useful for demand-dial routing connections, although you can use it for dial-up remote access connections if you know in advance all phone numbers in use by clients.

❏ **NAS Port Type** Applies the policy only if the Network Access Server (NAS) port type matches. Use this condition to restrict access to modems, wireless access points, or VPN connections. You can also configure NAS port type restrictions using the Constraints tab.

7. In the Constraints tab, you can set an idle timeout (which disconnects idle sessions, primarily for use with dial-up connections) or a session timeout (which ends a session after a specified amount of time, whether or not the connection is idle). You can also configure the Called Station ID, which identifies the phone number of the dial-up server (as opposed to the Calling Station ID condition, which identifies the phone number of the dial-up client). Additionally, although they are also available as conditions, you can configure authentication methods, day and time restrictions, and NAS port type constraints. Click OK.

8. In the Settings tab, you can configure NAP settings (described in Chapter 8, "Configuring Windows Firewall and Network Access Protection") and RADIUS attributes (which might be required by specific RADIUS clients but are not typically used). For dial-up connections, click Multilink And Bandwidth Allocation Protocol (BAP) to configure whether clients with access to multiple modems and multiple phone lines can establish multiple dial-up connections for increased bandwidth and at what bandwidth threshold you disconnect any unused circuits. To configure packet filtering for this connection type, click IP Filters. Click Encryption to configure encryption requirements. Click IP settings to specify whether the client may request an IP address (typically, you will not change the default setting of Server Settings Determine IP Address Assignment).

9. Click OK.

Testing Connectivity

After they are connected, most users want to immediately verify connectivity. The most straightforward and reliable way to check connectivity is to attempt to connect to an internal resource. For example, the user could open a Web browser and attempt to open an internal Web page. If the Web page opens, it shows that connectivity is in place, name resolution is occurring correctly, and internal services are accessible.

If application layer services are not available, begin by examining the current configuration. Then, use IP troubleshooting tools to isolate which components are working correctly and which are not.

IPConfig

IPConfig is a command-line tool for displaying the current IP address configuration. To quickly retrieve a list of IP addresses and default gateways for each network adapter (including dial-up and VPN connections), run the following command:

```
ipconfig
```

IPConfig displays output that resembles the following:

```
Windows IP Configuration

PPP adapter VPN Connection:
   Connection-specific DNS Suffix  . :
   IPv4 Address. . . . . . . . . . : 192.168.2.103
   Subnet Mask . . . . . . . . . . : 255.255.255.255
   Default Gateway . . . . . . . . :

Ethernet adapter Local Area Connection:
   Connection-specific DNS Suffix  . : hsd1.nh.contoso.com.
   IPv4 Address. . . . . . . . . . : 192.168.1.197
   Subnet Mask . . . . . . . . . . : 255.255.255.0
   Default Gateway . . . . . . . . : 192.168.1.1

Wireless LAN adapter Wireless Network Connection:
   Connection-specific DNS Suffix  . : hsd1.nh.contoso.com.
   Link-local IPv6 Address . . . . . : fe80::462:7ed4:795b:1c9f%8
   IPv4 Address. . . . . . . . . . : 192.168.1.142
   Subnet Mask . . . . . . . . . . : 255.255.255.0
   Default Gateway . . . . . . . . : 192.168.1.1
```

For more detailed configuration information, including DNS and DHCP servers, run the following command:

ipconfig /all

```
Windows IP Configuration

   Host Name . . . . . . . . . . . : ClientComputer
   Primary Dns Suffix  . . . . . . :
   Node Type . . . . . . . . . . . : Hybrid
   IP Routing Enabled. . . . . . . : No
   WINS Proxy Enabled. . . . . . . : No
   DNS Suffix Search List. . . . . : hsd1.nh.contoso.com.

PPP adapter VPN Connection:

   Connection-specific DNS Suffix  . :
   Description . . . . . . . . . . : VPN Connection
   Physical Address. . . . . . . . :
   DHCP Enabled. . . . . . . . . . : No
   Autoconfiguration Enabled . . . . : Yes
   IPv4 Address. . . . . . . . . . : 192.168.2.103(Preferred)
   Subnet Mask . . . . . . . . . . : 255.255.255.255
   Default Gateway . . . . . . . . :
   DNS Servers . . . . . . . . . . : 10.100.100.201
                                      10.100.100.204
   Primary WINS Server . . . . . . : 10.100.100.201
   Secondary WINS Server . . . . . : 10.100.100.204
   NetBIOS over Tcpip. . . . . . . : Enabled
```

```
Ethernet adapter Local Area Connection:

   Connection-specific DNS Suffix  . : hsd1.nh.contoso.com.
   Description . . . . . . . . . . : 57xx Gigabit Controller
   Physical Address. . . . . . . . : 00-15-C5-08-82-F3
   DHCP Enabled. . . . . . . . . . : Yes
   Autoconfiguration Enabled . . . . : Yes
   IPv4 Address. . . . . . . . . . : 192.168.1.197(Preferred)
   Subnet Mask . . . . . . . . . . : 255.255.255.0
   Lease Obtained. . . . . . . . . : Tuesday, November 06, 2007 6:16:30 AM
   Lease Expires . . . . . . . . . : Wednesday, November 07, 2007 6:16:29 AM
   Default Gateway . . . . . . . . : 192.168.1.1
   DHCP Server . . . . . . . . . . : 192.168.1.1
   DNS Servers . . . . . . . . . . : 192.168.1.1
   NetBIOS over Tcpip. . . . . . . : Enabled

Wireless LAN adapter Wireless Network Connection:

   Connection-specific DNS Suffix  . : hsd1.nh.contoso.com.
   Description . . . . . . . . . . : Wireless 3945ABG Network Connection
   Physical Address. . . . . . . . : 00-13-02-1E-E6-59
   DHCP Enabled. . . . . . . . . . : Yes
   Autoconfiguration Enabled . . . . : Yes
   Link-local IPv6 Address . . . . . : fe80::462:7ed4:795b:1c9f%8(Preferred)
   IPv4 Address. . . . . . . . . . : 192.168.1.142(Preferred)
   Subnet Mask . . . . . . . . . . : 255.255.255.0
   Lease Obtained. . . . . . . . . : Tuesday, November 06, 2007 6:19:17 AM
   Lease Expires . . . . . . . . . : Wednesday, November 07, 2007 6:19:16 AM
   Default Gateway . . . . . . . . : 192.168.1.1
   DHCP Server . . . . . . . . . . : 192.168.1.1
   DHCPv6 IAID . . . . . . . . . . : 101554242
   DNS Servers . . . . . . . . . . : 192.168.1.1
   NetBIOS over Tcpip. . . . . . . : Enabled

Tunnel adapter Local Area Connection*:

   Media State . . . . . . . . . . : Media disconnected
   Connection-specific DNS Suffix  . :
   Description . . . . . . . . . . : isatap.hsd1.nh.contoso.com.
   Physical Address. . . . . . . . : 00-00-00-00-00-00-00-E0
   DHCP Enabled. . . . . . . . . . : No
   Autoconfiguration Enabled . . . . : Yes
```

If you establish a connection but fail to retrieve an IP address from a DHCP server (a scenario that is more common on LANs than on VPNs), run the following commands to give up your current DHCP-assigned IP addresses and attempt to retrieve new addresses:

```
ipconfig /release
ipconfig /renew
```

Ping

The Ping tool uses Internet Control Message Protocol (ICMP) to contact remote hosts and show how long it took to receive a response from the remote host. Typically, you ping your default gateway, DNS server, or another server that you know responds to pings. For example:

ping 192.168.1.1

```
Pinging 192.168.1.1 with 32 bytes of data:
Reply from 192.168.1.1: bytes=32 time<1ms TTL=64
Reply from 192.168.1.1: bytes=32 time<1ms TTL=64
Reply from 192.168.1.1: bytes=32 time<1ms TTL=64
Reply from 192.168.1.1: bytes=32 time<1ms TTL=64

Ping statistics for 192.168.1.1:
    Packets: Sent = 4, Received = 4, Lost = 0 (0% loss),
Approximate round trip times in milli-seconds:
    Minimum = 0ms, Maximum = 0ms, Average = 0ms
```

This demonstrates that the host with an IP address of 192.168.1.1 is responding to network communications. The following output demonstrates that a host could not be reached, which might be a sign that the network has failed or that the remote host is offline:

ping 192.168.1.2

```
Pinging 192.168.1.2 with 32 bytes of data:
Request timed out.
Request timed out.
Request timed out.
Request timed out.
Ping statistics for 192.168.1.2:
    Packets: Sent = 4, Received = 0, Lost = 4 (100% loss),
```

If a host responds to pings, you know that host is at least connected to the network and online. If a host doesn't respond to pings, it could be any of the following:

- The host you are pinging is offline.
- The client is not connected to the network, or the client's network settings are misconfigured.
- The network has a problem, such as a routing error.

- The host you are pinging is configured to drop ICMP communications.
- A firewall between the client and the host you are pinging is configured to drop ICMP communications.

Familiarize yourself with hosts on your network that respond to pings so that you can ping those specific hosts and be sure that failure to respond to a ping is not caused by firewall configuration.

Tracert

Tracert performs Ping tests for every router between the client and destination host. This allows you to identify the path packets take, to isolate possible routing problems, and to determine the source of performance problems. For example:

tracert www.microsoft.com

```
Tracing route to www.microsoft.com [10.46.19.254]
over a maximum of 30 hops:

  1    22 ms    24 ms     7 ms  c-3-0-ubr01.winchendon.contoso.com [10.165.8.1]
  2     7 ms    19 ms    18 ms  ge-1-2-ur01.winchendon.contoso.com [10.87.148.129]
  3    13 ms     9 ms     9 ms  ge-1-1-ur01.gardner.contoso.com [10.87.144.225]
  4    10 ms    17 ms     9 ms  te-9-1-ur01.sterling.contoso.com [10.87.144.217]
  5     8 ms     8 ms     8 ms  te-9-2-ur01.marlboro.contoso.com [10.87.144.77]
  6    17 ms    17 ms    14 ms  te-8-1-ur01.natick.contoso.com [10.87.144.197]
  7    23 ms    38 ms    35 ms  te-8-3-ar02.woburn.contoso.com [10.87.145.9]
  8    23 ms    16 ms    18 ms  po-12-ar02.needham.contoso.com [10.87.146.45]
  9    16 ms    19 ms    13 ms  po-11-ar01.needham.contoso.com [10.87.146.37]
 10    13 ms    11 ms    14 ms  po-10-ar01.springfield.contoso.com [10.87.146.22]
 11    23 ms    15 ms    14 ms  po-11-ar01.chartford.contoso.com [10.87.146.26]
 12     *         *       16 ms  edge1.NewYork2.Fabricam.com [10.71.186.10]
 13    17 ms    17 ms    15 ms  edge1.NewYork2.Fabricam.com [10.71.186.9]
 14    22 ms    18 ms    16 ms  bbr2.NewYork1.Fabricam.com [10.68.16.130]
 15   109 ms   103 ms    98 ms  SanJose1.Fabricam.com [10.159.1.130]
 16    92 ms    91 ms   105 ms  SanJose1.Fabricam.com [10.68.18.62]
 17    90 ms    91 ms    91 ms  www.microsoft.com [10.68.123.2]
```

NOTE **Preventing Tracert from performing DNS lookups**

To improve Tracert performance, add the -d parameter before the IP address.

Each host that Tracert displays is a router that forwards packets between your computer and the destination. Typically, the first host will be your default gateway, and the last host will be the destination.

Tracert pings each host three times and reports the number of milliseconds the host took to respond. Typically, hosts farther down the list take longer to respond because they are farther away from your computer. An asterisk indicates that a host failed to respond. The last host will always be the target computer you specify. If that computer is offline or does not respond to ICMP requests, Tracert will display a series of Request Timed Out messages.

As an alternative to Tracert, you can use PathPing. The PathPing tool functions similarly but spends several minutes performing performance testing for more accurate latency information.

PRACTICE Establishing a Remote Access VPN Connection

In this practice, you configure a VPN server, and then connect to the VPN server from a client computer.

▶ **Exercise 1   Configure a VPN Server**

In this exercise, you configure Dcsrv1 as a VPN server to accept incoming connections. Dcsrv1 must have two network adapters: one network adapter that is connected to your internal network (or the public Internet) and a second, private network adapter. You will connect Boston, the VPN client, to the private network adapter and verify VPN connectivity by establishing a VPN connection and connecting to resources on the Internet.

This exercise assumes that you have completed Exercise 1 in the previous lesson. If you have not completed that exercise, add the Network Policy And Access Services role before completing this exercise with the Routing And Remote Access Services role service.

1. Using Server Manager on Dcsrv1, create a group named "VPN Users." Then, create a user account named VPNUser with a complex password. Add the VPNUser account to the Domain Users and VPN Users groups.

   Next, you need to enable demand-dial routing on the server by following these steps:

2. In Server Manager, right-click Roles\Network Policy And Access Services\Routing And Remote Access, and then choose Disable Routing And Remote Access (if necessary). Then, confirm the dialog box that appears. Disabling routing and remote access allows you to reconfigure it as if it were a newly configured computer.

3. Right-click Roles\Network Policy And Access Services\Routing And Remote Access, and then choose Configure And Enable Routing And Remote Access.

4. On the Welcome To The Routing And Remote Access Server Setup Wizard page, click Next.

5. On the Configuration page, select Remote Access, and then click Next.

6. On the Remote Access page, select VPN, and then click Next.

7. On the VPN Connection page, select the network adapter that connects the server to the Internet. Click Next.

8. On the Network Selection page, select the interface that connects the server to the internal network.

9. On the IP Address Assignment page, select Automatically, and then click Next. If you do not have a DHCP server, click From A Specified Range Of Addresses, click Next, complete the Address Range Assignment page, and click Next again.

10. On the Managing Multiple Remote Access Servers page, select No, and then click Next.

11. On the Completing The Routing And Remote Access Server Setup Wizard page, click Finish.

12. In the Routing And Remote Access dialog box, click OK.

13. Click the Roles\Network Policy And Access Services\Routing And Remote Access\Ports node to view the list of VPN ports available to accept incoming VPN connections.

▶ **Exercise 2 Configure a VPN Client**

In this exercise, you configure Boston as a VPN client.

1. On the Boston VPN client computer, click Start, and then choose Connect To.
   The Connect To A Network Wizard appears.

2. On the Disconnect Or Connect To Another Network page, click Set Up A Connection or Network.

3. On the Choose A Connection Option page, click Connect To A Workplace, and then click Next.

4. If the Do You Want To Use A Connection That You Already Have page appears, click No, Create A New Connection, and then click Next.

5. On the How Do You Want To Connect page, click Use My Internet Connection.

6. On the Type The Internet Address To Connect To page, type the IP address of your VPN server's network adapter that is connected to your internal network. Click Next.

7. On the Type Your User Name And Password page, type the user name, password, and domain. Select the Remember This Password check box. Then, click Connect.

8. After the connection is established, click Close.

9. On the Set Network Location page, click Work.

10. When prompted, click Close.

11. Open a command prompt and ping the internal interface on the VPN server—the IP address you did not connect directly to. The server should reply to the Ping request, indicating that you have successfully established a VPN connection and that the VPN server is routing communications correctly.

12. On the VPN server, in Server Manager, click Roles\Network Policy And Access Services \Routing And Remote Access\Remote Access Clients. Notice that the Details pane shows the single VPN connection. Right-click the connection, and then click Disconnect.

13. Notice that the client displays the Network Connections dialog box, prompting the user to reconnect.

You can also disconnect a VPN connection from the client by clicking Start, clicking Connect To, clicking the VPN connection, and then clicking the Disconnect button.

Lesson Summary

- Dial-up connections provide remote connectivity to your internal network without requiring you to connect to the Internet. VPN connections use the Internet to tunnel encryption communications from the client to the internal network.

- Windows Server 2008 can act as either a dial-up server or a RADIUS server to authenticate a separate dial-up server. To configure a Windows Server 2008 computer to accept dial-up connections, you must connect one or more modems to it.

- Windows Server 2008 can act as a VPN server and accept PPTP, L2TP, and SSTP connections. PPTP provides simple Windows authentication. L2TP, which is based on IPsec, requires client certificates for authentication and thus requires you to implement a PKI. SSTP is supported only by Windows Vista and Windows Server 2008, and it provides VPN connectivity across proxy servers and firewalls.

Lesson Review

You can use the following questions to test your knowledge of the information in Lesson 3, "Connecting to Remote Networks." The questions are also available on the companion CD if you prefer to review them in electronic form.

NOTE   Answers

Answers to these questions and explanations of why each answer choice is correct or incorrect are located in the "Answers" section at the end of the book.

---

1. You are a systems engineer for a paper sales company. Frequently, your sales staff travels overnight and needs to connect to resources on your protected intranet. After discussions with some of the sales staff, you discover that they frequently use their mobile computers to connect to the Internet using wireless networks. At other times, hotels offer Ethernet connections with Internet access. Frequently, however, they have access only to a phone line that they can use to establish a dial-up connection. At any given time, 100 salespeople might need to connect, and at most 30 would need dial-up connections. Your organization is near the end of its fiscal year, and capital budget is tight. Therefore, you need to minimize up-front costs. What is the best way to configure remote access for the sales staff while using existing Active Directory user credentials? (Choose all that apply.)

    A. Connect a Windows Server 2008 computer to both the public Internet and your intranet. Then, configure it to accept incoming VPN connections.

    B. Connect a Windows Server 2008 computer to the public Internet. Then, configure it as a RADIUS server. Configure the client computers to submit RADIUS authentication requests to the server when they connect to remote networks.

    C. Configure a Windows Server 2008 computer to accept dial-up connections. Lease a circuit from your local telecommunications provider for 30 PSTN connections. Purchase a modem bank capable of accepting 30 simultaneous connections and connect it to the Windows Server 2008 computer.

    D. Establish an agreement with an ISP to provide dial-up access to your users. Then, configure a Windows Server 2008 computer as a RADIUS server. Have the ISP configure its modem bank to submit authentication requests to the RADIUS server.

2. You are a systems engineer evaluating remote access technologies. Which of the following statements comparing dial-up connections to VPN connections are true? (Choose all that apply.)

    A. VPN connections typically provide better performance than dial-up connections. However, dial-up connections are adequate for common tasks, including e-mail and streaming video.

    B. VPN connections require an existing Internet connection, while dial-up connections can completely bypass the Internet.

    C. Data sent across a VPN connection can be intercepted and interpreted by an attacker who has access to the ISP's infrastructure, whereas dial-up connections provide a much higher level of security by using the PSTN.

    D. Both VPN and dial-up connections can authenticate to the same, central RADIUS server. That RADIUS server can be hosted on a computer running Windows Server 2008.

3. You are a systems administrator for a large fabric manufacturing company. You need to allow sales people to connect to your VPN server while traveling. Many sales people have complained that they are unable to connect at times, and you have isolated the problem as being caused by firewalls that do not allow PPTP or L2TP traffic through. You would like to recommend that the sales staff use SSTP VPN connections. Which operating systems support SSTP VPN connections? (Choose all that apply.)

    A. Windows XP Professional

    B. Windows 2000 Professional

    C. Windows Vista with Service Pack 1

    D. Windows Server 2008

Chapter Review

To further practice and reinforce the skills you learned in this chapter, you can

- Review the chapter summary.
- Review the list of key terms introduced in this chapter.
- Complete the case scenarios. These scenarios set up real-world situations involving the topics of this chapter and ask you to create a solution.
- Complete the suggested practices.
- Take a practice test.

Chapter Summary

- NAT allows clients on an intranet with private IP addresses to access the Internet. NAT works like a router but replaces the client computer's private source IP address with its own public IP address. When the NAT server receives return packets, it identifies which connection the packet is associated with, replaces the destination IP address with the client's private IP address, and forwards the packet to the client computer on the intranet. You can configure a Windows Server 2008 computer as a NAT server, but most organizations prefer a router, firewall, or dedicated network device.

- Wireless connectivity is now a requirement for many organizations. To minimize the inherent security risks, use WPA-EAP security. When a wireless access point is configured to use WPA-EAP security, it must forward authentication requests to a RADIUS server. You can configure Windows Server 2008 as a RADIUS server and authenticate users with either domain credentials or client computer certificates. If you have existing RADIUS servers, you can configure Windows Server 2008 as a RADIUS proxy and forward RADIUS requests to the appropriate RADIUS server based on criteria such as the realm of the RADIUS request.

- When away from the office, users can access internal resources using either a dial-up or VPN connection. Windows Server 2008 can act as either a dial-up server, a VPN server, or a RADIUS server that authenticates requests from other dial-up or VPN servers.

Key Terms

Do you know what this key term means? You can check your answer by looking up the term in the glossary at the end of the book.

- latency

Case Scenarios

In the following case scenarios, you will apply what you've learned about how to connect computers to networks. You can find answers to these questions in the "Answers" section at the end of this book.

Case Scenario 1: Connecting a Branch Office to the Internet

You are a systems administrator for City Power & Light. Because your organization acquired a large block of public IP addresses from the Internet Assigned Numbers Authority (IANA) in the early 1980s, all of your hosts are configured with routed public IP addresses.

Because of recent changes to government regulations, your organization needs to open a small branch office. Currently, all of your IP addresses are routed to the headquarters, and you do not have any public IP address blocks available to assign to the branch office. However, after contacting a local ISP in the area, you learn that the DSL connection you plan to use includes one public IP address. You plan to deploy at least 50 computers to the office. You do not plan to host any servers at the office, and the only incoming connection from the Internet you plan to use is a VPN connection.

Your manager asks you to come by his office to discuss connectivity for the branch office. Answer the following questions for your manager:

1. Can we, and should we, get a block of public IP addresses for the branch office?
2. If we use private addresses on the intranet, how will client computers communicate on the Internet?
3. If we choose to use NAT, what technology should we use to implement it?

Case Scenario 2: Planning Remote Access

You are a systems administrator working for Humongous Insurance. Although your organization has always had sales staff who traveled with laptops, they have traditionally called their administrative assistants at your headquarters when they needed to access internal resources. Even sales staff who used mobile computers lacked a way to connect to your intranet.

Recently, the IT department has been posting a great deal of valuable information on your intranet, and your sales staff has requested the ability to connect to that information while they travel. You do have an Internet connection at your headquarters, and several servers are currently connected to both the public Internet and your intranet. Your manager asks you to interview key people and then come to her office to answer her questions about your design choices.

Interviews

Following is a list of company personnel interviewed and their statements:

- **Salesperson**   "I don't normally take my laptop to customer sites, but I do use my computer in my hotel room. The phone always has a data connection with a picture of a computer, and sometimes they have a network cable there, too. I've seen signs at some front desks showing that they had a wireless network available."

- **Sales Manager**   "My sales staff aren't the most technically sophisticated group, overall. However, we do have several team members who are very competent with their computers. For example, while I'm on a customer premises, I often hop on their wireless network to check my personal e-mail. In fact, I have my admin forward my work e-mail to my personal e-mail so that I can more easily check it while I'm traveling."

Questions

1. Which remote access technologies should we use?

2. If we use a VPN server, how will we configure it? I want to make sure users don't have to remember a separate user name and password.

3. I'm guessing that we need to support about 50 dial-in users simultaneously. What are our options for making that happen?

4. If one of our sales staff connects to a wireless network, can that person connect to a VPN from there?

Suggested Practices

To successfully master the Configuring Network Access exam objective, complete the following tasks.

Configure Wireless Access

For this task, you should complete at least Practice 1. For more experience about real-world wireless security risks, complete Practice 2.

- **Practice 1** Configure a Windows Server 2008 computer as a RADIUS server for a wireless network. First, configure the RADIUS server to authenticate users with domain credentials and use a client computer to connect to the wireless network. Next, configure the RADIUS server to authenticate users with certificates. Change the SSID of the wireless network (so that the wireless client will see it as a new network) and connect to the wireless network. Examine the event logs and view the information that Windows Server 2008 recorded about the authentication.

- **Practice 2** Configure a wireless access point to use 64-bit WEP security. Using the Internet, identify software tools used for cracking WEP security. Attempt to connect to the wireless access point using only the cracking tools you can find freely available on the Internet.

Configure Remote Access

For this task, you should complete all four practices.

- **Practice 1** Connect a modem to a Windows Server 2008 computer and connect the modem to a phone line. From a different phone line, dial in to the Windows Server 2008 computer and verify that you can connect to network resources.

- **Practice 2** Configure a Windows 98, a Windows 2000 Professional, or a Windows XP computer to connect to both a dial-up server and a VPN server.

- **Practice 3** Configure filters on a Windows Server 2008 VPN server so that it replies to ping requests on the Internet interface.

- **Practice 4** Without connecting to a VPN, use Tracert to determine the path between a client computer and a server on the Internet (such as *www.microsoft.com*). Next, connect to a VPN (preferably at a different location) and perform the Tracert command again. Notice how the route changes.

- **Practice 5**   Connect a Windows Vista or Windows Server 2008 VPN client to a network with a very restrictive firewall. Attempt to establish a VPN connection using either PPTP and L2TP; if the firewall is genuinely restrictive, it will block the connection. Next, attempt the same VPN connection using SSTP. Does it work?
- **Practice 6**   Establish a VPN connection. Then, run Network Monitor (available at *http://www.microsoft.com*) and capture the VPN communications. Examine the communications and verify that the traffic is encrypted.

Configure Network Authentication

For this task, you should complete Practice 1. For more experience about real-world security risks, complete Practice 2.

- **Practice 1**   Configure a Windows Server 2008 computer as a VPN server. Experiment with the different authentication protocols. Test connectivity using both PPTP and L2TP.
- **Practice 2**   Use the Internet to find tools that can crack MS-CHAP protected credentials. Attempt to capture and crack credentials by intercepting network communications, as if you were attacking your own network.

Take a Practice Test

The practice tests on this book's companion CD offer many options. For example, you can test yourself on just the content covered in this chapter, or you can test yourself on all the 70-642 certification exam content. You can set up the test so that it closely simulates the experience of taking a certification exam, or you can set it up in study mode so that you can look at the correct answers and explanations after you answer each question.

MORE INFO   Practice tests

For details about all the practice test options available, see "How to Use the Practice Tests" in this book's Introduction.

Chapter 8

Configuring Windows Firewall and Network Access Protection

By their nature, networks can allow healthy computers to communicate with unhealthy computers and malicious tools to attack legitimate applications. This can result in costly security compromises, such as a worm that spreads rapidly through an internal network or a sophisticated attacker who steals confidential data across the network.

Windows Server 2008 supports two technologies that are useful for improving network security: Windows Firewall and Network Access Protection (NAP). Windows Firewall can filter incoming and outgoing traffic, using complex criteria to distinguish between legitimate and potentially malicious communications. NAP requires computers to complete a health check before allowing unrestricted access to your network and facilitates resolving problems with computers that do not meet health requirements.

This lesson describes how to plan and implement Windows Firewall and NAP using Windows Server 2008.

Exam objectives in this chapter:
- Configure Network Access Protection (NAP).
- Configure firewall settings.

Lessons in this chapter:

Before You Begin

To complete the lessons in this chapter, you should be familiar with Microsoft Windows networking and be comfortable with the following tasks:

- Adding roles to a Windows Server 2008 computer
- Configuring Active Directory domain controllers and joining computers to a domain
- Basic network configuration, including configuring IP settings

You will also need the following nonproduction hardware connected to test networks:

1. A computer named Dcsrv1 that is a domain controller in the Nwtraders.msft domain. This computer must have at least one network interface that you can connect to either the Internet or a private network.

NOTE   Computer and domain names

The computer and domain names you use will not affect these exercises. The practices in this chapter refer to these computer names for simplicity, however.

---

2. A computer named Boston that is a member of the Nwtraders.msft domain.

Real World

Tony Northrup

Security is rarely black and white. Instead of absolutes, security can be measured only in degrees of risk. Although NAP can't prevent a determined, skilled attacker from connecting to your network, NAP can improve your network security by helping keep computers up-to-date and ensuring that legitimate users do not accidentally connect to your internal network without meeting your security requirements.

When evaluating NAP as a way to protect against malicious attackers, remember that NAP trusts the System Health Agent (SHA) to report on the health of the client. The SHA is also running on the client computer. So it's a bit like airport security merely asking people if they are carrying any banned substances—people without any malicious intent would happily volunteer anything they accidentally brought. People with malicious intent would simply lie.

It's not *quite* as easy as simply lying because the SHA signs the Statement of Health (SoH) to help prove that the health report is genuine. Additional security measures, such as requiring IPsec connection security, can help further reduce the opportunity for attackers. Nonetheless, with some time and effort, it's entirely possible that someone will create a malicious SHA that impersonates a legitimate SHA.

Lesson 1: Configuring Windows Firewall

Windows Firewall filters incoming traffic to help block unwanted network traffic. Optionally, Windows Firewall can also filter outgoing traffic to help limit the risk of malware. Although Windows Firewall's default settings will work well with components built into Windows, they might prevent other applications from functioning correctly. Windows Firewall's default settings can also be significantly improved to provide even stronger protection by requiring authorization or limiting the scope of allowed connections.

After this lesson, you will be able to:
- Describe the purpose of firewalls.
- List the three firewall profiles and how each is used.
- Create a firewall rule to allow inbound traffic.
- Create a firewall rule to allow outbound traffic and enable outbound filtering.
- Configure the scope of a firewall rule to limit communications to specific subnets.
- Configure firewall rules to require IPsec connection security and, optionally, limit authorization to specific users and computers.
- Use Group Policy settings to configure firewall rules in an Active Directory domain environment.
- Enable Windows Firewall logging so you can isolate problems related to firewall rules.
- Identify network communications used by a specific application so that you can create rules for the application.

Estimated lesson time: 45 minutes

Why Firewalls Are Important

In networking, *firewalls* analyze communications and drop packets that haven't been specifically allowed. This is an important task because connecting to the Internet means any of the millions of other Internet-connected computers can attack you. A successful compromise can crash a service or computer, compromise confidential data, or even allow the attacker to take complete control of the remote computer. In the case of *worms*, automated software attacks computers across the Internet, gains elevated privileges, copies itself to the compromised computer, and then begins attacking other computers (typically at random).

The purpose of a firewall is to drop unwanted traffic, such as traffic from worms, while allowing legitimate traffic, such as authorized file sharing. The more precisely you use firewall rules to identify legitimate traffic, the less you risk exposure to unwanted traffic from worms.

Firewall Profiles

When you create firewall rules to allow or block traffic, you can separately apply them to the Domain, Private, and Public profiles. These profiles enable mobile computers to allow incoming connections while connected to a domain network (for example, to allow incoming Remote Desktop connections) but block connection attempts on less-secure networks (such as public wireless hotspots).

The firewall profiles are:

- **Domain**   Applies when a computer is connected to its Active Directory domain. Specifically, any time a member computer's domain controller is accessible, this profile will be applied.
- **Private**   Applies when a computer is connected to a private network location. By default, no networks are considered private—users must specifically mark a network location, such as their home office network, as private.
- **Public**   The default profile applied to all networks when a domain controller is not available. For example, the Public profile is applied when users connect to Wi-Fi hotspots at airports or coffee shops. By default, the Public profile allows outgoing connections but blocks all incoming traffic that is not part of an existing connection.

Most servers will always be connected to a domain environment. To ensure consistent operation even if a domain controller is not available, configure the same firewall rules for all three profiles when configuring a server.

Filtering Inbound Traffic

By default, Windows Firewall (as well as most other firewalls) blocks any inbound traffic that hasn't been specifically allowed. By default, the Public profile allows absolutely no incoming connections—this provides excellent security when connecting to public hotspots or other untrusted networks. The Domain and Private profiles allow some incoming connections, such as connections for file and printer sharing.

If you install or enable a Windows feature that requires incoming connections, Windows will automatically enable the required firewall rules. Therefore, you do not need to manually adjust the firewall rules. Figure 8-1 shows the default inbound firewall rules for a Windows Server 2008 computer configured as a domain controller. As you can see, rules exist to allow each of the protocols required for a domain controller.

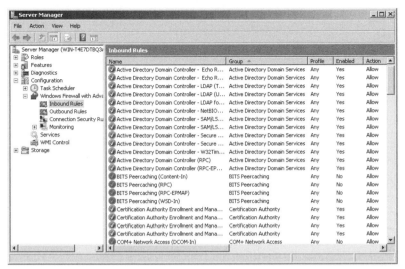

Figure 8-1   Default inbound firewall rules

If you install an application that does not automatically enable the required firewall rules, you will need to create the rules manually. You can create firewall rules using the stand-alone Windows Firewall With Advanced Security console, or you can apply the rules with Group Policy by using the same interface at Computer Configuration\Policies\Windows Settings\Security Settings\Windows Firewall With Advanced Security\Windows Firewall With Advanced Security.

To create an inbound filter, follow these steps:

1. In the Windows Firewall With Advanced Security snap-in, right-click Inbound Rules, and then choose New Rule.

   The New Inbound Rule Wizard appears.

2. On the Rule Type page, select one of the following options, and then click Next:

   ❑ **Program**   A rule that allows or blocks connections for a specific executable file, regardless of the port numbers it might use. You should use the Program rule type whenever possible. The only time it's not possible to use the Program rule type is when a service does not have its own executable.

   ❑ **Port**   A rule that allows or blocks communications for a specific TCP or UDP port number, regardless of the program generating the traffic.

❑ **Predefined**   A rule that controls connections for a Windows component, such as Active Directory Domain Services, File And Printer Sharing, or Remote Desktop. Typically, Windows enables these rules automatically.

❑ **Custom**   A rule that can combine program and port information.

3. Complete the following page or pages, which vary depending on the rule type you selected. Click Next.

4. On the Action page, select one of the following options, and then click Next.

   ❑ **Allow The Connection**   Allows any connection that matches the criteria you specified on the previous pages.

   ❑ **Allow The Connection If It Is Secure**   Allows connections that match the criteria you specified on the previous pages only if they are protected with IPsec. Optionally, you can select the Require The Connections To Be Encrypted check box, which requires encryption in addition to authentication. Selecting the Override Block Rules check box configures the rule to take precedence over other rules that might prevent a client from connecting. If you select this rule type, the wizard will also prompt you to select users and computers that are authorized to establish this type of connection.

   ❑ **Block The Connection**   Drops any connection attempt that matches the criteria you specified on the previous pages. Because inbound connections are blocked by default, you rarely need to create this rule type. However, you might use this action for an outbound rule if you specifically want to prevent an application from initiating outgoing connections.

5. On the Profile page, choose which profiles to apply the rule to. For servers, you should typically apply it to all three profiles because servers are typically continually connected to a single network. For mobile computers in domain environments, you typically need to apply firewall rules only to the Domain profile. If you do not have an Active Directory domain or if users need to use the firewall rule when connected to their home network, apply the rule to the Private profile. Avoid creating firewall rules on mobile computers for the Public profile because an attacker on an unprotected network might be able to exploit a vulnerability exposed by the firewall rule. Click Next.

6. On the Name page, type a name for the rule, and then click Finish.

The inbound rule takes effect immediately, allowing incoming connections that match the criteria you specified.

Filtering Outbound Traffic

By default, Windows Firewall allows all outbound traffic. Allowing outbound traffic is much less risky than allowing inbound traffic. However, outbound traffic still carries some risk:

- If malware infects a computer, it might send outbound traffic containing confidential data (such as content from a Microsoft SQL Server database, e-mail messages from a Microsoft Exchange server, or a list of passwords).
- Worms and viruses seek to replicate themselves. If they successfully infect a computer, they will attempt to send outbound traffic to infect other computers. After one computer on an intranet is infected, network attacks can allow malware to rapidly infect computers on an intranet.
- Users might use unapproved applications to send data to Internet resources and either knowingly or unknowingly transmit confidential data.

By default, all versions of Windows (including Windows Server 2008) do not filter outbound traffic. However, Windows Server 2008 does include outbound filters for core networking services, enabling you to quickly enable outbound filtering while retaining basic network functionality. By default, outbound rules are enabled for:

- Dynamic Host Configuration Protocol (DHCP) requests
- DNS requests
- Group Policy communications
- Internet Group Management Protocol (IGMP)
- IPv6 and related protocols

Blocking outbound communications by default will prevent many built-in Windows features, and all third-party applications you might install, from communicating on the network. For example, Windows Update will no longer be able to retrieve updates, Windows will no longer be able to activate across the Internet, and the computer will be unable to send SNMP alerts to a management host.

If you do enable outbound filtering, you must be prepared to test every application to verify that it runs correctly. Most applications are not designed to support outbound filtering and will require you to identify the firewall rules that need to be created and then create those rules.

To create an outbound filter, follow these steps:

1. In Windows Firewall With Advanced Security (which you can access in Server Manager under Configuration), right-click Outbound Rules, and then choose New Rule.
   The New Outbound Rule Wizard appears.

2. On the Rule Type page, select a rule type (as described in "Filtering Inbound Traffic" earlier in this lesson), and then click Next.

3. On the Program page, click This Program Path. In the box, type the path to the application's executable file. Click Next.

4. On the Action page, select an action type (as described in "Filtering Inbound Traffic" earlier in this lesson), and then click Next.

5. On the Profile page, select the check boxes for the profiles to apply the rule to, and then click Next.

6. On the Name page, type a name for the rule, and then click Finish.

The outbound rule takes effect immediately, allowing outgoing packets that match the criteria you specified.

To block outbound connections by default, first create and enable any outbound firewall rules so that applications do not immediately stop functioning. Then, follow these steps:

1. In Server Manager, right-click Configuration\Windows Firewall With Advanced Security, and then choose Properties.

2. Click the Domain Profile, Private Profile, or Public Profile tab.

3. From the Outbound Connections drop-down list, select Block. If necessary, return to the previous step to block outbound traffic for other profiles.

4. Click OK.

You will need to perform extensive testing to verify that all required applications function correctly when outbound connections are blocked by default. This testing should include background processes, such as Automatic Updates.

Configuring Scope

One of the most powerful ways to increase computer security is to configure firewall scope. Using scope, you can allow connections from your internal network and block connections from external networks. This can be used in the following ways:

■   For a server that is connected to the Internet, you can allow anyone on the Internet to connect to public services (such as the Web server) while allowing only users on your internal network to access private servers (such as Remote Desktop).

■   For internal servers, you can allow connections only from the specific subnets that contain potential users. When planning such scope limitations, remember to include remote access subnets.

■   For outgoing connections, you can allow an application to connect to servers only on specific internal subnets. For example, you might allow SNMP traps to be sent to only your SNMP management servers. Similarly, you might allow a network backup application to connect to only your backup servers.

■ For mobile computers, you can allow specific communications (such as Remote Desktop) from only the subnets you use for management.

To configure the scope of a rule, follow these steps:

1. In the Windows Firewall With Advanced Security snap-in, select Inbound Rules or Outbound Rules.
2. In the details pane, right-click the rule you want to configure, and then choose Properties.
3. Click the Scope tab. In the Remote IP Address group, select These IP Addresses.
4. In the Remote IP Address group, click Add.

NOTE Configuring scope for local IP addresses

The only time you would want to configure the scope using the Local IP Address group is when the computer is configured with multiple IP addresses, and you do not want to accept connections on all IP addresses.

---

5. In the IP Address dialog box, select one of the following three options, and then click OK:
   ❑ **This IP Address Or Subnet** Type an IP address (such as 192.168.1.22) or a subnet using Classless Inter-Domain Routing (CIDR) notation (such as 192.168.1.0/24) that should be allowed to use the firewall rule.
   ❑ **This IP Address Range** Using the From and To boxes, type the first and last IP address that should be allowed to use the firewall rule.
   ❑ **Predefined Set Of Computers.** Select a host from the list: Default Gateway, WINS Servers, DHCP Servers, DNS Servers, and Local Subnet.
6. Repeat steps 4 and 5 for any additional IP addresses that should be allowed to use the firewall rule.
7. Click OK.

Authorizing Connections

If you are using IPsec connection security in an Active Directory environment, you can also require the remote computer or user to be authorized before a connection can be established.

For example, imagine that your organization had a custom accounting application that used TCP port 1073, but the application had no access control mechanism—any user who connected to the network service could access confidential accounting data. Using Windows Firewall connection authorization, you could limit inbound connections to users who are members of the Accounting group—adding access control to the application without writing any additional code.

Most network applications do have access control built in, however. For example, you can configure Internet Information Server (a Web server installed as part of the Application Server role) to authenticate users and allow only authorized users to connect to a Web application. Similarly, if you share a folder on the network, you can use file permissions and share permissions to restrict who can access the folder. Application-layer authorization should always be your first layer of security; however, connection authorization using Windows Firewall can provide an additional layer of security. Using multiple layers of security, a technique known as *defense-in-depth*, reduces risk by providing protection even if one layer has a vulnerability.

To configure connection authorization for a firewall rule, follow these steps:

1. In Server Manager, select Configuration\Windows Firewall With Advanced Security\Inbound Rules or Configuration\Windows Firewall With Advanced Security\Outbound Rules.

2. In the details pane, right-click the rule you want to configure, and then choose Properties.

3. Click the General tab. Select Allow Only Secure Connections. Because the authorization relies on IPsec, you can configure authorization only on secure connections.

4. Click the Users And Computers tab for an inbound rule or the Computers tab for an outbound rule.

   ❑ **To allow connections only from specific computers**   Select the Only Allow Connections From These Computers check box for an inbound rule or the Only Allow Connections To These Computers check box for an outbound rule.

   ❑ **To allow connections only from specific users**   If you are editing an inbound rule, select the Only Allow Connections From These Users check box. You can use this option only for inbound connections.

5. Click Add and select the groups containing the users or computers you want to authorize. Figure 8-2 shows how the Users And Computers tab appears after you have configured connections for an inbound rule. Click OK.

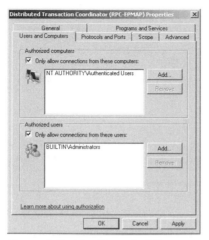

Figure 8-2   The Users And Computers tab

6.   Click OK again.

Any future connections that match the firewall rule will require IPsec for the connection to be established. Additionally, if the authenticated computer or user is not on the list of authorized computers and users that you specified, the connection will be immediately dropped.

Configuring Firewall Settings with Group Policy

You can configure Windows Firewall either locally, using Server Manager or the Windows Firewall With Advanced Security console in the Administrative Tools folder, or using the Computer Configuration\Policies\Windows Settings\Security Settings\Windows Firewall With Advanced Security\Windows Firewall With Advanced Security node of a Group Policy Object (GPO). Typically, you will configure policies that apply to groups of computers (including IPsec connection security policies) by using GPOs and edit server-specific policies (such as configuring the range of IP addresses a DNS server accepts queries from) by using local tools.

You can use Group Policy to manage Windows Firewall settings for computers running Windows Vista and Windows Server 2008 by using two nodes:

- **Computer Configuration\Policies\Windows Settings\Security Settings\Windows Firewall With Advanced Security\Windows Firewall With Advanced Security**   This node applies settings only to computers running Windows Vista and Windows Server 2008 and provides exactly the same interface as the same node in Server Manager. You should always use this node when configuring Windows Vista and Windows Server 2008 computers because it provides for more detailed configuration of firewall rules.

- **Computer Configuration\Policies\Administrative Templates\Network\Network Connections \Windows Firewall** This node applies settings to computers running Windows XP, Windows Server 2003, Windows Vista, and Windows Server 2008. This tool is less flexible than the Windows Firewall With Advanced Security console; however, settings apply to all versions of Windows that support Windows Firewall. If you are not using the new IPsec features in Windows Vista, you can use this node to configure all your clients.

For best results, create separate GPOs for Windows Vista/Windows Server 2008 and Windows XP/Windows Server 2003. Then, use WMI queries to target the GPOs to computers running only the appropriate version of Windows.

MORE INFO Creating WMI queries

For more information, read Microsoft Knowledge Base article 555253, "HOWTO: Leverage Group Policies with WMI Filters" at *http://support.microsoft.com/kb/555253*.

Enabling Logging for Windows Firewall

If you are ever unsure about whether Windows Firewall is blocking or allowing traffic, you should enable logging, re-create the problem you're having, and then examine the log files. To enable logging, follow these steps:

1. In the console tree of the Windows Firewall With Advanced Security snap-in, right-click Windows Firewall With Advanced Security, and then choose Properties.

   The Windows Firewall With Advanced Security Properties dialog box appears.

2. Select the Domain Profile, Private Profile, or Public Profile tab.

3. In the Logging group, click the Customize button.

   The Customize Logging Settings dialog box appears.

4. To log packets that Windows Firewall drops, from the Log Dropped Packets drop-down list, select Yes. To log connections that Windows Firewall allows, from the Log Successful Connections drop-down list, select Yes.

5. Click OK.

By default, Windows Firewall writes log entries to %SystemRoot%\System32\LogFiles \Firewall\Pfirewall.log and stores only the last 4 KB of data. In most production environments, this log will be almost constantly written to, which can cause a performance impact. For that reason, you should enable logging only when actively troubleshooting a problem and then immediately disable logging when you're done.

Identifying Network Communications

The documentation included with network applications often does not clearly identify the communication protocols the application uses. Fortunately, creating Program firewall rules allows any communications required by that particular program.

If you prefer to use Port firewall rules or if you need to configure a network firewall that can identify communications based only on port number and the application's documentation does not list the firewall requirements, you can examine the application's behavior to determine the port numbers in use.

The simplest tool to use is Netstat. On the server, run the application, and then run the following command to examine which ports are listening for active connections:

```
netstat -a -b
```

Any rows in the output with a State of LISTENING are attempting to receive incoming connections on the port number specified in the Local Address column. The executable name listed after the row is the executable that is listening for the connection. For example, the following output demonstrates that RpcSs, running under the SvcHost.exe process (which runs many services), is listening for connections on TCP port 135:

```
Active Connections

  Proto  Local Address          Foreign Address        State
  TCP    0.0.0.0:135            Dcsrv1:0               LISTENING
  RpcSs
  [svchost.exe]
```

Similarly, the following output demonstrates that the DNS service (Dns.exe) is listening for connections on TCP port 53:

```
Active Connections

  Proto  Local Address          Foreign Address        State
  TCP    0.0.0.0:53             Dcsrv1:0               LISTENING
  [dns.exe]
```

Although Windows Firewall has existing rules in place for these services (because they are built into Windows), the same technique would allow you to identify the port numbers used by any third-party application.

PRACTICE Configuring Windows Firewall

In this practice, you configure both inbound and outbound filtering. These are common tasks that occur when you install new applications in almost any network environment, from small businesses to large enterprises.

▶ **Exercise 1   Configure Inbound Filtering**

In this exercise, you will install the Telnet Server feature, which configures Windows Server 2008 to accept incoming connections on TCP port 23. Then, you will examine the incoming firewall rule that applies to the Telnet Server and adjust the rule configuration.

1. In the console tree of Server Manager, select Features. In the details pane, click Add Features.

   The Add Features Wizard appears.

2. On the Select Features page, select the Telnet Server check box. Click Next.

3. On the Confirm Installation Selections page, click Install.

4. On the Installation Results page, click Close.

5. In Server Manager, select Configuration\Services. Then, in the details pane, right-click the Telnet service and choose Properties. From the Startup Type drop-down list, select Manual. Click the Apply button. Then, click the Start button to start the Telnet Server. Click OK.

6. On a client computer, open a command prompt and run the following command (where *ip_address* is the Telnet Server's IP address):

   `telnet ip_address`

   The Telnet server should prompt you for a user name. This proves that the client was able to establish a TCP connection to port 23.

7. Press Ctrl+] to exit the Telnet session. Type **quit** and press Enter to close Telnet.

8. On the Telnet Server, in Server Manager, select Configuration\Windows Firewall With Advanced Security\Inbound Rules. In the details pane, right-click the Telnet Server rule, and then choose Properties.

NOTE   Automatically enabling required rules

Notice that the Telnet Server rule is enabled; the Add Features Wizard automatically enabled the rule when it installed the Telnet Server feature.

---

9. Click the Programs And Services tab. Notice that the default rule is configured to allow communications for %SystemRoot%\system32\TlntSvr.exe, which is the executable file for the Telnet Server service. Click the Settings button and verify that Telnet is selected. Click Cancel twice.

10. In Server Manager, right-click the Telnet Server rule, and then choose Disable Rule.

11. On the Telnet client computer, run the same Telnet command again. This time the command should fail because Windows Firewall is no longer allowing incoming Telnet requests.

12. Use Server Manager to remove the Telnet Server feature and restart the computer if necessary.

▶ **Exercise 2 Configure Outbound Filtering**

In this exercise, you configure Windows Server 2008 to block outbound requests by default. Then, you test it by attempting to visit a Web site with Internet Explorer. Next, you will create an outbound rule to allow requests from Internet Explorer and verify that the outbound rule works correctly. Finally, you will return your computer to its original state.

1. Open Internet Explorer and visit *http://www.microsoft.com*. If an Internet Explorer Enhanced Security Configuration dialog box appears, you can click Close to dismiss it.

2. In Server Manager, right-click Configuration\Windows Firewall With Advanced Security, and then choose Properties.

3. Click the Domain Profile tab. From the Outbound Connections drop-down list, select Block. Repeat this step for the Private Profile and Public Profile tabs.

4. Click OK.

5. Open Internet Explorer and attempt to visit *http://support.microsoft.com*.

6. You should be unable to visit the Web site because outbound filtering is blocking Internet Explorer's outgoing HTTP queries.

7. In Server Manager, below Configuration\Windows Firewall With Advanced Security, right-click Outbound Rules, and then choose New Rule.
   The New Outbound Rule Wizard appears.

8. On the Rule Type page, select Program. Then, click Next.

9. On the Program page, select This Program Path. In the box, type **%ProgramFiles% \Internet Explorer\iexplore.exe** (the path to the Internet Explorer executable file). Click Next.

10. On the Action page, select Allow The Connection. Then, click Next.

11. On the Profile page, accept the default selection of applying the rule to all three profiles. Click Next.

12. On the Name page, type **Allow Internet Explorer outgoing communications**. Then, click Finish.

13. Now, in Internet Explorer, attempt to visit *http://support.microsoft.com* again. This time the connection succeeds because you created an outbound filter specifically for Internet Explorer.

14. In Server Manager, disable outbound filtering by right-clicking Configuration\Windows Firewall With Advanced Security, and then choosing Properties. In the Domain Profile tab, click the Outbound Connections list, and then click Allow (Default). Repeat this step for the Private Profile and Public Profile tabs. Click OK.

Lesson Summary

- Firewalls are designed to drop unwanted communications (such as packets generated by a worm) while still allowing legitimate communications (such as packets generated by a network management tool).

- Windows Vista and Windows Server 2008 support three firewall profiles: Domain, Private, and Public. The Domain profile applies whenever a computer can communicate with its domain controller. The Private profile must be manually applied to a network. The Public profile applies any time a domain controller is not available, and a network has not been configured as Private.

- Use the Windows Firewall With Advanced Security snap-in to create an inbound firewall rule that allows a server application to receive incoming connections.

- Use the Windows Firewall With Advanced Security snap-in to create an outbound firewall rule that allows a client application to establish outgoing connections. You need to create outbound firewall rules only if you configure outbound connections to be blocked by default.

- You can edit the properties of a firewall rule to configure the scope, which limits the subnets an application can communicate with. Configuring scope can greatly reduce the risk of attacks from untrusted networks.

- If you use IPsec in your environment, you can configure firewall rules to allow only secure connections and to allow only connections for authorized users and computers.

- Group Policy is the most effective way to configure firewall settings for all computers in a domain. Using Group Policy, you can quickly improve the security of a large number of computers and control which applications are allowed to communicate on the network.

- Windows Firewall logging identifies connections that Windows Firewall allows or blocks. This information is very useful when troubleshooting a connectivity problem that might be caused by Windows Firewall.

- If an application must accept incoming connections but the developers have not documented the communication ports that it uses, you can use the Netstat tool to identify which ports the application listens on. With this information, you can then create Port firewall rules.

Lesson Review

You can use the following questions to test your knowledge of the information in Lesson 1, "Configuring Windows Firewall." The questions are also available on the companion CD if you prefer to review them in electronic form.

NOTE Answers

Answers to these questions and explanations of why each answer choice is correct or incorrect are located in the "Answers" section at the end of the book.

---

1. You are a systems administrator for a property management company. You need to install an internally developed automation tool on a computer running Windows Server 2008. The tool acts as a network client and needs to connect to a server on your intranet using TCP port 88 and to a server on the Internet using TCP port 290. Additionally, a client component you install on your workstation running Windows Vista will connect to the computer running Windows Server 2008 using TCP port 39. Windows Firewall is currently configured with the default settings on both computers. Which of the following changes do you need to make to allow the application to work?

   A. On the computer running Windows Server 2008, add a firewall rule to allow outbound connections on TCP port 290.

   B. On the computer running Windows Server 2008, add a firewall rule to allow inbound connections on TCP port 39.

   C. On the computer running Windows Server 2008, add a firewall rule to allow inbound connections on TCP port 290.

   D. On your workstation, add a firewall rule to allow outbound connections on TCP port 39.

2. You are a systems administrator for an enterprise manufacturing company specializing in water purification equipment. You have recently installed an internal server application on a computer running Windows Server 2008 that accepts incoming connections on TCP port 1036. The application does not include any access control capability. How can you configure the inbound firewall rule properties to allow connections only from authorized users in your domain? (Choose all that apply. Each answer forms part of the complete solution.)

    A. In the General tab, click Allow Only Secure Connections.

    B. In the Advanced tab, click These Profiles, and then select Domain.

    C. In the Users And Computers tab, select Only Allow Connections From These Users. Then, add the Domain Users group.

    D. In the Scope tab, in the Local IP Address group, select These IP Addresses. Then, add each of your internal networks.

3. You are a systems administrator for a medium-sized facilities management organization. You need to use Group Policy settings to configure firewall settings on your Windows XP and Windows Vista client computers. You would like to configure firewall rules using only the *Windows Firewall* node rather than the *Windows Firewall With Advanced Security* node. Which of the following features are NOT available when using the *Windows Firewall* node in Group Policy settings?

    A. Filtering UDP traffic

    B. Allowing a specific executable to accept incoming connections on any port number

    C. Dropping connections not originating from a specific subnet

    D. Requiring IPsec authentication for a connection

Lesson 2: Configuring Network Access Protection

Consider this common scenario: an enterprise has thousands of computers on a private network. Perimeter firewalls protect the network from Internet threats, including network attacks from worms. Suddenly, someone creates a worm that can exploit a vulnerability in Windows computers that do not have the latest security updates installed. The worm spreads quickly across the Internet, but the private network's perimeter firewalls protect the vulnerable computers on the internal network. A traveling salesperson then returns to the office with his mobile computer. While on his trip, he connected his computer to the wireless network at the hotel, where another guest's computer transmitted a worm across the network. When he connects to the private network, the worm immediately begins spreading to the vulnerable computers, completely bypassing the perimeter security. In a few hours, most of the computers on the internal network are infected.

Network Access Protection (NAP) can prevent this scenario. When computers connect to your local area network (LAN), they must meet specific health requirements, such as having recent updates installed. If they can't meet those health requirements, they can be quarantined to a network where they can download updates, install antivirus software, and obtain more information about how to meet the requirements of the LAN.

This lesson describes NAP and how you can deploy it on your network.

After this lesson, you will be able to:
- Describe how NAP works to protect your network.
- Plan a NAP deployment while minimizing the impact on users.
- Install and configure the Network Policy Service.
- Configure NAP enforcement.
- Configure various NAP components.
- Examine NAP log files.

Estimated lesson time: 90 minutes

Network Access Protection Concepts

As shown in Figure 8-3, NAP is designed to connect hosts to different network resources depending on their current health state. This division of network resources can be implemented using virtual LANs (VLANs, as Figure 8-3 demonstrates), IP filters, IP subnet assignment, static routes, or IPsec enforcement.

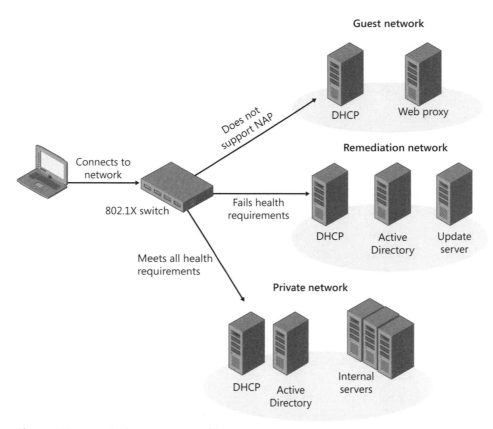

Figure 8-3   A typical NAP VLAN architecture

If you choose to provide a remediation network (rather than simply denying network access), you might need additional infrastructure servers for the remediation network. For example, if you configure an Active Directory domain controller on the remediation network, you should use a read-only domain controller to limit the risk if the domain controller is attacked. Similarly, you should provide separate DHCP and DNS servers from your infrastructure servers to reduce the risk that a noncompliant computer might spread malware to the production server.

Enforcement Types

For NAP to work, a network component must enforce NAP by either allowing or denying network access. The sections that follow describe the different NAP enforcement types you can use: IPsec connection security, 802.1X access points, VPN servers, and DHCP servers.

NOTE   Terminal Services Gateway

Terminal Services Gateway enforcement is not discussed in this book because it is not covered on the exam.

IPsec Connection Security   This enforcement type requires clients to perform a NAP health check before they can receive a health certificate. In turn, this health certificate is required for IPsec connection security before the client can connect to IPsec-protected hosts. IPsec enforcement allows you to require health compliance on a per-IP address or a per-TCP/UDP port number basis. For example, you could allow noncompliant computers to connect to a Web server but allow only compliant computers to connect to a file server—even if the two services are running on a single computer.

You can also use IPsec connection security to allow healthy computers to communicate only with other healthy computers. IPsec enforcement requires a CA running Windows Server 2008 Certificate Services and NAP to support health certificates. In production environments, you will need at least two CAs for redundancy. Other public key infrastructures (PKIs) will not work. IPsec enforcement provides a very high level of security, but it can protect only computers that are configured to support IPsec.

MORE INFO   Deploying a PKI

For more information about deploying a new Windows-based PKI in your organization, see Windows Server 2008 Help And Support, *http://www.microsoft.com/pki*, and *Windows Server 2008 PKI and Certificate Security* by Brian Komar (Microsoft Press, 2008).

802.1X Access Points   This enforcement type uses Ethernet switches or wireless access points that support 802.1X authentication. Compliant computers are granted full network access, and noncompliant computers are connected to a remediation network or completely prevented from connecting to the network. If a computer falls out of compliance after connecting to the 802.1X network, the 802.1X network access device can change the computer's network access. This provides some assurance of compliance for desktop computers, which might remain connected to the network indefinitely.

802.1X enforcement uses one of two methods to control which level of access compliant, noncompliant, and unauthenticated computers receive:

- **An access control list (ACL)** A set of Internet Protocol version 4 (IPv4) or Internet Protocol version 6 (IPv6) packet filters configured on the 802.1X access point. The 802.1X access point applies the ACL to the connection and drops all packets that are not allowed by the ACL. Typically, you apply an ACL to noncompliant computer connections and allow compliant computers to connect without an ACL (thus granting them unlimited network access). ACLs allow you to prevent noncompliant computers from connecting to one another, thus limiting the ability of a worm to spread, even among noncompliant computers.

- **A virtual local area network** A group of ports on the switch that are grouped together to create a separate network. VLANs cannot communicate with one another unless you connect them using a router. VLANs are identified using a VLAN identifier, which must be configured on the switch itself. You can then use NAP to specify in which VLAN the compliant, noncompliant, and unauthenticated computers are placed. When you place noncompliant computers into a VLAN, they can communicate with one another. This can allow a noncompliant computer infected with a worm to attack, and possibly infect, other noncompliant computers. Another disadvantage of using VLANs is that the client's network configuration must change when transitioning from being a noncompliant NAP client to being a compliant NAP client (for example, if they are able to successfully apply updates). Changing the network configuration during system startup and user logon can cause Group Policy updates or other boot processes to fail.

Your 802.1X access points may support ACLs, VLANs, or both. If they support both and you're already using either ACLs or VLANs for other purposes, use the same technique for 802.1X enforcement. If your 802.1X access point supports both ACLs and VLANs and you are not currently using either, use ACLs for 802.1X enforcement so you can take advantage of their ability to limit network access between noncompliant clients.

VPN Server This enforcement type enforces NAP for remote access connections using a VPN server running Windows Server 2008 and Routing and Remote Access (other VPN servers do not support NAP). With VPN server enforcement enabled, only compliant client computers are granted unlimited network access. The VPN server can apply a set of packet filters to connections for noncompliant computers, limiting their access to a remediation server group that you define. You can also define IPv4 and IPv6 packet filters, exactly as you would when configuring a standard VPN connection.

MORE INFO Configuring VPN connections

For more information about configuring VPN connections, refer to Chapter 7, "Connecting to Networks."

DHCP Server   This enforcement type uses a computer running Windows Server 2008 and the Dynamic Host Configuration Protocol (DHCP) Server service that provides IP addresses to intranet clients. Only compliant computers receive an IP address that grants full network access; noncompliant computers are granted an IP address with a subnet mask of 255.255.255.255 and no default gateway.

Additionally, noncompliant hosts receive a list of *host routes* (routes that direct traffic to a single IP address) for network resources in a remediation server group that you can use to allow the client to apply any updates required to become compliant. This IP configuration prevents noncompliant computers from communicating with network resources other than those you configure as part of a remediation server group.

If the health state of a NAP client changes (for example, if Windows Firewall is disabled), the NAP client performs a new health evaluation using a DHCP renewal. This allows clients that become noncompliant after successfully authenticating to the network to be blocked from further network access. If you change the health policy on NAP servers, the changes will not be enforced until the client's DHCP lease is renewed.

Although 802.1X network access devices and VPN servers are capable of disconnecting computers from the network and IPsec enforcement can allow connections only from healthy computers, DHCP server enforcement points can be bypassed by an attacker who manually configures an IP address. Nonetheless, DHCP server enforcement can reduce the risk from nonmalicious users who might attempt to connect to your network with a noncompliant computer.

System Health Agents and System Health Validators

NAP health validation takes place between two components:

- **System Health Agents (SHAs)**   The client components that create a Statement of Health (SoH) containing a description of the health of the client computer. Windows Vista, Windows Server 2008, and Windows XP with Service Pack 3 include an SHA that monitors Windows Security Center settings. Microsoft and third-party developers can create custom SHAs that provide more complex reporting.

- **System Health Validators (SHVs)**   The server components that analyze the SoH generated by the SHA and create a SoH Response (SoHR). The NAP health policy server uses the SoHR to determine the level of access the client computer should have and whether any remediation is necessary. Windows Server 2008 includes an SHV that corresponds to the SHA built into Windows Vista and Windows XP with Service Pack 3.

The NAP connection process is as follows:

1. The NAP client connects to a network that requires NAP.

2. Each SHA on the NAP client validates its system health and generates an SoH. The NAP client combines the SoHs from multiple SHAs into a System Statement of Health (SSoH), which includes version information for the NAP client and the set of SoHs for the installed SHAs.

3. The NAP client sends the SSoH to the NAP health policy server through the NAP enforcement point.

4. The NAP health policy server uses its installed SHVs and the health requirement policies that you have configured to determine whether the NAP client meets health requirements. Each SHV produces a Statement of Health Response (SoHR), which can contain remediation instructions (such as the version number of an antivirus signature file) if the client doesn't meet that SHV's health requirements.

5. The NAP health policy server combines the SoHRs from the multiple SHVs into a System Statement of Health Response (SSoHR).

6. The NAP health policy server sends the SSoHR back to the NAP client through the NAP enforcement point. The NAP enforcement point can now connect a compliant computer to the network or connect a noncompliant computer to a remediation network.

7. Each SHA on the NAP client processes the SoHR created by the corresponding SHV. If possible, any noncompliant SHAs can attempt to come into compliance (for example, by downloading updated antivirus signatures).

8. If any noncompliant SHAs were able to meet the requirements specified by the SHV, the entire process starts over again—hopefully with a successful result.

Quick Check

1. Which NAP enforcement types do not require support from your network infrastructure?

2. Which versions of Windows can act as NAP clients?

Quick Check Answers

1. IPSec connection security, DHCP, and VPN enforcement do not require support from your network infrastructure. They can be implemented using only Windows Server 2008. 802.1X provides very powerful enforcement, but requires a network infrastructure that supports 802.1X.

2. Windows XP with Service Pack 3, Windows Vista, and Windows Server 2008.

Planning a NAP Deployment

NAP has the potential to prevent legitimate users from accessing the network. Any security mechanism that reduces productivity will be quickly removed, so you must carefully plan a NAP deployment to minimize user impact.

Typically, a NAP deployment occurs in three phases:

- **Testing**   Test the NAP using examples of each different operating system, client computer configuration, and enforcement points in your environment.
- **Monitoring**   Deploy NAP in a monitoring-only mode that notifies administrators if a computer fails to meet health requirements but does not prevent the user from connecting to the network. This allows you to identify computers that are not meeting health requirements and to bring them into compliance. You could bring computers into compliance manually or by using automated tools, such as Microsoft Systems Management Server 2003 and Microsoft System Center Configuration Manager 2007. For more information, read the section entitled "Configuring NAP for Monitoring Only" later in this chapter.
- **Limited access**   If, during the monitoring phase, you reach a point where almost all of your computers are compliant, you can enable NAP enforcement to prevent noncompliant computers from connecting to your production network. Users can then use resources on the remediation network to bring their computers into compliance, if necessary. Typically, you will need to configure exceptions for computers that are not NAP-compliant.

Installing and Configuring the Network Policy Server

NAP depends on a Windows Server 2008 NAP health policy server, which acts as a RADIUS server, to evaluate the health of client computers. If you have existing RADIUS servers that are running Windows Server 2003 or Windows 2000 Server and Internet Authentication Service (IAS), you can upgrade them to Windows Server 2008 and configure them as NAP health policy servers. If you have RADIUS servers running any other operating system, you will need to configure new Windows Server 2008 NAP health policy servers, configure the health policy, and then migrate your existing RADIUS clients to the NAP health policy servers.

Typically, you will need to deploy at least two NAP health policy servers for fault tolerance. If you have only a single NAP health policy server, clients will be unable to connect to the network if it is offline. As described in Chapter 7, you can use connection request policies to allow a single RADIUS server to act as a NAP health policy server and authenticate requests from other RADIUS clients.

Installing NAP

To install NAP, follow these steps:

1. In the console tree of Server Manager, select Roles. In the details pane, click Add Roles. The Add Roles Wizard appears.
2. On the Before You Begin page, click Next.
3. On the Select Server Roles page, select the Network Policy And Access Services check box. Click Next.
4. On the Network Policy And Access Services page, click Next.
5. On the Select Role Services page, select the Network Policy Server check box. Click Next.
6. On the Confirmation page, click Install.
7. On the Results page, click Close.

This installs the core NPS service, which is sufficient for using the Windows Server 2008 computer as a RADIUS server for 802.1X, VPN, or DHCP enforcement.

Using the Configure NAP Wizard

After installing the Network Policy And Access Services role, follow these steps to configure NAP:

1. In Server Manager, select Roles\Network Policy And Access Services\NPS. You might need to close and reopen Server Manager if you recently installed the Network Policy And Access Services role.
2. In the details pane, select Network Access Protection, and then click Configure NAP. The Configure NAP Wizard appears.
3. On the Select Network Connection Method For Use With NAP page, choose your enforcement method. Then, click Next.
4. On the next page (whose title depends on the previously selected network connection method), you need to add any HRA servers (other than the local computer) and RADIUS clients. For example, if you are using 802.1X enforcement, you would need to add the IP address of each switch. If you are using VPN enforcement, add the IP address of each VPN server. If you are configuring DHCP servers, add each of your NAP-capable DHCP servers. Click Add for each host and configure a friendly name, address, and shared secret. Then, click OK. After you have configured any external HRA servers and RADIUS clients, click Next.
5. Depending on the network method you chose, you might be presented with additional page options, such as DHCP scopes or Terminal Service gateway options. Configure these options appropriately.

6. On the Configure User Groups And Machines page, you can accept the default settings to allow all users to connect. To grant or deny access to a group, click the Add Machine button. Then, select the group and click OK. Click Next.

7. The pages that follow vary depending on your NAP enforcement method. For example, for the 802.1X or VPN enforcement methods, you use the Configure An Authentication Method page (shown in Figure 8-4) to specify the NAP health policy server certificate and the EAP types to use for user or computer-level authentication. For the 802.1X enforcement method, you use the Configure Virtual LANs (VLANs) page to configure the unlimited VLAN and the restricted network VLAN.

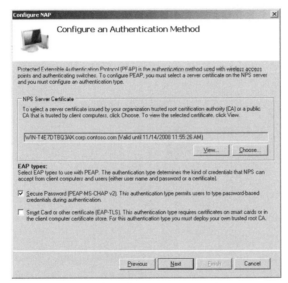

Figure 8-4   Configuring an 802.1X enforcement authentication method

8. On the Define NAP Health Policy page, you can select from the installed SHVs. By default, only the Windows Security Health Validator is installed. As shown in Figure 8-5, you should leave autoremediation enabled to allow client computers to automatically change settings to meet health requirements. During initial production deployments, select Allow Full Network Access To NAP-Ineligible Client Computers to configure NAP in monitoring-only mode. Noncompliant computers will generate an event in the event log, allowing you to fix noncompliant computers before they are prevented from connecting to the network. Click Next.

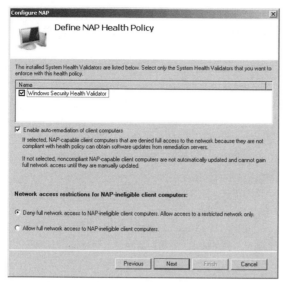

Figure 8-5 Defining NAP health policy

9. On the Completing NAP Enforcement Policy And RADIUS Client Configuration page, click Finish.

The Configure NAP Wizard creates:

- A connection request policy with the name specified on the Select Network Connection Method For Use With NAP page.

- Compliant and noncompliant health policies, based on the name specified on the Select Network Connection Method For Use With NAP page.

- Compliant and noncompliant network policies, based on the same name as the health policies.

Configuring NAP Enforcement

After you have installed and configured NAP, you must perform additional steps to enable NAP enforcement. The steps you follow vary depending on whether you are using IPsec, 802.1X, DHCP, or VPN enforcement. The sections that follow describe how to configure each of these enforcement types at a high level, cross-referencing other sections in this lesson for more detailed instructions.

Configuring IPsec Enforcement

Configuring IPsec enforcement requires the following high-level steps:

1. Install the HRA role service and the Certificate Services role (if it's not already present).

2. Use the Configure NAP Wizard to configure the connection request policy, network policy, and NAP health policy, as described in the section of this chapter entitled "Using the Configure NAP Wizard." Although you can configure these elements individually, it's much easier to use the wizard.

3. Configure HRA, as described in the sections that follow.

4. Enable the NAP IPsec Relying Party enforcement client and start the NAP service on NAP-capable client computers, as described later in this chapter in the sections entitled "Configuring Client Computers for IPsec Enforcement" and "Configuring NAP Clients."

5. Require IPsec connection security using health certificates for computers that should communicate only with other healthy computers, as described in the sections that follow.

The following sections describe these steps in more detail.

Installing the HRA Role Service   If you plan to use IPsec enforcement, you will also need to install the Health Registration Authority (HRA) role service. In production environments, you should always configure at least two HRAs for fault tolerance. Large networks might require additional HRAs to meet the performance requirements.

Installing the HRA role service configures the following:

- **A certification authority (if one does not already exist)**   HRA requires a certification authority running Windows Server 2008 Certificate Services, which can be an existing CA or a new CA. For a Windows Server 2003–based CA, you must manually create a System Health Authentication certificate template so that members of the IPsec exemption group can autoenroll a long-lived health certificate.

  MORE INFO   Configuring a CA for IPsec NAP enforcement

  For more information about configuring a Windows Server 2003–based CA, read "Step By Step Guide: Demonstrate IPsec NAP Enforcement in a Test Lab" at *http:// download.microsoft.com/download/d/2/2/d22daf01-a6d4-486c-8239-04db487e6413 /NAPIPsec_StepByStep.doc*.

- **A Web application**   The Add Role Services Wizard creates a Web application named DomainHRA under the default Web site in IIS.

You can install the HRA role service using the Add Roles Wizard by selecting the Health Registration Authority check box on the Select Role Services page and following the prompts that appear, or you can install the role service after installing the Network Policy And Access Services role by following these steps:

1. In Server Manager, right-click Roles\Network Policy and Access Services, and then choose Add Role Services.

The Add Role Services Wizard appears.

2. On the Select Role Services page, select the Health Registration Authority check box. When prompted, click Add Required Role Services. Click Next.

3. On the Choose The Certification Authority To Use With The Health Registration Authority page, select Install A Local CA To Issue Health Certificates For This HRA Server if you do not yet have a CA and you want to install one. If you have a CA installed on a remote server, select Use An Existing Remote CA. Click Next.

4. On the Choose Authentication Requirements For The Health Registration Authority page, select Yes if all client computers are a member of a trusted domain. If some computers are not members of a domain, you can select No—but you must accept slightly weaker security. Click Next.

5. On the Server Authentication Certificate page, you can select an SSL certificate to encrypt communications with the HRA server using one of the following three options. After you select an option, click Next.

   ❏ **Choose An Existing Certificate For SSL Encryption**   If you have an SSL certificate, select this option, and then select the certificate you want to use. If your certificate does not appear in the list, click Import.

   ❏ **Create A Self-Signed Certificate For SSL Encryption**   Clients do not trust self-signed certificates by default, which means you will need to manually configure the certificate on every client computer. For this reason, it is not a practical option in most circumstances.

   ❏ **Don't Use SSL Or Choose A Certificate For SSL Encryption Later**   If you are installing Certificate Services as part of this wizard, select this option so you can manually add an SSL certificate after you have completed the Certificate Services installation.

NOTE   Installing an SSL certificate after completing the wizard

You can install an SSL certificate later using the Internet Information Services Manager. Right-click Sites\Default Web Site, and then choose Edit Bindings. In the Site Bindings dialog box, click Add and create an HTTPS binding with your SSL certificate.

---

6. On the Server Authentication Certificate page, you can select an SSL certificate to encrypt communications with the HRA server. After you select an option, click Next.

7. If you are installing the Windows Server 2008 Certificate Services role at this time, the Active Directory Certificate Services page appears. If it does not appear, skip to step 16. On this page, click Next.

8. On the Role Services page, click Next.

9. On the Setup Type page, select whether to configure an enterprise or stand-alone CA. In Active Directory environments, configuring an Enterprise CA is much easier because you can automatically issue certificates to client computers. Click Next.

10. On the CA Type page, select Root CA if this is your first CA. If you have an existing PKI, select Subordinate CA. The remainder of these steps assume you are configuring a root CA; some pages are different if you configure a subordinate CA. Click Next.

11. On the Private Key page, click Next.

12. On the Cryptography page, click Next.

13. On the CA Name page, you can type a new common name for the CA. This name must be the name clients will use to connect to the server. The default will typically work. Click Next.

14. On the Validity Period page, click Next.

15. On the Certificate Database page, click Next.

16. On the Web Server page, click Next.

17. On the Role Services page, click Next.

18. On the Confirmation page, click Install.

19. On the Results page, click Close.

Configuring the NAP Wizard   Next, follow the steps in "Using The Configure NAP Wizard" and, on the Select Network Connection Method For Use With NAP page, select IPsec With Health Registration Authority. Completing the wizard creates the following:

- A connection request policy named NAP IPsec With HRA (at Roles\Network Policy And Access Server\NPS\Policies\Connection Request Policies in Server Manager). This connection request policy configures the local server to process NAP IPsec requests using the HRA.

- A health policy named NAP IPsec With HRA Compliant (at Roles\Network Policy And Access Server\NPS\Policies\Health Policies in Server Manager). This health policy applies to compliant computers that pass all SHV checks.

- A network policy named NAP IPsec With HRA Compliant (at Roles\Network Policy And Access Server\NPS\Policies\Network Policies in Server Manager). This network policy grants access to compliant computers.

- A health policy named NAP IPsec With HRA Noncompliant (at Roles\Network Policy And Access Server\NPS\Policies\Heath Policies in Server Manager). This health policy applies to noncompliant computers that fail one or more SHV checks.

- A network policy named NAP IPsec With HRA Noncompliant (at Roles\Network Policy And Access Server\NPS\Policies\Network Policies in Server Manager). This network policy grants limited network access to noncompliant computers. Specifically, noncompliant computers will be able to access only remediation servers. You should never set the Access Permission to Deny Access because that prevents the health check from being performed.

Configuring HRA   Now you can configure HRA settings using Server Manager by selecting the Roles\Network Policy And Access Services\NPS\Health Registration Authority node. Before you can use IPsec enforcement, you must configure a CA (such as Windows Server 2008 Certificate Services) that will issue health certificates.

To configure the CA that will be used to issue health certificates for IPsec enforcements, follow these steps:

1. In Server Manager, right-click Roles\Network Policy And Access services\Health Registration Authority\Certification Authority, and then choose Add Certification Authority.

2. In the Add Certification Authority dialog box, click Browse to select an enterprise CA. Select the appropriate server, and then click OK. Alternatively, you can type the fully qualified domain name (FQDN) of your CA. Figure 8-6 shows the Add Certification Authority dialog box with an enterprise CA selected.

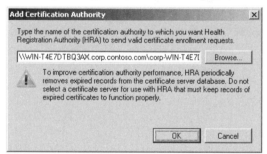

Figure 8-6   Selecting a CA for IPsec enforcement

3. Click OK.

4. Right-click Roles\Network Policy And Access Services\Health Registration Authority \Certification Authority, and then click Properties.

   The Certification Authorities Properties dialog box appears.

5. If you are using an enterprise CA, select Use Enterprise Certification Authority. Then, click OK.

The CA appears in the details pane when you select the Roles\Network Policy And Access Services\Health Registration Authority\Certification Authority node in Server Manager. You can repeat the previous steps to add CAs, which allows for fault tolerance. If you have only a single CA and it goes offline, clients will be unable to undergo a NAP health check. If you have NAP enforcement enabled, this means clients will be unable to connect to the network.

You can also configure the mechanisms used for IPsec enforcement using the Roles\Network Policy And Access Services\Health Registration Authority\Certification Authority node in Server Manager. However, the default settings are typically sufficient.

Configuring Client Computers for IPsec Enforcement   After configuring the NPS server for IPsec enforcement, you must configure client computers for IPsec enforcement. First, configure clients to use IPsec, as described in Chapter 6, "Configuring IPsec." Then, configure the client by following these steps:

1. Use the Group Policy Management Editor to open the GPO you want to use to apply the NAP enforcement client settings.

2. Right-click the Computer Configuration\Policies\Windows Settings\Security Settings \Network Access Protection\NAP Client Configuration\Health Registration Settings \Trusted Server Groups node, and then choose New.

   The New Trusted Server Group Wizard appears.

3. On the Group Name page, type a name that describes the group of HRA servers you will use for IPsec enforcement. Click Next.

4. On the Add Servers page, type the URL for each HRA. If you have an SSL certificate (that clients trust) installed on the server, type the URL as **https://**_servername_, where _servername_ matches the common name on the SSL certificate. If you do not have an SSL certificate, clear the Require Server Verification check box and type the URL as **https:// servername**. Click Add and repeat the process for any additional HRAs. NAP clients always start with the first HRA and continue through the list until an HRA can be contacted. Click Finish.

Now that you have configured clients to trust your HRAs, you should enable IPsec enforcement.

1. Select the Computer Configuration\Policies\Windows Settings\Security Settings\Network Access Protection\NAP Client Configuration\Enforcement Clients node.

2. In the Details pane, double-click IPsec Relying Party.

3. In the IPsec Relying Party Properties dialog box, select the Enable This Enforcement Client check box. Then, click OK.

Additionally, follow the steps described in "Configuring NAP Clients" later in this chapter.

Configuring IPsec Connection Security Rules   Next, configure any servers that should be accessed only by compliant computers to require IPsec for inbound (but not outbound) connections. Note that this will prevent network communications from all computers that are not NAP-compliant or NAP-capable. In the Windows Firewall With Advanced Security snap-in, follow these steps:

1. Right-click Connection Security Rules, and then choose New Rule.

The New Connection Security Rule Wizard page appears.

2. On the Rule Type page, select Isolation. Then, click Next.

3. On the Requirements page, select Require Authentication For Inbound Connections And Request Authentication For Outbound Connections. Click Next.

4. On the Authentication Method page, select Computer Certificate. Then, click Browse and select the CA used to generate the certificate for your HRA. Click OK. Select the Only Accept Health Certificates check box, as shown in Figure 8-7. Then, click Next.

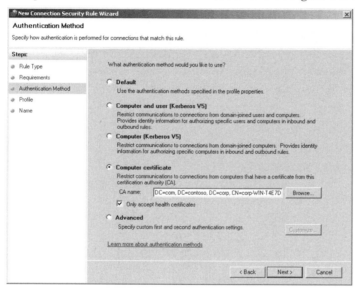

Figure 8-7 Requiring health certificates for a server

5. On the Profile page, click Next.

6. On the Name page, type a name, and then click Finish.

After the policy is applied to computers, only clients with a valid health certificate will be able to communicate. For this reason, you can't require health certificates for your HRA server, or clients would be unable to retrieve their health certificates.

For the HRA server, remediation servers, and any other computer that should be accessible by either noncompliant or non-NAP-capable computers, configure an IPsec connection security rule to request, but not require, security for inbound connections. For more information, read Chapter 6, "Configuring IPsec."

For NAP clients running Windows XP SP3, you will need to configure the equivalent policies using the IP Security Polices snap-in, available in Group Policy at Computer Configuration \Policies\Windows Settings\IP Security Policies. To c onfigure a Windows XP SP3–based

NAP client to use its health certificate for IPsec authentication, you must set the HKEY_LOCAL_MACHINE\SYSTEM\CurrentControlSet\Services\PolicyAgent\Oakley \IKEFlags registry value to 0x1c.

Configuring 802.1X Enforcement

Configuring 802.1X enforcement requires the following high-level steps:

1. Use the Configure NAP Wizard to configure the connection request policy, network policy, and NAP health policy, as described in the section of this chapter entitled "Using the Configure NAP Wizard." Although you can configure these elements individually, it's much easier to use the wizard. On the Configure Virtual LANs page, you will need to specify the ACLs or VLANs for both compliant and noncompliant NAP clients, as shown in Figure 8-8. Refer to your switch documentation for information about which RADIUS attributes to use to specify the VLAN or ACL.

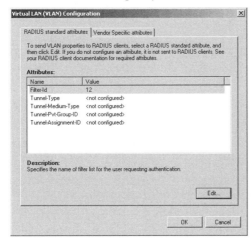

Figure 8-8 Configuring the VLAN for unrestricted network access

2. Configure your 802.1X authenticating switches to perform Protected Extensible Authentication Protocol (PEAP)-based authentication (either PEAP-MS-CHAP v2 or PEAP-TLS) and submit RADIUS requests to your NAP server. Additionally, configure a reauthentication interval to require authenticated client computers that remain connected to the network to be reauthenticated regularly. Microsoft suggests a reauthentication interval of four hours. Refer to your switch documentation for instructions.

3. If you plan to use certificates for authentication (using either PEAP-TLS or EAP-TLS), deploy a PKI such as the Certificate Services role and distribute certificates to client computers using a mechanism such as Active Directory autoenrollment. For more information, refer to Chapter 7, "Connecting to Networks." If you plan to use PEAP-MS-CHAP v2 domain authentication, use a PKI to issue server certificates to the NAP server.

4. Create NAP exemptions for computers that cannot complete a NAP health evaluation by creating a network policy that grants wireless or wired access and uses the Windows Groups condition set to the security group for the exempted computers but does not use the Health Policy condition. For more information, read "Configuring Network Policies" later in this lesson.

5. Enable the NAP EAP Quarantine Enforcement Client and start the NAP service on NAP-capable client computers. For more information, read "Configuring NAP Clients" later in this lesson.

Configuring DHCP Enforcement

Configuring DHCP enforcement requires the following high-level steps:

1. Use the Configure NAP Wizard to configure the connection request policy, network policy, and NAP health policy, as described in the section of this chapter entitled "Using the Configure NAP Wizard." Although you can configure these elements individually, it's much easier to use the wizard.

2. Configure remediation servers to define the computers noncompliant clients can access. For more information, read "Configuring Remediation" later in this lesson.

3. Configure a DHCP server. For more information, refer to Chapter 4, "Installing and Configuring a DHCP Server." NPS must be installed on the DHCP server. If your DHCP and primary NPS servers are different computers, configure NPS on the remote DHCP NPS server as a RADIUS proxy to forward connection requests to the primary NPS server. For more information about configuring RADIUS proxies, refer to Chapter 7, "Connecting to Networks."

4. In the DHCP console, enable NAP for individual scopes or for all scopes on the DHCP server, as described in the sections that follow.

5. Enable the NAP DHCP Quarantine Enforcement Client and start the NAP service on NAP-capable client computers. For more information, read "Configuring NAP Clients" later in this chapter.

Enabling NAP on All DHCP Scopes   To enable NAP for all DHCP scopes on a DHCP server, follow these steps:

1. In Server Manager, right-click Roles\DHCP Server\<*Computer Name*>\IPv4, and then choose Properties.

2. In the Network Access Protection tab (as shown in Figure 8-9), click Enable On All Scopes. Then, select one of the following options:

    ❑ **Full Access** Enables NAP for monitoring only. Noncompliant clients will be granted full network access.

❑ **Restricted Access** Enables NAP enforcement. Noncompliant clients will be assigned an IP address configuration that grants access only to servers listed in the remediation server group.

❑ **Drop Client Packet** Ignores DHCP requests from noncompliant clients. Windows clients will then automatically assign themselves an Automatic Private IP Addressing (APIPA) address in the 169.254.0.0/16 network, where they will be able to communicate only with other APIPA computers.

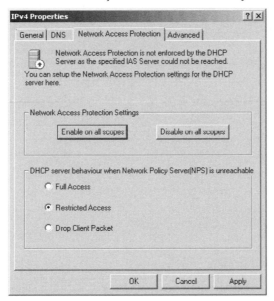

Figure 8-9 Configuring NAP on a DHCP server

3. Click OK.

Enabling NAP on a Single DHCP Scope To enable NAP for a single DHCP scope, follow these steps:

1. In Server Manager, right-click Roles\DHCP Server\<*Computer Name*>\IPv4\<*Scope Name*>, and then choose Properties.

2. In the Network Access Protection tab, select Enable For This Scope. Then, click OK.

Repeat these steps for each scope that you want to protect using NAP. For more information, read Chapter 4, "Installing and Configuring a DHCP Server."

Configuring VPN Enforcement

Configuring VPN enforcement requires the following high-level steps:

1. Use the Configure NAP Wizard to configure the connection request policy, network policy, and NAP health policy, as described in the section of this chapter entitled "Using the Configure NAP Wizard." Although you can configure these elements individually, it is much easier to use the wizard.

2. Configure remediation servers to define the computers that noncompliant clients can access. For more information, read "Configuring Remediation" later in this lesson.

3. Configure your VPN servers to perform PEAP-based authentication (either PEAP-MS-CHAP v2 or PEAP-TLS) and submit RADIUS requests to your NAP server. For more information, refer to Chapter 7, "Connecting to Networks."

4. If you plan to use certificates for authentication (using either PEAP-TLS or EAP-TLS), deploy a PKI such as the Certificate Services role and distribute certificates to client computers using a mechanism such as Active Directory autoenrollment. For more information, refer to Chapter 7, "Connecting to Networks." If you plan to use PEAP-MS-CHAP v2 domain authentication, use a PKI to issue server certificates to the NAP server.

5. Enable the NAP Remote Access Quarantine Enforcement Client and start the NAP service on NAP-capable client computers. For more information, read "Configuring NAP Clients" in the next section of this chapter.

Configuring NAP Components

Depending on the NAP enforcement type and your organization's specific requirements, you will need to configure SHVs, NAP client settings, and health requirement policies. Additionally, during the initial deployment phase, you will need to configure NAP for monitoring only. The sections that follow describe these tasks in detail.

Configuring NAP Clients

After configuring the NPS server, you must configure client computers for NAP. The easiest way to do this is to use GPO settings in the Computer Configuration\Policies\Windows Settings\Security Settings\Network Access Protection\NAP Client Configuration node. You can configure client NAP settings using the three subnodes:

- **Enforcement Clients**   You must enable one policy to configure clients to use that enforcement type.
- **User Interface Settings**   Configure the User Interface Settings policy to provide customized text (and, optionally, an image) that users will see as part of the NAP client interface.

- **Health Registration Settings**   Use the Request Policy subnode to configure crypto-graphic settings for NAP clients (the default settings are typically fine). Use the Trusted Server Group subnode to configure an HRA for IPsec NAP clients to use.

Additionally, you must start the Network Access Protection Agent service on all client comput-ers. You can do this manually, but it is easiest if you use Group Policy settings. In your GPO, select the Computer Configuration\Policies\Windows Settings\Security Settings\System Ser-vices node. Then, double-click the Network Access Protection Agent service. Define the policy and set it to start automatically, as shown in Figure 8-10.

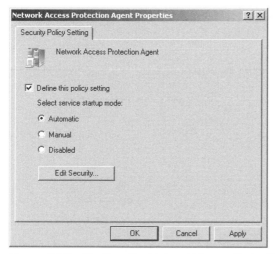

Figure 8-10   Starting the Network Access Protection Agent service automatically

Finally, to allow managed clients to use the default Windows SHV, you must enable Security Center by enabling the Computer Configuration\Policies\Administrative Templates\Windows Components\Security Center\Turn On Security Center policy.

NOTE   Configuring a working NAP environment

NAP configuration is complex, and this lesson has shown you many ways to configure NAP. Be sure to complete the practice at the end of this lesson to complete a NAP implementation from start to finish.

You can quickly verify a client's configuration by running the following command at a com-mand prompt:

```
netsh nap client show state
```

The following output shows a client that has the Network Access Protection Agent service started and only the IPsec enforcement agent enabled:

```
Client state:
----------------------------------------------------
Name                    = Network Access Protection Client
Description             = Microsoft Network Access Protection Client
Protocol version        = 1.0
Status                  = Enabled
Restriction state       = Not restricted
Troubleshooting URL     =
Restriction start time  =

Enforcement client state:
----------------------------------------------------
Id                      = 79617
Name                    = DHCP Quarantine Enforcement Client
Description             = Provides DHCP based enforcement for NAP
Version                 = 1.0
Vendor name             = Microsoft Corporation
Registration date       =
Initialized             = No

Id                      = 79618
Name                    = Remote Access Quarantine Enforcement Client
Description             = Provides the quarantine enforcement for RAS Client
Version                 = 1.0
Vendor name             = Microsoft Corporation
Registration date       =
Initialized             = No

Id                      = 79619
Name                    = IPSec Relying Party
Description             = Provides IPSec based enforcement for Network Access Protection
Version                 = 1.0
Vendor name             = Microsoft Corporation
Registration date       =
Initialized             = Yes

Id                      = 79621
Name                    = TS Gateway Quarantine Enforcement Client
Description             = Provides TS Gateway enforcement for NAP
Version                 = 1.0
Vendor name             = Microsoft Corporation
Registration date       =
Initialized             = No

Id                      = 79623
Name                    = EAP Quarantine Enforcement Client
```

```
Description              = Provides EAP based enforcement for NAP
Version                  = 1.0
Vendor name              = Microsoft Corporation
Registration date        =
Initialized              = No

System health agent (SHA) state:
--------------------------------------------------
Id                       = 79744
Name                     = Windows Security Health Agent

Description              = The Windows Security Health Agent checks the compliance of a computer
with an administrator-defined policy.

Version                  = 1.0

Vendor name              = Microsoft Corporation

Registration date        =
Initialized              = Yes
Failure category         = None
Remediation state        = Success
Remediation percentage = 0
Fixup Message            = (3237937214) - The Windows Security Health Agent has finished updating
its security state.

Compliance results       =
Remediation results      =

Ok.
```

If applying Group Policy settings is not convenient, you can use the SHA ID numbers to enable a NAP client at the command line (or from within a script). For example, to enable the DHCP Quarantine enforcement client (which has an ID of 79617), run the following command:

```
netsh nap client set enforcement 79617 enable
```

Configuring a Health Requirement Policy

Health requirement policies determine which clients must meet health requirements, what those health requirements are, and what happens if a client cannot comply. A health requirement policy is a combination of the following:

- **Connection request policy** Determines whether a request should be processed by NPS.
- **System health validators** Define which health checks a client must meet to be considered compliant. For example, with the default Windows SHV, you can configure whether not having a firewall enabled makes a client noncompliant.

- **Remediation server group**   A group of servers that noncompliant clients can access. These servers should provide clients with DNS and Active Directory services, as well as access to resources that will allow the client to become compliant, such as an update server.

- **Health policy**   Defines health requirements using SHV settings. Separate health policies must exist for both compliant and noncompliant clients.

- **Network policy**   Defines the level of network access clients get based on which health policy they match. You also use network policies to define the remediation servers clients with limited access can connect to. As shown in Figure 8-11, you can specify network policy conditions that cause the network policy to apply to a client based on matching a specific health policy, operating system, or whether the client supports NAP.

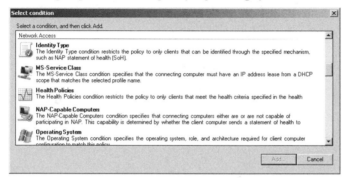

Figure 8-11   Configuring conditions for a network policy

Configuring SHVs   Windows Server 2008 includes only the Windows Security Health Validator SHV. Either Microsoft or third parties can supply additional SHVs that you would need to install on every NPS server.

After installing SHVs, configure them (including the Windows SHV, described in the next section, "Configuring the Windows Security Health Validator") by following these steps:

1. In Server Manager, select the Roles\Network Policy And Access Services\NPS\Network Access Protection\System Health Validators node.

2. In the Details pane, right-click the SHV, and then choose Properties.

3. First, configure the Error Code Resolution settings, as shown in Figure 8-12. For each of the six settings, you can define whether clients are compliant or noncompliant. Typically, you should leave these set to Noncompliant. However, if you experience a problem with clients receiving an error code when they should be compliant (for example, if an SHV or SHA needs to contact external services and cannot because of intermittent connectivity problems), you can change the error code resolution to Compliant.

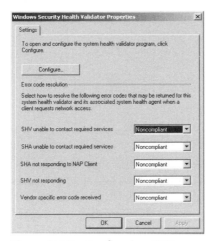

Figure 8-12   Configuring SHV error code resolution

4. Click the Configure button to configure settings specific to that SHV, and then click OK. This dialog box is different for every SHV.

5. Click OK again to save the SHV configuration settings.

Configuring the Windows Security Health Validator   By default, Windows Server 2008 includes a single SHV: the Windows SHV. The Windows SHV performs many of the same checks as the Security Center:

- Verifies that a firewall (such as Windows Firewall) is enabled for all network connections. Windows XP and Windows Vista include Windows Firewall, which fulfills this requirement.

- Verifies that antivirus software is present and that the signatures are up to date. Because Windows does not include antivirus software, this check will cause Windows computers to fail by default.

- For Windows Vista computers, verifies that antispyware software is present and the signatures are up to date. Windows Vista includes Windows Defender, which fulfills this requirement. You can also install Windows Defender on Windows XP computers, but the Windows Security Health Validator does not support checking antispyware software for computers running Windows XP.

- Automatic Updating is enabled.

Additionally, you can restrict access for clients that do not have all recent security updates installed and what level of security updates are required: Critical Only, Important And Above, Moderate And Above, Low And Above, or All. Figure 8-13 shows the Windows Security Health

Validator properties with its default settings. The Windows XP tab applies only to Windows XP clients with Service Pack 3 installed.

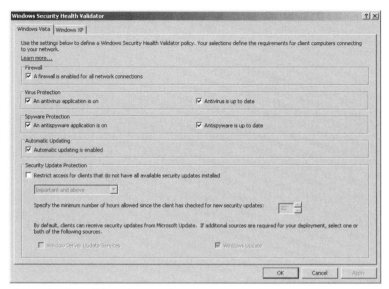

Figure 8-13   Editing the Windows SHV properties

To configure the Windows SHV, select NPS\Network Access Protection\System Health Validators in the Network Policy And Access Services snap-in. Then, in the Details pane, double-click Windows Security Health Validator. In the Windows Security Health Validator properties dialog box, click Configure.

Configuring Remediation   To provide assistance to users of noncompliant computers when requiring NAP health enforcement, you can configure a remediation server group and troubleshooting URL that will be available to users if they fail the compliance check. The remediation server group is used only for DHCP and VPN enforcement types; 802.1X and IPsec enforcement use different technologies to limit network access. Remediation servers are not required if you are using reporting mode because computers that fail the health check will still be allowed to connect to the network.

Although your exact remediation servers will vary depending on the requirements of your SHVs (the remediation servers should allow a noncompliant computer to enter compliance), remediation servers typically consist of the following:

■ DHCP servers to provide IP configuration

■ DNS servers, and optionally WINS servers, to provide name resolution

- Active Directory domain controllers, preferably configured as read-only, to minimize security risks
- Internet proxy servers—so that noncompliant NAP clients can access the Internet
- HRAs—so that noncompliant NAP clients can obtain a health certificate for the IPsec enforcement method
- A troubleshooting URL server, which provides a Web page users can access to view more information about the problem
- Antivirus update servers to retrieve updated antivirus signatures (if required by the health policy)
- Antispyware update servers to retrieve updated antispyware signatures (if required by the health policy)
- Software update servers

To configure these settings, follow these steps:

1. In Server Manager, select Roles\Network Policy And Access Services\NPS\Policies\Network Policies.

2. In the details pane, double-click the compliance policy that applies to noncompliant computers.

3. In the properties dialog box, click the Settings tab. In the Settings list, select NAP Enforcement. Then, click the Configure button.

4. In the Remediation Servers And Troubleshooting URL dialog box, do one or both of the following:

   ❑ Use the Remediation Server Group list to select a remediation server group. If you haven't created a remediation server group, click the New Group button. Name the group, and then click the Add button to add each server that should be accessible to clients who fail the compliance check. One remediation server group might be enough, but you can create separate remediation server groups for noncompliant NAP clients and non-NAP-capable clients. Click OK.

   NOTE Updating the remediation server group

   You can update your remediation server group later using Server Manager by selecting the Roles\Network Policy And Access Services\NPS\Network Access Protection\Remediation Server Groups node.

   ❑ In the Troubleshooting URL group, type the internal URL to a Web page that provides users with more information about why they can't connect to the network, how they can bring their computers into compliance, and whom they can call for assistance. A noncompliant computer visits this URL when a user clicks More Information in the Network Access Protection dialog box that appears when a user attempts to troubleshoot a failed connection, as shown in Figure 8-14. On the Web page, you should provide information that the user can employ to determine how to update the computer so that it is compliant or to troubleshoot network access. This URL is also visible when a user runs the *netsh nap client show state* command. The Web server you specify in the URL should be part of the Remediation Server Group list so that the client computer can access it.

Figure 8-14   Information provided to a noncompliant NAP client

5. Click OK.

Configuring Network Policies   Network policies determine whether a connection request matches specific conditions (such as a health policy, a client operating system, or whether a computer is NAP-capable). They then grant full or limited network access to the client.

To add a network policy, follow these steps:

1. In Server Manager, right-click Roles\Network Policy And Access Services\NPS\Policies\Network Policies, and then choose New.

   The New Network Policy Wizard appears.

2. On the Specify Network Policy Name And Connection Type page, type a policy name, and then select a network access server type. For IPsec enforcement, select Health Registration Authority. For 802.1X or VPN enforcement, select Remote Access Server. For DHCP enforcement, select DHCP Server. If you plan to use the Health Credential Authorization Protocol (HCAP) to integrate with Cisco Network Access Control, select HCAP server. Click Next.

Exam Tip   For the exam, don't worry about HCAP. Instead, focus on the other enforcement types.

---

3. On the Specify Conditions page, click the Add button to create any conditions you require, as shown in Figure 8-15, and then click Next. The most useful conditions for NAP are:

- ❑ **Health Policies**   Specifies that a client must meet the conditions specified in a health policy.
- ❑ **NAP-Capable Computers**   Allows you to match either computers that support NAP or computers that do not support NAP.
- ❑ **Operating System**   Allows you to apply the network policy to NAP-capable computers with specific operating system version numbers or computer architectures (such as 32-bit or 64-bit computers). This condition is not used as frequently as Health Policies and NAP-Capable Computers.
- ❑ **Policy Expiration**   Use this condition if you want to apply different conditions based on the current date and time. For example, if you are creating a temporary policy that applies only for the next week, you would add the Policy Expiration condition. You should create a second network policy to apply after the Policy Expiration condition expires.
- ❑ **Location Groups and HCAP User Groups**   These two conditions are useful if you are using NAP with Cisco Network Access Control. HCAP is not discussed in detail in this book.

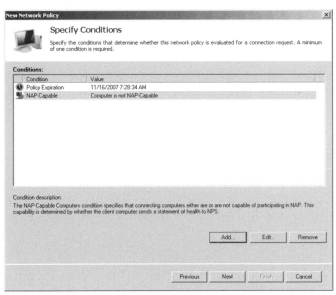

Figure 8-15   Specifying network policy conditions

4. On the Specify Access Permission page, select Access Granted. You should never select Access Denied for NPS policies because it prevents the health check from occurring. Click Next.

5. On the Configure Authentication Methods page, click Next. For NAP, authentication methods are selected in the Connection Request Policy.

6. On the Configure Constraints page, click Next. NAP rarely uses constraints, although you could use the Day And Time Restrictions constraints to apply the network policy at only specific times. Click Next.

7. On the Configure Settings page, select NAP Enforcement. Then, select one of the following options and click Next:

   ❑ **Allow Full Network Access**   Grants full access. Use this option if you are creating a network policy for healthy computers.

   ❑ **Allow Full Network Access For A Limited Time**   Grants full access up to a specific date and then restricts access to the selected Remediation Server Group. Use this option during the initial NAP deployment if you want to offer a grace period for noncompliant computers. When selecting this option, click the Configure button to select a remediation server group and specify a troubleshooting URL. If you select this option when using VPN enforcement, VPN clients are disconnected when the expiration time is reached.

   ❑ **Allow Limited Access**   Limits access to the servers specified in the selected remediation server group. Use this option when creating a network policy for noncompliant computers. When selecting this option, click the Configure button to select a remediation server group and specify a troubleshooting URL.

NOTE **The Extended State setting**

This page also includes the Extended State setting. This setting is used only if you are using HCAP with Cisco Network Admission Control. Otherwise, leave this setting at the default.

---

8. On the Completing New Network Policy Wizard page, click Finish.

Now, right-click the network policy and choose Move Up or Move Down to prioritize it. Higher network policies are evaluated first, and the first network policy with criteria that match a client is applied.

Configuring NAP for Monitoring Only

During your initial NAP deployment, you should allow noncompliant computers to connect to all network resources, even if they fail the NAP health check. To do this, modify the noncompliant health policy to allow full network access by following these steps:

1. In Server Manager, select Roles\Network Policy And Access Services\NPS\Policies\Network Policies. In the Details pane, double-click the noncompliant policy. For example, if you specified "NAP IPsec with HRA" as the name on the Select Network Connection Method For Use With NAP page of the NAP Wizard, the network policy for noncompliant NAP clients would have the name "NAP IPsec with HRA Noncompliant."

2. Click the Settings tab, and then select NAP Enforcement.

3. In the network policy properties dialog box, in the Details pane, select Allow Full Network Access, and then click OK.

To reenable NAP enforcement, change the setting to Allow Limited Access.

NAP Logging

NAP logging allows you to identify noncompliant computers. This is particularly important during the initial stages of a NAP deployment, when you will be using NAP only to gather information about the compliance level of the computers on your network. Using NAP logging, you can identify computers that are not compliant and resolve the problem before you enable NAP enforcement and prevent the computer from connecting to your network. NAP logging also enables you to identify computers that would be unable to connect to the network if NAP enforcement were enabled.

To configure NAP logging, right-click Roles\Network Policy And Access Services\NPS, and then choose Properties. In the General tab, select or clear the Rejected Authentication Requests and Successful Authentication Requests check boxes, as shown in Figure 8-16.

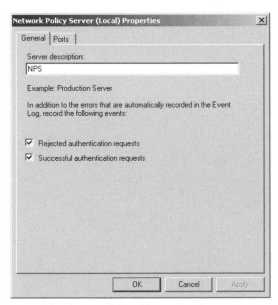

Figure 8-16   Configuring NPS logging

On the NAP server, you can use the Windows Logs\Security event log, available in Server Manager at Diagnostics\Event Viewer\Windows Logs\Security, to view NPS events. These events will reveal which NAP clients are not compliant. Figure 8-17 shows an event that indicates a computer that failed to pass the NAP health check.

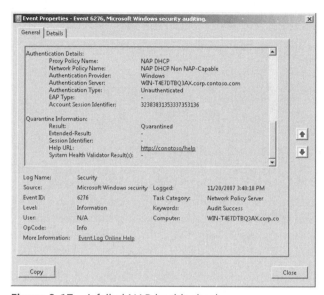

Figure 8-17   A failed NAP health check

Figure 8-18 shows a computer that passed the NAP health check.

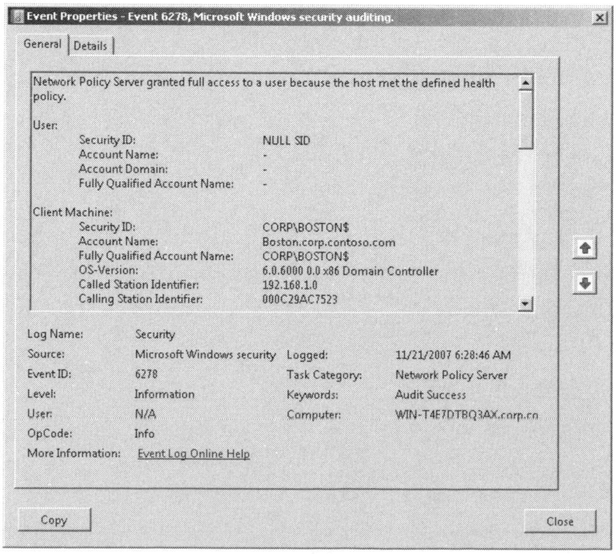

Figure 8-18   A successful NAP health check

On Windows Vista and Windows Server 2008 NAP clients, use the Event Viewer console to examine the Applications and Services Logs\Microsoft\Windows\Network Access Protection\Operational log. On NAP clients running Windows XP With Service Pack 3, use the Event Viewer console to examine the System event log.

Additionally, you can enable tracing for the Network Access Protection Agent service to gather extremely detailed information, which is typically required only when troubleshooting complex network problems. To enable tracing, run the following command:

```
netsh nap client set tracing enable level=verbose
```

The trace log files are stored in the %SystemRoot%\Tracing folder.

For more information about NAP logging, refer to Chapter 7, "Connecting to Networks" (NAP performs the same logging when used as a RADIUS server).

PRACTICE Configuring DHCP NAP Enforcement

In this practice, you configure DHCP NAP enforcement and test it with both a compliant and noncompliant NAP client. Although DHCP NAP enforcement is the least secure, it is used as an example here because the configuration is the easiest to demonstrate. To prepare for the exam, you should configure each of the different NAP enforcement types in a lab environment.

Configuring NAP DHCP enforcement is a common scenario for networks with hardware that does not support 802.1X and where IPsec is not available. Although DHCP enforcement does not prevent knowledgeable attackers from connecting to your network, it does inform users who are unaware that their computer does not meet your security requirements of the problem. In production environments, you would typically implement NAP for monitoring-only before enabling NAP enforcement.

▶ Exercise 1   Add the NPS and DHCP Server Roles

In this exercise, you will add the Network Policy And Access Services and DHCP Server roles to Dcsrv1. If either of these roles already exists (for example, if you added one or both in a previous exercise), remove the roles before continuing.

1. Configure Dcsrv1 with a static IP address of 192.168.1.2, a subnet mask of 255.255.255.0, and a DNS server address of 192.168.1.2.

2. In Server Manager, on Dcsrv1, select Roles. In the Details pane, click Add Roles. The Add Roles Wizard appears.

3. On the Before You Begin page, click Next.

4. On the Select Server Roles page, select the Network Policy And Access Services and DHCP Server check boxes. Click Next.

5. On the Network Policy And Access Services page, click Next.

6. On the Select Role Services page, select the Network Policy Server check box. Click Next.

7. On the DHCP Server page, click Next.

8. On the Network Connection Bindings page, click Next.

9. On the IPv4 DNS Settings page, click Next.

10. On the IPv4 WINS Settings page, click Next.

11. On the DHCP Scopes page, click Add. Complete the Add Scope dialog box, as shown in Figure 8-19. Name the scope NAP Clients. Provide an IP address range of 192.168.1.10 to 192.168.1.100. In the Subnet Mask box, type **255.255.255.0**. In the Default Gateway box, type **192.168.1.1** (even though that IP address does not exist). In the Subnet Type list, select Wireless. Selecting Wireless simply specifies a shorter lease duration, which requires NAP clients to process any health policy updates more regularly. Click OK, and then click Next.

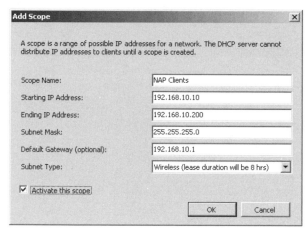

Figure 8-19 Configuring a DHCP scope

12. On the Configure DHCPv6 Stateless Mode page, click Next.

13. On the IPv6 DNS Settings page, click Next.

14. On the DHCP Server Authorization page, click Next.

15. On the Confirmation page, click Install.

16. On the Results page, click Close.

This installs DHCP and the core NPS service.

▶ **Exercise 2   Configure NAP on the DHCP Server**

In this exercise, you must configure NAP on the DHCP server to enforce health checks before assigning client computers an IP address that provides unlimited network access.

1. If Server Manager is already open, close it, and then reopen it. In Server Manager on Dcsrv1, select Roles\Network Policy And Access Services\NPS.

2. In the Details pane, under Standard Configuration, in the drop-down list, select Network Access Protection (NAP), and then click Configure NAP.

3. On the Select Network Connection Method For Use With NAP page, under Network Connection Method, select Dynamic Host Configuration Protocol (DHCP). Click Next.

4. On the Specify NAP Enforcement Servers Running DHCP Server page, click Add. In the New RADIUS Client dialog box, type **Dcsrv1** in the Friendly Name box and type Dcsrv1's IPv4 address (**192.168.1.2**) in the Address box. Click OK, and then click Next.

5. On the Specify DHCP Scopes page, click Next to apply NAP to all DHCP scopes.

6. On the Configure User Groups and Machine Groups page, click Next to apply the policy to all users.

7. On the Specify A NAP Remediation Server Group And URL page, click New Group. In the New Remediation Server Group dialog box, type a Group Name of DHCP Remediation Servers. Then, click Add and provide a Friendly Name of NAP and Dcsrv1's IPv4 address (192.168.1.2). Click OK twice. Notice that you can also type a troubleshooting URL in this dialog box if you had set up a Web page for this purpose and added that server to the remediation server group. For now, type a troubleshooting URL of **http://contoso/help**. Although this URL will not work, it will allow you to see how the troubleshooting URL is used. Click Next.

8. On the Define NAP Health Policy page, click Next to accept the default settings.

9. On the Completing NAP Enforcement Policy And RADIUS Client Configuration page, click Finish.

10. In Server Manager, select Roles\Network Policy And Access Services\NPS\Policies\Connection Request Policies. Verify that the NAP DHCP policy exists and that it is the first policy listed. If other NAP connection request policies exist, remove them. Similarly, if other network policies exist, you should remove them, too.

    Now you need to enable NAP enforcement on the DHCP server by following these steps:

11. In Server Manager, right-click Roles\DHCP Server\<*Computer Name*>\IPv4, and then choose Properties.

12. In the Network Access Protection tab, click Enable On All Scopes. Then, select Restricted Access. Click OK.

▶ **Exercise 3   Configure NAP Client Group Policy Settings**

After configuring the NPS server, you must configure client computers for NAP by following these steps:

1. Click Start, Administrative Tools, and then Group Policy Management.

   The Group Policy Management console appears.

2. Right-click Group Policy Management\Forest\Domains\<*Domain Name*>\Default Domain Policy, and then click Edit.

   The Group Policy Management Editor console appears.

3. Select the Computer Configuration\Policies\Windows Settings\Security Settings\Network Access Protection\NAP Client Configuration\Enforcement Clients node.

4. In the Details pane, double-click DHCP Quarantine Enforcement Client. Select the Enable This Enforcement Client check box, and then click OK.

5. Select the Computer Configuration\Policies\Windows Settings\System Services node. Then, in the Details pane, double-click Network Access Protection Agent. Select the Define This Policy Setting check box, and then select Automatic. Click OK.

6. Select the Computer Configuration\Policies\Administrative Templates\Windows Components\Security Center node. In the Details pane, double-click Turn On Security Center. Select Enabled, and then click OK.

▶ **Exercise 4   Test a Noncompliant Client**

In this exercise, you will connect a noncompliant computer to the network and determine whether it receives an IP address intended for compliant or noncompliant computers.

1. On Boston, open a command prompt with administrative credentials and run the command **gpupdate /force**. This retrieves the updated Group Policy settings from the domain controller, verifying that the changes you made for NAP clients are applied correctly. Verify that the Network Access Protection Agent service is started.

2. On Boston, run the command **netsh nap client show state** to verify that the DHCP Quarantine enforcement agent is enabled. If it is not, run the command **netsh nap client set enforcement 79617 enable** to manually enable it.

3. Disable any DHCP servers other than Dcsrv1. If you are using virtual machines, you can create a virtual network and connect both Dcsrv1 and Boston to the virtual network.

4. Connect Boston to the same network as Dcsrv1.

5. On Boston, open a command prompt with administrative privileges. Then, run the following commands to retrieve new IP address settings from the DHCP server:

```
ipconfig /release
ipconfig /renew
```

6. The client computer should display a new IP address configuration, with an IP address of 192.168.1.10 and a subnet mask of 255.255.255.255. Because the subnet mask is invalid (it should be 255.255.255.0), this indicates that the client computer failed the NAP health check.

7. At a command prompt, run the command **route print**. In the IPv4 Route Table, you should see a route with a Network Destination of 192.168.1.2. This address corresponds to the remediation server you configured.

8. At a command prompt, run the command **ping 192.168.1.2** (the IP address of Dcsrv1). Dcsrv1 should respond to the ping, verifying that the remediation server is accessible.

9. At a command prompt, run the command **ping 192.168.1.1** The command fails with a Transmit Failed error because there is no valid route to the destination.

10. Notice that a notification bubble appears in the system tray, indicating that there was a problem. Click the link to view the details of the error. Notice that the error specifies that Windows did not detect an antivirus program. Click the More Information button to attempt to open the *http://contoso/help* page. Click Close.

11. On Dcsrv1, check the System event log. Find the event indicating that the client computer failed the NAP health check. If you had implemented NAP in monitoring-only mode, this would be the only sign that a computer did not meet the health requirements.

▶ **Exercise 5   Update a Health Policy**

In this exercise, you change the health policy to allow the client computer to pass the health check.

1. On Dcsrv1, in Server Manager, select Roles\Network Policy And Access Services\NPS \Network Access Protection\System Health Validators. In the Details pane, double-click Windows Security Health Validator.

2. Click Configure to open the Windows Security Health Validator dialog box. In the Windows Vista tab, clear the An Antivirus Application Is On check box. Then, clear the Automatic Updating Is Enabled check box. Click OK twice.

The Boston client computer will be able to pass the remaining health validation tests.

▶ **Exercise 6   Test a Compliant Client**

In this exercise, you will connect a compliant computer to the network and determine whether it receives an IP address intended for compliant or noncompliant computers.

1. On Boston, open a command prompt with administrative privileges. Then, run the following commands to retrieve new IP address settings from the DHCP server:

```
ipconfig /release
ipconfig /renew
```

2. The client computer should display a new IP address configuration, with an IP address of 192.168.1.10, a subnet mask of 255.255.255.0 and a default gateway of 192.168.1.1. Because the subnet mask is now valid, it will be able to connect to other computers on the subnet (if any were available). A notification bubble will also appear, indicating that you have met the network's requirements.

3. On Boston, open Event Viewer and view the Applications and Services Logs\Microsoft \Windows\Network Access Protection\Operational log. Examine the events for both the unsuccessful and successful NAP health checks.

4. On Dcsrv1, open Event Viewer and view the Windows Logs\Security log. Examine the events for both the unsuccessful and successful NAP health checks.

You can now remove NAP from Dcsrv1 and remove the DHCP enforcement client configuration from Boston.

Lesson Summary

■ Network Access Protection (NAP) allows you to verify that computers meet specific health requirements before granting them unlimited access to your internal network. You can enforce NAP by using IPsec, 802.1X access points, VPN servers, or DHCP servers.

■ When deploying NAP, plan to implement it in monitoring-only mode first. This will allow you to identify and fix noncompliant computers before preventing them from connecting to your network.

■ You can use Server Manager to install and configure Network Policy Server.

■ Although the Configure NAP Wizard performs much of the configuration, each of the different NAP enforcement methods requires customized configuration steps.

■ Before NAP takes effect, you must configure NAP clients. Additionally, when using IPsec enforcement, you must configure a health requirement policy.

■ By default, NAP adds events to the Security event log on the NAP server each time a computer passes or fails a NAP health check. You can use the Security event log for auditing and to identify noncompliant computers that require manual configuration to become compliant.

Lesson Review

You can use the following questions to test your knowledge of the information in Lesson 2, "Configuring Network Access Protection." The questions are also available on the companion CD if you prefer to review them in electronic form.

NOTE Answers

Answers to these questions and explanations of why each answer choice is correct or incorrect are located in the "Answers" section at the end of the book.

1. You are a systems administrator for an enterprise company. You are currently configuring NAP enforcement in a lab environment. You need to create a network policy that prevents noncompliant computers from connecting to the network. How should you configure the network policy properties?

    A. In the Settings tab, set NAP Enforcement to Allow Limited Access.

    B. In the Overview tab, set Access Permission to Deny Access.

    C. In the Constraints tab, set the Session Timeout to 0.

    D. In the Settings tab, create an IP filter that drops all traffic.

2. You are a systems engineer developing NAP scenarios for future deployment within your organization. You want to configure a set of remediation servers that should be accessible for clients that do not support NAP. Which of the following do you need to do? (Choose all that apply.)

    A. Create a health policy and set it to Client Fails All SHV Checks.

    B. Create a network policy with a Condition type of NAP-Capable Computers.

    C. Create a remediation server group with the servers that should be accessible.

    D. Create a connection request policy with a Condition type of NAP-Capable Computers.

3. You are a systems administrator configuring NAP using DHCP enforcement. You plan to run NPS and DHCP on separate computers. Which of the following requirements do you need to fulfill? (Choose all that apply.)

    A. Configure a RADIUS proxy on the DHCP server.

    B. Install NPS on the DHCP server.

    C. Install HRA on the DHCP Server.

    D. Configure Certificate Services on the DHCP server.

Chapter Review

To further practice and reinforce the skills you learned in this chapter, you can

- Review the chapter summary.
- Review the list of key terms introduced in this chapter.
- Complete the case scenarios. These scenarios set up real-world situations involving the topics of this chapter and ask you to create a solution.
- Complete the suggested practices.
- Take a practice test.

Chapter Summary

- Windows Firewall is enabled by default to block most unwanted incoming connections. With additional configuration, you can limit the incoming connections that are allowed to specific subnets, user groups, or computer groups. Additionally, you can control which applications can initiate outgoing connections.
- Network Access Protection (NAP) is not enabled by default and requires complex planning and configuration to implement. After you deploy it, however, NAP provides network-level protection by allowing only clients that pass a health check to connect to your network.

Key Terms

Do you know what these key terms mean? You can check your answers by looking up the terms in the glossary at the end of the book.

- defense-in-depth
- firewall
- host route
- worm

Case Scenarios

In the following case scenarios, you will apply what you've learned about how to plan and deploy Windows Firewall and NAP. You can find answers to these questions in the "Answers" section at the end of this book.

Case Scenario 1: Evaluate Firewall Settings

You are a systems administrator for Fabrikam, Inc. Recently, your IT development department created a new client/server application that uses a Web service. Your manager asks you to interview key people and then come to his office to answer his questions about the changes you will need to make to the Windows Firewall configuration.

Interviews

Following is a list of company personnel interviewed and their statements:

- **Developer** "It's a Web service application, but it doesn't use IIS. Instead, it's its own service and listens for connections on TCP port 81. We need the server part of the application installed on Server1, and all client computers in the Accounting department should receive the client application. The client app just connects to the server on TCP port 81."
- **Lead systems engineer** "We use the default settings for Windows Firewall, so just let me know what I need to change."

Questions

Answer the following questions for your manager:

1. What type of firewall rule will you need to create to Windows Firewall on Server1?
2. What type of firewall rule will you need to create on the Windows Vista client computers in the Accounting department?

Case Scenario 2: Planning NAP

You are a systems administrator at Contoso, Inc., an enterprise that manufactures large-scale farm equipment. Last night the news carried a story of corporate espionage—and your organization was the victim. According to the story, an employee of your biggest competitor gained access to your internal network six months ago, stole confidential plans for new equipment, and used them to improve their own designs. Last week, a disgruntled employee contacted the media and told the entire story.

Apparently, your competitor's employee waited patiently at a coffee shop near your offices. When he saw someone come in with a laptop and a Contoso badge, he waited for the employee to connect to the wireless network. He then exploited a known network vulnerability (which had been fixed several months earlier but had not been updated on the employee's computer) in the user's Windows XP computer to install a tool that would automatically gather and forward documents from your company's internal network.

Your Chief Executive Officer (CEO) blames your Chief Security Officer (CSO), who in turn holds your Chief Information Officer (CIO) responsible. The CIO blames your manager, and your manager needs your help to create a plan to prevent this from happening again.

Answer the following questions for your manager:

1. Why would the attacker have been able to exploit a network vulnerability? How can that be prevented?

2. Is there some way we could have prevented the malware application from transmitting the confidential documents to a server on the Internet?

3. We can never guarantee that mobile computers will receive updates and won't be infected. After all, some of our staffers stay disconnected from the internal network for weeks at a time. So how can we keep these computers from connecting to our internal network and potentially doing damage?

4. If we suddenly turn on NAP, won't that cause problems for many of our client computers? How can we prevent that?

5. Which NAP enforcement method should we use?

Suggested Practices

To successfully master the Configure Network Access Protection (NAP) and Configure Firewall Settings exam objectives, complete the following tasks.

Configure Firewall Settings

For this task, you should complete all four practices to gain real-world experience working with Windows Firewall.

- **Practice 1** Configure outbound filtering to block requests by default. Then, create firewall rules to allow common applications, including Internet Explorer and Microsoft Office, to connect to the Internet. Verify that Windows Update can retrieve updates from Microsoft.

- **Practice 2** Using a computer that is connected to the public Internet, enable firewall logging. Wait several hours, and then examine the firewall log. What types of requests were dropped? What might have happened if the firewall were not enabled?

- **Practice 3** On your organization's production network, examine the inbound firewall rules. How can you adjust the scope of these rules to minimize security risks?

- **Practice 4** Watch the "Windows Vista Firewall And IPSec Enhancements" presentation by Steve Riley at *http://www.microsoft.com/emea/spotlight/sessionh.aspx?videoid=352*.

Configure Network Access Protection (NAP)

For this task, you should complete all four practices to gain experience using Network Access Protection in a variety of scenarios.

- **Practice 1** In a lab environment, deploy NAP using 802.1X, VPN, and IPsec. First, deploy NAP in monitoring-only mode. Then, switch to NAP enforcement.
- **Practice 2** Create a Web page that you could specify in the Troubleshooting URL, providing all the information the user of a noncompliant computer needs to remedy a problem and connect to the network.
- **Practice 3** Create a NAP test environment, including remediation servers. Using a noncompliant computer and any NAP enforcement technique, verify that you can bring the computer into compliance using just the resources provided by your remediation servers.
- **Practice 4** Watch the "Security and Policy Enforcement: Network Accesss Protection" presentation by Graziano Galante at *http://www.microsoft.com/emea/spotlight/sessionh .aspx?videoid=491.*

Take a Practice Test

The practice tests on this book's companion CD offer many options. For example, you can test yourself on just the content covered in this chapter, or you can test yourself on all the 70-642 certification exam content. You can set up the test so that it closely simulates the experience of taking a certification exam, or you can set it up in study mode so that you can look at the correct answers and explanations after you answer each question.

MORE INFO   Practice tests

For details about all the practice test options available, see "How to Use the Practice Tests" in this book's Introduction.

Chapter 9
Managing Software Updates

Over the years, computers have become much easier to manage. Hardware and software are more reliable, operating systems are easier to use, and many management tasks (for example, defragmentation) are now completely automated. However, there remains one area that requires constant, ongoing maintenance: software updates.

Unfortunately, the penalty for not installing software updates can be severe. If computers do not have recent updates installed, it's much more likely that an attacker will exploit a software vulnerability. This in turn can lead to extended downtime, additional computers being compromised, and confidential information leaving your internal network.

To help you distribute updates throughout your organization while minimizing the management time required, Microsoft provides Windows Server Update Services (WSUS). WSUS allows you to download, approve (after you've tested the updates), and distribute updates throughout your organization—no matter how many client computers you manage.

The lessons in this chapter provide an overview of WSUS to enable you to plan an update infrastructure deployment, along with detailed information about configuring WSUS.

Exam objectives in this chapter:
- Configure Windows Server Update Services (WSUS) server settings.

Lessons in this chapter:

Before You Begin

To complete the lessons in this chapter, you should be familiar with Microsoft Windows networking and be comfortable with the following tasks:

- Adding roles to a Windows Server 2008 computer
- Configuring Active Directory domain controllers and joining computers to a domain
- Basic network configuration, including configuring IP settings

You will also need the following nonproduction hardware, connected to test networks:

■   A computer named Dcsrv1 that is a domain controller in the Nwtraders.msft domain.

NOTE   Computer and domain names

The computer and domain names you use will not affect these exercises. The practices in this chapter refer to these computer names for simplicity, however.

■   A computer named Boston that is a member of the Nwtraders.msft domain.

Real World

Tony Northrup

Deploying updates can take a lot of time. You need to test the update against all applicable operating systems and the applications that you run on that operating system. When you deploy it, client computers often need to be restarted—which can interrupt user productivity. Additionally, any update can cause compatibility problems, even with proper testing. As you can see, deploying updates has a significant cost, but it doesn't provide any new functionality.

The truth is, it's all too easy to fall behind when distributing security updates. If Microsoft releases a new security update and you do absolutely nothing with it, you'll *probably* be fine. After all, many vulnerabilities can be exploited only if multiple layers of protection have been bypassed, and, even when exploited, the attacker might not be able to take any significant action on the compromised computer.

Several times a year, however, someone releases malicious software to exploit a known vulnerability for which an update already exists. These exploits can devastate organizations, costing millions of dollars in lost productivity. You can typically avoid these losses by installing a single update prior to the release of the malicious software, but you never know which update will be the important one.

The only way to be sure you're protected from the next big exploit is to promptly test and install all security updates. Adding Network Access Protection (NAP) to provide an additional layer of protection for unpatched computers helps, too.

Lesson 1: Understanding Windows Server Update Services

Before deploying Windows Server Update Services (WSUS), you must understand how both the client and server components should be configured for different environments. Without proper planning, updates can take too long to distribute, waste large amounts of your limited Internet and wide area network (WAN) bandwidth, or fail to install correctly. This lesson provides background and planning information on WSUS.

NOTE   **New features**

If you are familiar with earlier versions of WSUS, WSUS 3.0 with Service Pack 1 (included with Windows Server 2008) provides a significant amount of new functionality. Most significantly, there is now a console to manage WSUS; you no longer need to manage it using a Web browser. Additionally, you have more flexibility for controlling which computers receive which updates.

> **After this lesson, you will be able to:**
> - Describe the purpose of WSUS.
> - Configure the WSUS client.
> - Design a WSUS architecture to meet the needs of both small and large organizations.
> - List the client and server requirements for WSUS.
> - Describe the tools you can use to identify computers that are missing important updates.
>
> **Estimated lesson time: 15 minutes**

WSUS Overview

Windows Server Update Services (WSUS) is a private version of the Microsoft Update service from which Windows computers automatically download updates. Because you can run WSUS on your own internal network and use it to distribute updates to your computers, you can use bandwidth more efficiently and maintain complete control over the updates installed on your client computer.

When you run WSUS, it connects to the Microsoft Update site, downloads information about available updates, and adds them to a list of updates that require administrative approval. After an administrator approves and prioritizes these updates (a process that you can entirely automate), WSUS automatically makes them available to Windows computers. The Windows Update client (when properly configured) then checks the WSUS server and automatically downloads and, optionally, installs approved updates. You can distribute WSUS across multiple servers and locations to scale from small business to enterprise needs.

Windows Update Client

The Windows Update client is the component of WSUS clients that retrieves software from the WSUS server, verifies the digital signature and the Secure Hash Algorithm (SHA1) hash, notifies the user that the update is available, and installs the software (if configured to do so). The Windows Update client installs updates at a scheduled time and can automatically restart the computer if necessary. If the computer is turned off at that time, the updates can be installed as soon as the computer is turned on. If the computer's hardware supports it, Windows Update can wake a computer from sleep and install the updates at the specified time.

NOTE   WSUS client in earlier versions of Windows

In Windows XP and Windows 2000, the client component of WSUS is called the Automatic Updates client.

Because Windows Update settings should be applied to all computers in your organization, Group Policy is typically the best way to distribute the settings. Windows Update settings are located at Computer Configuration\Policies\Administrative Templates\Windows Components\Windows Update. The Windows Update Group Policy settings are:

- **Specify Intranet Microsoft Update Service Location**   Specifies the location of your WSUS server.

- **Configure Automatic Updates**   Specifies whether client computers will receive security updates and other important downloads through the Windows Update service. You also use this setting to configure whether the user is prompted to install updates or the Windows Update client automatically installs them (and at what time of day the installation occurs).

- **Automatic Updates Detection Frequency**   Specifies how frequently the Windows Update client checks for new updates. By default, this is a random time between 17 and 22 hours.

- **Allow Non-Administrators To Receive Update Notifications**   Determines whether all users or only administrators will receive update notifications. Nonadministrators can install updates using the Windows Update client.

- **Allow Automatic Updates Immediate Installation**   Specifies whether Windows Update will immediately install updates that don't require the computer to be restarted.

- **Turn On Recommended Updates Via Automatic Updates** Determines whether client computers install both critical and recommended updates, which might include updated drivers.

- **No Auto-Restart For Scheduled Automatic Updates Installations** Specifies that to complete a scheduled installation, Windows Update will wait for the computer to be restarted by any user who is logged on instead of causing the computer to restart automatically.

- **Re-Prompt For Restart With Scheduled Installations** Specifies how often the Windows Update client prompts the user to restart. Depending on other configuration settings, users might have the option of delaying a scheduled restart. However, the Windows Update client will automatically remind them to restart based on the frequency configured in this setting.

- **Delay Restart For Scheduled Installations** Specifies how long the Windows Update client waits before automatically restarting.

- **Reschedule Automatic Updates Scheduled Installations** Specifies the amount of time for Windows Update to wait, following system startup, before continuing with a scheduled installation that was missed previously. If you don't specify this amount of time, a missed scheduled installation will occur one minute after the computer is next started.

- **Enable Client-Side Targeting** Specifies which group the computer is a member of. This option is useful only if you are using WSUS; you cannot use this option with Software Update Services (SUS), the predecessor to WSUS.

- **Enabling Windows Update Power Management To Automatically Wake Up The System To Install Scheduled Updates** If people in your organization tend to shut down their computers when they leave the office, enable this setting to configure computers with supported hardware to automatically start up and install an update at the scheduled time. Computers will not wake up unless there is an update to be installed. If the computer is on battery power, the computer will automatically return to sleep after two minutes.

- **Allow Signed Updates From An Intranet Microsoft Update Service Location** Specifies whether Windows XP with Service Pack 1 or later will install updates signed using a trusted certificate even if the certificate is not from Microsoft. This is not a commonly used setting.

Additionally, the following two settings are available at the same location under User Configuration (which you can use to specify per-user settings) in addition to Computer Configuration:

- **Do Not Display 'Install Updates And Shut Down' Option In Shut Down Windows Dialog Box** Specifies whether Windows XP with Service Pack 2 or later shows the Install Updates And Shut Down option.

- **Do Not Adjust Default Option To 'Install Updates And Shut Down' In Shut Down Windows Dialog Box**   Specifies whether Windows XP with Service Pack 2 or later automatically changes the default shutdown option to Install Updates And Shut Down when Windows Update is waiting to install an update.

Finally, the last user setting is available only at User Configuration\Administrative Templates \Windows Components\Windows Update:

- **Remove Access To Use All Windows Update Features**   When enabled, prevents a user from accessing the Windows Update interface.

WSUS Architecture

WSUS can scale from small organizations to multinational enterprises. In general, you'll need a single WSUS server for each regional office with more than 10 computers and a separate WSUS server for each different IT department that requires control over how updates are approved.

Typically, redundancy is not required for WSUS servers; however, you should back up the WSUS database and be prepared to repair or replace the server within a week of failure. If a WSUS server fails, there's no direct impact on users, and updates are rarely so time-critical that there would be any impact if it took even a few days to restore a WSUS server.

The sections that follow describe how to design WSUS architectures for different types of offices.

Organizations with One Office

If you have only one location, you can use a single WSUS server—regardless of the total number of client computers. The Windows Update client is designed to share bandwidth and wait when your network is busy, so network impact should be minimal.

Organizations with Multiple Offices

If you were to use a single WSUS server to support clients at multiple offices, each client computer would need to download updates across your WAN connection. Updates, especially service packs, can be several hundred megabytes. Because WAN connections tend to have lower bandwidth than LAN connections, downloading large updates across the WAN could affect overall WAN performance. If your WAN is low-bandwidth or highly busy, clients might not be able to retrieve updates promptly.

To allow clients to retrieve updates from your LAN, configure one WSUS server at each regional location and configure the WSUS servers to retrieve updates in a hierarchy from their parent servers. For best results, use a hierarchy that mirrors your WAN architecture while minimizing the number of levels in the hierarchy. Figure 9-1 illustrates a typical WAN architecture, and Figure 9-2 demonstrates an efficient WSUS design for that architecture.

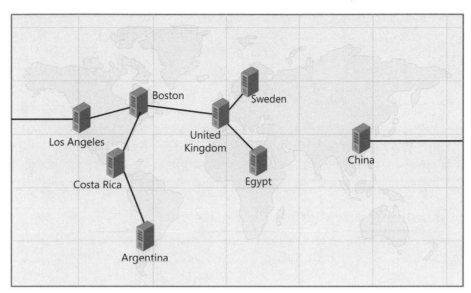

Figure 9-1   A typical WAN architecture

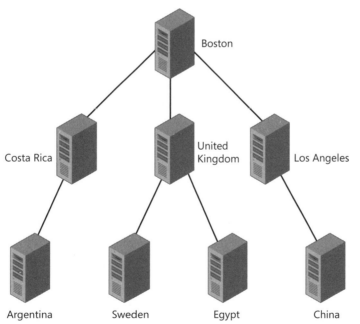

Figure 9-2   An efficient WSUS architecture for the previous sample WAN

In this architecture, only the Boston WSUS server would retrieve updates directly from Microsoft. All update management would be performed on the Boston WSUS server, and all other WSUS servers would be configured as replicas. The downstream servers would pull updates from the upstream servers; for example, Los Angeles (the downstream server) would pull updates from Boston (the upstream server). Similarly, Argentina is considered a downstream server to Costa Rica.

To provide updates for small offices that cannot support a local WSUS server, configure client computers to download updates from the nearest WSUS server. If the office has a fast Internet connection, consider deploying a WSUS replica that does not store updates locally and instead directs client computers to retrieve updates directly from Microsoft.

Organizations with Multiple IT Departments

The architecture demonstrated in the previous section shows an ideal that is rarely realistic: an entire multinational company managed by a single IT department. Most organizations have separate IT departments, with their own processes and guidelines, who will insist on controlling which updates are deployed to the client computers they manage.

In organizations with distributed IT departments, you can design the WSUS architecture exactly as described in the previous section. The only difference is in the configuration—instead of configuring each WSUS server as a replica, configure the WSUS servers as autonomous, which allows for approvals and management at each specific server. The configuration steps required are described in Lesson 2, "Using Windows Server Update Services."

WSUS Requirements

When planning your WSUS deployment, keep the following requirements in mind:

- The WSUS server must establish HTTP connections to the Internet (specifically, to the Microsoft Update Web site). If the connection uses a proxy server, you must provide credentials (if required).
- Downstream WSUS servers must establish connections to upstream WSUS servers using either HTTP (and TCP port 80) or, if you have an SSL certificate installed, HTTPS (and TCP port 443).
- Client computers must connect from your intranet using either HTTP or HTTPS.
- The client computer operating system must be one of the following:
    - Windows 2000 with Service Pack 3 or Service Pack 4
    - Windows XP Professional
    - Windows Vista

❑ Windows Server 2003

❑ Windows Server 2008

■ If client computers are disconnected from your network for an extended period of time (for example, if a professor leaves on sabbatical or an employee works from home for months and does not connect to the virtual private network [VPN]), the client will not be able to download updates. Consider configuring the computer to automatically install updates directly from Microsoft or, using NAP, to require computers to have updates before connecting to your intranet. For more information about NAP, read Chapter 8, "Configuring Windows Firewall and Network Access Protection."

Planning the WSUS Installation

During the WSUS installation process, you will need to make several critical decisions:

■ **Update source**   WSUS can retrieve updates either directly from Microsoft Update or from another WSUS server on your own network. Typically, you should choose the method that is most bandwidth efficient. If two WSUS servers are connected by a high-speed local area network (LAN), have one of those servers retrieve updates from Microsoft Update and the second server retrieve updates from the first. If you have WSUS servers in three remote offices that are linked using VPNs across the Internet, it would be more efficient for each to download updates directly from Microsoft—because the updates would need to cross the individual Internet connections anyway. Your WSUS architecture defines the exact arrangement, with downstream servers configured to retrieve updates from upstream servers.

■ **Approval and configuration replication**   If you have multiple WSUS servers and you configure servers to retrieve updates from one of your WSUS servers, you can choose to also synchronize approvals, settings, computers, and groups from the parent WSUS server. Essentially, this makes the child WSUS server a perfect replica. If you configure a server as a replica, you do not need to approve updates on the replica server. If you configure a server as autonomous, you must manually approve updates on the WSUS servers—which is useful for giving multiple IT departments independent control.

■ **Update storage**   WSUS can either copy updates from Microsoft and store them locally or direct client computers to download updates directly from Microsoft. If you choose to store updates locally, the WSUS server will require at least 6 GB of free disk space (although the actual amount can be much greater, depending on how many updates Microsoft releases and how many languages you require). Storing updates locally can greatly reduce your Internet bandwidth update by allowing clients to retrieve updates across the LAN.

■ **Database**   By default, WSUS will store the list of updates (including which updates you want to deploy and other settings) in a Windows Internal Database. The WSUS setup process requires at least 3 GB of free disk space to store the Windows Internal Database, although the actual size is typically closer to 1 GB. The Windows Internal Database works for most purposes, but you can also use an existing database server (such as a Microsoft SQL Server) on the local computer or a remote computer.

NOTE   Default WSUS database location

By default, the database is located at C:\WSUS\UpdateServicesDbFiles\SUSDB.mdf.

■ **Web site selection**   WSUS requires IIS because client computers retrieve updates using HTTP or HTTPS (if you have an SSL certificate, such as one purchased from a public certification authority or generated by a Windows Server 2008 certification authority). If you do not use IIS for any other purposes on the WSUS server, you can use the existing IIS default Web site. Otherwise, you can create a new Web site specifically for WSUS.

■ **Languages**   Many updates are language-specific. To minimize disk space usage, you should choose to download only languages that are required by client computers that will access the WSUS server. You should avoid selecting all languages, because the total storage space and bandwidth required will be very high.

■ **Products**   Microsoft Update can provide updates for a wide variety of products other than core Windows operating systems. For example, Microsoft Update distributes updates for Exchange Server, ISA Server, SQL Server, and Office. Select only the applications and operating systems used within your organization to minimize the disk space required.

Auditing Updates

After deploying WSUS, some client computers might still be missing updates because the update installation fails, the client computer is misconfigured (or is not part of your Active Directory domain), or the client computer has been disconnected from your network for a long time. You can use several techniques to identify computers that are missing updates:

■ **Windows Update console**   You can use the *Computers And Reports* node to identify WSUS clients that have not installed approved updates.

■ **Microsoft System Center Configuration Manager 2007 (Configuration Manager 2007)** Configuration Manager 2007 is the latest version of Microsoft Systems Management Server (SMS). Configuration Manager 2007, like SMS, can provide detailed information about the updates and applications installed on managed computers. Configuration Manager 2007 is best suited to enterprises with an Active Directory domain. For more information about Configuration Manager 2007, visit *http://www.microsoft.com/smserver/*.

- **Microsoft Baseline Security Analyzer (MBSA)** MBSA is an automated security auditing tool that identifies missing updates and configurations that might lead to security vulnerabilities. MBSA can scan entire networks, enabling you to identify unmanaged computers on your network. This provides a significant advantage over the Windows Update console, which can report only on clients that are configured to use the WSUS server. For more information about MBSA and to download the free tool, visit *http://www.microsoft.com/mbsa/*.
- **Network Access Protection (NAP)** NAP, when combined with the standard Windows System Health Validator (as described in Chapter 8, "Configuring Windows Firewall and Network Access Protection"), can verify that computers have recent updates installed each time they connect to your network. In monitoring-only mode, NAP adds an event to the event log that you can monitor, allowing you to identify out-of-date computers. If you enable NAP enforcement, client computers that do not meet your health requirements can be connected to a remediation network, where they must apply required updates before gaining access to the private network.

Lesson Summary

- WSUS allows you to store and distribute software updates from Microsoft across your internal network, reducing Internet bandwidth usage. Additionally, WSUS gives you complete control over when updates are deployed to client computers, allowing you to test updates prior to release.
- The Windows Update client retrieves updates from the WSUS server. Depending on how you have configured the Windows Update client, it can notify the user that the update is available for installation or automatically install the update without interacting with the user. You can configure the Windows Update client using Group Policy settings.
- A single WSUS server is sufficient for most organizations that have a single location. Typically, you will want to deploy a separate WSUS server to each office to minimize Internet and WAN usage. Additional WSUS servers can be configured as replicas (which copy their configuration from the upstream WSUS server) or can be autonomous (which allows separate IT departments to make their own decisions about when updates are deployed).
- Several types of problems can prevent WSUS clients from installing updates. To identify these updates, you can use the Update Services console, Configuration Manager 2007, MBSA, and NAP.

Lesson Review

You can use the following questions to test your knowledge of the information in Lesson 1, "Understanding Windows Server Update Services." The questions are also available on the companion CD if you prefer to review them in electronic form.

NOTE Answers

Answers to these questions and explanations of why each answer choice is correct or incorrect are located in the "Answers" section at the end of the book.

---

1. You are a systems engineer for an enterprise video production company. Your organization has six offices and a centralized IT department that manages all of the 1200 client computers. Each of the offices has about 200 computers. The WAN uses a hub-and-spoke architecture, with each of the five remote offices connected directly to the headquarters. How would you design the WSUS architecture?

   A. Deploy a WSUS server to each office. Configure the WSUS servers to be managed by each office's local IT support department.

   B. Deploy a WSUS server at the headquarters. Configure all client computers to retrieve updates directly from Microsoft.

   C. Deploy a WSUS server at the headquarters. Configure all client computers to retrieve updates directly from the WSUS server.

   D. Deploy a WSUS server to each office. Configure the WSUS servers at the remote offices to be replicas of the WSUS server at the headquarters.

2. You are a systems administrator configuring an update infrastructure for your organization. You need to use Group Policy settings to configure client computers to download updates and install them automatically without prompting the user. Which Group Policy setting should you enable and configure?

   A. Allow Automatic Updates Immediate Installation

   B. Configure Automatic Updates

   C. No Auto-Restart For Scheduled Automatic Updates

   D. Enable Client-Side Targeting

3. You are currently evaluating which of the computers in your environment will be able to download updates from WSUS. Which of the following operating systems can act as WSUS clients (even if they require a service pack)? (Choose all that apply.)

   A. Windows 95

   B. Windows 98

   C. Windows 2000 Professional

   D. Windows XP Professional

Lesson 2: Using Windows Server Update Services

With Windows Server 2008, you can install WSUS using Server Manager and manage it with the Update Services console. This newest version of WSUS includes a significant number of new features and user interface changes, and, even if you are familiar with earlier versions, you should complete this lesson so that you understand exactly how to manage the software.

After this lesson, you will be able to:
- Install WSUS on a computer running Windows Server 2008.
- Configure computer groups, approve updates, and view WSUS reports.
- Troubleshoot both client and server problems installing updates.
- Manually remove problematic updates from client computers.

Estimated lesson time: 40 minutes

How to Install Windows Server Update Services

WSUS is a free download available at *http://www.microsoft.com/wsus*. Follow the instructions available at that Web page to install the latest version of WSUS for Windows Server 2008.

After installation you must synchronize the updates from Microsoft Update by following these steps:

1. Click Start, Administrative Tools, and then Microsoft Windows Server Update Services. The Update Services console appears.

2. In the console tree, select the server name. In the details pane, click the Synchronize Now link.

Synchronization will take several minutes (and could take more than an hour). After synchronization completes, you can begin to manage WSUS.

How to Configure Windows Server Update Services

After installing WSUS and beginning synchronization, configure WSUS by following these steps:

1. Fine-tune the WSUS configuration by editing WSUS options.

2. Configure computer groups to allow you to distribute updates to different sets of computers at different times.

3. Configure client computers to retrieve updates from your WSUS server.

4. After testing updates, approve or decline them.

5. View reports to verify that updates are being distributed successfully and identify any problems.

The sections that follow describe each of these steps in more detail.

How to Configure WSUS Options

Though the setup wizard prompts you to configure the most important WSUS options, you can configure other options after the initial configuration by selecting the *Options* node in the Update Services console, as shown in Figure 9-3.

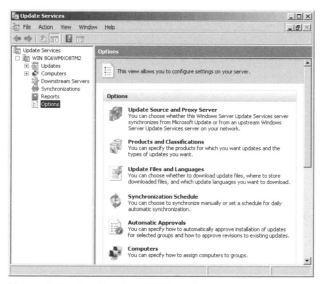

Figure 9-3 Configuring WSUS options

You can configure options in the following categories:

■ **Update Source And Proxy Server** Configure the upstream WSUS server or configure the WSUS server to retrieve updates from Microsoft. You configure this during installation and rarely need to change it unless you modify your WSUS architecture.

■ **Products And Classifications** Choose the Microsoft products that WSUS will download updates for. You should update these settings when you begin supporting a new product or stop supporting an existing product (such as an earlier version of Microsoft Office).

■ **Update Files And Languages** Select where updates are stored and which languages to download updates for.

- **Synchronization Schedule**   Configure whether WSUS automatically synchronizes updates from the upstream server and how frequently.

- **Automatic Approvals**   Configure updates for automatic approval. For example, you can configure critical updates to be automatically approved. You should use this only if you have decided not to test updates for compatibility—a risky decision that can lead to compatibility problems with production computers.

- **Computers**   Choose whether to place computers into groups using the Update Services console or Group Policy and registry settings. For more information, read the following section, "How to Configure Computer Groups."

- **Server Cleanup Wizard**   Over time, WSUS will accumulate updates that are no longer required and computers that are no longer active. This wizard helps you remove these outdated and unnecessary updates and computers, freeing disk space (if you store updates locally) and reducing the size of the WSUS database.

- **Reporting Rollup**   By default, downstream servers push reporting information to upstream servers, aggregating reporting data. You can use this option to configure each server to manage its own reporting data.

- **E-Mail Notifications**   WSUS can send an e-mail when new updates are synchronized, informing administrators that they should be evaluated, tested, and approved. In addition to configuring those e-mail notifications, you can use this option to send daily or weekly status reports.

- **Microsoft Update Improvement Program**   Disabled by default, you can enable this option to send Microsoft some high-level details about updates in your organization, including the number of computers and how many computers successfully or unsuccessfully install each update. Microsoft can use this information to improve the update process.

- **Personalization**   On this page you can configure whether the server displays data from downstream servers in reports. You can also select which items are shown in the To Do list that appears when you select the WSUS server name in the Update Services console.

- **WSUS Server Configuration Wizard**   Allows you to reconfigure WSUS using the wizard interface used for initial configuration. Typically, it's easier to configure the individual settings you need.

How to Configure Computer Groups

In most environments, you will not deploy all updates to all clients at once. To give you control over when computers receive updates, WSUS 3.0 allows you to configure groups of computers and deploy updates to one or more groups. You might create additional groups for different models of computers or different organizations, depending entirely on the process you use for deploying updates. Typically, you will create computer groups for each stage of your update deployment process, which should resemble this:

- **Testing** Deploy updates to computers in a lab environment. This will allow you to verify that the update distribution mechanism works properly. Then you can test your applications on a computer after the updates have been installed.
- **Pilot** After testing, you will deploy updates to a pilot group. Typically, the pilot group is a set of computers belonging to your IT department or another computer-savvy group that is able to identify and work around problems.
- **Production** If the pilot deployment goes well and there are no reported problems after a week or more, you can deploy updates to your production computers with less risk of compatibility problems.

You can configure computer groups in one of two ways:

- **Server-side Targeting** Best suited for small organizations, you add computers to computer groups manually using the Update Services console.
- **Client-side Targeting** Better suited for larger organizations, you use Group Policy settings to configure computers as part of a computer group. Computers automatically add themselves to the correct computer group when they connect to the WSUS server.

Whichever approach you use, you must first use the Update Services console to create computer groups. By default, a single computer group exists: All Computers. To create additional groups, follow these steps:

1. Click Start, Administrative Tools, and then Microsoft Windows Server Update Services. The Update Services console appears.
2. In the console tree, expand Computers, and then right-click All Computers (or the computer group you want to nest the new computer group within). Choose Add Computer Group.
   The Add Computer Group dialog box appears.
3. Type a name for the computer group, and then click Add.
4. Repeat steps 2 and 3 to create as many computer groups as you need.

Server-side Targeting To add computers to a group using server-side targeting, follow these steps:

1. In the console tree of the Update Services console, expand Computers, All Computers, and then select Unassigned Computers. Then, in the details pane, right-click the computer you want to assign to a group (you can also select multiple computers by Ctrl-clicking) and choose Change Membership.

2. In the Set Computer Group Membership dialog box, select the check box for each group that you want to assign the computer or computers to. Click OK.

The computers you selected will be moved to the specified computer groups.

Client-side Targeting   You use Group Policy objects (GPOs) to add computers to computer groups when you enable client-side targeting. First, configure the WSUS server for client-side targeting by following these steps:

1. Click Start, Administrative Tools, and then Microsoft Windows Server Update Services. The Update Services console appears.
2. In the console tree, select Options. In the details pane, click Computers.
3. In the Computers dialog box, select Use Group Policy Or Registry Settings On Computers. Then, click OK.

Next, configure GPOs to place computers in the correct computer group. You will need to create separate GPOs for each computer group and configure each to apply only to the appropriate computers.

1. Open the GPO in the Group Policy Management Editor.
2. In the console tree, select the Computer Configuration\Policies\Administrative Templates\Windows Components\Windows Update node.
3. In the details pane, double-click the Enable Client-Side Targeting policy.
4. In the Enable Client-Side Targeting Properties dialog box, select Enabled. Then, type the name of the computer group you want to add the computer to and click OK.

After the client computers apply the Group Policy settings, restart the Windows Update services, and contact the WSUS server; they will place themselves in the specified group.

Quick Check

1. What protocol do Windows Update clients use to retrieve updates from an update server?
2. Should an enterprise use client-side targeting or server-side targeting?

Quick Check Answers

1. HTTP.
2. Enterprises should use client-side targeting, which leverages Group Policy settings to configure which updates client computers retrieve.

How to Configure Client Computers

The section "Windows Update Client" in Lesson 1, "Understanding Windows Server Update Services," described the different Group Policy settings available to configure how clients retrieve updates. The following steps provide instructions for performing the minimal amount of configuration necessary (which is sufficient for many organizations) for WSUS clients to download updates from your WSUS server.

1. Open the GPO you want to use to distribute the configuration settings. In the Group Policy Management Editor, select the Computer Configuration\Policies\Administrative Templates\Windows Components\Windows Update node.

2. In the details pane, double-click Specify Intranet Microsoft Update Service Location.

   The Specify Intranet Microsoft Update Service Location Properties dialog box appears.

3. Select Enabled. In both the Set The Intranet Update Service For Detecting Updates box and the Set The Intranet Statistics Server box, type **http://WSUS_Computer_Name**. Click OK.

4. Double-click Configure Automatic updates.

   The Configure Automatic updates Properties dialog box appears.

5. Select Enabled. Configure the automatic update settings. For example, to have updates automatically installed, from the Configure Automatic Updating drop-down list select 4 - Auto Download And Schedule The Install. Click OK.

With these Group Policy settings enabled, clients will retrieve and optionally install updates from your WSUS server.

How to Approve Updates

Unless you have configured automatic approval, updates are not approved by default. To manually approve updates, follow these steps:

1. Click Start, Administrative Tools, and then Microsoft Windows Server Update Services.

   The Update Services console appears.

2. In the console tree, expand the server name, and then expand Updates. Select one of the following options:

   - **All Updates**   Displays all updates. This is the most convenient option for approving updates.
   - **Critical Updates**   Displays only critical updates, which are high-priority updates, such as bug fixes, that are not security related.
   - **Security Updates**   Displays only updates that fix known security problems.
   - **WSUS Updates**   Displays updates related to the update process.

3. On the toolbar at the top of the details pane, from the Approval drop-down list, select Unapproved, as shown in Figure 9-4. You can also use this list to view updates that you have approved or declined.

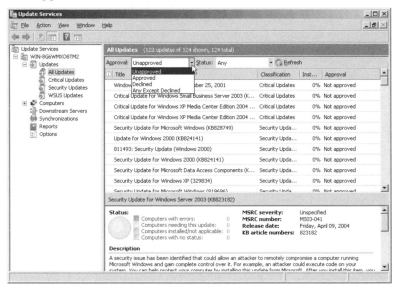

Figure 9-4   Viewing updates that require approval

4. From the Status drop-down list, select Any. Click Refresh to display the updates.

NOTE   Sorting updates

To sort updates so that newer updates appear first in the list, right-click the column headings, and then select the Release Date column. Then, click the Release Date column header to sort by that date.

---

5. Select the updates that you want to approve. You can select multiple updates by Ctrl-clicking each update. Alternatively, you can select many updates by clicking the first update and then shift-clicking the last update. Press Ctrl+A to select all updates. Right-click the selected updates, and then choose either Approve (to distribute the update to clients the next time they check for updates) or Decline (to prevent the update from being distributed).

6. If the Approve Updates dialog box appears, select the computer group you want to apply the updates to, and then choose Approved For Install. Repeat to apply the update to multiple computers. Click OK when you are done.

7. To define a deadline (after which an update must be installed and users will not be given the option of delaying the update), right-click the computer group, choose Deadline, and then select the deadline.

8. Click OK.

9. If a license agreement appears, click I Accept.

NOTE Removing updates

If you've previously applied updates to computers, you can choose Approved For Removal to remove the update. Most updates do not support automated removal, however, and WSUS will report an error in the Approval Progress dialog box. To remove these updates, follow the instructions in "How to Remove Updates" later in this lesson.

The Approval Progress dialog box appears as WSUS applies the updates.

10. Examine any errors displayed in the Approval Progress dialog box, and then click Close.

How to Decline Updates

After approving necessary updates, you can decline updates that you do not want to install on computers. Declining updates does not directly affect client computers; it only helps you organize updates in the WSUS console.

To decline updates, follow these steps:

1. In the Update Services console, right-click the update you want to decline, and then choose Decline.

2. In the Decline Update dialog box, click Yes.

To review updates that have been declined, from the Approval drop-down list in the Windows Update console, select Declined. Then click Refresh.

How to View Reports

You can view detailed information about updates, computers, and synchronization using the *Reports* node in the Update Services console, as shown in Figure 9-5.

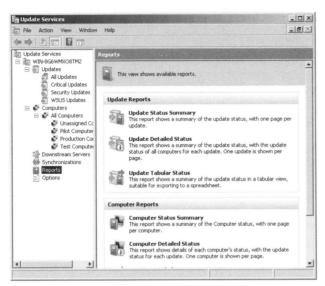

Figure 9-5 WSUS reports

WSUS provides the following reports:

■ **Update Status Summary**   As shown in Figure 9-6, this report displays detailed information about every update that you choose to report on, including the full description (provided by Microsoft), the computer groups the update has been approved for, and the number of computers the update has been installed on.

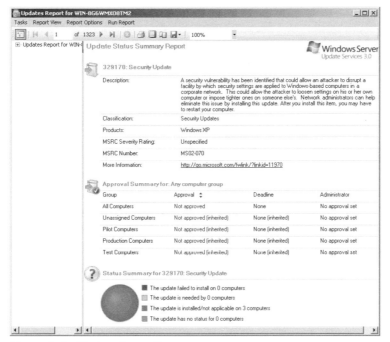

Figure 9-6   Update Status Summary report

- **Update Detailed Status**   In addition to the information shown for the Update Status Summary report (which is shown on odd-numbered pages), this report shows the update status for all computers for each update on even-numbered pages, allowing you to determine exactly which computers have the update installed. This report is useful if you determine that a security exploit has been released and you need to quickly identify any computers that might be vulnerable because a critical update has not been applied.

- **Update Tabular Status**   This report provides data similar to the previous two reports but uses a table format that can be exported to a spreadsheet.

- **Computer Status Summary**   Displays update information for every computer in your organization. This report is useful if you are interested in auditing specific computers.

- **Computer Detailed Status**   In addition to the information shown for the Computer Status Summary report, this report shows whether each update has been installed on each of your computers.

- **Computer Tabular Status**   This report provides data similar to the previous two reports but uses a table format that can be exported to a spreadsheet.

- **Synchronization Results**   Displays the results of the last synchronization.

When you open a report, you can configure options to filter the information shown in the report. For example, for update reports you can choose which products to display updates for. After configuring the options, click Run Report to display the report. The last page of the report displays a summary of settings used to generate the report.

How to Manage Synchronizations

The *Synchronizations* node in the Update Services console displays a list showing every time WSUS has retrieved a list of updates from the upstream server. You can right-click any synchronization and then choose Synchronization Report for detailed information. Use this node to verify that synchronizations are occurring and new updates are being found.

How to Troubleshoot Problems Installing Updates

Occasionally, you might experience a problem installing an update. You can use the WSUS console to identify clients that have updates installed, as well as clients that have been unable to install updates. To gather more information about a specific failed installation, you can troubleshoot the problem at the client computer.

The sections that follow describe how to troubleshoot server-side and client-side problems.

How to Troubleshoot WSUS

WSUS creates three logs files that can be useful in troubleshooting. The default locations are:

- **The Application event log**   This log stores events related to synchronization, Update Services console errors, and WSUS database errors with a source of Windows Server Update Services. Most events provide detailed information about the cause of the problem and guidance for further troubleshooting the problem. For additional help with specific errors, search for the error at *http://support.microsoft.com*. The Application event log should always be the first place you check when troubleshooting WSUS errors.

- **C:\Program Files\Update Services\LogFiles\Change.txt**   A text file that stores a record of every update installation, synchronization, and WSUS configuration change. The log entries aren't detailed, however. For example, if an administrator changes a configuration setting, WSUS records only "WSUS configuration has been changed" in the log file.

- **C:\Program Files\Update Services\LogFiles\SoftwareDistribution.txt**   An extremely detailed text log file used primarily for debugging purposes by Microsoft support.

How to Troubleshoot the Windows Update Client

To identify the source of the problem causing an update to fail, follow these steps:

1. Examine the %SystemRoot%\WindowsUpdate.log file to verify that the client is contacting the correct update server and to identify any error messages. For detailed information about how to read the WindowsUpdate.log file, refer to Microsoft Knowledge Base article 902093 at *http://support.microsoft.com/kb/902093/*.

2. Verify that the client can connect to the WSUS server by opening a Web browser and visiting http://<*WSUSServerName*>/iuident.cab. If you are prompted to download the file, this means that the client can reach the WSUS server and it is not a connectivity issue. Otherwise, you could have a name resolution or connectivity issue or WSUS is not configured correctly.

3. If you use Group Policy to configure the Windows Update client, use the Resultant Set of Policy (RSOP) tool (Rsop.msc) to verify the configuration. Within RSOP, browse to the Computer Configuration\Administrative Templates\Windows Components\Windows Update node and verify the configuration settings.

If you have identified a problem and made a configuration change that you hope will resolve it, restart the Windows Update service on the client computer to make the change take effect and begin another update cycle. You can do this using the Services console or by running the following two commands:

```
net stop wuauserv
net start wuauserv
```

Within 6 to 10 minutes, Windows Update will attempt to contact your update server.

To make Windows Update begin querying the WSUS server, run the following command:

```
wuauclt /a
```

Although the WindowsUpdate.log file provides the most detailed information and should typically be the first place you look when troubleshooting, you can view high-level Windows Update-related events in the System event log, with a source of WindowsUpdateClient. The Windows Update service adds events each time an update is downloaded or installed and when a computer needs to be restarted to apply an update. The Windows Update service also adds a Warning event (with Event ID 16) when it cannot connect to the automatic updates service, a sign that the client cannot reach your WSUS server.

Even more detailed information can be found in the Applications And Services Logs\Microsoft\Windows\WindowsUpdateClient\Operational log. The Windows Update service adds an event to this log each time it connects to or loses connectivity with a WSUS server, checks for updates (even if no updates are available), as shown in Figure 9-7, and experiences an error.

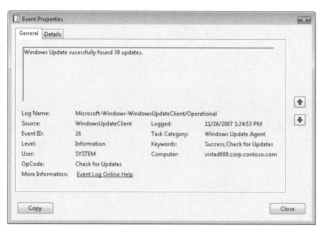

Figure 9-7 Verifying that the Windows Update client found available updates

To view which updates have been installed on a computer running Windows Vista or Windows Server 2008, follow these steps:

1. Click Start and then Control Panel. Click the System And Maintenance link, and then click the Windows Update link.
2. Click View Update History.

Windows Update displays the complete list of installed updates, as demonstrated by Figure 9-8. You can double-click any update to view more detailed information.

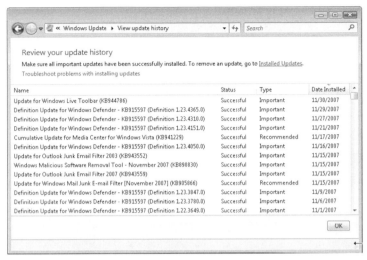

Figure 9-8   Viewing installed updates

How to Remove Updates

Occasionally, an update might cause a compatibility problem. If you experience a problem with an application or a Windows feature after installing updates and one of the updates was directly related to that problem, you can uninstall the update to determine whether it is related to the problem.

To remove an update, follow these steps:

Use Windows Update to view the update history, as described in "How to Troubleshoot the Windows Update Client" in the previous section. View the details of each update to identify the update that might be causing a problem. Make note of the Knowledge Base (KB) number for the update.

1. Click Start, and then click Control Panel.
2. Under Programs, click the Uninstall A Program link.
3. Under Tasks (in the upper-left corner of the window), click the View Installed Updates link.
4. Select the update you want to remove by using the KB number you noted in step 1. Then click Uninstall.
5. Follow the prompts that appear and restart the computer if required.

If removing the update does not resolve the problem, you should reapply the update. Then contact the application developer (in the case of a program incompatibility) or your Microsoft support representative to inform them of the incompatibility.

PRACTICE Deploying Updates with WSUS

In this practice, you configure WSUS on a server, use Group Policy settings to configure client computers, and then approve and distribute updates.

▶ **Exercise 1   Install WSUS**

In this exercise, you will add WSUS to a server. To minimize storage requirements, you will configure the WSUS server to direct clients to retrieve updates directly from Microsoft.

1. Download and install WSUS on Dcsrv1 by following the instructions at *http://www.microsoft.com/wsus*.

2. Click Start, Administrative Tools, and then Microsoft Windows Server Update Services.

3. The Update Services console appears.

4. Select the computer name, Dcsrv1. In the Details pane, click Synchronize Now.

Synchronization will take several minutes (and could take more than an hour).

▶ **Exercise 2   Configure Client Computers to Retrieve Updates**

In this exercise, you will update Group Policy settings to configure client computers to retrieve updates from your WSUS server, rather than directly from Microsoft.

1. Open the GPO you want to use to distribute the configuration settings. In the Group Policy Management Editor, select the Computer Configuration\Policies\Administrative Templates\Windows Components\Windows Update node.

2. In the details pane, double-click Specify Intranet Microsoft Update Service Location. The Specify Intranet Microsoft Update Service Location Properties dialog box appears.

3. Select Enabled. In both the Set The Intranet Update Service For Detecting Updates box and the Set The Intranet Statistics Server box, type **http://Dcsrv1**. Click OK.

4. Double-click Configure Automatic Updates. The Configure Automatic Updates Properties dialog box appears.

5. Select Enabled. Configure the automatic update settings. For example, to have updates automatically installed, from the Configure Automatic Updating drop-down list, select 3 - Auto Download And Notify For Install. Click OK.

Next, log on to Boston as a member of the Administrators group. Run the command *gpupdate /force* to cause the client computer to apply the updated Group Policy settings. Then, restart the Windows Update service to cause Boston to immediately connect to the WSUS server.

▶ **Exercise 3   Approve Updates**

In this exercise, you will approve an update to be deployed to your client computer, Boston.

1. On Dcsrv1, in the Update Services console, expand Dcsrv1 and Updates. Then, select All Updates.

2. On the toolbar at the top of the details pane, from select the Approval drop-down list, select Unapproved.

3. From the Status drop-down list, select Any. Click Refresh to display the updates.

4. Select a recent update that would apply to Boston (your client computer). Right-click the selected updates, and then choose Approve.

NOTE Removing the update for testing purposes

If the update has already been applied to Boston, remove the update using the Programs tool in Control Panel.

---

5. In the Approve Updates dialog box, select the All Computers computer group, and then choose Approved For Install. In a production environment, you would typically have created several computer groups. Click OK.

6. If a license agreement appears, click I Accept.

The Approval Progress dialog box appears as WSUS applies the updates.

7. Examine any errors displayed in the Approval Progress dialog box to verify that the update can be applied to Boston, and then click Close.

8. In the Update Services console, select the Computers\All Computers node. Then, select Any on the Status drop-down list and click the Refresh button. The Boston client computer should appear on the list, having had sufficient time to connect to the WSUS server after refreshing Group Policy. If it has not appeared yet, wait another few minutes.

On the Boston client computer, restart the Windows Update service. Wait 15 minutes or more, and Windows Update should display a notification that an update is available. For detailed information, examine the System log on Boston for Windows Update events.

Lesson Summary

- You can download WSUS from Microsoft.com.
- After installing WSUS and synchronizing updates from the upstream server, you should configure computer groups to allow you to selectively distribute updates to clients. Next, approve or decline updates and wait for them to be distributed to clients. Use reports to verify that the update process is successful and identify any clients who have been unable to install important updates.
- If you experience problems with WSUS, examine the Application event log on the WSUS server. Although WSUS also creates two text-based log files, the Application event log contains the most useful troubleshooting information. If a client experiences problems connecting to the WSUS server or installing updates, begin troubleshooting by examining the %SystemRoot%\WindowsUpdate.log file.
- Although you can remove some updates using WSUS, you typically need to manually remove updates from client computers using the Programs tool in Control Panel.

Lesson Review

You can use the following questions to test your knowledge of the information in Lesson 2, "Using Windows Update Services." The questions are also available on the companion CD if you prefer to review them in electronic form.

NOTE   Answers

Answers to these questions and explanations of why each answer choice is correct or incorrect are located in the "Answers" section at the end of the book.

---

1. You are a systems administrator at an enterprise home audio equipment design firm. Recently, you used MBSA to audit your client computers for the presence of specific security updates. You found several computers that did not have the updates installed. How can you determine why the update installation failed? (Choose all that apply.)

   A. Examine the System log on the client computer.

   B. Examine the Applications And Services Logs\Microsoft\Windows\Windows UpdateClient\Operational on the client computer.

   C. Examine the System log on the WSUS server.

   D. Examine the %SystemRoot%\WindowsUpdate.log file.

2. You are a systems administrator for an architecture firm. You have recently deployed WSUS, and you need to verify that updates are being distributed successfully. Which of the following pieces of information can you get from the Update Status Summary report?

   A. Which computer groups a particular update has been approved for

   B. Which computers have successfully installed an update

   C. Whether an update can be removed using WSUS

   D. The number of computers that failed to install an update

3. You are in the process of deploying WSUS to your organization. Currently, you are configuring client computers to be members of different computer groups so that you can stagger update deployments. How can you configure the computer group for a computer? (Choose all that apply.)

   A. Enable the Configure Automatic Updates policy.

   B. Configure the Enable Client-Side Targeting Group Policy setting.

   C. In the Update Services console, right-click the computer, and then choose Change Membership.

   D. In the Update Services console, drag the computers to the appropriate computer group.

Chapter Review

To further practice and reinforce the skills you learned in this chapter, you can

- Review the chapter summary.
- Review the list of key terms introduced in this chapter.
- Complete the case scenarios. These scenarios set up real-world situations involving the topics of this chapter and ask you to create a solution.
- Complete the suggested practices.
- Take a practice test.

Chapter Summary

- WSUS gives you control over the approval and distribution of updates from Microsoft to your client computers. A WSUS server can copy updates from Microsoft and store them locally. Then client computers will download updates from your WSUS server instead of downloading them from Microsoft across the Internet. To support organizations with multiple offices, downstream WSUS servers can synchronize updates, approvals, and configuration settings from upstream WSUS servers, allowing you to design a hierarchy that can scale to any capacity.
- Installing WSUS also requires installing IIS, but WSUS can coexist with other IIS Web sites. After WSUS is installed, you can manage WSUS with the Windows Update console, available from the Administrative Tools menu on the WSUS server. First, you should begin synchronizing the WSUS server with updates from Microsoft. Then, create the different computer groups you will use to deploy updates selectively to different computers. Next, configure client computers to contact your local WSUS servers instead of the Microsoft Update servers on the Internet and add client computers to the appropriate computer groups.

Key Terms

Do you know what these key terms mean? You can check your answers by looking up the terms in the glossary at the end of the book.

- downstream server
- upstream server
- Windows Server Update Services (WSUS)

Case Scenarios

In the following case scenarios, you will apply what you've learned about how to design and configure a WSUS infrastructure. You can find answers to these questions in the "Answers" section at the end of this book.

Case Scenario 1: Planning a Basic WSUS Infrastructure

You are a systems engineer for City Power & Light. Currently, you have configured all client computers to download updates directly from Microsoft and automatically install them. However, after a recent service pack release, you notice that the bill from your Internet service provider (ISP) for Internet bandwidth jumped significantly after Microsoft released a large service pack to Windows Update (you pay per usage with your contract).

You'd like to use WSUS to reduce your bandwidth usage to your headquarters, where you have approximately 250 computers. Eventually, you'd like to begin testing updates before deploying them. However, you do not have the staff to perform the testing, so for the time being you want updates to be automatically approved and installed.

You go into your manager's office to discuss the ISP bill and how you can avoid it in the future. Answer the following questions for your manager:

1. How can WSUS reduce your bandwidth utilization?
2. How many WSUS servers will you need?
3. How can you configure WSUS to automatically approve updates?

Case Scenario 2: Planning a Complex WSUS Infrastructure

You are a systems engineer working for Northwind Traders, an international company with offices around the globe. Your headquarters are in London, and you have branch offices in New York, Mexico City, Tokyo, and Casablanca. All offices have high-speed Internet connections, and they are interconnected with VPNs using a full-mesh architecture. In other words, each of the five offices is connected directly to the other four offices.

Currently, the London IT department manages both the London and New York offices. The Mexico City, Tokyo, and Casablanca offices each have their own IT departments. As you are beginning to deploy Windows Server 2008, you are evaluating WSUS and would like to create an architecture that will meet the needs of each of your five locations.

Interviews

Following is a list of company personnel interviewed and their statements:

- **Mexico City IT Manager** "I talked with the IT managers in Tokyo and Casablanca, and we each have unique technical requirements, languages, client operating systems, and testing procedures. Therefore, we need to be able to manage our own update approvals. However, we're open to synchronizing updates from a central server, if that's your preference."

- **Your Manager** "It doesn't matter to me whether you synchronize updates between offices or from the Internet. Since we're using a VPN, it all crosses the same Internet connection anyway. So it's up to you."

Questions

Answer the following questions for your manager:

1. How many WSUS server do you need, and where will you locate them?
2. Which of the WSUS servers will be replicas, and which will be managed independently?

Suggested Practices

To successfully master the Monitoring and Managing a Network Infrastructure exam objective, complete the following tasks.

Configure Windows Server Update Services (WSUS) Server Settings

For this task, you should complete at least Practices 1 and 3. If your organization currently uses WSUS, also complete Practice 2.

- **Practice 1** Examine the WindowsUpdate.log file on your computer (or any production computer that has been running for a long time). When did failures occur and what caused them? Were the failed updates successfully installed later?

- **Practice 2** If your organization currently uses WSUS, view the different reports that are available to determine how many computers are up to date and which updates failed most often during installation.

- **Practice 3** Consider your organization's current network, including any remote offices, and the WAN connections. How would you design a WSUS infrastructure to most efficiently distribute updates? If you currently use WSUS, is the design optimal?

Take a Practice Test

The practice tests on this book's companion CD offer many options. For example, you can test yourself on just the content covered in this chapter, or you can test yourself on all the 70-642 certification exam content. You can set up the test so that it closely simulates the experience of taking a certification exam, or you can set it up in study mode so that you can look at the correct answers and explanations after you answer each question.

MORE INFO   Practice tests

For details about all the practice test options available, see "How to Use the Practice Tests" in this book's Introduction.

Chapter 10
Monitoring Computers

A solid understanding of how to monitor computers in your organization is vital for both quickly troubleshooting problems and responding to problems before they become critical. For troubleshooting problems, monitoring allows you to gather detailed information about a computer's state, such as the processor, memory, and disk utilization. Monitoring can also allow you to be proactive and identify warning signs that indicate an impending problem before the problem becomes serious.

This chapter describes three useful monitoring techniques: event forwarding, performance monitoring, and network monitoring.

Exam objectives in this chapter:
- Capture performance data.
- Monitor event logs.
- Gather network data.

Lessons in this chapter:

Before You Begin

To complete the lessons in this chapter, you should be familiar with Microsoft Windows networking and be comfortable with the following tasks:

- Adding roles to a Windows Server 2008 computer.
- Configuring Active Directory domain controllers and joining computers to a domain.
- Basic network configuration, including configuring IP settings.

You will also need the following nonproduction hardware, connected to test networks:

- A computer named Dcsrv1 that is a domain controller in the Nwtraders.msft domain. This computer must have at least one network interface that is connected to the Internet.

NOTE   Computer and domain names

The computer and domain names you use will not affect these exercises. The practices in this chapter refer to these computer names for simplicity, however.

- A computer named Boston that is a member of the Nwtraders.msft domain.

Real World

Tony Northrup

What Process Monitor (available at *http://www.microsoft.com/technet/sysinternals/File AndDisk/processmonitor.mspx*) is to troubleshooting application problems, Network Monitor is to troubleshooting network problems.

When errors occur, applications often present useless messages. For example, consider an e-mail client that is unable to connect to a server. The e-mail client is likely to show the user a message such as, "Unable to connect to server. Please contact your network administrator." If you use Network Monitor to capture the unsuccessful connection attempt, you can quickly determine whether the cause of the problem is connectivity, name resolution, authentication, or something else.

When I worked with the original version of Network Monitor, network administrators weren't as concerned about security. As a result, communications were rarely encrypted and Network Monitor could capture traffic in clear text. This made troubleshooting network problems easy—but it also made it easy to collect people's passwords on the network.

To address that privacy risk, most applications that transfer private data now provide some form of application-layer security (including e-mail) and more organizations are using IPsec to encrypt data at the network layer. Encrypted packets appear as garbage in Network Monitor, which can interpret only the headers. If you need to troubleshoot a network problem and encryption is preventing you from interpreting the data, consider temporarily disabling IPsec or application-layer encryption until you have isolated the problem.

Lesson 1: Monitoring Event Logs

Windows has always stored a great deal of important information in the event logs. Unfortunately, with versions of Windows released prior to Windows Vista, that information could be very hard to access. Event logs were always stored on the local computer, and finding important events among the vast quantity of informational events could be very difficult.

With Windows Vista, Windows Server 2008, and Windows Server 2003 R2, you can collect events from remote computers (including computers running Windows XP) and detect problems, such as low disk space, before they become more serious. Additionally, Windows now includes many more event logs to make it easier to troubleshoot problems with a specific Windows component or application. This lesson will describe how to manage events in Windows Server 2008 and Windows Vista.

> **After this lesson, you will be able to:**
> - Describe how event forwarding works.
> - Configure computers to support event forwarding and create a subscription.
>
> **Estimated lesson time: 25 minutes**

Event Forwarding Concepts

With event forwarding, you can send events that match specific criteria to an administrative computer, allowing you to centralize event management. This allows you to view a single log and see the most important events from computers anywhere in your organization, rather than needing to connect to the local event logs on individual computers. With event forwarding, the critical information in the event log becomes much more accessible.

Event forwarding uses Hypertext Transfer Protocol (HTTP) or HTTPS (Hypertext Transfer Protocol Secure) to send events from a forwarding computer to a collecting computer. Because event forwarding uses the same protocols used to browse Web sites, it works through most firewalls and proxy servers. Whether event forwarding uses HTTP or HTTPS, it is encrypted.

How to Configure Event Forwarding

Using event forwarding requires you to configure both the forwarding and collecting computers. First, you must start the following services on both the forwarding and collecting computer:

- Windows Remote Management
- Windows Event Collector

Additionally, the forwarding computer must have a Windows Firewall exception for the HTTP protocol. As described later in this lesson, you might also need to create a Windows Firewall exception on the collecting computer, depending on the delivery optimization technique you choose. Only Windows Vista, Windows Server 2008, and Windows Server 2003 R2 can act as collecting computers. Only Windows XP with Service Pack 2, Windows Server 2003 with Service Pack 1 or 2, Windows Server 2003 R2, Windows Vista, and Windows Server 2008 can act as forwarding computers.

NOTE **Forwarding events from Windows XP and Windows Server 2003**

Before computers running Windows XP or Windows Server 2003 can act as forwarding computers, you must install WS-Management 1.1. For more information, see *http://go.microsoft.com/fwlink/ ?LinkId=100895*.

The sections that follow describe step-by-step how to configure computers for event forwarding.

Configuring the Forwarding Computer

To configure a computer running Windows Vista or Windows Server 2008 to forward events, follow these steps:

1. At a command prompt with administrative privileges, run the following command to configure the Windows Remote Management service:

   `winrm quickconfig`

   Windows displays a message similar to the following (other changes might be required, depending on how the operating system is configured):

   ```
   WinRM is not set up to allow remote access to this machine for management.
   The following changes must be made:

   Create a WinRM listener on HTTP://* to accept WS-Man requests to any IP on this
   machine.
   Enable the WinRM firewall exception.

   Make these changes [y/n]?
   ```

2. Type **Y**, and then press Enter.

   WinRM (the Windows Remote Management command-line tool) configures the computer to accept WS-Management requests from other computers. Depending on the current configuration, this might involve making the following changes:

   ❑ On Windows Vista computers, setting the Windows Remote Management (WS-Management) service to Automatic (Delayed Start) and starting the service. This service is already started on Windows Server 2008 computers.

❑ Configuring a Windows Remote Management HTTP listener.

❑ Creating a Windows Firewall exception to allow incoming connections to the Windows Remote Management service using HTTP. This exception applies only to the Domain and Private profiles; traffic will still be blocked while the computer is connected to Public networks.

Next, you must add the computer account of the collector computer to the local Event Log Readers group on each of the forwarding computers. You can do this manually or automatically from a script or command prompt by running the following command:

```
net localgroup "Event Log Readers" <computer_name>$@<domain_name> /add
```

For example, to add the computer SERVER1 in the contoso.com domain, you would run the following command:

```
net localgroup "Event Log Readers" server1$@contoso.com /add
```

Configuring the Collecting Computer

To configure a computer running Windows Vista or Windows Server 2008 to collect events, open a command prompt with administrative privileges. Then, run the following command to configure the Windows Event Collector service:

```
wecutil qc
```

In Windows Server 2008 you can also simply select the *Subscriptions* node in the console tree of Event Viewer. Event Viewer will prompt you to configure the Windows Event Collector service to start automatically, as shown in Figure 10-1.

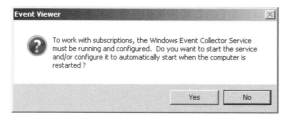

Figure 10-1 Event Viewer prompting the user to configure the computer as a collector

---

Quick Check

1. What command should you run to configure a forwarding computer?
2. What command should you run to configure a collecting computer?

Quick Check Answers
1. You should run **winrm quickconfig**.
2. You should run **wecutil qc**.

Creating an Event Subscription

To create a subscription on a Windows Server 2008 collecting computer, follow these steps (the steps on a Windows Vista computer are similar but slightly different):

1. In Event Viewer (under the *Diagnostics* node in Server Manager), right-click Subscriptions, and then choose Create Subscription.
2. In the Event Viewer dialog box, click Yes to configure the Windows Event Collector service (if prompted).

   The Subscription Properties dialog box appears, as shown in Figure 10-2.

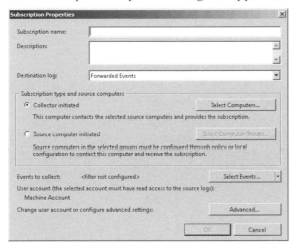

Figure 10-2 The Subscription Properties dialog box

3. In the Subscription Name box, type a name for the subscription. Optionally, type a description.
4. You can create two types of subscriptions:
   - ❑ **Collector initiated** The collecting computer contacts the source computers to retrieve events. Click the Select Computers button. In the Computers dialog box, click Add Domain Computers, choose the computers you want to monitor, and then click OK. Click the Test button to verify that the source computer is properly configured, and then click OK. If you have not run the *winrm quickconfig* command

on the source computer, the connectivity test will fail. Click OK to return to the Subscription Properties dialog box.

❑ **Source computer initiated**   The forwarding computers contact the collecting computer. Select Source Computer Initiated, and then click Select Computer Groups. Click Add Domain Computers or Add Non-Domain Computers to add either type of computer. If you add nondomain computers, they need to have a computer certificate installed. Click Add Certificates to add the certification authority (CA) that issued the certificate to the nondomain computer.

5. Click the Select Events button to open the Query Filter dialog box. Use this dialog box to define the criteria that forwarded events must match. Figure 10-3 shows an example configuration. Then click OK.

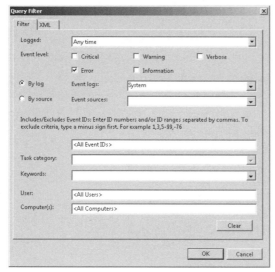

Figure 10-3   The Query Filter dialog box

6. Optionally, click the Advanced button to open the Advanced Subscription Settings dialog box. You can configure three types of subscriptions:

❑ **Normal**   This option ensures reliable delivery of events and does not attempt to conserve bandwidth. It is the appropriate choice unless you need tighter control over bandwidth usage or need forwarded events delivered as quickly as possible. It uses pull delivery mode (where the collecting computer contacts the forwarding computer) and downloads five events at a time unless 15 minutes pass, in which case it downloads any events that are available.

❑ **Minimize Bandwidth**   This option reduces the network bandwidth consumed by event delivery and is a good choice if you are using event forwarding across a wide area network (WAN) or on a large number of computers on a local area network (LAN). It uses push delivery mode (where the forwarding computer contacts the collecting computer) to forward events every six hours.

❑ **Minimize Latency**   This option ensures that events are delivered with minimal delay. It is an appropriate choice if you are collecting alerts or critical events. It uses push delivery mode and sets a batch timeout of 30 seconds.

Additionally, if you use a collector initiated subscription, you can use this dialog box to configure the user account the subscription uses. Whether you use the default Machine Account setting or specify a user, you will need to ensure that the account is a member of the forwarding computer's Event Log Readers group.

7. In the Subscription Properties dialog box click OK to create the subscription.

By default, normal event subscriptions check for new events every 15 minutes. You can decrease this interval to reduce the delay in retrieving events. However, there is no graphical interface for configuring the delay; you must use the command-line Wecutil tool that you initially used to configure the collecting computer.

To adjust the event subscription delay, first create your subscription using Event Viewer. Then run the following two commands at a command prompt with administrative privileges:

```
wecutil ss <subscription_name> /cm:custom
wecutil ss <subscription_name> /hi:<milliseconds_delay>
```

For example, if you created a subscription named "Disk Events" and you wanted the delay to be two minutes, you would run the following commands:

```
wecutil ss "Disk Events" /cm:custom
wecutil ss "Disk Events" /hi:12000
```

If you need to check the interval, run the following command:

```
wecutil gs "<subscription_name>"
```

For example, to verify that the interval for the "Disk Events" subscription is one minute, you would run the following command and look for the HeartbeatInterval value:

```
wecutil gs "Disk Events"
```

The Minimize Bandwidth and Minimize Latency options both batch a default number of items at a time. You can determine the value of this default by typing the following command at a command prompt:

```
winrm get winrm/config
```

Configuring Event Forwarding to Use HTTPS

Although standard HTTP transport uses encryption for forwarded events, you can configure event forwarding to use the encrypted HTTPS protocol. In addition to those described in the section entitled "Configuring the Forwarding Computer" earlier in this chapter, you must:

■ Configure the computer with a computer certificate. You can do this automatically in Active Directory environments by using an enterprise CA.

■ Create a Windows Firewall exception for TCP port 443. If you have configured Minimize Bandwidth or Minimize Latency Event Delivery Optimization for the subscription, you must also configure a computer certificate and an HTTPS Windows Firewall exception on the collecting computer.

■ Run the following command at a command prompt with administrative privileges:

```
winrm quickconfig –transport:https
```

On the collecting computer you must view the Advanced Subscription Settings dialog box for the subscription and set the Protocol box to HTTPS, as shown in Figure 10-4. Additionally, the collecting computer must trust the CA that issued the computer certificate (which happens automatically if an enterprise CA issued the certificate and both the forwarding computer and the collecting computer are part of the same Active Directory domain).

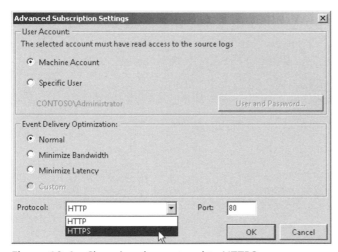

Figure 10-4   Changing the protocol to HTTPS

PRACTICE Collecting Events

In this practice you configure a computer, Boston, to forward events to the domain controller, Dcsrv1.

▶ **Exercise 1   Configuring a Computer to Collect Events**

In this exercise you configure the computer Dcsrv1 to collect events.

1. Log on to Dcsrv1 using a domain account with administrative privileges.
2. At a command prompt, run the following command to configure the Windows Event Collector service:

    ```
    wecutil qc
    ```

3. When prompted to change the service startup mode to Delay-Start, type **Y** and press Enter.

    Exam Tip   You could also do this by responding to the prompt that appears when you attempt to create the first subscription. However, the exam expects you to be familiar with the command-line tools for configuring computers for subscriptions.

▶ **Exercise 2   Configuring a Computer to Forward Events**

In this exercise you configure Boston to forward events to the collecting computer. To complete this exercise, you must have completed Exercise 1.

1. Log on to Boston using a domain account with administrative privileges.
2. At a command prompt, run the following command to configure the Windows Remote Management service:

    ```
    winrm quickconfig
    ```

3. When prompted to change the service startup mode, create the WinRM listener, enable the firewall exception, type **Y**, and press Enter.
4. Verify that the Windows Remote Management service is configured to automatically start by selecting the Configuration\Services node in Server Manager, selecting the Windows Remote Management (WS-Management) service, and verifying that it is started and that the Startup Type is set to Automatic (Delayed Start).
5. Run the following command at the command prompt to grant Dcsrv1 access to the event log. If your collecting computer has a different name or domain name, replace Dcsrv1 with the correct name and nwtraders.msft with the correct domain name.

    ```
    net localgroup "Event Log Readers" Dcsrv1@nwtraders.msft /add
    ```

▶ **Exercise 3   Configuring an Event Subscription**

In this exercise you create an event subscription on Dcsrv1 to gather events from Boston. To complete this exercise, you must have completed Exercises 1 and 2.

1. Log on to Dcsrv1. In Server Manager, right-click Diagnostics\Event Viewer\Subscriptions, and then choose Create Subscription.

2. In the Event Viewer dialog box, click Yes to configure the Windows Event Collector service (if prompted).

   The Subscription Properties dialog box appears.

3. In the Subscription Name box, type **Kernel Events**.

4. Click the Select Computers button. In the Computers dialog box, click Add Domain Computers. Type **Boston**. Then click OK.

5. In the Computers dialog box, click Test. Click OK when Event Viewer verifies connectivity. Then click OK to close the Computers dialog box.

6. Click the Select Events button. In the Query Filter dialog box, select the Error, Critical, Warning, and Information check boxes. Select By Source. Then from the Event Sources drop-down list, select the Kernel-General check box. Click OK.

7. Click the Advanced button to open the Advanced Subscription Settings dialog box. Note that it is configured to use the Machine Account by default. This will work because we have added this computer's domain account to the forwarding computer's Event Log Readers local group. Also note that the subscription is configured by default to use Normal Event Delivery Optimization using the HTTP protocol. Click OK.

8. In the Subscription Properties dialog box, click OK.

Next, generate a Kernel event on Boston by following these steps:

1. Log on to Boston. Right-click the clock on the system tray, and then choose Adjust Date/Time.

2. In the Date And Time dialog box, click Change Date And Time.

3. Change the time, and then click OK twice.

4. While still using Boston, open Event Viewer and check the System log. You should see an Information event with a source of Kernel-General.

5. Using Dcsrv1, select the Forwarded Events event log (located below Windows Logs). If you don't immediately see the event, wait a few minutes—it might take up to 15 minutes for the event to appear.

Lesson Summary

- Event forwarding uses HTTP or HTTPS to send events that match a filter you create to a collecting computer. Using event forwarding, you can centralize event management and better track critical events that occur on client and server computers.

- To use event forwarding, you must configure both the collecting and forwarding computers. On the forwarding computer, run the command *winrm quickconfig*. On the collecting computer, run the command *wecutil qc*. Then you can configure the event subscription on the collecting computer.

Lesson Review

You can use the following questions to test your knowledge of the information in Lesson 1, "Monitoring Event Logs." The questions are also available on the companion CD if you prefer to review them in electronic form.

NOTE Answers

Answers to these questions and explanations of why each answer choice is right or wrong are located in the "Answers" section at the end of the book.

---

1. You are configuring a computer named Server to collect events from a computer named Client. Both computers are in the Nwtraders.msft domain. Which of the following commands would you run on the collecting computer?

    A. wecutil qc

    B. winrm quickconfig

    C. net localgroup "Event Log Readers" Server$@nwtraders.msft /add

    D. net localgroup "Event Log Readers" Client$@nwtraders.msft /add

2. You are configuring a computer named Server to collect events from a computer named Client. Both computers are in the Nwtraders.msft domain. Which of the following commands would you run on the forwarding computer? (Choose all that apply.)

    A. wecutil qc

    B. winrm quickconfig

    C. net localgroup "Event Log Readers" Server$@nwtraders.msft /add

    D. net localgroup "Event Log Readers" Client$@nwtraders.msft /add

3. You need to configure an event subscription to update every minute. Which tool should you use?

    A. Wecutil

    B. WinRM

    C. Net

    D. The Event Viewer console

Lesson 2: Monitoring Performance and Reliability

Performance and reliability monitoring is useful in several scenarios:

- Improving the performance of servers by identifying the performance bottleneck and then upgrading the bottlenecked resource.
- Identifying the source of critical performance problems that make services unusable or completely unavailable.
- Correlating events, such as application installations, with failures.

This lesson describes how to use three tools that provide performance and reliability monitoring: Performance Monitor, Reliability Monitor, and Data Collector Sets.

After this lesson, you will be able to:
- Use Performance Monitor to view real-time or recorded performance data.
- Use Reliability Monitor to examine failures and software installations.
- Use Data Collector Sets to record information about a computer's current state for later analysis.

Estimated lesson time: 30 minutes

Performance Monitor

Performance Monitor graphically shows real-time performance data, including processor utilization, network bandwidth usage, and thousands of other statistics. Figure 10-5 shows an example.

To use Performance Monitor, follow these steps:

1. In Server Manager, select Diagnostics\Reliability And Performance\Monitoring Tools \Performance Monitor.
2. Add counters to the real-time graph by clicking the green plus button on the toolbar. You can also display data from other computers on the network.

Each line on the graph appears in a different color. To make it easier to view a specific line, select a counter and press Ctrl+H. The selected counter appears bold and in black on the graph.

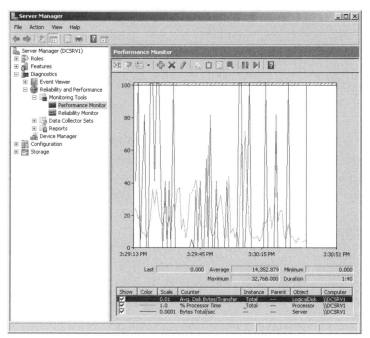

Figure 10-5   Performance Monitor showing real-time data

To change the appearance and refresh rate of the chart, right-click Performance Monitor, and then choose Properties. The five tabs of the Performance Monitor Properties dialog box provide access to different configuration options:

- **General**   In the Graph Elements group, adjust the Sample Every box to change how frequently the graph updates. Use a longer interval to show a smoother, less jagged graph that is updated less frequently and uses less bandwidth. Adjust the Duration box to change how much data is displayed in the graph before Performance Monitor begins overwriting the graph on the left portion of the chart. A Duration of 3,600 displays one hour of data in the graph, and a Duration of 86,400 displays one full day.

- **Source**   Choose whether to display current activity in real time or show log files that you have saved using a Data Collector Set. If you display a log file, you can use this tab to control the time range that is displayed in the Performance Monitor window.

- **Data**   In the Counters list select the counter you want to configure. Then adjust the Color, Width, and Style. Increase or decrease the Scale value to change the height of the graph for a counter. You can also adjust the scale for all counters by clicking the Graph tab and changing the Maximum and Minimum values in the Vertical Scale group.

- **Graph**   By default, Performance Monitor begins overwriting graphed data on the left portion of the chart after the specified duration has been reached. When graphing data over a long period of time, it's typically easier to see the chart scroll from right to left, similar to the way that Task Manager shows data. To do this, in the Scroll Style group, select Scroll. Although the line chart shows the most information, you can select from the following chart types by clicking the Change Graph Type button on the toolbar or by pressing Ctrl+G:
  - ❑ **Line**. The default setting, this shows values over time as lines on the chart.
  - ❑ **Histogram bar**. This shows a bar graph with the most recent values for each counter displayed. If you have a large number of values and you're primarily interested in the current value (rather than the value of each counter over time), this will be earlier to read than the line chart.
  - ❑ **Report**. This text report lists each current value.
- **Appearance**   If you keep multiple Performance Monitor windows open simultaneously, you can make it easier to quickly distinguish between the windows by using this tab to change the color of the background or other elements.

Reliability Monitor

Reliability Monitor tracks a computer's stability. Computers that have no new software installations or failures are considered stable and can achieve the maximum system stability index of 10. The more installations and failures that occur on a computer, the lower the system stability index drops toward a minimum value of 0.

Reliability Monitor is useful for diagnosing intermittent and long-term problems. For example, if you were to install an application that caused the operating system to fail once a week, it would be very difficult to correlate the failures with the application installation. With Reliability Monitor, as shown in Figure 10-6, you can quickly browse both failures and the application installations over time. If recurring failures begin shortly after an application installation, the two might be related.

To open Reliability Monitor, select the Diagnostics\Reliability And Performance\Monitoring Tools\Reliability Monitor node in Server Manager.

The chart at the top of Reliability Monitor shows one data point for each day. The rows below the chart show icons for successful and unsuccessful software installations, application failures, hardware failures, Windows failures, and other miscellaneous failures. Click a day to view the day's details in the System Stability Report below the chart.

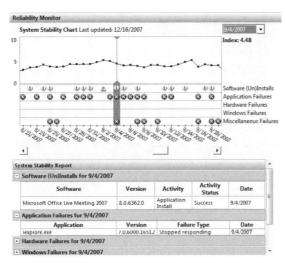

Figure 10-6 Reliability Monitor showing historical data

The Reliability Monitor displays data gathered by the Reliability Analysis Component (RAC), which is implemented using RACAgent.exe. RACAgent.exe runs once an hour using a hidden scheduled task. To view the scheduled task, browse to Configuration\Task Scheduler\Task Scheduler Library\Microsoft\Windows\RAC. Then click the View menu and select Show Hidden Tasks.

Data Collector Sets

Data Collector Sets gather system information, including configuration settings and performance data, and store it in a data file. You can later use the data file to examine detailed performance data in Performance Monitor or view a report that summarizes the information.

The sections that follow describe how to create Data Collector Sets and how to view reports.

Built-in Data Collector Sets

Windows Server 2008 includes several built-in Data Collector Sets located at Data Collector Sets\System:

- **Active Directory Diagnostics** Present only on domain controllers, this Data Collector Set logs kernel trace data, Active Directory trace data, performance counters, and Active Directory registry configuration.
- **LAN Diagnostics** Logs network performance counters, network configuration data, and important diagnostics tracing. Use this Data Collector Set when troubleshooting

complex network problems, such as network time-outs, poor network performance, or virtual private network (VPN) connectivity problems.

- **System Performance** Logs processor, disk, memory, and network performance counters and kernel tracing. Use this Data Collector Set when troubleshooting a slow computer or intermittent performance problems.

- **System Diagnostics** Logs all the information included in the System Performance Data Collector Set, plus detailed system information. Use this Data Collector Set when troubleshooting reliability problems such as problematic hardware, driver failures, or Stop errors (also known as blue screens). The report generated by the Data Collector Set provides a summary of error conditions on the system without requiring you to manually browse Event Viewer and Device Manager.

- **Wireless Diagnostics** Present only on computers with wireless capabilities, this Data Collector Set logs the same information as the LAN Diagnostics Data Collector Set, plus information relevant to troubleshooting wireless network connections. Use this Data Collector Set only when troubleshooting network problems that occur when connected to a wireless network.

To use a Data Collector Set, right-click it, and then choose Start. The System Performance and System Diagnostics Data Collector Sets stop automatically after a minute, the Active Directory Diagnostics Data Collector Set stops automatically after five minutes, and the LAN Diagnostics and Wireless Diagnostics Data Collector Sets run until you stop them. If you are troubleshooting a network problem, you should attempt to reproduce the problem after starting the Data Collector Set. To manually stop a Data Collector Set, right-click it, and then click Stop.

After running a Data Collector Set, you can view a summary of the data gathered in the Reliability And Performance\Reports node. To view the most recent report for a Data Collector Set, right-click the Data Collector Set, and then choose Latest Report. Reports are automatically named using the format *yyyymmdd-####*.

To minimize the performance impact of data logging, log the least amount of information required. For example, you should use System Performance instead of System Diagnostics whenever possible because System Performance includes fewer counters.

How to Create a Data Collector Set

When you use Performance Monitor, you can see performance counters in real time. Data Collector Sets can record this data so that you can analyze it later in Performance Monitor.

If you either have a performance problem or you want to analyze and possibly improve the performance of a server, you can create a Data Collector Set to gather performance data. However, for the analysis to be useful, you should always create a baseline by logging performance data before you make any changes. Then you can compare the performance before and after your adjustments.

To create a custom Data Collector Set, follow these steps:

1. Right-click Data Collector Sets\User Defined, choose New, and then choose Data Collector Set.

   The Create New Data Collector Set Wizard appears.

2. On the How Would You Like To Create This New Data Collector Set page, type a name for the set. Make sure Create From A Template is selected. Then click Next.

3. On the Which Template Would You Like To Use page, as shown in Figure 10-7, choose from one of the standard templates (which can vary depending on the computer's configuration) and click Next:

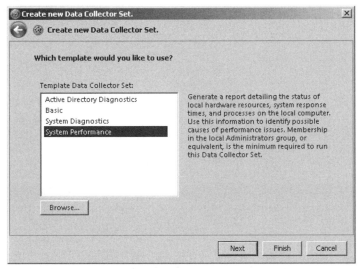

Figure 10-7   Creating a new Data Collector Set based on a template

❑ **Active Directory Diagnostics**   Collects Active Directory configuration information and performance counters.

❑ **Basic**   Logs all Processor performance counters, stores a copy of the HKLM \Software\Microsoft\Windows NT\CurrentVersion registry key, and performs a Windows Kernel trace.

❑ **System Diagnostics**   Logs 13 useful performance counters (including processor, disk, memory, and network counters), stores a copy of dozens of important configuration settings, and performs a Windows Kernel trace. By default, System Diagnostics logs data for one minute, giving you a snapshot of the computer's status.

❑ **System Performance**   Logs 14 useful performance counters (including the same counters logged by the System Diagnostics template) and performs a Windows Kernel trace. System Performance logs data for one minute.

4. On the Where Would You Like The Data To Be Saved page, click Next to accept the default location for the data (%SystemDrive%\perflogs\Admin\).

5. On the Create New Data Collector Set page, leave Run As set to <Default> to run it using the current user's credentials or click the Change button to specify other administrative credentials. Select one of three options before clicking the Finish button:

❑ **Open Properties For This Data Collector Set**   Immediately customize the Data Collector Set.

❑ **Start This Data Collector Set Now**   Immediately begin logging data without customizing the Data Collector Set.

❑ **Save And Close**   Close the Data Collector Set without starting it. You can edit the properties and start it at any time after saving it.

Custom Data Collector Sets are available under the User Defined node within Data Collector Sets.

How to Customize a Data Collector Set

By default, a custom Data Collector Set logs only the data sources defined in the template you chose. To add your own data sources to a Data Collector Set, you must update it after creating it.

To add a data source to a Data Collector Set, right-click the Data Collector Set, choose New, and then choose Data Collector to open the Create New Data Collector Wizard. On the What Type Of Data Collector Would You Like To Create page, type a name for the Data Collector, select the type, and then click Next.

You can choose from the following types of Data Collectors (each of which provides different options in the Create New Data Collector Wizard):

■ **Performance Counter Data Collector**   Logs data for any performance counter available when using the Performance Monitor console. You can add as many counters as you like to a Data Collector. You can assign a sample interval (15 seconds by default) to the Data Collector.

■ **Event Trace Data Collector**   Stores events from an event trace provider that match a particular filter. Windows provides hundreds of event trace providers that are capable of logging even the minutest aspects of the computer's behavior. For best results, add every event trace providers that might relate to the problem you are troubleshooting.

- **Configuration Data Collector**   Stores a copy of specific registry keys, Windows Management Instrumentation (WMI) management paths, files, or the system state. After creating the Data Collector, edit the Data Collector's properties to add configuration data other than registry keys. If you are troubleshooting application problems or if you need to be aware of application settings, add the registry keys using a configuration Data Collector.
- **Performance Counter Alert**   Generates an alert when a performance counter is above or below a specified threshold. By viewing the Data Collector's properties after you create it, you can log an entry in the Application event log or run a task when the alert is triggered.

You can add as many Data Collectors to a Data Collector Set as required. To edit a Data Collector, select the Data Collector Set within the Data Collector Sets\User Defined node. Then in the Details pane, right-click the Data Collector and choose Properties.

How to Save Performance Data

After creating a Data Collector Set, you can gather the data specified in the Data Collector Set by right-clicking it and choosing Start. Depending on the settings configured in the Stop Condition tab of the Data Collector Set's properties dialog box, the logging might stop after a set amount of time or it might continue indefinitely. If it does not stop automatically, you can manually stop it by right-clicking it and clicking Stop.

How to View Saved Performance Data in a Report

After using a Data Collector Set to gather information and then stopping the Data Collector Set, you can view a summary by right-clicking the Data Collector Set and then choosing Latest Report. As shown in Figure 10-8, the console selects the report generated when the Data Collector Set last ran. You can expand each section to find more detailed information.

If the Data Collector Set included performance counters, you can also view them using the Performance Monitor snap-in by right-clicking the report, choosing View, and then choosing Performance Monitor. Figure 10-9 shows performance data gathered using the standard Active Directory Diagnostics report.

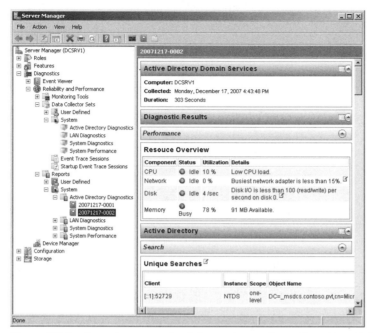

Figure 10-8 Reports summarize information gathered by a Data Collector Set

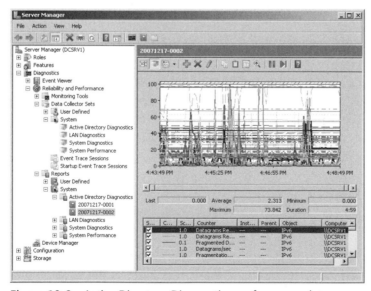

Figure 10-9 Active Directory Diagnostics performance data

Now Performance Monitor shows the logged data instead of real-time data. To narrow the time range shown, click and drag your cursor over the graph to select a time range. Then, right-click the graph and choose Zoom To, as shown in Figure 10-10. The horizontal bar beneath the graph illustrates the currently selected time range. Drag the left and right sides of the bar to expand the selected time range. Then, right-click the graph and choose Zoom To again to change the selection.

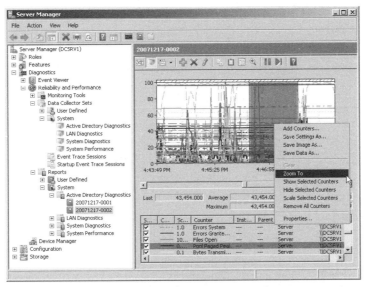

Figure 10-10   Using the Zoom To feature to analyze a narrow time span

PRACTICE Run a Data Collector Set and Analyze the Results

In this practice you will run a standard Data Collector Set and then analyze the results.

1. On Dcsrv1, open Server Manager. Right-click Diagnostics\Reliability And Performance\Data Collector Sets\System\System Performance, and then choose Start.

   Wait one minute for the Data Collector Set to gather information about the system. When the minute has passed, the green icon will disappear from the *System Performance* node.

2. Right-click the *System Performance* node, and then choose Latest Report.

   Server Manager displays the report you just generated.

3. Examine the report. In particular, look for any warnings, such as the warning shown in Figure 10-11 that shows a report run on a system with insufficient memory.

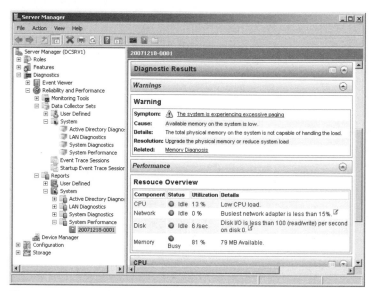

Figure 10-11 The report detects high paging due to insufficient memory

4. Right-click the report, choose View, and then choose Performance Monitor.

5. Drag your cursor across the graph to select approximately 30 seconds out of the full minute of data that was collected. Then right-click the selected area and choose Zoom To.

6. Select each of the four performance counters and view the average, minimum, and maximum values for the time range.

Lesson Summary

- You can use Performance Monitor to view thousands of performance counters in real time. After running a Data Collector Set, you can also use Performance Monitor to analyze logged data.

- Reliability Monitor records application installations and different types of failures. You can use this tool to quickly view a computer's history, which is useful for correlating software installations with recurring problems.

- Data Collector Sets record configuration settings, performance data, and events. By creating your own Data Collector Set, you can quickly gather information about a computer's current state for later analysis.

Lesson Review

You can use the following questions to test your knowledge of the information in Lesson 2, "Monitoring Performance and Reliability." The questions are also available on the companion CD if you prefer to review them in electronic form.

NOTE Answers

Answers to these questions and explanations of why each answer choice is right or wrong are located in the "Answers" section at the end of the book.

1. A computer running Windows Server 2008 has been experiencing intermittent performance problems. You think the problems might be caused by an application that was installed last week. Which tool would you use to determine exactly when the application was installed?

   A. Performance Monitor

   B. Reliability Monitor

   C. Data Collector Sets

   D. Network Monitor

2. Users are complaining that e-mail is very slow at peak usage times in the middle of the day. At night performance seems adequate. You would like to determine what resources are limiting performance by recording performance data overnight and during the day and then comparing them. Which tools should you use to accomplish this? (Choose all that apply.)

   A. Performance Monitor

   B. Reliability Monitor

   C. Data Collector Sets

   D. Network Monitor

3. Which of the following types of information might be stored in Reliability Monitor? (Choose all that apply.)

   A. A Web site configuration error

   B. An application that was uninstalled

   C. A service that was stopped

   D. A device driver that failed

Lesson 3: Using Network Monitor

Troubleshooting complex problems requires gaining insight into the inner workings of an application. When you are troubleshooting network problems, one of the best ways to gain insight is to capture and analyze the network communications using a protocol analyzer. Microsoft provides Network Monitor, a powerful protocol analyzer, as a free download. This lesson explains how to use Network Monitor to record and analyze network traffic.

> **After this lesson, you will be able to:**
> - Download and install Network Monitor.
> - Capture, filter, and analyze network communications.
>
> **Estimated lesson time: 30 minutes**

Installing Network Monitor

Network Monitor is not included with Windows, but you can download it for free from the Microsoft Download Center at *http://www.microsoft.com/downloads*. After visiting that page, search for "Network Monitor." The installation is Windows Installer-based and uses a standard wizard interface.

The installation process adds the Network Monitor 3 Driver to each network adapter, as shown in Figure 10-12, including VPN and remote access adapters. You must install and enable this driver before Network Monitor can collect data from a network adapter.

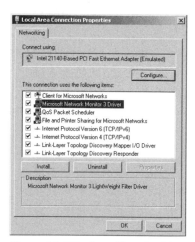

Figure 10-12   Installing the Network Monitor 3 Driver enables Network Monitor to collect data from a network adapter

Capturing and Analyzing Network Communications

To start Network Monitor, follow these steps:

1. Click Start, All Programs, Microsoft Network Monitor 3.1 (or the current version), and then choose Microsoft Network Monitor.

2. If prompted, choose whether to automatically check for updates. On Windows Vista and Windows Server 2008, this is unnecessary because Windows Update will automatically retrieve updates for Network Monitor.

The sections that follow describe how to capture, analyze, and filter network communications.

Capturing Network Data

After you start Network Monitor, you can capture network traffic by following these steps:

1. In the Start Page tab, in the Select Networks pane, select the network adapters that you want to monitor, as shown in Figure 10-13.

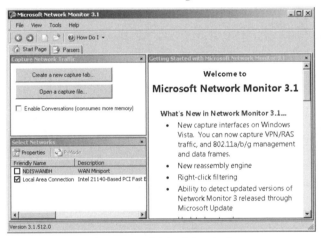

Figure 10-13   The Network Monitor window

2. After selecting the network adapters in the Select Networks pane, you can configure different options by selecting the network adapter and then clicking the Properties button. For wired network connections, you can enable P-Mode (promiscuous-mode) to capture frames sent to computers other than your own (which will not work in environments with Layer 2 switches). For wireless network connections, you can switch to Monitor Mode, which functions similar to P-Mode for wireless connections.

3. In the Capture Network Traffic pane, select the Enable Conversations check box. Then click Create A New Capture Tab.

   Network Monitor creates and selects a new capture tab.

4. On the toolbar, click the Start Capture button (a green play icon).

   Network Monitor begins to capture network traffic and displays it in the Frame Summary pane, as shown in Figure 10-14.

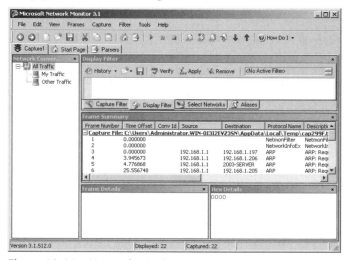

Figure 10-14   Network Monitor actively capturing data

5. If you are troubleshooting a network problem, you should re-create the problem while Network Monitor is capturing data. To stop capturing data, click the Stop Capture button on the toolbar (a blue stop icon).

You can configure the size of the temporary capture file and where it is stored by clicking the Tools menu and then choosing Options. The Capture tab of the Options dialog box, shown in Figure 10-15, allows you to configure settings related to the temporary capture file.

Network Monitor can capture only traffic that the network adapter receives. Most modern networks connect wired computers to a Layer 2 switch, which sends only computer traffic that the computer needs to receive: broadcasts and messages unicast to the computer's Media Access Control (MAC) address. Therefore, even if you have P-Mode enabled, Network Monitor will not be able to capture unicast communications sent between other computers.

Many Layer 2 switches can be configured with a *monitoring port*. The switch forwards all communications to the monitoring port. If you need to use Network Monitor to capture communications between two other hosts and your network uses a Layer 2 switch, you will need to enable the monitoring port and connect the computer running Network Monitor to that port.

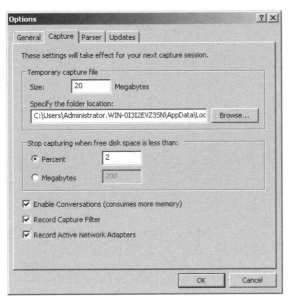

Figure 10-15   Configuring capture file settings

If your network uses hubs (a technology that predates Layer 2 switches but which is still commonly in use), any computer can receive any other computer's communications if P-Mode is enabled. Therefore, if your computer is connected to a hub and one of the computers you are monitoring is connected to the same hub, you do not need to enable a monitoring port. This is also an important security concern: any user with a protocol analyzer, such as Network Monitor, can capture communications between other computers. For this reason it's especially important to use encryption, such as that provided by IPsec (discussed in Chapter 8, "Configuring Windows Firewall and Network Access Protection").

Capturing Network Data Using a Command Prompt

To capture network traffic from a command prompt, switch to the Network Monitor installation folder (C:\Program Files\Microsoft Network Monitor 3 by default) and run the following command:

```
NMCap /network * /capture /file filename.cap
```

This captures all traffic on all network interfaces and saves it to a file named *filename*.cap. When you are done capturing, press Ctrl+C. You can then analyze the capture file using Network Monitor by clicking the Open A Capture File button in the Start Page tab.

To use a filter capture, type the filter capture in quotation marks after the /capture parameter. For example, the following command captures only DNS traffic:

```
NMCap /network * /capture "DNS" /file filename.cap
```

To capture in P-Mode (capturing all traffic that is visible to the computer, not just broadcast traffic and traffic sent to or from the computer), use the /DisableLocalOnly parameter, as shown in the following example:

```
NMCap /network * /DisableLocalOnly /capture /file filename.cap
```

NOTE   Automating the capture of network data

For more information about capturing with NMCap, read "NMCap: the Easy Way to Automate Capturing" at *http://blogs.technet.com/netmon/archive/2006/10/24/nmcap-the-easy-way-to-automate-capturing.aspx.*

Because Network Monitor and NMCap require the Network Monitor driver to be installed, you cannot simply copy NMCap.exe to a computer that you need to capture from. If you need to quickly capture traffic on a computer that does not have Network Monitor installed, you can run Network Monitor OneClick, available for download at *http://www.microsoft.com/downloads/details.aspx?FamilyID=9f37302e-d491-4c69-b7ce-410c8784fd0c.* As shown in Figure 10-16, OneClick can capture traffic without requiring a complete Network Monitor installation. After completing the capture, OneClick automatically removes itself from the computer.

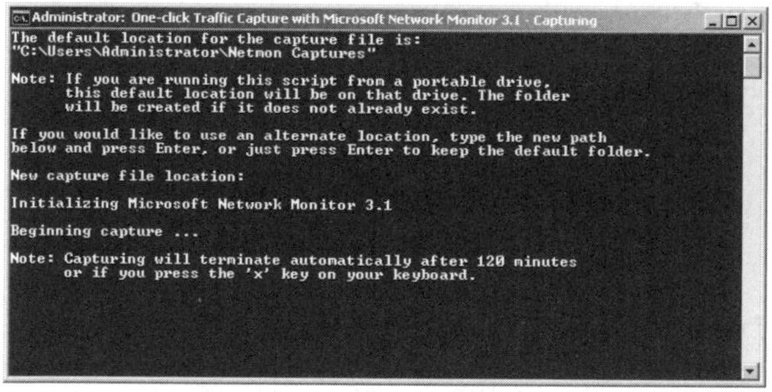

Figure 10-16   Capturing traffic with OneClick

Analyzing Network Data

After creating a capture, you can analyze the network data using the same capture tab. Browse the captured data in the Frame Summary pane and select any frame to view the data. As shown in Figure 10-17, the Frame Details pane summarizes the data in the frame and the Hex Details pane shows the raw data.

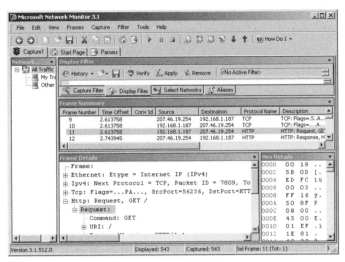

Figure 10-17 Examining captured data

NOTE Packet and frames

A frame isn't exactly like a packet, but it's similar. Technically, a frame includes Layer 2 data, such as the Ethernet header. Packets are Layer 3 units and start with the IP header.

Typically, the Frame Details pane is much more useful than the Hex Details pane because it shows frame data by layer. For example, Figure 10-18 shows just the Frame Details pane. As you can see by examining the HTTP layer of the frame, that particular frame was requesting the file /downloads/ from the host www.microsoft.com. To provide more display area, you can right-click any frame in the Frame Summary pane and then choose View Selected Frame(s) In A New Window.

```
Frame Details
  Frame:
  Ethernet: Etype = Internet IP (IPv4)
  Ipv4: Next Protocol = TCP, Packet ID = 8187, Total IP Length = 505
  Tcp: Flags=...PA..., SrcPort=56258, DstPort=HTTP(80), Len=465, Seq=3865462997 - 3865463462, Ack=1911
  Http: Request, GET /downloads/
    Request:
       Command: GET
       URI: /downloads/
       ProtocolVersion: HTTP/1.1
       Accept: image/gif, image/x-xbitmap, image/jpeg, image/pjpeg, */*
       Accept-Language: en-us
       UA-CPU: x86
       Accept-Encoding: gzip, deflate
       UserAgent: Mozilla/4.0 (compatible; MSIE 7.0; Windows NT 6.0; SLCC1; .NET CLR 2.0.50727)
       Host: www.microsoft.com
       Connection: Keep-Alive
       Cookie: MUID=250628CBFD2A4A9B8F15E25F8950B06C; MC1=GUID=93b5a5ed54ce874c89781d66c7a918f0&HASH=
       HeaderEnd: CRLF
```

Figure 10-18 Details of an HTTP request

Filtering Network Data

A busy server can transfer hundreds of frames a second, making it difficult to isolate the specific frames you need to analyze. To narrow down the data, you can use a capture filter (which filters frames before they are captured) or a display filter (which filters frames after they are captured).

You must create capture filters before capturing data. If you want to filter data from an existing capture, create a display filter. To create a filter using standard filters, in the Capture Filter or Display Filter pane click the Load Filter button. Then choose Standard Filters and choose one of the built-in filters. Finally, click the Apply button. The most useful filters include:

- **BaseNetworkTShoot**   Shows only frames that might be related to low-level network problems, including ICMP, ARP, and TCP resets. Use this filter if you are experiencing general network problems and you want to try and identify the specific host causing the problems.
- **Broadcasts and No-Broadcasts**   Broadcasts shows only broadcast frames. No-Broadcasts removes all broadcast frames.
- **DNS**   Shows only DNS traffic.
- **NameResolution**   Shows all name resolution traffic, including DNS, NetBIOS name resolution, and ARP requests.
- **HttpWebpageSearch**   Shows requests for specific Web pages. This is useful for determining which computers on a network are requesting a specific page, particularly if the page you are searching for is a malformed path that might be involved in an attack against a Web server (and thus might not be stored in the log files).
- **MyIPv4Address and MyIPv6Address**   Shows only requests sent to or from the current computer.
- **IPv4Address, IPv4DestinationAddress, IPv4SourceAddress, IPv4SourceAndDestination**   Shows only requests sent to or from specific IPv4 addresses.
- **IPv6Address, IPv6DestinationAddress, IPv6SourceAddress**   Shows only requests sent to or from specific IPv6 addresses.
- **IPv4SubNet**   Shows only requests sent to or from a specific subnet.

Many of the standard filters require editing. For example, if you add the IPv4DestinationAddress standard filter, you will need to change the sample IPv4 address to the IPv4 address that you want to filter for.

You can create more complex filters by combining multiple standard filters using binary operators. Separating two filters with the && operator requires frames to match both filters, while separating two filters with the || operator shows frames that match either filter. You can use parentheses to group multiple parameters. Prefix a parameter with an exclamation point to capture traffic that does not match the parameter. For example, the filter "!(tcp.port == 3389)" captures all traffic except Remote Desktop traffic (which uses TCP port 3389), which is useful when logging on to a computer remotely to capture traffic.

NOTE   Other filter operators

You can also use the operators AND and OR instead of && and ||.

For example, if you were to capture traffic on a DNS server, the following filter would show all DNS traffic from the host at 192.168.10.123:

```
DNS && IPv4.SourceAddress == 192.168.10.123
```

The following filter would capture all Web requests for either the page named Page1.htm or Page2.htm:

```
contains(Http.Request.URI,"Page1.htm") || contains(Http.Request.URI,"Page2.htm")
```

If you have an existing capture, you can create a display filter based on an existing frame by right-clicking the frame in the Frame Summary window and then choosing Add Cell To Display Filter. Then click Apply. Network Monitor will show only frames that match that exact description.

When creating custom filters, use the Verify button to check that your syntax is correct. The Display Filter pane will highlight any errors and allow you to correct them. For detailed information about creating custom filters, refer to the topic "Using Filters" in Network Monitor Help.

Exam Tip   For the exam, know how to create filters and how to capture network data at a command prompt using NMCap.

PRACTICE **Capture and Analyze Network Traffic**

In this practice you will capture communications using both graphical and command-line tools and work with both capture and display filters.

▶ **Exercise 1   Capture Traffic Using Graphical Tools**

In this exercise you must capture communications with Network Monitor. Then you will use a display filter to view only the frames you are most interested in.

1.   Download and install the latest version of Network Monitor.
2.   Start Network Monitor by clicking Start, All Programs, Microsoft Network Monitor 3.1 (or the current version) and then clicking Microsoft Network Monitor.

3. If prompted, choose not to automatically check for updates.

4. In the Start Page tab, in the Select Networks pane, select only the network adapter that is connected to the Internet.

5. In the Capture Network Traffic pane, select the Enable Conversations check box. Then click Create A New Capture Tab.

6. In the new capture tab that appears, click the Start Capture button on the toolbar.

7. Open Internet Explorer and visit *http://www.microsoft.com*. After the page appears, return to Network Monitor and click the Stop Capture button.

8. Use the Frame Summary pane to examine the captured data. You should see the following sequence (each step probably generated multiple frames):

   ❑ **ARP**   The computer might have generated an ARP request to identify the MAC address of its DNS server. If the DNS server is on another subnet, the computer would need to identify the MAC address of the default gateway. If no ARP requests were captured, the computer had previously cached the MAC address.

   ❑ **DNS**   The computer would need to identify the IP address associated with the host name www.microsoft.com.

   ❑ **TCP**   The computer establishes a TCP connection to the IP address that www.microsoft.com resolved to. This requires a total of three frames.

   ❑ **HTTP**   Using the newly established TCP connection to www.microsoft.com, the computer can now query the Web site for the "/" URI, which is the default page. After the first HTTP requests, several other DNS queries, TCP connections, and HTTP sessions were probably captured as the computer downloaded objects embedded into the www.microsoft.com Web site.

9. In the Display Filter pane, type **HTTP && IPv4.SourceAddress == IpConfig .LocalIpv4Address**. Then click Apply.

10. Browse the frames displayed in the Frame Summary pane to see every HTTP request required to open the default page at www.microsoft.com.

▶ **Exercise 2   Capture Traffic at the Command Line**

In this exercise you must capture network communications at a command prompt using a capture filter. Then you will examine the communications using Network Monitor.

1. Open a command prompt with administrative credentials and run the following commands:

```
cd %ProgramFiles%\Microsoft Network Monitor 3
NMCap /network * /capture "DNS" /StopWhen /TimeAfter 2 min /file DNS.cap
```

2. Now open a second command prompt and run the following commands:

   ```
   ping www.contoso.com
   nslookup www.fabrikam.com
   ```

3. Open Internet Explorer and visit *http://www.microsoft.com*.

4. Wait until two minutes have passed and the NMCap capture completes.

5. Open Network Monitor. In the Start Page tab, click Open A Capture File.

6. In the Open dialog box, select C:\Program Files\Microsoft Network Monitor 3\DNS.cap.

7. In the capture tab that appears, examine the Frame Summary pane. Notice that only DNS frames were captured—the HTTP requests associated with opening the Web site were not captured because they did not match the capture filter you specified. Select each frame and examine the Frame Details pane to determine whether the frame is a query or a response and what host name each query was attempting to identify.

Lesson Summary

- Network Monitor is a free download available from Microsoft.com.

- You can capture data using either the graphical Network Monitor tool or the command-line NMCap tool. All analysis must be done using the graphical Network Monitor tool, however. Especially on a busy server, you will need to use filters to reduce the number of frames not related to the application you are examining. Capture filters are applied while data is captured, and display filters are applied after the data has been captured.

Lesson Review

You can use the following questions to test your knowledge of the information in Lesson 3, "Using Network Monitor." The questions are also available on the companion CD if you prefer to review them in electronic form.

NOTE   Answers

Answers to these questions and explanations of why each answer choice is right or wrong are located in the "Answers" section at the end of the book.

---

1. You need to use Network Monitor to capture communications between two computers, HostA and HostB. In which of the following scenarios will you be able to capture the communications? (Choose all that apply.)

   A. You are running Network Monitor on HostA, but HostB does not have Network Monitor installed.

   B. You are running Network Monitor on HostC, with P-Mode enabled. HostA is connected to the same Layer 2 switch as HostC. HostB is connected to a different network.

   C. You are running Network Monitor on HostC, with P-Mode enabled. HostA is connected to the same hub as HostC. HostB is connected to a different network.

   D. You are running Network Monitor on HostC, with P-Mode enabled. HostA is connected to the same hub as HostB. HostC is connected to a Layer 2 switch.

2. You need to create a Network Monitor capture file from a command prompt. Which tool should you use?

   A. Netmon

   B. NMCap

   C. Nmconfig

   D. Nmwifi

3. A client computer with the IP address 192.168.10.12 is having a problem retrieving Web pages from a Web server you manage. You use Network Monitor to capture network traffic while the client computer submits a request. However, you also captured hundreds of other requests. Which display filter should you use to view just the communications sent to and from the client computer?

   A. HTTP || IPv4.SourceAddress == 192.168.10.12

   B. HTTP && IPv4.SourceAddress == 192.168.10.12

   C. HTTP || IPv4.Address == 192.168.10.12

   D. HTTP && IPv4.Address == 192.168.10.12

Chapter Review

To further practice and reinforce the skills you learned in this chapter, you can

- Review the chapter summary.
- Review the list of key terms introduced in this chapter.
- Complete the case scenarios. These scenarios set up real-world situations involving the topics of this chapter and ask you to create a solution.
- Complete the suggested practices.
- Take a practice test.

Chapter Summary

- You can use event forwarding to centralize event management. Event forwarding uses HTTP or HTTPS to forward specific events from computers distributed throughout your organization to a central computer. To use event forwarding, you must configure both the collecting and forwarding computers. On the forwarding computer, run the command *winrm quickconfig*. On the collecting computer, run the command *wecutil qc*. Then you can configure the event subscription on the collecting computer.

- You can use Performance Monitor to analyze resource utilization on a computer, either in real time or using data logged by a Data Collector Set. Reliability Monitor records application installations and different types of failures. You can use this tool to quickly view a computer's history, which is useful for correlating software installations with recurring problems. Data Collector Sets record configuration settings, performance data, and events. By creating your own Data Collector Set, you can quickly gather information about a computer's current state for later analysis.

- Network Monitor is a free protocol analyzer that can record and analyze network communications. To capture data from a command prompt, use the NMCap tool and then analyze the communications using the graphical Network Monitor tool. Use filters to restrict which packets are captured and displayed.

Key Terms

Do you know what these key terms mean? You can check your answers by looking up the terms in the glossary at the end of the book.

- monitoring port
- P-Mode

Case Scenarios

In the following case scenarios you will apply what you've learned about how to monitor computers. You can find answers to these questions in the "Answers" section at the end of this book.

Case Scenario 1: Troubleshooting a Network Performance Problem

You are a systems administrator at A. Datum Corporation. Recently, users have been complaining about intermittent performance problems when accessing a file server. Another systems administrator has been trying to isolate the problem but has failed. You discuss the problem with your manager and the system administrator who worked on the problem.

Interviews

Following is a list of company personnel interviewed and their statements:

- **Your Manager**   "David's had this ticket open for a week and hasn't made any progress, so I'm going to assign it to you. Talk to David, and then we'll meet again to discuss the best way to isolate the cause of the performance problems."

- **David, Systems Administrator**   "What an awful ticket. When I get a complaint from a user, I connect to the server and run Task Manager, but the processor utilization is fine. So I don't know what the problem could be. I hope you have better luck than I did."

Questions

Now that you have talked with David, answer the following questions for your manager:

1. How can you analyze disk, network, processor, and memory resources both when the problem is occurring and when performance is normal?
2. If the problem is network related, how can you analyze the network traffic?

Case Scenario 2: Monitoring Computers for Low Disk Space

You are a systems administrator for Proseware, Inc. Recently, the CEO of your company called because he couldn't download his e-mail. The help support technician identified the source of the problem as low disk space, helped the CEO clear sufficient free space, and resolved the problem.

The CEO would like your department to develop a proactive way to identify low disk space problems on computers so that you can free more disk space before the condition causes application failures.

Answer the following questions for your manager:

1. How can you monitor client computers for low disk space events?
2. Which client operating systems can you monitor?

Suggested Practices

To successfully master the Monitoring and Managing a Network Infrastructure exam objective, complete the following tasks.

Monitor Event Logs

For this task, you should complete both Practices 1 and 2.

- **Practice 1** Configure a forwarding computer to send events to a collecting computer using each of the three bandwidth optimization techniques. Then use Wecutil to customize the event forwarding configuration by reducing the time required to forward events by half.

- **Practice 2** Examine the event logs on several production client computers in your organization. Identify several events that IT might want to be aware of. Then configure those computers to forward events to a central computer and monitor the central event log.

Capture Performance Data

For this objective you should complete all three practices to gain experience in troubleshooting performance and reliability problems.

- **Practice 1** Run each standard Data Collector Set and analyze the report generated by each.

- **Practice 2** On several production Windows Vista or Windows Server 2008 computers that have been online for more than a month, run Reliability Monitor. How stable are the computers? Can you identify the cause of any stability problems?

- **Practice 3** Using several applications that your organization uses internally, create a Data Collector Set that gathers each of the application's configuration settings.

Gather Network Data

For this task, you should complete all three practices.

■ **Practice 1**   Have a friend (with the friend's permission) visit several Web sites and run other network applications while you record the frames using Network Monitor. Then, analyze the frames and determine what applications your friend used. Can you determine which Web sites and Web pages your friend visited? Are any passwords visible in the raw communications?

■ **Practice 2**   Copy Network Monitor OneClick to a USB flash drive. Then connect the USB flash drive to a computer that does not have Network Monitor installed and capture network data to the USB flash drive. Return the USB flash drive to your own computer and analyze the .CAP file.

■ **Practice 3**   Write a batch file that runs NMCap and captures data for five minutes. Then use Network Monitor to analyze the .CAP file.

Take a Practice Test

The practice tests on this book's companion CD offer many options. For example, you can test yourself on just the content covered in this chapter, or you can test yourself on all the 70-642 certification exam content. You can set up the test so that it closely simulates the experience of taking a certification exam, or you can set it up in study mode so that you can look at the correct answers and explanations after you answer each question.

MORE INFO   Practice tests

For details about all the practice test options available, see "How to Use the Practice Tests" in this book's Introduction.

Chapter 11
Managing Files

Many types of documents, including financial spreadsheets, business plans, and sales presentations, must be shared on your network while remaining protected from unauthorized access. Windows Server 2008 offers a suite of technologies to provide both availability and security for documents.

To control access, use NTFS file permissions and Encrypting File System (EFS). To provide redundancy, create a Distributed File System (DFS) namespace and use replication to copy files between multiple servers. You can use quotas to ensure that no single user consumes more than his or her share of disk space (which might prevent other users from saving files). Shadow copies and backups allow you to quickly recover from data corruption and hardware failures. This chapter describes how to use each of these technologies and explains the new Windows Server 2008 File Services server role.

Exam objectives in this chapter:
- Configure a file server.
- Configure Distributed File System (DFS).
- Configure shadow copy services.
- Configure backup and restore.
- Manage disk quotas.

Lessons in this chapter:

Before You Begin

To complete the lessons in this chapter, you should be familiar with Microsoft Windows networking and be comfortable with the following tasks:

- Adding roles to a Windows Server 2008 computer
- Configuring Active Directory directory service domain controllers and joining computers to a domain
- Basic network configuration, including configuring IP settings

You will also need the following nonproduction hardware, connected to test networks:

- A computer named Dcsrv1 that is a domain controller in the Nwtraders.msft domain. This computer must have at least one network interface. Dcsrv1 must have at least two hard disks for this chapter because Lesson 3, "Backing Up and Restoring Files," requires you to back up the system disk to a second hard disk.

NOTE Computer and domain names

The computer and domain names you use will not affect these practices. The practices in this chapter refer to these computer names for simplicity, however.

- A computer named Boston that is a member of the Nwtraders.msft domain.

Real World

Tony Northrup

Adding quotas can reduce disk performance, but you'll probably never notice it. According to a December 6, 2005, chat transcript, Ran Kalach at Microsoft feels that the performance impact should be 10 percent at most. Because the performance impact of quotas is so minimal, users should never notice this difference.

According to the same chat transcript, file screening should not have a noticeable impact. File screening checks file extensions only when new files are created or existing files are renamed—tasks that typically do not happen frequently.

Enabling EFS does have a performance impact because additional processing time is required for decryption when reading files. Although the exact impact varies widely depending on the type of file access and the processing capabilities of the computers, studies have found a performance decrease of 10 percent to 60 percent.

Lesson 1: Managing File Security

Much of an organization's most confidential data is stored in files and folders. Windows Server 2008, along with most recent business versions of Windows, provide two technologies for controlling access to files and folders: NTFS file permissions and EFS. The sections that follow give more information about these two technologies.

After this lesson, you will be able to:
- Use NTFS file permissions to control user access to files and folders.
- Use EFS to protect files from offline attacks.

Estimated lesson time: 40 minutes

NTFS File Permissions

NTFS file permissions determine which users can view or update files. For example, you would use NTFS file permissions to grant your Human Resources group access to personnel files while preventing other users from accessing those files.

The default NTFS file permissions for user and system folders are designed to meet basic needs. These default permissions for different file types are:

- **User files**   Users have full control permissions over their own files. Administrators also have full control. Other users who are not administrators cannot read or write to a user's files.
- **System files**   Users can read, but not write to, the %SystemRoot% folder and subfolders. Administrators can add and update files. This allows administrators, but not users, to install updates and applications.
- **Program files**   Similar to the system files permissions, the %ProgramFiles% folder permissions are designed to allow users to run applications and allow only administrators to install applications. Users have read access, and administrators have full control.

Additionally, any new folders created in the root of a disk will grant administrators full control and users read access.

The default file and folder permissions work well for desktop environments. File servers, however, often require you to grant permissions to groups of users to allow collaboration. For example, you might want to create a folder that all Marketing users can read and update but that users outside the Marketing group cannot access. Administrators can assign users or groups any of the following permissions to a file or folder:

- **List Folder Contents**   Users can browse a folder but not necessarily open the files in it.
- **Read**   Users can view the contents of a folder and open files. If a user has Read but not Read & Execute permission for an executable file, the user will not be able to start the executable.
- **Read & Execute**   In addition to the Read permission, users can run applications.
- **Write**   Users can create files in a folder but not necessarily read them. This permission is useful for creating a folder in which several users can deliver files but not access each other's files or even see what other files exist.
- **Modify**   Users can read, edit, and delete files and folders.
- **Full Control**   Users can perform any action on the file or folder, including creating and deleting it and modifying its permissions.

To protect a file or folder with NTFS, follow these steps:

1. Open Windows Explorer (for example, by clicking Start and then choosing Computer).
2. Right-click the file or folder, and then choose Properties.
   The Properties dialog box for the file or folder appears.
3. Click the Security tab.
4. Click the Edit button.
   The Permissions dialog box appears.
5. If the user you want to configure access for does not appear in the Group Or User Names list, click Add. Type the user name, and then click OK.
6. Select the user you want to configure access for. Then, select the check boxes for the desired permissions in the Permissions For *user or group name* list, as shown in Figure 11-1. Denying access always overrides allowed access. For example, if Mary is a member of the Marketing group and you allow full control access for Mary and then deny full control access for the Marketing group, Mary's effective permissions will be to deny full control.

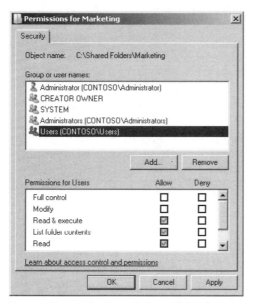

Figure 11-1 The permissions dialog box

Exam Tip When taking the exam, expect questions where a user is granted access to a file but denied access through a group membership. Remember that although permission assignments are cumulative, denied access overrides all other permissions.

---

7. Repeat steps 5 and 6 to configure access for additional users.
8. Click OK twice.

Additionally, there are more than a dozen special permissions that you can assign to a user or group. To assign special permissions, click the Advanced button in the Security tab of the file or folder Properties dialog box, as shown in Figure 11-2.

To configure NTFS file permissions from a command prompt or script, use the Icacls command. For complete usage information, type **icacls /?** at a command prompt.

NTFS file permissions are in effect whether users are logged on locally or accessing folders across the network.

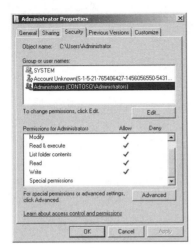

Figure 11-2   The Security tab

Encrypting File System

NTFS provides excellent protection for files and folders as long as Windows is running. However, an attacker who has physical access to a computer can start the computer from a different operating system (or simply reinstall Windows) or remove the hard disk and connect it to a different computer. Any of these very simple techniques would completely bypass NTFS security, granting the attacker full access to files and folders.

EFS protects files and folders by encrypting them on the disk. If an attacker bypasses the operating system to open a file, the file appears to be random, meaningless bytes. Windows controls access to the decryption key and provides it only to authorized users.

NOTE   EFS support

Windows 2000 and later versions of Windows support EFS.

The sections that follow describe how to configure EFS.

How to Protect Files and Folders with EFS

To protect a file or folder with EFS, follow these steps:

1. Open Windows Explorer (for example, by clicking Start and then choosing Computer).
2. Right-click the file or folder, and then click Properties.
    The Properties dialog box appears.

3. In the General tab, click Advanced.

   The Advanced Attributes dialog box appears.

4. Select the Encrypt Contents To Secure Data check box.

5. Click OK twice.

If you encrypt a folder, Windows automatically encrypts all new files in the folder. Windows Explorer shows encrypted files in green.

The first time you encrypt a file or folder, Windows might prompt you to back up your file encryption key, as shown in Figure 11-3. Choosing to back up the key launches the Certificate Export Wizard, which prompts you to password-protect the exported key and save it to a file. Backing up the key is very important for stand-alone computers because if the key is lost, the files are inaccessible. In Active Directory environments, you should use a data recovery agent (DRA), as described later in this section, to recover files.

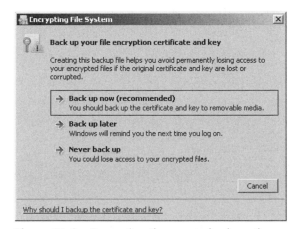

Figure 11-3   Prompting the user to back up the encryption key

How to Share Files Protected with EFS

If you need to share EFS-protected files with other users on your local computer, you need to add their encryption certificates to the file. You do not need to follow these steps to share files across a network; EFS only affects files that are accessed on the local computer because Windows automatically decrypts files before sharing them.

To share an EFS-protected file, follow these steps:

1. Open the Properties dialog box for an encrypted file.

2. In the General tab, click Advanced.

   The Advanced Attributes dialog box appears.

3. Click the Details button.

    The User Access dialog box appears, as shown in Figure 11-4.

Figure 11-4   The User Access dialog box

4. Click the Add button.

    The Encrypting File System dialog box appears.

5. Select the user you want to grant access to, and then click OK.

6. Click OK three more times to close all open dialog boxes.

The user you selected will now be able to open the file when logged on locally.

How to Configure EFS Using Group Policy Settings

Users can selectively enable EFS on their own files and folders. However, most users are not aware of the need for encryption and will never enable EFS on their own. Rather than relying on users to configure their own data security, you should use Group Policy settings to ensure that domain member computers are configured to meet your organization's security needs.

Within the Group Policy Management Editor, you can configure EFS settings by right-clicking the Computer Configuration\Policies\Windows Settings\Security Settings\Public Key Policies \Encrypting File System node and then choosing Properties to open the Encrypting File System Properties dialog box, as shown in Figure 11-5.

Figure 11-5   Defining EFS properties

This dialog box allows you to configure the following options:

- **File Encryption Using Encrypting File System (EFS)**   By default, EFS is allowed. If you select Don't Allow, users will be unable to encrypt files with EFS.
- **Encrypt The Contents Of The User's Documents Folder**   Enable this option to automatically encrypt the user's Documents folder. Although many other folders contain confidential information, encrypting the Documents folder significantly improves security, especially for mobile computers, which are at a higher risk of theft.

NOTE   **Preventing attackers from bypassing EFS**

EFS protects files when the operating system is offline. Therefore, if someone steals an employee's laptop at an airport, the thief won't be able to access EFS-encrypted files—unless the user is currently logged on. If you enable EFS, you should also configure the desktop to automatically lock when not in use for a few minutes.

- **Require A Smart Card For EFS**   Select this check box to prevent the use of software certificates for EFS. Enable this if users have smart cards and you want to require the user to insert the smart card to access encrypted files. This can add security, assuming the user does not always leave the smart card in the computer.
- **Create Caching-Capable User Key From Smart Card**   If this and the previous option are enabled, users need to insert a smart card only the first time they access an encrypted file during their session. If this option is disabled, the smart card must be present every time the user accesses a file.

- **Enable Pagefile Encryption**   Encrypts the page file. Windows uses the page file to store a copy of data that is stored in memory, and, as a result, it might contain unencrypted copies of EFS-encrypted files. Therefore, a very skillful attacker might find unencrypted data in the page file if this option is disabled. Encrypting the page file can impact performance.

- **Display Key Backup Notifications When User Key Is Created or Changed**   If enabled, Windows prompts the user to back up EFS keys when encryption keys are created or changed.

- **Allow EFS To Generate Self-Signed Certificates When A Certification Authority Is Not Available**   If disabled, client computers will need to contact your certification authority (CA) the first time an EFS file is encrypted. This would prevent users who are disconnected from your network from enabling EFS for the first time. To allow EFS to retrieve a certificate from a CA instead of generating a self-signed certificate, you should configure a CA and enable autoenrollment. For detailed instructions, perform Practice 1 in this lesson.

Additionally, you should consider configuring the following EFS-related Group Policy settings:

- **Computer Configuration\Policies\Administrative Templates\Network\Offline Files\Encrypt The Offline Files Cache**   Enable this setting to encrypt Offline Files. Offline Files are discussed in Lesson 2, "Sharing Folders."

- **Computer Configuration\Policies\Administrative Templates\Windows Components\Search \Allow Indexing Of Encrypted Files**   If you index encrypted files, an attacker might be able to see the contents of an encrypted file by examining the index. Disabling indexing of encrypted files improves security but prevents users from searching those files.

How to Configure a Data Recovery Agent

An encrypted file is inaccessible to anyone who lacks the decryption key, including system administrators and, if they lose their original key, users who encrypted the files. To enable recovery of encrypted files, EFS supports DRAs. DRAs can decrypt encrypted files. In enterprise Active Directory environments, you can use Group Policy settings to configure one or more user accounts as DRAs for your entire organization. To configure an enterprise DRA, follow these steps:

1. Configure an enterprise CA. For example, you can install the Windows Server 2008 Active Directory Certificate Services server role. The default settings work well.

2. Create a dedicated user account to act as the DRA. Although you could use an existing user account, the DRA has the ability to access any encrypted file—an almost unlimited

power that must be carefully controlled in most organizations. Log on using the DRA account.

IMPORTANT   Avoid giving one person too much power

For the DRA user account, or any highly privileged account, have two people type half the account's password. Then have each user write down half of the password and give the password halves to different managers to protect. This requires at least two people to work together to access the DRA account—a security concept called *collusion*. Collusion greatly reduces the risk of malicious use by requiring attackers to trust each other and work together.

---

3. Open the Group Policy Object in the Group Policy Management Editor.
4. Right-click Computer Configuration\Policies\Windows Settings\Security Settings\Public Key Policies\Encrypting File System, and then choose Create Data Recovery Agent.

   The Group Policy Management Editor creates a file recovery certificate for the DRA account.

DRAs can automatically open encrypted files just like any other file—exactly as if they had encrypted it with their own user certificate. You can create multiple DRAs.

PRACTICE Encrypt and Recover Files

In this practice, you create two user accounts: a user account that will encrypt a file with EFS and a DRA that will access the encrypted file. Then, you will encrypt a file, verify that other user accounts cannot access it, and finally recover the encrypted file using the DRA.

▶ **Exercise 1   Configure a DRA**

In this exercise, you create accounts that represent a traditional EFS user and a DRA.

1. Add the Active Directory Certificate Services role using the default settings to Dcsrv1 to configure it as an enterprise CA.
2. Create a domain user account named EFSUser and make the account a member of the Domain Admins group so that it can log on to the domain controller. You will use this account to create and encrypt a file.
3. Create a domain user account named DRA and make the account a member of the Domain Admins group. Log on using the DRA account.
4. In Server Manager, right-click Features\Group Policy Management\Forest: nwtraders.msft \Domains\nwtraders.msft\Default Domain Policy, and then choose Edit.

   The Group Policy Management Editor appears.

5. In the console tree, expand Computer Configuration\Policies\Windows Settings\Security Settings, and then select Public Key Policies. In the details pane, double-click the Certificate Services Client – Auto-Enrollment policy. Set the Configuration Model to Enabled, and then click OK.

6. Right-click Computer Configuration\Policies\Windows Settings\Security Settings\Public Key Policies\Encrypting File System, and then choose Create Data Recovery Agent.

The account you are currently logged on with, DRA, is now configured as a DRA.

▶ **Exercise 2 Encrypt a File**

In this exercise, you use the newly created EFSUser account to create an encrypted text file.

1. On Dcsrv1, log on using the EFSUser account.

2. Click Start, and then choose Documents.

3. In the Documents window, right-click Documents, and then choose Properties. Do not right-click the Documents shortcut listed in the Favorite Links pane; doing so will modify the shortcut and not the folder.

4. In the General tab of the Documents Properties dialog box, click Advanced. Select the Encrypt Contents To Secure Data check box, and then click OK three times.

5. Right-click the details pane, choose New, and then choose Text Document. Name the document Encrypted. Notice that it appears in green in Windows Explorer because it is encrypted.

6. Open the encrypted document and add the text "Hello, world." Save and close the document.

▶ **Exercise 3 Attempt to Access an Encrypted File**

In this exercise, you use the Administrator account (which is not configured as a DRA) to simulate an attacker attempting to access a file that another user has encrypted.

1. On Dcsrv1, log on using the Administrator account. This account has administrative privileges to Dcsrv1, but it is not configured as a DRA.

2. Click Start, and then choose Computer.

3. In the Computer window, browse to C:\Users\EFSUser\Documents.

4. Double-click the Encrypted document in the details pane. Notice that Notepad displays an Access Is Denied error. You would see this same error even if you reinstalled the operating system or connected the hard disk to a different computer.

▶ **Exercise 4   Recover an Encrypted File**

In this exercise, you use the DRA account to access the encrypted file and then remove the encryption from the file so that other users can access it.

1. On Dcsrv1, log on using the DRA account. This account is configured as a DRA.
2. Click Start, and then choose Computer.
3. In the Computer window, browse to C:\Users\EFSUser\Documents. Respond to any User Account Control (UAC) prompts that appear.
4. Double-click the Encrypted document in the Details pane. Notice that Notepad displays the file because the DRA account is configured as a DRA. Close Notepad.
5. In Windows Explorer, right-click the Encrypted file, and then choose Properties. In the General tab, click Advanced. Clear the Encrypt Contents To Secure Data check box, and then click OK twice. Respond to the UAC prompts that appear. DRA accounts can remove encryption, allowing other accounts to access previously encrypted files.

Lesson Summary

- NTFS file permissions control access to files when Windows is running, whether users access files locally or across the network. NTFS file permissions allow you to grant users and groups read access, write access, or full control access (which allows users to change permissions). If you deny a user NTFS file permissions, it overrides any other assigned permissions. If a user does not have any NTFS file permissions assigned, that user is denied access.

- EFS encrypts files, which protects them when Windows is offline. Although encryption provides very strong security, users will be unable to access encrypted files if they lose the encryption key. To protect against this, use Active Directory Group Policy settings to configure a DRA that can recover encrypted files.

Lesson Review

You can use the following questions to test your knowledge of the information in Lesson 1, "Managing File Security." The questions are also available on the companion CD if you prefer to review them in electronic form.

NOTE   Answers

Answers to these questions and explanations of why each answer choice is correct or incorrect are located in the "Answers" section at the end of the book.

1. You create a folder named Marketing on a computer named FileServer and configure NTFS permissions to grant the Domain Users group Read permission and the Marketing group Modify permission. You share the folder and grant the Everyone group Reader permission. Mary, a user account who is a member of both the Marketing group and the Domain Users group, logs on locally to the FileServer computer to access the Marketing folder. What effective permissions will Mary have?

   A. No access

   B. Read

   C. Write

   D. Full Control

2. You have a folder protected with EFS that contains a file you need to share across the network. You share the folder and assign NTFS and share permissions to allow the user to open the file. What should you do to allow the user to access the encrypted file without decreasing the security?

   A. Right-click the file, and then choose Properties. In the Security tab, add the user's account.

   B. Right-click the file, and then choose Properties. In the General tab, click Advanced. Click the Details button, and then add the user's account.

   C. Right-click the file, and then choose Properties. In the General tab, click Advanced. Clear the Encrypt Contents To Secure Data check box.

   D. Do nothing.

Lesson 2: Sharing Folders

One of the most common ways for users to collaborate is by storing documents in shared folders. Shared folders allow any user with access to your network and appropriate permissions to access files. Shared folders also allow documents to be centralized, where they are more easily managed than if they were distributed to thousands of client computers.

Although all versions of Windows since Windows For Workgroups 3.11 have supported file sharing, Windows Server 2008 adds the File Services server role, which includes a robust set of features for sharing folders and managing shared files. With the improved disk quota capability, Windows can notify users and administrators if individual users consume too much disk space. DFS provides a centralized directory structure for folders shared from multiple computers and is capable of automatically replicating files between folders for redundancy. Offline Files automatically copy shared files to mobile computers so that users can access the files while disconnected from the network.

After this lesson, you will be able to:
- Install the File Services server role.
- Use quotas to notify you when users consume more than an allotted amount of disk space.
- Share folders across the network.
- Use DFS to create a namespace of shared folders on multiple servers.
- Use Offline Files to grant mobile users access to copies of network files and folders while they are disconnected from the network.

Estimated lesson time: 55 minutes

Installing the File Services Server Role

Windows Server 2008 can share folders without adding any server roles. However, adding the File Services server role adds useful management tools along with the ability to participate in DFS namespaces, configure quotas, generate storage reports, and other capabilities. To install the File Services server role, follow these steps:

1. In Server Manager, select and then right-click Roles. Choose Add Role.
   The Add Roles Wizard appears.
2. On the Before You Begin page, click Next.
3. On the Server Roles page, select the File Services check box. Click Next.
4. On the File Services page, click Next.

5. On the Select Role Services page, select from the following roles:
    - ❑ **File Server**   Although not required to share files, adding this core role service allows you to use the Share And Storage Management snap-in.
    - ❑ **Distributed File System**   Enables sharing files using the DFS namespace and replicating files between DFS servers. If you select this role service, the wizard will prompt you to configure a namespace.
    - ❑ **File Server Resources Manager**   Installs tools for generating storage reports, configuring quotas, and defining file screening policies. If you select this role service, the wizard will prompt you to enable storage monitoring on the local disks.
    - ❑ **Services for Network File System**   Provides connectivity for UNIX client computers that use Network File System (NFS) for file sharing. Note that most modern UNIX operating systems can connect to standard Windows file shares, so this service is typically not required.
    - ❑ **Windows Search Service**   Indexes files for faster searching when clients connect to shared folders. This role service is not intended for enterprise use. If you select this role service, the wizard will prompt you to enable indexing on the local disks.
    - ❑ **Windows Server 2003 File Services**   Provides services compatible with computers running Windows Server 2003.
6. Respond to any roles service wizard pages that appear.
7. On the Confirmation page, click Install.
8. On the Results page, click Close.

You can access the File Services tools using the Roles\File Services node in Server Manager.

Using Quotas

When multiple users share a disk, whether locally or across the network, the disk will quickly become filled—usually because one or two users consume far more disk space than the rest. Disk quotas make it easy to monitor users who consume more than a specified amount of disk space. Additionally, you can enforce quotas to prevent users from consuming more disk space (although this can cause applications to fail and is not typically recommended).

With Windows Server 2008 you should use the Quota Management console to configure disk quotas. You can also configure quotas using the DirQuota command-line tool. Additionally, you can configure disk quotas by using Group Policy settings or by using Windows Explorer. The sections that follow describe each of these techniques.

Configuring Disk Quotas Using the Quota Management Console

After installing the File Server Resource Manager role service, you can manage disk quotas using the Quota Management console. In Server Manager, you can access the snap-in at Roles\File Services\Share And Storage Management\File Server Resource Manager\Quota Management. The Quota Management console provides more flexible control over quotas and makes it easier to notify users or administrators that a user has exceeded a quota threshold or to run an executable file that automatically clears up disk space.

Creating Quota Templates The Quota Management snap-in supports the use of quota templates. You can use a quota template to apply a set of quotas and response behavior to volumes. Windows Server 2008 includes the following standard templates:

- **100 MB Limit** Defines a *hard quota* (a quota that prevents the user from creating more files) of 100 MB per user, with e-mail warnings sent to the user at 85 percent and 95 percent. At 100 percent of the quota, this template sends an e-mail to the user and to administrators.

- **200 MB Limit Reports To User** Defines a hard quota of 200 MB per user, with e-mail warnings sent to the user at 85 percent and 95 percent. At 100 percent of the quota, this template sends an e-mail to the user and to administrators and sends a report to the user.

- **200 MB Limit With 50 MB Extension** Defines a 200 MB quota. When the 200MB quota is reached, the computer sends an e-mail to the user and administrators and then applies the 250 MB Extended Limit quota to grant the user additional capacity.

- **250 MB Extended Limit** Primarily used with the previous quota template to provide the user an additional 50 MB of capacity. This template prevents the user from exceeding 250 MB.

- **Monitor 200 GB Volume Usage** Provides e-mail notifications when utilization reaches 70 percent, 80 percent, 90 percent, and 100 percent of the 200 GB soft quota.

- **Monitor 500 MB Share** Provides e-mail notifications when utilization reaches 80 percent, 100 percent, and 120 percent of the 500 MB soft quota.

These standard templates are provided as examples. To create your own quota templates, right-click Quota Templates in the Quota Management console, and then choose Create Quota Template. In the Create Quota Template dialog box, select a standard template you want to base your new template on, and then click Copy. Figure 11-6 demonstrates copying a quota template.

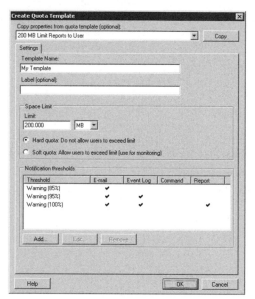

Figure 11-6   Creating a quota template

Thresholds define what happens when a user reaches a quota (or a percentage of a quota). To add a threshold, edit a quota template or a quota, and then click Add. The Add Threshold dialog box has four tabs:

■ **E-mail Message**   Sends an e-mail notification to administrators or to the user. You can define the [Admin Email] variable and other e-mail settings by right-clicking File Server Resource Manager and then choosing Configure Options.

■ **Event Log**   Logs an event to the event log, which is useful if you have management tools that process events.

■ **Command**   Runs a command or a script when a threshold is reached. You can use this to run a script that automatically compresses files, removes temporary files, or allocates more disk space for the user.

■ **Report**   Generates a report that you can e-mail to administrators or the user. You can choose from a number of reports.

Use thresholds to notify users or administrators that a user has consumed a specific amount of disk space.

Creating Quotas   To apply quotas consistently, you should always create a quota template first and then create a quota based on that template. To create a quota, follow these steps:

1. Select and right-click the *Quotas* node in Server Manager, and then choose Create Quota. The Create Quota dialog box appears, as shown in Figure 11-7.

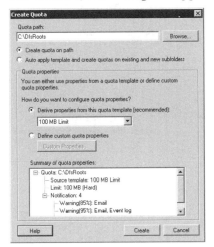

Figure 11-7   Creating a quota

2. Click the Browse button to select a folder to apply the quota to, and then click OK.

3. Optionally, select Auto Apply Template And Create Quotas On Existing And New Sub-folders. Selecting this option applies a template to any new folders created within the parent folder you select.

4. Select the Derive Properties From This Quota Template option, and then select the quota template from the drop-down list. Otherwise, you can select the Define Custom Quota Properties option and then click the Custom Properties button to define a quota not based on an existing template.

5. Click Create.

The Quotas snap-in shows the newly created quota, which is immediately in effect.

Configuring Disk Quotas at a Command Prompt or Script

You can use the DirQuota command to configure disk quotas at the command prompt or from a script. For example, the following command applies the standard 200 MB Limit Reports To User template to the C:\Shared folder:

```
dirquota quota add /Path:C:\Shared /SourceTemplate:"200 MB Limit Reports To User"
```

To create a hard limit of 100 MB, run the following command:

```
dirquota quota add /Path:C:\Shared /Limit:100MB /Type:Hard
```

Although you can create multiple thresholds and notifications using the *DirQuota* command, it is typically easier to create templates and use DirQuota to apply the templates. For complete usage information, type the command **DirQuota /?**.

Configuring Disk Quotas Using Windows Explorer

Although you should always use the Quota Management console to configure quotas in Windows Server 2008, the operating system continues to support quota management using Windows Explorer, using the same interface as earlier versions of Windows. To configure disk quotas on a local computer using Windows Explorer, follow these steps:

1. Open Windows Explorer (for example, by clicking Start and then choosing Computer).

2. Right-click the disk you want to configure quotas for, and then choose Properties. You cannot configure quotas for individual folders.

   The disk properties dialog box appears.

3. In the Quota tab, select the Enable Quota Management check box, as shown in Figure 11-8.

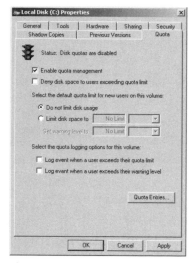

Figure 11-8 Enabling quota management

4. Select the Limit Disk Space To option. Specify the limit and warning levels. Windows does not notify users if they exceed either threshold. In fact, if you choose not to enforce quota limits, the only difference between the two thresholds is the event ID that is added to the System event log.

5. To add an event for the warning or limit levels, select the Log Event When A User Exceeds Their Quota Limit check box or the Log Event When A User Exceeds Their Warning Level check box. Events are added to the System event log with a source of

NTFS. Event ID 36 indicates that a user reached the warning level, and event ID 37 indicates a user reached the quota limit. Use event triggers to send an e-mail or run a program when these events are added so that systems administrators can address the problem. For more information about event triggers, read Chapter 10, "Monitoring Computers."

6. Optionally, select the Deny Disk Space To Users Exceeding Quota Limit check box. If you select this check box, users will be unable to save or update files when they exceed their quota limit. For this reason, you should typically not select this option—the potential harm to user productivity is rarely worth it. Instead, create an event trigger that notifies IT when a user exceeds the quota limit so that IT can follow up with the user.

7. Click Quota Entries to view the current disk usage, as shown in Figure 11-9. In the Quota Entries window, double-click a user to configure a user-specific quota that differs from the default settings for the disk.

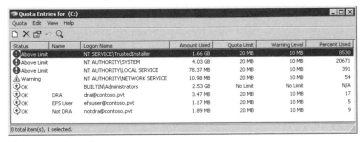

Figure 11-9   Viewing quota entries

8. Click OK to close the Quota Settings For *user name* dialog box, close the Quota Entries For *drive letter* window, and then click OK again to close the Local Disk Properties dialog box. If prompted, click OK to enable system quotas.

Configuring Disk Quotas Using Group Policy

You can also configure simple disk quotas using Group Policy settings. In the Group Policy Management Editor, select the Computer Configuration\Policies\Administrative Templates\System\Disk Quotas node to define these policy settings:

- **Enable Disk Quotas**   You must enable this policy to use disk quotas.
- **Enforce Disk Quota Limit**   Equivalent to selecting the Deny Disk Space To Users Exceeding Quota Limit check box when configuring local disk quotas.
- **Default Quota Limit And Warning Level**   Defines the quota limit and warning levels, exactly as you can when configuring disk quotas using Windows Explorer.
- **Log Event When Quota Limit Exceeded**   Equivalent to selecting the Log Event When A User Exceeds Their Quota Limit check box in Windows Explorer.

- **Log Event When Quota Warning Level Exceeded** Equivalent to selecting the Log Event When A User Exceeds Their Warning Level check box in Windows Explorer.
- **Apply Policy To Removable Media** Defines whether quotas are applied to removable media. Typically, this policy should be disabled.

Sharing Folders

You can share folders across the network to allow other computers to access them, as if the computers were connected to a local disk.

Sharing Folders from Windows Explorer

The simplest way to share a folder is to right-click the folder in Windows Explorer and then choose Share. As shown in Figure 11-10, the File Sharing dialog box appears and allows you to select the users who will have access to the folder. Click Share to create the shared folder, and then click Done.

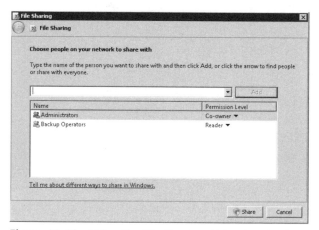

Figure 11-10 Using the File Sharing dialog box to share a folder

Using this interface you can select four permission levels:

- **Reader** Provides read-only access. This is equivalent to the Read share permission.
- **Contributor** Provides read and write access. This is equivalent to the Change share permission.
- **Co-owner** Enables the user to change file permissions, as well as granting full read and write access. This is equivalent to the Full Control share permission.
- **Owner** Assigned to the user who creates the share and allows changing file permissions and read and write files. This is equivalent to the Full Control share permission.

Sharing Folders Using the Provision A Shared Folder Wizard

Using the Provision A Shared Folder Wizard, you can share folders, configure quotas, and specify security by following these steps:

1. In Server Manager, right-click Roles\File Services\Share And Storage Management, and then choose Provision Share.

   The Provision A Shared Folder Wizard appears.

2. On the Shared Folder Location page, click the Browse button to select the folder to share. Click OK. Click Next.

3. On the NTFS Permissions page, select Yes, Change NTFS Permissions and then, if necessary, click Edit Permissions. Configure the NTFS permissions as necessary, and then click OK. Click Next.

4. On the Share Protocols page you can choose whether to share the folder using Windows protocol (indicated as SMB, which stands for Server Message Block) or using a UNIX protocol (indicated as NFS, or Network File System). Typically, SMB will suffice, even for UNIX clients. NFS is available only if the Services For Network File System role service is installed. Click Next.

5. On the SMB Settings page, click Advanced if you want to change the default settings for the number of simultaneous users permitted or Offline Files. Click Next.

6. On the SMB Permissions page, as shown in Figure 11-11, select the permissions you want to assign. To define custom permissions, select Users And Groups Have Custom Share Permissions, and then click the Permissions button. Click Next.

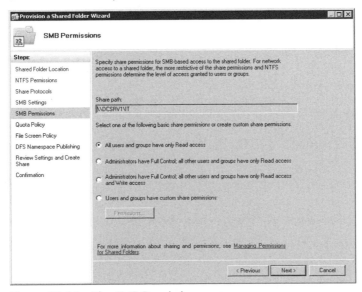

Figure 11-11 The SMB Permissions page

7. On the Quota Policy page, select the Apply Quota check box if you want to define a quota. Then, select a quota template. Click Next.

8. On the File Screen Policy page, select the Apply File Screen check box if you want to allow only specific types of files in the folder. Then, select the file screen you want to use. Click Next.

NOTE Configuring file screening

You can configure file screening using the Roles\File Services\Share And Storage Management\File Server Resource Manager\File Screening Management node of Server Manager. You can use the FileScrn.exe command-line tool in scripts or when running Windows Server 2008 Server Core.

---

9. On the DFS Namespace Publishing page, select the Publish The SMB Share To A DFS Namespace check box if desired. Then, provide the DFS namespace information. Click Next.

10. On the Review Settings And Create Share page, click Create.

11. Click Close.

Sharing Folders from a Command Prompt or Script

You can share folders from a script or a command prompt (for example, when running Server Core) using the *net share* command.

To view existing shares, type the following command:

```
net share
```

To create a share, use the following syntax:

```
net share ShareName=Path [/GRANT:user,[READ|CHANGE|FULL]]
[/CACHE:Manual|Documents|Programs|None]
```

For example, to share the C:\Shared folder using the share name Files, type the following command:

```
net share Files=C:\Shared
```

To share the same folder with read access for everyone but disallow Offline Files, type the following command:

```
net share Files=C:\Shared /GRANT:Everyone,Read /CACHE:None
```

To remove a share, specify the share name and the /DELETE parameter. The following example would remove the share named Files:

```
net share Files /DELETE
```

For complete usage information, tyep the following command:

```
net share /?
```

Connecting to Shared Folders

Client computers connect to shared folders across the network by using the Universal Naming Convention (UNC) format: \\<*server_name*>\<*share_name*>. For example, if you share the folder MyDocs from the server MyServer, you would connect to it by typing **MyServer \MyDocs**.

You can use UNC format just as you would specify any folder name. For example, you could open a file in Notepad by providing the path \\MyServer\MyDocs\MyFile.txt. At a command prompt, you could view the contents of the shared folder by running the following command:

```
dir \\MyServer\MyDocs
```

Most users prefer to access shared folders using a network drive. Network drives map a drive letter to a shared folder. For example, although the C drive is typically a local hard disk, you could assign the Z drive to a shared folder. Client computers can connect to shared folders from Windows Explorer by clicking the Map Network Drive button or by clicking the Tools menu and then choosing Map Network Drive. Alternatively, you can map a network drive using the Net command at a command prompt with the following syntax:

```
net use <drive_letter>: \\<server_name>\<share_name>
```

For example, the following command would map the Z drive to the \\MyServer\MyDocs shared folder:

```
net use Z: \\MyServer\MyDocs
```

DFS Overview

Large organizations often have dozens, or even hundreds, of file servers. This can make it very difficult for users to remember which file server specific files are stored on.

DFS provides a single namespace that allows users to connect to any shared folder in your organization. With DFS, all shared folders can be accessible using a single network drive letter in Windows Explorer. For example, if your Active Directory domain is contoso.com, you could create the DFS namespace \\contoso.com\dfs. Then, you could create the folder \\contoso.com\dfs\marketing and map it to shared folders (known as *targets*) at both \\server1\marketing and \\server2\marketing.

Besides providing a single namespace to make it easier for users to find files, DFS can provide redundancy for shared files using replication. Replication also allows you to host a shared folder on multiple servers and have client computers automatically connect to the closest available server.

Installing DFS

You can install DFS when adding the File Services server role using the Add Roles Wizard, or you can add the role service later using Server Manager by right-clicking Roles\File Services and then choosing Add Role Services. Whichever method you use, follow these steps to complete the wizard pages:

1. On the DFS Namespaces page, choose whether to create a namespace. Click Next.
2. If the Namespace Type page appears, choose whether to use a domain-based namespace (for Active Directory environments) or a stand-alone namespace (for workgroup environments). If all DFS servers for the namespace are running Windows Server 2008, enable Windows Server 2008 mode. Click Next.
3. If the Namespace Configuration page appears, you can click the Add button to add folders. You can also do this later using the DFS Management snap-in. Click Next.

If you don't create a DFS namespace or add folders, you can add them later using the DFS Management console in Server Manager.

Creating a DFS Namespace

The DFS namespace forms the root of shared folders in your organization. Although you might need only a single DFS namespace, you can create multiple DFS namespaces. To create a DFS namespace, follow these steps:

1. In Server Manager, right-click Roles\File Services\DFS Management\Namespaces, and then choose New Namespace.

    The New Namespace Wizard appears.
2. On the Namespace Server page, type the name of the server that will host the namespace. You can add servers later to host the namespace for redundancy. Users do not reference the server name when accessing the DFS namespace. Click Next.
3. On the Namespace Name And Settings page, type a name. This name acts as the share name when users access the DFS namespace—for example, *domain_name* *namespace_name*. Click the Edit Settings button to configure the permissions for the namespace. Click Next.

4. On the Namespace Type page, choose whether to create a domain-based namespace or a stand-alone namespace. Domain-based namespaces use the Active Directory domain name as their root, and stand-alone namespaces use the server as their root. Click Next.

5. On the Review Settings And Create Namespace page, click Create.

6. On the Confirmation page, click Close.

After creating a namespace, you can adjust settings by right-clicking it and then choosing Properties. The Properties dialog box for the namespace has three tabs:

- **General**   Allows you to type a description for the namespace.
- **Referrals**   When a client accesses the root of a namespace or a folder with targets, the client receives a referral from the domain controller. Clients always attempt to access the first target computer in the referral list and, if the first target computer does not respond, access computers farther down the list. This tab gives you control over how multiple targets in a referral list are ordered. Select Random Order from the Ordering Method drop-down list to distribute referrals evenly among all targets (with targets in the same site listed first). Select Lowest Cost to direct clients to the closest target computer first using site link costs (which you can define using the Active Directory Sites And Services console). If you would rather have clients fail instead of accessing a target in a different Active Directory site, select Exclude Targets Outside Of The Client's Site. Folders inherit the ordering method from the namespace root by default, but you can also edit the properties of individual folders. The Cache Duration setting defines how long clients wait before requesting a new referral.

Exam Tip   Know the different referral order types for the exam!

- **Advanced**   Choose from two polling configurations: Optimize For Consistency or Optimize For Scalability. Optimize For Consistency configures namespace servers to query the primary domain controller (PDC) each time the namespace changes, which reduces the time it takes for changes to the namespace to be visible to users. Optimize For Scalability reduces the number of queries (thus improving performance and reducing utilization of your PDC) by querying the closest domain controller at regular intervals.

Adding Folders to a DFS Namespace

Before your namespace is useful, you must add folders to it. Folders can be organizational, which means they exist only within the DFS namespace, or they can be associated with a shared folder on a server. When users connect to a DFS namespace, these folders appear exactly like folders in a traditional file system.

To add folders to a DFS namespace, follow these steps:

1. In Server Manager, select Roles\File Services\DFS Management\Namespaces.
2. In the details pane, right-click the namespace, and then choose New Folder. The New Folder dialog box appears.
3. Type the name for the folder. If the folder is to be used only for organizational purposes (for example, it will contain only other folders), you can click OK. If you want the folder to contain files, click the Add button to associate it with a shared folder. If you add multiple folder targets, you can configure automatic replication between the folders.
4. Click OK.

Configuring DFS from a Command Prompt or Script

You can use the DFSUtil tool to configure DFS from a command prompt or script. For example, to view the DFS roots in a domain, run the following command:

```
dfsutil domain <domain_name>
```

To view the roots on a specific server, run the following command:

```
dfsutil server <server_name>
```

To view the targets in a namespace, run the following command:

```
dfsutil target \\<domain_name>\<namespace_root>
```

To view the targets for a folder, run the following command:

```
dfsutil link \\<domain_name>\<namespace_root>\<folder>
```

To view which Active Directory site a client participates in, run the following command:

```
dfsutil client siteinfo <client_name>
```

For complete usage information, type **dfsutil /?** at a command prompt. To troubleshoot DFS, use the DFSDiag command-line tool. For more information, type **dfsdiag /?** at a command prompt.

Offline Files

Mobile users might need access to shared folders even when they're disconnected from your internal network. Offline Files makes this possible by allowing client computers to automatically cache a copy of files on shared folders and by providing transparent access to the files when the user is disconnected from the network. The next time the user connects to the network, Offline Files synchronizes any updates and prompts the user to manually resolve any conflicts.

Server administrators can configure Offline Files at the shared folder, and users of client computers can configure Offline Files when connected to a shared folder. To configure Offline Files caching behavior for a shared folder, follow these steps:

1. In Server Manager, select Roles\File Services\Share And Storage Management.
2. In the details pane, right-click the share you want to configure, and then choose Properties.
3. In the Sharing tab, click Advanced.
4. In the Advanced dialog box, click the Caching tab, as shown in Figure 11-12. Select one of the following three options, and then click OK twice:

   ❑ **Only The Files And Programs That Users Specify Are Available Offline** Users must manually select the files they want to access while offline. This option works well when users understand how to use Offline Files.

   ❑ **All Files And Programs That Users Open From The Share Are Automatically Available Offline** Files that users access while connected to the network are automatically cached for a limited amount of time. This option works well when users do not understand how to use Offline Files.

   ❑ **No Files Or Programs From The Share Are Available Offline** Prevents users from accessing Offline Files. This option is the best choice for confidential documents that should not be stored on mobile computers.

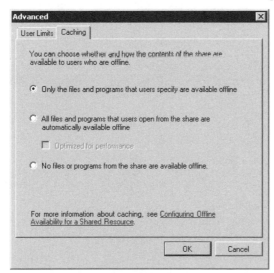

Figure 11-12 Configuring Offline Files behavior for a shared folder

You can also access the same settings from Windows Explorer by clicking Advanced Sharing in the Sharing tab of the shared folder's properties dialog box and then clicking the Caching button.

If you choose Only The Files And Programs That Users Specify Are Available Offline, users must configure mapped drives for use with Offline Files. In Windows Vista, configure a mapped drive for Offline Files by following these steps:

1. In Windows Explorer, right-click the network folder or file, and then choose Properties.
2. On the Offline Files tab, select the Always Available Offline check box. Then, click OK.

NOTE   Using Offline Files in Windows Vista

In Windows Vista, you can right-click a network file or folder and then select Always Available Offline.

Windows immediately synchronize the file or folder. Users can return to the Offline Files tab later and click Synch Now to copy the latest version of the file.

PRACTICE **Working with Shared Folders**

In this practice, you create a redundant DFS namespace.

▶ Exercise 1   Add the Distributed File System Role Service

In this exercise, you must add the File Services server role and Distributed File System role service on both Dcsrv1 and Boston. Then, you will create a DFS namespace that is hosted on both computers and create shared folders that will be part of that namespace. The shared folders will automatically replicate files between each other, providing redundancy for clients who need to access the files.

To complete this exercise, Dcsrv1 should be configured as a domain controller and Boston should be configured as a domain member.

1. On Dcsrv1, in Server Manager, right-click Roles, and then choose Add Roles.
   The Add Roles Wizard appears.
2. On the Before You Begin page, click Next.
3. On the Server Roles page, select the File Services check box. Click Next.
4. On the File Services page, click Next.
5. On the Select Role Services page, select the role services File Server, Distributed File System, and File Server Resource Manager check boxes. Click Next.
6. On the Create A DFS Namespace page, type the namespace name **Public**. Click Next.
7. On the Namespace Type page, leave the default settings selected. Click Next.
8. On the Namespace Configuration page, click Next.

9. On the Configure Storage Usage Monitoring page, select the check boxes for all local disks, and then click Next.
10. On the Report Options page, click Next.
11. On the Confirmation page, click Install.
12. On the Results page, click Close.

Repeat the previous steps on Boston, except do not create a namespace on the Create A DFS Namespace page.

▶ **Exercise 2   Add a Server to the DFS Namespace**

Now, add a replicated folder to the DFS namespace by following these steps:

1. On Dcsrv1, in Server Manager, right-click Roles\File Services\DFS Management\ NameSpaces\\\<*domain*>\Public, and then choose Add Namespace Server.

    The Add Namespace Server dialog box appears.

2. Click the Browse button. In the Select Computer dialog box, type **Boston**, and then click OK. If you're prompted to start the DFS Namespace service on Boston, click Yes. Click OK again to close the Add Namespace Server dialog box.

3. In the details pane, click the Namespace Servers tab. Note that both servers are listed. If one of the servers is offline, clients will be able to connect to the second server. This provides redundancy for critical DFS namespaces.

▶ **Exercise 3   Add a Replicated Folder to the DFS Namespace**

Now that you have created the DFS namespace and hosted it on two servers, you will create a shared folder named Files on both Dcsrv1 and Boston, add the shared folder to the DFS namespace, and configure it for replication.

1. On Dcsrv1, in Server Manager, right-click Roles\File Services\Share And Storage Management, and then click Provision Share.

    The Provision A Shared Folder Wizard appears.

2. On the Shared Folder Location page, type **C:\Files**. Click Next. When prompted, click Yes to create the folder.

3. On the NTFS Permissions page, select Yes, Change NTFS Permissions. Click Edit Permissions and grant the Users group Allow Modify permissions. Click OK. Then, click Next.

4. On the Share Protocols page, type a share name of **Files**. Click Next.

5. On the SMB Settings page, click Advanced. In the Caching tab, select No Files Or Programs From The Share Are Available Offline. This prevents mobile computers from keeping a locally cached copy of files. Click OK, and then click Next.

6. On the SMB Permissions page, select Administrators Have Full Control; All Other Users And Groups Have Only Read Access. Click Next.

7. On the Quota Policy page, select the Apply Quota check box. Select Auto Apply Template To Create Quotas On Existing And New Subfolders. Then, in the Derive Properties From This Quota Template drop-down list, select 200 MB Limit With 50 MB Extension. Click Next.

8. On the File Screen Policy page, select the Apply File Screen check box. In the Derive Properties From This File Screen Template drop-down list, select Block Executable Files. Click Next.

9. On the DFS Namespace Publishing page, select the Publish The SMB Share To A DFS Namespace check box. In the Parent Folder In Namespace box, type **nwtraders.msft** **Public** (or substitute your domain name). In the New Folder Name box, type **Files**. Click Next.

10. On the Review Settings And Create Share page, click Create.

11. Click Close.

12. On Boston, open a command prompt with administrative privileges and run the following commands to create a folder, assign Users the Modify NTFS permission, and then share the folder. This duplicates the shared folder you created on Dcsrv1 using the Provision A Shared Folder Wizard.

```
mkdir C:\Files
icacls C:\Files\ /grant users:M
net share Files=C:\Files /GRANT:Users,READ /GRANT:Administrators,FULL /CACHE:None
```

Now, on Dcsrv1, add the \\Boston\Files shared folder as a folder target for the \\nwtraders.msft\Public\Files folder.

1. On Dcsrv1, in Server Manager, right-click \\nwtraders.msft\Public, and then choose Refresh.

2. In Server Manager, right-click \\nwtraders.msft\Public\Files, and then choose Add Folder Target.

3. In the New Folder Target dialog box, type **Boston\Files**. Click OK.

4. In the Replication dialog box, click Yes to create a replication group between the Dcsrv1 and Boston servers.

   The Replicate Folder Wizard appears.

5. On the Replication Group And Replicated Folder Name page, click Next.

6. On the Replication Eligibility page, click Next.

7. On the Primary Member page, select Dcsrv1. Click Next.

8. On the Topology Selection page, select Full Mesh. Click Next. Note that if you have more than two or three replication partners and you will always be updating one server, a hub and spoke topology can be more efficient.

9. On the Replication Group Schedule And Bandwidth page, click Next. Note that you have the option to limit bandwidth (to reduce impact on other network applications) or to replicate only during nonpeak hours.

10. On the Review Settings And Create Replication Group page, click Create.

11. On the Confirmation page, click Close.

12. In the Replication Delay dialog box, click OK.

13. In Server Manager, select the DFS Management\Namespaces\\\nwtraders.msft\Public \Files folder, and then select the Replication tab in the details pane. Note that both Dcsrv1 and Boston are listed as replication members.

14. In Server Manager, select the DFS Management\Replication\nwtraders.msft\public \files node. In the details pane, browse each of the four tabs to view more information about the replication group that the Replicate Folder Wizard automatically created.

▶ **Exercise 4   Test DFS Replication**

In this exercise, you connect to the DFS namespace and create a file to verify that it automatically replicates.

1. On Dcsrv1, while logged on as any account other than Administrator, click Start, and then choose Computer.

2. In the Computer window, click Map Network Drive on the toolbar.

3. In the Map Network Drive window, type **\\nwtraders.msft\Public\Files**. Then, click Finish. Windows Explorer maps the Z drive to the shared folder.

4. In the new mapped drive, create a text file by right-clicking the details pane, choosing New, and then choosing Text Document. Because UAC limits your privileges to those of a standard user and the Users group has only the Read share permission (even though Users have Modify NTFS permissions), you will be unable to create the file.

5. In the Windows Explorer window, select the C:\Files folder. Then, right-click the details pane, choose New, and choose Text Document. Assign the document the name Text File. Then, open the file and type "Hello, world." Save and close the file.

6. On Boston, open Windows Explorer and view the C:\Files folder. Notice that the Text File has been replicated (this might take a few minutes). Open the file to verify that it contains the text you typed.

Lesson Summary

■ The File Services server role installs tools for managing shared folders, disk quotas, file screening, and storage reports.

■ You can define quota thresholds to notify users and administrators when a user consumes more than a specified amount of disk space. Although they will cause applications to fail, you can create hard quotas to block users from saving files once they exceed a limit that you define. You can manage quotas using Windows Explorer, the Quota Management console, or the DirQuota command-line tool.

■ DFS defines a namespace that can consist of different shared folders located throughout your organization. By adding multiple targets for a single folder, you can replicate files between multiple file servers, providing redundancy and allowing users to connect to the shared folder even if one of the servers fails.

■ Offline Files is a Windows feature that copies network files and folders to the local computer so that users can access them when disconnected from the network. Offline Files can automatically synchronize files when the user is online.

Lesson Review

You can use the following questions to test your knowledge of the information in Lesson 2, "Sharing Folders." The questions are also available on the companion CD if you prefer to review them in electronic form.

NOTE   Answers

Answers to these questions and explanations of why each answer choice is correct or incorrect are located in the "Answers" section at the end of the book.

---

1. You create a folder named Marketing and configure NTFS permissions to grant the Domain Users group Read permission and the Marketing group Modify permission. You share the folder and grant the Everyone group the Reader share permission. Mary, a user account who is a member of both the Marketing group and the Domain Users group, needs to access files in the folder from across the network. What effective permissions will Mary have?

   A. No Access

   B. Read

   C. Write

   D. Full Control

2. You are running Windows Server 2008 Server Core. You need to create a shared folder. Which command should you use?

    A. Net

    B. Netsh

    C. Share

    D. Ipconfig

3. Your organization has a central headquarters with seven regional offices. You deploy a DFS server to the headquarters and each regional office and add a DFS namespace that is hosted on each of the DFS servers. You want clients to connect to their local DFS server if it is available and then connect to any other DFS server if the local DFS server is not available. Which ordering method should you choose?

    A. Random Order

    B. Lowest Cost

    C. Excludes Targets Outside Of The Client's Site

    D. Clients Fall Back To Preferred Targets

4. To better control disk utilization, you need to use disk quotas to send an e-mail to users when they have consumed 80 MB of disk space and to prevent users from consuming more than 100 MB of disk space. What is the most efficient way to do this?

    A. Create a hard quota with a 80 MB limit and a second hard quota with a 100 MB limit.

    B. Create a soft quota with a 80 MB limit and a second soft quota with a 100 MB limit.

    C. Create a single hard quota with a 100 MB limit. Create a warning at 80 percent.

    D. Create a single soft quota with a 100 MB limit. Create a warning at 80 percent.

5. You need to configure quotas on a computer running Windows Server 2008 Server Core. Which tool should you use?

    A. FileScrn

    B. DirQuota

    C. StorRept

    D. Net

Lesson 3: Backing Up and Restoring Files

With previous versions of Windows, administrators needed to rely on non-Microsoft software to back up servers. With Windows Server 2008, the operating system has useful backup capabilities built in. Although Windows Server Backup cannot meet all your disaster recovery needs (for example, network backup capabilities are limited and you will still need to provide off-site backups), it can back up and recover files and entire volumes.

After this lesson, you will be able to:

- Manage shadow copy storage.
- Use Windows Server Backup to restore files and volumes.

Estimated lesson time: 30 minutes

Shadow Copies

Shadow copies allow backup software to access files that are in use. If backup software (including Windows Server Backup and non-Microsoft applications) needs to access a file that's in use by a different application, Volume Shadow Copy creates a shadow copy of the file in its current state and then gives the backup process access to the shadow copy. This allows the application that's using the file to make updates without affecting the backup.

If an application updates a file after a shadow copy is made, Windows must store both the original and changed portion of the file. Because shadow copies store only changes to files, the storage requirements are significantly less than the full size of files being accessed.

Managing Shadow Copies from Windows Explorer

You can manage shadow copies using the Windows Explorer interface. Follow these steps:

1. In Windows Explorer, right-click a volume, and then choose Configure Shadow Copies. The Shadow Copies dialog box appears.
2. In the Select A Volume list, select the volume you want to configure. Then, do any of the following:
3. Click Enable, and then click Yes to enable shadow copies on the volume. Similarly, you can click Disable and then click Yes to turn shadow copies back off.
4. Click Settings to define where shadow copies are stored, how much space they will consume, and how often they will be created.
5. Click Create Now to immediately create a shadow copy.
6. Click OK.

Managing Shadow Copies from a Command Prompt

You can manage shadow copies from the command prompt using the VSSAdmin tool. For example, to create a shadow copy of the C:\ volume, run the following command with administrative privileges:

```
vssadmin create shadow /For=C:
```

To view the storage currently allocated to shadow copies, run the following command:

```
vssadmin list shadowstorage
```

To view available shadow copies and the time they were created, run the following command:

```
vssadmin list shadows
```

That command lists shadow copy IDs, which you need to specify when reverting to a shadow copy. For example, if a shadow copy ID is {56036723-cdcc-49ef-98a4-445b1645770e}, you could revert to the shadow copy using the following command:

```
vssadmin revert shadow /Shadow={56036723-cdcc-49ef-98a4-445b1645770e}
```

For complete usage information, type **VSSAdmin /?** at a command prompt.

Windows Server Backup

Windows Server Backup copies an entire disk volume (for example, the volume Windows is installed on) to a .vhd file on a second local disk. After performing a backup, you can restore individual files or an entire volume. If Windows cannot start (for example, if the system volume has failed), you can start the computer from the Windows installation media, restore the system volume from the backup, and have the operating system up and running in less than an hour.

The sections that follow describe how to install the Windows Server Backup features, manually initiate a backup, schedule automatic backups, and recover files and volumes.

Installing Windows Server Backup Features

To install the Windows Server Backup Features, follow these steps:

1. In Server Manager, right-click Features, and then choose Add Features.
   The Add Features Wizard appears.
2. On the Features page, expand Windows Server Backup Features. Then, select either the Windows Server Backup check box (for graphical tools) or the Command-Line Tools check box (to script backups), or both check boxes. If you're prompted to install additional features to support the Command-Line Tools, click Add Required Features. Click Next.

3. On the Confirmation page, click Install.

4. On the Results page, click Close.

Now you can access the Windows Server Backup tool from the Administrative Tools folder on the Start menu and run the Wbadmin backup tool from a command prompt or script.

Manually Performing a Backup

To manually perform a backup, follow these steps:

1. Click Start, choose Administrative Tools, and then choose Windows Server Backup. Click Continue in the UAC dialog box.

    The Windows Server Backup console appears.

2. In the Actions pane, click Backup Once.

    The Backup Once Wizard appears.

3. On the Backup Options page, choose whether to use the same or new options, and then click Next. If you choose to use the same options, you will skip to step 9.

4. On the Server Backup Configuration page, choose whether to back up the full server or select Custom to select specific volumes. If you are backing up to a local disk, you should select Custom so that you can exclude the backup volume from the backup. Click Next.

5. If the Select Backup Items page appears, select the check boxes for the volumes you want to back up, and then click Next.

6. On the Specify Destination Type page, choose whether to back up locally (for example, to a different volume) or to a shared folder on the network. Click Next.

7. On the Select Backup Destination page, choose where to save the backup file. Click Next.

8. On the Specify Advanced Option page, leave the default setting of VSS Copy Backup selected to protect VSS log files that might be used by other backup applications. If you do not use another backup application, select VSS Full Backup. Click Next.

9. On the Confirmation page, click Backup.

10. On the Backup Progress page, you can watch the backup progress (as shown in Figure 11-13) or click Close to allow the backup to continue in the background.

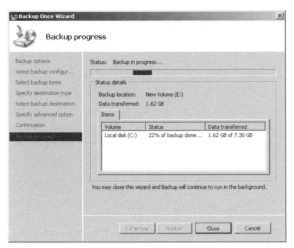

Figure 11-13   Manually running a backup

Backups are saved using the same format as the Complete PC backups provided by Windows Vista. Windows creates a WindowsImageBackup folder in the root of the backup media. Inside that folder, it creates a folder with the current computer's name. It then creates a Catalog folder containing the GlobalCatalog and BackupGlobalCatalog files and a "Backup *<year>*-*<month>*-*<date>* *<time>*" folder containing the .vhd disk image file. The format is exactly the same as a Complete PC backup created in Windows Vista.

MORE INFO   **Installing VHDMount**

Microsoft Virtual Server 2005 R2 SP1 includes VHDMount, a command-line tool for mounting .vhd files so that you can browse their contents. This is an excellent way to extract files from a Windows Server backup. For instructions on how to install VHDMount without installing Virtual Server 2005 R2 SP1, read "VHDMount Without Virtual Server" at *http://blogs.technet.com/daven/archive/2006/12 /15/vhdmount-without-virtual-server.aspx*.

Scheduling Backups

Scheduling backups requires a dedicated local disk. You cannot use the Backup Schedule Wizard to back up to a disk that will be used by other applications, and you cannot back up to a shared folder on the network. After running the Backup Schedule Wizard, the backup target disk will not be visible in Windows Explorer.

To schedule a backup to run automatically, follow these steps:

1. Click Start, choose Administrative Tools, and then choose Windows Server Backup. The Windows Server Backup console appears.

2. In the Actions pane, click Backup Schedule.

   The Backup Schedule Wizard appears.

3. On the Getting Started page, click Next.

4. On the Select Backup Configuration page, choose whether to back up the full server or select Custom to select specific volumes. If you are backing up to a local disk, you should select Custom so that you can exclude the backup volume from the backup.

5. If the Select Backup Items page appears, select the check boxes for the volumes you want to back up, and then click Next.

6. On the Specify Backup Time page, select the time and frequency of your backups, as shown in Figure 11-14. Click Next.

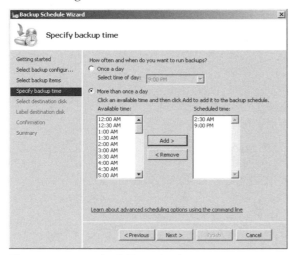

Figure 11-14   Scheduling a backup

7. On the Select Destination Disk page, choose where to save the backup file. This disk will be reformatted, and all data will be lost. Click Next.

8. Click Yes when prompted.

9. On the Label Destination Disk page, click Next.

10. On the Confirmation page, click Finish.

11. On the Summary page, the Backup Schedule Wizard formats the backup destination disk. Click Close.

You can view the scheduled task that initiates the backup using the Task Scheduler console. The backup task is available in the \Configuration\Task Scheduler Library\Microsoft\Windows \Backup node in Server Manager and calls the Wbadmin tool to perform the backup.

Performing Backups from a Command Prompt or Script

You can use the Wbadmin tool to initiate backups from a script or at a command prompt (such as when using Windows Server 2008 Server Core). For example, to initiate a backup of the C drive to the L drive, you would run the following command prompt from an elevated command prompt:

```
wbadmin start backup -backupTarget:L: -include:C: -quiet
```

The output resembles the following:

```
wbadmin 1.0 - Backup command-line tool
(C) Copyright 2004 Microsoft Corp.

Retrieving volume information...

This would backup volume Local Disk(C:) to L:.

Backup to L: is starting.

Running shadow copy of volumes requested for backup.
Running backup of volume Local Disk(C:), copied (0%).
Running backup of volume Local Disk(C:), copied (18%).
Running backup of volume Local Disk(C:), copied (40%).
Running backup of volume Local Disk(C:), copied (77%).
Running backup of volume Local Disk(C:), copied (98%).
Backup of volume Local Disk(C:) completed successfully.
Backup completed successfully.

Summary of backup:
------------------

Backup of volume Local Disk(C:) completed successfully.
```

To perform a backup of the system state, type **Wbadmin** with the **start systemstaterecovery** parameters. To schedule a backup, type **Wbadmin** with the **Enable backup** parameters. For complete usage information, type **wbadmin /?** at a command prompt.

Quick Check

1. What command should you run to configure shadow copies?
2. What command should you run to initiate a backup?

> **Quick Check Answers**
> 1. You should run **vssadmin**.
> 2. You shoud run **wbadmin**.

Recovering Individual Files

You can restore individual files from a backup or a recent shadow copy by following these steps:

1. In Windows Explorer, right-click a file you want to restore, and then choose Restore Previous Versions.

    The properties dialog box appears with the Previous Versions tab selected.
2. As shown in Figure 11-15, select the version you want to restore, and then click Restore.

Figure 11-15   Restoring a file with Previous Versions

3. When prompted, click Restore.
4. Click OK twice.

The previous version of the file will be restored.

Recovering Files or Volumes

To recover a server from a backup, follow these steps:

1. Click Start, choose Administrative Tools, and then choose Windows Server Backup.
    The Windows Server Backup console appears.

2. In the Actions pane, click Recover.

   The Recovery Wizard appears.

3. On the Getting Started page, select the server to recover, and then click Next.

4. On the Select Backup Date page, choose the backup from which to recover. Click Next.

5. On the Select Recovery Type page, choose one of the following three options, and then click Next:

   ❑ **Files And Folders**   Browse files that have been backed up and select specific files, folders, or both to be recovered.

   ❑ **Applications**   Applications can register with Windows Server Backup to store application-specific data. This option allows you to selectively restore application data.

   ❑ **Volumes**   Allows you to restore an entire volume. However, you cannot use this to restore the operating system volume. To do that, follow the instructions in the next section of this lesson, "Recovering from a Backup When Windows Will Not Start."

6. If the Select Items To Recover page appears, browse the backup to select a folder or files to recover, as shown in Figure 11-16. Then, click Next. If a dialog box appears, click OK.

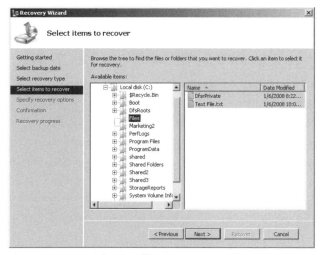

Figure 11-16   Selecting files to recover

7. If the Specify Recovery Options page appears, as shown in Figure 11-17, choose the backup destination and whether existing files will be overwritten. Click Next.

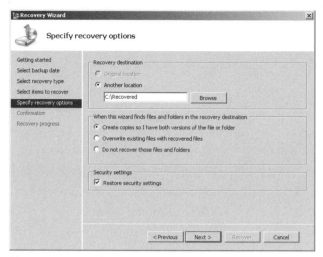

Figure 11-17   Selecting recovery options

8. If the Select Volumes page appears, select the volume check box, and then click Next.

9. On the Confirmation page, click Recover.

10. On the Recovery Progress page, click Close.

Recovering from a Backup When Windows Will Not Start

If Windows cannot start or if you need to recover the entire system volume from a backup, you can start the computer from the Windows Server 2008 DVD and use the Windows Complete PC Restore Wizard to recover the operating system. Follow these steps:

1. Insert the Windows Server 2008 media and restart the computer.

2. When the Press Any Key To Boot From The CD prompt appears, press a key.
    After a brief delay, the Install Windows Wizard appears.

3. On the language selection page, click Next.

4. Click Repair Your Computer, as shown in Figure 11-18.

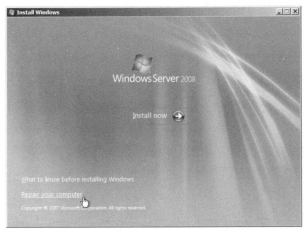

Figure 11-18 Choosing to repair your computer from the Windows Server 2008 DVD

5. On the System Recovery Options dialog box, select the operating system instance, and then click Next.

6. Click Windows Complete PC Restore.

The Windows Complete PC Restore Wizard appears.

7. On the Restore Your Entire Computer From A Backup, use the default setting to restore the most recent backup. Alternatively, click Restore A Different Backup if you need to restore an older backup (for example, if the most recent backup is corrupted or if you need to restore to a date prior to a security compromise). Click Next.

8. On the Choose How To Restore The Backup page, click Next.

9. On the final page, click Finish.

10. In the dialog box, select the I Confirm check box, and then click OK.

Windows restores your backup by overwriting the volumes you are recovering. After the restoration is complete, Windows automatically restarts using the state it was in at the time of the backup.

PRACTICE Backing Up and Restoring Files

In this practice, you back up and restore files using shadow copies and Windows Server Backup.

▶ **Exercise 1 Restore a File from a Shadow Copy**

In this exercise, you create a file, perform a volume shadow copy, and then restore the file.

1. Create a text document on your desktop. Open the text document, add the text "Before," and save and close the document.

2. Open a command prompt with administrative privileges. Then, run the following command to create a shadow copy of your C drive:

   `vssadmin create shadow /For=C:`

3. Open the text document that you saved to the desktop. Change the text to "After" and save and close the document.

4. Right-click the document, and then choose Restore Previous Versions.

   The properties dialog box appears with the Previous Versions tab selected.

5. Select the most recent version (there will probably be only one because the file is new), and then click Restore.

6. When prompted, click Restore.

7. Click OK twice.

8. Open the text file to verify that the document was restored to the state it was in before you created the shadow copy.

▶ **Exercise 2   Back Up and Restore Files**

In this exercise, you must back up Dcsrv1, restore individual files, and then restore the entire system volume. Prior to performing this exercise, configure Dcsrv1 with a second hard disk to provide a backup target.

1. On Dcsrv1, log on using the Administrator account. Click Start, choose Administrative Tools, and then choose Windows Server Backup.

   The Windows Server Backup console appears.

2. In the Actions pane, click Backup Schedule.

   The Backup Schedule Wizard appears.

3. On the Getting Started page, click Next.

4. On the Select Backup Configuration page, select Custom.

5. On the Select Backup Items page, select only the system volume check box, and then click Next.

6. On the Specify Backup Time page, specify a time approximately five minutes in the future. Click Next.

7. On the Select Destination Disk page, select the backup target disk. Click Next.

8. Click Yes when prompted.

9. On the Label Destination Disk page, click Next.

10. On the Confirmation page, click Finish.

11. On the Summary page, the Backup Schedule Wizard formats the backup destination disk. Click Close.

Wait until the backup begins and completes. You can monitor the backup progress using the Windows Server Backup console.

After the backup has completed, follow these steps to remove, and then restore a file. These steps assume you have completed the Lesson 1 practice. If you have not, you can delete any file on the disk instead of the suggested files.

1. Delete the C:\Users\EfsUser\Documents folder.
2. Click Start, choose Administrative Tools, and then choose Windows Server Backup.
   The Windows Server Backup console appears.
3. In the Actions pane, click Recover.
   The Recovery Wizard appears.
4. On the Getting Started page, click Next.
5. On the Select Backup Date page, notice that the most recent backup is already selected. Click Next.
6. On the Select Recovery Type page, select Files And Folders, and then click Next.
7. If the Select Items To Recover page appears, browse the backup to select the C:\Users \EfsUser\Documents folder. Then, click Next. If a dialog box appears, click OK.
8. If the Specify Recovery Options page appears, specify the backup destination C:\Users \EfsUser. Click Next.
9. On the Confirmation page, click Recover.
10. On the Recovery Progress page, click Close.

Now open Windows Explorer to verify that the C:\Users\EfsUser\Documents folder has been recovered. Then delete the C:\Users\EfsUser\Documents folder again and perform the following steps to restore the entire Windows system volume. This simulates a complete recovery—for example, a recovery from a failed hard disk.

1. Insert the Windows Server 2008 media and restart the computer.
2. When the Press Any Key To Boot From The CD prompt appears, press a key.
   After a brief delay, the Install Windows Wizard appears.
3. On the language selection page, click Next.
4. Click Repair Your Computer.
5. In the System Recovery Options dialog box, select the operating system instance, and then click Next.
6. Click Windows Complete PC Restore.
   The Windows Complete PC Restore Wizard appears.

7. On the Restore Your Entire Computer From A Backup page, click Next.

8. On the Choose How To Restore The Backup page, click Next.

9. On the final page, click Finish.

10. In the dialog box, select the I Confirm check box, and then click OK.

Wait several minutes for the volume to be rewritten from the backup. After Windows restarts, verify that the C:\Users\EfsUser\Documents folder was recovered. The restore would have been successful even if a new hard disk had been used.

Lesson Summary

- Windows automatically creates shadow copies when backup software needs to access files that are in use. Although you might never need to manage shadow copies, you can use the VSSAdmin tool to manually create shadow copies or manage the shadow copy storage space.

- Windows Server Backup creates a .vhd image file containing a copy of the disk volume being backed up. You can then restore individual files or the entire volume. Use the Wbadmin tool to manage backups from a command prompt.

Lesson Review

You can use the following questions to test your knowledge of the information in Lesson 3, "Backing Up and Restoring Files." The questions are also available on the companion CD if you prefer to review them in electronic form.

NOTE Answers

Answers to these questions and explanations of why each answer choice is correct or incorrect are located in the "Answers" section at the end of the book.

---

1. You are planning to modify several critical configuration files on a computer running Windows Server 2008. Which tool can you use to allow you to restore files to their previous state if necessary?

   A. StorRept

   B. FileScrn

   C. DirQuota

   D. VSSAdmin

2. You use the Windows Server Backup tool to manually perform a backup to the D drive on a computer named FileServer. In which folder is the backup stored?

   A. D:\WindowsFileBackup\FileServer\

   B. D:\WindowsImageBackup\FileServer\

   C. D:\WindowsImage\Backup\FileServer\

   D. D:\FileServer\WindowsImage\Backup\

3. You are using the Windows Server Backup tool to restore data. Which of the following tasks can you perform? (Choose all that apply.)

   A. Restore individual files

   B. Restore the system volume

   C. Restore a nonsystem volume

   D. Overwrite files that are currently in use

Chapter Review

To further practice and reinforce the skills you learned in this chapter, you can

- Review the chapter summary.
- Review the list of key terms introduced in this chapter.
- Complete the case scenarios. These scenarios set up real-world situations involving the topics of this chapter and ask you to create a solution.
- Complete the suggested practices.
- Take a practice test.

Chapter Summary

- NTFS file permissions provide access control while the operating system is online, and EFS protects files from unauthorized access if an attacker bypasses the operating system. Use NTFS file permissions as the primary method for file security, and use EFS to protect mobile computers that might be stolen or computers that otherwise might be physically accessible to an attacker.

- Windows Server 2008 provides much more powerful shared folder capabilities. After installing the File Services server role, you can manage disk quotas for individual folders, automatically notifying users and administrators when a user exceeds a specified threshold. You can now provision shared folders, complete with quotas and file security, using a simplified wizard interface. With DFS you can create a single namespace that provides users access to all the shared folders in your organization. Mobile users can enable Offline Files to configure Windows to automatically create a local copy of shared files so they can be accessed while the user is disconnected from the network.

- Shadow copies allow backup software to access files that are currently in use, and they can be used to create quick backups on the local disk. The Windows Server Backup tool provides powerful backup capabilities that allow you to restore individual files or entire volumes.

Key Terms

Do you know what these key terms mean? You can check your answers by looking up the terms in the glossary at the end of the book.

- hard quota
- referral
- soft quota
- targets

Case Scenarios

In the following case scenarios, you will apply what you've learned about how to plan and deploy file services. You can find answers to these questions in the "Answers" section at the end of this book.

Case Scenario 1: Planning File Services

You are a systems engineer for City Power & Light. Currently, your organization uses departmental servers for file sharing. Because each department has its own file server, your organization has hundreds of shared folders. Users are easily confused about which mapped drives contain the files they need, and systems administrators have a difficult time providing security for folders. Additionally, if a departmental server fails, the shared folder is offline until the server can be restored from a backup.

Answer the following questions for your manager:

1. How can you reduce the number of shared folders users must connect to?
2. If you use a DFS namespace, how can you ensure users do not connect to other department's shared folders?
3. How can you provide redundancy?

Case Scenario 2: Planning Disaster Recovery

You are a systems administrator for Northwind Traders. Your organization is beginning to deploy servers running Windows Server 2008. Your manager is very concerned about recovering a server that fails because of a failed hard disk.

Answer the following questions for your manager:

1. When purchasing servers, what are the hardware requirements for scheduling backups using Windows Server Backup?

2. After performing a backup, how will you recover a server with a failed system disk?

3. Can the same backup be used to restore files that become corrupted or are accidentally deleted?

Suggested Practices

To successfully master the Configure File And Print Services exam objective, complete the following tasks.

Configure a File Server

For this task, you should complete both practices.

- **Practice 1**   Use EFS to encrypt a file. Then, either start the computer from a CD that allows you to view files or reinstall Windows. Attempt to access the encrypted file.

- **Practice 2**   Log on using standard user privileges and attempt to edit files in your own user folders, other users' folders, program files folders, and Windows system folders. Examine the NTFS file permissions for each folder.

Configure Distributed File System

For this task, you should complete Practices 1 and 2 to gain practical experience with DFS. For practice working with the DFSUtil command-line tool, complete Practice 3. Complete Practice 4 to gain experience troubleshooting DFS problems.

- **Practice 1**   Create a DFS namespace in your production environment and add shared folders to the namespace.

- **Practice 2**   Create a shared folder with three or more target folders and configure replication between the folders. Add files of different sizes and determine how long it takes for files to replicate.

- **Practice 3**   Use DFSUtil to configure a complete DFS namespace, complete with multiple targets and folders.

- **Practice 4**   Use DFSDiag to diagnose problems with your DFS namespace.

Configure Shadow Copy Services

For this task you should complete Practices 1 and 2 on a computer in a practice environment. For additional practice working with VSSAdmin, complete Practice 3.

- **Practice 1** Use VSSAdmin to decrease the storage space allowed for shadow copies.
- **Practice 2** Use VSSAdmin to remove all shadow copies.
- **Practice 3** Use Restore Previous Versions to restore a file of more than 200 MB from a shadow copy. While the restoration is taking place, type the command **Vssadmin Query Reverts /For=C:** to view the status.

Configure Backup and Restore

For this task you, should complete all three practices to gain experience using the Wbadmin command-line tool for managing backup and restore actions.

- **Practice 1** Schedule a daily backup using the *Wbadmin* command.
- **Practice 2** Use the *Wbadmin* command to back up system state, and then restore it.
- **Practice 3** Using an installation of Windows Server 2008 Server Core, use *Wbadmin* to back up the system volume. Then, restore a specific file from the backup.
- **Practice 4** Watch the "New Backup and Offline Files Features in Windows Vista" from TechEd 2006 at *http://www.microsoft.com/emea/spotlight/sessionh.aspx?videoid=219*.

Configure Disk Quotas

For this task you should complete both practices to gain experience working with disk quotas.

- **Practice 1** Create a custom quota template to send an e-mail notification to the user when the user consumes 80 MB, send an e-mail notification to both the user and administrators when they consume 90 MB, and prevent the user from saving more data when the user consumes 100 MB. Apply the quota template, and then test it to verify that it works as expected and you receive the notifications. Notice the behavior of different applications as you try to save a file to the folder protected by the quota.
- **Practice 2** Apply the template you created in Practice 1 using the DirQuota command-line tool.

Take a Practice Test

The practice tests on this book's companion CD offer many options. For example, you can test yourself on just the content covered in this chapter, or you can test yourself on all the 70-642 certification exam content. You can set up the test so that it closely simulates the experience of taking a certification exam, or you can set it up in study mode so that you can look at the correct answers and explanations after you answer each question.

MORE INFO   **Practice tests**

For details about all the practice test options available, see "How to Use the Practice Tests" in this book's Introduction.

Chapter 12

Managing Printers

Printers are one of an organization's most complex management challenges. Because printers must be located physically near users, they're impossible to centralize. Printers require almost constant maintenance because ink must be replaced, paper must be refilled, and hardware must be fixed.

Although printers will always be a challenge, Windows Server 2008 provides sophisticated tools to improve manageability and to allow you to quickly detect problems. This chapter describes how to install, share, and manage printers.

Exam objectives in this chapter:
- Configure and monitor print services.

Lessons in this chapter:

Before You Begin

To complete the lesson in this chapter, you should be familiar with Microsoft Windows networking and be comfortable with the following tasks:

- Adding roles to a Windows Server 2008 computer
- Configuring Active Directory directory service domain controllers and joining computers to a domain
- Basic network configuration, including configuring IP settings

You will also need the following nonproduction hardware, connected to test networks:

1. A computer named Dcsrv1 that is a domain controller in the Nwtraders.msft domain. This computer must have at least one network interface.

NOTE   **Computer and domain names**

The computer and domain names you use will not affect these exercises. The practices in this chapter refer to these computer names for simplicity, however.

---

2. A computer named Boston that is a member of the Nwtraders.msft domain.
3. Optionally, one or more printers.

Real World

Tony Northrup

Because they are full of moving parts and must be physically distributed, printers are always going to be a management challenge. Use these best practices to minimize print management costs:

■ Deploy two or more identical printers to each location and configure them as printer pools. Printer pools allow users to continue printing even if one printer fails–and hardware problems are extremely common with printers.

■ Try to use only one or two printer models throughout your organization. This will simplify the ink and replacement parts you need to stock, as well as minimize your employees' training requirements.

■ Connect printers directly to wired networks instead of connecting them to servers. This will provide more flexibility for choosing the location of your printers and allow you to physically secure your servers.

■ Train users to perform basic printer management tasks, including refilling paper, replacing ink, and fixing jammed paper. This will reduce the number of printer-related support calls.

Lesson 1: Managing Printers

Windows Server 2008 includes the Print Services server role, which provides sophisticated printer management capabilities using the Print Management snap-in. There are also a variety of command-line tools for scripting print management tasks and managing computers running Windows Server 2008 Server Core. Although you can still use the Control Panel to install, share, and manage printers, the Print Management snap-in provides a more full-featured user interface. This lesson describes how to use the Control Panel, the Print Management snap-in, and command-line tools to manage printers.

After this lesson, you will be able to:
- Install the Print Services server role.
- Install printers using either the Control Panel or the Print Management snap-in.
- Share printers across the network.
- Configure printer permissions to limit who can print to or manage a printer.
- Add printer drivers to allow different platforms to automatically install required software.
- Configure multiple printers into a printer pool.
- Use printer priorities to allow higher-priority documents to print before lower-priority documents.
- Enable Internet Printing to print using Web protocols.
- Generate e-mail notifications when printers have problems.
- Deploy printers to clients using Group Policy settings.
- Migrate printers from one server to another.
- Configure printers from a command prompt or script.
- Monitor printers using the Performance Monitor snap-in.

Estimated lesson time: 45 minutes

Installing the Print Services Server Role

Windows Server 2008 can share printers without adding any server roles. However, adding the Print Services server role adds the Print Management snap-in, which simplifies printer configuration. To install the Print Services server role, follow these steps:

1. In Server Manager, right-click Roles, and then choose Add Roles.
   The Add Roles Wizard appears.
2. On the Before You Begin page, click Next.
3. On the Server Roles page, select the Print Services check box. Click Next.

4. On the Print Services page, click Next.

5. On the Select Role Services page, select the appropriate check boxes for the following roles, and then click Next:
   - ❑ **Print Server**   Installs the Print Management snap-in, described later in this lesson. This is sufficient for allowing Windows and many non-Windows clients to print.
   - ❑ **LPD Service**   Allows clients to print using the *Line Printer Daemon (LPD)* protocol, which is commonly used by UNIX clients.
   - ❑ **Internet Printing**   Allows clients to print using *Internet Printing Protocol (IPP)* and creates a Web site where users can manage print jobs using their Web browser. This role service requires Internet Information Services (IIS).

6. If you are prompted to install the Web Server (IIS) role service, click Add Required Role Services, and then click Next.

7. If the Web Server (IIS) page appears because you selected the Internet Printing role service, click Next. Then, on the Select Role Services page, configure the required IIS role services and click Next again.

8. On the Confirm Installation Selections page, click Install.

9. On the Installation Results page, click Close.

Before attempting to use the Print Services management tools, close and reopen Server Manager. You can access the Print Services tools using the Roles\Print Services node in Server Manager.

Installing Printers

To allow printers to be physically accessible to users while keeping print servers secured, most modern printers are connected to the network. Although users can print directly to network printers, using a print server gives you stronger management capabilities. The following sections describe how to install printers using either the Control Panel or the Print Management snap-in.

Installing a Printer Using Control Panel

After connecting a printer either to the network or to a server, follow these steps to install it using Control Panel (the exact steps vary depending on the type of printer you install):

1. Click Start, and then choose Control Panel.

2. In the Control Panel Home view of Control Panel, below Hardware And Sound, click Printer.

3. Double-click Add Printer.

   The Add Printer wizard appears.

4. On the Choose A Local Or Network Printer page, if the printer is attached directly to the server, click Add A Local Printer. If the printer is wireless or attached to the network, click Add A Network, Wireless, Or Bluetooth Printer.

5. If the Choose A Printer Port page appears, select the physical port to which the printer is attached, as shown in Figure 12-1. Click Next.

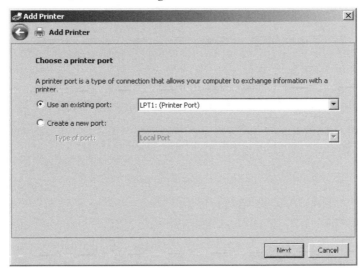

Figure 12-1   The Choose A Printer Port page

6. If you are installing a network printer, select the printer or click The Printer That I Want Isn't Listed and specify the network location of the printer. Click Next.

7. If you are installing a network printer and you select Add A Printer Using A TCP/IP Address Or Hostname, you next see the Type A Printer Hostname Or IP Address page. In the Hostname Or IP Address text box, type the name or IP address of the printer. Click Next.

NOTE   Searching for network printers

The Network Printer Installation Wizard, described in the following section, "Installing a Printer Using the Print Management Snap-in," does a much better job of finding network printers.

---

8. If the Install The Printer Driver page appears, select a manufacturer and printer to use a driver included with Windows Server 2008. To retrieve updated drivers from the Microsoft Web site, click Windows Update. To use a driver included with the printer or downloaded from the manufacturer's Web site, click Have Disk, select the driver, and then click OK. Click Next.

9. On the Type A Printer Name page, type a name for the printer, and then click Next.

10. On the Printer Sharing page, choose whether to share the printer. If you do share the printer, type a location that will allow users to physically find the printer. Click Next.

11. Click Finish.

The printer is immediately available for use from the server. If you chose to share the printer, it is also accessible to authorized users.

Installing a Printer Using the Print Management Snap-in

After connecting a printer either to the network or to a server, follow these steps to install it using the Print Management snap-in (the exact steps vary depending on the type of printer you install):

1. In Server Manager, right-click Roles\Print Services\Print Management\Print Servers *<Server>*, and then choose Add Printer.

   The Network Printer Installation Wizard appears.

2. On the Printer Installation page, as shown in Figure 12-2, choose an installation method, and then click Next.

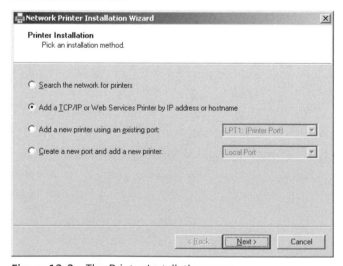

Figure 12-2   The Printer Installation page

3. The pages that follow will vary depending on the printer installation method you chose. For example, if you chose to search for a network printer, the Network Printer Search page (as shown in Figure 12-3) appears. Respond to the prompts and click Next.

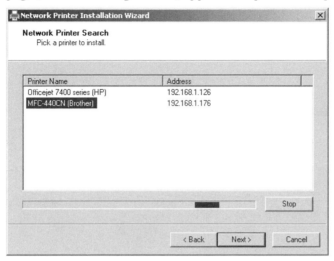

Figure 12-3   The Network Printer Search page

4. On the Printer Driver page, choose whether to use an existing driver, install a new driver, or use the printer driver that the wizard selected. Then, click Next.

5. If you choose to install a new driver, the Printer Installation page appears. Select a driver by first selecting the appropriate manufacturer and then selecting the printer model. Click Next.

6. On the Printer Name And Sharing Settings page, type a name for the printer. To immediately share the printer, select the Share This Printer check box and type a name and location. Click Next.

7. On the Printer Found page, click Next.

8. Depending on the type of printer, you might also be prompted to perform printer-specific configuration, as demonstrated by Figure 12-4.

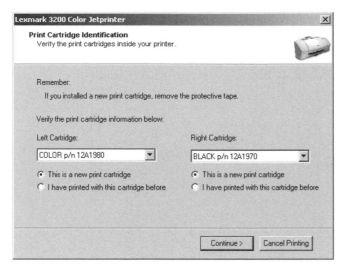

Figure 12-4   Performing printer-specific configuration

9. On the Completing The Network Printer Installation Wizard page, click Finish.

After completing the wizard, the printer is ready to be used.

Sharing Printers

The simplest way to share a printer is to right-click the printer in Control Panel and then choose Sharing. In the Print Management snap-in, right-click the printer, and then choose Manage Sharing. As shown in Figure 12-5, you can select the Share This Printer check box to allow other users to connect to the printer. Select the Render Print Jobs On Client Computers check box to allow clients to handle the processor-intensive rendering process or clear the check box to push the processing to the print server. Select the List In The Directory check box to allow the printer to be found in Active Directory.

If the client's operating system uses the same driver as the server, the client can automatically download the driver the first time the client connects to the printer. If a client requires a different driver—for example, if a client computer uses a 32-bit version of Windows and the server uses a 64-bit version of Windows—you should install the additional driver on the server to allow the client to automatically install the driver. From the Sharing tab, click the Additional Drivers button, select the check boxes for the platforms you want to support (as shown in Figure 12-6), click OK, and then select the printer driver.

Figure 12-5   The Sharing tab

Figure 12-6   The Additional Drivers dialog box

Configuring Printer Permissions

In a manner that is similar to configuring NTFS file permissions, you can configure printer permissions to control which users can print and manage printers from the Security tab of a printer's properties dialog box. For example, you could use printer permissions to grant only your Human Resources group access to print to a departmental printer and grant IT the right to manage the printer.

By default, everyone can print to a printer. Users can manage their own documents in the print queue but not other users' documents. Administrators can manage any user's documents in the print queue and configure the printer itself. You can configure the following permissions:

- **Print** Users can print.
- **Manage Printers** Users can change printer configuration settings.
- **Manage Documents** Users can remove documents that have been submitted to the printer.

Printer permissions are in effect whether users are logged on locally or are accessing folders across the network.

Adding Printer Drivers

You should install drivers for all client platforms you intend to support so that clients can automatically download and install the printer the first time they connect. To add printer drivers using the Print Management snap-in, follow these steps:

1. In Server Manager, right-click Roles\Print Services\Print Management\Print Servers \\<*ServerName*>\Drivers, and then choose Add Driver.

   The Add Printer Driver Wizard appears.

2. On the Welcome To The Add Printer Driver Wizard page, click Next.

3. On the Processor And Operating System Selection page, select the check boxes for the processors and operating systems that will be using the driver. Click Next.

4. On the Printer Driver Selection page, click the Have Disk button, select the folder containing the printer driver, and then click OK. Select the printer, and then click Next.

NOTE Finding printer drivers

Typically, you can find the latest driver at the printer manufacturer's Web site. You can also find drivers for a different Windows platform (for example, a 64-bit version of Windows) from that platform's installation media.

---

5. On the Completing The Add Printer Driver Wizard page, click Finish.

If the driver is not digitally signed, the Add Printer Driver Wizard will warn you that the driver might be dangerous. Drivers can be unreliable or malicious, and using digitally signed drivers significantly reduces those risks. If you choose to use drivers that are not signed, be certain you trust the source.

The Add Printer Driver Wizard might prompt you to install drivers for different versions of Windows, as shown in Figure 12-7. If prompted, provide the path to the driver files, and then click OK.

Figure 12-7   Providing drivers for different versions of Windows

If a user connects to a shared printer and you have not added the required driver, the user will be prompted to install the driver, as shown in Figure 12-8. You can disable the Computer Configuration\Policies\Windows Settings\Security Settings\Local Policies\Security Options\ Devices: Prevent Users From Installing Printer Drivers policy to allow users to install printer drivers without administrative privileges.

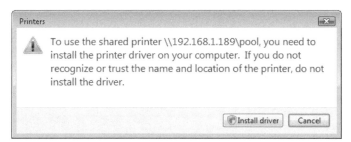

Figure 12-8   Prompting the user to confirm a driver installation

Configuring Printer Pooling

A printer pool consists of two or more identical printers that users can print to as if they were a single printer. Typically, you should physically locate the printers next to each other. Although any single print job will always print through a single printer, having multiple printers reduces the likelihood that users will need to wait for a large print job to complete before retrieving their print jobs.

Printers in a printer pool should use the same print driver. Although the printers do not have to be identical, client computers will install only a single driver for all printers in the print pool. Sometimes a single printer driver will work with multiple printer models from a single manufacturer, allowing you to use different printers as part of a single printer pool.

To create a printer pool, follow these steps:

1. Install each of the printers that will be in the pool.
2. In Server Manager, select Print Services\Print Management\Print Servers\<*Server-Name*>\Printers. In the details pane, right-click one of the printers in the pool, and then choose Properties.

   The printer properties dialog box appears.
3. Click the Ports tab and select the Enable Printer Pooling check box.
4. Select the port check box for each printer in the printer pool, as shown in Figure 12-9. Click OK.

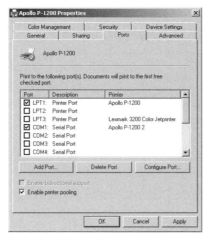

Figure 12-9   Enabling printer pooling

You need to share only the printer for which you enabled printer pooling. The reason is that any print jobs submitted to that shared printer will be sent to the first available printer in the printer pool. If you share individual printers in the printer pool, users can print to a specific printer, bypassing the pool.

Configuring Printer Priorities

When several documents are in a printer queue, you can use printer priorities to print higher-priority documents before lower-priority ones. For example, you could use this capability to allow documents printed by members of the Managers group to print before documents printed by members of the Employees group.

To configure printer priorities, follow these steps:

1. Install the printer that will have multiple priorities. Then, install the same printer again using the same port. You should have one logical printer for each priority level you need, even though you have only a single physical printer. You will assign each of the logical printers a different priority level.

2. In Server Manager, right-click one of the logical printers, and then choose Properties. The printer properties dialog box appears.

3. Click the Advanced tab and specify a priority for the logical printer. All print jobs sent to a higher-priority logical printer will print before any lower-priority logical printer begins to print its jobs. The highest priority is 99; the lowest is 1.

4. Repeat steps 2 and 3 for each of the logical printers.

5. Connect higher-priority users to the higher-priority logical printer and lower-priority users to the lower-priority logical printer. Configure printer permissions to restrict access to specific groups.

Although higher-priority print jobs are always placed above lower-priority print jobs in the print queue, after a print job begins printing, it cannot be interrupted. For example, if a user prints a 100-page document to a low-priority logical printer and no higher-priority documents are in the print queue, the printer immediately begin printing the document. If another user then submits a higher-priority print job, the 100-page low-priority document will finish printing before the higher-priority document is printed.

Managing Internet Printing

If you install the Internet Printing role service, you can manage printers by using a Web browser to visit the URL http://*<ServerName>*/Printers. As shown in Figure 12-10, the Web page lists the printers shared by a server and their current status.

Figure 12-10   Managing printers from a Web browser

Click a printer to view more detailed information about that printer, including the current print queue, and to pause, resume, or cancel printing. As shown in Figure 12-11, clicking Connect prompts the user to install the printer if it is not already installed. To connect to the printer, Internet Explorer must be configured to allow add-ons to run. Connecting to a printer using a Web browser is convenient for guests, but you should use Group Policy settings to configure printers for client computers that you manage. For more information, read "Deploying Printers with Group Policy" later in this lesson.

To connect directly to a printer shared with Internet printing, provide the URL in the format http://<*ServerName*>/Printers/<*PrinterName*>/.printer.

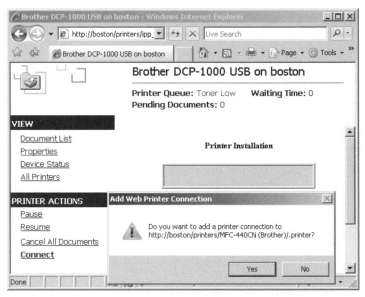

Figure 12-11   Installing a printer from a Web browser

Generating Notifications

You can use custom filters to generate e-mail notifications or to automatically run scripts when specific conditions are met on a printer. For example, you could send an e-mail to a printer administrator when a printer is out of paper or jammed.

First, create a custom filter by following these steps:

1. In Server Manager, right-click Roles\Print Services\Print Management\Custom Filters, and then choose Add New Printer Filter.

    The New Printer Filter Wizard appears.

2. On the Printer Filter Name And Description page, type a name for the filter, and then click Next.

3. On the Define A Printer Filter page, configure the Filter Criteria, one row at a time, as described here:

   ❑ **Field**   Defines the criteria being compared. The most useful Field is Queue Status, which indicates the printer's current state.

   ❑ **Condition**   Conditions vary depending on the value you select for Field, but they can be "is exactly," "is not exactly," "begins with," "contains," and many others.

   ❑ **Value**   The value the Field and Condition must match for a printer to meet the filter criteria.

4. When you have configured the filter criteria, click Next. Figure 12-12 shows a filter criteria that would match only shared printers with paper jams with a location beginning with Boston.

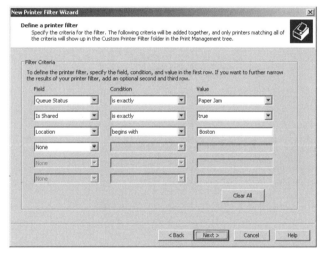

Figure 12-12   Defining a printer filter

5. On the Set Notifications (Optional) page, choose whether to send an e-mail notification, whether to run a script when a printer matches the criteria you defined on the previous page, or both. For example, if you configured the filter as shown in Figure 12-12, you could use this page to send an e-mail notification to an administrator in Boston who could then fix the paper jam. Click Finish.

Deploying Printers with Group Policy

Enterprise environments should use Group Policy settings to deploy shared printers to clients. To deploy a printer with Group Policy settings, follow these steps:

1. In Server Manager, select Roles\Print Services\Print Management\Print Servers\<*Server-Name*>\Printers. In the details pane, right-click the printer, and then choose Deploy With Group Policy.

2. In the Deploy With Group Policy dialog box, click the Browse button to select the Group Policy object (GPO) that you want to use. Then, click OK.

3. To deploy the printer to all users who log on to a particular computer, select the The Computers That This GPO Applies To check box. To deploy the printer to specific users regardless of which computers they log on to, select the The Users That This GPO Applies To check box. You can select both check boxes to deploy the printer using both the *Computer Configuration* and *User Configuration* nodes in a GPO.

4. Click the Add button to add the GPO to the list, as demonstrated in Figure 12-13.

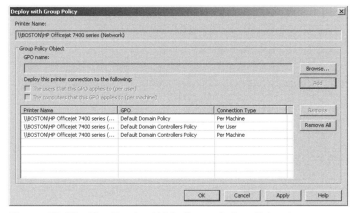

Figure 12-13 The Deploy With Group Policy dialog box

5. Repeat steps 2 and 3 to deploy the printer to additional GPOs.

6. Click OK.

7. Click OK to confirm that the printers were successfully added to the GPO, and then click OK again to close the Deploy With Group Policy dialog box.

The next time computers refresh Group Policy settings, the printer will be added to the list of available printers. You can view the deployed printers by editing a GPO in the Group Policy Management Editor and selecting the Policies\Windows Settings\Deployed Printers node in either the *Computer Configuration* (for printers deployed to computers) or *User Configuration* (for printers deployed to users) node.

Migrating Printers

To allow you to quickly migrate a print server from one computer to another, you can export a list of printers and drivers from the current print server and then import them into the new print server. You can automatically migrate all configuration settings, including whether a printer is published in the Active Directory. The sections that follow describe how to export and then import printers.

Exporting Printers

To export print queues and printer settings to a file, follow these steps:

1. In Server Manager, right-click Print Management, and then choose Migrate Printers. The Printer Migration wizard appears.
2. On the Getting Started With Printer Migration page, select Export Printer Queues And Printer Drivers To A File. Click Next.
3. On the Select A Print Server page, select a server, and then click Next.
4. On the Review The List Of Items To Be Exported page, click Next.
5. On the Select The File Location page, type a filename, and then click Next.
6. On the final page, click Finish.

You can also export printers at a command prompt or from a script using the PrintBRM tool, which is located in the %SystemRoot%\System32\spool\tools\ folder. To export printers to a file, run PrintBRM with the -B parameter, as the following example demonstrates:

```
printbrm -b -f printers.printerexport
```

For complete usage information, type **PrintBRM -?**.

Importing Printers

To import print queues and printer settings from a file, follow these steps:

1. In Server Manager, right-click Print Management, and then choose Migrate Printers. The Printer Migration wizard appears.
2. On the Getting Started With Printer Migration page, select Import Printer Queues And Printer Drivers From A File. Click Next.
3. On the Select The File Location page, type the name of the exported file, and then click Next.
4. On the Review The List Of Items To Be Imported page, click Next.
5. On the Select A Print Server page, select a server, and then click Next.

6. On the Select Import Options page, as shown in Figure 12-14, click the Import Mode drop-down list to choose whether to keep or overwrite existing printers. Then, choose whether to list the imported printers in the Active Directory. Click Next.

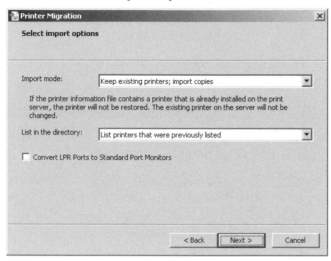

Figure 12-14   The Select Import Options page

7. On the final page, click Open Event Viewer to review any errors that might have occurred during the import process (all errors will have the source PrintBRM). Then, click Finish.

You can also simply double-click the .PrinterExport file created when you exported the printers and follow the prompts that appear.

To import printers at a command prompt or from a script, run *PrintBRM* with the -R parameter, as the following example demonstrates:

```
printbrm -r -f printers.printerexport
```

For complete usage information, type **PrintBRM -?**.

Managing Printers from a Command Prompt or Script

Windows Server 2008 includes seven tools for managing printers from a command prompt. The following scripts are stored in the %SystemRoot%\System32\Printing_Admin_Scripts\en-US\ folder:

- **PrnMngr.vbs**   Adds and removes printers.
- **PrnCnfg.vbs**   Configures printers. For example, you can change printer names or locations, configure a separator page, or grant print permissions to users.

- **PrnDrvr.vbs**   Adds, removes, or lists printer drivers. For example, you can add a driver to make it available for automatic installation by a client.
- **PrnJobs.vbs**   Manages print jobs. For example, you can list and cancel documents in the print queue.
- **PrnPort.vbs**   Manages printer ports. For example, you can create a port for a network printer.
- **PrnQctl.vbs**   Prints a test page, pauses or resumes a printer, and clears a printer queue.
- **PubPrn.vbs**   Publishes a printer to the Active Directory.

Each of these tools is a Visual Basic script. To use them, run the *Cscript* command and pass the full path to the script file as the first parameter. Then, provide any script parameters. For example, to view usage information for the PrnCnfg.vbs script, run the following command:

```
cscript %SystemRoot%\System32\Printing_Admin_Scripts\en-US\prncnfg.vbs -?
```

To add a printer named Printer1 that is connected to LPT1 on the local computer and requires a printer driver called Printer Driver1, type:

```
Cscript %SystemRoot%\System32\Printing_Admin_Scripts\en-US\prnmngr.vbs -a -p Printer1 -m
"Printer Driver1" -r lpt1:
```

To configure a printer named MyPrinter so that the spooler in the remote computer named MyServer keeps print jobs after they have been printed, type:

```
cscript %SystemRoot%\System32\Printing_Admin_Scripts\en-US\prncnfg.vbs -t -s MyServer -p
MyPrinter +keepprintedjobs
```

To list all drivers on the \\PrintServer1 server, type:

```
Cscript %SystemRoot%\System32\Printing_Admin_Scripts\en-US\prndrvr.vbs -l -s \\PrintServer1
```

To add a version 3 Windows x64 printer driver for the "Laser Printer Model 1" model of printer using the C:\temp\LaserPrinter1.inf driver information file for a driver stored in the C:\temp folder, type:

```
Cscript %SystemRoot%\System32\Printing_Admin_Scripts\en-US\prndrvr.vbs -a -m "Laser Printer
Model 1" -v 3 -e "Windows x64" -i c:\temp\LaserPrinter1.inf -h c:\temp
```

Quick Check

1. Which role service should you install to allow clients to manage printers using their Web browser?
2. What script would you run to publish a printer to Active Directory?

Quick Check Answers
1. The Internet Printing role service.
2. The PubPrn.vbs script.

Monitoring Printers

You can monitor printer usage in real time using the Performance Monitor snap-in. The most useful counters offered by the Print Queue object are:

- **Job Errors and Out Of Paper Errors**   The total number of job errors or out of paper errors since the last restart.
- **Jobs and Jobs Spooling**   The number of jobs currently in a print queue. You can monitor these counters to determine if a particular printer is being overused and might need to be replaced with a faster printer or added to a printer pool.
- **Total Pages Printed and Total Jobs Printed**   The total number of pages and jobs printed by a printer.

You can view the counters for a specific printer by selecting the printer below Instances Of Selected Object in the Add Counters dialog box. For detailed information about using Performance Monitor, read Lesson 2 "Monitoring Performance and Reliability," in Chapter 10, "Monitoring Computers."

PRACTICE Install and Share a Printer

In this practice, you will share a printer pool from Dcsrv1 and then connect and print to it from Boston.

▶ **Exercise 1   Install the Print Services Server Role**

In this exercise, you will install the Print Services server role with the Print Server and Internet Printing role services.

1. On Dcsrv1, in Server Manager, right-click Roles, and then choose Add Roles.
   The Add Roles Wizard appears.
2. On the Before You Begin page, click Next.
3. On the Server Roles page, select the Print Services check box. Click Next.
4. On the Print Services page, click Next.
5. On the Select Role Services page, select the Print Server and Internet Printing check boxes. Click Next.

6. If IIS isn't currently installed, in the Add Roles Wizard dialog box, click Add Required Role Services.

7. On the Select Role Services page, click Next.

8. On the Web Server (IIS) page, click Next.

9. On the Select Role Services page, you're prompted to select the role services you want to install to support IIS. Click Next to accept the default settings.

10. On the Confirmation page, click Install.

11. On the Results page, click Close.

▶ **Exercise 2   Install Two Printers**

In this exercise, you will install two printers. If you have a printer (either a network printer or a printer connected directly to your server), you can substitute that printer for the nonexistent printer described in this exercise.

1. On Dcsrv1, close and then reopen Server Manager. In Server Manager, right-click Roles \Print Services\Print Management\Print Servers\Dcsrv1\Printers, and then choose Add Printer.

   The Network Printer Installation Wizard appears.

2. On the Printer Installation page, select Add A New Printer Using An Existing Port. Select the LPT:1 port, which corresponds to the parallel port present on most computers. Click Next.

3. On the Printer Driver page, select Install A New Driver. Click Next.

4. On the Printer Installation page, select the Apollo P-1200 driver. Click Next.

5. On the Printer Name And Sharing Settings page, select the Share This Printer check box. Click Next.

6. On the Printer Found page, click Next.

7. On the Completing The Network Printer Installation Wizard page, select the Add Another Printer check box. Click Finish.

8. On the Printer Installation page, select Add A New Printer Using An Existing Port. Select the LPT2 port, and then click Next.

9. On the Printer Driver page, select Use An Existing Printer Driver On The Computer. Select Apollo P-1200 and then click Next.

10. On the Printer Name And Sharing Settings page, clear the Share This Printer check box. Click Next.

11. On the Printer Found page, click Next.

12. On the Completing The Network Printer Installation Wizard page, click Finish.

Now you have configured Dcsrv1 to simulate having two identical printers connected to LPT1 and LPT2.

▶ **Exercise 3   Configure a Printer Pool**

In this exercise, you configure a printer pool on Dcsrv1.

    1. On Dcsrv1, in Server Manager, select Roles\Print Services\Print Management\Print Servers\Dcsrv1\Printers. In the details pane, right-click Apollo P-1200, and then choose Properties.

    2. Select the Ports tab. Select the Enable Printer Pooling check box. Then, select both LPT1 and LPT2. Click OK.

Now, any print jobs submitted to the first Apollo P-1200 printer will be sent to either of the two printers you created, depending on which printer is available.

▶ **Exercise 4   Print to the Printer Pool**

In this exercise, you will install a network printer and then print to the printer pool from Boston.

    1. On Boston, click Start, and then choose Control Panel.

    2. In Control Panel, click Printer.

    3. Double-click Add Printer.

        The Add Printer wizard appears.

    4. On the Choose A Local Or Network Printer page, click Add A Network, Wireless, Or Bluetooth Printer.

    5. Click The Printer That I Want Isn't Listed.

    6. On the Find A Printer By Name Or TCP/IP Address page, select Select A Shared Printer By Name. Type **\\Dcsrv1\Apollo P-1200**. Click Next. Notice that the printer driver is automatically installed.

    7. On the Type A Printer Name page, click Next.

    8. On Dcsrv1, select the Apollo P-1200 printer in the Print Management snap-in and watch the job queue. On Boston, click Print A Test Page several times to watch the client submit the jobs to the printer. Click Finish.

▶ **Exercise 5   Use Group Policy Settings to Configure a Client Printer**

In this exercise, you will use Group Policy settings to configure Boston with a connection to a shared printer.

    1. On Dcsrv1, in Server Manager, select Roles\Print Services\Print Management\Print Servers\Dcsrv1\Printers. In the details pane, right-click Apollo P-1200 (Copy 1), and then choose Deploy With Group Policy.

2. In the Deploy With Group Policy dialog box, click the Browse button. Select Default Domain Policy, and then click OK.

3. Select both the The Computers That This GPO Applies To (Per Machine) and The Users That This GPO Applies To (Per User) check boxes.

4. Click the Add button to add the GPO to the list.

5. Click OK.

6. Click OK to confirm that the printers were successfully added to the GPO. Then, click OK one more time to close the Deploy With Group Policy dialog box.

Restart Boston. When it restarts, log on and open Control Panel\Printers and verify that the second copy of the Apollo P-1200 printer was added using Group Policy.

▶ **Exercise 6   Manage Internet Printing**

In this exercise, you will use a Web browser to manage a shared printer from a remote computer.

1. On Boston, click Start, and then choose Internet Explorer.

2. In the Address bar, type **http://Dcsrv1/Printers**, and then press Enter.

3. On the All Printers On Dcsrv1 page, click Apollo P-1200.

4. Click the different links in the left pane to view more information about the printer and to pause and resume the printer.

Lesson Summary

- You can use Server Manager to install the Print Services server role, which adds the Print Management snap-in.

- Installing a printer requires you to select a port (which can be a physical or network port) and a print driver.

- Sharing printers allows users to print from across the network.

- You can use printer permissions to control which users can print to and manage a printer.

- Different Windows platforms require different drivers. For example, 32-bit and 64-bit versions of Windows require separate drivers. To allow clients to automatically download and install the correct driver, you should install drivers for all Windows platforms that you support.

- A printer pool uses a single logical printer to print to multiple physical printers. Windows will print to the first available printer.

- You can prioritize documents by creating multiple logical printers for a single physical printer and then assigning different priorities to each of the logical printers. Documents sent to the high-priority logical printer will always complete before any documents sent to the low-priority logical printer are processed. Use printer permissions to control who can print to the high-priority logical printer.

- If you install the Internet Printing Protocol (IPP) role service, clients can use HTTP to submit print jobs and manage print queues.

- You can use custom filters to generate notifications when specific printers have problems.

- Use Group Policy settings to configure clients to connect to shared printers.

- Windows Server 2008 includes both graphical and command-line tools to migrate printers from one server to another.

- To manage printers from a command prompt, use the scripts provided in the %SystemRoot%\System32\Printing_Admin_Scripts\en-US\ folder.

- You can monitor printers using the Performance Monitor snap-in.

Lesson Review

You can use the following questions to test your knowledge of the information in Lesson 1, "Managing Printers." The questions are also available on the companion CD if you prefer to review them in electronic form.

NOTE Answers

Answers to these questions and explanations of why each answer choice is correct or incorrect are located in the "Answers" section at the end of the book.

---

1. Currently, you manage eight Windows Server 2008 print servers. You plan to centralize management by moving all printers to a single print server running Windows Server 2008 Server Core. After exporting the printers on each of the eight original print servers, how can you import them on the new print server?

   A. printui -b -f *<filename>*

   B. printbrm -r -f *<filename>*

   C. printbrmengine -r -f *<filename>*

   D. netsh print import *<filename>*

2. You need to write a script to publish several printers to the Active Directory. Which tool should you use?

   A. PrnMngr.vbs

   B. PrnCnfg.vbs

   C. PrnQctl.vbs

   D. PubPrn.vbs

3. You share a printer, MyPrinter, from a computer named MyServer. MyServer runs Windows Server 2008 and has the Internet Printing role service installed. You need to configure a client computer to print to the shared printer from behind a firewall that allows only Web connections. When configuring the client, what path to the printer should you provide?

   A. http://MyServer/Printers/MyPrinter/.printer

   B. http://MyServer/MyPrinter

   C. \\MyServer\Printers\MyPrinter\.printer

   D. \\MyServer\MyPrinter

4. You would like to be notified by e-mail when a specific printer runs out of paper or has a paper jam. How can you do this?

   A. Configure a notification from the driver properties.

   B. Use the PrintBRM tool to configure an e-mail notification.

   C. Configure a notification from the printer properties.

   D. Create a custom filter.

Chapter Review

To further practice and reinforce the skills you learned in this chapter, you can

- Review the chapter summary.
- Review the list of key terms introduced in this chapter.
- Complete the case scenarios. These scenarios set up real-world situations involving the topics of this chapter and ask you to create a solution.
- Complete the suggested practices.
- Take a practice test.

Chapter Summary

- To install, share, and manage printers connected to a Windows Server 2008 computer, install the Print Services server role. This adds the Print Management snap-in to the Server Manager console. You can also manage printers from Control Panel or by using command-line tools.

Key Terms

Do you know what these key terms mean? You can check your answers by looking up the terms in the glossary at the end of the book.

- Internet Printing Protocol (IPP)
- Line Printer Daemon (LPD)

Case Scenario

In the following case scenario, you will apply what you've learned about how to plan and deploy printer sharing. You can find answers to these questions in the "Answers" section at the end of this book.

Case Scenario: Managing Network Printers

You are a systems administrator for Northwind Traders, a medium-sized organization with approximately 200 employees in a single facility. The employees share about 20 printers. Most of the printers are for general use by any employee, but each of the five executives has an office printer that should be accessible only to the executive and the executive's assistant.

Currently, client computers print directly to the network printers, but managing the printers has been a challenge. If a printer jams or runs out of paper, nobody is notified—and users often simply choose to print to a different printer rather than solve the problem. Another challenge is that the Marketing department often creates large print jobs of more than 100 pages, requiring other users to wait until the print job completes to retrieve their documents. Several executives have complained that other employees print to their private printers because the printers show up when users search the network for a printer.

Your manager calls you into her office to discuss possible solutions to these problems.

Answer the following questions for your manager:

1. How can we centralize management of the network printers?
2. How can we notify an administrator if a printer runs out of paper or is jammed?
3. How can you control access to private printers?
4. How can you reduce the impact of large print jobs?

Suggested Practices

To successfully master the Configuring File and Print Services exam objective, complete the following tasks.

Configure and Monitor Print Services

For this task, you should complete Practices 1, 2, and 3. Although clusters will probably not be covered on your exam, you can complete Practice 4 to gain experience creating highly available print servers.

- **Practice 1** Install Windows Server 2008 Server Core and use command-line tools to configure the server as a print server and share a printer.

- **Practice 2** If you have multiple printers that use the same driver (or two printers that are the same model), configure them as a printer pool. Then, print several documents of different lengths in rapid succession and examine how Windows Server 2008 distributes the print jobs.

- **Practice 3** Install and share a printer. Then, use Performance Monitor to monitor usage of the printer. Submit several print jobs to the printer.

- **Practice 4** If you have the hardware available, configure a print server failover cluster to provide redundancy if a print server fails. For detailed instructions, read "Step-by-Step Guide for Configuring a Two-Node Print Server Failover Cluster in Windows Server 2008" at *http://technet2.microsoft.com/windowsserver2008/en/library/71b0e978-d1ff-47a2-b4bd-1f4d19280dbe1033.mspx*.

Take a Practice Test

The practice tests on this book's companion CD offer many options. For example, you can test yourself on just the content covered in this chapter, or you can test yourself on all the 70-642 certification exam content. You can set up the test so that it closely simulates the experience of taking a certification exam, or you can set it up in study mode so that you can look at the correct answers and explanations after you answer each question.

MORE INFO   Practice tests

For details about all the practice test options available, see "How to Use the Practice Tests" in this book's Introduction.

Answers

Chapter 1: Lesson Review Answers

Lesson 1

1. **Correct Answer: A**
   - A. **Correct:** The address shown is an APIPA address, which is assigned automatically to a DHCP client if a DHCP server cannot be found. An APIPA address usually results in a loss of connectivity to network resources. To fix the problem, you should first attempt to obtain a new address from a DHCP server. To do that, use the *Ipconfig /renew* command.
   - B. **Incorrect:** This command will merely verify that you can connect to your own address. It will not help establish network connectivity.
   - C. **Incorrect:** This command will merely verify that you can trace a path to your own address. It will not help establish network connectivity.
   - D. **Incorrect:** This command displays the list of IP address-to-MAC address mappings stored on the computer. It will not fix any problems in network connectivity.

2. **Correct Answer: D**
   - A. **Incorrect:** You should not configure a DNS server as a DHCP client. A DNS server needs the most stable address available, which is a manually configured static address.
   - B. **Incorrect:** An APIPA address is an address that signifies a network problem. It is not a stable address and should not be assigned to a server.
   - C. **Incorrect:** An alternate configuration is not a stable address because it can be replaced by a DHCP-assigned address. You should assign the most stable address type—a static address—to a DNS server.
   - D. **Correct:** The addresses of infrastructure servers such as DHCP and DNS servers should never change. Therefore, these server types should be assigned manual or static addresses because these address types do not change.

Lesson 2

1. **Correct Answer: D**
   - A. **Incorrect:** A /23 network can support 512 addresses but only 510 devices.
   - B. **Incorrect:** A /22 network can support 1024 addresses but only 1022 devices.

    C. **Incorrect:** A /23 network can support 510 devices, but a /22 network can support more.

    D. **Correct:** A /22 network can support 1024 addresses but only 1022 devices because two addresses in every block are reserved for network communications.

2. **Correct Answer: B**

    A. **Incorrect:** A /28 network supports 16 addresses and 14 computers. You need to support 18 addresses and 16 computers.

    B. **Correct:** You need to support 18 addresses and 16 computers. A /27 network supports 32 addresses and 30 computers. This is the smallest option that provides you with the address space you need.

    C. **Incorrect:** A /26 network supports 64 addresses and 62 computers. This is larger than you need, so it would violate company policy.

    D. **Incorrect:** The current /29 network supports eight addresses and six computers. It cannot support the 16 computers you need.

Lesson 3

1. **Correct Answer: A**

    A. **Correct:** Global addresses are routable addresses that can communicate directly with IPv6-only hosts on public networks. This is the kind of address you need if you want a static IPv6 address to which other computers can connect from across the IPv6 Internet.

    B. **Incorrect:** A link-local address is not routable and cannot be used on a public network.

    C. **Incorrect:** A unique-local address is routable but cannot be used on a public network.

    D. **Incorrect:** A site-local address is a version of a unique local address, but these address types are being phased out.

2. **Correct Answer: C**

    A. **Incorrect:** You would need global addresses only if you wanted your network to connect to the public IPv6 network.

    B. **Incorrect:** Link-local addresses are not routable so they would not allow your subnets to intercommunicate.

    C. **Correct:** Unique local addresses resemble private address ranges in IPv4. They are used for private routing within organizations.

    D. **Incorrect:** Site-local addresses were once defined as a way to provide routing within a private network, but this address type has been deprecated.

Chapter 1: Case Scenario Answers

Case Scenario: Working with IPv4 Address Blocks

1. /29 (255.255.255.248)
2. You need a /28 network (subnet mask 255.255.255.240).
3. This address block would support 16 addresses and 14 hosts.

Chapter 2: Lesson Review Answers

Lesson 1

1. **Correct Answer: A**
   A. **Correct:** This command flushes the DNS server cache. If you know that a DNS server is responding to queries with outdated cache data, it's best to clear the server cache. This way, the next time the DNS server receives a query for the name, it will attempt to resolve that name by querying other computers.
   B. **Incorrect:** Restarting the DNS Client service will flush the DNS client cache on the computer in question. It won't affect the way the DNS server responds to the query for that computer's name.
   C. **Incorrect:** Typing **ipconfig /flushdns** simply clears the DNS client cache. It won't affect the way the DNS server responds to the query for that computer's name.
   D. **Incorrect:** Restarting all client computers will not fix the problem. It merely has the effect of clearing the DNS client cache on all computers. This could fix problems related to outdated client cache data, but it will not fix the problem on the DNS server itself.

2. **Correct Answer: D**
   A. **Incorrect:** When you enable IPv6 on a computer running Windows Server 2008, no extra functionality is enabled in connections to a computer running Windows XP.
   B. **Incorrect:** IPv6 never blocks network functionality, so disabling it would never enable a feature like connectivity through a UNC.
   C. **Incorrect:** Enabling LLMNR on WS08A could enable UNC connectivity to another computer running Windows Server 2008 or Windows Vista, but it would not enable UNC connectivity to a computer running Windows XP.
   D. **Correct:** If NetBIOS were disabled, it would block UNC connectivity to a computer running Windows XP.

Lesson 2

1. **Correct Answer: A**

   A. **Correct:** The file Cache.dns, located in the %systemroot%\system32\dns\ folder, contains the list of the root DNS servers that the local DNS server will query if it cannot itself answer a query. By default, this file contains the list of Internet root servers, but you can replace it with the list of your company root servers.

   B. **Incorrect:** A HOSTS file specifies a list of resolved names that are preloaded into the DNS client cache. It does not specify root servers.

   C. **Incorrect:** The Lmhosts file is used to resolve NetBIOS names. It does not specify DNS root servers.

   D. **Incorrect:** Specifying a forwarder is not the same as specifying root servers. If the connection to a forwarder fails, a DNS server will query its root servers.

2. **Correct Answer: C**

   A. **Incorrect:** This option does not provide a way to resolve Internet names. It also does not provide a way for the New York DNS servers to resolve the names in the Sacramento office.

   B. **Incorrect:** This option does not provide a way for computers in each office to resolve names of the computers in the other office.

   C. **Correct:** This is the only solution that enables the DNS servers to effectively resolve names in the local domain, in the remote domain, and on the Internet.

   D. **Incorrect:** This option does not provide an effective way for computers to resolve Internet names.

Lesson 3

1. **Correct Answer: B**

   A. **Incorrect:** Configuring conditional forwarding would allow computers in one domain to resolve names in the other domain. However, the question states that this functionality is already being achieved. Conditional forwarding by itself would not enable clients to connect to resources by using a single-tag name.

   B. **Correct:** If you specify west.cpandl.com on the DNS suffix search list, that suffix will be appended to a DNS query. This option would enable a user to submit a single-tag name query in a UNC path and have the client automatically append the name of the west.cpandl.com domain.

   C. **Incorrect:** This option merely ensures that the client's own name is registered in DNS. It does not enable a user to connect to resources in the remote domain.

    D. **Incorrect:** By default, the client will append a single-tag name query with the client's own domain name. If that query fails, the client will append the single-tag name query with the parent domain name. Neither of these options would enable the query for a computer in the remote domain to be resolved properly.

2. **Correct Answer: D**

    A. **Incorrect:** Merely configuring a connection-specific suffix does not enable a computer to register with DNS if all the other settings are left at the default values.

    B. **Incorrect:** Enabling this option registers a connection-specific suffix only if one is configured. If the other settings are left at the default values for a non-DHCP client, this setting would have no effect.

    C. **Incorrect:** This option is already enabled if the DNS client settings are left at the default values.

    D. **Correct:** This answer choice provides the only solution that is not a default value and that, when configured, enables a DNS client to register its static address with a DNS server.

Chapter 2: Case Scenario Answers

Case Scenario 1: Troubleshooting DNS Clients

1. Enable the Use This Connection's DNS Suffix In DNS Registration.

2. Configure the Windows Vista clients with the address of the WINS server.

Case Scenario 2: Deploying a Windows Server

1. You should deploy a caching-only server.

2. Configure conditional forwarding so that all queries for the fabrikam.com network are directed to DNS servers on the internal network at the main office.

Chapter 3: Lesson Review Answers

Lesson 1

1. **Correct Answer: D**

    A. **Incorrect:** If you disable scavenging on the zone, it will affect all records. You want to prevent a single record from being scavenged.

B. **Incorrect:** If you disable scavenging on the server, it will prevent all records on the server from being scavenged. You want to prevent only a single record from being scavenged.

C. **Incorrect:** Computers with a static address register their addresses in the same way that the DHCP clients do.

D. **Correct:** Manually created records are never scavenged. If you need to prevent a certain record from being scavenged in a zone, the best way to achieve that is to delete the original record and re-create it manually.

2. **Correct Answers: A, B, F**

A. **Correct:** To prevent computers outside of the Active Directory domain from registering with a DNS server, you need to configure the zone to accept secure dynamic updates only. You can configure a zone to accept secure dynamic updates only if you store it in Active Directory. You can store a zone in Active Directory only if you create the zone on a domain controller.

B. **Correct:** To prevent computers outside of the Active Directory domain from registering with a DNS server, you need to configure the zone to accept secure dynamic updates only. This option is available only if you store the DNS zone in Active Directory, and this last option is available only if you create the zone on a domain controller.

C. **Incorrect:** If you don't store the zone in Active Directory, you won't be able to require secure updates for the zone.

D. **Incorrect:** If you disable dynamic updates for the zone, no computers will be able to register and you will have to create and update every record manually. This is not the best way to solve this problem because it creates too much administrative overhead.

E. **Incorrect:** You don't want to choose this option because you want to prevent non-secure updates. When you allow nonsecure updates, you allow computers outside of the local Active Directory domain to register in the zone.

F. **Correct:** To prevent computers outside of the Active Directory domain from registering with a DNS server, you need to configure the zone to accept secure dynamic updates only. This option is available only if you store the DNS zone in Active Directory, and this last option is available only if you create the zone on a domain controller.

Lesson 2

1. **Correct Answer: A**
   A. **Correct:** This is the only solution that will improve name resolution response times, keep an updated list of remote name servers, and minimize zone transfer traffic.
   B. **Incorrect:** Conditional forwarding would improve name resolution response times and minimize zone transfer traffic, but it would not allow you to keep an updated list of remote name servers.
   C. **Incorrect:** A secondary zone would improve name resolution response times and allow you to keep an updated list of remote name servers, but it would not minimize zone transfer traffic because the entire zone would need to be copied periodically from the remote office.
   D. **Incorrect:** You cannot perform a delegation in this case. You can perform a delegation only for a child domain in the DNS namespace. For example, a child domain of the ny.us.nwtraders.msft domain might be uptown.ny.us.nwtraders.msft.

2. **Correct Answer: C**
   A. **Incorrect:** When you choose this option, computers running Windows 2000 Server cannot see the ForestDnsZones partition in which zone data is stored.
   B. **Incorrect:** When you choose this option, computers running Windows 2000 Server cannot see the DomainDnsZones partition in which zone data is stored.
   C. **Correct:** When you choose this option, zone data is stored in the domain partition, which is visible to computers running Windows 2000 Server.
   D. **Incorrect:** Computers running Windows 2000 Server would not be able to see any new application directory partitions that you create, so creating one and choosing the associated option would not resolve the problem.

Chapter 3: Case Scenario Answers

Case Scenario 1: Managing Outdated Zone Data

1. The best way to remove stale records that you know to be outdated is to delete them manually.
2. You can enable aging and scavenging on each server and in the zone to prevent the accumulation of such records in the future.
3. The No-Refresh interval should be left at the default of seven days. The Refresh interval should be configured as 14 days.

Case Scenario 2: Configuring Zone Transfers

1. You should host a secondary zone at the Rochester site.

2. Configure notifications on the primary zone at the headquarters so that the server hosting the secondary zone is notified whenever changes occur.

Chapter 4: Lesson Review Answers

Lesson 1

1. **Correct Answer: A**

   A. **Correct:** If computers cannot communicate beyond the local subnet even when you specify an IP address, the problem is most likely that the computers do not have a default gateway specified. To assign a default gateway address to DHCP clients, configure the 003 Router option.

   B. **Incorrect:** If the DHCP clients needed to have a DNS server assigned to them, they would be able to connect to computers when specified by address but not by name.

   C. **Incorrect:** The 015 Domain Name option provides DHCP clients with a connection-specific DNS suffix assigned to them. If clients needed such a suffix, the problem reported would be that clients could not connect to servers when users specified a single-label computer name such as "Server1" (instead of a fully qualified domain name [FQDN] such as "Server1.contoso.com").

   D. **Incorrect:** The 044 WINS/NBNS Server option configures DHCP clients with the address of a WINS server. A WINS server would not enable you to connect to computers on remote subnets when you specify those computers by address.

2. **Correct Answer: C**

   A. **Incorrect:** We know that clients are already configured as DHCP clients because they have received addresses in the APIPA range of 169.254.0.0/16.

   B. **Incorrect:** Dhcp1 does not need to be running the DHCP client service because it is not acting as a DHCP client.

   C. **Correct:** If you want the DHCP server to assign addresses to computers on the local subnet, the server needs to be assigned an address that is also located on the same subnet. With its current configuration, the server is configured with an address in the 10.10.0.0/24 subnet but is attempting to lease addresses in the 10.10.1.0/24 range. To fix this problem, you can either change the address of the DHCP server or change the address range of the scope.

    D. **Incorrect:** This command would enable other computers to connect to Dhcp1 if a user specified Dhcp1 by name. However, the ability to connect to a DHCP server by specifying its name is not a requirement for DHCP to function correctly. DHCP exchanges do not rely on computer names.

Lesson 2

1. **Correct Answer: D**

    A. **Incorrect:** Configuring a scope option that assigns clients the DNS server address does nothing to prevent the potential conflict of the scope leasing out the same address owned by the DNS server.

    B. **Incorrect:** It is not recommended to assign reservations to infrastructure servers such as DNS servers. DNS servers should be assigned static addresses.

    C. **Incorrect:** You can configure only one contiguous address range per scope.

    D. **Correct:** Creating an exclusion for the DNS server address is the simplest way to solve the problem. When you configure the exclusion, the DHCP server will not lease the address and the DNS server preserves its static configuration.

2. **Correct Answer: B**

    A. **Incorrect:** This command configures the DHCP Server service to start automatically when Windows starts.

    B. **Correct:** This is a command you can use on a Server Core installation of Windows Server 2008 to install the DHCP Server role.

    C. **Incorrect:** This command starts the DHCP Server service after it is already installed.

    D. **Incorrect:** You can use this command on a full installation of Windows Server 2008 to install the DHCP Server role. You cannot use this command on a Server Core installation.

Chapter 4: Case Scenario Answers

Case Scenario 1: Deploying a New DHCP Server

1. Configure the scope with a default gateway option (the 015 Router option).
2. Delete the leases. This will force the DHCP clients to renew their leases and obtain a default gateway address.

Case Scenario 2: Configuring DHCP Options

1. You should configure these options at the server level (the Server Options folder) because they apply to all scopes.

2. Create a new user class for these 30 computers. In the user class, configure the 015 DNS Domain Name option that specifies the special connection-specific suffix. On the 30 clients use the *Ipconfig /setclassid* command to configure those clients as members of the class.

Chapter 5: Lesson Review Answers

Lesson 1

1. **Correct Answer: B**

   A. **Incorrect:** This answer has the incorrect router. The router with the IP address 192.168.1.1 is currently the default gateway, so all traffic will be sent to that router anyway.

   B. **Correct:** When using the *Route Add* command, specify the destination network first and then the subnet mask. Finally, provide the router that will be used to access the remote network.

   C. **Incorrect:** In this answer the parameters are reversed—the destination network should be listed as the first parameter after *Route Add*.

   D. **Incorrect:** In this answer the parameters are reversed and the wrong router is listed.

2. **Correct Answers: A and D**

   A. **Correct:** PathPing uses ICMP to detect routers between your computer and a specified destination. Then PathPing computes the latency to each router in the path.

   B. **Incorrect:** Ping tests connectivity to a single destination. You cannot easily use Ping to determine the routers in a path.

   C. **Incorrect:** Although you can use Ipconfig to determine the default gateway, you cannot use it to determine all routers in a path.

   D. **Correct:** TraceRt provides very similar functionality to PathPing, using ICMP to contact every router between your computer and a specified destination. The key different between TraceRt and PathPing is that PathPing computes accurate performance statistics over a period of time, while TraceRt sends only three packets to each router in the path and displays the latency for each of those three packets.

3. **Correct Answer: C**

    A. **Incorrect:** Network Address Translation (NAT) allows clients with private IP addresses to connect to computers on the public Internet. NAT does not automatically configure routing.

    B. **Incorrect:** Although OSPF is a routing protocol and would meet the requirements of this scenario, Windows Server 2008 does not support OSPF. Earlier versions of Windows do support OSPF.

    C. **Correct:** RIP is a routing protocol. Routing protocols allow routers to communicate a list of subnets that each router provides access to. If you enable RIP on a computer running Windows Server 2008, it can automatically identify neighboring routers and forward traffic to remote subnets.

    D. **Incorrect:** Although you could use static routes to reach remote subnets, the question requires you to configure Windows Server 2008 to automatically identify the remote networks.

Chapter 5: Case Scenario Answers

Case Scenario 1: Adding a Second Default Gateway

1. If the computers are configured with static IP addresses, you can use the Advanced TCP/IP Settings dialog box to configure multiple default gateways. If the computers are configured with dynamically assigned DHCP IP addresses, you can define multiple default gateways using DHCP scope options. Clients will automatically detect a failed default gateway and send traffic through the second default gateway.

Case Scenario 2: Adding a New Subnet

1. Yes, you can create a static route on the client computers specifying that the router with IP address 192.168.1.2 is the correct path to the 192.168.2.0/24 network. As long as 192.168.1.1 remains the default gateway, all other communications will be sent to 192.168.1.1.

2. You should run the following command:

```
route -p add 192.168.2.0 MASK 255.255.255.0 192.168.1.2
```

Chapter 6: Lesson Review Answers

Lesson 1

1. **Correct Answer: B**

   A. **Incorrect:** AH provides data authentication but not data encryption.

   B. **Correct:** ESP is the protocol that provides encryption for IPsec.

   C. **Incorrect:** Using IPsec with both AH and ESP is not the best answer because only ESP is needed to encrypt data. Using AH with ESP increases the processing overhead unnecessarily.

   D. **Incorrect:** Tunnel mode is used to provide compatibility for some gateway-to-gateway VPN communications.

2. **Correct Answer: A**

   A. **Correct:** If both domains are in the same Active Directory forest, you can use the Kerberos protocol built into Active Directory to provide authentication for IPsec communication.

   B. **Incorrect:** You do not need to configure certificates for authentication. Active Directory already provides the Kerberos protocol that you can use with IPsec.

   C. **Incorrect:** You do not need to configure a preshared key as the authentication method. The Kerberos protocol is already available, and it is more secure than a preshared key.

   D. **Incorrect:** NTLM is a backup authentication method for Active Directory, but it is not a valid authentication method for IPsec.

Chapter 6: Case Scenario Answers

Case Scenario: Implementing IPsec

1. Kerberos (because the IPsec communications are limited to an Active Directory environment).

2. Assign the Client (Respond Only) IPsec policy.

Chapter 7: Lesson Review Answers

Lesson 1

1. **Correct Answers: A and C**

   A. **Correct:** Enabling ICS changes the IP address of the internal network adapter to 192.168.0.1.

   B. **Incorrect:** Enabling ICS does not change the IP address of the external network adapter, which is typically a public IP address defined by your ISP.

   C. **Correct:** Enabling ICS automatically enables a DHCP server on your internal interface, so that clients on the internal network can receive the proper IP configuration.

   D. **Incorrect:** Enabling ICS enables a DHCP server on your internal interface, but not on your external interface.

2. **Correct Answer: A**

   A. **Correct:** By default, NAT does not allow connections from the Internet to the intranet. You can support them, however, by configuring port forwarding on the NAT server. With port forwarding, the NAT device accepts the TCP connection and forwards it to a specific server on the intranet.

   B. **Incorrect:** NAT allows clients to establish TCP connections to servers on the Internet.

   C. **Incorrect:** Streaming video often uses User Datagram Protocol (UDP), which often fails when a NAT device is in use. However, streaming video connections that use TCP should always work. For that reason, most streaming media protocols support both UDP (for performance) and TCP (for compatibility with NAT).

   D. **Incorrect:** HTTPs functions exactly like any other TCP connection. Therefore, NAT clients do not have any problem establishing an HTTPS connection to a server on the Internet.

3. **Correct Answer: C**

   A. **Incorrect:** The Internet network adapter should have the IP address that was assigned by your ISP, not the internal network adapter.

   B. **Incorrect:** You should configure the ICS server to send queries to the DNS server and client computers to send DNS queries to the ICS server. However, you should not configure the internal network adapter with the DNS server's IP address.

   C. **Correct:** ICS always assigns the IP address 192.168.0.1 to the internal network adapter.

   D. **Incorrect:** 192.168.0.0/24 is the internal network that ICS assigns to clients. 192.168.0.0 is not a valid IP address, however.

Lesson 2

1. **Correct Answer: D**

   A. **Incorrect:** 802.11b is one of the original wireless standards, and newer standards, including both 802.11g and 802.11n, provide much better performance with backward-compatibility.

   B. **Incorrect:** 802.11g provides better performance than 802.11b and is backward-compatible. However, 802.11n provides even better performance than 802.11g.

   C. **Incorrect:** 802.11a uses a different frequency from 802.11b and thus would not provide compatibility with your 802.11b clients.

   D. **Correct:** 802.11n provides the highest performance of the wireless protocols listed, and it is capable of providing backward compatibility with 802.11b clients.

2. **Correct Answer: C**

   A. **Incorrect:** The wireless client cannot log detailed information about authentication failures because RADIUS does not provide detailed information about why credentials were rejected. Instead, you should examine the Security event log on the RADIUS server.

   B. **Incorrect:** Same as answer A.

   C. **Correct:** The Windows Server 2008 RADIUS service adds events to the local Security event log. These events have information useful for identifying the cause of the problem, such as the user name submitted.

   D. **Incorrect:** The Windows Server 2008 RADIUS service adds events to the local Security event log, not to the System event log.

3. **Correct Answer: D**

   A. **Incorrect:** 128-bit WEP provides much better security than 64-bit WEP. However, 128-bit WEP is still considered extremely unsecure because it uses static keys and can be cracked in a relatively short time.

   B. **Incorrect:** WPA-PSK uses static keys, making it vulnerable to brute force attacks. WPA-PSK should be used only for testing.

   C. **Incorrect:** 64-bit WEP is the original wireless security standard, and it is now considered outdated. 64-bit WEP uses small, static keys and contains several cryptographic weaknesses that allow it to be cracked in a short time.

   D. **Correct:** WPA-EAP (and WPA2-EAP) provide the highest level of security by authenticating users to a central RADIUS server, such as a server running Windows Server 2008. As of the time of this writing, breaking WPA-EAP security using brute force techniques would be much more difficult than any other wireless security standard.

Lesson 3

1. **Correct Answers: A and D**
   A. **Correct:** A VPN server allows clients on the public Internet to connect to your intranet while providing authentication and encryption.
   B. **Incorrect:** Clients never submit requests directly to a RADIUS server. Instead, a wireless access point, VPN server, or other access provider submits authentication requests to the RADIUS server on the client's behalf. Additionally, without a VPN connection, client computers would not have access to the internal network.
   C. **Incorrect:** Configuring your own modem bank and telephone circuits would provide the required connectivity. However, the capital expense would be significant. A more cost-effective alternative is to outsource the dial-up access to an ISP.
   D. **Correct:** ISPs can provide dial-up access with integrated VPN connections to clients and authenticate to your internal RADIUS server. With Windows Server 2008, the RADIUS server can, in turn, authenticate to an Active Directory domain controller.

2. **Correct Answers: B and D**
   A. **Incorrect:** VPN connections almost always provide better performance than dial-up connections. However, dial-up connections are not adequate for streaming video.
   B. **Correct:** Dial-up connections can connect directly to a server on your intranet, bypassing the Internet entirely.
   C. **Incorrect:** VPNs include encryption, preventing an attacker with access to the transmission from interpreting the data.
   D. **Correct:** Both VPN and dial-up servers can authenticate to a central RADIUS server.

3. **Correct Answers: C and D**
   A. **Incorrect:** Windows XP Professional does not support SSTP.
   B. **Incorrect:** Windows 2000 Professional does not support SSTP.
   C. **Correct:** Windows Vista with Service Pack 1 supports being an SSTP VPN client. It does not support being a VPN server. Windows Vista without Service Pack 1 does not support SSTP.
   D. **Correct:** Windows Server 2008 supports being either an SSTP VPN client or server.

Chapter 7: Case Scenario Answers

Case Scenario 1: Connecting a Branch Office to the Internet

1. The ISP might be able to provide you with a block of more than 50 IP addresses. However, the additional cost probably wouldn't be worth it because you do not need to accept incoming connections. Although you always need at least one public IP address, additional IP addresses are required only if you plan to host a server that will be accessible from the Internet.

2. You should configure a NAT server on the boundary between the public Internet and your intranet. The NAT server can translate the private IP addresses to its public IP address, allowing complete connectivity for outgoing connections.

3. Typically, for an office with only 50 computers you would choose a router that has NAT capabilities built in. Alternatively, you could choose to deploy NAT using a Windows Server 2008 computer. That would be advisable only if you planned to connect the server to the Internet anyway.

Case Scenario 2: Planning Remote Access

1. The sales staff will need dial-up access because they might be in hotel rooms that have only an analog modem connection. For better performance, you should also recommend supporting a VPN server.

2. The VPN server will need to be connected to both the Internet and your private intranet. You already have several servers that are configured this way, so you could configure an existing server to accept VPN connections and route the communications to the intranet. To address the concerns about maintaining a separate user name and password, you could authenticate users to the Active Directory domain controller (for PPTP connections) or using client certificates (for L2TP connections).

3. You could choose to connect a bank of 50 modems to a dial-up server that is connected to your private intranet, you could purchase a separate modem bank and have it authenticate to a RADIUS server, or you could establish a service agreement with a dial-up ISP and have the ISP authenticate against your RADIUS server.

4. Probably, because most wireless networks connect to the Internet. The firewall might block VPN connections, however. In that case, SSTP connections (available for only Windows Vista and Windows Server 2008 clients) might be compatible with the firewall.

Chapter 8: Lesson Review Answers

Lesson 1

1. **Correct Answer: B**
    A. **Incorrect:** The computer running Windows Server 2008 will need to make outbound connections on TCP port 290; however, Windows Firewall allows outbound connections by default. Therefore, you do not need to create a firewall rule.
    B. **Correct:** By default, Windows Server 2008 will block inbound connections that do not have a firewall rule. There is no firewall rule for TCP port 39 by default. Therefore, you will need to add one.
    C. **Incorrect:** The computer running Windows Server 2008 needs to make outbound connections on TCP port 290, but it does not need to allow inbound connections on that port.
    D. **Incorrect:** Windows Vista allows any outbound connection by default. Therefore, you do not need to create a firewall rule to allow outbound connections.

2. **Correct Answers: A and C**
    A. **Correct:** Selecting Allow Only Secure Connections requires IPsec, which you must use to require domain authentication at the firewall level.
    B. **Incorrect:** Specifying a profile for the firewall rule simply means the rule won't apply if the server isn't connected to the domain network. You can't use profiles to require client connection authentication.
    C. **Correct:** After requiring IPsec on the General tab, you can use this tab to limit connections only to users who are members of specific groups.
    D. **Incorrect:** Configuring scope can be a very powerful tool for limiting connections from users. Although it might be advisable to also limit scope to connections from client computers on your internal network, that doesn't necessarily require users to be a member of your domain. Additionally, you would need to configure the Remote IP Address settings, not the Local IP Address settings.

3. **Correct Answer: D**
    A. **Incorrect:** Both Windows XP (configured using the Windows Firewall node) and Windows Vista (configured using either the Windows Firewall node or the Windows Firewall With Advanced Security node) support filtering UDP traffic.
    B. **Incorrect:** Both the Windows Firewall and the Windows Firewall With Advanced Security nodes support creating a rule for an executable.
    C. **Incorrect:** Both the Windows Firewall and the Windows Firewall With Advanced Security nodes support configuring scope for a rule.

   D. **Correct:** The Windows Firewall With Advanced Security node supports firewall features available only for Windows Vista and Windows Server 2008, not Windows XP. One of the most important features is the ability to require IPsec connection security and to authenticate and authorize users or computers using IPsec.

Lesson 2

1. **Correct Answer: A**

   A. **Correct:** Setting NAP Enforcement to Allow Limited Access limits the client to the remediation servers you list. If you do not list any remediation servers, clients will be completely denied network access.

   B. **Incorrect:** Setting the Access Permission to Deny Access prevents clients from performing a health check. Therefore, both compliant and noncompliant clients will be blocked.

   C. **Incorrect:** The Session Timeout disconnects remote access connections after a specific amount of time. You cannot set a Session Timeout of 0.

   D. **Incorrect:** IP filters should be used for remote access connections. They do not apply to NAP network policies.

2. **Correct Answers: B and C**

   A. **Incorrect:** Health policies apply only to NAP-capable computers.

   B. **Correct:** Computers that do not support NAP require a separate network policy with a NAP-Capable Computers condition that matches Only Computers That Are Not NAP-Capable.

   C. **Correct:** Remediation server groups define the servers that are accessible to computers with limited access. To meet the requirements of this scenario, you would need to create a network policy with a NAP-Capable Computers condition matching Only Computers That Are Not NAP-Capable, set the NAP Enforcement for that network policy to Allow Limited Access, and then configure the network policy with the new remediation server group.

   D. **Incorrect:** You can use a single connection request policy for computers that both are and are not NAP-capable. Therefore, you do not need to create a new connection request policy. Additionally, the NAP-Capable Computers condition is not available for connection request policies.

3. **Correct Answers: A and B**

   A. **Correct:** Because NPS and DHCP are running on separate computers, you must install NPS on the DHCP server and then configure a RADIUS proxy on the DHCP server to forward RADIUS requests to the primary NPS server.

B. **Correct:** Same as answer A.

C. **Incorrect:** HRA is required only for IPsec enforcement.

D. **Incorrect:** DHCP enforcement does not require certificate services.

Chapter 8: Case Scenario Answers

Case Scenario 1: Evaluate Firewall Settings

1. You will need to create a Program firewall rule that allows inbound connections for the Web service. Although you could create a Port firewall rule that allows inbound connections for TCP port 81, it's typically more efficient to create a Program firewall rule.

2. You do not need to create a firewall rule on the client computers because they allow outbound connections by default.

Case Scenario 2: Planning NAP

1. The Windows XP computer didn't have an important update installed, and the attacker exploited a vulnerability. It could have been prevented in a couple of ways. First, if the Windows XP computer had been recently updated, the vulnerability would have been removed. Second, if the Windows XP computer had been updated to Windows Vista, which supports a public Windows Firewall profile that automatically drops all unrequested incoming connections when connected to untrusted networks, the attack would have been dropped regardless of whether the update were applied.

2. Yes, you could enable outbound firewall rules and block outbound traffic by default. This would require you to create firewall rules for all applications that are allowed to communicate on your network.

3. NAP can be used to perform health checks on client computers before granting them network access. The default SHV can verify that Windows Firewall is enabled, recent updates have been installed, and antivirus software is running. NAP could have prevented the infected computer from connecting to the internal network and accessing confidential documents.

4. Probably, because most organizations have computers that would not meet even the most basic health checks. To prevent that, implement NAP in monitoring-only mode. After you have identified computers that fail health checks, you can update them and verify that they now pass the health check. There will probably be computers that cannot pass the health check or are not NAP-capable. You will need to create exceptions to allow those computers to connect to your network.

5. You will probably need to use a combination of several NAP enforcement methods. IPsec and 802.1X enforcement provide excellent security. To protect remote access connections, you will need to use VPN enforcement. If you have networks that cannot support IPsec or 802.1X enforcement, you can make use of DHCP enforcement.

Chapter 9: Lesson Review Answers

Lesson 1

1. **Correct Answer: D**
   A. **Incorrect:** Because you have a centralized IT department, having local IT departments manage the WSUS servers would be inefficient. Instead, you should configure the remote offices as replicas of the WSUS server at the headquarters, allowing you to manage all updates using a single WSUS server.
   B. **Incorrect:** Although this architecture would work, it would be extremely wasteful of Internet bandwidth. The bandwidth required for 1200 client computers to each download a service pack from the Internet would be so extreme that for many computers the updates might never succeed.
   C. **Incorrect:** Like answer B, this architecture would work. However, the WAN links would likely be saturated with update traffic as every computer at each remote office transfers large updates. To resolve this, place WSUS servers at each office.
   D. **Correct:** To make best use of WAN and Internet bandwidth, configure a WSUS server at each office and have each computer download updates from your central WSUS server.

2. **Correct Answer: B**
   A. **Incorrect:** Enabling this setting configures the Windows Update client to immediately install updates that do not require the computer to be restarted.
   B. **Correct:** This Group Policy setting allows you to configure whether updates are installed automatically and when they are installed. By default, however, Windows Update clients will notify users of the updates and prompt them to perform the installation.
   C. **Incorrect:** Enabling this setting prevents the Windows Update client from automatically restarting the computer. By default, this setting is disabled, which is required for automatically restarting computers, as outlined in the scenario.
   D. **Incorrect:** You can use this setting to configure client computers as members of a computer group. It has no impact on how updates are installed.

3. **Correct Answers: C and D**

   A. **Incorrect:** Windows 95 does not support acting as a WSUS client.

   B. **Incorrect:** Windows 98 does not support acting as a WSUS client.

   C. **Correct:** Windows 2000, with Service Pack 3 or later, can act as a WSUS client.

   D. **Correct:** Windows XP can act as a WSUS client without any service pack.

Lesson 2

1. **Correct Answers: A, B, and D**

   A. **Correct:** The System log contains high-level information generated by the Windows Update client.

   B. **Correct:** The Windows Update Operational log contains detailed information generated by the Windows Update client.

   C. **Incorrect:** In this scenario, only the client computer would be able to report on the cause of the error. Therefore, the information cannot be available on the WSUS server.

   D. **Correct:** The WindowsUpdate.log file has extremely detailed information generated by the Windows Update client.

2. **Correct Answers: A and D**

   A. **Correct:** The Update Status Summary report shows a description of every update and which computer groups the update is approved for.

   B. **Incorrect:** The Update Status Summary report does not show specifically which computers installed an update, though it does provide the total number of computers. However, the Update Detailed Status report does provide this information.

   C. **Incorrect:** The Update Status Summary report does not show whether an update can be removed using WSUS.

   D. **Correct:** The Update Status Summary report shows a pie chart with the number of computers the update failed and succeeded for.

3. **Correct Answers: B and C**

   A. **Incorrect:** You can use the Configure Automatic Updates policy to control whether client computers download updates and notify users or automatically install updates. You cannot use the policy to define computer group memberships, however.

   B. **Correct:** Configuring the Enable Client-Side Targeting Group Policy setting and then specifying a target group name for the computer will place all computers the GPO is applied to in the specified computer group.

    C. **Correct:** Selecting Change Management allows you to specify the computer groups a computer will be placed in.

    D. **Incorrect:** You cannot use the drag-and-drop feature to move computers in the Update Services console.

Chapter 9: Case Scenario Answers

Case Scenario 1: Planning a Basic WSUS Infrastructure

1. WSUS can act as a distribution point for updates on your LAN. Clients can then retrieve the updates without connecting to Microsoft on the Internet. Although the WSUS server will still need to download updates across the Internet, it will use much less bandwidth than 250 computers individually would.

2. A single WSUS server can serve all 250 computers on your LAN. Although you could configure two WSUS servers redundantly (by configuring a round-robin DNS entry that contained the IP addresses of both WSUS servers), it's typically unnecessary because a WSUS server can go offline for short periods without affecting client computers.

3. Click the *Options* node in the Update Services console. Then, in the Details pane, click Automatic Approvals. You can simply enable the Default Automatic Approval Rule (which approves all critical and security updates), or you can create your own customized rules.

Case Scenario 2: Planning a Complex WSUS Infrastructure

1. Each of the five offices should have a WSUS server.

2. The New York City office can be a replica of the London office. However, the other three offices will need to have an independently managed WSUS server.

Chapter 10: Lesson Review Answers

Lesson 1

1. **Correct Answer: A**

    A. **Correct:** You can use the Wecutil utility to automatically configure a computer to collect events.

    B. **Incorrect:** This command should be run on the forwarding computer.

    C. **Incorrect:** This command should be run on the forwarding computer.

      D. **Incorrect:** You don't need to add the forwarding computer to the Event Log Readers group. Only the collecting computer should be a member of that group.

2. **Correct Answers: B and C**

      A. **Incorrect:** You should run this command on the collecting computer.

      B. **Correct:** You should run this command on the forwarding computer.

      C. **Correct:** You should run this command on the forwarding computer.

      D. **Incorrect:** You don't need to add the forwarding computer to the Event Log Readers group. Only the collecting computer should be a member of that group.

3. **Correct Answer: A**

      A. **Correct:** As described in "Creating an Event Subscription," you should use the Wecutil tool to customize a subscription interval.

      B. **Incorrect:** WinRM is used to configure the forwarding computer.

      C. **Incorrect:** The Net tool is useful for stopping and starting services and for changing group memberships at the command line. It cannot configure subscriptions.

      D. **Incorrect:** The Event Viewer console allows you to configure many aspects of a subscription, but it does not allow you to customize the subscription interval.

Lesson 2

1. **Correct Answer: B**

      A. **Incorrect.** You can use Performance Monitor to view performance counters in real time or to analyze performance data saved as part of a Data Collector Set. However, Performance Monitor cannot tell you when an application was installed.

      B. **Correct:** Reliability Monitor tracks application installations (assuming they use Windows Installer). With a few clicks, you can determine whether any applications were installed recently and exactly when the installation occurred.

      C. **Incorrect:** Data Collector Sets capture current performance and configuration data. They cannot tell you when an application was installed.

      D. **Incorrect:** Network Monitor, discussed in Lesson 3, "Using Network Monitor," captures network traffic. It does not have information about application installations.

2. **Correct Answers: A and C**

      A. **Correct:** Performance Monitor views real-time data by default, but you can also use it to view data recorded using a Data Collector Set.

      B. **Incorrect:** Reliability Monitor records and displays application installations and various type of failures. It does not record performance data.

C. **Correct:** Data Collector Sets record performance data. Once the data is recorded, you can view it using the Performance Monitor tool. To be able to analyze two sets of data against each other, create a custom Data Collector Set that records the necessary performance information. Then run the Data Collector Set during peak usage times and at night. You can then open two instances of Performance Monitor to view each of the reports and compare them to each other.

D. **Incorrect:** Network Monitor, discussed in Lesson 3, "Using Network Monitor," captures network traffic. It does not record performance data.

3. **Correct Answers: B and D**

A. **Incorrect:** Although application failures are recorded, errors within an application (that do not cause an application to fail) are not recorded in Reliability Monitor.

B. **Correct:** Application installs and uninstalls are recorded in Reliability Monitor.

C. **Incorrect:** Services starting and stopping are typically recorded in the event log but are not tracked by Reliability Monitor.

D. **Correct:** Reliability Monitor records device driver failures.

Lesson 3

1. **Correct Answers: A and C**

A. **Correct:** Regardless of the network infrastructure, you can always capture communications to and from your local computer.

B. **Incorrect:** By default, Layer 2 switches will not send HostC any communications between HostA and HostYou would need to enable the port HostC is connected to as a monitoring port.

C. **Correct:** All computers connected to a hub can see all other computer's communications. Therefore, with P-Mode enabled, HostC would be able to capture communications sent to HostA.

D. **Incorrect:** HostC must be connected to the same hub as either HostA or HostThe switch would not forward communications destined for either HostA or HostB to HostC.

2. **Correct Answer: B**

A. **Incorrect:** Netmon is the Network Monitor executable file, and it starts the graphical tool. You cannot run it from a command prompt.

B. **Correct:** NMCap allows you to capture communications from a command prompt and save them to a .CAP file.

C. **Incorrect:** Nmconfig is used to install and uninstall Network Monitor. You cannot use it to capture data.

      D. **Incorrect:** Nmwifi.com configures wireless scanning options, and you typically access it by viewing a wireless network adapter's properties from within Network Monitor.

3. **Correct Answer: D**

      A. **Incorrect:** This filter would show all HTTP communications and any communications that came from the IP address 192.168.10.12.

      B. **Incorrect:** This filter would show only HTTP communications from the IP address 192.168.10.1 The scenario requires you to view communications sent both to and from the client computer, and this filter would not show communications sent to the client computer (which would have a destination IP address of 192.168.10.12).

      C. **Incorrect:** This filter would show all HTTP communications and any communications that came from or were sent to the IP address 192.168.10.12.

      D. **Correct:** The && operator requires that both parameters be met for a frame to be shown. In this case the filter meets your requirements because the frames must be HTTP and must have either a source or destination IP address of 192.168.10.12. The IPv4.Address parameter can match either the source or destination IP address.

Chapter 10: Case Scenario Answers

Case Scenario 1: Troubleshooting a Network Performance Problem

1. You can use Data Collector Sets to record a baseline when the server is performing normally. Then run the same Data Collector Set when the performance problem occurs. You can then use Performance Monitor to analyze the two sets of results and identify the factors that differentiate the two.

2. A protocol analyzer, such as Network Monitor, would allow you to analyze the individual frames.

Case Scenario 2: Monitoring Computers for Low Disk Space

1. You can use event forwarding to send low disk space events to a central computer. Then the IT department can monitor that single event log to identify computers with low disk space conditions.

2. Windows XP, Windows Server 2003, Windows Vista, and Windows Server 2008 can support event forwarding. Windows XP must have Service Pack 2 and WS-Management 1.1 installed. Windows Server 2003 must be either Windows Server 2003 R2 or have Service Pack 1 or later installed. Windows Server 2003 also requires WS-Management 1.1.

Chapter 11: Lesson Review Answers

Lesson 1

1. **Correct Answer: C**
   A. **Incorrect:** Users have No Access permission if no access control entry applies to them or if they explicitly have a Deny permission assigned. In this case, Mary has Write access because she has the Modify NTFS permission assigned.
   B. **Incorrect:** Share permissions apply only when users access a folder across the network. Because Mary is accessing the folder from the local computer, only NTFS permissions apply. The Marketing group is granted Modify NTFS permissions, which allows Mary to write to the folder (in addition to being able to read the contents of the folder).
   C. **Correct:** Through Mary's membership in the Marketing group, Mary has the Modify NTFS permission. Because Mary is not accessing the files using the share, share permissions do not affect Mary's effective permissions. Therefore, Mary can write to the folder.
   D. **Incorrect:** Full Control permissions allow users to change permissions. Having this level of access would require Mary to have Full Control NTFS permissions.

2. **Correct Answer: D**
   A. **Incorrect:** This procedure would add NTFS permissions for the user. However, the user already has the necessary NTFS permissions.
   B. **Incorrect:** This is the correct procedure for allowing local users to share EFS-encrypted files. However, it is not necessary when users connect across the network.
   C. **Incorrect:** Although removing encryption would allow the user to access the file, it would also reduce security.
   D. **Correct:** EFS affects only users who access files locally. Therefore, because the user is connecting across the network, you do not need to make any changes.

Lesson 2

1. **Correct Answer: B**
   A. **Incorrect:** Users have No Access permission if no access control entry applies to them or if they explicitly have a Deny permission assigned. In this case, Mary has Read access because she has both NTFS and share permissions assigned.
   B. **Correct:** When connecting to a shared folder, users always have the fewest privileges allowed by both share permissions and NTFS permissions. In this case, the

only share permission grants the Everyone group Reader access—which limits Mary's permission to read-only.

C. **Incorrect:** If Mary were to log on locally to the computer and access the files on the local hard disk, share permissions would not be a factor and Mary would be able to update the files. However, because Mary is accessing the folder using a share and the share has only Reader permissions assigned, Mary will be able to only read the files.

D. **Incorrect:** Full Control permissions allow users to change permissions. Having this level of access would require Mary to have both Full Control NTFS permissions and Co-owner share permissions.

2. **Correct Answer: A**

A. **Correct:** You can use the *Net Share* command to create shared folders.

B. **Incorrect:** You can use *Netsh* for a wide variety of network configuration tasks, but you cannot use it to share folders.

C. **Incorrect:** Share is an executable program used for file locking by legacy MS-DOS applications.

D. **Incorrect:** The Ipconfig tool displays IP configuration information, but it cannot be used to add shares.

3. **Correct Answer: A**

A. **Correct:** Random Order configures clients to connect to DFS servers at their local site first. If no local DFS server is available, clients randomly choose another DFS server.

B. **Incorrect:** The Lowest Cost algorithm uses Active Directory site costs to determine which DFS server to connect to if no DFS server is available at the local site. Although this algorithm is often more efficient than Random Order, the scenario requires clients to randomly connect to DFS servers at different sites.

C. **Incorrect:** This algorithm prevents clients from connecting to DFS servers at different sites.

D. **Incorrect:** Selecting this check box configures how clients connect to DFS servers when a DFS server is offline and then later online. It does not configure how clients initially select a DFS server

4. **Correct Answer: C**

A. **Incorrect:** Creating a hard quota at 80 MB would prevent the user from saving more than 80 MB of files, which does not meet your requirements.

B. **Incorrect:** Creating a soft quota with a 100 MB limit would not prevent users from exceeding the quota.

C.   **Correct:** The most efficient way to meet your requirements is to create a single hard quota with a 100 MB limit. The hard quota prevents users from saving files if they exceed their quota limit. Creating a warning at 80 percent would allow you to configure the quota to send an e-mail to the user when the user has consumed 80 MB of disk space.

D.   **Incorrect:** Soft quotas allow the user to continue to save files once the user has exceeded the quota. For this reason, it would not meet your requirements.

5.   **Correct Answer: B**

A.   **Incorrect:** Use the FileScrn tool to configure file screening for folders, which configures Windows to block specific file types.

B.   **Correct:** You can use the DirQuota tool configure disk quotas from the command prompt.

C.   **Incorrect:** The StorRept tool configures storage reports from the command prompt.

D.   **Incorrect:** You can use the Net tool to configure folder sharing from the command prompt. It cannot configure disk quotas.

Lesson 3

1.   **Correct Answer: D**

A.   **Incorrect:** The StorRept tool configures storage reports from the command prompt.

B.   **Incorrect:** FileScrn is a command-line tool for configuring file screening. It cannot be used to create backups.

C.   **Incorrect:** You can use DirQuota to configure disk quotas. It does not create backups, however.

D.   **Correct:** VSSAdmin allows you to initiate a shadow copy, which you can use to restore files after they have been modified.

2.   **Correct Answer: B**

A.   **Incorrect:** Refer to the explanation for answer B for more information.

B.   **Correct:** Windows creates a WindowsImageBackup folder in the root of the backup media. Inside that folder, it creates a folder with the current computer's name.

C.   **Incorrect:** Refer to the explanation for answer B for more information.

D.   **Incorrect:** Refer to the explanation for answer B for more information.

3. **Correct Answers: A and C**

    A. **Correct:** You can use the Windows Server Backup tool to restore individual files. You can also simply right-click a file and then choose Restore Previous Versions.

    B. **Incorrect:** Windows cannot overwrite system files while the operating system is running. Therefore, to restore the system volume you must perform a recovery by starting the computer from the Windows Server 2008 installation media.

    C. **Correct:** You can restore nonsystem volumes while the operating system is running.

    D. **Incorrect:** Windows Server Backup cannot overwrite files that are currently in use. Instead, you will be prompted to save the recovered files to a different folder.

Chapter 11: Case Scenario Answers

Case Scenario 1: Planning File Services

1. You can create a DFS namespace that contains multiple shared folders even if they're hosted by different servers. Then, users can map a network drive to the namespace and use the single network drive to connect to any shared folder.

2. You can use share permissions and NTFS file permissions.

3. You can add multiple targets to a shared folder and enable replication between them. Users who connect to the shared folder can automatically be connected to the server at their local site. If that server is unavailable, the client computer can connect to another target server and access the same files.

Case Scenario 2: Planning Disaster Recovery

1. You will need an additional hard disk with sufficient capacity to store a backup of the system volume and any other volumes that you plan to back up.

2. After replacing the failed disk, you will need to start the computer from the Windows Server 2008 installation media and then use the system recovery tools to restore the system volume.

3. Yes, if you restore the file before another backup is performed. If a backup is performed after the file becomes corrupted, the corrupted file might overwrite the valid version of the file.

Chapter 12: Lesson Review Answers

Lesson 1

1. **Correct Answer: B**

   A. **Incorrect:** The *PrintUI* command is a graphical interface and cannot be called from a command line. Also, the -b parameter is used to export printer configurations, not to import them.

   B. **Correct:** You use the *PrintBRM* command to export and import printer settings from a command prompt. Use the -R parameter to specify an import.

   C. **Incorrect:** The PrintBRMEngine executable file is used by PrintBRM and PrintBM-RUI, but it cannot be directly called.

   D. **Incorrect:** *Netsh* is used to configure network settings and cannot be used to import or export printer settings.

2. **Correct Answer: D**

   A. **Incorrect:** The PrnMngr.vbs tool adds and removes printers.

   B. **Incorrect:** The PrnCnfg.vbs tool configures printer names, locations, permissions, and other basic configuration settings.

   C. **Incorrect:** The PrnQctrl.vbs tool prints a test page, pauses or resumes a printer, and clears the print queue.

   D. **Correct:** The PubPrn.vbs tool publishes a printer to the Active Directory.

3. **Correct Answer: A**

   A. **Correct:** To allow a client to connect from behind a firewall that allows only Web connections, you will need to use Internet printing. To connect to printers shared with Internet printing, specify the path in the format http://<*ServerName*>/Printers/<*PrinterName*>/.printer.

   B. **Incorrect:** Although connecting through the firewall will require you to use HTTP, you must specify the URL using the format http://<*ServerName*>/Printers/<*Printer Name*>/.printer.

   C. **Incorrect:** You do not need to specify the Printers folder or the printer name as part of a Universal Naming Convention (UNC) path. Also, a UNC path would not allow you to bypass the firewall.

   D. **Incorrect:** This would be the correct format if you were connecting to a printer across a local area network using a standard Universal Naming Convention (UNC) path. However, you must specify a URL to use Internet printing, which will allow you to bypass the firewall.

4. **Correct Answer: D**

   A. **Incorrect:** You cannot configure notifications directly from the driver's properties. Instead, you should create a custom filter and then create a notification for the filter.

   B. **Incorrect:** PrintBRM is used to export and import printer settings and cannot configure e-mail notifications.

   C. **Incorrect:** You cannot configure notifications directly from the printer's properties. Instead, you should create a custom filter and then create a notification for the filter.

   D. **Correct:** You can create a custom filter with criteria that match the printer name and a problem status. Then, you can create a notification for the custom filter to send an e-mail.

Chapter 12: Case Scenario Answers

Case Scenario: Managing Network Printers

1. You can use Windows Server 2008 as a print server. If you install each of the network printers and then share them, users can connect to the Windows Server 2008 computer and submit print jobs to the server. The server can then manage the print queues for each of the printers.

2. You can create custom filters that match printers with problems and then configure an e-mail notification to be sent to an administrator. Alternatively, you can use the notification to run a script or executable file that is integrated into a custom management infrastructure.

3. Windows Server 2008 supports using permissions to control which users can print to and manage printers. You can deny access to all users except the executive, the assistant, and the IT personnel who need to manage the printer. This wouldn't, however, prevent users from connecting directly to printers. To control direct access, you would need to modify the printer's configuration to allow connections only from the print server. Alternatively, if your network supports virtual local area networks (VLANs) or another access control technology, you could restrict access to the printers using your network infrastructure.

4. You could configure multiple similar printers as part of a printer pool. Any print jobs submitted to the printer pool would be sent to the first available printer. This would allow small print jobs to print to one printer while another printer handled the large print job.

Glossary

address block   A group of contiguous addresses that can be expressed with a single network address and a subnet mask. An example of an address block is 10.10.10.192 /26.

aging   The process of tracking the age of resource records in a zone.

application directory partition   A partition in Active Directory that is reserved for use with a specific application, such as DNS. In Windows Server 2003 and Windows Server 2008, domain controllers that are DNS servers include two application directory partitions by default: DomainDnsZones and ForestDnsZones.

Authentication Header (AH)   The security protocol in IPsec that ensures data authentication and integrity.

Automatic Private IP Addressing (APIPA)   An autoconfigured IPv4 address in the range 169.254.0.0 /16. An APIPA address offers limited connectivity and is normally a sign that a DHCP server cannot be reached.

broadcast   A type of network transmission in which a signal is sent to all computers on a local subnet.

Default User class   An options class to which all DHCP clients belong. When you assign a DHCP option to the Default User class, all DHCP clients receive the option.

defense-in-depth   A security technique that reduces risk by providing multiple layers of protection. With defense-in-depth, if one security layer fails, another layer continues to provide protection.

Domain Name System (DNS)   The hierarchical (multitag) naming and name resolution system used on the Internet and in Windows networks.

downstream server   The server that synchronizes updates from an upstream server when you are designing WSUS architectures.

dynamic updates   The feature in which DNS clients can automatically register and update their own resource records in DNS.

Encapsulating Security Payload (ESP)   The security protocol in IPsec that provides data encryption.

exclusion   An IP address that falls within the range of a DHCP server scope but that is configured not to be leased to DHCP clients.

firewall   A security tool used to filter unwanted traffic while allowing legitimate traffic.

forwarder   A DNS server (not a root server) to which unresolved queries are sent by a forwarding DNS server.

forwarding   For a DNS server, the process of sending to another specified DNS server (not the root server) any query that the original DNS server cannot answer.

fully qualified domain name (FQDN)   A computer's host name concatenated with its DNS suffix. An FQDN is a name that can be queried for in a DNS infrastructure. An example of an FQDN is server1.contoso.com.

gateway   A synonym for router; a device that forwards communications between networks.

hard quota   A storage limit that prevents users from creating more files after they reach a threshold.

hop   A router or gateway.

host name In DNS, the first or single-tag name assigned to a computer. For example, "clientA" is a host name.

host route A route that directs traffic to a single IP address. DHCP NAP enforcement uses host routes to allow a noncompliant computer to access remediation resources

HOSTS A manually configured file sometimes used by the local system to map DNS names to IP addresses.

Internet Control Message Protocol (ICMP) The messaging protocol built into IP on which the Ping and Tracert utilities are based.

Internet Printing Protocol (IPP) A printing protocol that uses Hypertext Transfer Protocol (HTTP). HTTP can work through most proxy servers and firewalls.

Internet Protocol Security (IPsec) An Internet Engineering Task Force (IETF) standards-based suite of protocols whose purpose is to provide data authentication and encryption for IP networks.

IPv4 The Layer 3 protocol that currently forms the backbone of the Internet and almost every computer network in the world. IPv4 provides addressing and routing services, but its addresses are becoming exhausted.

IPv6 A Layer 3 protocol that offers a virtually unlimited supply of addresses and that, in the long term, will replace IPv4 on public networks.

iteration For a DNS client or server, the process of making multiple queries to servers in a DNS namespace. Iteration is performed on the basis of referrals received from queried servers.

Kerberos The data authentication protocol native to Active Directory.

latency The delay that occurs when a packet travels from a client to a server.

lease The use of an IP address that is assigned to a DHCP client by a DHCP server. An address lease has a finite length and must be renewed periodically.

Line Printer Daemon (LPD) A printing protocol commonly used by older UNIX operating systems. Most newer operating systems, including UNIX, can connect to shared printers using standard Windows sharing.

Link Local Multicast Name Resolution (LLMNR) A name resolution service for IPv6-enabled computers running Windows Vista or Windows Server 2008. LLMNR resolves names only on the local subnet.

Lmhosts A manually configured file sometimes used by the local system to map NetBIOS names to IP addresses.

master zone A zone, usually a primary zone, from which a transfer is performed to a secondary or stub zone.

monitoring port A port on a Layer 2 switch that receives all communications even if they are not directed to that port. You can use a monitoring port with Network Monitor to capture communications between other computers.

name resolution The process of translating a computer name into a computer address.

NetBIOS An older set of network services still present in Windows networks today. NetBIOS includes, among other features, a naming system and a name resolution system.

Network Address Translation (NAT) A technology deployed on a router that hides the addresses on one network and allows computers on private ranges to communicate with computers on the Internet.

options class A category of DHCP clients that enables a DHCP server to assign options only to particular clients within a scope.

P-Mode When using Network Monitor, a promiscuous mode that records communications sent between hosts other than the computer running Network Monitor. P-Mode is disabled by default.

Preshared Key A shared password that is also used to encrypt and decrypt data.

primary DNS suffix The main domain name assigned to a computer. The primary DNS suffix is tied to domain membership and enables automatic DNS registration in a zone.

primary zone A read-write copy of a zone that provides the original source data for a portion of a DNS namespace.

private address ranges Specific IPv4 ranges that can be employed by any organization for private use.

recursion For a DNS server, the process of accepting a name query from a client and then querying other servers on behalf of the client.

referral A list of servers, provided by an Active Directory domain controller, that can serve a DFS request.

referrals Resource records that are provided in a response to DNS clients or servers after a query and that specify another DNS server to contact to resolve the queried-for name.

replication The automatic synchronization of data that occurs among domain controllers in an Active Directory domain.

reservation An IP address that is configured always to be assigned to a DHCP client by a DHCP server.

resolver In general, a service that resolves names for a computer. In Windows, the resolver is the DNS Client service.

root hints A file that contains the list of root servers in a DNS namespace. The root servers are queried by default when a DNS server cannot itself answer a query.

router A device that forwards communications between networks.

routing table A list of IP destinations and how a computer can reach each destination.

scavenging The process of deleting outdated records in a zone.

secondary zone A standard zone stored in a text file that provides a read-only copy of zone data.

Security Association (SA) A set of security standards agreed upon by two computers communicating through IPsec.

soft quota A storage limit that allows users to create more files after they reach a threshold. Soft quotas are used to send notifications or add events.

stub zone A zone that includes only a list of servers authoritative for names in a specific DNS domain.

subnet mask A 32-bit number used by a host on an IPv4 network to differentiate the network ID portion of an IPv4 address from the host ID portion.

targets Destination shared folders referenced by nodes in a DFS namespace.

Time to Live (TTL) The number of seconds for which a resource record is configured to remain in a DNS cache.

Transport mode The traditional mode of IPsec that provides end-to-end security between computers on a network.

Tunnel mode A mode of IPsec that provides compatibility for some VPN gateways.

upstream server The server that provides update files to all downstream servers when you are designing WSUS architectures. Microsoft's own Microsoft Update servers are the final upstream servers.

user class A user-defined options class that is populated by DHCP clients sharing a particular class ID set by an administrator.

vendor class   A options class that is made up of members belonging to a vendor group. "Microsoft Windows 2000 Options" is an example of a vendor class.

Windows Server Update Services (WSUS)   Software that provides automated support for installing the latest critical updates and security updates to Windows 2000 and later versions of Windows.

WINS server   A name server used to resolve NetBIOS names on Windows networks.

worm   A type of malware that replicates by attacking vulnerable computers across a network.

zone   A database on a DNS server that includes the authoritative data for computer name-to-address mappings of a particular portion of a DNS namespace. A zone is assigned the same names as the domain for which it contains the data.

zone transfers   The periodic zone copies that must occur between a master and a secondary zone in order to keep zone data current.

Index

Symbols and Numbers

802.1X
Access Points, 395
configuring 802.1X enforcement, 409–410

A

A or AAAA resource records, 178
Access Client IPv4 Address and Access Client IPv6
  Address, 360
access control list (ACL), 396
accomodating physical topology, 56–57
ACL (access control list), 396
Active Directory Zone Replication Scope, 166–167
Active Directory–integrated zones, 192–198
  choosing zone replication scope, 194–197
  creating custom application directory partitions,
    197–198
  re-creating DomainDnsZones and
    ForestDnsZones, 197
  replication and application directory partitions,
    193–194
ad hoc mode, wireless networks, 325
Add Or Edit DHCP Scopes, 225–227
  activate this scope, 227
  default gateway, 227
  scope name, 227
  starting and ending IP address, 227
  subnet mask, 227
  subnet type, 227
Add Roles Wizard
  Add Or Edit DHCP Scopes, 225–227
  Authorize DHCP Server, 230
  Configure DHCPv6 Stateless Mode, 228–229
  Configure IPv6 DNS Server Settings, 230
  Enable DHCPv6 Stateless Mode For This Server,
    229
  Select Network Connection Bindings, 223

Specify IPv4 DNS Server Settings, 223–224
Specify IPv4 WINS Server Settings, 225
adding DHCP server role
  Add Or Edit DHCP Scopes, 225–227
  Authorize DHCP Server, 230
  Configure DHCPv6 Stateless Mode, 228–229
  Configure IPv6 DNS Server Settings, 230
  Dynamic Host Configuration Protocol (DHCP)
    servers, installing, 221–231
  Enable DHCPv6 Stateless Mode For This Server,
    229
  Select Network Connection Bindings, 223
  Specify IPv4 DNS Server Settings, 223–224
  Specify IPv4 WINS Server Settings, 225
adding DNS servers to domain controllers, 170
adding folders to DFS namespace, 537–538
adding printer drivers, 574–575
address assignment, DHCP servers, 218–221
  address leases, 219–220
  DHCP options, 220–221
  scopes, 220
address blocks
  determining number of addresses per, 51–52
  subnets and, 50
address configuration, viewing, 18–20
address exclusions, creating (DHCP), 235–236
address ranges, IPv4, 48–54
  address blocks and subnets, 50
  determining block size requirements, 53–54
  determining host capacity per block, 53
  determining number of addresses per address
    block, 51–52
  private addresses, 49
  public addresses, 49
Address Resolution Protocol (ARP), 31–32
adjusting lease durations, DHCP, 238–239
aging and scavenging, 182–186
  enabling aging, 182–183

System Requirements

We recommend that you use an isolated network that is not part of your production network to do the practice exercises in this book. The computer that you use to perform practices requires Internet connectivity. It is possible to perform all of the practices in this training kit if you decide to use a virtual machine instead of standard computer hardware.

Hardware Requirements

To complete most of the practices in this book, you need two computers or virtual machines running Windows Server 2008 using the default settings. Some exercises (specifically, those in Chapter 6, "Protecting Network Traffic with IPSec") require a third computer or virtual machine. Your computers or virtual machines should meet (at a minimum) the following hardware specifications:

- Personal computer with a 1-GHz or faster processor
- 512 MB of RAM
- 20 GB of available hard disk space
- DVD-ROM drive
- Super VGA (800 x 600) or higher-resolution monitor
- Keyboard and Microsoft mouse or compatible pointing device

Software Requirements

The following software is required to complete the practice exercises:

- Windows Server 2008 Standard or Enterprise. (A 60-day evaluation edition of Windows Server 2008 Enterprise—the only Windows Server 2008 evaluation software available as of this writing—is included with this book. You can use this evaluation edition for all of the practices.)
- To run computers as virtual machines within Windows, you can use Virtual PC, Virtual Server 2005 R2, Hyper-V, or third-party virtual machine software. To download Virtual PC 2007, visit *http://www.microsoft.com/windows/downloads/virtualpc*. To download an evaluation edition of, and for more information about, Virtual Server 2005 R2, visit *http://www.microsoft.com/virtualserver*. For more information about Hyper-V, visit *http://www.microsoft.com/hyperv*.

What do you think of this book?

We want to hear from you!

Do you have a few minutes to participate in a brief online survey?

Microsoft is interested in hearing your feedback so we can continually improve our books and learning resources for you.

To participate in our survey, please visit:

www.microsoft.com/learning/booksurvey/

...and enter this book's ISBN-10 or ISBN-13 number (located above barcode on back cover*). As a thank-you to survey participants in the United States and Canada, each month we'll randomly select five respondents to win one of five $100 gift certificates from a leading online merchant. At the conclusion of the survey, you can enter the drawing by providing your e-mail address, which will be used for prize notification only.

Thanks in advance for your input. Your opinion counts!

* Where to find the ISBN on back cover

ISBN-13: 000-0-0000-0000-0
ISBN-10: 0-0000-0000-0

0 000000 000000
00000

Example only. Each book has unique ISBN.

Microsoft®
Press